ESSAYS

ON

THE ACTIVE POWERS OF THE HUMAN MIND;

AN INQUIRY INTO THE HUMAN MIND ON THE PRINCIPLES
OF COMMON SENSE;

AND AN

ESSAY ON QUANTITY.

BY

THOMAS REID, D.D. F.R.S.E.

PROFESSOR OF MORAL PHILOSOPHY IN THE UNIVERSITY OF GLASGOW.

AND

A MEMOIR OF THE AUTHOR,

BY DUGALD STEWART.

WITH NOTES, SECTIONAL HEADS, AND A SYNOPTICAL TABLE
OF CONTENTS,

BY THE

REV. G. N. WRIGHT, M.A. &c.

LONDON:

PRINTED FOR THOMAS TEGG, CHEAPSIDE;
R. GRIFFIN AND CO., GLASGOW; T. MESSURIER, DUBLIN;
J. AND S. A. TEGG, SYDNEY AND HOBART TOWN.

MDCCCXLIII.

EDITOR'S PREFACE.

GREATER typographical accuracy is not the only advantage to which this edition of the author's works is entitled; it possesses the still further recommendation of being the only complete and perfect collection of his writings yet published. In the first volume are included, "An Account of Dr. Reid's Life and Writings," from the classic pen of Dugald Stewart; "Essays on the Active Powers of the Human Mind;" "An Inquiry into the Human Mind, on the Principles of Common Sense;" and "An Essay on Quantity:" the last has hitherto only appeared in the "Philosophical Transactions." The second volume contains the author's *præclarum opus*, "Essays on the Intellectual Powers of Man," together with his "View" or "Analysis of Aristotle's Logic," first published in the works of Lord Kames, and subsequently in a separate volume.

In the preparation of these Essays for the press and the public, one uniform method has been observed. Where it had not been previously done by the author, the chapters are divided, with scrupulous attention to each pause, or interruption in the chain of reasoning, into sections; and to every section, whether original or newly separated, *headings* are prefixed. These headings present a condensed view of the contents, argument, or arguments, in each section; and, as far as it could be done, they are so linked together in meaning as to afford a tolerably full, correct, and continuous synopsis of the author's theory. In these introductions, perhaps, consist the chief merit which this edition can claim. To facilitate, however, the interpretation of abstruse passages, brackets are employed, italic letters frequently used, and forcible examples marked by indices; besides which those arguments that support any theory or fact, and which are scattered over many pages or chapters, or even Essays, are indicated and connected by the numerals of some one particular fount; and attention called to this connexion by notes, sometimes containing a complete recapitulation.

In those parts of the author's writings that are of a mixed character—moral and metaphysical—numerous quotations from the works of ancient philosophers occur in the original languages. All such extracts have been translated, not literally, but appropriately; and given, not in substitution, but in addition to the originals.

Hitherto the philosophical labours of this able and excellent man, the bold assailant of Locke, lay, like the Sibyl's leaves, where the winds had carried them. Henceforth, it is hoped, their connexion, an end so valuable in such serious investigations, will be unequivocally perceived; and some of the difficulties that have obstructed the study of pneumatology thereby alleviated, if not entirely removed.

G. N. W.

Coed Celyn, Llanrwst, Denbighshire.
1843.

SYNOPTICAL TABLE OF CONTENTS.

ESSAYS ON THE ACTIVE POWERS OF THE MIND.

	Page
Life of Dr. Reid	1
Introduction	77

ESSAY I.
OF ACTIVE POWER IN GENERAL.
CHAPTER I.
OF THE NOTION OF ACTIVE POWER . . 79
Sec. 1. An explanation of the meaning of "active power" necessary . . . ib.
2. The Aristotelian definition of motion . . . ib.
3. Of our conception of active power . . . 80
4. Power not an object of consciousness . . . ib.
   But a relative conception . 81
6. There are some things of which we can have both a direct and a relative conception . . . 82
7. Our conception of power is relative to its exertions or effects . . . 83
8. Our idea of power . . ib.

CHAPTER II.
THE SAME SUBJECT . . 85
Sec. 1. Distinction of "action and passion" coeval with the origin of languages . ib.
2. Objection . . . ib.
6. Active verbs appear plainly to have been first contrived to express action . . 88

CHAPTER III.
OF MR. LOCKE'S ACCOUNT OF OUR IDEA OF POWER . . 91
2. Objections to Mr. Locke's origin of our idea of power ib.

CHAPTER IV.
OF MR. HUME'S OPINION OF THE IDEA OF POWER . . 93
Sec. 1. Induction, by which Mr. Hume attempts to explain the origin of our simple ideas, imperfect . . ib.
4. Of the two principles which Hume opposes to Locke . 96

CHAPTER V.
WHETHER BEINGS THAT HAVE NO WILL NOR UNDERSTANDING MAY HAVE ACTIVE POWER? . 97
Sec. 1. The question perplexed by the ambiguity of certain terms . . . ib.
4. Volition necessary to the operation of power . 99
6. Our conception of active power relative . . 101

CHAPTER VI.
OF THE EFFICIENT CAUSES OF THE PHENOMENA OF NATURE . 103
Sec. 1. Of powers ascribed to matter ib.

CHAPTER VII.
OF THE EXTENT OF HUMAN POWER. 107
Sec. 1. Power an attribute of accountable beings . . ib.
8. Human power entirely dependent upon God and the laws of nature . . 113

ESSAY II.
OF THE WILL.
CHAPTER I.
OBSERVATIONS CONCERNING THE WILL 114

	Page
Sec. 1. Volition and will different	114
2. The term will, how used	ib.
3. Its definition	115
5. Of command, will, and desire	117

CHAPTER II.
OF THE INFLUENCE OF INCITEMENTS AND MOTIVES UPON THE WILL 119

Sec. 1. Instinct	ib.
2. Judgment not necessary to instinct	ib.
3. The exercise of judgment distinct from the impulse of appetite	121
4. Taste and judgment differ	122
5. Of passion and reason	ib.

CHAPTER III.
OF OPERATIONS OF MIND WHICH MAY BE CALLED VOLUNTARY . 126

Sec. 1. Of attention, deliberation, and resolution	ib.
2. Of genius	127
3. Deliberation	129
6. Resolution	131
7. The virtue and affection of benevolence different	132

CHAPTER IV.
COROLLARIES . . . 135

Sec. 1. Of transient and momentary acts of the will . . ib.

ESSAY III.
OF THE PRINCIPLES OF ACTION.

PART I.
OF THE MECHANICAL PRINCIPLES OF ACTION.

CHAPTER I.
OF THE PRINCIPLES OF ACTION IN GENERAL . . . 138

Sec. 1. Actions of men classified	ib.
2. Knowledge of the principles of action important	ib.
3. Difficulties attending an investigation of the principles of human actions	139
4. Third cause of the difficulty of tracing the principles of action in man	140

CHAPTER II.
OF INSTINCT . . . 142

Sec. 1. Of instinct in man . ib.

	Page
Sec. 2. Of instinct in inferior animals	143
3. Some human instincts transitory, others permanent	145
6. Fourth case in which instinct, probably, is requisite	147
7. Judgment and belief influenced, to a certain extent, by instinct	148

CHAPTER III.
OF HABIT 151

Sec. 1. Vulgar definition of habit	ib.
2. The art of speaking, the strongest illustration of the force of habit	152

PART II.
OF ANIMAL PRINCIPLES OF ACTION.

CHAPTER I.
OF APPETITES . . . 154

Sec. 1. Definition of animal principles of action	ib.
5. The principle of activity belongs to every period of life	157
7. The government of appetites gives a superiority to man over brute animals	159

CHAPTER II.
OF DESIRES 160

Sec. 1. Distinction between appetites and desires twofold	ib.
2. Of esteem and contempt	ib.
5. Such natural desires not selfish principles	162
6. Our desires auxiliary to the maintenance of morals	ib.
9. Of acquired desires	165

CHAPTER III.
OF BENEVOLENT AFFECTION IN GENERAL . . . 166

Sec. 2. Objects of our desires and our affections different . 167

CHAPTER IV.
OF THE PARTICULAR BENEVOLENT AFFECTIONS . . . 171

Sec. 1. Of natural affection	ib.
2. Duration of parental affection limited in inferior animals; not so in the human species	172
3. Parental affection the effect of our natural constitution	173
4. Further uses of parental affection	ib.

Sec. 11. Necessity for submitting public spirit to the control of reason and virtue, evident . . . 179

CHAPTER V.
OF MALEVOLENT AFFECTION . 182
Sec. 1. Of emulation and resentment . . . ib.
4. Effects of emulation in brute-animals . . 185
5. Definition of resentment . ib.
7. Children and rude nations generally ascribe life and intelligence to inanimate things . . . 188
9. Agreements and disagreements between deliberate and mere animal resentment . . . 189

CHAPTER VI.
OF PASSION . . . 190
Sec. 1. Passion, Disposition, Opinion . . . ib.
2. Definition of passion . 191
5. Hume's paradoxes generally reducible to abuses of words 193
6. Common division of the passions . . . ib.
7. Influence of passion . 194

CHAPTER VII.
OF DISPOSITION . . 198
Sec. 3. The excellent consequences of good humour . 199
5. Elation, magnanimity, a sense of honour and pride 200
6. Depression, humility, meanness . . . ib.

CHAPTER VIII.
OF OPINION . . . 202
Sec. 1. Influence of opinion upon our animal principles . ib.
4. Analogy between the discipline of body and mind . 203
5. Man actuated by no sense of duty, considered . 204

PART III.
OF THE RATIONAL PRINCIPLES OF ACTION.

CHAPTER I.
THERE ARE RATIONAL PRINCIPLES OF ACTION IN MAN . . 206
Sec. 2. Hume's error as to one of the chief offices of reason . 207

CHAPTER II.
OF REGARD TO OUR GOOD ON THE WHOLE . . . 208
Sec. 1. Chief spring of our early actions . . . ib.
2. The conception of what is good or ill for us upon the whole, the offspring of reason . . . 209
4. Office of practical reason . 211

CHAPTER III.
THE TENDENCY OF THIS PRINCIPLE 213
Sec. 1. Question of the ancient moralists, "What is the greatest good?" . . ib.
2. Fallacy of the Epicurean doctrine . . . ib.
3. Doctrine of the Stoics not original . . . 214
4. Recapitulation of what has been advanced relative to the rational principles of action . . . 216

CHAPTER IV.
DEFECTS OF THIS PRINCIPLE . 217
Sec. 1. The rational principle of action not the only regulator of human conduct . ib.

CHAPTER V.
OF THE NOTION OF DUTY, RECTITUDE, MORAL OBLIGATION . 221
Sec. 1. A sense of interest, or a sense of duty, or both, necessary to the social state . ib.
2. Of a sense of duty only . ib.
3. The notion of this principle invariable, its extent not so 223
4. Reality of moral distinctions . . . ib.
6. Moral obligation a relation 225

CHAPTER VI.
OF THE SENSE OF DUTY . . 227
Sec. 1. The moral sense,—the moral faculty,—conscience . ib.
2. This analogy excusable . ib.
3. Further shown . . 228
5. Universality of first principles . . . 230
6. The first principles of morals are the immediate dictates of the moral faculty . 230
7. Recapitulation . . 231

CHAPTER VII.
OF MORAL APPROBATION AND DISAPPROBATION . . . 231

viii SYNOPTICAL TABLE

Sec. 1. Of affections and feelings included in our moral judgments . . . 231
3. Moral disapprobation . 233
6. Social ties auxiliary to virtue, unfavourable to vice . 235
7. Consequences of remorse . ib.
8. Operations of the faculty called moral sense . . 236

CHAPTER VIII.
OBSERVATIONS CONCERNING CONSCIENCE . . . 237
Sec. 1. Our judgment of moral conduct advances from infancy by insensible degrees . ib.
3. Scepticism twofold . . 238
8. The intention or end of our active powers obvious . 241
9. Office of conscience . 242
10. Stoical perfection ideal . 243
12. Extravagance of Mysticism ib.

ESSAY IV.
ON THE LIBERTY OF MORAL AGENTS.

CHAPTER I.
THE NOTIONS OF MORAL LIBERTY AND NECESSITY STATED . 246
Sec. 1. Moral liberty . . ib.
2. The voluntary actions of brutes, determined by the present predominant passion . . . 247
7. Three additional meanings of the word *liberty* . 249

CHAPTER II.
OF THE WORDS CAUSE AND EFFECT, ACTION, AND ACTIVE POWER . 251
Sec. 1. The use of ambiguous terms has impeded our reasonings about moral liberty . ib.
2. Active power . . 252
5. Recapitulation . . 254

CHAPTER III.
CAUSES OF THE AMBIGUITY OF THOSE WORDS . . . 255
Sec. 1. Premature conclusion as to objects indued with motion ib.
6. A chief cause of the imperfection of language . 257
8. Absurd theories of philosophers to explain causation 259
9. Not mischievous . . ib.

Sec. 10. Proof of a Deity on these principles presents no difficulty . . . 260

CHAPTER IV.
OF THE INFLUENCE OF MOTIVES . 261
Sec. 6. Motives of the same kind may be compared . . 264
8. Animal test of the strength of motives . . . 265
9. Rational motives defined . 266
10. Rational test of the strength of motives . . . ib.
14. The supposition of necessity precludes rewards and punishments — liberty gives efficacy to both . . 268

CHAPTER V.
LIBERTY CONSISTENT WITH GOVERNMENT . . . 269
Sec. 1. Mechanical and moral government . . . ib.
7. The moral government of God consistent with liberty 273

CHAPTER VI.
FIRST ARGUMENT . . . 275
Sec. 3. The belief of acting freely is coeval with our reason, universal, and necessary . 278
5. Exceptions . . . 279

CHAPTER VII.
SECOND ARGUMENT . . 282
Sec. 1. Certain first principles universally conceded . . ib.

CHAPTER VIII.
THIRD ARGUMENT . . . 286
Sec. 2. Argument from analogy . 286
3. Its application . . 287
4. Objection and answer . ib.

CHAPTER IX.
OF ARGUMENTS FOR NECESSITY . 289
Sec. 1. Three classes of arguments against human liberty . ib.
2. Boast of Leibnitz . . ib.
3. Identity of indiscernibles . 290
4. Leibnitz' proof of the truth of his principle only a petitio principii . . ib.
5. Three meanings of the principle of "a sufficient reason" applied to the determinations of the will . . 291
6. The principle further examined . . . ib.

	Page
Sec. 9. Four consequences of this definition of a cause	. 294

CHAPTER X.
THE SAME SUBJECT . . 297
Sec. 2. Third class of arguments against human liberty . 298

CHAPTER XI.
OF THE PERMISSION OF EVIL . 303
Sec. 2. Scientia media . . ib.
3. Prescience of the Deity indisputable. . . 304

ESSAY V.
OF MORALS.

CHAPTER I.
OF THE FIRST PRINCIPLES OF MORALS 312
Sec. 1. First principles . . ib.
4. Another class of axioms in morals . . . 317
5. Conclusion . . 319

CHAPTER II.
OF SYSTEMS OF MORALS . . 319
Sec. 1. Instruction in morals necessary . . . ib
3. Necessity of instruction in morals shown from the evidence of history . . 321
6. Morals have been methodized in different ways . 322

CHAPTER III.
OF SYSTEMS OF NATURAL JURISPRUDENCE . . . 323
Sec. 1. Jurisprudence and morals closely related . . ib.
5. True origin of systems of natural jurisprudence . 326

CHAPTER IV.
WHETHER AN ACTION DESERVING MORAL APPROBATION, MUST BE DONE WITH THE BELIEF OF ITS BEING MORALLY GOOD . 329
Sec. 9. Conscience, or moral sense 337

CHAPTER V.
WHETHER JUSTICE BE A NATURAL OR AN ARTIFICIAL VIRTUE . 338
Sec. 1. Hume consistent as a writer on morals . . . ib.
3. Hume agrees with the Epicureans in one respect . 339
4. Disagrees in another . 340
5. Effect of this doctrine . ib.
6. Natural and artificial virtues . . . ib.
8. Esteem . . . 341
9. The merit of justice, according to Hume . . 342
17. Six branches of justice . 349
20. Mr. Hobbes' system . 350
26. This argument would prove all social virtues to be artificial, as well as justice . 357
28. Obvious defect in Mr. Hume's reasoning as to the standard of justice generally . . . 358
29. Standard of justice among the ancients . . 359

CHAPTER VI.
OF THE NATURE AND OBLIGATION OF A CONTRACT . . 361
Sec. 1. Promise and contract different . . . ib.
2. Definition of a contract . 362
5. Contracts and promises have a foundation in nature . 367
7. Natural tendency of Mr. Hume's principles . 370
8. Mr. Hume's practice probably contradicted his principles . . . 371
10. Origin of the contradictions in Mr. Hume's arguments 374

CHAPTER VII.
THAT MORAL APPROBATION IMPLIES A REAL JUDGMENT . 376
Sec. 4. Of feeling and judgment . 377
8. Improper use of words has impeded the study of moral philosophy . . 384
10. Impiety of the assertion, that moral judgment is merely a feeling . . . 392

AN INQUIRY INTO THE HUMAN MIND ON THE PRINCIPLES OF COMMON SENSE.

	Page
DEDICATION TO LORD DESKFOORD	395

CHAPTER I.

INTRODUCTION	399
Sec. 1. The importance of the subject, and the means of prosecuting it	ib.
2. The impediments to our knowledge of the mind	400
3. The present state of this part of philosophy. Of Des Cartes, Malebranche, and Locke	403
4. Apology for these philosophers	405
5. Of Bishop Berkeley; the "Treatise of Human Nature;" and of scepticism	406
6. Of the "Treatise of Human Nature"	408
7. The system of all these authors is the same, and leads to scepticism	409
8. We ought not to despair of a better	410

CHAPTER II.

OF SMELLING	411
Sec. 1. The order of proceeding. Of the medium and organ of smell	ib.
2. The sensation considered abstractly	412
3. Sensation and its remembrance natural principles of belief	413
4. Judgment and belief in some cases precede simple apprehension	415
5. Two theories of the nature of belief refuted. Conclusions from what hath been said	415
6. Apology for metaphysical absurdities. Sensation without a sentient, a consequence of the theory of ideas. Consequences of this strange opinion	418
7. The conception and belief of a sentient being or mind, is suggested by our constitution. The notion of relations not always got by comparing the related ideas	422
8. There is a quality or virtue in bodies, which we call their smell. How this is connected in the imagination with the sensation	424
9. That there is a principle in human nature, from which the notion of this, as well as all other natural virtues or causes, is derived	425
10. Whether in sensations the mind is active or passive	428

CHAPTER III.

OF TASTING	430

CHAPTER IV.

OF HEARING	433
Sec. 1. Variety of sounds. Their place and distance learned by custom, without reasoning	ib.
2. Of natural language	434

CHAPTER V.

OF TOUCH	437
Sec. 1. Of heat and cold	ib.
2. Of hardness and softness	438
3. Of natural signs	441
4. Of hardness, and other primary qualities	444
5. The distinction betwixt primary and secondary qualities hath had several revolutions	ib.
6. Of extension	445
7. Of extension	447
8. Of the existence of a material world	449
9. Of the systems of philosophers concerning the senses	454

CHAPTER VI.

OF SEEING	457
Sec. 1. The excellence and dignity of this faculty	ib.
2. Sight discovers almost nothing which the blind may not comprehend. The reason of this	459

	Page		Page
Sec. 3. Of the visible appearances of objects	. 462	Sec. 16. Facts relating to squinting	524
4. That colour is a quality of bodies, not a sensation of the mind	. 465	17. Of the effect of custom in seeing objects single	. 526
5. First inference from the preceding	. 467	18. Of Dr. Porterfield's account of single and double vision	532
6. Second.—That none of our sensations are resemblances of any of the qualities of bodies	. 470	19. Of Dr. Briggs's theory, and Sir Isaac Newton's conjecture on this subject	. 534
7. Of visible figure and extension	. 474	20. Of perception in general	. 542
8. Some queries concerning visible figure answered	. 477	21. Of the process of nature in perception	. 548
9. Of the geometry of visibles	482	22. Of the signs by which we learn to perceive distance from the eye	. 552
10. Of the parallel motion of the eyes	. 490	23. Of the signs used in these acquired perceptions	. 561
11. Of our seeing objects erect by inverted images	. 492	24. Of the analogy between perception and the credit we give to human testimony	563
12. The same subject continued	497		
13. Of seeing objects single with two eyes	. 509		

CHAPTER VII.

CONCLUSION . . . 575

14. Of the laws of vision in brute animals . 514	
15. The phenomena of squinting considered hypothetically 516	Sec. 1. Containing reflections upon the opinions of philosophers on this subject . 575

AN ESSAY ON QUANTITY.

	Page		Page
Sec. 1. What quantity is	. 591	Sec. 6. Of the Newtonian measure of force	. 596
2. Of proper and improper quantity	. 592	7. Of the Leibnitzian measure of force	. 597
3. Corollary 1	. 594	8. Reflections on this controversy	. 598
4. Corollary 2	. ib.		
5. Corollary 3	. 595		

ACCOUNT

OF

THE LIFE AND WRITINGS

OF

THOMAS REID, D.D.

SECTION I.

FROM DR. REID'S BIRTH TILL THE DATE OF HIS LATEST PUBLICATION.

THE life of which I am now to present to the Royal Society a short account, although it fixes an era in the history of modern philosophy, was uncommonly barren of those incidents which furnish materials for biography; strenuously devoted to truth, to virtue, and to the best interests of mankind; but spent in the obscurity of a learned retirement, remote from the pursuits of ambition, and with little solicitude about literary fame. After the agitation, however, of the political convulsions which Europe has witnessed for a course of years, the simple record of such a life may derive an interest even from its uniformity; and when contrasted with the events of the passing scene, may lead the thoughts to some views of human nature, on which it is not ungrateful to repose.

THOMAS REID, D.D., late Professor of Moral Philosophy in the University of Glasgow, was born on the 26th of April, 1710, at Strachan in Kincardineshire, a country parish situated about twenty miles from Aberdeen, on the north side of the Grampian Mountains.

His father, the Reverend Lewis Reid, was minister of this parish for fifty years. He was a clergyman, according to his son's account of him, respected by all who knew him, for his piety, prudence, and benevolence; inheriting from his ancestors (most of whom, from the time of the Protestant establishment, had been ministers of the Church of Scotland) that purity and simplicity of manners which became his station; and a love of letters, which, without attracting the notice of the world, amused his leisure, and dignified his retirement.

For some generations before his time, a propensity to literature, and to the learned professions,—a propensity which, when it has once become characteristical of a race, is peculiarly apt to be propagated by the influence of early associations and habits,—may be traced in several individuals among his kindred. One of his ancestors, James Reid, was the first minister of Banchory-Ternan after the Reformation; and transmitted to four sons a predilection for those studious habits which formed his own happiness. He was himself a younger son of Mr. Reid of Pitfoddels, a gentleman of a very ancient and respectable family in the county of Aberdeen.

James Reid was succeeded as minister of Banchory by his son Robert. Another son, Thomas, rose to considerable distinction both as a philosopher and a poet; and seems to have wanted neither ability nor inclination to turn his attainments to the best advantage. After travelling over Europe, and maintaining, as was the custom of his age, public disputations in several universities, he collected into a volume the theses and dissertations which had been the subjects of his literary contests; and also published some Latin poems, which may be found in the collection entitled "Deliciæ Poëtarum Scotorum." On his return to his native country, he fixed his residence in London, where he was appointed secretary in the Greek and Latin tongues to King James the First of England, and lived in habits of intimacy with some of the most distinguished characters of that period.—Little more, I believe, is known of Thomas Reid's history, excepting that he bequeathed to the Marischal College of Aberdeen a curious collection of books and manuscripts, with a fund for establishing a salary to a librarian.

Alexander Reid, the third son, was physician to King Charles the First, and published several books on surgery and medicine. The fortune he acquired in the course of his practice was considerable, and enabled him (beside many legacies to his relations and friends) to leave various lasting and honourable memorials, both of his benevolence, and of his attachment to letters.

A fourth son, whose name was Adam, translated into English, "Buchanan's History of Scotland." Of this translation, which was never published, there is a manuscript copy in the possession of the University of Glasgow.

A grandson of Robert, the eldest of these sons, was the third minister of Banchory after the Reformation, and was great-grandfather of Thomas Reid, the subject of this memoir.*

* In the account given in the text, of Dr. Reid's ancestors, I have followed scrupulously the information contained in his own memorandums. I have some suspicion, however, that he has committed a mistake with respect to the name of the translator of Buchanan's History; which would appear, from the MS. in Glasgow College, to have been—not Adam, but John. At the same time, as this last statement rests on an authority altogether unknown, (being written in a hand different from the rest of the MS.,) there is a possibility that Dr. Reid's account may be correct; and therefore I have thought it advisable, in a matter of so very trifling consequence, to adhere to it in preference to the other.

The following particulars, with respect to Thomas Reid may, perhaps, be acceptable to some of my readers. They are copied from Dempster, a contemporary writer; whose details concerning his countrymen, it must, however, be confessed, are not always to be implicitly relied on.

"Thomas Reidus Aberdonensis, pueritiæ meæ et infantilis otii sub Thoma Cargillo collega, Lovanii literas in schola Lipsii serió didicit, quas magno nomine in Germania docuit, carus Principibus. Londini diu in comitatu humanissimi ac clarissimi viri Fulconis Grevilli, Regii Consiliarii Interioris et Angliæ Proquæstoris, egit: tum ad amicitiam Regis, eodem Fulcone deducente, evectus, inter Palatinos admissus, à literis Latinis Regi fuit. Scripsit multa, ut est magnâ indole et variâ eruditione," &c.—"Ex aula se, nemine conscio, nuper proripuit, dum illi omnia festinati honoris augmenta singuli ominarentur, nec quid deinde egerit aut quó locorum se contulerit quisquam indicare potuit. Multi suspicabantur, tædio aulæ affectum, monasticæ quieti seipsum tradidisse, sub annum 1618. Rumor postea fuit in aulam rediisse, et meritissimis honoribus redditum, sed nunquam id consequetur quod virtus promeretur."—*Hist. Ecclesiastica Gentis Scotorum,* lib. xvi. p. 576.

What was the judgment of Thomas Reid's own times with respect to his genius, and what their hopes of his posthumous fame, may be collected from an elegy on his death by his learned countryman Robert Aytoun. Already, before the lapse of two hundred years, some apology, alas! may be thought necessary for an attempt to rescue his name from total oblivion.

Aytoun's elegy on Reid is referred to in terms very flattering both to its author and to its subject, by the editor of the Collection, entitled, "Poëtarum Scotorum Musæ Sacræ." "In obitum Thomæ Rheidi epicedium extat elegan-

The particulars hitherto mentioned, are stated on the authority of some short memorandums written by Dr. Reid a few weeks before his death. In consequence of a suggestion of his friend Dr. Gregory, he had resolved to amuse himself with collecting such facts as his papers or memory could supply, with respect to his life, and the progress of his studies; but, unfortunately, before he had fairly entered on the subject, his design was interrupted by his last illness. If he had lived to complete it, I might have entertained hopes of presenting to the public some details with respect to the history of his opinions and speculations on those important subjects to which he dedicated his talents;—the most interesting of all articles in the biography of a philosopher, and of which, it is to be lamented, that so few authentic records are to be found in the annals of letters. All the information, however, which I have derived from these notes, is exhausted in the foregoing pages; and I must content myself, in the continuation of my narrative, with those indirect aids which tradition, and the recollection of a few old acquaintances, afford; added to what I myself have learned from Dr. Reid's conversation, or collected from a careful perusal of his writings.

His mother, Margaret Gregory, was a daughter of David Gregory, Esq., of Kinnairdie, in Banffshire; elder brother of James Gregory, the inventor of the reflecting telescope, and the antagonist of Huyghens. She was one of twenty-nine children; the most remarkable of whom was David Gregory, Savilian Professor of Astronomy at Oxford, and an intimate friend of Sir Isaac Newton. Two of her younger brothers were at the same time professors of mathematics; the one at St. Andrew's, the

tissimum Roberti Aytoni, viri literis ac dignitate clarissimi, in Deliciis Poëtarum Scotorum, ubi et ipsius quoque poëmata, paucula quidem illa, sed venusta, sed elegantia, comparent."

The only works of Alexander Reid of which I have heard, are " Chirurgical Lectures on Tumors and Ulcers," London, 1635 ; and a " Treatise of the first part of Chirurgerie," London, 1638. He appears to have been the physician and friend of the celebrated mathematician Thomas Harriott, of whose interesting history so little was known, till the recent discovery of his manuscripts, by Mr. Zach, of Saxe-Gotha.

A remarkable instance of the careless or capricious orthography formerly so common in writing proper names, occurs in the different individuals to whom this note refers. Sometimes the family name is written—*Reid;* on other occasions, *Riede, Read, Rhead* or *Rhaid.*

other at Edinburgh; and were the first persons who taught the Newtonian philosophy in our northern universities. The hereditary worth and genius which have so long distinguished, and which still distinguish, the descendants of this memorable family, are well known to all who have turned their attention to Scottish biography; but it is not known so generally, that through the female line, the same characteristical endowments have been conspicuous in various instances; and that to the other monuments which illustrate the race of the Gregories, is to be added *the Philosophy of Reid.*

With respect to the earlier part of Dr. Reid's life, all that I have been able to learn amounts to this, that after two years spent at the parish school of Kincardine, he was sent to Aberdeen, where he had the advantage of prosecuting his classical studies under an able and diligent teacher; that, about the age of twelve or thirteen, he was entered as a student in Marischal College; and that his master in philosophy, for three years, was Dr. George Turnbull, who afterwards attracted some degree of notice as an author; particularly by a book entitled " Principles of Moral Philosophy," and by a voluminous treatise (long ago forgotten) on Ancient Painting.* The sessions of the College were, at that time, very short, and the education (according to Dr. Reid's own account) slight and superficial.

It does not appear from the information which I have received, that he gave any early indications of future eminence. His industry, however, and modesty, were conspicuous from his childhood; and it was foretold of him, by the parish school-

* Dr. Turnbull's work on Moral Philosophy was published at London in 1740. As I have only turned over a few pages, I cannot say any thing with respect to its merits. The mottos on the title-page are curious, when considered in connexion with those inquiries which his pupil afterwards prosecuted with so much success; and may, perhaps, without his perceiving it, have had some effect in suggesting to him that plan of philosophizing which he so systematically and so happily pursued.

" If Natural Philosophy, in all its parts, by pursuing this method, shall at length be perfected, the bounds of Moral Philosophy will also be enlarged."— *Newton's Optics.*

" Account for moral, as for natural things."—*Pope.*

For the opinion of a very competent judge with respect to the Treatise on Ancient Painting, vide Hogarth's print, entitled, " Beer-lane."

master who initiated him in the first principles of learning, " That he would turn out to be a man of good and well wearing parts;" a prediction which touched, not unhappily, on that capacity of "patient thought" which so peculiarly characterised his philosophical genius.

His residence at the university was prolonged beyond the usual term, in consequence of his appointment to the office of librarian, which had been endowed by one of his ancestors about a century before. The situation was acceptable to him, as it afforded an opportunity of indulging his passion for study, and united the charms of a learned society, with the quiet of an academical retreat.

During this period, he formed an intimacy with John Stewart, afterwards Professor of Mathematics in Marischal College, and author of a commentary on Newton's " Quadrature of Curves." His predilection for mathematical pursuits was confirmed and strengthened by this connexion. I have often heard him mention it with much pleasure, while he recollected the ardour with which they both prosecuted these fascinating studies, and the lights which they imparted mutually to each other, in their first perusal of the " Principia," at a time when a knowledge of the Newtonian discoveries was only to be acquired in the writings of their illustrious author.

In 1736, Dr. Reid resigned his office of librarian, and accompanied Mr. Stewart on an excursion to England. They visited, together, London, Oxford, and Cambridge, and were introduced to the acquaintance of many persons of the first literary eminence. His relation to Dr. David Gregory procured him a ready access to Martin Folkes, whose house concentrated the most interesting objects which the metropolis had to offer to his curiosity. At Cambridge he saw Dr. Bentley, who delighted him with his learning, and amused him with his vanity; and enjoyed repeatedly the conversation of the blind mathematician, Saunderson; a phenomenon in the history of the human mind, to which he has referred more than once, in his philosophical speculations.

With the learned and amiable man who was his companion in this journey, he maintained an uninterrupted friendship till 1766, when Mr. Stewart died of a malignant fever. His death was accompanied with circumstances deeply afflicting to Dr. Reid's sensibility; the same disorder proving fatal to his wife and daughter, both of whom were buried with him in one grave.

In 1737, Dr. Reid was presented, by the King's College of Aberdeen, to the living of New-Machar in the same county; but the circumstances in which he entered on his preferment were far from auspicious. The intemperate zeal of one of his predecessors, and an aversion to the law of patronage, had so inflamed the minds of his parishioners against him, that, in the first discharge of his clerical functions, he had not only to encounter the most violent opposition, but was exposed to personal danger. His unwearied attention, however, to the duties of his office; the mildness and forbearance of his temper, and the active spirit of his humanity, soon overcame all these prejudices; and, not many years afterwards, when he was called to a different situation, the same persons who had suffered themselves to be so far misled as to take a share in the outrages against him, followed him, on his departure, with their blessings and tears.

Dr. Reid's popularity at New-Machar (as I am informed by the respectable clergyman* who now holds that living) increased greatly after his marriage, in 1740, with Elizabeth, daughter of his uncle, Dr. George Reid, physician in London. The accommodating manners of this excellent woman, and her good offices among the sick and necessitous, are still remembered with gratitude; and so endeared the family to the neighbourhood, that its removal was regarded as a general misfortune. The simple and affecting language in which some old men expressed themselves on this subject, in conversing with the present minister, deserves to be recorded. " We fought *against* Dr. Reid when he came, and would have fought *for* him when he went away."

In some notes relative to the earlier part of his history, which have been kindly communicated to me by the Reverend Mr. Davidson, minister of Rayne, it is mentioned as a proof of his uncommon modesty and diffidence, that long after he became minister of New-Machar, he was accustomed, from a distrust in his own powers, to preach the sermons of Dr. Tillotson and of Dr. Evans. I have heard also, through other channels, that he had neglected the practice of composition to a more than ordinary

* The Reverend William Stronach.

degree, in the earlier part of his studies. The fact is curious, when contrasted with that ease, perspicuity, and purity of style, which he afterwards attained. From some information, however, which has been lately transmitted to me by one of his nearest relations, I have reason to believe, that the number of original discourses which he wrote, while a country clergyman, was not inconsiderable.

The satisfaction of his own mind was probably, at this period, a more powerful incentive to his philosophical researches, than the hope of being able to instruct the world as an author. But, whatever his views were, one thing is certain, that during his residence at New-Machar, the greater part of his time was spent in the most intense study; more particularly in a careful examination of the laws of external perception, and of the other prinples which form the groundwork of human knowledge. His chief relaxations were gardening and botany, to both of which pursuits he retained his attachment even in old age.

A paper which he published in the Philosophical Transactions of the Royal Society of London, for the year 1748, affords some light with respect to the progress of his speculations about this period. It is entitled, " An Essay on Quantity, occasioned by reading a Treatise, in which Simple and Compound Ratios are applied to Virtue and Merit;" and shows plainly, by its contents, that, although he had not yet entirely relinquished the favourite researches of his youth, he was beginning to direct his thoughts to other objects.

The treatise alluded to in the title of this paper, was manifestly the " Inquiry into the Origin of our Ideas of Beauty and Virtue," by Dr. Hutcheson of Glasgow. According to this very ingenious writer, the *moment* of public good produced by an individual, depending partly on his *benevolence,* and partly on his *ability*, the relation between these different moral ideas may be expressed in the technical form of algebraists, by saying, that the first is in the compound proportion of the two others. Hence, Dr. Hutcheson infers, that " *the benevolence* of an agent (which in this system is synonymous with his *moral merit*) is proportional to a fraction, having the moment of good for the numerator, and the ability of the agent for the denominator." Various other examples of a similar nature occur in the same work; and are stated with a gravity not altogether worthy of the author. It is probable, that they were intended merely as *illustrations* of his general reasonings, not as *media* of investigation for the discovery of new conclusions; but they appeared to Dr. Reid to be an innovation which it was of importance to resist, on account of the tendency it might have (by confounding the evidence of different branches of science) to retard the progress of knowledge. The very high reputation which Dr. Hutcheson then possessed in the universities of Scotland, added to the recent attempts of Pitcairn and Cheyne to apply mathematical reasoning to medicine, would bestow, it is likely, an interest on Dr. Reid's Essay at the time of its publication, which it can scarcely be expected to possess at present. Many of the observations, however, which it contains, are acute and original; and all of them are expressed with that clearness and precision, so conspicuous in his subsequent compositions. The circumstance which renders a subject susceptible of mathematical consideration, is accurately stated; and the proper province of that science defined in such a manner, as sufficiently to expose the absurdity of those abuses of its technical phraseology which were at that time prevalent. From some passages in it, there is, I think, ground for concluding, that the author's reading had not been very extensive previous to this period. The enumeration, in particular, which he has given of the different kinds of *proper quantity*, affords a proof, that he was not acquainted with the refined yet sound disquisitions concerning the nature of *number* and of *proportion*, which had appeared almost a century before, in the "Mathematical Lectures" of Dr. Barrow; nor with the remarks on the same subject introduced by Dr. Clarke in one of his controversial letters addressed to Leibnitz.

In the same paper, Dr. Reid takes occasion to offer some reflections on the dispute between the Newtonians and Leibnitzians concerning the measure of forces. The fundamental idea on which these reflections proceed, is just and important; and it leads to the correction of an error, committed very generally by the partizans of both opinions; that, of mistaking a question concerning the comparative advantages of two *definitions*, for a difference of statement with respect to a *physical fact*. It must, I think, be acknowledged, at the same time, that the whole merits of the controversy are not here exhausted; and that the honour of placing this very subtle and abstruse question in a point of view calculated to reconcile completely the contending parties, was reserved for M. D'Alembert. To have fallen short of the success which attended the inquiries of that eminent man, on a subject so congenial to his favourite habits of study, will not reflect any discredit on the powers of Dr. Reid's mind, in the judgment of those who are at all acquainted with the history of this celebrated discussion.

In 1752, the professors of King's College elected Dr. Reid Professor of Philosophy, in testimony of the high opinion they had formed of his learning and abilities. Of the particular plan which he followed in his academical lectures, while he held this office, I have not been able to obtain any satisfactory account; but the department of science which was assigned to him by the general system of education in that university, was abundantly extensive; comprehending mathematics and physics, as well as logic and ethics. A similar system was pursued formerly in the other universities of Scotland; the same professor then conducting his pupils through all those branches of knowledge which are now appropriated to different teachers. And where he happened fortunately to possess those various accomplishments which distinguished Dr. Reid in so remarkable a degree, it cannot be doubted that the unity and comprehensiveness of method, of which such academical courses admitted, must necessarily have possessed important advantages over that more minute subdivision of literary labour which has since been introduced. But as public establishments ought to adapt themselves to what is ordinary, rather than to what is possible, it is not surprising, that experience should have gradually suggested an arrangement more suitable to the narrow limits which commonly circumscribe human genius.

Soon after Dr. Reid's removal to Aberdeen, he projected (in conjunction with his friend Dr. John Gregory) a literary society, which subsisted for many years, and which seems to have had the happiest effects in awakening and directing that spirit of philosophical research, which has since reflected so much lustre on the north of Scotland. The meetings of this society were held weekly; and afforded the members (beside the advantages to be derived from a mutual communication of their sentiments on the common objects of their pursuit) an opportunity of subjecting their intended publications to the test of friendly criticism. The number of valuable works which issued nearly about the same time, from individuals connected with this institution, more particularly the writings of Reid, Gregory, Campbell, Beattie, and Gerard, furnish the best panegyric on the enlightened views of those under whose direction it was originally formed.

Among these works, the most original and profound was, unquestionably, the "Inquiry into the Human Mind," published by Dr. Reid in 1764. The plan appears to have been conceived, and the subject deeply meditated, by the author long before; but it is doubtful whether his modesty would have ever permitted him to present to the world the fruits of his solitary studies, without the encouragement which he received from the general acquiescence of his associates, in the most important conclusions to which he had been led.

From a passage in the dedication, it would seem that the speculations which terminated in these conclusions had commenced as early as the year 1739; at which period the publication of Mr. Hume's "Treatise of Human Nature" induced him, for the first time, as he himself informs us, "to call in question the principles commonly received with regard to the human understanding." In his "Essays on the Intellectual Powers," he acknowledges, that, in his youth he had, without examination, admitted the established opinions on which Mr. Hume's system of scepticism was raised; and that it was the consequences which these opinions seemed to involve, which roused his suspicions concerning their truth. "If I may presume," says he, "to speak my own sentiments, I once believed the doctrine of ideas so firmly, as to embrace the whole of Berkeley's system along with it; till finding other consequences to follow from it, which gave me more uneasiness than the want of a material world, it came into my mind more than forty years ago, to put the question, What evidence have I for this doctrine, that all the objects of my knowledge are ideas in my own mind? From that time to the present, I have been candidly and impartially, as I think, seeking for the evidence of this principle; but can find none, excepting the authority of philosophers."

In following the train of Dr. Reid's researches, this last extract merits attention, as it contains an explicit avowal, on his own part, that, at one period of his life, he had been led, by Berkeley's reasonings, to abandon the belief of the existence of *matter*. The avowal does honour to his candour, and the fact reflects no discredit on his sagacity. The truth is, that this article of the Berkleian system, however contrary to the conclusions of a sounder philosophy, was the error of no common mind. Considered in contrast with that theory of materialism which the excellent author was anxious to supplant, it possessed important advantages, not only in its tendency, but in its scientific consistency; and it afforded a proof, wherever it met with a favourable reception, of an understanding superior to those casual associations, which, in the apprehensions of most men, blend indissolubly the phenomena of thought with the objects of external perception. It is recorded as a saying of M. Turgot, (whose philosophical opinions in some important points approached very nearly to those of Dr. Reid,[*]) that " he who had never doubted of the existence of matter, might be assured he had no turn for metaphysical disquisitions."

As the refutation of Mr. Hume's sceptical theory was the great and professed object of Dr. Reid's "Inquiry," he was anxious, before taking the field as a controversial writer, to guard against the danger of misapprehending or misrepresenting the meaning of his adversary, by submitting his reasonings to Mr. Hume's private examination. With this view, he availed himself of the good offices of Dr. Blair, with whom both he and Mr. Hume had long lived in habits of friendship. The communications which he at first transmitted, consisted only of detached parts of the work; and appear evidently, from a correspondence which I have perused, to have conveyed a very imperfect idea of his general system. In one of Mr. Hume's letters to Dr. Blair, he betrays some want of his usual good humour, in looking forward to his new antagonist. " I wish," says he, " that the parsons would confine themselves to their old

[*] See, in particular, the article " Existence," in the *Encyclopédie*.

occupation of worrying one another, and leave philosophers to argue with temper, moderation, and good manners." After Mr. Hume, however, had read the manuscript, he addressed himself directly to the author, in terms so candid and liberal, that it would be unjust to his memory to withhold from the public so pleasing a memorial of his character.

"By Dr. Blair's means, I have been favoured with the perusal of your performance, which I have read with great pleasure and attention. It is certainly very rare, that a piece so deeply philosophical is wrote with so much spirit, and affords so much entertainment to the reader; though I must still regret the disadvantages under which I read it, as I never had the whole performance at once before me, and could not be able fully to compare one part with another. To this reason, chiefly, I ascribe some obscurities, which, in spite of your short analysis or abstract, still seem to hang over your system. For I must do you the justice to own, that when I enter into your ideas, no man appears to express himself with greater perspicuity than you do; a talent which, above all others, is requisite in that species of literature which you have cultivated. There are some objections which I would willingly propose to the chapter, 'Of Sight,' did I not suspect that they proceed from my not sufficiently understanding it; and I am the more confirmed in this suspicion, as Dr. Blair tells me, that the former objections I made had been derived chiefly from that cause. I shall therefore forbear till the whole can be before me, and shall not at present propose any farther difficulties to your reasonings. I shall only say, that if you have been able to clear up these abstruse and important subjects, instead of being mortified, I shall be so vain as to pretend to a share of the praise; and shall think, that my errors, by having at least some coherence, had led you to make a more strict review of my principles, which were the common ones, and to perceive their futility.

"As I was desirous to be of some use to you, I kept a watchful eye all along over your style; but it is really so correct, and so good English, that I found not any thing worth the remarking. There is only one passage in this chapter, where you make use of the phrase *hinder to do,* instead of *hinder from doing,* which is the English one; but I could not find the passage when I sought for it. You may judge how unexceptionable the whole appeared to me, when I could remark so small a blemish. I beg my compliments to my friendly adversaries, Dr. Campbell and Dr. Gerard; and also to Dr. Gregory, whom I suspect to be of the same disposition, though he has not openly declared himself such."—

Of the particular doctrines contained in Dr. Reid's "Inquiry," I do not think it necessary here to attempt any abstract; nor indeed do his speculations (conducted as they were in strict conformity to the rules of inductive philosophizing) afford a subject for the same species of rapid outline, which is so useful in facilitating the study of a merely hypothetical theory. Their great object was to record and to classify the phenomena which the operations of the human mind present to those who reflect carefully on the subjects of their consciousness; and of such a history, it is manifest, that no abridgment could be offered with advantage. Some reflections on the peculiar plan adopted by the author, and on the general scope of his researches in this department of science, will afterwards find a more convenient place, when I shall have finished my account of his subsequent publications.

The idea of prosecuting the study of the human mind, on a plan analogous to that which had been so successively adopted in physics by the followers of Lord Bacon, if not first conceived by Dr. Reid, was at least first carried successfully into execution in his writings. An attempt had long before been announced by Mr. Hume, in the title-page of his "Treatise of Human Nature," to introduce the experimental method of reasoning into moral subjects; and some admirable remarks are made in the introduction to that work, on the errors into which his predecessors had been betrayed by the spirit of hypothesis; and yet it is now very generally admitted, that the whole of his own system rests on a principle for which there is no evidence but the authority of philosophers; and it is certain, that in no part of it has he aimed to investigate by a systematical analysis, those general principles of our constitution which can alone afford a synthetical explanation of its complicated phenomena.

I have often been disposed to think, that Mr. Hume's inattention to those rules of philosophizing which it was his professed, intention to exemplify, was owing in part to some indistinctness in his notions concerning their import. It does not appear, that, in the earlier part of his studies, he had paid much attention to the models of investigation exhibited in the writings of Newton and of his successors; and that he was by no means aware of the extraordinary merits of Bacon as a philosopher, nor of the influence which his writings have had on the subsequent progress of physical discovery, is demonstrated by the cold and qualified encomium which is bestowed on his genius, in one of the most elaborate passages of the " History of England."

In these respects, Dr. Reid possessed important advantages; familiarized from his early years to those experimental inquiries which, in the course of the two last centuries, have exalted natural philosophy to the dignity of a science; and determined strongly, by the peculiar bent of his genius, to connect every step in the progress of discovery with the history of the human mind. The influence of the general views opened in the " Novum Organon," may be traced in almost every page of his writings; and indeed, the circumstance by which these are so strongly and characteristically distinguished, is, that they exhibit the first systematical attempt to exemplify, in the study of human nature, the same plan of investigation which conducted Newton to the properties of light, and to the law of gravitation. It is from a steady adherence to this plan, and not from the superiority of his inventive powers, that he claims to himself any merit as a philosopher; and he seems even willing (with a modesty approaching to a fault) to abandon the praise of what is commonly called *genius*, to the authors of the systems which he was anxious to refute. " It is genius," he observes in one passage, " and not the want of it, that adulterates philosophy, and fills it with error and false theory. A creative imagination disdains the mean offices of digging for a foundation, of removing rubbish, and carrying materials: leaving these servile employments to the drudges of science, it plans a design, and raises a fabric. Invention supplies materials where they are wanting, and fancy adds colouring and every befitting ornament. The work pleases the eye, and wants nothing but solidity and a good foundation. It seems even to vie with the works of nature, till some succeeding architect blows it into ruins, and builds as goodly a fabric of his own in its place."

"Success in an inquiry of this kind," he observes farther, "it is not in human power to command; but perhaps it is possible, by caution and humility, to avoid error and delusion. The labyrinth may be too intricate, and the thread too fine, to be traced through all its windings; but, if we stop where we can trace it no farther, and secure the ground we have gained, there is no harm done; a quicker eye may in time trace it farther."

The unassuming language with which Dr. Reid endeavours to remove the prejudices naturally excited by a new attempt to philosophize on so unpromising, and hitherto so ungrateful a subject, recalls to our recollection those passages in which Lord Bacon—filled as his own imagination was with the future grandeur of the fabric founded by his hand—bespeaks the indulgence of his readers, for an enterprise apparently so hopeless and presumptuous. The apology he offers for himself, when compared with the height to which the structure of physical knowledge has since attained, may perhaps have some effect in attracting a more general attention to pursuits still more immediately interesting to mankind; and, at any rate, it forms the best comment on the prophetic suggestions in which Dr. Reid occasionally indulges himself concerning the future progress of moral speculation.

" Si homines per tanta annorum spatia viam veram inveniendi et colendi scientias tenuissent, nec tamen ulterius progredi potuissent, audax procul dubio et temeraria foret opinio, posse rem in ulterius provehi. Quod si in *via* ipsa erratum sit, atque hominum opera in iis consumpta in quibus minime oportebat, sequitur ex eo, non in rebus ipsis difficultatem oriri, quæ potestatis nostræ non sunt; sed in intellectu humano, ejusque usu et applicatione, quæ res remedium et medicinam suscipit."* . . . " De nobis ipsis silemus: de re autem quæ agitur, petimus; ut homines eam non opinionem, sed opus esse cogitent; ac pro certo habeant, non sectæ nos alicujus, aut placiti, sed utilitatis et amplitudinis humanæ fundamenta moliri. Præterea, ut bene sperent; neque Instaurationem nostram ut quiddam infinitum et ultra mortale fingant, et animo concipiant; quum revera sit infiniti erroris finis et terminus legitimus."†

* Nov. Org. 94. † Instaur. Mag.—Præfat.

The impression produced on the minds of speculative men by the publication of Dr. Reid's "Inquiry," was fully as great as could be expected from the nature of his undertaking. It was a work neither addressed to the multitude, nor level to their comprehension; and the freedom with which it canvassed opinions sanctioned by the highest authorities, was ill calculated to conciliate the favour of the learned. A few, however, habituated, like the author, to the analytical researches of the Newtonian school, soon perceived the extent of his views, and recognised in his pages the genuine spirit and language of inductive investigation. Among the members of this university, Mr. Ferguson was the first to applaud Dr. Reid's success; warmly recommending to his pupils a steady prosecution of the same plan, as the only effectual method of ascertaining the general principles of the human frame; and illustrating happily, by his own profound and eloquent disquisitions, the application of such studies, to the conduct of the understanding, and to the great concerns of life. I recollect, too, when I attended (about the year 1771) the lectures of the late Mr. Russell, to have heard high encomiums on the philosophy of Reid, in the course of those comprehensive discussions concerning the objects and the rules of experimental science, with which he so agreeably diversified the particular doctrines of physics. Nor must I omit this opportunity of paying a tribute to the memory of my old friend, Mr. Stevenson, then professor of logic, whose candid mind, at the age of seventy, gave a welcome reception to a system subversive of the theories which he had taught for forty years; and whose zeal for the advancement of knowledge prompted him, when his career was almost finished, to undertake the laborious task of new-modelling that useful compilation of elementary instruction, to which a singular diffidence of his own powers limited his literary exertions.

It is with no common feelings of respect and of gratitude, that I now recall the names of those to whom I owe my first attachment to these studies, and the happiness of a liberal occupation superior to the more aspiring aims of a servile ambition.

From the University of Glasgow, Dr. Reid's "Inquiry" received a still more substantial testimony of approbation; the author having been invited, in 1763, by that learned body, to the professorship of moral philosophy, then vacant by the resignation of Mr. Smith. The preferment was in many respects advantageous; affording an income considerably greater than he enjoyed at Aberdeen; and enabling him to concentrate to his favourite objects' that attention which had been hitherto distracted by the miscellaneous nature of his academical engagements. It was not, however, without reluctance, that he consented to tear himself from a spot where he had so long been fastening his roots; and, much as he loved the society in which he passed the remainder of his days, I am doubtful if, in his mind, it compensated the sacrifice of earlier habits and connexions.

Abstracting from the charm of local attachment, the University of Glasgow, at the time when Dr. Reid was adopted as one of its members, presented strong attractions to reconcile him to his change of situation. Robert Simson, the great restorer of ancient geometry, was still alive; and, although far advanced in years, preserved unimpaired his ardour in study, his relish for social relaxation, and his amusing singularities of humour. Dr. Moor combined with a gaiety and a levity foreign to this climate, the profound attainments of a scholar and of a mathematician. In Dr. Black, to whose fortunate genius a new world of science had just opened, Reid acknowledged an instructor and a guide; and met a simplicity of manners congenial to his own. The Wilsons (both father and son) were formed to attach his heart by the similarity of their scientific pursuits, and an entire sympathy with his views and sentiments. Nor was he less delighted with the good-humoured opposition which his opinions never failed to encounter in the acuteness of Millar,—then in the vigour of youthful genius, and warm from the lessons of a different school. Dr. Leechman, the friend and biographer of Hutcheson, was the official head of the college; and added the weight of a venerable name to the reputation of a community, which he had once adorned in a more active station.*

* James Moor, LL.D., author of a very ingenious fragment on Greek grammar, and of other philological essays. He was also distinguished by a profound acquaintance with ancient geometry. Dr. Simson, an excellent judge of his merits both in literature and science, has somewhere honoured him with

Animated by the zeal of such associates, and by the busy scenes which his new residence presented in every department of useful industry, Dr. Reid entered on his functions at Glasgow, with an ardour not common at the period of life which he had now attained. His researches concerning the human mind, and the principles of morals, which had occupied but an inconsiderable space in the wide circle of science, allotted to him by his former office, were extended and methodized in a course, which employed five hours every week, during six months of the year: the example of his illustrious predecessor, and the prevailing topics of conversation around him, occasionally turned his thoughts to commercial politics, and produced some ingenious essays on different questions connected with trade, which were communicated to a private society of his academical friends: his early passion for the mathematical sciences was revived by the conversation of Simson, Moor, and the Wilsons; and, at the age of fifty-five, he attended the lectures of Black, with a juvenile curiosity and enthusiasm.

As the substance of Dr. Reid's lectures at Glasgow (at least of that part of them which was most important and original) has been since given to the public in a more improved form, it is unnecessary for me to enlarge on the plan which he followed in the discharge of his official duties. I shall therefore only observe, that beside his " Speculations on the Intellectual and Active Powers of Man," and a " System of Practical Ethics," his course comprehended some general views with respect to natural jurisprudence, and the fundamental principles of politics. A few lectures on rhetoric, which were read, at a separate hour, to a more advanced class of students, formed a voluntary addition to the appropriate functions of his office, to which, it is probable, he was prompted, rather by a wish to supply what was then a deficiency in the established course of education, than by any predilection for a branch of study so foreign to his ordinary pursuits.

the following encomium: " Tum in Mathesi, tum in Græcis literis multum et feliciter versatus."

Alexander Wilson, M.D., and Patrick Wilson, Esq.; well known over Europe by their " Observations on the Solar Spots;" and many other valuable memoirs.

The merits of Dr. Reid, as a public teacher, were derived chiefly from that rich fund of original and instructive philosophy which is to be found in his writings; and from his unwearied assiduity in inculcating principles which he conceived to be of essential importance to human happiness. In his elocution and mode of instruction, there was nothing peculiarly attractive. He seldom, if ever, indulged himself in the warmth of extempore discourse; nor was his manner of reading calculated to increase the effect of what he had committed to writing. Such, however, was the simplicity and perspicuity of his style; such the gravity and authority of his character; and such the general interest of his young hearers in the doctrines which he taught, that by the numerous audiences to which his instructions were addressed, he was heard uniformly with the most silent and respectful attention. On this subject, I speak from personal knowledge; having had the good fortune, during a considerable part of the winter of 1772, to be one of his pupils.

It does not appear to me, from what I am now able to recollect of the order which he observed in treating the different parts of his subject, that he had laid much stress on systematical arrangement. It is probable, that he availed himself of whatever materials his private inquiries afforded, for his academical compositions; without aiming at the merit of combining them into *a whole*, by a comprehensive and regular design;—an undertaking, to which, if I am not mistaken, the established forms of his university, consecrated by long custom, would have presented some obstacles. One thing is certain, that neither he nor his immediate predecessor ever published any general *prospectus* of their respective plans; nor any *heads* or *outlines* to assist their students in tracing the trains of thought which suggested their various transitions.

The interest, however, excited by such details as these, even if it were in my power to render them more full and satisfactory, must necessarily be temporary and local; and I therefore hasten to observations of a more general nature, on the distinguishing characteristics of Dr. Reid's philosophical genius, and on the spirit and scope of those researches which he has bequeathed to posterity, concerning the phenomena and laws of the human mind. In mentioning his first performance on this subject, I have already anticipated a few remarks which are equally applicable to his subsequent publications; but the hints then suggested were too slight, to place in so strong a light as I could wish, the peculiarities of that mode of investigation, which it was the great object of his writings to recommend and to exemplify. His own anxiety, to neglect nothing that might contribute to its farther illustration, induced him, while his health and faculties were yet entire, to withdraw from his public labours; and to devote himself, with an undivided attention, to a task of more extensive and permanent utility. It was in the year 1781, that he carried this design into execution, at a period of life (for he was then upwards of seventy) when the infirmities of age might be supposed to account sufficiently for his retreat; but when, in fact, neither the vigour of his mind nor of his body seemed to have suffered any injury from time. The works which he published not many years afterwards, afford a sufficient proof of the assiduity with which he had availed himself of his literary leisure; his "Essays on the Intellectual Powers of Man" appearing in 1785; and those on the "Active Powers" in 1788.

As these two performances are, both of them, parts of one great work, to which his "Inquiry into the Human Mind" may be regarded as the introduction, I have reserved for this place whatever critical reflections I have to offer on his merits as an author; conceiving that they would be more likely to produce their intended effect, when presented at once in a connected form, than if interspersed, according to a chronological order, with the details of a biographical narrative.

SECTION II.

OBSERVATIONS ON THE SPIRIT AND SCOPE OF DR. REID'S PHILOSOPHY.

I HAVE already observed, that the distinguishing feature of Dr. Reid's philosophy, is the systematical steadiness, with which he has adhered in his inquiries, to that plan of investigation which is delineated in the "Novum Organon," and which has been so happily exemplified in physics by Sir Isaac Newton and his followers. To recommend this plan as the only effectual method of enlarging our knowledge of nature, was the favourite aim of all his studies, and a topic on which he thought he could not enlarge too much, in conversing or corresponding with his younger friends. In a letter to Dr. Gregory, which I have perused, he particularly congratulates him, upon his acquaintance with Lord Bacon's works; adding, " I am very apt to measure a man's understanding, by the opinion he entertains of that author."

It were perhaps to be wished, that he had taken a little more pains to illustrate the fundamental rules of that logic, the value of which he estimated so highly; more especially, to point out the modifications with which it is applicable to the science of mind. Many important hints, indeed, connected with this subject, may be collected from different parts of his writings; but I am inclined to think, that a more ample discussion of it in a preliminary dissertation, might have thrown light on the scope of many of his researches, and obviated some of the most plausible objections which have been stated to his conclusions.

It is not, however, my intention at present, to attempt to supply a desideratum of so great a magnitude;—an undertaking which, I trust, will find a more convenient place, in the farther prosecution of those speculations with respect to the intellectual powers which I have already submitted to the public. The detached remarks which follow, are offered merely as a supplement to what I have stated concerning the nature and object of this branch of study, in the introduction to the " Philosophy of the Human Mind."

The influence of Bacon's genius on the subsequent progress of physical discovery, has been seldom fairly appreciated; by some writers almost entirely overlooked; and by others considered as the sole cause of the reformation in science which has since taken place. Of these two extremes, the latter certainly is the least wide of the truth; for, in the whole history of letters, no other individual can be mentioned whose exertions have had so indisputable an effect in forwarding the intellectual progress of mankind. On the other hand, it must be acknowledged, that before the era when Bacon appeared, various philosophers in different parts of Europe had struck into the right path; and it may perhaps be doubted, whether any one important rule with respect to the true method of investigation be contained in his works, of which no hint can be traced in those of his predecessors. His great merit lay in concentrating their feeble and scattered lights; fixing the attention of philosophers on the distinguishing characteristics of true and of false science, by a felicity of illustration peculiar to himself, seconded by the commanding powers of a bold and figurative eloquence. The method of investigation which he recommended had been previously followed in every instance in which any solid discovery had been made with respect to the laws of nature; but it had been followed accidentally, and without any regular, preconceived design; and it was reserved for him to reduce to rule and method what others had effected, either fortuitously, or from some momentary glimpse of the truth. It is justly observed by Dr. Reid, that "the man who first discovered that cold freezes water, and that heat turns it into vapour, proceeded on the same general principle by which Newton discovered the law of gravitation and the properties of light. His 'Regulæ Philosophandi' are maxims of common sense, and are practised every day in common life; and he who philosophizes by other rules, either concerning the material system or concerning the mind, mistakes his aim."

These remarks are not intended to detract from the just glory of Bacon; for they apply to all those, without exception, who have systematized the principles of any of the arts. Indeed, they apply less forcibly to him than to any other philosopher whose studies have been directed to objects analogous to his; inasmuch as we know of no art, of which the rules have been reduced successfully into a didactic form, when the art itself was as much in infancy as experimental philosophy was when Bacon wrote. Nor must it be supposed that the utility was small of thus attempting to systematize the accidental processes of unenlightened ingenuity, and to give to the noblest exertions of human reason the same advantages of scientific method which have contributed so much to ensure the success of genius in pursuits of inferior importance. The very philosophical motto which Reynolds has so happily prefixed to his "Academical Discourses," admits, on this occasion, of a still more appropriate application: "Omnia fere quæ præceptis continentur ab ingeniosis hominibus fiunt; sed casu quodam magis quam scientia. Ideoque doctrina et animadversio adhibenda est, ut ea quæ interdum sine ratione nobis occurrunt, semper in nostra potestate sint; et quoties res postulaverit, a nobis ex præparato adhibeantur."—Almost all things set forth in precepts are produced by men of high intellectual powers; but it is rather by chance than through science. Wherefore learning and attention should be applied that we may have command even over those things which occur sometimes to us without reasoning; so that we may be prepared to make use of them when necessary.

But although a few superior minds seem to have been in some measure predisposed for that revolution in science which Bacon contributed so powerfully to accomplish, the case was very different with the great majority of those who were then most distinguished for learning and talents. His views were plainly too advanced for the age in which he lived; and, that he was sensible of this himself, appears from those remarkable passages in which he styles himself "the servant of posterity," and "bequeaths his fame to future times." Hobbes, who in his early youth had enjoyed his friendship, speaks, a considerable time after Bacon's death, of experimental philosophy in terms of contempt; influenced probably, not a little, by the tendency he perceived in the inductive method of inquiry, to undermine the foundations of that fabric of scepticism which it was the great object of his labours to rear. Nay, even during the course of the last century, it has been less from Bacon's own speculations than from the examples of sound investigation exhibited by a few eminent men, who professed to follow him as their guide, that the practical spirit of his writings has been caught by the multitude of physical experimentalists over Europe; truth and good sense descending gradually, in this as in other instances, by the force of imitation and of early habit, from the higher orders of intellect to the lower. In some parts of the continent, more especially, the circulation of Bacon's philosophical works has been surprisingly slow. It is doubtful whether Des Cartes himself ever perused them; and, as late as the year 1759, if we may credit Montucla, they were very little known in France. The introductory discourse prefixed by D'Alembert to the "Encyclopédie," first recommended them in that country to general attention.

The change which has taken place during the two last centuries in the plan of physical research, and the success which has so remarkably attended it, could not fail to suggest an idea, that something analogous might probably be accomplished at a future period, with respect to the phenomena of the intellectual world. And accordingly, various hints of this kind may be traced in different authors, since the era of Newton's discoveries. A memorable instance occurs in the prediction with which that great man concludes his " Optics : "—" That if natural philosophy in all its parts, by pursuing the inductive method, shall at length be perfected, the bounds of moral philosophy will also be enlarged." Similar remarks may be found in other publications; particularly in Mr. Hume's " Treatise of Human Nature," where the subject is enlarged on with much ingenuity. As far, however, as I am able to judge, Dr. Reid was the first who conceived justly and clearly the analogy between these two different branches of human knowledge, defining with precision the distinct provinces of observation and of reflection, in furnishing the data of all our reasonings concerning matter and mind; and demonstrating the necessity of a careful separation between the phenomena which they respectively exhibit, while we adhere to the same mode of philosophizing in investigating the laws of both.

That so many philosophers should have thus missed their aim, in prosecuting the study of the human mind, will appear the less surprising, when we consider in how many difficulties, peculiar to itself, this science is involved. It is sufficient at present to mention those which arise,—from the metaphorical origin of all the words which express the intellectual phenomena,—from the subtle and fugitive nature of the objects of our reasonings,—from the habits of inattention we acquire in early life, to the subjects of our consciousness,—and from the prejudices which early impressions and associations create to warp our opinions. It must be remembered, too, that in the science of mind (so imperfectly are its logical rules as yet understood) we have not the same checks on the abuses of our reasoning powers, which serve to guard us against error in our other researches. In physics, a speculative mistake is abandoned when contradicted by facts which strike the senses. In mathematics, an absurd or inconsistent conclusion is admitted as a demonstrative proof of a faulty hypothesis. But, in those inquiries which relate to the principles of human nature, the absurdities and inconsistencies to which we are led by almost all the systems hitherto proposed, instead of suggesting corrections and improvements on these systems, have too frequently had the effect of producing scepticism with respect to all of them alike. How melancholy is the confession of Hume!—" The intense view of these manifold contradictions and imperfections in human reason has so wrought upon me and heated my brain, that I am ready to reject all belief and reasoning, and can look upon no opinion even as more probable or likely than another."

Under these discouragements to this branch of study, it affords us some comfort to reflect on the great number of important facts with respect to the mind which are scattered in the writings of philosophers. As the subject of our inquiry here lies within our own breast, a considerable mixture of truth may be expected even in those systems which are most erroneous; not only because a number of men can scarcely be long imposed on by an hypothesis which is perfectly groundless, concerning the objects of their own consciousness; but because it is generally by an alliance with truth and with the original principles of human nature, that prejudices and associations produce their effects. Perhaps it may even be affirmed, that our progress in this research depends less on the degree of our industry and invention than on our sagacity and good sense in separating old discoveries from the errors which have been blended with them; and on that candid and dispassionate temper that may prevent us from being led astray by the love of novelty, or the affectation of singularity. In this respect, the science of mind possesses a very important advantage over that which relates to the laws of the material world. The former has been cultivated with more or less success in all ages and countries: the facts which serve as the basis of the latter have, with a very few exceptions, been collected during the course of the two last centuries. An observation similar to this is applied to systems of ethics by Mr. Smith, in his account of the theory of Mandeville; and the illustration he gives of it may be extended with equal propriety to the science of mind in general. " A system of natural philosophy," he remarks, " may appear very plausible, and be, for a long time, very generally received in the world, and yet have no foundation in nature, nor any sort of resemblance to the truth. But it is otherwise with systems of moral philosophy. When a traveller gives an account of some distant country, he may impose upon our credulity the most groundless and absurd fictions as the most certain matters of fact. But when a person pretends to inform us of what passes in our neighbourhood, and of the affairs of the very parish we live in, though here too, if we are so careless as not to examine things with our own eyes, he may deceive us in many respects; yet the greatest falsehoods which he imposes on us must bear some resemblance to the truth, and must even have a considerable mixture of truth in them."

These considerations demonstrate the essential importance, in this branch of study, of forming, at the commencement of our inquiries, just notions of the criteria of true and false science, and of the rules of philosophical investigation. They demonstrate, at the same time, that an attention to the rules of philosophizing, as they are exemplified in the physical researches of Newton and his followers, although the best of all preparations for an examination of the mental phenomena, is but one of the steps necessary to ensure our success. On an accurate comparison of the two subjects, it might probably appear, that after this preliminary step has been gained, the most arduous part of the process still remains. One thing is certain, that it is not from any defect in the power of ratiocination or deduction, that our speculative errors chiefly arise,—a fact of which we have a decisive proof in the facility with which most students may be taught the mathematical and physical sciences, when compared with the difficulty of leading their minds to the truth on questions of morals and politics.

The logical rules which lay the foundation of sound and useful conclusions concerning the laws of this internal world, although not altogether overlooked by Lord Bacon, were plainly not the principal object of his work; and what he has written on the subject, consists chiefly of detached hints dropt casually in the course of other speculations. A comprehensive view of the sciences and arts dependent on the philosophy of the human mind, exhibiting the relations which they bear to each other, and to the general system of human knowledge, would form a natural and useful introduction to the study of these logical principles; but such a view remains still a desideratum, after all the advances made towards it by Bacon and D'Alembert. Indeed, in the present improved state of things, much is wanting to complete and perfect that more simple part of their intellectual map which relates to the material universe.—Of the inconsiderable progress hitherto made towards a just delineation of the method to be pursued in studying the mental phenomena, no other evidence is necessary than this, That the sources of error and false judgment, so peculiarly connected, in consequence of the association of ideas, with studies in which our best interests are immediately and deeply concerned, have never yet been investigated with such accuracy, as to afford effectual aid to the student, in his attempts to counteract their influence. One of these sources alone,—that which arises from the imperfections of language,—furnishes an exception to the general remark. It attracted, fortunately, the particular notice of Locke, whose observations with respect to it, compose, perhaps, the most valuable part of his philosophical writings; and, since the time of Condillac, the subject has been still more deeply analyzed by others. Even on this article, much yet remains to be done; but enough has been already accomplished to justify the profound aphorism in which Bacon pointed it out to the attention of his followers:— " Credunt homines rationem suam verbis imperare; sed fit etiam ut verba vim suam super rationem retorqueant."*—Men suppose that their reason has command over words. Still it also happens that words exercise reaction on reason. (Nov. Organ. lix.)

Into these logical discussions concerning the means of advancing the philosophy of human nature, Dr. Reid has seldom entered; and still more rarely has he indulged himself in tracing the numerous relations, by which this philosophy is connected with the practical business of life. But he has done what was still more essential at the time he wrote; he has exemplified, with the happiest success, that method of investigation by which alone any solid progress can be made; directing his inquiries to a subject which forms a necessary groundwork for the labours of his successors,—an analysis of the various powers and principles belonging to our constitution. Of the importance of this undertaking, it is sufficient to observe, that it stands somewhat, although I confess not altogether, in the same relation to the different branches of intellectual and moral science, (such as gram-

* This passage of Bacon forms the motto to a very ingenious and philosophical dissertation, published by M. Prevost of Geneva,) entitled, " Des Signes envisagés relativement à leur Influence sur la Formation des Idées." Paris, an 8.

mar, rhetoric, logic, ethics, natural theology, and politics,) in which the anatomy of the human body stands to the different branches of physiology and pathology. And as a course of medical education naturally, or rather necessarily, begins with a general survey of man's animal frame; so, I apprehend, that the proper, or rather the essential preparation for those studies which regard our nobler concerns, is an examination of the principles which belong to man as an intelligent, active, social, and moral being. Nor does the importance of such an analysis rest here; it exerts an influence over all those sciences and arts which are connected with the material world; and the philosophy of Bacon itself, while it points out the road to physical truth, is but a branch of the philosophy of the human mind.

The substance of these remarks is admirably expressed by Mr. Hume in the following passage,—allowances being made for a few trifling peculiarities of expression, borrowed from the theories which were prevalent at the time when he wrote: " 'Tis evident, that all the sciences have a relation, greater or less, to human nature, and that, however wide any of them may seem to run from it, they still return back by one passage or another. Even mathematics, natural philosophy, and natural religion, are in some measure dependent on the science of man; since they lie under the cognizance of men, and are judged of by their powers and faculties. It is impossible to tell what changes and improvements we might make in these sciences, were we thoroughly acquainted with the extent and force of human understanding, and could explain the nature of the ideas we employ, and of the operations we perform in our reasonings.

" If, therefore, the sciences of mathematics, natural philosophy, and natural religion, have such a dependence on the knowledge of man, what may be expected in the other sciences, whose connexion with human nature is more close and intimate? The sole end of logic is to explain the principles and operations of our reasoning faculty, and the nature of our ideas: morals and criticism regard our tastes and sentiments: and politics consider men as united in society, and dependent on each other. In these four sciences of logic, morals, criticism, and politics, is comprehended almost every thing which it can any way import us to be acquainted with, or which can tend either to the improvement or ornament of the human mind.

"Here, then, is the only expedient from which we can hope for success in our philosophical researches; to leave the tedious, lingering method, which we have hitherto followed; and, instead of taking, now and then, a castle or village on the frontier, to march up directly to the capital or centre of these sciences, to human nature itself; which being once masters of, we may every where else hope for an easy victory. From this station, we may extend our conquests over all those sciences which more intimately concern human life, and may afterwards proceed at leisure to discover more fully those which are the objects of pure curiosity. There is no question of importance, whose decision is not comprised in the science of man; and there is none which can be decided with any certainty, before we become acquainted with that science."

To prepare the way for the accomplishment of the design so forcibly recommended in the foregoing quotation, by exemplifying, in an analysis of our most important intellectual and active principles, the only method of carrying it successfully into execution, was the great object of Dr. Reid, in all his various philosophical publications. In examining these principles, he had chiefly in view a vindication of those fundamental laws of belief which form the groundwork of human knowledge, against the attacks made on their authority in some modern systems of scepticism; leaving to his successors the more agreeable task of applying the philosophy of the mind to its practical uses. On the *analysis* and classification of our powers, which he has proposed, much room for improvement must have been left in so vast an undertaking; but imperfections of this kind do not necessarily affect the justness of his conclusions, even where they may suggest to future inquirers the advantages of a simpler arrangement, and a more definite phraseology. Nor must it be forgotten, that, in consequence of the plan he has followed, the mistakes which may be detected in particular parts of his works, imply no such weakness in the fabric he has reared, as might have been justly apprehended, had he presented a connected system founded on gratuitous hypotheses, or on arbitrary definitions. The detections, on the contrary, of his occasional errors, may be expected, from the invariable consistency and harmony of truth, to throw new lights on those parts of his work, where his inquiries have been more successful; as the correction of a particular misstatement in an authentic history, is often found, by completing an imperfect link, or reconciling a seeming contradiction, to dispel the doubts which hung over the most faithful and accurate details of the narrative.

In Dr. Reid's first performance, he confined himself entirely to the five senses, and the principles of our nature necessarily connected with them; reserving the further prosecution of the subject for a future period. At that time, indeed, he seems to have thought, that a more comprehensive examination of the mind was an enterprise too great for one individual. "The powers," he observes, "of memory, of imagination, of taste, of reasoning, of moral perception, the will, the passions, the affections, and all the active powers of the soul, present a boundless field of philosophical disquisition, which the author of this 'Inquiry' is far from thinking himself able to explore with accuracy. Many authors of ingenuity, ancient and modern, have made incursions into this vast territory, and have communicated useful observations; but there is reason to believe, that those who have pretended to give us a map of the whole, have satisfied themselves with a very inaccurate and incomplete survey. If Galileo had attempted a complete system of natural philosophy, he had probably done little service to mankind; but, by confining himself to what was within his comprehension, he laid the foundation of a system of knowledge, which rises by degrees, and does honour to the human understanding. Newton, building upon this foundation, and in like manner, confining his inquiries to the law of gravitation, and the properties of light, performed wonders. If he had attempted a great deal more, he had done a great deal less, and perhaps nothing at all. Ambitious of following such great examples, with unequal steps, alas! and unequal force, we have attempted an inquiry into one little corner only, of the human mind; that corner which seems to be most exposed to vulgar observation, and to be most easily comprehended; and yet, if we have delineated it justly, it must be acknowledged, that the accounts heretofore given of it were very lame, and wide of the truth."

From these observations, when compared with the magnitude of the work which the author lived to execute, there is some ground for supposing, that, in the progress of his researches, he became more and more sensible of the mutual connexion and dependence which exist among the conclusions we form concerning the various principles of human nature; even concerning those which seem, on a superficial view, to have the most remote relation to each other: and it was fortunate for the world, that, in this respect, he was induced to extend his views so far beyond the limits of his original design. His examination, indeed, of the powers of external perception, and of the questions immediately connected with them, bears marks of a still more minute diligence and accuracy than appear in some of his speculations concerning the other parts of our frame; and what he has written on the former subject, in his " Inquiry into the Human Mind," is evidently more highly finished both in matter and form, than the volumes which he published in his more advanced years. The value, however, of these is inestimable to future adventurers in the same arduous undertaking; not only, in consequence of the aids they furnish as a rough draught of the field to be examined, but, by the example they exhibit of a method of investigation on such subjects, hitherto very imperfectly understood by philosophers. It is by the originality of this method, so systematically pursued in all his researches, still more than by the importance of his particular conclusions, that he stands so conspicuously distinguished among those who have hitherto prosecuted analytically the study of man.

I have heard it sometimes mentioned, as a subject of regret, that the writers who have applied themselves to this branch of knowledge, have, in general, aimed at a great deal more than it was possible to accomplish; extending their researches to all the different parts of our constitution, while a long life might be well employed in examining and describing the phenomena connected with any one particular faculty. Dr. Reid, in a passage already quoted from his " Inquiry," might have been supposed to give some countenance to this opinion; if his own subsequent labours did not so strongly sanction the practice in question. The truth, I apprehend, is, that such detached researches concerning the human mind, can seldom be attempted with much hope of success; and that those who have recommended them, have not attended sufficiently to the circumstances which so remarkably distinguish this study from that which has for its object the philosophy of the material world. A few remarks in illustration of this proposition seem to me to be necessary, in order to justify the reasonableness of Dr. Reid's undertaking; and they will be found to apply with still greater force, to the labours of such as may wish to avail themselves of a similar analysis in explaining the varieties of human genius and character, or in developing the latent capacities of the youthful mind.

One consideration of a more general nature is, in the first place, worthy of notice; that in the infancy of every science, the grand and fundamental desideratum is a bold and comprehensive outline:—somewhat for the same reason, that, in the cultivation of an extensive country, forests must be cleared, and wildernesses reclaimed, before the limits of private property are fixed with accuracy; and long before the period, when the divisions and subdivisions of separate possessions give rise to the details of a curious and refined husbandry. The speculations of Lord Bacon embraced all the objects of human knowledge. Those of Newton and Boyle were confined to physics; but included an astonishing range of the material universe. The labours of their successors, in our own times, have been employed with no less zeal, in pursuing those more particular, but equally abstruse investigations, in which they were unable to engage, for want of a sufficient stock, both of facts and of general principles; and which did not perhaps interest their curiosity in any considerable degree.

If these observations are allowed to hold to a certain extent with respect to all the sciences, they apply in a more peculiar manner to the subjects treated of in Dr. Reid's writings;—subjects which are all so intimately connected, that it may be doubted, if it be possible to investigate any one completely, without some general acquaintance, at least, with the rest. Even the theory of the understanding may receive important lights from an examination of the active and the moral powers; the state of which in the mind of every individual, will be found to have a powerful influence on his intellectual character:—while, on the other hand, an accurate analysis of the faculties of the understanding, would probably go far to obviate the sceptical difficulties which have been started concerning the origin of our moral ideas. It appears to me, therefore, that, whatever be the department of mental science that we propose more particularly to cultivate, it is necessary to begin with a survey of human nature in all its various parts; studying these parts, however, not so much on their own account, as with a reference to the applications of which our conclusions are susceptible to our favourite purpose. The researches of Dr. Reid, when considered carefully in the relation which they bear to each other, afford numberless illustrations of the truth of this remark. His leading design was evidently to overthrow the modern system of scepticism; and at every successive step of his progress, new and unexpected lights break in on his fundamental principles.

It is, however, chiefly in their practical application to the conduct of the understanding, and the culture of the heart, that such partial views are likely to be dangerous; for here, they tend not only to mislead our theoretical conclusions, but to counteract our improvement and happiness. Of this I am so fully convinced, that the most faulty theories of human nature, provided only they embrace the whole of it, appear to me less mischievous in their probable effects, than those more accurate and microscopical researches which are habitually confined to one particular corner of our constitution. It is easy to conceive, that where the attention is wholly engrossed with the intellectual powers, the moral principles will be in danger of running to waste: and it is no less certain, on the other hand, that, by confining our care to the moral constitution alone, we may suffer the understanding to remain under the influence of unhappy prejudices, and destitute of those just and enlightened views, without which the worthiest dispositions are of little use, either to ourselves or to society. An exclusive attention to any one of the subordinate parts of our frame,—to the culture of taste (for example) or of the argumentative powers, or even to the refinement of our moral sentiments and feelings,—must be attended with a hazard proportionally greater.

"In forming the human character," says Bacon, in a passage which Lord Bolingbroke has pronounced to be one of the finest and deepest in his writings, "we must not proceed, as a statuary does in forming a statue, who works sometimes on the face, sometimes on the limbs, sometimes on the folds of the drapery;

but we must proceed (and it is in our power to proceed) as nature does in forming a flower, or any other of her productions;—she throws out altogether, and at once, the whole system of being, and the rudiments of all the parts. 'Rudimenta partium omnium simul parit et producit.'" *

Of this passage, so strongly marked with Bacon's capacious intellect, and so richly adorned with his " philosophical fancy," I will not weaken the impression by any comment; and, indeed, to those who do not intuitively perceive its evidence, no comment would be useful.

In what I have hitherto said of Dr. Reid's speculations, I have confined myself to such general views of the scope of his researches, and of his mode of philosophizing, as seemed most likely to facilitate the perusal of his works to those readers who have not been much conversant with these abstract disquisitions. A slight review of some of the more important and fundamental objections which have been proposed to his doctrines, may, I hope, be useful as a farther preparation for the same course of study.

Of these objections, the four following appear to me to be chiefly entitled to attention.

1. That he has assumed gratuitously in all his reasonings, that theory concerning the human soul, which the scheme of materialism calls in question.

2. That his views tend to damp the ardour of philosophical curiosity, by stating as ultimate facts, phenomena which may be resolved into principles more simple and general.

3. That, by an unnecessary multiplication of original or instinctive principles, he has brought the science of mind into a state more perplexed and unsatisfactory, than that in which it was left by Locke and his successors.

4. That his philosophy, by sanctioning an appeal from the decisions of the learned to the voice of the multitude, is unfavourable to a spirit of free inquiry, and lends additional stability to popular errors.

1. With respect to Dr. Reid's supposed assumption of a

* In the foregoing paragraph, I have borrowed (with a very trifling alteration) Lord Bolingbroke's words, in a beautiful paraphrase on Bacon's remark. —See his " Idea of a Patriot King."

doubtful hypothesis concerning the nature of the thinking and sentient principle, it is almost sufficient for me to observe, that the charge is directed against that very point of his philosophy in which it is most completely invulnerable. The circumstance which peculiarly characterises the inductive science of mind is, that it professes to abstain from all speculations concerning its nature and essence; confining the attention entirely to *phenomena,* for which we have the evidence of consciousness, and to the laws by which these phenomena are regulated. In this respect, it differs equally, in its scope, from the pneumatological discussions of the schools; and from the no less visionary theories, so loudly vaunted by the physiological metaphysicians of more modern times. Compared with the first, it differs, as the inquiries of the *mechanical* philosophers concerning the laws of moving bodies, differ from the discussions of the ancient sophists concerning the existence and the nature of motion. Compared with the other, the difference is analogous to what exists between the conclusions of Newton concerning the law of gravitation, and his *query* concerning the invisible ether of which he supposed it might, possibly, be the effect. The facts which this inductive science aims at ascertaining, rest on their own proper evidence;—an evidence unconnected with all these hypotheses, and which would not, in the smallest degree, be affected, although the truth of any one of them should be fully established. It is not, therefore, on account of its inconsistency with any favourite opinions of my own, that I would oppose the disquisitions either of scholastic pneumatology, or of physiological metaphysics; but because I consider them as an idle waste of time and genius on questions where our conclusions can neither be verified nor overturned by an appeal to experiment or observation. Sir Isaac Newton's query concerning the cause of gravitation was certainly not *inconsistent* with his own discoveries concerning its laws; but what would have been the consequences to the world, if he had indulged himself in the prosecution of hypothetical theories with respect to the former, instead of directing his astonishing powers to an investigation of the latter?

That the general spirit of Dr. Reid's philosophy is hostile to the conclusions of the materialists, is indeed a fact: not, however, because his system rests on the contrary hypothesis as a fundamental principle, but because his inquiries have a powerful tendency to wean the understanding gradually from those obstinate associations and prejudices, to which the common mechanical theories of mind owe all their plausibility. It is, in truth, much more from such examples of sound research concerning the laws of thought, than from any direct metaphysical refutation, that a change is to be expected in the opinions of those who have been accustomed to confound together two classes of phenomena, so completely and essentially different.—But this view of the subject does not belong to the present argument.

It has been recommended of late, by a medical author of great reputation, to those who wish to study the human mind, to begin with preparing themselves for the task by the study of anatomy. I must confess, I cannot perceive the advantages of this order of investigation; as the anatomy of the body does not seem to me more likely to throw light on the philosophy of the mind, than an analysis of the mind to throw light on the physiology of the body. To ascertain, indeed, the general laws of their connexion from facts established by observation or experiment, is a reasonable and most interesting object of philosophical curiosity; and in this inquiry, (which was long ago proposed and recommended by Lord Bacon,) a knowledge of the constitution both of mind and body is indispensably requisite; but even here, if we wish to proceed on firm ground, the two classes of facts must be kept completely distinct; so that neither of them may be warped or distorted, in consequence of theories suggested by their supposed relations or analogies.* Thus, in many of the phenomena connected with custom and habit, there is ample scope for investigating general laws, both with respect to our mental and our corporeal frame; but what light do we derive from such information concerning this part of our constitution as is contained in the following sentence of Locke? "Habits seem to be but trains of motion in the animal spirits, which, once set a-going, continue in the same steps they had been used to, which by often treading are worn into a smooth path." In like manner, the laws which regulate the connexion between the mind and our external organs, in the case of perception, have furnished a very fertile subject of examination to some

* Elements of the Philosophy of the Human Mind, pp. 11, 12, 2nd edit.

of the best of our modern philosophers; but how impotent does the genius of Newton itself appear, when it attempts to shoot the gulf which separates the sensible world, and the sentient principle? " Is not the sensorium of animals," he asks in one of his queries, " the place where the sentient substance is present, and to which the sensible species of things are brought through the nerves and brain, that they may be perceived by the mind present in that place?"

It ought to be remembered also, that this inquiry, with respect to the laws regulating the connexion between our bodily organization, and the phenomena subjected to our own consciousness, is but one particular department of the philosophy of the mind; and that there still remains a wide and indeed boundless region, where all our data must be obtained from our own mental operations. In examining, for instance, the powers of judgment and reasoning, let any person of sound understanding, after perusing the observations of Bacon on the different classes of our prejudices, or those of Locke on the abuse of words, turn his attention to the speculations of some of our contemporary theorists; and he will at once perceive the distinction between the two modes of investigation which I wish at present to contrast. " Reasoning," says one of the most ingenious and original of these, " is that operation of the sensorium, by which we excite two or many tribes of ideas; and then re-excite the ideas, in which they differ or correspond. If we determine this difference, it is called Judgment; if we in vain endeavour to determine it, it is called Doubting.—If we re-excite the ideas in which they differ, it is called Distinguishing; if we re-excite those in which they correspond, it is called Comparing."*—In what acceptation the word *idea* is to be understood in the foregoing passage, may be learned from the following definition of the same author :— " The word *idea* has various meanings in the writers of metaphysics: it is here used simply for those notions of external things, which our organs of sense bring us acquainted with originally; and is defined, a contraction, or motion, or configuration, of the fibres, which constitute the immediate organ of sense."† Mr. Hume, who was less of a physiologist than Dr. Darwin, has made use of a language by no means so theoretical

* Zoonomia, vol. i. p. 181, 3rd edit. † Ibid. vol. i. pp. 11, 12.

and arbitrary; but still widely removed from the simplicity and precision essentially necessary in studies, where everything depends on the cautious use of terms. "Belief," according to him, is "a lively idea related to or associated with a present impression; memory is the faculty by which we repeat our impressions, so as that they retain a considerable degree of their first vivacity, and are somewhat intermediate betwixt an idea and an impression."

According to the views of Dr. Reid, the terms which express the simple powers of the mind, are considered as unsusceptible of definition or explanation; the words, feeling, for example, knowledge, will, doubt, belief, being, in this respect, on the same footing with the words, green or scarlet, sweet or bitter. To the names of these mental operations, all men annex some notions, more or less distinct; and the only way of conveying to them notions more correct, is by teaching them to exercise their own powers of reflection. The definitions quoted from Hume and Darwin, even if they were more unexceptionable in point of phraseology, would, for these reasons, be unphilosophical, as attempts to simplify what is incapable of analysis; but, as they are actually stated, they not only envelop truth in mystery, but lay a foundation, at the very outset, for an erroneous theory. It is worth while to add, that of the two theories in question, that of Darwin, how inferior soever, in the estimation of competent judges, as a philosophical work, is by far the best calculated to impose on a very wide circle of readers, by the mixture it exhibits of crude and visionary metaphysics, with those important facts and conclusions which might be expected from the talents and experience of such a writer, in the present advanced state of medical and physiological science. The questions which have been hitherto confined to a few, prepared for such discussions by habits of philosophical study, are thus submitted to the consideration,—not only of the cultivated and enlightened minds, which adorn the medical profession,—but of the half-informed multitude who follow the medical trade. Nor is it to be doubted, that many of these will give the author credit upon subjects of which they feel themselves incompetent to judge, for the same ability which he displays within their own professional sphere. The hypothetical principles assumed by

Hume are intelligible to those only who are familiarized to the language of the schools; and his ingenuity and elegance, captivating as they are to men of taste and refinement, possess slight attractions to the majority of such as are most likely to be misled by his conclusions.

After all, I do not apprehend that the physiological theories concerning the mind, which have made so much noise of late, will produce a very lasting impression. The splendour of Dr. Darwin's accomplishments could not fail to bestow a temporary importance on whatever opinions were sanctioned by his name; as the chemical discoveries which have immortalized that of Priestley, have, for a while, recalled from oblivion the reveries of Hartley. But, abstracting from these accidental instances, in which human reason seems to have held a retrograde course, there has certainly been, since the time of Des Cartes, a continual, and, on the whole, a very remarkable approach to the inductive plan of studying human nature. We may trace this in the writings even of those who profess to consider *thought* merely as *an agitation of the brain;* in the writings more particularly of Hume and of Helvetius; both of whom, although they may have occasionally expressed themselves in an unguarded manner concerning the nature of mind, have, in their most useful and practical disquisitions, been prevented, by their own good sense, from blending any theory with respect to the *causes* of the intellectual phenomena with the history of facts, or the investigation of general laws. The authors who form the most conspicuous exceptions to this gradual progress, consist chiefly of men whose errors may be easily accounted for, by the prejudices connected with their circumscribed habits of observation and inquiry; of physiologists, accustomed to attend to that part alone of the human frame which the knife of the anatomist can lay open; or of chemists, who enter on the analysis of thought, fresh from the decompositions of the laboratory; carrying into the theory of mind itself (what Bacon expressively calls) " the smoke and tarnish of the furnace." Of the value of such pursuits, none can think more highly than myself; but I must be allowed to observe, that the most distinguished pre-eminence in them does not necessarily imply a capacity of collected and abstracted reflection, or an understanding superior to the prejudices of early association, and the illusions of popular language. I will not go so far as Cicero, when he ascribes to those who possess these advantages a more than ordinary vigour of intellect: " Magni est ingenii revocare mentem a sensibus, et cogitationem a consuetudine abducere." "It is characteristic of great genius to be able to call away the mind from objects of sense, and abstract the thoughts from those that are customary." I would only claim for them the merit of patient and cautious research; and would exact from their antagonists the same qualifications.*

In offering these remarks, I have no wish to exalt any one branch of useful knowledge at the expense of another, but to combat prejudices equally fatal to the progress of them all. With the same view, I cannot help taking notice of a prevailing, but very mistaken idea, that the formation of a hypothetical system is a stronger proof of inventive genius than the patient investigation of nature, in the way of induction. To form a system, appears to the young and inexperienced understanding a species of creation; to ascend slowly to general conclusions, from the observation and comparison of particular facts, is to comment servilely on the works of another.

No opinion surely can be more groundless. To fix on a few principles, or even on a single principle as the foundation of a theory; and, by an artful statement of supposed facts, aided by a dexterous use of language, to give a plausible explanation, by means of it, of an immense number of phenomena; is within the reach of most men whose talents have been a little exercised among the subtleties of the schools: whereas, to follow nature through all her varieties with a quick yet an exact eye; to re-

* A writer of great talents (after having reproached Dr. Reid with " a gross ignorance, disgraceful to the university of which he was a member,") boasts of the trifling expense of time and thought which it had cost himself to overturn his philosophy. " Dr. Oswald is pleased to pay me a compliment in saying, that ' I might employ myself to more advantage to the public, by pursuing other branches of science, than by deciding rashly on a subject which he sees I have not studied.' In return to this compliment, I shall not affront him by telling him how very little of my time this business has hitherto taken up. If he alludes to my *experiments*, I can assure him that I have lost no time at all; for having been intent upon such as require the use of a burning lens, I believe I have not lost one hour of sunshine on this account. And the public may perhaps be informed, some time or other, of what I have been doing in the *sun*, as well as in the *shade*."—Examination of Reid's Inquiry, &c. p. 357. See also pp. 101, 102, of the same work.

cord faithfully what she exhibits, and to record nothing more;—to trace, amidst the diversity of her operations, the simple and comprehensive laws by which they are regulated, and sometimes to guess at the beneficent purposes to which they are subservient,—may be safely pronounced to be the highest effort of a created intelligence. And, accordingly, the number of ingenious theorists has, in every age, been great; that of sound philosophers has been wonderfully small, or rather, they are only beginning now to have a glimpse of their way, in consequence of the combined lights furnished by their predecessors.

Des Cartes aimed at a complete system of physics, deduced *à priori* from the abstract suggestions of his own reason: Newton aspired no higher than at a faithful " interpretation of nature," in a few of the more general laws which she presents to our notice; and yet the intellectual power displayed in the voluminous writings of the former vanishes into nothing, when compared with what we may trace in a single page of the latter. On this occasion a remark of Lord Bacon appears singularly apposite; that " Alexander and Cæsar, though they acted without the aid of magic or prodigy, performed exploits that are truly greater than what fable reports of King Arthur or Amadis de Gaul."

I shall only add farther on this head, that the last observation holds more strictly with respect to the philosophy of the human mind than any other branch of science; for there is no subject whatever on which it is so easy to form theories calculated to impose on the multitude; and none where the discovery of truth is attended with so many difficulties. One great cause of this is, the analogical or theoretical terms employed in ordinary language to express every thing relating either to our intellectual or active powers; in consequence of which, specious explanations of the most mysterious phenomena may be given to superficial inquirers; while, at the same time, the labour of just investigation is increased to an incalculable degree.

2. To allege, that in this circumscription of the field of our inquiries concerning the mind, there is any tendency to repress a reasonable and philosophical curiosity, is a charge no less unfounded than the former; inasmuch as every physical inquiry concerning the material world is circumscribed by limits precisely analogous. In all our investigations, whatever their subject may be, the business of philosophy is confined to a reference

of particular facts to other facts more general; and our most successful researches must at length terminate in some law of nature, of which no explanation can be given. In its application to Dr. Reid's writings, this objection has, I think, been more pointedly directed against his reasonings concerning the process of nature in perception; a part of his writings which (as it is of fundamental importance in his general system) he has laboured with peculiar care. The result is, indeed, by no means flattering to the pride of those theorists who profess to explain every thing; for it amounts to an acknowledgment, that, after all the lights which anatomy and physiology supply, the information we obtain, by means of our senses, concerning the existence and the qualities of matter, is no less incomprehensible to our faculties than it appears to the most illiterate peasant; and that all we have gained is a more precise and complete acquaintance with some particulars in our animal economy,—highly interesting indeed when regarded in their proper light, as accessions to our physical knowledge, but, considered in connexion with the philosophy of the mind, affording only a more accurate statement of the astonishing phenomena which we would vainly endeavour to explain. This language has been charged, but most unjustly and ignorantly, with *mysticism;* for the same charge may be brought, with equal fairness, against all the most important discoveries in the sciences. It was in truth the very objection urged against Newton, when his adversaries contended, that *gravity* was to be ranked with the *occult qualities* of the schoolmen, till its mechanical cause should be assigned; and the answer given to this objection by Sir Isaac Newton's commentator, Mr. Maclaurin, may be literally applied, in the instance before us, to the inductive philosophy of the human mind.

"The opponents of Newton, finding nothing to object to his observations and reasonings, pretended to find a resemblance between his doctrines and the exploded tenets of the scholastic philosophy. They triumphed mightily in treating gravity as an occult quality, because he did not pretend to deduce this principle fully from its cause. I know not that ever it was made an objection to the circulation of the blood, that there is no small difficulty in accounting for it mechanically. They, too, who first extended gravity to air, vapour, and to all bodies round the earth, had their praise; though the cause of gravity was as obscure as before; or *rather appeared more mysterious*, after they had shown, that there was no body found near the earth, exempt from gravity, that might be supposed to be its cause. Why then were his admirable discoveries, by which this principle was extended over the universe, so ill relished by some philosophers? The truth is, he had, with great evidence, overthrown the boasted schemes by which they pretended to unravel all the mysteries of nature; and the philosophy he introduced, in place of them, carrying with it a sincere confession of our being far from a complete and perfect knowledge of it, could not please those who had been accustomed to imagine themselves possessed of the eternal reasons and primary causes of all things.

" It was, however, no new thing that this philosophy should meet with opposition. All the useful discoveries that were made in former times, and particularly in the seventeenth century, had to struggle with the prejudices of those who had accustomed themselves, not so much as to think but in a certain systematic way; who could not be prevailed on to abandon their favourite schemes, while they were able to imagine the least pretext for continuing the dispute. Every art and talent was displayed to support their falling cause; no aid seemed foreign to them that could in any manner annoy their adversary; and such often was their obstinacy, that truth was able to make little progress, till they were succeeded by younger persons, who had not so strongly imbibed their prejudices."

These excellent observations are not the less applicable to the subject now under consideration, that the part of Dr. Reid's writings which suggested the quotation, leads only to the correction of an inveterate prejudice, not to any new general conclusion. It is probable, indeed, (now that the Ideal Theory has in a great measure disappeared from our late metaphysical systems,) that those who have a pleasure in detracting from the merits of their predecessors, may be disposed to represent it as an idle waste of labour and ingenuity to have entered into a serious refutation of an hypothesis at once gratuitous and inconceivable. A different judgment, however, will be formed by such as are acquainted with the extensive influence which, from the earliest accounts of science, this single prejudice has had in vitiating almost every branch of the philosophy of the mind; and who, at the same time, recollect the names of the illustrious men, by whom, in more modern times, it has been adopted as an incontrovertible principle. It is sufficient for me to mention those of Berkeley, Hume, Locke, Clarke, and Newton. To the two first of these, it has served as the basis of their sceptical conclusions, which seem indeed to follow from it as necessary consequences; while the others repeatedly refer to it in their reasonings, as one of those facts concerning the mind, of which it would be equally superfluous to attempt a proof or a refutation.

I have enlarged on this part of Dr. Reid's writings the more fully as he was himself disposed, on all occasions, to rest upon it his chief merit as an author. In proof of this, I shall transcribe a few sentences from a letter of his to Dr. Gregory, dated 20th August, 1790.

" It would be want of candour not to own, that I think there is some merit in what you are pleased to call *my philosophy ;* but I think it lies chiefly in having called in question the common theory of *ideas or images of things in the mind* being the only objects of thought; a theory founded on natural prejudices, and so universally received as to be interwoven with the structure of language. Yet were I to give you a detail of what led me to call in question this theory, after I had long held it as self-evident and unquestionable, you would think, as I do, that there was much of chance in the matter. The discovery was the birth of time, not of genius; and Berkeley and Hume did more to bring it to light than the man that hit upon it. I think there is hardly any thing that can be called *mine* in the philosophy of the mind which does not follow with ease from the detection of this prejudice.

" I must, therefore, beg of you most earnestly, to make no contrast in my favour to the disparagement of my predecessors in the same pursuit. I can truly say of them, and shall always avow, what you are pleased to say of me, that but for the assistance I have received from their writings, I never could have wrote or thought what I have done."

3. Somewhat connected with the last objection are the censures which have been so frequently bestowed on Dr. Reid for an unnecessary and unsystematical multiplication of original or instinctive principles.

In reply to these censures, I have little to add to what I have remarked on the same topic, in the "Philosophy of the Human Mind." That the fault which is thus ascribed to Dr. Reid has been really committed by some ingenious writers in this part of the island, I most readily allow; nor will I take upon me to assert, that he has in no instance fallen into it himself. Such instances, however, will be found, on an accurate examination of his works, to be comparatively few, and to bear a very trifling proportion to those in which he has most successfully and decisively displayed his acuteness in exposing the premature and flimsy generalizations of his predecessors.

A certain degree of leaning to that extreme to which Dr. Reid seems to have inclined, was, at the time when he wrote, much safer than the opposite bias. From the earliest ages, the sciences in general, and more particularly the science of the human mind, have been vitiated by an undue love of simplicity; and in the course of the last century this disposition, after having been long displayed in subtile theories concerning the active powers, or the principles of human conduct, has been directed to similar refinements with respect to the faculties of the understanding, and the truths with which they are conversant. Mr. Hume himself has coincided so far with the Hartleian school, as to represent the "principle of union and cohesion among our simple ideas as a kind of *attraction*, of as universal application in the mental world as in the natural;"* and Dr. Hartley, with a still more sanguine imagination, looked forward to an era "when future generations shall put all kinds of evidences and inquiries into mathematical forms, reducing Aristotle's ten categories, and Bishop Wilkins's forty summa genera, to the head of quantity alone, so as to make mathematics and logic, natural history and civil history, natural philosophy and philosophy of all other kinds, coincide omni exparte."†

It is needless to remark the obvious tendency of such premature generalizations to withdraw the attention from the study of particular phenomena; while the effect of Reid's mode of philosophizing, even in those instances where it is carried to an excess, is to detain us, in this preliminary step, a little longer

* Treatise of Human Nature, vol. i. p. 30.
† Hartley on Man, p. 207, London, 1791.

than is absolutely necessary. The truth is, that when the phenomena are once ascertained, generalization is here of comparatively little value, and a task of far less difficulty than to observe facts with precision, and to record them with fairness.

In no part of Dr. Reid's writings, I am inclined to think, could more plausible criticisms be made on this ground, than in his classification of our active principles; but even there, the facts are always placed fully and distinctly before the reader. That several of the benevolent affections which he has stated as ultimate facts in our constitution, might be analyzed into the same general principle differently modified, according to circumstances, there can, in my opinion, be little doubt. This, however, (as I have elsewhere observed,*) notwithstanding the stress which has been sometimes laid upon it, is chiefly a question of arrangement. Whether we suppose these affections to be all ultimate facts, or some of them to be resolvable into other facts more general; they are equally to be regarded as constituent parts of human nature; and, upon either supposition, we have equal reason to admire the wisdom with which that nature is adapted to the situation in which it is placed. The laws which regulate the acquired perceptions of sight, are surely as much a part of our frame as those which regulate any of our original perceptions; and, although they require, for their development, a certain degree of experience and observation in the individual, the uniformity of the result shows, that there is nothing arbitrary nor accidental in their origin. In this point of view, what can be more philosophical, as well as beautiful, than the words of Mr. Ferguson, that "natural affection springs up in the soul of the mother, as the milk springs in her breast, to furnish nourishment to her child!"—" The effect is here to the race," as the same author has excellently observed, "what the vital motion of the heart is to the individual; too necessary to the preservation of nature's works, to be intrusted to the precarious will or intention of those most nearly concerned."†

The question, indeed, concerning the origin of our different

* Outlines of Moral Philosophy, pp. 79, 80, 2nd edit. Edin. 1801.

† Principles of Moral and Political Science, Part i. chap. i. sect. 3, "Of the principles of society in human nature."—The whole discussion unites, in a singular degree, the soundest philosophy with the most eloquent description.

affections, leads to some curious analytical disquisitions; but is of very subordinate importance to those inquiries which relate to their laws, and uses, and mutual references. In many ethical systems, however, it seems to have been considered as the most interesting subject of disquisition which this wonderful part of our frame presents.

In Dr. Reid's "Essays on the Intellectual Powers of Man," and in his "Inquiry into the Human Mind," I recollect little that can justly incur a similiar censure; notwithstanding the ridicule which Dr. Priestley has attempted to throw on the last of these performances, in his "Table of Reid's Instinctive Principles."* To examine all the articles enumerated in that table, would require a greater latitude of disquisition than the limits of this memoir allow; and, therefore, I shall confine my observations to a few instances, where the precipitancy of the general criticism seems to me to admit of little dispute. In this light I cannot help considering it, when applied to those dispositions or determinations of the mind, to which Dr. Reid has given the names of the "principle of credulity," and the "principle of veracity." How far these titles are happily chosen, is a question of little moment; and on that point I am ready to make every concession. I contend only for what is essentially connected with the objection which has given rise to these remarks.

"That any man," says Dr. Priestley, "should imagine that a peculiar instinctive principle was necessary to explain our giving credit to the relations of others, appears to me, who have been used to see things in a different light, very extraordinary; and yet this doctrine is advanced by Dr. Reid, and adopted by Dr. Beattie. But really," he adds, "what the former says in favour of it, is hardly deserving of the slightest notice.†"

The passage quoted by Dr. Priestley, in justification of this very peremptory decision, is as follows: "If credulity were the effect of reasoning and experience, it must grow up and gather strength in the same proportion as reason and experience do. But if it is the gift of nature, it will be the strongest in childhood, and limited and restrained by experience; and the most superficial view of human life shows that this last is the case, and not the first."

* Examination of Reid's Inquiry, &c. London, 1774.   † Ibid. p. 82.

To my own judgment, this argument of Dr. Reid's, when connected with the excellent illustrations which accompany it, carries complete conviction; and I am confirmed in my opinion by finding that Mr. Smith (a writer inferior to none in acuteness, and strongly disposed by the peculiar bent of his genius, to simplify, as far as possible, the philosophy of human nature,) has, in the latest edition of his "Theory of Moral Sentiments," acquiesced in this very conclusion; urging in support of it the same reasoning which Dr. Priestley affects to estimate so lightly. " There seems to be in young children an instinctive disposition to believe whatever they are told. Nature seems to have judged it necessary for their preservation that they should, for some time at least, put implicit confidence in those to whom the care of their childhood, and of the earliest and most necessary part of their education, is intrusted. Their credulity, accordingly, is excessive, and it requires long and much experience of the falsehood of mankind to reduce them to a reasonable degree of diffidence and distrust."*—That Mr. Smith's opinion also coincided with Dr. Reid's, in what he has stated concerning the "principle of veracity," appears evidently from the remarks which immediately follow the passage just quoted.—But I must not add to the length of this memoir by unnecessary citations.

Another instinctive principle mentioned by Reid is, "our belief of the continuance of the present course of nature."— " All our knowledge of nature," he observes, " beyond our original perceptions, is got by experience, and consists in the interpretation of natural signs. The appearance of the sign is followed by the belief of the thing signified. Upon this principle of our constitution, not only acquired perception, but also inductive reasoning, and all reasoning from analogy, is grounded; and, therefore, for want of a better name, we shall beg leave to call it the "inductive principle." It is from the force of this principle that we immediately assent to that axiom, upon which all our knowledge of nature is built, that effects of the same kind must have the same cause. Take away the light of this inductive principle, and experience is as blind as a mole. She may, indeed, feel what is present, and what immediately touches her,

---

* Smith's "Theory," last edit. Part VII. sect. 4.

but she sees nothing that is either before or behind, upon the right hand or upon the left, future or past."

On this doctrine, likewise, the same critic has expressed himself with much severity; calling it "a mere quibble;" and adding, "Every step that I take among this writer's sophisms, raises my astonishment higher than before." In this, however, as in many other instances, he has been led to censure Dr. Reid, not because he was able to see farther than his antagonist, but because he did not see quite so far. Turgot, in an article inserted in the French "Encyclopédie," and Condorcet, in a discourse prefixed to one of his mathematical publications,* have, both of them, stated the fact with a true philosophical precision; and, after doing so, have deduced from it an inference, not only the same in substance with that of Dr. Reid, but almost expressed in the same form of words.

In these references, as well as in that already made to Mr. Smith's "Theory," I would not be understood to lay any undue stress on authority in a philosophical argument. I wish only, by contrasting the modesty and caution resulting from habits of profound thought, with that theoretical intrepidity which a blindness to insuperable difficulties has a tendency to inspire, to invite those whose prejudices against this part of Reid's system rest chiefly on the great names to which they conceive it to be hostile, to re-examine it with a little more attention, before they pronounce finally on its merits.

The prejudices which are apt to occur against a mode of philosophizing so mortifying to scholastic arrogance, are encouraged greatly by that natural disposition to refer particular facts to general laws, which is the foundation of all scientific arrangement; a principle of the utmost importance to our intellectual constitution, but which requires the guidance of a sound and experienced understanding to accomplish the purposes for which it was destined. They are encouraged, also, in no inconsiderable degree, by the acknowledged success of mathematicians, in raising, on the basis of a few simple data, the most magnificent, and at the same time the most solid fabric of science, of which

---

* Essai sur l'Application de l'Analyse à la Probabilité des Decisions rendues à la Pluralité des Voix.—Paris, 1785.

human genius can boast. The absurd references which logicians are accustomed to make to Euclid's "Elements of Geometry," as a model which cannot be too studiously copied, both in physics and in morals, have contributed, in this as in a variety of other instances, to mislead philosophers from the study of facts into the false refinements of hypothetical theory.

On these misapplications of mathematical method to sciences which rest ultimately on experiment and observation, I shall take another opportunity of offering some strictures. At present, it is sufficient to remark the peculiar nature of the truths about which pure or abstract mathematics are conversant. As these truths have all a necessary connexion with each other, (all of them resting ultimately on those definitions or hypotheses which are the principles of our reasoning,) the beauty of the science cannot fail to increase in proportion to the simplicity of the data, compared with the incalculable variety of consequences which they involve. And to the simplifications and generalizations of theory on such a subject, it is perhaps impossible to conceive any limit. How different is the case in those inquiries where our first principles are not *definitions* but *facts;* and where our business is not to trace necessary connexions, but the laws which regulate the established order of the universe!

In various attempts which have been lately made, more especially on the Continent, towards a systematical exposition of the elements of physics, the effects of the mistake I am now censuring are extremely remarkable. The happy use of mathematical principles exhibited in the writings of Newton and his followers, having rendered an extensive knowledge of them an indispensable preparation for the study of the mechanical philosophy, the early habits of thought acquired in the former pursuit are naturally transferred to the latter. Hence the illogical and obscure manner in which its elementary principles have frequently been stated; an attempt being made to deduce from the smallest possible number of data the whole system of truths which it comprehends. The analogy existing among some of the fundamental laws of mechanics, bestows, in the opinion of the multitude, an appearance of plausibility on such attempts; and their obvious tendency is to withdraw the attention from that unity of design which it is the noblest employment of philosophy to illustrate, by disguising it under the semblance of an eternal and necessary order, similar to what the mathematician delights to trace among the mutual relations of quantities and figures.

These slight hints may serve as a reply in part to what Dr. Priestley has suggested with respect to the consequences likely to follow, if the spirit of Reid's philosophy should be introduced into physics.* One consequence would unquestionably be, a careful separation between the principles which we learn from experience alone, and those which are fairly resolvable by mathematical or physical reasoning, into other facts still more general; and, of course, a correction of that false logic, which, while it throws an air of mystery over the plainest and most undeniable facts, levels the study of nature, in point of moral interest, with the investigations of the geometer or of the algebraist.

It must not, however, be supposed, that, in the present state of natural philosophy, a false logic threatens the same dangerous effects as in the philosophy of the mind. It may retard somewhat the progress of the student at his first outset; or it may confound, in his apprehensions, the harmony of systematical order with the consistency and mutual dependency essential to a series of mathematical theorems: but the fundamental truths of physics are now too well established, and the checks which it furnishes against sophistry are too numerous and palpable to admit the possibility of any permanent error in our deductions. In the philosophy of the mind, so difficult is the acquisition of those habits of reflection which can alone lead to a correct knowledge of the intellectual phenomena, that a faulty hypothesis, if skilfully fortified by the imposing, though illusory strength of arbitrary definitions and a systematical phraseology, may maintain its ground for a succession of ages.

It will not, I trust, be inferred from any thing I have here advanced, that I mean to offer an apology for those who, either in physics or morals, would presumptuously state their own opinions with respect to the laws of nature, as a bar against future attempts to simplify and generalize them still farther. To assert, that none of the mechanical explanations yet given of

* Examination of Dr. Reid's Inquiry, p. 110.

gravitation are satisfactory, and even to hint, that ingenuity might be more profitably employed than in the search of such a theory, is something different from a gratuitous assumption of ultimate facts in physics; nor does it imply an obstinate determination to resist legitimate evidence, should some fortunate inquirer—contrary to what seems probable at present—succeed where the genius of Newton has failed. If Dr. Reid has gone farther than this in his conclusions concerning the principles which he calls original or instinctive, he has departed from that guarded language in which he commonly expresses himself; for all that it was of importance for him to conclude was, that the theories of his predecessors were, in these instances, exceptionable; and the doubts he may occasionally insinuate, concerning the success of future adventurers, so far from betraying any overweening confidence in his own understanding, are an indirect tribute to the talents of those, from whose failure he draws an argument against the possibility of their undertaking.

The same eagerness to simplify and to generalize, which led Priestley to complain of the number of Reid's instinctive principles, has carried some later philosophers a step farther. According to them, the very word *instinct* is unphilosophical; and every thing either in man or brute which has been hitherto referred to this mysterious source, may be easily accounted for by experience or imitation. A few instances in which this doctrine appears to have been successfully verified, have been deemed sufficient to establish it without any limitation.

In a very original work, on which I have already hazarded some criticisms, much ingenuity has been employed in analysing the wonderful efforts which the human infant is enabled to make for its own preservation the moment after its introduction to the light. Thus, it is observed, that the fœtus, while still in the uterus, learns to perform the operation of swallowing; and also learns to relieve itself, by a change of posture, from the irksomeness of continued rest: and, therefore, (if we admit these propositions,) we must conclude, that some of the actions which infants are vulgarly supposed to perform in consequence of instincts coeval with birth, are only a continuation of actions to which they were determined at an earlier period of their being. The remark is ingenious, and it may, perhaps, be just; but it does not prove, that *instinct* is an unphilosophical term; nor does it render the operations of the infant less mysterious than they seem to be on the common supposition. How far soever the analysis, in such instances, may be carried, we must at last arrive at some phenomenon no less wonderful than that we mean to explain: in other words, we must still admit, as an ultimate fact, the existence of an original determination to a particular mode of action salutary or necessary to the animal; and all we have accomplished is to connect the origin of this instinct with an earlier period in the history of the human mind.

The same author has attempted to account, in a manner somewhat similar, for the different degrees in which the young of different animals are able, at the moment of birth, to exert their bodily powers. Thus, calves and chickens are able to walk almost immediately; while the human infant, even in the most favourable situations, is six or even twelve months old before he can stand alone. For this, Dr. Darwin assigns two causes. 1. That the young of some animals come into the world in a more complete state than that of others:—the colt and lamb (for example) enjoying, in this respect, a striking advantage over the puppy and the rabbit. 2. That the mode of walking of some animals coincides more perfectly than that of others, with the previous motions of the *foetus in utero*. The struggles of all animals, he observes, in the womb, must resemble their manner of swimming, as by this kind of motion they can best change their attitude in water. But the swimming of the calf and of the chicken resembles their ordinary movements on the ground, which they have thus learned in part to execute, while concealed from our observation; whereas, the swimming of the human infant differing totally from his manner of walking, he has no opportunity of acquiring the last of these arts till he is exposed to our view.—The theory is extremely plausible, and does honour to the author's sagacity; but it only places in a new light that provident care which Nature has taken of all her offspring in the infancy of their existence.

Another instance may contribute towards a more ample illustration of the same subject. A lamb, not many minutes after it is dropped, proceeds to search for its nourishment in that spot where alone it is to be found; applying both its limbs and its eyes to their respective offices. The peasant observes the fact, and gives the name of *instinct*, or some corresponding term, to the unknown principle by which the animal is guided. On a more accurate examination of circumstances, the philosopher finds reason to conclude, that it is by the sense of smelling, it is thus directed to its object. In proof of this, among other curious facts, the following has been quoted. " On dissecting," says Galen, " a goat great with young, I found a brisk embryon, and having detached it from the matrix, and snatching it away before it saw its dam, I brought it into a room where there were many vessels; some filled with wine, others with oil, some with honey, others with milk, or some other liquor; and in others there were grains and fruits. We first observed the young animal get upon its feet and walk; then it shook itself, and afterwards scratched its side with one of its feet: then we saw it smelling to every one of those things that were set in the room; and when it had smelt to them all, it drank up the milk."* Admitting this very beautiful story to be true, (and, for my own part, I am far from being disposed to question its probability,) it only enables us to state the fact with a little more precision, in consequence of our having ascertained, that it is to the sense of smelling, the instinctive determination is attached. The conclusion of the peasant is not here at variance with that of the philosopher. It differs only in this, that he expresses himself in those general terms which are suited to his ignorance of the particular process by which Nature in this case accomplishes her end; and, if he did otherwise, he would be censurable for prejudging a question of which he is incompetent to form an accurate opinion.

The application of these illustrations to some of Dr. Reid's conclusions concerning the instinctive principles of the human mind, is, I flatter myself, sufficiently manifest. They relate, indeed, to a subject which differs, in various respects, from that which has fallen under his more particular consideration; but the same rules of philosophizing will be found to apply equally to both.

4. The criticisms which have been made on what Dr. Reid has written concerning the intuitive truths which he distinguishes

* Darwin, vol. i. pp. 195, 196.

by the title of "Principles of Common Sense," would require a more ample discussion than I can now bestow on them;—not that the importance of these criticisms (of such of them, at least, as I have happened to meet with) demands a long or elaborate refutation; but because the subject, according to the view I wish to take of it, involves some other questions of great moment and difficulty, relative to the foundations of human knowledge. Dr. Priestley, the most formidable of Dr. Reid's antagonists, has granted as much in favour of this doctrine as it is worth while to contend for, on the present occasion. "Had these writers," he observes with respect to Dr. Reid and his followers, "assumed, as the elements of their common sense, certain truths which are so plain that no man could doubt of them, (without entering into the ground of our assent to them,) their conduct would have been liable to very little objection. All that could have been said would have been, that, without any necessity, they had made an innovation in the received use of a term. For no person ever denied, that there *are* self-evident truths, and that these must be assumed as the foundation of all our reasoning. I never met with any person who did not acknowledge this, or heard of any argumentative treatise that did not go upon the supposition of it."* After such an acknowledgment, it is impossible to forbear asking (with Dr. Campbell), "What is the great point which Dr. Priestley would controvert? Is it, whether such self-evident truths shall be denominated principles of common sense, or be distinguished by some other appellation?"†

* Examination of Dr. Reid's Inquiry, &c. p. 119.

† The following strictures on Dr. Priestley's "Examination," &c. are copied from a very judicious note in Dr. Campbell's "Philosophy of Rhetoric," vol. i. p. 111.

"I shall only subjoin two remarks on this book. The first is, that the author, through tne whole, confounds two things totally distinct,—certain associations of ideas, and certain judgments implying belief, which, though in *some*, are not in *all* cases, and therefore not *necessarily* connected with association. And if so, merely to account for the association, is in no case to account for the belief with which it is attended. Nay, admitting his plea, (p. 86,) that by the principle of association, not only the ideas, but the concomitant belief may be accounted for, even this does not invalidate the doctrine he impugns. For, let it be observed, that it is one thing to assign a cause, which, from the me-

That the doctrine in question has been, in some publications, presented in a very exceptionable form, I most readily allow; nor would I be understood to subscribe to it implicitly, even as it appears in the works of Dr. Reid. It is but an act of justice to him, however, to request, that his opinions may be judged of from his own works alone, not from those of others who may have happened to coincide with him in certain tenets, or in certain modes of expression; and that, before any ridicule be attempted on his conclusions concerning the authority of common sense, his antagonists would take the trouble to examine in what acceptation he has employed that phrase.

The truths which Dr. Reid seems, in most instances, disposed to refer to the judgment of this tribunal, might, in my opinion, be denominated more unexceptionably, " fundamental laws of human belief." They have been called by a very ingenious foreigner, (M. Trembley of Geneva,) but certainly with a singular infelicity of language, *Préjugés Légitimes*.—Of this kind are the following propositions: " I am the same person to-day that

chanism of our nature, has given rise to a particular tenet of belief, and another thing to produce a reason by which the understanding has been convinced. Now, unless this be done as to the principles in question, they must be considered as primary truths in respect of the understanding, which never deduced them from other truths, and which is under a necessity, in all her moral reasonings, of founding upon them. In fact, to give any other account of our conviction of them, is to confirm, instead of confuting, the doctrine, that in all argumentation they must be regarded as primary truths, or truths which reason never inferred through any medium, from other truths previously perceived. My second remark is, that though this examiner has, from Dr. Reid, given us a catalogue of first principles, which he deems unworthy of the honourable place assigned them, he has no where thought proper to give us a list of those self-evident truths, which, by his own account, and in his own express words, 'must be assumed as the foundation of all our reasoning.' How much light might have been thrown upon the subject by the contrast! Perhaps we should have been enabled, on the comparison, to discover some distinctive characters in his genuine axioms, which would have preserved us from the danger of confounding them with their spurious ones. Nothing is more evident than that, in whatever regards matter of fact, the mathematical axioms will not answer. These are purely fitted for evolving the abstract relations of quantity. This he in effect owns himself (p. 39.) It would have been obliging, then, and would have greatly contributed to shorten the controversy, if he had given us, at least, a specimen of those self-evident principles, which, in his estimation, are the *non plus ultra* of moral reasoning."

I was yesterday;" " The material world has an existence independent of that of percipient beings;" " There are other intelligent beings in the universe beside myself;" " The future course of nature will resemble the past." Such truths no man but a philosopher ever thinks of stating to himself in words; but all our conduct and all our reasonings proceed on the supposition that they are admitted. The belief of them is essential for the preservation of our animal existence: and it is accordingly coeval with the first operations of the intellect.

One of the first writers who introduced the phrase *common sense* into the technical or appropriate language of logic, was Father Buffier, in a book entitled, " Traité des Premières Verités." It has since been adopted by several authors of note in this country; particularly by Dr. Reid, Dr. Oswald, and Dr. Beattie; by all of whom, however, I am afraid, it must be confessed, it has been occasionally employed without a due attention to precision. The last of these writers uses it* to denote that power by which the mind perceives the truth of any intuitive proposition; whether it be an axiom of abstract science; or a statement of some fact resting on the immediate information of consciousness of perception, or of memory; or one of those fundamental laws of belief which are implied in the application of our faculties to the ordinary business of life. The same extensive use of the word may, I believe, be found in the other authors just mentioned. But no authority can justify such a laxity in the employment of language in philosophical discussions; for, if mathematical axioms be (as they are manifestly and indisputably) a class of propositions essentially distinct from the other kinds of intuitive truths now described, why refer them all indiscriminately to the same principle in our constitution? If this phrase, therefore, be at all retained, precision requires, that it should be employed in a more limited acceptation; and accordingly, in the works under our consideration, it is appropriated most frequently, though by no means uniformly, to that class of intuitive truths which I have already called " fundamental laws of belief."† When thus restricted, it con-

* Essay on Truth, second edition, p. 40, et seq.; also p. 166, et seq.

† This seems to be nearly the meaning annexed to the phrase, by the learned and acute author of " The Philosophy of Rhetoric," vol. i. p. 109, et seq.

veys a notion, unambiguous at least, and definite; and, consequently, the question about its propriety or impropriety turns entirely on the coincidence of this definition with the meaning of the word as employed in ordinary discourse. Whatever objections, therefore, may be stated to the expression as now defined, will apply to it with additional force, when used with the latitude which has been already censured.

I have said, that the question about the propriety of the phrase *common sense* as employed by philosophers, must be decided by an appeal to general practice: for, although it be allowable and even necessary for a philosopher to limit the acceptation of words which are employed vaguely in common discourse, it is always dangerous to give to a word a scientific meaning essentially distinct from that in which it is usually understood. It has, at least, the effect of misleading those who do not enter deeply into the subject; and of giving a paradoxical appearance to doctrines, which, if expressed in more unexceptionable terms, would be readily admitted.

It appears to me, that this has actually happened in the present instance. The phrase *common sense*, as it is generally understood, is nearly synonymous with *mother-wit;* denoting that degree of sagacity (depending partly on original capacity, and partly on personal experience and observation,) which qualifies an individual for those simple and essential occupations which all men are called on to exercise habitually by their common nature. In this acceptation, it is opposed to those mental acquirements which are derived from a regular education, and from the study of books; and refers, not to the speculative convictions of the understanding, but to that prudence and discretion which are the foundation of successful conduct. Such is the idea which Pope annexes to the word, when, speaking of good sense, (which means only a more than ordinary share of common sense,) he calls it

"the gift of Heaven,
And though no science, fairly worth the seven."

To speak, accordingly, of appealing from the conclusions of philosophy to common sense, had the appearance, to title-page readers, of appealing from the verdict of the learned to the voice of the multitude; or of attempting to silence free discussion, by a reference to some arbitrary and undefinable standard, distinct from any of the intellectual powers hitherto enumerated by logicians. Whatever countenance may be supposed to have been given by some writers to such an interpretation of this doctrine, I may venture to assert that none is afforded by the works of Dr. Reid. The standard to which he appeals, is neither the creed of a particular sect, nor the inward light of enthusiastic presumption; but that constitution of human nature without which all the business of the world would immediately cease;— and the substance of his argument amounts merely to this, that those essential laws of belief to which sceptics have objected, when considered in connexion with our scientific reasonings, are implied in every step we take as active beings; and if called in question by any man in his practical concerns, would expose him universally to the charge of insanity.

In stating this important doctrine, it were perhaps to be wished, that the subject had been treated with somewhat more of analytical accuracy; and it is certainly to be regretted, that a phrase should have been employed, so well calculated by its ambiguity to furnish a convenient handle to misrepresentations: but in the judgment of those who have perused Dr. Reid's writings with an intelligent and candid attention, these misrepresentations must recoil on their authors; while they who are really interested in the progress of useful science, will be disposed rather to lend their aid in supplying what is defective in his views, than to reject hastily a doctrine which aims, by the development of some logical principles, overlooked in the absurd systems which have been borrowed from the schools, to vindicate the authority of truths intimately and extensively connected with human happiness.

In the prosecution of my own speculations on the human mind, I shall have occasion to explain myself fully concerning this as well as various other questions connected with the foundations of philosophical evidence. The new doctrines, and new phraseology on that subject, which have lately become fashionable among some metaphysicians in Germany, and which, in my opinion, have contributed not a little to involve it in additional obscurity, are a sufficient proof that this essential and fundamental article of logic is not as yet completely exhausted.

In order to bring the foregoing remarks within some compass, I have found it necessary to confine myself to such objections as strike at the root of Dr. Reid's philosophy, without touching on any of his opinions on particular topics, however important. I have been obliged also to compress what I have stated within narrower limits than were, perhaps, consistent with complete perspicuity; and to reject many illustrations which crowded upon me at almost every step of my progress.

It may not, perhaps, be superfluous to add, that, supposing some of these objections to possess more force than I have ascribed to them in my reply, it will not therefore follow, that little advantage is to be derived from a careful perusal of the speculations against which they are directed. Even they who dissent the most widely from Dr. Reid's conclusions, can scarcely fail to admit that, as a writer, he exhibits a striking contrast to the most successful of his predecessors, in a logical precision and simplicity of language; his statement of facts being neither vitiated by physiological hypothesis, nor obscured by scholastic mystery. Whoever has reflected on the infinite importance, in such inquiries, of a skilful use of words as the essential instrument of thought, must be aware of the influence which his works are likely to have on the future progress of science, were they to produce no other effect than a general imitation of his mode of reasoning, and of his guarded phraseology.

It is not indeed every reader to whom these inquiries are accessible; for habits of attention in general, and still more habits of attention to the phenomena of thought, require early and careful cultivation: but those who are capable of the exertion, will soon recognise, in Dr. Reid's statements, the faithful history of their own minds, and will find their labours amply rewarded by that satisfaction which always accompanies the discovery of useful truth. They may expect, also, to be rewarded by some intellectual acquisitions not altogether useless in their other studies. An author well qualified to judge, from his own experience, of whatever conduces to invigorate or to embellish the understanding, has beautifully remarked, that, "by turning the soul inward on itself, its forces are concentred, and are fitted for stronger and bolder flights of science; and that, in such pursuits, whether we take, or whether we lose the game, the chase is certainly of service."* In this respect, the philosophy of the mind (abstracting entirely from that pre-eminence which belongs to it in consequence of its practical applications) may claim a distinguished rank among those preparatory disciplines which another writer of no less eminence has happily compared to "the crops which are raised, not for the sake of the harvest, but to be ploughed in as a dressing to the land."†

SECTION III.

CONCLUSION OF THE NARRATIVE.

THE three works to which the foregoing remarks refer, together with the "Essay on Quantity," published in the "Philosophical Transactions of the Royal Society of London," and a short but masterly "Analysis of Aristotle's Logic," which forms an appendix to the third volume of Lord Kames's "Sketches," comprehend the whole of Dr. Reid's publications. The interval between the dates of the first and last of these amounts to no less than forty years, although he had attained to the age of thirty-eight before he ventured to appear as an author.

With the "Essays on the Active Powers of Man" he closed his literary career; but he continued, notwithstanding, to prosecute his studies with unabated ardour and activity. The more modern improvements in chemistry attracted his particular notice; and he applied himself, with his wonted diligence and success, to the study of its new doctrines and new nomenclature. He amused himself, also, at times, in preparing for a philosophical society, of which he was a member, short essays on particular topics, which happened to interest his curiosity, and on which he thought he might derive useful hints from friendly discussion. The most important of these were, "An Examination of Priestley's Opinions concerning Matter and Mind;" "Observations on the Utopia of Sir Thomas More;" and "Physiological Reflections on Muscular Motion." This last essay appears to have been written in the eighty-sixth year of his age, and was

---

* Preface to Mr. Burke's "Essay on the Sublime and Beautiful."
† Bishop Berkeley's "Querist."

read by the author to his associates a few months before his death. His " thoughts were led to the speculations it contains," (as he himself mentions in the conclusion,) " by the experience of some of the effects which old age produces on the muscular motions."—-"As they were occasioned, therefore," he adds, " by the infirmities of age, they will, I hope, be heard with the greater indulgence."

Among the various occupations with which he thus enlivened his retirement, the mathematical pursuits of his earlier years held a distinguished place. He delighted to converse about them with his friends, and often exercised his skill in the investigation of particular problems. His knowledge of ancient geometry had not probably been, at any time, very extensive; but he had cultivated diligently those parts of mathematical science which are subservient to the study of Sir Isaac Newton's works. He had a predilection, more particularly, for researches requiring the aid of arithmetical calculation, in the practice of which he possessed uncommon expertness and address. I think I have sometimes observed in him a slight and amiable vanity connected with this accomplishment.

The revival, at this period, of Dr. Reid's first scientific propensity, has often recalled to me a favourite remark of Mr. Smith's, that of all the amusements of old age, the most grateful and soothing is a renewal of acquaintance with the favourite studies and favourite authors of our youth; a remark which, in his own case, seemed to be more particularly exemplified, while he was re-perusing, with the enthusiasm of a student, the tragic poets of ancient Greece. I heard him at least repeat the observation more than once, while Sophocles or Euripides lay open on his table.

In the case of Dr. Reid, other motives perhaps conspired with the influence of the agreeable associations to which Mr. Smith probably alluded. His attention was always fixed on the state of his intellectual faculties; and for counteracting the effects of time on these, mathematical studies seem to be fitted in a peculiar degree. They are fortunately, too, within the reach of many individuals, after a decay of memory disqualifies them for inquiries which involve a multiplicity of details. Such detached problems, more especially, as Dr. Reid commonly selected for his consideration; problems where all the data are brought at once under the eye, and where a connected train of thinking is not to be carried on from day to day, will be found, (as I have witnessed with pleasure, in several instances,) by those who are capable of such a recreation, a valuable addition to the scanty resources of a life protracted beyond the ordinary limit.

While he was thus enjoying an old age, happy in some respects beyond the usual lot of humanity, his domestic comfort suffered a deep and incurable wound by the death of Mrs. Reid. He had had the misfortune, too, of surviving, for many years, a numerous family of promising children; four of whom (two sons and two daughters) died after they attained to maturity. One daughter only was left to him when he lost his wife; and of her affectionate good offices he could not always avail himself, in consequence of the attentions which her own husband's infirmities required. Of this lady, who is still alive, (the widow of Patrick Carmichael, M.D.,*) I shall have occasion again to introduce the name, before I conclude this narrative.

A short extract from a letter addressed to myself by Dr. Reid, not many weeks after his wife's death, will, I am persuaded, be acceptable to many, as an interesting relic of the writer.

" By the loss of my bosom-friend, with whom I lived fifty-two years, I am brought into a kind of new world, at a time of life when old habits are not easily forgot, or new ones acquired. But every world is God's world, and I am thankful for the comforts he has left me. Mrs. Carmichael has now the care of two old deaf men, and does every thing in her power to please them; and both are very sensible of her goodness. I have more health than at my time of life I had any reason to expect. I walk about; entertain myself with reading what I soon forget; can converse with one person, if he articulates distinctly, and is within ten inches of my left ear; go to church, without hearing one word of what is said. You know, I never had any pretensions to vivacity, but I am still free from languor and ennui.

* A learned and worthy physician, who, after a long residence in Holland, where he practised medicine, retired to Glasgow. He was a younger son of Professor Gerschom Carmichael, who published, about the year 1720, an edition of Puffendorf, "De Officio Hominis et Civis," and who is pronounced by Dr. Hutcheson, " by far the best commentator on that book."

" If you are weary of this detail, impute it to the anxiety you express to know the state of my health. I wish you may have no more uneasiness at my age,—being yours most affectionately."

About four years after this event, he was prevailed on by his friend and relation Dr. Gregory, to pass a few weeks, during the summer of 1796, at Edinburgh. He was accompanied by Mrs. Carmichael, who lived with him in Dr. Gregory's house; a situation which united, under the same roof, every advantage of medical care, of tender attachment, and of philosophical intercourse. As Dr. Gregory's professional engagements, however, necessarily interfered much with his attentions to his guest, I enjoyed more of Dr. Reid's society than might otherwise have fallen to my share. I had the pleasure, accordingly, of spending some hours with him daily, and of attending him in his walking excursions, which frequently extended to the distance of three or four miles. His faculties (excepting his memory, which was considerably impaired,) appeared as vigorous as ever; and, although his deafness prevented him from taking any share in general conversation, he was still able to enjoy the company of a friend. Mr. Playfair and myself were both witnesses of the acuteness which he displayed on one occasion, in detecting a mistake, by no means obvious, in a manuscript of his kinsman David Gregory, on the subject of " Prime and Ultimate Ratios." Nor had his temper suffered from the hand of time, either in point of gentleness or of gaiety. " Instead of repining at the enjoyments of the young, he delighted in promoting them; and, after all the losses he had sustained in his own family, he continued to treat children with such condescension and benignity, that some very young ones noticed the peculiar kindness of his eye."* In apparent soundness and activity of body, he resembled more a man of sixty than of eighty-seven.

He returned to Glasgow in his usual health and spirits; and continued, for some weeks, to devote, as formerly, a regular portion of his time to the exercise both of body and of mind. It appears, from a letter of Dr. Cleghorn's to Dr. Gregory, that he

* I have borrowed this sentence from a just and elegant character of Dr. Reid, which appeared, a few days after his death, in one of the Glasgow journals. I had occasion frequently to verify the truth of the observation during his last visit to Edinburgh.

was still able to work with his own hands in his garden; and he was found by Dr. Brown occupied in the solution of an algebraical problem of considerable difficulty, in which, after the labour of a day or two, he at last succeeded. It was in the course of the same short interval that he committed to writing those particulars concerning his ancestors which I have already mentioned.

His active and useful life was now, however, drawing to a conclusion. A violent disorder attacked him about the end of September; but does not seem to have occasioned much alarm to those about him, till he was visited by Dr. Cleghorn, who soon after communicated his apprehensions in a letter to Dr. Gregory. Among other symptoms, he mentioned particularly, " that alteration of voice and features, which, though not easily described, is so well known to all who have opportunities of seeing life close." Dr. Reid's own opinion of his case was probably the same with that of his physician; as he expressed to him on his first visit, his hope that he was " soon to get his dismission." After a severe struggle, attended with repeated strokes of palsy, he died on the 7th of October following. Dr. Gregory had the melancholy satisfaction of visiting his venerable friend on his death-bed, and of paying him this unavailing mark of attachment, before his powers of recollection were entirely gone.

The only surviving descendant of Dr. Reid is Mrs. Carmichael, a daughter worthy in every respect of such a father—long the chief comfort and support of his old age, and his anxious nurse in his last moments.*

* Dr. Reid's father, the Rev. Lewis Reid, married, for his second wife, Janet, daughter of Mr. Fraser, of Phopachy, in the county of Inverness. A daughter of this marriage survived Dr. Reid; the wife of the Rev. Alexander Leslie, and the mother of the Rev. James Leslie, ministers of Fordoun. To the latter of these gentlemen, I am indebted for the greater part of the information I have been able to collect with respect to Dr. Reid, previous to his removal to Glasgow; Mr. Leslie's regard for the memory of his uncle having prompted him, not only to transmit to me such particulars as had fallen under his own knowledge, but some valuable letters on the same subject, which he procured from his relations and friends in the North.

For all the members of this most respectable family, Dr. Reid entertained the strongest sentiments of affection and regard. During several years before his death, a daughter of Mrs. Leslie's was a constant inmate of his house, and added much to the happiness of his small domestic circle.

Another daughter of Mr. Lewis Reid was married to the Rev. John Rose,

In point of bodily constitution, few men have been more indebted to nature than Dr. Reid. His form was vigorous and athletic; and his muscular force (though he was somewhat under the middle size) uncommonly great; advantages to which his habits of temperance and exercise, and the unclouded serenity of his temper, did ample justice. His countenance was strongly expressive of deep and collected thought; but when brightened up by the face of a friend, what chiefly caught the attention was, a look of good-will and of kindness. A picture of him, for which he consented, at the particular request of Dr. Gregory, to sit, to Mr. Raeburn, during his last visit to Edinburgh, is generally and justly ranked among the happiest performances of that excellent artist. The medallion of Tassie, also, for which he sat in the eighty-first year of his age, presents a very perfect resemblance.

I have little to add to what the foregoing pages contain with respect to his character. Its most prominent features were,—intrepid and inflexible rectitude;—a pure and devoted attachment to truth;—and an entire command (acquired by the unwearied exertions of a long life) over all his passions. Hence, in those parts of his writings where his subject forces him to dispute the conclusions of others, a scrupulous rejection of every expression calculated to irritate those whom he was anxious to convince; and a spirit of liberality and good-humour towards

minister of Udny. She died in 1793. In this connexion, Dr. Reid was no less fortunate than in the former; and to Mr. Rose I am indebted for favours of the same kind with those which I have already acknowledged from Mr. Leslie.

The widow of Mr. Lewis Reid died in 1798, in the eighty-seventh year of her age, having survived her step-son, Dr. Reid, more than a year.

The limits within which I was obliged to confine my biographical details, prevented me from availing myself of many interesting circumstances which were communicated to me through the authentic channels which I have now mentioned. But I cannot omit this opportunity of returning to my different correspondents my warmest acknowledgments for the pleasure and instruction which I received from their letters.

Mr. Jardine, also, the learned Professor of Logic in the University of Glasgow, a gentleman, who, for many years, lived in habits of the most confidential intimacy with Dr. Reid and his family, is entitled to my best thanks for his obliging attention to various queries, which I took the liberty to propose to him, concerning the history of our common friend.

his opponents, from which no asperity on their part could provoke him, for a moment, to deviate. The progress of useful knowledge, more especially in what relates to human nature and to human life, he believed to be retarded rather than advanced by the intemperance of controversy; and to be secured most effectually when intrusted to the slow but irresistible influence of sober reasoning. That the argumentative talents of the disputants might be improved by such altercations, he was willing to allow; but, considered in their connexion with the great objects which all classes of writers profess equally to have in view, he was convinced "that they have done more harm to the practice, than they have done service to the theory of morality."*

In private life, no man ever maintained, more eminently or more uniformly, the dignity of philosophy; combining with the most amiable modesty and gentleness, the noblest spirit of independence. The only preferments which he ever enjoyed, he owed to the unsolicited favour of the two learned bodies who successively adopted him into their number; and the respectable rank which he supported in society was the well-earned reward of his own academical labours. The studies in which he delighted were little calculated to draw on him the patronage of the great; and he was unskilled in the art of courting advancement, by "fashioning his doctrines to the varying hour."

As a philosopher, his genius was more peculiarly characterised by a sound, cautious, distinguishing judgment; by a singular patience and perseverance of thought; and by habits of the most fixed and concentrated attention to his own mental operations; endowments which, although not the most splendid in the estimation of the multitude, would seem entitled, from the history of science, to rank among the rarest gifts of the mind.

With these habits and powers, he united (what does not always accompany them) the curiosity of a naturalist, and the eye of an observer; and, accordingly, his information about every thing relating to physical science and to the useful arts, was extensive and accurate. His memory for historical details was not so remarkable; and he used sometimes to regret the imperfect degree in which he possessed this faculty. I am inclined, however, to

* Preface to Pope's "Essay on Man."

think, that, in doing so, he underrated his natural advantages; estimating the strength of memory, as men commonly do, rather by the recollection of particular facts, than by the possession of those general conclusions, from a subserviency to which, such facts derive their principal value.

Towards the close of life, indeed, his memory was much less vigorous than the other powers of his intellect; in none of which could I ever perceive any symptom of decline. His ardour for knowledge, too, remained unextinguished to the last; and, when cherished by the society of the young and inquisitive, seemed even to increase with his years. What is still more remarkable, he retained in extreme old age all the sympathetic tenderness, and all the moral sensibility of youth; the liveliness of his emotions, wherever the happiness of others was concerned, forming an affecting contrast to his own unconquerable firmness under the severest trials.

Nor was the sensibility which he retained, the selfish and sterile offspring of taste and indolence. It was alive and active, wherever he could command the means of relieving the distresses, or of adding to the comforts of others; and was often felt in its effects where he was unseen and unknown. Among the various proofs of this which have happened to fall under my own knowledge, I cannot help mentioning particularly (upon the most unquestionable authority) the secrecy with which he conveyed his occasional benefactions to his former parishioners at New-Machar, long after his establishment at Glasgow. One donation, in particular, during the scarcity of 1782,—a donation which, notwithstanding all his precautions, was distinctly traced to his beneficence,—might perhaps have been thought disproportionate to his limited income, had not his own simple and moderate habits multiplied the resources of his humanity.

His opinions on the most important subjects are to be found in his works; and that spirit of piety which animated every part of his conduct, forms the best comment on their practical tendency. In the state in which he found the philosophical world, he believed, that his talents could not be so usefully employed, as in combating the schemes of those who aimed at the complete subversion of religion, both natural and revealed; convinced with Dr. Clarke, that " as Christianity presupposes the truth of natural religion, whatever tends to discredit the latter, must have a proportionally greater effect in weakening the authority of the former."* In his views of both, he seems to have coincided nearly with Bishop Butler, an author whom he held in the highest estimation. A very careful abstract of the treatise entitled " Analogy," drawn up by Dr. Reid, many years ago, for his own use, still exists among his manuscripts; and the short " Dissertation on Virtue," which Butler has annexed to that work, together with the " Discourses on Human Nature," published in his volume of Sermons, he used always to recommend as the most satisfactory account that has yet appeared on the fundamental principles of morals; nor could he conceal his regret, that the profound philosophy which these discourses contain, should of late have been so generally supplanted in England, by the speculations of some other moralists, who, while they profess to idolize the memory of Locke, " approve little or nothing in his writings, but his errors."†

Deeply impressed, however, as he was with his own principles, he possessed the most perfect liberality towards all whom he believed to be honestly and conscientiously devoted to the search of truth. With one very distinguished character, the late Lord Kames, he lived in the most cordial and affectionate friendship, notwithstanding the avowed opposition of their sentiments on some moral questions, to which he attached the greatest importance. Both of them, however, were the friends of virtue and of mankind; and both were able to temper the warmth of free discussion, with the forbearance and good-humour founded on reciprocal esteem. No two men, certainly, ever exhibited a more striking contrast in their conversation, or in their constitutional tempers: the one, slow and cautious in his decisions, even on those topics which he had most diligently studied; reserved and silent in promiscuous society; and retaining, after all his literary eminence, the same simple and unassuming manners which he brought from his country residence: the other, lively, rapid,

---

* Collection of papers which passed between Leibnitz and Clarke.—See Dr. Clarke's Dedication.

† I have adopted here the words which Dr. Clarke applied to some of Mr. Locke's earlier followers. They are still more applicable to many writers of the present times.—See Clarke's first Reply to Leibnitz.

and communicative; accustomed, by his professional pursuits, to wield with address the weapons of controversy, and not averse to a trial of his powers on questions the most foreign to his ordinary habits of inquiry. But these characteristical differences, while to their common friends they lent an additional charm to the distinguishing merits of each, served only to enliven their social intercourse, and to cement their mutual attachment.

I recollect few, if any, anecdotes of Dr. Reid, which appear to me calculated to throw additional light on his character; and I suspect strongly that many of those which are to be met with in biographical publications are more likely to mislead than to inform. A trifling incident, it is true, may sometimes paint a peculiar feature better than the most elaborate description; but a selection of incidents really characteristical, presupposes, in the observer, a rare capacity to discriminate and to generalize ; and where this capacity is wanting, a biographer, with the most scrupulous attention to the veracity of his details, may yet convey a very false conception of the individual he would describe. As, in the present instance, my subject afforded no materials for such a choice, I have attempted, to the best of my abilities, (instead of retailing detached fragments of conversations, or recording insulated and unmeaning occurrences,) to communicate to others the general impressions which Dr. Reid's character has left on my own mind. In this attempt I am far from being confident that I have succeeded; but, how barren soever I may have thus rendered my pages in the estimation of those who consider biography merely in the light of an amusing tale, I have, at least, the satisfaction to think that my picture, though faint in the colouring, does not present a distorted resemblance of the original.

The confidential correspondence of an individual with his friends, affords to the student of human nature, materials of far greater authenticity and importance; more particularly the correspondence of a man like Dr. Reid, who will not be suspected by those who knew him of accommodating his letters (as has been alleged of Cicero) to the humours and principles of those whom he addressed. I am far, at the same time, from thinking, that the correspondence of Dr. Reid would be generally interesting; or even that he excelled in this species of writing; but few men, I sincerely believe, who have written so much, have left behind them such unblemished memorials of their virtue.

At present I shall only transcribe two letters, which I select from a considerable number now lying before me, as they seem to accord, more than the others, with the general design of this memoir. The first (which is dated 13 January, 1779,) is addressed to the Reverend William Gregory, (afterwards Rector of St. Andrew's, Canterbury,) then an undergraduate in Balliol College, Oxford. It relates to a remarkable peculiarity in Dr. Reid's physical temperament, connected with the subject of dreaming; and is farther interesting as a genuine record of some particulars in his early habits, in which it is easy to perceive the openings of a superior mind.

"The fact which your brother the Doctor desires to be informed of, was as you mention it. As far as I remember the circumstances, they were as follow:

"About the age of fourteen I was, almost every night, unhappy in my sleep from frightful dreams. Sometimes hanging over a dreadful precipice, and just ready to drop down; sometimes pursued for my life, and stopped by a wall, or by a sudden loss of all strength; sometimes ready to be devoured by a wild beast. How long I was plagued with such dreams I do not now recollect. I believe it was for a year or two at least; and I think they had quite left me before I was fifteen. In those days I was much given to what Mr. Addison, in one of his 'Spectators,' calls *Castle-building;* and in my evening solitary walk, which was generally all the exercise I took, my thoughts would hurry me into some active scene, where I generally acquitted myself much to my own satisfaction; and in these scenes of imagination I performed many a gallant exploit. At the same time, in my dreams I found myself the most arrant coward that ever was. Not only my courage, but my strength, failed me in every danger; and I often rose from my bed in the morning, in such a panic, that it took some time to get the better of it. I wished very much to get free of these uneasy dreams, which not only made me unhappy in sleep, but often left a disagreeable impression in my mind for some part of the following day. I thought it was worth trying whether it was possible to recollect that it was all a dream, and that I was in no real danger. I often went to sleep with my mind as strongly impressed as I could with this thought, that I never in my lifetime was in any real danger, and that every fright I had was a dream. After many fruitless endeavours to recollect this when the danger appeared, I effected it at last, and have often, when I was sliding over a precipice into the abyss, recollected that it was all a dream, and boldly jumped down. The effect of this commonly was, that I immediately awoke. But I awoke calm and intrepid, which I thought a great acquisition. After this, my dreams were never very uneasy; and in a short time I dreamed not at all.

"During all this time I was in perfect health; but whether my ceasing to dream was the effect of the recollection above mentioned, or of any change in the habit of my body, which is usual about that period of life, I cannot tell. I think it may more probably be imputed to the last. However, the fact was, that for at least forty years after, I dreamed none, to the best of my remembrance: and finding, from the testimony of others, that this is somewhat uncommon, I have often, as soon as I awoke, endeavoured to recollect, without being able to recollect, any thing that passed in my sleep. For some years past I can sometimes recollect some kind of dreaming thoughts, but so incoherent that I can make nothing of them.

"The only distinct dream I ever had since I was about sixteen, as far as I remember, was about two years ago. I had got my head blistered for a fall. A plaster which was put upon it after the blister, pained me excessively for a whole night. In the morning I slept a little, and dreamed very distinctly that I had fallen into the hands of a party of Indians, and was scalped.

"I am apt to think, that as there is a state of sleep, and a state wherein we are awake, so there is an intermediate state, which partakes of the other two. If a man peremptorily resolves to rise at an early hour for some interesting purpose, he will of himself awake at that hour. A sick-nurse gets the habit of sleeping in such a manner that she hears the least whisper of the sick person, and yet is refreshed by this kind of half sleep. The same is the case of a nurse who sleeps with a child in her arms. I have slept on horseback, but so as to preserve my balance; and if the horse stumbled, I could make the exertion necessary for saving me from a fall, as if I was awake.

"I hope the sciences at your good university are not in this state. Yet, from so many learned men, so much at their ease, one would expect something more than we hear of."

For the other letter, I am indebted to one of Dr. Reid's most intimate friends, to whom it was addressed, in the year 1784, on occasion of the melancholy event to which it alludes.

"I sympathize with you very sincerely in the loss of a most amiable wife. I judge of your feelings by the impression she made upon my own heart, on a very short acquaintance. But all the blessings of this world are transient and uncertain; and it would be but a melancholy scene if there were no prospect of another.

"I have often had occasion to admire the resignation and fortitude of young persons, even of the weaker sex, in the views of death, when their imagination is filled with all the gay prospects which the world presents at that period. I have been witness to instances of this kind, which I thought truly heroic, and I hear Mrs. Gregory gave a remarkable one.

"To see the soul increase in vigour and wisdom, and in every amiable quality, when health and strength and animal spirits decay; when it is to be torn by violence from all that filled the imagination, and flattered hope, is a spectacle truly grand and instructive to the surviving. To think that the soul perishes in that fatal moment, when it is purified by this fiery trial, and fitted for the noblest exertions in another state, is an opinion which I cannot help looking down upon with contempt and disdain.

"In old people there is no more merit in leaving this world with perfect acquiescence than in rising from a feast after one is full. When I have before me the prospect of the infirmities, the distresses, and the peevishness of old age, and when I have already received more than my share of the good things of this life, it would be ridiculous indeed to be anxious about prolonging it; but when I was four-and-twenty, to have had no anxiety for its continuance, would, I think, have required a noble effort. Such efforts, in those that are called to make them, surely shall not lose their reward."

* * * * *

I HAVE now finished all that the limits of my plan permit me

to offer here, as a tribute to the memory of this excellent person. In the details which I have stated, both with respect to his private life and his scientific pursuits, I have dwelt chiefly on such circumstances as appeared to me most likely to interest the readers of his works, by illustrating his character as a man, and his views as an author. Of his merits as an instructor of youth, I have said but little; partly from a wish to avoid unnecessary diffuseness; but chiefly from my anxiety to enlarge on those still more important labours, of which he has bequeathed the fruits to future ages. And yet, had he left no such monument to perpetuate his name, the fidelity and zeal with which he discharged, during so long a period, the obscure but momentous duties of his official station, would, in the judgment of the wise and good, have ranked him in the first order of useful citizens.—
" Nec enim is solus reipublicæ prodest, qui candidatos extrahit, et tuetur reos, et de pace belloque censet; sed qui juventutem exhortatur; qui, in tantâ bonorum præceptorum inopiâ, virtute instruit animos; qui, ad pecuniam luxuriamque cursu ruentes prensat ac retrahit, et, si nihil aliud, certe moratur: in privato, publicum negotium agit," Seneca, De Tranquill. An. cap. 3.—
" For neither is he alone of service to the republic who induces candidates to come forward, and defends the accused, and gives his opinion concerning peace and war; but he who admonishes the young; who in such a dearth of good precepts disciplines their minds with virtuous precepts; who checks and draws back those eagerly rushing to money and dissipation, and retards them, if nothing more; who in a private station forwards the public good."

In concluding this memoir, I trust I shall be pardoned, if, for once, I give way to a personal feeling, while I express the satisfaction with which I now close finally, my attempts as a biographer. Those which I have already made, were imposed on me by the irresistible calls of duty and attachment; and, feeble as they are, when compared with the magnitude of subjects so splendid and so various, they have encroached deeply on that small portion of literary leisure which indispensable engagements allow me to command. I cannot, at the same time, be insensible to the gratification of having endeavoured to associate in some degree, my name with three of the greatest which have adorned this age;—happy, if without deviating intentionally from truth, I may have succeeded, however imperfectly, in my wish, to gratify, at once, the curiosity of the public, and to soothe the recollections of surviving friends.——But I, too, have designs and enterprises of my own; and the execution of these (which alas! swell in magnitude, as the time for their accomplishment hastens to a period,) claims at length, an undivided attention. Yet I should not look back on the past with regret, if I could indulge the hope, that the facts which it has been my province to record,—by displaying those fair rewards of extensive usefulness, and of permanent fame, which talents and industry, when worthily directed, cannot fail to secure,—may contribute, in one single instance, to foster the proud and virtuous independence of genius; or, amidst the gloom of poverty and solitude, to gild the distant prospect of the unfriended scholar, whose laurels are now slowly ripening in the unnoticed privacy of humble life.

ESSAYS

ON THE

ACTIVE POWERS OF THE HUMAN MIND.

INTRODUCTION.

THE division of the faculties of the human mind into *Understanding* and *Will* is very ancient, and has been very generally adopted; the former comprehending all our speculative, the latter all our active powers.

It is evidently the intention of our Maker, that man should be an active and not merely a speculative being. For this purpose, certain active powers have been given him, limited indeed in many respects, but suited to his rank and place in the creation.

Our business is to manage these powers, by proposing to ourselves the best ends, planning the most proper system of conduct that is in our power, and executing it with industry and zeal. This is true wisdom; this is the very intention of our being.

Every thing virtuous and praiseworthy must lie in the right use of our power; every thing vicious and blameable in the abuse of it. What is not within the sphere of our power cannot be imputed to us either for blame or praise. These are self-evident truths, to which every unprejudiced mind yields an immediate and invincible assent.

Knowledge derives its value from this, that it enlarges our power, and directs us in the application of it. For in the right employment of our active power consists all the honour, dignity, and worth of a man, and, in the abuse and perversion of it, all the vice, corruption, and depravity.

We are distinguished from the brute animals, not less by our active than by our speculative powers.

The brutes are stimulated to various actions by their instincts, by their appetites, by their passions. But they seem to be necessarily determined by the strongest impulse, without any capacity of self-government. Therefore we do not blame them for what they do; nor have we any reason to think that they blame themselves. They may be trained up by discipline, but cannot be governed by law. There is no evidence that they have the conception of a law, or of its obligation.

Man is capable of acting from motives of a higher nature. He perceives a dignity and worth in one course of conduct, a demerit and turpitude in another, which brutes have not the capacity to discern.

He perceives it to be his duty to act the worthy and the honourable part, whether his appetites and passions incite him to it, or to the contrary. When he sacrifices the gratification of the strongest appetites or passions to duty, this is so far from diminishing the merit of his conduct, that it greatly increases it, and affords upon reflection, an inward satisfaction and triumph, of which brute animals are not susceptible. When he acts a contrary part, he has a consciousness of demerit, to which they are no less strangers.

Since, therefore, the active powers of man make so important a part of his constitution, and distinguish him so eminently from his fellow-animals, they deserve no less to be the subject of philosophical disquisition than his intellectual powers.

A just knowledge of our powers, whether intellectual or active, is so far of real importance to us, as it aids us in the exercise of them. And every man must acknowledge, that to act properly is much more valuable than to think justly or reason acutely.

ESSAY I.

OF ACTIVE POWER IN GENERAL.

CHAPTER I.

OF THE NOTION OF ACTIVE POWER.

I. *An explanation of the meaning of "active power" necessary.*—To consider gravely what is meant by active power, may seem altogether unnecessary, and to be mere trifling. It is not a term of art, but a common word in our language, used every day in discourse, even by the vulgar. We find words of the same meaning in all other languages; and there is no reason to think that it is not perfectly understood by all men who understand the English language.

I believe all this is true, and that an attempt to explain a word so well understood, and to show that it has a meaning, requires an apology.

[The apology is, that *this term*, so well understood by the vulgar, *has been darkened by philosophers*, who, in this, as in many other instances, have found great difficulties about a thing which, to the rest of mankind, seems perfectly clear.]

This has been the more easily effected, because power is a thing so much of its own kind, and so simple in its nature, as not to admit of a logical definition.

It is well known, that there are many things perfectly understood, and of which we have clear and distinct conceptions, which cannot be logically defined. No man ever attempted to define magnitude; yet there is no word whose meaning is more distinctly or more generally understood. We cannot give a logical definition of thought, of duration, of number, or of motion.

When men attempt to define such things, they give no light. They may give a synonymous word or phrase, but it will probably be a worse for a better. If they will define, the definition will either be grounded upon a hypothesis, or it will darken the subject rather than throw light upon it.

II. The *Aristotelian definition of motion*, that it is " actus entis in potentia, quatenus in potentia," has been justly censured by modern philosophers; yet I think it is matched by what a celebrated modern philosopher has given us, as the most accurate definition of belief, to wit, " that it is a lively idea related to or associated with a present impression." (Treatise of Human Nature, Vol. I. p. 172.) "Memory," according to the same philosopher, "is the faculty by which we repeat our impressions, so as that they retain a considerable degree of their first vivacity, and are somewhat intermediate betwixt an idea and an impression."

Euclid, if his editors have not done him injustice, has attempted to define a right line, to define unity, ratio, and number. But these definitions are good for nothing. We may, indeed, suspect them not to be Euclid's, because they are never once quoted in the " Elements," and are of no use.

I shall not, therefore, attempt to define active power, that I may not be liable to the same censure; but shall offer some observations that may lead us to attend to the conception we have of it in our own minds.

III. *Of our conception of active power.*—1. *Power is not an object* of any of our external senses, nor even an object *of consciousness.*

That it is not seen, nor heard, nor touched, nor tasted, nor smelt, needs no proof. That we are not conscious of it, in the proper sense of that word, will be no less evident, if we reflect, that consciousness is that power of the mind by which it has an immediate knowledge of its own operations. Power is not an operation of the mind, and therefore no object of consciousness. Indeed, every operation of the mind is the exertion of some power of the mind; but we are conscious of the operation only, the power lies behind the scene; and though we may justly infer the power from the operation, it must be remembered, that inferring is not the province of consciousness, but of reason.

I acknowledge, therefore, that our having any conception or idea of power is repugnant to Mr. Locke's theory, that all our simple ideas are got either by the external senses, or by consciousness. Both cannot be true. Mr. Hume perceived this repugnancy, and consistently maintained, that we have no idea of power. Mr. Locke did not perceive it. If he had, it might have led him to suspect his theory; for when theory is repugnant to fact, it is easy to see which ought to yield. I am conscious that I have a *conception* or *idea* of power, but, strictly speaking, I am not conscious that I have *power*.

IV. *Power not an object of consciousness.*—I shall have occasion to show, that we have very early, from our constitution, a conviction or belief of some degree of active power in ourselves. This belief, however, is not consciousness: for we may be deceived in it; but the testimony of consciousness can never deceive. Thus, a man who is struck with a palsy in the night, commonly knows not that he has lost the power of speech till he attempts to speak; he knows not whether he can move his hands and arms till he makes the trial; and if, without making trial, he consults his consciousness ever so attentively, it will give him no information whether he has lost these powers, or still retains them.

From this we must conclude, that the *powers* we have *are not an object of consciousness,* though it would be foolish to censure this way of speaking in popular discourse, which requires not accurate attention to the different provinces of our various faculties. The testimony of consciousness is always unerring, nor was it ever called in question by the greatest sceptics, ancient or modern.

But a relative conception.—[2. A *second* observation is, that as there are some things of which we have a direct, and others of which we have only *a relative conception,* power belongs to the latter class.]

As this distinction is overlooked by most writers in logic, I shall beg leave to illustrate it a little, and then shall apply it to the present subject.

Of some things, we know what they are in themselves; our conception of such things I call *direct*. Of other things, we know not what they are in themselves, but only that they have certain properties or attributes, or certain relations to other things; of these our conception is only *relative*.

☞ To illustrate this by some examples: in the university-library, I call for the book, press L, shelf 10, No. 10; the library-keeper must have such a conception of the book I want, as to be able to distinguish it from ten thousand that are under his care. But what conception does he form of it from my words? They inform him neither of the author, nor the subject, nor the language, nor the size, nor the binding, but only of its mark and place. His conception of it is merely relative to these circumstances; yet this relative notion enables him to distinguish it from every other book in the library.

There are other relative notions that are not taken from accidental relations, as in the example just now mentioned, but from qualities or attributes essential to the thing.

☞ Of this kind are our notions both of body and mind. What is body? It is, say philosophers, *that which is extended, solid, and divisible.* Says the querist, I do not ask what the properties of body are, but what is the thing itself? let me first know directly what body is, and then consider its properties. To this demand I am afraid the querist will meet with no satisfactory answer; because our notion of body is not direct, but relative to its qualities. We know that it is something extended, solid, and divisible, and we know no more.

G

☞ Again, if it should be asked, What is mind? *It is that which thinks.* I ask not what it does, or what its operations are, but what it is? To this I can find no answer; our notion of mind being not direct, but relative to its operations, as our notion of body is relative to its qualities.

☞ There are even many of the qualities of body, of which we have only a relative conception. What is heat in a body? It is *a quality which affects the sense of touch* in a certain way. If you want to know, not how it affects the sense of touch, but what it is in itself; this I confess I know not. My conception of it is not direct, but relative to the effect it has upon bodies. The notions we have of all those qualities which Mr. Locke calls secondary, and of those he calls powers of bodies, such as the power of the magnet to attract iron, or of fire to burn wood, are relative.

V. Having given examples of things of which our conception is only *relative*, it may be proper to mention some of which it is *direct*. Of this kind, are (1) all the primary qualities of body; figure, extension, solidity, hardness, fluidity, and the like. Of these we have a direct and immediate knowledge from our senses. To this class belong also (2) all the operations of mind of which we are conscious. I know what thought is, what memory, what a purpose, what a promise.

VI. *There are some things of which we can have both a direct and a relative conception.* I can directly conceive ten thousand men or ten thousand pounds, because both are objects of sense, and may be seen. But whether I see such an object, or directly conceive it, my notion of it is indistinct; it is only that of a great multitude of men, or of a great heap of money; and a small addition or diminution makes no perceptible change in the notion I form in this way. ☞ But I can form a *relative* notion of the same number of men or of pounds, by attending to the relations which this number has to other numbers, greater or less. Then I perceive that the relative notion is distinct and scientific. For the addition of a single man, or a single pound, or even of a penny, is easily perceived.

☞ In like manner, I can form a *direct* notion of a polygon of a thousand equal sides and equal angles. This direct notion cannot be more distinct, when conceived in the mind, than that which I get by sight, when the object is before me; and I find it so indistinct, that it has the same appearance to my eye, or to my direct conception, as a polygon of a thousand and one, or of nine hundred and ninety-nine sides. But when I form a relative conception of it, by attending to the relation it bears to polygons of a greater or less number of sides, my notion of it becomes distinct and scientific, and I can demonstrate the properties by which it is distinguished from all other polygons. From these instances it appears, that our relative conceptions of things are not always less distinct, nor less fit materials for accurate reasoning, than those that are direct; and that the contrary may happen in a remarkable degree.

VII. *Our conception of power is relative to its exertions or effects.*—Power is one thing; its exertion is another thing. It is true, there can be no exertion without power; but there may be power that is not exerted. Thus a man may have power to speak when he is silent; he may have power to rise and walk when he sits still.

But, though it be one thing to speak, and another to have the power of speaking, I apprehend we conceive of the power as something which has a certain relation to the effect. And of every power we form our notion by the effect which it is able to produce.

3. It is evident that power is a quality, and cannot exist without a subject to which it belongs.

That power may exist without any being or subject to which that power may be attributed, is an absurdity, shocking to every man of common understanding.

It is a quality which may be varied, not only in degree, but also in kind; and we distinguish both the kinds and degrees by the effects which they are able to produce.

Thus a power to fly, and a power to reason, are different kinds of power, their effects being different in kind. But a power to carry one hundred weight, and a power to carry two hundred, are different degrees of the same kind.

4. We cannot conclude the want of power from its not being exerted; nor from the exertion of a less degree of power, can we conclude that there is no greater degree in the subject. Thus, though a man on a particular occasion said nothing, we cannot conclude from that circumstance, that he had not the power of speech; nor from a man's carrying ten pound weight, can we conclude that he had not power to carry twenty.

5. There are some qualities that have a contrary, others that have not; power is a quality of the latter kind.

Vice is contrary to virtue, misery to happiness, hatred to love, negation to affirmation; but *there is no contrary to power*. Weakness or impotence are defects or privations of power, but not contraries to it.

If what has been said of power be easily understood, and readily assented to, by all who understand our language, as I believe it is, we may from this justly conclude, that we have a distinct notion of power, and may reason about it with understanding, though we can give no logical definition of it.

VIII. *Our idea of power.*—If power were a thing of which we have no idea, as some philosophers have taken much pains to prove, that is, if power were a word without any meaning, we could neither affirm nor deny any thing concerning it with understanding. We should have equal reason to say that it is a substance, as that it is a quality; that it does not admit of degrees, as that it does. If the understanding immediately assents to one of these assertions, and revolts from the contrary, we may conclude with certainty, that we put some meaning upon the word *power*, that is, that *we have some idea of it*. And it is chiefly for the sake of this conclusion, that I have enumerated so many obvious things concerning it.

IX. The term *active power is used*, I conceive, *to distinguish it from speculative powers*. As all languages distinguish action from speculation, the same distinction is applied to the powers by which they are produced. The powers of seeing, hearing, remembering, distinguishing, judging, reasoning, are speculative powers; the power of executing any work of art or labour is active power.

There are many things related to power, in such a manner, that we can have no notion of them if we have none of power.

The exertion of active power we call *action;* and as every action produces some change, so every change must be caused by some exertion, or by the cessation of some exertion of power. That which produces a change by the exertion of its power, we call the *cause* of that change; and the change produced, the *effect* of that cause.

When one being, by its active power, produces any change upon another, the last is said to be *passive*, or to be acted upon. Thus we see, that action and passion, cause and effect, exertion and operation, have such a relation to active power, that if it be understood, they are understood of consequence; but if power be a word without any meaning, all those words which are related to it, must be words without any meaning. They are, however, common words in our language; and equivalent words have always been common in all languages.

It would be very strange indeed, if mankind had always used these words so familiarly, without perceiving that they had no meaning; and that this discovery should have been first made by a philosopher of the present age.

With equal reason it might be maintained, that though there are words in all languages to express sight, and words to signify the various colours which are objects of sight; yet that all mankind, from the beginning of the world, had been blind, and never had an idea of sight or of colour. But there are no absurdities so gross as those which philosophers have advanced concerning ideas.

CHAPTER II.

THE SAME SUBJECT.

I. *Distinction of " action and passion" coeval with the origin of languages.*—[THERE are, I believe, *no abstract notions,* that are to be found more early, or *more universally, in the minds of men, than* those of *acting, and being acted upon.*] Every child that understands the distinction between striking and being struck, must have the conception of action and passion.

We find, accordingly, that there is no language so imperfect, but that it has active and passive verbs, and participles; the one signifying some kind of action; the other, the being acted upon. *This distinction enters into the original contexture of all languages.*

Active verbs have a form and construction proper to themselves; passive verbs a different form and a different construction. In all languages, the nominative to an active verb is the agent; the thing acted upon is put in an oblique case. In passive verbs, the thing acted upon is the nominative, and the agent, if expressed, must be in an oblique case; as in this example: *Raphael drew the Cartoons; the Cartoons were drawn by Raphael.*

Every distinction which we find in the structure of all languages, must have been familiar to those who framed the languages at first, and to all who speak them with understanding.

II. *Objection.*—[It may be objected to this argument, taken from the structure of language, in the use of active and passive verbs, (1) that active verbs are not always used to denote an action; (2) nor is the nominative before an active verb conceived in all cases to be an agent, in the strict sense of that word; (3) that there are many passive verbs which have an active signification, and active verbs which have a passive.] From these facts, it may be thought a just conclusion, that in contriving the different forms of active and passive verbs, and their different construction, men have not been governed by a regard to any distinction between action and passion, but by chance, or some accidental cause.

III. In *answer to this objection,* the fact on which it is founded must be admitted; but I think the conclusion not justly drawn from it, for the following reasons:

[1. It seems *contrary to reason,* to attribute to chance or accident, what is subject to rules, even though there may be exceptions to the rule.] The exceptions may, in such a case, be attributed to accident, but the rule cannot. There is perhaps hardly anything in language so general, as not to admit of exceptions. It cannot be denied to be a general rule, that verbs and participles have an active and a passive voice; and as this is a general rule, not in one language only, but in all the languages we are acquainted with, it shows evidently that men, in the earliest stages, and in all periods of society, have distinguished action from passion.

[2. It is to be observed, that *the forms of language are often applied to purposes different from those for which they were originally intended.* The varieties of a language, even the most perfect, can never be made equal to all the variety of human conceptions.] The forms and modifications of language must be confined within certain limits, that they may not exceed the capacity of human memory. Therefore, in all languages, there must be a kind of frugality used, to make one form of expression serve many different purposes, like Sir Hudibras' dagger, which, though made to stab or break a head, was put to many other uses. Many examples might be produced of this frugality in language. Thus the Latins and Greeks had five or six cases of nouns, to express all the various relations that one thing could bear to another. The genitive case must have been at first intended to express some one capital relation, such as that of possession or of property: but it would be very difficult to enumerate all the relations which, in the progress of language, it was used to express. The same observation may be applied to other cases of nouns.

The slightest similitude or analogy is thought sufficient to justify the extension of a form of speech beyond its proper meaning, whenever the language does not afford a more proper form. In the moods of verbs, a few of those which occur most frequently are distinguished by different forms, and these are made to supply all the forms that are wanting. The same observation may be applied to what is called the *voices* of verbs. An active and a passive are the capital ones; some languages have more, but no language so many as to answer to all the variations of human thought. We cannot always coin new ones, and therefore must use some one or other of those that are to be found in the language, though at first intended for another purpose.

[3. A third observation in answer to the objection is, That *we can point out a cause of the frequent misapplication of active verbs,* to things which have no proper activity:] a cause which extends to the greater part of such misapplications, and which confirms the account I have given of the proper intention of active and passive verbs.

As there is no principle that appears to be more universally acknowledged by mankind, from the first dawn of reason, than, that every change we observe in nature must have a cause; so this is no sooner perceived, than there arises in the human mind a strong desire to know the causes of those changes that fall within our observation. "Felix qui potuit rerum cognoscere causas," is the voice of nature in all men. Nor is there any thing that more early distinguishes the rational from the brute creation, than this avidity to know the causes of things, of which I see no sign in brute animals.

IV. It must surely be admitted, that in those periods wherein languages are formed, men are but poorly furnished for carrying on this investigation with success. We see, that the experience of thousands of years is necessary to bring men into the right track in this investigation, if indeed they can yet be said to be brought into it. What innumerable errors rude ages must fall into, with regard to causes, from impatience to judge, and inability to judge right, we may conjecture from reason, and may see from experience; from which I think it is evident, that supposing active verbs to have been originally intended to express what is properly called action, and their nominatives to express the agent; yet, in the rude and barbarous state wherein languages are formed, there must be innumerable misapplications of such verbs and nominatives, and many things spoken of as active, which have no real activity.

To this we may add, [that it is *a general prejudice of our early years*, and of rude nations, when we perceive any thing to be changed, and do not perceive any other thing which we can believe to be the cause of that change, *to impute it to the thing itself*, and conceive it to be active and animated, so far as to have the power of producing that change in itself.] ☞ Hence to a child, or to a savage, all nature seems to be animated; the sea, the earth, the air, the sun, moon, and stars, rivers, fountains, and groves, are conceived to be active and animated beings. As this is a sentiment natural to man in his rude state, it has, on that account, even in polished nations, the verisimilitude that is required in poetical fiction and fable, and makes personification one of the most agreeable figures in poetry and eloquence.

V. *The origin of this prejudice* probably is, that we judge of other things by ourselves, and therefore are disposed to ascribe to them that life and activity which we know to be in ourselves.

☞ A little girl ascribes to her doll the passions and sentiments she feels in herself. Even brutes seem to have something of this nature. A young cat, when she sees any brisk motion in a feather or a straw, is prompted, by natural instinct, to hunt it as she would hunt a mouse.

Whatever be the origin of this prejudice in mankind, it has a powerful influence upon language, and leads men, in the structure of language, to ascribe action to many things that are merely passive; because, when such forms of speech were invented, those things were really believed to be active. Thus we say, the wind blows, the sea rages, the sun rises and sets, bodies gravitate and move.

When experience discovers that these things are altogether inactive, it is easy to correct our opinion about them; but it is not so easy to alter the established forms of language. The most perfect and the most polished languages are like old furniture, which is never perfectly suited to the present taste, but retains something of the fashion of the times when it was made.

☞ Thus, though all men of knowledge believe that the succession of day and night is owing to the rotation of the earth round its axis, and not to any diurnal motion of the heavens; yet we find ourselves under a necessity of speaking in the old style, of the sun's rising and going down, and coming to the meridian. And this style is used, not only in conversing with the vulgar, but when men of knowledge converse with one another. And if we should suppose the vulgar to be at last so far enlightened, as to have the same belief with the learned, of the cause of day and night, the same style would still be used.

From this instance we may learn, that the language of mankind may furnish good evidence of opinions which have been early and universally entertained, and that the forms contrived for expressing such opinions may remain in use after the opinions which gave rise to them have been greatly changed.

VI. *Active verbs appear plainly to have been first contrived to express action.*—They are still in general applied to this purpose. And though we find many instances of the application of active verbs to things which we now believe not to be active, this ought to be ascribed to men's having once had the belief that those things are active, and perhaps, in some cases, to this, that forms of expression are commonly extended, in course of time, beyond their original intention, either from analogy, or because more proper forms for the purpose are not found in the language.

[(1) Even the misapplication of this notion of action and active power shows that *there is such a notion in the human mind*, and shows the necessity there is in philosophy of distinguishing the proper application of these words, from the vague and improper application of them, founded on common language, or on popular prejudice.]

[(2) Another argument to show that *all men have a notion* or idea *of active power* is, that there are many operations of mind common to all men who have reason, and necessary in the ordinary conduct of life, which imply a belief of active power in ourselves and in others.]

All our volitions and efforts to act, all our deliberations, our purposes and promises, imply a belief of active power in ourselves: our counsels, exhortations, and commands, imply a belief of active power in those to whom they are addressed.

☞ If a man should make an effort to fly to the moon; if he should even deliberate about it, or resolve to do it, we should conclude him to be lunatic; and even lunacy would not account for his conduct, unless it made him believe the thing to be in his power.

If a man promises to pay me a sum of money to-morrow, without believing that it will then be in his power, he is not an honest man: and, if I did not believe that it will then be in his power, I should have no dependence on his promise.

All our power is, without doubt, derived from the Author of our being, and, as he gave it freely, he may take it away when he will. No man can be certain of the continuance of any of his powers of body or mind for a moment; and, therefore, in every promise there is a condition understood, to wit, if we live, if we retain that health of body and soundness of mind which is necessary to the performance, and if nothing happen, in the providence of God, which puts it out of our power. The rudest savages are taught by nature to admit these conditions in all promises, whether they be expressed or not; and no man is charged with breach of promise, when he fails through the failure of these conditions.

It is evident, therefore, that, without the belief of some active power, no honest man would make a promise, no wise man would trust to a promise; and it is no less evident, that the belief of active power, in ourselves, or in others, implies an idea or notion of active power.

The same reasoning may be applied to every instance wherein we give counsel to others, wherein we persuade or command. As long, therefore, as mankind are beings who can deliberate, and resolve, and will; as long as they can give counsel, and exhort, and command, they must believe the existence of active power in themselves, and in others, and therefore must have a notion or idea of active power.

VII. [It might further be observed, that *power is the proper and immediate object of ambition*, one of the most universal passions of the human mind, and that which makes the greatest figure in the history of all ages.] Whether Mr. Hume, in defence of his system, would maintain that there is no such passion in mankind as ambition, or that ambition is not a vehement desire of power, or that men may have a vehement desire of power, without having any idea of power, I will not pretend to divine.

I cannot help repeating my apology for insisting so long in the refutation of so great an absurdity. It is a capital doctrine in a late celebrated system of human nature, that we have no idea of power, not even in the Deity; that we are not able to discover a single instance of it, either in body or spirit, either in superior or inferior natures; and that we deceive ourselves when we imagine that we are possessed of any idea of this kind.

To support this important doctrine, and the out-works that are raised in its defence, a great part of the first volume of the "Treatise of Human Nature" is employed. That system abounds with conclusions the most absurd that ever were advanced by any philosopher, deduced with great acuteness and ingenuity from principles commonly received by philosophers. To reject such conclusions as unworthy of a hearing, would be disrespectful to the ingenious author; and to refute them is difficult, and appears ridiculous.

It is difficult, because we can hardly find principles to reason from, more evident than those we wish to prove; and it appears ridiculous, because, as this author justly observes, next to the ridicule of denying an evident truth, is that of taking much pains to prove it.

☞ Protestants complain, with justice, of the hardship put upon them by Roman Catholics, in requiring them to prove that bread andwine is not flesh and blood. They have, however, submitted to this hardship for the sake of truth. I think it is no less hard to be put to prove that men have an idea of power.

[What convinces myself that I have an idea of power is, *that I am conscious that I know what I mean by that word*, and, while I have this *consciousness*, I disdain equally to hear arguments for or against my having such an idea.] But if we would convince those who, being led away by prejudice, or by authority, deny that they have any such idea, we must condescend to use such arguments as the subject will afford, and such as we should use with a man who should deny that mankind have any idea of magnitude or of equality.

VIII. *The arguments* I have *adduced are taken from* these *five topics:* 1. That there are many things that we can affirm or deny concerning power, with understanding. 2. That there are, in all languages, words signifying, not only power, but signifying many other things that imply power, such as action and passion, cause and effect, energy, operation, and others. 3. That in the structure of all languages, there is an active and passive form in verbs and participles, and a different construction adapted to these forms, of which diversity no account can be given, but that it has been intended to distinguish action from passion. 4. That there are many operations of the human mind familiar to every man come to the use of reason, and necessary in the ordinary conduct of life, which imply a conviction of some degree of power in ourselves and in others. 5. That the desire of power is one of the strongest passions of human nature.

CHAPTER III.

OF MR. LOCKE'S ACCOUNT OF OUR IDEA OF POWER.

1. This author, having refuted the Cartesian doctrine of innate ideas, took up, perhaps too rashly, an opinion that all our simple ideas are got, either by sensation or by reflection; that is, by our external senses, or by consciousness of the operations of our own minds.

Through the whole of his Essay, he shows a fatherly affection to this opinion, and often strains very hard to reduce our simple ideas to one of those sources, or both. Of this, several instances might be given, in his account of our idea of substance, of duration, of personal identity. Omitting these, as foreign to the present subject, I shall only take notice of the account he gives of our idea of power.

The sum of it is, that observing, by our senses, various changes in objects, we collect a possibility in one object to be changed, and in another a possibility of making that change, and so come by that idea which we call power.

Thus we say the fire has a power to melt gold, and gold has power to be melted; the first he calls active, the second passive power.

He thinks, however, that we have the most distinct notion of active power, by attending to the power which we ourselves exert, in giving motion to our bodies when at rest, or in directing our thoughts to this or the other object, as we will. And this way of forming the idea of power he attributes to reflection, as he refers the former to sensation.*

II. *Objections to Mr. Locke's origin of our idea of power.*—On this account of the origin of our idea of power, I would beg leave to make two remarks, with the respect that is most justly due to so great a philosopher, and so good a man.

[1. Whereas he distinguishes power into *active* and *passive*, I conceive passive power is no power at all. He means by it, the possibility of being changed. To call this *power*, seems to be a misapplication of the word. I do not remember to have met with the phrase *passive power* in any other good author.] Mr. Locke seems to have been unlucky in inventing it; and it deserves not to be retained in our language.

Perhaps he was unwarily led into it, as an opposite to active

---

* "Observing *in ourselves*, that we do and can think; and that we can at pleasure move several parts of our bodies which were at rest: the effects, also, that *natural bodies* are able to produce in one another, occurring every moment to our senses, we *both* these ways get the idea of power."—Essay, Book ii. chap. vii. sect. 8.

power. But I conceive we call certain powers *active*, to distinguish them from other powers that are called *speculative*. As all mankind distinguish action from speculation, it is very proper to distinguish the powers by which those different operations are performed, into active and speculative. Mr. Locke, indeed, acknowledges that active power is more properly called power; but I see no propriety at all in passive power; it is a powerless power, and a contradiction in terms.

[2. I would observe, that *Mr. Locke seems to have imposed upon himself*, in attempting to reconcile this account of the idea of power to his favourite doctrine, that all our simple ideas are ideas of sensation, or of reflection.]

There are two steps, according to his account, which the mind takes in forming this idea of power; *first*, it observes changes in things; and, *secondly*, from these changes, it infers a cause of them, and a power to produce them.

If both these steps are operations of the external senses, or of consciousness, then the idea of power may be called an idea of sensation, or of reflection. But, if either of those steps requires the co-operation of other powers of the mind, it will follow, that the idea of power cannot be got by sensation, nor by reflection, nor by both together. Let us, therefore, consider each of these steps by itself.

First, we observe various changes in things. And Mr. Locke takes it for granted, that changes in external things are observed by our *senses*, and that changes in our thoughts are observed by *consciousness*.

I grant that it may be said, that changes in things are observed by our senses, when we do not mean to exclude every other faculty from a share in this operation. And it would be ridiculous to censure the phrase, when it is so used in popular discourse. But it is necessary to Mr. Locke's purpose, that changes in external things should be observed by the senses *alone*, excluding every other faculty; because every faculty that is necessary in order to observe the change, will claim a share in the origin of the idea of power.

Now, it is evident, that *memory* is *no less necessary than the senses*, in order to our observing changes in external things, and therefore the idea of power, derived from the changes observed, may as justly be ascribed to memory as to the senses.

Every change supposes two states of the thing changed. Both these states may be past; one of them at least must be past; and one only can be present. By our senses we may observe the present state of the thing; but memory must supply us with the past; and, unless we remember the past state, we can perceive no change.

[The same observation may be applied to consciousness. The

truth, therefore, is, that *by the senses alone*, without memory, or by consciousness alone, without memory, *no change can be observed*.] Every idea, therefore, that is derived from observing changes in things, must have its origin, partly from memory, and not from the senses alone, nor from consciousness alone, nor from both together.

The *second* step made by the mind in forming this idea of power is this: from the changes observed, we collect a cause of those changes, and a power to produce them.

Here one might ask Mr. Locke, whether it is by our senses that we draw this conclusion, or is it by consciousness? Is reasoning the province of the senses, or is it the province of consciousness? If the senses can draw one conclusion from premises, they may draw five hundred, and demonstrate the whole Elements of Euclid.

Thus, I think, it appears, that [the account which Mr. Locke himself gives of the origin of our idea of power, cannot be reconciled to his favourite doctrine, that all our simple ideas have their origin from sensation or reflection; and that, in attempting to derive the idea of power from these two sources only, he unawares *brings in our memory and our reasoning power for a share in its origin.*]

CHAPTER IV.

OF MR. HUME'S OPINION OF THE IDEA OF POWER.

I. *Induction, by which Mr. Hume attempts to explain the origin of our simple ideas, imperfect.*—THIS very ingenious author adopts the principle of Mr. Locke before mentioned,—That all our simple ideas are derived either from sensation or reflection. This he seems to understand, even in a stricter sense than Mr. Locke did; for he will have all our simple ideas to be copies of preceding impressions, either of our external senses or of consciousness. "After the most accurate examination," says he, "of which I am capable, I venture to affirm, that the rule here holds without any exception, and that every simple idea has a simple impression which resembles it, and every simple impression a correspondent idea. Every one may satisfy himself in this point, by running over as many as he pleases."

[I observe here, by the way, that this conclusion is formed by the author rashly and unphilosophically. For it is a conclusion that admits of no proof but by induction; and it is upon this ground that he himself founds it. *The induction cannot be perfect till every simple idea that can enter into the human mind be examined*, and be shown to be copied from a resembling impression of sense or of consciousness.] No man can pretend to have made this examination of all our simple ideas without exception; and, therefore, no man can, consistently with the rules of philosophizing, assure us, that this conclusion holds without any exception.

The author professes, in his title-page, to introduce into moral subjects the experimental method of reasoning. This was a very laudable attempt; but he ought to have known, that it is a rule in the experimental method of reasoning, That conclusions, established by induction, ought never to exclude exceptions, if any such should afterwards appear from observation or experiment. Sir Isaac Newton, speaking of such conclusions, says, " Et si quando in experiundo postea reperiatur aliquid, quod a parte contraria faciat; tum demum, non sine istis exceptionibus affirmetur conclusio opportebit." " And if at any time, in the course of experimenting, a contrary instance occur, then the conclusion must necessarily be affirmed subject to such exception." " But," says our author, " I will venture to affirm, that the rule here holds without any exception."

Accordingly, throughout the whole treatise, this general rule is considered as of sufficient authority, in itself, to exclude, even from a hearing, every thing that appears to be an exception to it. This is contrary to the fundamental principles of the experimental method of reasoning, and therefore may be called rash and unphilosophical.

II. [Having thus established this general principle, the author does great execution by it among our ideas. He finds, (1) that we have no idea of substance, material or spiritual; (2) that body and mind are only certain trains of related impressions and ideas; (3) that we have no idea of space or duration; and (4) no idea of power, active or intellective.]

Mr. Locke used his principle of sensation and reflection with greater moderation and mercy. Being unwilling to thrust the ideas we have mentioned into the limbo of non-existence, he stretches sensation and reflection to the very utmost, in order to receive these ideas within the pale; and draws them into it, as it were, by violence.

But this author, instead of showing them any favour, seems fond to get rid of them.

Of the ideas mentioned, it is only that of power that concerns our present subject. And, with regard to this, the author boldly affirms, " That we never have any idea of power; that we deceive ourselves when we imagine we are possessed of any idea of this kind."

He begins with observing, " That the terms *efficacy, agency, power, force, energy*, are all nearly synonymous; and therefore it is an absurdity to employ any of them in defining the rest. By this observation," says he, " we reject at once all the vulgar definitions which philosophers have given of *power* and *efficacy*."

Surely this author was not ignorant, that there are many things of which we have a clear and distinct conception, which are so simple in their nature, that they cannot be defined any other way than by synonymous words. It is true that this is not a logical definition; but that there is, as he affirms, an absurdity in using it, when no better can be had, I cannot perceive.

He might here have applied to *power* and *efficacy* what he says, in another place, of *pride* and *humility*. " The passions of *pride* and *humility*," he says, " being simple and uniform impressions, it is impossible we can ever give a just definition of them. As the words are of general use, and the things they represent the most common of any, every one, of himself, will be able to form a just notion of them without danger of mistake."

He mentions Mr. Locke's account of the idea of power, That, observing various changes in things, we conclude that there must be somewhere a power capable of producing them, and so arrive at last, by this reasoning, at the idea of power and efficacy.

" But," says he, " to be satisfied that this explication is more popular than philosophical, we need but reflect on two very obvious principles : *first*, That reason alone can never give rise to any original idea; and, *secondly*, That reason, as distinguished from experience, can never make us conclude that a cause, or productive quality, is absolutely requisite to every beginning of existence."*

III. Before we consider the *two principles* which our author opposes to the popular opinion of Mr. Locke, I observe,

First, That there are some *popular* opinions, which, on that very account, deserve more regard from philosophers than this author is willing to bestow.

That things cannot begin to exist, nor undergo any change, without a cause that hath power to produce that change, is indeed so popular an opinion, that, I believe, this author is the first of mankind that ever called it in question. It is so popular, that there is not a man of common prudence who does not act from this opinion, and rely upon it every day of his life. And any man who should conduct himself by the contrary opinion, would soon be confined as insane, and continue in that state, till a sufficient cause was found for his enlargement.

Such a popular opinion as this stands upon a higher authority than that of philosophy, and philosophy must strike sail to it, if she would not render herself contemptible to every man of common understanding.

* Vide Essay IV., chap. ix. sec. 9.

For though, in matters of deep speculation, the multitude must be guided by philosophers, yet, in things that are within the reach of every man's understanding, and upon which the whole conduct of human life turns, the philosopher must follow the multitude, or make himself perfectly ridiculous.

Secondly, I observe, that whether this popular opinion be true or false, it follows from men's having this opinion, that they have an idea of power. A false opinion about power, no less than a true, implies an idea of power; for how can men have any opinion, true or false, about a thing of which they have no idea?

IV. *Of the two principles which Mr. Hume opposes to Mr. Locke.*
—[The *first* of the very obvious principles which the author opposes to Mr. Locke's account of the idea of power, is, That *reason alone can never give rise to any original idea.*]

This appears to me so far from being a very obvious principle, that the contrary is very obvious.

Is it not our reasoning faculty that gives rise to the idea of reasoning itself? As our idea of sight takes its rise from our being endowed with that faculty, so does our idea of reasoning. Do not the ideas of demonstration, of probability, our ideas of a syllogism, of major, minor and conclusion, of an enthymeme, dilemma, sorites, and all the various modes of reasoning, take their rise from the faculty of reason? Or is it possible, that a being, not endowed with the faculty of reasoning, should have these ideas? This principle, therefore, is so far from being obviously true, that it appears to be obviously false.

[The *second* obvious principle is, That *reason*, as *distinguished from experience, can never make us conclude, that a cause,* or productive quality, *is absolutely requisite to every beginning of existence.*]

In some " Essays on the Intellectual Powers of Man," I had occasion to treat of this principle, That every change in nature must have a cause; and, to prevent repetition, I beg leave to refer the reader to what is said upon this subject, Essay vi. chap. 6. I endeavoured to show, that it is a first principle, evident to all men come to years of understanding. Besides its having been universally received, without the least doubt, from the beginning of the world, it has this sure mark of a first principle, that the belief of it is absolutely necessary in the ordinary affairs of life, and, without it, no man could act with common prudence, or avoid the imputation of insanity. Yet a philosopher, who acted upon the firm belief of it every day of his life, thinks fit, in his closet, to call it in question.

[He insinuates here, that we may know it from *experience*. I endeavoured to show, that we do not learn it from experience, for two reasons.]

[*First*, Because it is *a necessary truth*, and has always been received as a necessary truth. Experience gives no information of what is necessary, or of what must be.]

We may know from experience, what is, or what was, and from that may probably conclude what shall be in like circumstances; but with regard to what must necessarily be, experience is perfectly silent.

☞ Thus we know, by unvaried experience, from the beginning of the world, that the sun and stars rise in the east and set in the west. But no man believes that it could not possibly have been otherwise, or that it did not depend upon the will and power of Him who made the world, whether the earth should revolve to the east or to the west.

In like manner, if we had experience, ever so constant, that every change in nature we have observed, actually had a cause, this might afford ground to believe, that, for the future, it shall be so; but no ground at all to believe that it must be so, and cannot be otherwise.

[*Another reason* to show that this principle is not learned from experience is, *That experience does not show us a cause* of one in a hundred of those changes which we observe, and therefore *can never teach us that there must be a cause of all.*]

Of all the paradoxes this author has advanced, there is not one more shocking to the human understanding than this, That things may begin to exist without a cause. This would put an end to all speculation, as well as to all the business of life. The employment of speculative men, since the beginning of the world, has been to investigate the causes of things. What pity is it, they never thought of putting the previous question, Whether things have a cause or not? This question has at last been started; and what is there so ridiculous as not to be maintained by some philosopher?

Enough has been said upon it, and more, I think, than it deserves. But being about to treat of the active powers of the human mind, I thought it improper to take no notice of what has been said by so celebrated a philosopher, to show that there is not, in the human mind, any idea of power.

CHAPTER V.

WHETHER BEINGS THAT HAVE NO WILL NOR UNDERSTANDING MAY HAVE ACTIVE POWER?

I. *The question perplexed by the ambiguity of certain terms.*— That active power is an attribute, which cannot exist but in some being possessed of that power, and the subject of that attribute, I take for granted as a self-evident truth. Whether there can be active power in a subject which has no thought, no understanding, no will, is not so evident.

[The ambiguity of the words *power, cause, agent,* and of all the words related to these, tends to perplex this question.] The weakness of human understanding, which gives us only an indirect and relative conception of power, contributes to darken our reasoning, and should make us cautious and modest in our determinations.

We can derive little light in this matter from the events which we observe in the course of nature. We perceive changes innumerable in things without us. We know that those changes must be produced by the active power of some agent; but we neither perceive the agent nor the power, but the change only. Whether the things be active, or merely passive, is not easily discovered. And though it may be an object of curiosity to the speculative few, it does not greatly concern the many.

To know the event and the circumstances that attended it, and to know in what circumstances like events may be expected, may be of consequence in the conduct of life; but to know the real efficient, whether it be matter or mind, whether of a superior or inferior order, concerns us little.

Thus it is with regard to all the effects we ascribe to nature.

II. *Nature* is the name we give to the efficient cause of innumerable effects which fall daily under our observation. But if it be asked what nature is?—whether the first universal cause, or a subordinate one, whether one or many, whether intelligent or unintelligent?—upon these points we find various conjectures and theories, but no solid ground upon which we can rest; and I apprehend the wisest men are they who are sensible that they know nothing of the matter.

From the course of events in the natural world, we have sufficient reason to conclude the existence of an eternal intelligent First Cause. But whether he acts immediately in the production of those events, or by subordinate intelligent agents, or by instruments that are unintelligent, and what the number, the nature, and the different offices of those agents or instruments may be; these I apprehend to be mysteries placed beyond the limits of human knowledge. We see an established order in the succession of natural events, but we see not the bond that connects them together.

III. [Since we derive so little light, with regard to efficient causes and their active power, from attention to the *natural* world, let us next attend to the *moral,* I mean, to *human actions and conduct.*]

Mr. Locke observes very justly, "That, from the observation of the operation of bodies by our senses, we have but a very imperfect obscure idea of active power, since they afford us not any idea in themselves of the power to *begin* any action, either of motion or thought." He adds, " That we find in ourselves a power to begin or forbear, continue or end several actions of our minds and motions of our bodies, barely by a thought or preference of the mind, ordering, or, as it were, commanding the doing or not doing such a particular action. This power which the mind has thus to order the consideration of any idea, or the forbearing to consider it, or to prefer the motion of any part of the body to its rest, and *vice versa*, in any particular instance, is that which we call *the will.* The actual exercise of that power, by directing any particular action, or its forbearance, is that which we call *volition* or *willing.*"

According to Mr. Locke, therefore, the only clear notion or idea we have of active power, is taken from the power which we find in ourselves to give certain motions to our bodies, or a certain direction to our thoughts; and this power in ourselves can be brought into action only by willing or volition.

IV. *Volition necessary to the operation of power.*—[From this, I think, it follows, that, if we had not *will*, and that degree of understanding which will necessarily implies, we could exert no active power, and consequently could have none: for power that cannot be exerted is no power. It follows also, that the active power, of which only we can have any distinct conception, can be only in beings that have understanding and will.]

Power to produce any effect implies power not to produce it. We can conceive no way in which power may be determined to one of these rather than the other, in a being that has no will.

[Whatever is the effect of active power must be something that is *contingent*. Contingent existence is that which depended upon the power and will of its cause. Opposed to this, is *necessary* existence, which we ascribe to the Supreme Being, because his existence is not owing to the power of any being. The same distinction there is between contingent and necessary truth.]

☞ That the planets of our system go round the sun from west to east, is a contingent truth; because it depended upon the power and will of him who made the planetary system, and gave motion to it. That a circle and a right line can cut one another only in two points, is a truth which depends upon no power nor will, and therefore is called necessary and immutable. Contingency, therefore, has a relation to active power, as all active power is exerted in contingent events; and as such events can have no existence, but by the exertion of active power.

☞ When I observe a plant growing from its seed to maturity, I know that there must be a cause that has power to produce this effect. But I see neither the cause nor the manner of its operation.

But in certain motions of my body and directions of my thought, I know, not only that there must be a cause that has power to produce these effects, but that I am that cause; and I am conscious of what I do in order to the production of them.

From the consciousness of our own activity, seems to be derived, not only the clearest, but the only conception we can form of activity, or the exertion of active power.

As I am unable to form a notion of any intellectnal power different in kind from those I possess, the same holds with respect to active power. If all men had been blind, we should have had no conception of the power of seeing, nor any name for it in language. If man had not the powers of abstraction and reasoning, we could not have had any conception of these operations. In like manner, if he had not some degree of active power, and if he were not conscious of the exertion of it in his voluntary actions, it is probable he could have no conception of activity, or of active power.

A train of events following one another ever so regularly, could never lead us to the notion of a cause, if we had not, from our constitution, a conviction of the necessity of a cause to every event.

And of the manner in which a cause may exert its active power, we can have no conception but from consciousness of the manner in which our own active power is exerted.

With regard to the operations of nature, it is sufficient for us to know, that, whatever the agents may be, whatever the manner of their operation, or the extent of their power, they depend upon the First Cause, and are under his control; and this indeed is all that we know; beyond this we are left in darkness. But, in what regards human actions, we have a more immediate concern.

It is of the highest importance to us, as moral and accountable creatures, to know what actions are in our own power, because it is for these only that we can be accountable to our Maker, or to our fellow-men in society; by these only we can merit praise or blame; in these only all our prudence, wisdom and virtue must be employed; and, therefore, with regard to them, the wise Author of nature has not left us in the dark.

Every man is led by nature to attribute to himself the free determinations of his own will, and to believe those events to be in his power which depend upon his will. On the other hand, it is self-evident, that nothing is in our power that is not subject to our will.

We grow from childhood to manhood, we digest our food, our blood circulates, our heart and arteries beat, we are sometimes sick and sometimes in health; all these things must be done by the power of some agent; but they are not done by our power.

How do we know this? Because they are not subject to our will. This is the infallible criterion by which we distinguish what is our doing from what is not; what is in our power from what is not.

[*Human power*, therefore, *can only be exerted by will*, and we are unable to conceive any active power to be exerted without will. Every man knows infallibly that what is done by his *conscious will* and *intention*, is to be imputed to him as the agent or cause; and that whatever is done without his will and intention, cannot be imputed to him with truth.]

We judge of the actions and conduct of other men by the same rule as we judge of our own. In morals, it is self-evident that no man can be the object either of approbation or of blame for what he did not. But how shall we know whether it is his doing or not? If the action depended upon his will, and if he intended and willed it, it is his action in the judgment of all mankind. But if it was done without his knowledge, or without his will and intention, it is as certain that he did it not, and that it ought not to be imputed to him as the agent.

When there is any doubt to whom a particular action ought to be imputed, the doubt arises only from our ignorance of facts; when the facts relating to it are known, no man of understanding has any doubt to whom the action ought to be imputed.

V. [The general rules of *imputation* are self-evident. They have been the same in all ages, and among all civilized nations.] No man blames another for being black or fair, for having a fever or the falling sickness; because these things are believed not to be in his power; and they are believed not to be in his power, because they depend not upon his will. [We can never conceive that a man's duty goes beyond his power, or that his power goes beyond what depends upon his will.]

Reason leads us to ascribe unlimited power to the Supreme Being. But what do we mean by unlimited power? It is power to do whatsoever he wills. To suppose him to do what he does not will to do, is absurd.

VI. *Our conception of active power relative.*—[The only distinct conception I can form of active power is, that it is an attribute in a being by which he can do certain things if he wills. This, after all, is only a *relative* conception. It is relative to the effect, and to the will of producing it.] Take away these, and the conception vanishes. They are the handles by which the mind takes hold of it. When they are taken away, our hold is gone. The same is the case with regard to other relative conceptions. Thus velocity is a real state of a body, about which philosophers reason with the force of demonstration; but our conception of it is relative to space and time. What is velocity in a body? It is a state in which it passes through a certain space in a certain time. Space and time are very different from velocity; but we cannot conceive it but by its relation to them. The effect produced, and the will to produce it, are things different from active power, but we can have no conception of it, but by its relation to them.

Whether the conception of an efficient cause, and of real activity, could ever have entered into the mind of man, if we had not had the experience of activity in ourselves, I am not able to determine with certainty. The origin of many of our conceptions, and even of many of our judgments, is not so easily traced as philosophers have generally conceived. No man can recollect the time when he first got the conception of an efficient cause, or the time when he first got the belief that an efficient cause is necessary to every change in nature. The conception of an efficient cause may very probably be derived from the experience we have had in very early life of our own power to produce certain effects. But the belief, that no event can happen without an efficient cause, cannot be derived from experience. We may learn from experience what is, or what was, but no experience can teach us what necessarily must be.

In like manner, we probably derive the conception of pain from the experience we have had of it in ourselves; but our belief that pain can only exist in a being that hath life, cannot be got by experience, because it is a necessary truth; and no necessary truth can have its attestation from experience.

If it be so that the conception of an efficient cause enters into the mind, only from the early conviction we have that we are the efficients of our own voluntary actions, (which I think is most probable,) the notion of efficiency will be reduced to this,— That it is a relation between the cause and the effect, similar to that which is between us and our voluntary actions. This is surely the most distinct notion, and, I think, the only notion we can form of real efficiency.

Now it is evident, that, to constitute the relation between me and my action, my conception of the action, and will to do it, are essential. For what I never conceived, nor willed, I never did.

If any man, therefore, affirms, that a being may be the efficient cause of an action, and have power to produce it, which that being can neither conceive nor will, he speaks a language which I do not understand. If he has a meaning, his notion of power and efficiency must be essentially different from mine; and, until he conveys his notion of efficiency to my understanding, I can no more assent to his opinion, than if he should affirm, that a being without life may feel pain.

It seems, therefore, to me most probable, that such beings only as have some degree of understanding and will, can possess active power: and that inanimate beings must be merely passive, and have no real activity. Nothing we perceive without us affords any good ground for ascribing active power to any inanimate being; and every thing we can discover in our own constitution, leads us to think, that active power cannot be exerted without will and intelligence.

CHAPTER VI.
OF THE EFFICIENT CAUSES OF THE PHENOMENA OF NATURE.

I. *Of powers ascribed to matter.*—IF active power, in its proper meaning, requires a subject endowed with will and intelligence, what shall we say of those active powers which philosophers teach us to ascribe to matter; the powers of corpuscular attraction, magnetism, electricity, gravitation, and others? Is it not universally allowed, that heavy bodies descend to the earth by the power of gravity; that, by the same power, the moon, and all the planets and comets, are retained in their orbits? Have the most eminent natural philosophers been imposing upon us, and giving us words instead of real causes?

In answer to this, I apprehend, that the principles of natural philosophy have, in modern times, been built upon a foundation that cannot be shaken, and that they can be called in question only by those who do not understand the evidence on which they stand. [But the ambiguity of the words *cause, agency, active power*, and the other words related to these, has led many to understand them, when used in natural philosophy, in a wrong sense, and in a sense which is neither necessary for establishing the true principles of natural philosophy, nor was ever meant by the most enlightened in that science.]

To be convinced of this, we may observe, that those very philosophers who attribute to matter the power of gravitation, and other active powers, teach us, at the same time, that matter is a substance altogether inert, and merely passive; that gravitation, and the other attractive or repulsive powers which they ascribe to it, are not inherent in its nature, but impressed upon it by some external cause, which they do not pretend to know, or to explain. Now, when we find wise men ascribing action and active power to a substance which they expressly teach us to consider as merely passive, and acted upon by some unknown cause, we must conclude that the action and active power ascribed to it are not to be understood strictly, but in some popular sense.

II. It ought likewise to be observed, that although philosophers, for the sake of being understood, must speak the language of the vulgar, as when they say, the sun rises and sets, and goes through all the signs of the zodiac, yet they often think differently from the vulgar. Let us hear what the greatest of natural philosophers says, in the 8th definition prefixed to his " Principia," " Voces autem attractionis, impulsus, vel propensionis cujuscunque in centrum, indifferenter et pro se mutuo promiscue usurpo; has voces non physicè sed mathematicè considerando. Unde caveat lector, ne per hujus modi voces cogitet me speciem vel modum actionis, causamve aut rationem physicam, alicubi definire; vel centris (quæ sunt puncta mathematica) vires vere et physice tribuere, si forte centra trahere, aut vires centrorum esse, dixero."

" But I use the words attraction, impulse, or propensity of any sort towards a centre, promiscuously and indifferently one for another, considering those forces not physically but mathematically. Therefore if I happen to speak of centres as attracting, or as endued with attractive powers, let the reader beware lest he imagine, that I anywhere take upon me to define the kind, or the manner of the action; or the cause or physical reason thereof; or that I attribute forces in a true and physical sense, to certain centres which are only mathematical points."

[In all languages, *action is attributed to many things* which all men of common understanding believe to be *merely passive;* thus we say, the wind blows, the rivers flow, the sea rages, the fire burns, bodies move, and impel other bodies.]

Every object which undergoes any change, must be either active or passive in that change. This is self-evident to all men from the first dawn of reason; and therefore the change is always expressed in language, either by an active or a passive verb. Nor do I know any verb, expressive of a change, which does not imply either action or passion. The thing either changes, or it is changed. [But it is remarkable in language, that *when an external cause of the change is not obvious, the change is always imputed to the thing changed,* as if it were animated, and had active power to produce the change in itself. So we say, the moon changes, the sun rises and goes down.]

Thus active verbs are very often applied, and active power imputed to things, which a little advance in knowledge and experience teaches us to be merely passive. This property, common to all languages, I endeavoured to account for in the second chapter of this Essay, to which the reader is referred.

III. A like irregularity may be observed in the use of the word signifying *cause,* in all languages, and of the words related to it.

Our knowledge of causes is very scanty in the most advanced state of society, much more is it so in that early period in which language is formed. A strong desire to know the causes of things, is common to all men in every state; but the experience of all ages shows that this keen appetite, rather than go empty, will feed upon the husks of real knowledge where the fruit cannot be found.

While we are very much in the dark with regard to the real agents or causes which produce the phenomena of Nature, and have, at the same time, an avidity to know them, ingenious men frame conjectures, which those of weaker understanding take for truth. The fare is coarse, but appetite makes it go down.

Thus, in a very ancient system, love and strife were made the causes of things. Plato made the causes of things to be matter, ideas, and an efficient architect. Aristotle, matter, form, and privation. Des Cartes thought matter, and a certain quantity of motion given it by the Almighty at first, to be all that is necessary to make the material world. Leibnitz conceived the whole universe, even the material part of it, to be made up of *monades*, each of which is active and intelligent, and produces in itself, by its own active power, all the changes it undergoes from the beginning of its existence to eternity.

In common language, we give the name of a *cause* to a reason, a motive, an end, to any circumstance which is connected with the effect, and goes before it.

IV. [Aristotle, and the schoolmen after him, *distinguished four kinds of causes, the efficient, the material, the formal, and the final.*] This, like many of Aristotle's distinctions, is only a distinction of the various meanings of an ambiguous word; for the efficient, the matter, the form, and the end, have nothing common in their nature, by which they may be accounted species of the same *genus;* but the Greek word which we translate *cause,* had these four different meanings in Aristotle's days, and we have added other meanings. We do not indeed call the matter or the form of a thing its cause; but we have final causes, instrumental causes, occasional causes, and I know not how many others.

Thus the word *cause* has been so hackneyed, and made to have so many different meanings in the writings of philosophers, and in the discourse of the vulgar, that its original and proper meaning is lost in the crowd.

With regard to the phenomena of nature, the important end of knowing their causes, besides gratifying our curiosity, is, that we may know when to expect them, or how to bring them about. This is very often of real importance in life; and this purpose is served, by knowing what, by the course of nature, goes before them and is connected with them; and this, therefore, we call the *cause* of such a phenomenon.

☞ If a magnet be brought near to a mariner's compass, the needle, which was before at rest, immediately begins to move, and bends its course towards the magnet, or perhaps the contrary way. If an unlearned sailor is asked the cause of this motion of the needle, he is at no loss for an answer. He tells you it is the magnet; and the proof is clear; for, remove the magnet, and the effect ceases; bring it near, and the effect is again produced. It is, therefore, evident to sense, that the magnet is the cause of this effect.

A Cartesian philosopher enters deeper into the cause of this phenomenon. He observes, that the magnet does not touch the needle, and therefore can give it no impulse. He pities the ignorance of the sailor. The effect is produced, says he, by magnetic effluvia, or subtile matter, which passes from the magnet to the needle, and forces it from its place. He can even show you, in a figure, where these magnetic effluvia issue from the magnet, what round they take, and what way they return home again. And thus he thinks he comprehends perfectly how, and by what cause, the motion of the needle is produced.

A Newtonian philosopher inquires what proof can be offered for the existence of magnetic effluvia, and can find none: he therefore holds it as a fiction, a *hypothesis;* and he has learned that hypotheses ought to have no place in the philosophy of nature. He confesses his ignorance of the real cause of this motion, and thinks that his business, as a philosopher, is only to find from experiment the laws by which it is regulated in all cases.

These three persons differ much in their sentiments with regard to the real cause of this phenomenon; and the man who knows most is he who is sensible that he knows nothing of the matter. Yet all the three speak the same language, and acknowledge that the cause of this motion is the attractive or repulsive power of the magnet.

V. What has been said of this, may be applied to every phenomenon that falls within the compass of natural philosophy. We deceive ourselves, if we conceive that we can point out the real efficient cause of any one of them.

[The grandest discovery ever made in natural philosophy, was that of the *law of gravitation*, which opens such a view of our planetary system, that it looks like something divine. But the author of this discovery was perfectly aware that he discovered no real cause, but only the law or rule according to which the unknown cause operates.]

Natural philosophers, who think accurately, have a precise meaning to the terms they use in the science; and when they pretend to show the cause of any phenomenon of nature, they mean by the cause, a law of nature of which that phenomenon is a necessary consequence.

The whole object of natural philosophy, as Newton expressly

teaches, is reducible to these two heads: first, by just *induction* from experiment and observation, to discover the laws of Nature, and then to apply those laws to the *solution* of the phenomena of Nature. This was all that this great philosopher attempted, and all that he thought attainable. And this indeed he attained in a great measure, with regard to the motions of our planetary system, and with regard to the rays of light.

But supposing that all the phenomena that fall within the reach of our senses were accounted for from general laws of nature, justly deduced from experience; that is, supposing natural philosophy brought to its utmost perfection, it does not discover the efficient cause of any one phenomenon in nature.

The laws of nature are the rules according to which the effects are produced; but there must be a cause which operates according to these rules. The rules of navigation never navigated a ship. The rules of architecture never built a house.

Natural philosophers, by great attention to the course of nature, have discovered many of her laws, and have very happily applied them to account for many phenomena; but they have never discovered the efficient cause of any one phenomenon; nor do those who have distinct notions of the principles of the science, make any such pretence.

Upon the theatre of nature we see innumerable effects, which require an agent, endowed with active power; but the agent is behind the scene. [Whether it be (1) the Supreme Cause alone, or (2) a subordinate cause or causes, and (3) if subordinate causes be employed by the Almighty, what their nature, their number, and their different offices may be, are things hid, for wise reasons without doubt, from the human eye.]

It is only in human actions, that may be imputed for praise or blame, that it is necessary for us to know who is the agent; and in this, nature has given us all the light that is necessary for our conduct.

CHAPTER VII.

OF THE EXTENT OF HUMAN POWER.

I. *Power an attribute of accountable beings.*—Every thing laudable and praiseworthy in man, must consist in the proper exercise of that power which is given him by his Maker. This is the talent which he is required to occupy, and of which he must give an account to him who committed it to his trust.

[To some persons more power is given than to others; and to the same person more at one time and less at another. Its existence, its extent, and its continuance, depend solely upon the pleasure of the Almighty; but *every man that is accountable must have more or less of it.* For, to call a person to account, to approve or disapprove of his conduct, who had no power to do good or ill, is absurd.] No axiom of Euclid appears more evident than this.

As power is a valuable gift, to under-rate it is ingratitude to the giver; to over-rate it, begets pride and presumption, and leads to unsuccessful attempts. It is therefore, in every man, a point of wisdom to make a just estimate of his own power. " Quid ferre recusent, quid valeant humeri."

II. [We can only speak of the power of man in general; and as *our notion of power is relative* to its effects, we can estimate its extent only by the effects which it is able to produce.]

It would be wrong to estimate the extent of human power by the effects which it has actually produced. For every man had power to do many things which he did not, and not to do many things which he did; otherwise he could not be an object either of approbation or of disapprobation, to any rational being.

The effects of human power are either immediate, or they are more remote.

The immediate effects, I think, are reducible to two heads. We can give certain motions to our own bodies; and we can give a certain direction to our own thoughts.

Whatever we can do beyond this, must be done by one of these means, or both.

We can produce no motion in any body in the universe, but by moving first our own body as an instrument. Nor can we produce thought in any other person, but by thought and motion in ourselves.

Our power to move our own body is not only limited in its extent, but in its nature is subject to mechanical laws. It may be compared to a spring endowed with the power of contracting or expanding itself, but which cannot contract without drawing equally at both ends, nor expand without pushing equally at both ends; so that every action of the spring is always accompanied with an equal re-action in a contrary direction.

We can conceive a man to have power to move his whole body in any direction, without the aid of any other body, or a power to move one part of his body without the aid of any other part. But philosophy teaches us that man has no such power.

If he carries his whole body in any direction with a certain quantity of motion, this he can do only by pushing the earth, or some other body, with an equal quantity of motion in the contrary direction. If he but stretch out his arm in one direction, the rest of his body is pushed with an equal quantity of motion in the contrary direction.

This is the case with regard to all animal and voluntary motions, which come within the reach of our senses. They are performed by the contraction of certain muscles; and a muscle, when it is contracted, draws equally at both ends. As to the motions antecedent to the contraction of the muscle, and consequently upon the volition of the animal, we know nothing, and can say nothing about them.

We know not even how those immediate effects of our power are produced by our willing them. We perceive not any necessary connexion between the volition and exertion on our part, and the motion of our body that follows them.

☞ Anatomists inform us, that every voluntary motion of the body is performed by the contraction of certain muscles, and that the muscles are contracted by some influence derived from the nerves. But, without thinking in the least either of muscles or nerves, we will only the external effect, and the internal machinery, without our call, immediately produces that effect.

This is one of the wonders of our frame, which we have reason to admire; but to account for it is beyond the reach of our understanding.

That there is an established harmony between our willing certain motions of our bodies, and the operation of the nerves and muscles which produces those motions, is a fact known by experience. This volition is an act of the mind. But whether this act of the mind have any physical effect upon the nerves and muscles, or whether it be only an occasion of their being acted upon by some other efficient, according to the established laws of nature, is hid from us. So dark is our conception of our own power when we trace it to its origin.

III. [We have good reason to believe, that *matter had its origin from mind,* as well as all its motions; but how, or in what manner, it is moved by mind, we know as little as how it was created.]

It is possible, therefore, for any thing we know, that what we call the immediate effects of our power, may not be so in the strictest sense. Between the will to produce the effect, and the production of it, there may be agents or instruments of which we are ignorant.

This may leave some doubt, whether we be, in the strictest sense, the efficient cause of the voluntary motions of our own body. But it can produce no doubt with regard to the moral estimation of our actions.

The man who knows that such an event depends upon his will, and who deliberately wills to produce it, is, in the strictest moral sense, the cause of the event; and it is justly imputed to him, whatever physical causes may have concurred in its production.

☞ Thus, he who maliciously intends to shoot his neighbour dead, and voluntarily does it, is undoubtedly the cause of his death, though he did no more to occasion it than draw the trigger of the gun. He neither gave to the ball its velocity, nor to the powder its expansive force, nor to the flint and steel the power to strike fire; but he knew that what he did must be followed by the man's death, and did it with that intention; and therefore he is justly chargeable with the murder.

Philosophers may therefore dispute innocently, whether we be the proper efficient causes of the voluntary motions of our own body; or whether we be only, as Malebranche thinks, the occasional causes. The determination of this question, if it can be determined, can have no effect on human conduct.

IV. The other branch of what is immediately in our power, is *to give a certain direction to our own thoughts.* This, as well as the first branch, is limited in various ways. It is greater in some persons than in others, and in the same person is very different, according to the health of his body, and the state of his mind. [But that men, when free from disease of body and of mind, have a considerable degree of power of this kind, and that it may be greatly increased by practice and habit, is sufficiently evident from experience, and from the natural conviction of all mankind.]

[Were we to examine minutely (1) into the connexion between our volitions, and the *direction of our thoughts* which obey these volitions; were we to consider (2) how we are able to give attention to an object for a certain time, and turn our attention to another when we choose, we might perhaps find it difficult to determine, whether *the mind* itself be *the sole efficient cause* of the voluntary changes in the direction of our thoughts, or whether it requires the aid of other efficient causes.]

I see no good reason why the dispute about efficient and occasional causes may not be applied to the power of directing our thoughts, as well as to the power of moving our bodies. In both cases, I apprehend, the dispute is endless, and, if it could be brought to an issue, would be fruitless.

Nothing appears more evident to our reason, than that there must be an efficient cause of every change that happens in nature. But when I attempt to comprehend the manner in which an efficient cause operates, either upon body or upon mind, there is a darkness which my faculties are not able to penetrate.

V. [However small the *immediate* effects of human power seem to be, its *more remote* effects are very considerable.]

☞ In this respect, the power of man may be compared to the Nile, the Ganges, and other great rivers, which make a figure upon the globe of the earth, and, traversing vast regions, bring sometimes great benefit, at other times great mischief, to many nations; yet, when we trace those rivers to their source, we find them to rise from inconsiderable fountains and rills.

☞ The command of a mighty prince, what is it but the sound of his breath, modified by his organs of speech? But it may have great consequences; it may raise armies, equip fleets, and spread war and desolation over a great part of the earth.

The meanest of mankind has considerable power to do good, and more to hurt himself and others.

From this I think we may conclude, that although the degeneracy of mankind be great, and justly to be lamented, yet, men in general are more disposed to employ their power in doing good, than in doing hurt to their fellow-men. The last is much more in their power than the first; and, if they were as much disposed to it, human society could not subsist, and the species must soon perish from the earth.

VI. We may *first consider the effects which may be produced by human power upon the material system.*

It is confined indeed to the planet which we inhabit; we cannot remove to another; nor can we produce any change in the annual or diurnal motions of our own.

But, by human power, great changes may be made upon the face of the earth; and those treasures of metals and minerals that are stored up in its bowels, may be discovered and brought forth.

The Supreme Being could, no doubt, have made the earth to supply the wants of man without any cultivation by human labour. Many inferior animals, who neither plant, nor sow, nor spin, are provided for by the bounty of Heaven. But this is not the case with man.

He has active powers and ingenuity given him, by which he can do much for supplying his wants; and his labour is made necessary for that purpose.

His wants are more than those of any other animal that inhabits this globe; and his resources are proportioned to them, and put within the sphere of his power.

☞ The earth is left by nature in such a state as to require cultivation for the accommodation of man.

It is capable of cultivation, in most places, to such a degree, that, by human labour, it may afford subsistence to an hundred times the number of men it could in its natural state.

Every tribe of men, in every climate, must labour for their subsistence and accommodation; and their supply is more or less comfortable, in proportion to the labour properly employed for that purpose.

It is evidently the intention of nature that man should be laborious, and that he should exert his powers of body and mind for his own and for the common good. And, by his power properly applied, he may make great improvement upon the fertility of the earth, and a great addition to his own accommodation and comfortable state.

By clearing, tilling, and manuring the ground, by planting and sowing, by building cities and harbours, draining marshes and lakes, making rivers navigable, and joining them by canals, by manufacturing the rude materials which the earth, duly cultivated, produces in abundance, by the mutual exchange of commodities and of labour, he may make the barren wilderness the habitation of rich and populous states.

If we compare the city of Venice, the province of Holland, the empire of China, with those places of the earth which never felt the hand of industry, we may form some conception of the extent of human power upon the material system, in changing the face of the earth, and furnishing the accommodations of human life.

VII. But, in order *to produce those happy changes, man himself must be improved.*

[His *animal faculties* are sufficient for the preservation of the species; *they grow up of themselves*, like the trees of the forest, which require only the force of nature and the influences of heaven.

His *rational and moral faculties*, like the earth itself, are rude and barren by nature, but capable of a high degree of culture; and *this culture he must receive from parents*, from instructors, from those with whom he lives in society, joined with his own industry.]

If we consider the changes that may be produced by man upon his own mind, and upon the minds of others, they appear to be great.

Upon his own mind he may make great improvement, in acquiring the treasures of useful knowledge, the habits of skill in arts, the habits of wisdom, prudence, self-command, and every other virtue. It is the constitution of nature, that such qualities as exalt and dignify human nature are to be acquired by proper exertions; and, by a contrary conduct, such qualities as debase it below the condition of brutes.

Even upon the minds of others, great effects may be produced by means within the compass of human power; by means of good education, of proper instruction, of persuasion, of good example, and by the discipline of laws and government.

That these have often had great and good effects on the civilization and improvement of individuals, and of nations, cannot be doubted. But what happy effects they might have, if applied universally with the skill and address that is within the reach of human wisdom and power, is not easily conceived, or to what pitch the happiness of human society, and the improvement of the species, might be carried.

What a noble, what a divine employment of human power is here assigned us! How ought it to rouse the ambition of parents, of instructors, of lawgivers, of magistrates, of every man in his station, to contribute his part towards the accomplishment of so glorious an end!

VIII. *Human power entirely dependent upon God and the laws of nature.*—[*The power of man* over his own and other minds, when we trace it to its origin, *is involved in darkness*, no less than his power to move his own and other bodies.]

How far we are properly *efficient* causes, how far *occasional* causes, I cannot pretend to determine.

We know that (1) *habit* produces great changes in the mind; but how it does so, we know not. We know that (2) *example* has a powerful, and, in the early period of life, almost an irresistible effect; but we know not how it produces this effect. (3) The *communication of thought*, sentiment, and passion, from one mind to another, has something in it as mysterious as the communication of motion from one body to another.

We perceive one event to follow another, according to established laws of nature, and we are accustomed to call the first the (4) *cause, and* the last the EFFECT, without knowing what is the bond that unites them. In order to produce a certain event, we use means which, by laws of nature, are connected with that event; and we call ourselves the cause of that event, though other efficient causes may have had the chief hand in its production.

Upon the whole, [human power, in its (1) existence, in its (2) extent, and in its (3) exertions, is entirely dependent upon God, and upon the laws of nature which he has established.] This ought to banish pride and arrogance from the most mighty of the sons of men. At the same time, that degree of power which we have received from the bounty of Heaven, is one of the noblest gifts of God to man; of which we ought not to be insensible, that we may not be ungrateful, and that we may be excited to make the proper use of it.

IX. *The extent of human power is perfectly suited to the state of man,* as a state of improvement and discipline. It is sufficient to animate us to the noblest exertions. By the proper exercise of this gift of God, human nature, in individuals and in societies, may be exalted to a high degree of dignity and felicity, and the earth become a paradise. On the contrary, its perversion and abuse is the cause of most of the evils that afflict human life.

ESSAY II.

OF THE WILL.

CHAPTER I.

OBSERVATIONS CONCERNING THE WILL.

I. *Volition and will different.*—EVERY man is conscious of a power to determine, in things which he conceives to depend upon his determination. To this power we give the name of *will;* and, as it is usual, in the operations of the mind, to give the same name to the power and to the act of that power, the term *will* is often put to signify the act of determining, which more properly is called *volition.*

[*Volition*, therefore, *signifies the act of willing* and determining; and *will* is put indifferently to signify *either the power* of willing, *or the act.*]

But the term *will* has very often, especially in the writings of philosophers, a more extensive meaning, which we must carefully distinguish from that which we have now given.

In the general division of our faculties into understanding and will, our passions, appetites, and affections, are comprehended under the will; and so it is made to signify, not only our determination to act or not to act, but every motive and incitement to action.

It is this, probably, that has led some philosophers to represent desire, aversion, hope, fear, joy, sorrow, all our appetites, passions, and affections, as different modifications of the will, which, I think, tends to confound things which are very different in their nature.

The advice given to a man, and his determination consequent to that advice, are things so different in their nature, that it would be improper to call them modifications of one and the same thing. In like manner, the motives to action, and the determination to act or not to act, are things that have no common nature, and therefore ought not to be confounded under one name, or represented as different modifications of the same thing.

II. *The term will, how used.*—[For this reason, in speaking of the will in this Essay, I do not comprehend under that term any of the incitements or motives which may have an influence upon our determinations, but solely *the determination itself*, and *the power to determine.*]

Mr. Locke has considered this operation of the mind more attentively, and distinguished it more accurately, than some very ingenious authors who wrote after him.

He defines volition* to be, " an act of the mind knowingly exerting that dominion it takes itself to have over any part of the man, by employing it in, or withholding it from, any particular action."†

III. *Its definition.*—[It may more briefly be defined, *the determination of the mind to do or not to do something which we conceive to be in our power.*]

If this were given as a strictly logical definition, it would be liable to this objection, that the determination of the mind is only another term for volition. But it ought to be observed, that the most simple acts of the mind do not admit of a logical definition. The way to form a clear notion of them is, to reflect attentively upon them as we feel them in ourselves. Without this reflection, no definition can give us a distinct conception of them.

For this reason, rather than sift any definition of the will, I shall make some observations upon it, which may lead us to reflect upon it, and to distinguish it from other acts of mind, which, from the ambiguity of words, are apt to be confounded with it.

[*First*, every act of will must have an *object*. He that wills, must will something; and that which he wills is called the object of his volition. As a man cannot think without thinking of something, nor remember without remembering something, so neither can he will without willing something.] Every act of will, therefore, must have an object; and the person who wills must have some conception, more or less distinct, of what he wills.

By this, things done voluntarily are distinguished from things done merely from instinct, or merely from habit.

☞ A healthy child, some hours after its birth, feels the sensation of hunger, and, if applied to the breast, sucks and swallows its food very perfectly. We have no reason to think, that, before it ever sucked, it has any conception of that complex operation, or how it is performed. It cannot, therefore, with propriety, be said, that it wills to suck.

---

* " The actual exercise of that power, by directing any particular action or its forbearance, is that which we call *volition*, or *willing*."—Book II. chap. xxi. sect. 5.

† Book II. chap. xxi. sect. 15.

Numberless instances might be given of things done by animals without any previous conception of what they are to do—without the intention of doing it. They act by some inward blind impulse, of which the efficient cause is hid from us; and though there is an end evidently intended by the action, this intention is not in the animal, but in its Maker.

Other things are done by habit, which cannot properly be called voluntary. We shut our eyes several times every minute while we are awake; no man is conscious of willing this every time he does it.

[A *second* observation is, that the immediate object of will must be *some action of our own*.

By this, will is distinguished from two acts of the mind, which sometimes take its name, and thereby are apt to be confounded with it; these are, *desire* and *command*.]

IV. The *distinction between will and desire* has been well explained by Mr. Locke; yet many later writers have overlooked it, and have represented desire as a modification of will.

[Desire and will *agree* in this, that both must have an object, of which we must have some conception; and therefore both must be accompanied with some degree of understanding. But they *differ* in several things.]

The object of desire may be any thing which appetite, passion, or affection, leads us to pursue; it may be any event which we think good for us, or for those to whom we are well affected. I may desire meat, or drink, or ease from pain: but to say that I will meat, or will drink, or will ease from pain, is not English. There is, therefore, a distinction in common language between desire and will. And the distinction is, that what we will must be an action, and our own action; what we desire may not be our own action, it may be no action at all.

A man desires that his children may be happy, and that they may behave well. Their being happy is no action at all; their behaving well is not his action, but theirs.

With regard to our own actions, we may desire what we do not will, and will what we do not desire; nay, what we have a great aversion to.

A man a-thirst has a strong desire to drink, but, for some particular reason, he determines not to gratify his desire. A judge, from a regard to justice, and to the duty of his office, dooms a criminal to die, while, from humanity or particular affection, he desires that he should live. A man, for health, may take a nauseous draught, for which he has no desire, but a great aversion. [Desire, therefore, even when its object is some action of our own, is only an *incitement* to will, but it is *not volition*.] The determination of the mind may be, not to do what we desire to do. But as desire is often accompanied by will, we are apt to overlook the distinction between them.

V. *Of command, will, and desire.*—[The *command* of a person *is sometimes called* his *will*, sometimes his *desire;* but when these words are used properly, they signify *three* different acts of the mind.

The immediate object of will is some action of our own; the object of a command is some action of another person, over whom we claim authority; the object of desire may be no action at all.]

In giving a command, all these acts concur; and as they go together, it is not uncommon in language to give to one the name which properly belongs to another.

A command being a voluntary action, there must be a will to give the command: some desire is commonly the motive to that act of will, and the command is the effect of it.

Perhaps it may be thought that a command is only a desire expressed by language, that the thing commanded should be done. But it is not so. For a desire may be expressed by language when there is no command; and there may possibly be a command without any desire that the thing commanded should be done. There have been instances of tyrants who have laid grievous commands upon their subjects, in order to reap the penalty of their disobedience, or to furnish a pretence for their punishment.

We might further observe, that *a command is a social act* of the mind. It can have no existence but by a communication of thought to some intelligent being; and therefore implies a belief that there is such a being, and that we can communicate our thoughts to him.

Desire and will are solitary acts, which do not imply any such communication or belief.

The immediate object of volition, therefore, must be some action, and our own action.

[A *third* observation is, That the object of our volition must be *something* which we believe to be *in our power*, and to depend upon our will.]

A man may desire to make a visit to the moon, or to the planet Jupiter, but he cannot will or determine to do it; because he knows it is not in his power. If an insane person should make an attempt, his insanity must first make him believe it to be in his power.

A man in his sleep may be struck with a palsy, which deprives him of the power of speech; when he awakes, he attempts to speak, not knowing that he has lost the power. But when he knows by experience that the power is gone, he ceases to make the effort.

The same man, knowing that some persons have recovered

the power of speech after they had lost it by a paralytic stroke, may now and then make an effort. In this effort, however, there is not properly a will to speak, but a will to try whether he can speak or not.

In like manner, a man may exert his strength to raise a weight which is too heavy for him. But he always does this, either from the belief that he can raise the weight, or for a trial whether he can or not. It is evident, therefore, that what we will must be believed to be in our power, and to depend upon our will.

[The *next* observation is, That when we will to do a thing immediately, the *volition is accompanied with an effort to execute* that which we will.]

If a man wills to raise a great weight from the ground by the strength of his arm, he makes an effort for that purpose proportioned to the weight he determines to raise. A great weight requires a great effort; a small weight a less effort. We say, indeed, that to raise a very small body requires no effort at all. But this, I apprehend, must be understood either as a figurative way of speaking, by which things very small are accounted as nothing; or it is owing to our giving no attention to very small efforts, and therefore having no name for them.

Great efforts, whether of body or mind, are attended with difficulty, and, when long continued, produce lassitude, which requires that they should be intermitted. This leads us to reflect upon them, and to give them a name. The name *effort* is commonly appropriated to them; and those that are made with ease, and leave no sensible effect, pass without observation and without a name, though they be of the same kind, and differ only in degree from those to which the name is given.

This effort we are conscious of, if we will but give attention to it; and there is nothing in which we are in a more strict sense active.

[The *last* observation is, That in all determinations of the mind that are of any importance, *there must be something in the preceding state of the mind that* disposes or *inclines us to that determination.*]

If the mind were always in a state of perfect indifference, without any incitement, motive, or reason, to act, or not to act, to act one way rather than another, our active power, having no end to pursue, no rule to direct its exertions, would be given in vain. We should either be altogether inactive, and never will to do any thing, or our volitions would be perfectly unmeaning and futile, being neither wise nor foolish, virtuous nor vicious.

We have reason, therefore, to think, that to every being to whom God hath given any degree of active power, he hath also given some principles of action, for the direction of that power to the end for which it was intended.

It is evident that, in the constitution of man, there are various principles of action suited to our state and situation. A particular consideration of these is the subject of the next Essay; in this we are only to consider them in general, with a view to examine the relation they bear to volition, and how it is influenced by them.

CHAPTER II.

OF THE INFLUENCE OF INCITEMENTS AND MOTIVES UPON THE WILL.

I. *Instinct.*—WE come into the world ignorant of every thing, yet we must do many things in order to our subsistence and wellbeing. A new-born child may be carried in arms, and kept warm by his nurse, but he must suck and swallow his food for himself. And this must be done before he has any conception of sucking or swallowing, or of the manner in which they are to be performed. [He is led by nature to do these actions, without knowing for what end, or what he is about. This we call *instinct.*]

In many cases, there is no time for voluntary determination. The motions must go on so rapidly, that the conception and volition of every movement cannot keep pace with them. In some cases of this kind, instinct, in others habit, comes in to our aid.

☞ When a man stumbles and loses his balance, the motion necessary to prevent his fall would come too late, if it were the consequence of thinking what is fit to be done, and making a voluntary effort for that purpose. He does this instinctively.

When a man beats a drum or plays a tune, he has not time to direct every particular beat or stop by a voluntary determination; but the habit which may be acquired by exercise answers the purpose as well.

[By instinct, therefore, and by habit, we do many things *without* any exercise either of *judgment or will.*]

In other actions, the will is exerted, but without judgment.

Suppose a man to know that, in order to live, he must eat. What shall he eat? How much? And how often? His reason can answer none of these questions; and therefore can give no direction how he should determine. Here again nature, as an indulgent parent, supplies the defects of his reason; giving him appetite, which shows him when he is to eat, how often, and how much; and taste, which informs him what he is and what he is not to eat. And by these principles he is much better directed than he could be, without them, by all the knowledge he can acquire.

II. *Judgment not necessary to instinct.*—As the Author of

nature has given us some principles of action to supply the defects of our knowledge, he has given others to supply the defects of our wisdom and virtue.

The natural desires, affections, and passions, which are common to the wise and to the foolish, to the virtuous and to the vicious, and even to the more sagacious brutes, serve very often to direct the course of human actions. By these principles, men may perform the most laborious duties of life, without any regard to duty; and do what is proper to be done, without regard to propriety, ☞ like a vessel that is carried on in her proper course by a prosperous gale, *without the* skill or *judgment* of those that are aboard.

Appetite, affection, or passion, give an impulse to a certain action. In this impulse there is no judgment implied. It may be weak or strong; we can even conceive it irresistible. In the case of madness, it is so. Madmen have their appetites and passions; but they want the power of self-government; and therefore we do not impute their actions to the man, but to the disease.

In actions that proceed from appetite or passion, we are passive in part, and only in part active. They are therefore partly imputed to the passion; and if it is supposed to be irresistible, we do not impute them to the man at all.

Even an American savage judges in this manner: when in a fit of drunkenness, he kills his friend: as soon as he comes to himself, he is very sorry for what he has done; but pleads, that drink, and not he, was the cause.

We conceive brute animals to have no superior principle to control their appetites and passions. On this account, their actions are not subject to law. Men are in a like state in infancy, in madness, and in the delirium of a fever. They have appetites and passions, but they want that which makes them moral agents, accountable for their conduct, and objects of moral approbation or of blame.

In some cases, a stronger impulse of appetite or passion may oppose a weaker. Here also there may be determination and action without judgment.

Suppose a soldier ordered to mount a breach, and certain of present death if he retreats: this man needs not courage to go on; fear is sufficient. The certainty of present death if he retreats, is an overbalance to the probability of being killed if he goes on. The man is pushed by contrary forces, and it requires neither judgment nor exertion to yield to the strongest.

A hungry dog acts by the same principle, if meat is set before him, with a threatening to beat him if he touch it. Hunger pushes him forward, fear pushes him back with more force, and the strongest force prevails.

Thus we see, that, in many even of our voluntary actions, we may act from the impulse of appetite, affection, or passion, without any exercise of judgment, and much in the same manner as brute animals seem to act.

III. *The exercise of judgment distinct from the impulse of appetite.*—[Sometimes, however, there is a calm in the mind from the gales of passion or appetite, and the man is left to work his way, in the voyage of life, *without those impulses* which they give.] Then he calmly weighs goods and evils, which are at too great a distance to excite any passion. He judges what is best upon the whole, without feeling any bias drawing him to one side. He judges for himself as he would do for another in his situation; and the determination is wholly imputable to the man, and not in any degree to his passion.

Every man come to years of understanding, who has given any attention to his own conduct, and to that of others, has, in his mind, a scale or measure of goods and evils, more or less exact. He makes an estimate of the value of health, of reputation, of riches, of pleasure, of virtue, of self-approbation, and of the approbation of his Maker. These things, and their contraries, have a comparative importance in his cool and deliberate judgment.

[When a man considers whether health ought to be preferred to bodily strength, fame to riches,—whether a good conscience and the approbation of his Maker, to every thing that can come in competition with it,—this appears to me to be *an exercise of judgment*, and *not any impulse of* passion or *appetite*.]

Every thing worthy of pursuit must be so, either intrinsically, and upon its own account, or as the means of procuring something that is intrinsically valuable. That it is by judgment that we discern the fitness of means for attaining an end, is self-evident; and in this, I think, all philosophers agree. But that it is the office of judgment to appreciate the value of an end, or the preference due to one end above another, is not granted by some philosophers.

In determining what is good or ill, and, of different goods, which is best, they think we must be guided, not by judgment, but by some natural or acquired taste, which makes us relish one thing and dislike another.

Thus, if one man prefers cheese to lobsters, another lobsters to cheese, it is vain, say they, to apply judgment to determine which is right. In like manner, if one man prefers pleasure to virtue, another virtue to pleasure, this is a matter of taste, judgment has nothing to do in it. This seems to be the opinion of some philosophers.

I cannot help being of a contrary opinion. I think we may

form a judgment, both in the question about cheese and lobsters, and in the more important question about pleasure and virtue.

When one man feels a more agreeable relish in cheese, another in lobsters, this, I grant, requires no judgment; it depends only upon the constitution of the palate. But, if we would determine which of the two has the best taste, I think the question must be determined by judgment; and that, with a small share of this faculty, we may give a very certain determination, to wit, that the two tastes are equally good, and that both of the persons do equally well, in preferring what suits their palate and their stomach.

Nay, I apprehend, that the two persons who differ in their taste will, notwithstanding that difference, agree perfectly in their judgment, that both tastes are upon a footing of equality, and that neither has a just claim to preference.

IV. *Taste and judgment differ.*—[Thus it appears, that, in this instance, the office of taste is very different from that of judgment; and that men, who differ most in taste, may agree perfectly in their judgment, even with respect to the tastes wherein they differ.]

To make the other case parallel with this, it must be supposed that the man of pleasure and the man of virtue agree in their judgment, and that neither sees any reason to prefer the one course of life to the other.

If this be supposed, I shall grant, that neither of these persons has reason to condemn the other. Each chooses according to his taste, in matters which his best judgment determines to be perfectly indifferent.

But it is to be observed, that this supposition cannot have place when we speak of men, or indeed of moral agents. The man who is incapable of perceiving the obligation of virtue, when he uses his best judgment, is a man in name, but not in reality. He is incapable either of virtue or vice, and is not a moral agent.

Even the man of pleasure, when his judgment is unbiassed, sees, that there are certain things which a man ought not to do, though he should have a taste for them. If a thief breaks into his house, and carries off his goods, he is perfectly convinced that he did wrong, and deserves punishment, although he had as strong a relish for the goods as he himself has for the pleasures he pursues.

V. *Of passion and reason.*—[It is evident, that mankind, in all ages, have conceived two parts in the human constitution that may have influence upon our voluntary actions. These we call by the general names of *passion* and *reason;* and we shall find, in all languages, names that are equivalent.]

Under the former, we comprehend various principles of action, similar to those we observe in brute animals, and in men who have not the use of reason. *Appetites, affections, passions*, are the names by which they are denominated; and these names are not so accurately distinguished in common language, but that they are used somewhat promiscuously. This, however, is common to them all, that they draw a man toward a certain object, without any farther view, by a kind of violence; a violence which indeed may be resisted if the man is master of himself, but cannot be resisted without a struggle.

Cicero's phrase for expressing their influence is, " Hominem huc et illuc rapiunt." Dr. Hutcheson uses a similar phrase, " Quibus agitatur mens et bruto quodam impetu fertur." There is no exercise of reason or judgment necessary in order to feel their influence.

With regard to this part (passion) of the human constitution, I see no difference between the vulgar and philosophers.

As to the other part of our constitution, which is commonly called *reason*, as opposed to passion, there have been very subtle disputes among modern philosophers, whether it ought to be called reason, or be not rather some *internal sense* or taste.

Whether it ought to be called reason, or by what other name, I do not here inquire, but what kind of influence it has upon our voluntary actions.

As to this point, I think, all men must allow that this is the *manly* part of our constitution, the other the *brute* part. This operates in a calm and dispassionate manner; a manner so like to judgment or reason, that even those who do not allow it to be called by that name, endeavour to account for its having always had the name, because, in the manner of its operation, it has a similitude to reason.

As the similitude between this principle and reason has led mankind to give it that name, so the dissimilitude between it and passion has led them to set the two in opposition. They have considered this *cool principle* as having an influence upon our actions so different from passion, that what a man does coolly and deliberately, without passion, is imputed solely to the man, whether it have merit or demerit; whereas, what he does from passion is imputed in part to the passion. If the passion be conceived to be irresistible, the action is imputed solely to it, and not at all to the man. If he had power to resist, and ought to have resisted, we blame him for not doing his duty; but, in proportion to the violence of the passion, the fault is alleviated.

By this cool principle, we judge what ends are most worthy to be pursued, how far every appetite and passion may be indulged, and when it ought to be resisted.

It directs us, not only to resist the impulse of passion when it would lead us wrong, but to avoid the occasions of inflaming it; ☞ like Cyrus, who refused to see the beautiful captive princess. In this he acted the part both of a wise and a good man; firm in the love of virtue, and, at the same time, conscious of the weakness of human nature, and unwilling to put it to too severe a trial. In this case, the youth of Cyrus, the incomparable beauty of his captive, and every circumstance which tended to inflame his desire, exalts the merit of his conduct in resisting it.

It is in such actions that the superiority of human nature appears, and the specific difference between it and that of brutes. In them we may observe one passion combating another, and the strongest prevailing; but we perceive no calm principle in their constitution, that is superior to every passion, and able to give law to it.

VI. The difference between these two parts of our constitution may be farther illustrated by an instance or two wherein passion prevails.

☞ If a man, upon great provocation, strike another when he ought to keep the peace, he blames himself for what he did, and acknowledges that he ought not to have yielded to his passion. Every other person agrees with his sober judgment: they think he did wrong in yielding to his passion, when he might and ought to have resisted its impulse. If they thought it impossible to bear the provocation, they would not blame him at all; but believing that it was in his power, and was his duty, they impute to him some degree of blame, acknowledging, at the same time, that it is alleviated in proportion to the provocation; so that the trespass is imputed, partly to the man, and partly to the passion. But if a man deliberately conceives a design of mischief against his neighbour, contrives the means, and executes it, the action admits of no alleviation, it is perfectly voluntary, and he bears the whole guilt of the evil intended and done.

If a man, by the agony of the rack, is made to disclose a secret of importance, with which he is intrusted, we pity him more than we blame him. We consider, that such is the weakness of human nature, that the resolution, even of a good man, might be overcome by such a trial. But if he have strength of mind, which even the agony of the rack could not subdue, we admire his fortitude as truly heroical.

Thus, I think, it appears, that the common sense of men (which, in matters of common life, ought to have great authority) has led them to distinguish two parts in the human constitution, which have influence upon our voluntary determinations. There is an irrational part, common to us with brute animals, consisting of appetites, affections, and passions; and there is a cool and rational part. The first, in many cases, gives a strong impulse, but without judgment, and without authority. The second is always accompanied with authority. All wisdom and virtue consist in following its dictates; all vice and folly in disobeying them. We may resist the impulses of appetite and passion, not only without regret, but with self-applause and triumph; but the calls of reason and duty can never be resisted without remorse and self-condemnation.

VII. [The ancient philosophers agreed with the vulgar, in making this distinction of the principles of action.] The irrational part the Greeks called ὁρμή; Cicero calls it *appetitus*, taking that word in an extensive sense, so as to include every propensity to action which is not grounded on judgment.

The other principle the Greeks called νους; Plato calls it the ἡγημονικον, or leading principle. "Duplex enim est vis animorum atque naturæ," says Cicero, "una pars in appetitu posita est, quæ est ὁρμή Græcè, quæ hominem huc et illuc rapit; altera in ratione, quæ docet, et explanat, quid faciendum fugiendumve sit; ita fit ut ratio præsit, appetitus obtemperet."

The reason of explaining this distinction here is, that these two principles influence the will in different ways. Their influence differs, not in degree only, but in kind. This difference we feel, though it may be difficult to find words to express it. We may perhaps more easily form a notion of it by a similitude.

It is one thing to push a man from one part of the room to another: it is a thing of a very different nature to use arguments to persuade him to leave his place, and go to another. He may yield to the force which pushes him, without any exercise of his rational faculties; nay, he must yield to it, if he do not oppose an equal or a greater force. His liberty is impaired in some degree; and, if he has not power sufficient to oppose, his liberty is quite taken away, and the motion cannot be imputed to him at all. The influence of appetite or passion seems to me to be very like to this. If the passion be supposed irresistible, we impute the action to it solely, and not to the man. If he had power to resist, but yields after a struggle, we impute the action partly to the man and partly to the passion.

If we attend to the other case, when the man is only urged by arguments to leave his place, this resembles the operation of the cool or rational principle. It is evident that, whether he yields to the arguments or not, the determination is wholly his own act, and is entirely to be imputed to him. Arguments, whatever be the degree of their strength, diminish not a man's liberty; they may produce a cool conviction of what we ought to do, and they can do no more. But appetite and passion give an impulse to act and impair liberty, in proportion to their strength.

With most men, the impulse of passion is more effectual than bare conviction; and, on this account, orators, who would persuade, find it necessary to address the passions, as well as to convince the understanding; and, in all systems of rhetoric, these two have been considered as different intentions of the orator, and to be accomplished by different means.

CHAPTER III.

OF OPERATIONS OF MIND WHICH MAY BE CALLED VOLUNTARY.

I. *Of attention, deliberation, and resolution.*—THE faculties of understanding and will are easily distinguished in thought, but very rarely, if ever, disjoined in operation.

In most, perhaps in all the operations of mind for which we have names in language, both faculties are employed, and we are both intellective and active.

Whether it be possible that intelligence may exist without some degree of activity, or impossible, is perhaps beyond the reach of our faculties to determine; but I apprehend that, in fact, they are always conjoined in the operations of our minds.

It is probable, I think, that there is some degree of activity in those operations which we refer to the understanding; accordingly, they have always, and in all languages, been expressed by active verbs; as, I see, I hear, I remember, I apprehend, I judge, I reason. And it is certain that every act of will must be accompanied by some operation of the understanding; for he that wills must apprehend what he wills, and apprehension belongs to the understanding.

The operations I am to consider in this chapter, I think, have commonly been referred to the understanding; but we shall find that the will has so great a share in them, that they may, with propriety, be called *voluntary*. They are these three,—*attention, deliberation*, and *fixed purpose*, or *resolution*.

[*Attention* may be given to any object, either of sense or of intellect, in order to form a distinct notion of it, or to discover its nature, its attributes, or its relations. And *so great is the effect of attention*, that, without it, it is impossible to acquire or retain a distinct notion of any object of thought.]

If a man hear a discourse without attention, what does he carry away with him? If he see St. Peter's or the Vatican without attention, what account can he give of it? While two persons are engaged in interesting discourse, the clock strikes within their hearing, to which they give no attention: what is the consequence? The next minute they know not whether the clock struck or not. Yet their ears were not shut. The usual impression was made upon the organ of hearing, and upon the auditory nerve and brain; but from inattention the sound either was not perceived, or passed in the twinkling of an eye, without leaving the least vestige in the memory.

A man sees not what is before his eyes when his mind is occupied about another object. In the tumult of a battle, a man may be shot through the body without knowing anything of the matter, till he discover it by the loss of blood or of strength.

The most acute sensation of pain may be deadened, if the attention can be vigorously directed to another object. A gentleman of my acquaintance, in the agony of a fit of the gout, used to call for the chess-board. As he was fond of that game, he acknowledged that, as the game advanced and drew his attention, the sense of pain abated, and the time seemed much shorter.

☞ Archimedes, it is said, being intent upon a mathematical proposition, when Syracuse was taken by the Romans, knew not the calamity of the city, till a Roman soldier broke in upon his retirement, and gave him a deadly wound; on which he lamented only that he had lost a fine demonstration.

It is needless to multiply instances to show, that when one faculty of the mind is intensely engaged about any object, the other faculties are laid, as it were, fast asleep.

II. *Of genius.*—It may be farther observed, that [if there be any thing that can be called *genius*, in matters of mere judgment and reasoning, it seems to consist chiefly in being able to give that attention to the subject which keeps it steady in the mind, till we can survey it accurately on all sides.]

There is a talent of imagination, which bounds from earth to heaven, and from heaven to earth, in a moment. This may be favourable to wit and imagery; but the powers of judging and reasoning depend chiefly upon keeping the mind to a clear and steady view of the subject.

Sir Isaac Newton, to one who complimented him upon the force of genius, which had made such improvements in mathematics and natural philosophy, is said to have made this reply, which was both modest and judicious, that, if he had made any improvements in those sciences, it was owing more to patient *attention* than to any other talent.

Whatever be the effects which attention may produce, (and I apprehend they are far beyond what is commonly believed,) it is for the most part in our power.

Every man knows that he can turn his attention to this subject or to that, for a longer or a shorter time, and with more or less intenseness, as he pleases. It is a voluntary act, and depends upon his will.

But what was before observed of the will in general, is applicable to this particular exertion of it, that the mind is rarely in a state of indifference, left to turn its attention to the object which to reason appears most deserving of it. There is, for the most part, a bias to some particular object more than to any other; and this not from any judgment of its deserving our attention more, but from some impulse or propensity, grounded on nature or habit.

It is well known, that things new and uncommon, things grand, and things that are beautiful, draw our attention, not in proportion to the interest we have, or think we have in them, but in a much greater proportion.

Whatever moves our passions or affections draws our attention, very often, more than we wish.

You desire a man not to think of an unfortunate event which torments him. It admits of no remedy. The thought of it answers no purpose but to keep the wound bleeding. He is perfectly convinced of all you say. He knows that he would not feel the affliction, if he could only not think of it; yet he hardly thinks of any thing else. Strange! when happiness and misery stand before him, and depend upon his choice, he chooses misery, and rejects happiness with his eyes open!

Yet he wishes to be happy, as all men do. How shall we reconcile this contradiction between his judgment and his conduct?

The account of it seems to me to be this: the afflicting event draws his attention so strongly, by a natural and blind force, that he either hath not the power, or hath not the vigour of mind, to resist its impulse, though he knows that to yield to it is misery, without any good to balance it.

Acute bodily pain draws our attention, and makes it very difficult to attend to any thing else, even when attention to the pain serves no other purpose but to aggravate it tenfold.

The man who played a game at chess in the agony of the gout, to engage his attention to another object, acted the reasonable part, and consulted his real happiness; but it required a great effort to give that attention to his game which was necessary to produce the effect intended by it.

Even when there is no particular object that draws away our attention, there is a desultoriness of thought in man, and in some more than in others, which makes it very difficult to give that fixed attention to important objects which reason requires.

It appears, I think, from what has been said, that the attention we give to objects is for the most part voluntary; that a great part of wisdom and virtue consists in giving a proper direction to our attention; and that however reasonable this appears to the judgment of every man, yet, in some cases, it requires an effort of self-command no less than the most heroic virtues.

III. *Deliberation.*—[Another operation that may be called *voluntary*, is deliberation about what we are to do or to forbear.]

Every man knows that it is in his power to deliberate or not to deliberate about any part of his conduct; to deliberate for a shorter, or a longer time, more carelessly, or more seriously; and when he has reason to suspect that his affection may bias his judgment, he may either honestly use the best means in his power to form an impartial judgment, or he may yield to his bias, and only seek arguments to justify what inclination leads him to do. In all these points, he determines, he wills, the right or the wrong.

IV. [The general *rules of deliberation* are perfectly evident to reason when we consider them abstractly. They are axioms in morals.]

(1) *We ought not to deliberate in cases that are perfectly clear.*—[No man deliberates whether he ought to choose happiness or misery. No honest man deliberates whether he shall steal his neighbour's property.] [(2) *When the case is not clear*, when it is of importance, and when there is time for deliberation, *we ought to deliberate* with more or less care, in proportion to the importance of the action.] [(3) In deliberation, *we ought* to weigh things in an even balance, and to allow to every consideration the weight which, in sober judgment, we think it ought to have, and no more. This is *to deliberate impartially*.] [(4) Our deliberation should be brought to an issue *in due time*, so that we may not lose the opportunity of acting while we deliberate.]

The axioms of Euclid do not appear to me to have a greater degree of self-evidence, than these rules of deliberation. And as far as a man acts according to them, his heart approves of him, and he has confidence of the approbation of the Searcher of hearts.

But though the manner in which we ought to deliberate be evident to reason, it is not always easy to follow it. Our appetites, our affections, and passions, oppose all deliberation, but that which is employed in finding the means of their gratification. Avarice may lead to deliberate upon the ways of making money, but it does not distinguish between the honest and the dishonest.

We ought surely to deliberate how far every appetite and passion may be indulged, and what limits should be set to it. But our appetites and passions push us on to the attainment of their objects, in the shortest road, and without delay.

Thus it happens, that, if we yield to their impulse, we shall often transgress those rules of deliberation which reason approves. In this conflict between the dictates of reason and the blind impulse of passion, we must voluntarily determine. When we take part with our reason, though in opposition to passion, we approve of our own conduct.

[What we call *a fault of ignorance*, is always owing to the *want of due deliberation*. When we do not take due pains to be rightly informed, there is a fault, not indeed in acting according to the light we have, but in not using the proper means to get light. For if we judge wrong, after using the proper means of information, there is no fault in acting according to that wrong judgment; the error is invincible.]

The natural consequence of deliberation on any part of our conduct, is a determination how we shall act; and if it is not brought to this issue it is lost labour.

V. [There are two cases in which *a determination* may take place; (1) when the opportunity of putting it in execution is *present*, and (2) when it is *at a distance*.]

When the opportunity is present, the determination to act is immediately followed by the action. Thus, if a man determine to rise and walk, he immediately does it, unless he is hindered by force, or has lost the power of walking. And if he sit still when he has power to walk, we conclude infallibly that he has not determined or willed to walk immediately.

Our determination or will to act is not always the result of deliberation; it may be the effect of some passion or appetite, without any judgment interposed. And when judgment is interposed, we may determine and act either according to that judgment, or contrary to it.

When a man sits down hungry to dine, he eats from appetite, very often without exercising his judgment at all; nature invites, and he obeys the call, as the ox, or the horse, or as an infant does.

When we converse with persons whom we love or respect, we say and do civil things merely from affection or from respect. They flow spontaneously from the heart, without requiring any judgment. In such cases, we act as brute-animals do, or as children before the use of reason. We feel an impulse in our nature, and we yield to it.

When a man eats merely from appetite, he does not consider the pleasure of eating, or its tendency to health. These considerations are not in his thoughts. But we can suppose a man who eats with a view to enjoy the pleasure of eating. Such a man reasons and judges. He will take care to use the proper means of procuring an appetite. He will be a critic in tastes, and make nice discriminations. This man uses his rational faculties even in eating. And however contemptible this application of them may be, it is an exercise of which, I apprehend, brute-animals are not capable.

In like manner, a man may say or do civil things to another, not from affection, but in order to serve some end by it, or because he thinks it his duty.

To act with a view to some distant interest, or to act from a sense of duty, seems to be proper to man as a reasonable being; but to act merely from passion, from appetite, or from affection, is common to him with the brute-animals. In the last case there is no judgment required, but in the first there is.

To act against what one judges to be for his real good upon the whole, is folly. To act against what he judges to be his duty, is immorality. It cannot be denied, that there are too many instances of both in human life. " Video meliora proboque, deteriora sequor,"—" I see and approve of better things, I follow worse,"—is neither an impossible nor an unfrequent case.

While a man does what he really thinks wisest and best to be done, the more his appetites, his affections, and passions, draw him the contrary way, the more he approves of his own conduct, and the more he is entitled to the approbation of every rational being.

VI. *Resolution.*—[The *third* operation of mind I mentioned, which may be called voluntary, is, a fixed purpose, or *resolution*, with regard to our future conduct.]

This naturally takes place, when any action, or course of action, about which we have deliberated, is not immediately to be executed, the occasion of acting being at some distance.

[A *fixed purpose* to do, some time hence, something which we believe shall then be in our power, *is strictly* and properly *a determination of will*, no less than a determination to do it instantly.] Every definition of volition agrees to it. Whether the opportunity of doing what we have determined to do be present or at some distance, is an accidental circumstance which does not affect the nature of the determination, and no good reason can be assigned why it should not be called *volition* in the one case, as well as in the other. A purpose or resolution, therefore, is truly and properly an act of will.

Our purposes are of two kinds. We may call the one *particular*, the other *general*. By a *particular* purpose, I mean that which has for its object an individual action, limited to one time and place; by a *general* purpose, that of a course or train of action, intended for some general end, or regulated by some general rule.

Thus, I may purpose to go to London next winter. When the time comes, I execute my purpose, if I continue of the same mind; and the purpose, when executed, is no more. Thus it is with every particular purpose.

A general purpose may continue for life; and, after many particular actions have been done in consequence of it, may remain and regulate future actions.

Thus, a young man proposes to follow the profession of law,

of medicine, or of theology. This general purpose directs the course of his reading and study. It directs him in the choice of his company and companions, and even of his diversions. It determines his travels and the place of his abode. It has influence upon his dress and manners, and a considerable effect in forming his character.

There are other fixed purposes which have a still greater effect in forming the character. I mean such as regard our moral conduct.

Suppose a man to have exercised his intellectual and moral faculties, so far as to have distinct notions of justice and injustice, and of the consequences of both, and, after due deliberation, to have formed a fixed purpose to adhere inflexibly to justice, and never to handle the wages of iniquity.

Is not this the man whom we should call a just man? We consider the moral virtues as inherent in the mind of a good man, even when there is no opportunity of exercising them. And what is it in the mind which we can call the virtue of justice, when it is not exercised? It can be nothing but a fixed purpose, or determination, to act according to the rules of justice, when there is opportunity.

The Roman law defined justice, *a steady and perpetual will to give to every man his due*. When the opportunity of doing justice is not present, this can mean nothing else than a steady purpose, which is very properly called will. Such a purpose, if it is steady, will infallibly produce just conduct; for every known transgression of justice demonstrates a change of purpose, at least for that time.

What has been said of justice, may be so easily applied to every other moral virtue, that it is unnecessary to give instances. They are all fixed purposes of acting according to a certain rule.

VII. *The virtue and affection of benevolence different.*—By this, the virtues may be easily distinguished, in thought at least, from natural affections that bear the same name. Thus, benevolence is a capital virtue, which, though not so necessary to the being of society, is entitled to a higher degree of approbation than even justice. But *there is a natural affection of benevolence*, common to good and bad men, to the virtuous and to the vicious. How shall these be distinguished?

In practice, indeed, we cannot distinguish them in other men, and with difficulty in ourselves; but in theory, nothing is more easy. [*The virtue of benevolence is a fixed purpose* or resolution to do good when we have opportunity, from a conviction that it is right, and is our duty. *The affection of benevolence is a propensity* to do good, from natural constitution or habit, without regard to rectitude or duty.]

There are good tempers and bad, which are a part of the constitution of the man, and are really involuntary, though they often lead to voluntary actions. A good natural temper is not virtue, nor is a bad one vice. Hard would it be indeed to think, that a man should be born under a decree of reprobation, because he has the misfortune of a bad natural temper.

The physiognomist saw, in the features of Socrates, the signatures of many bad dispositions, which that good man acknowledged he felt within him; but the triumph of his virtue was the greater in having conquered them.

In men who have no fixed rules of conduct, no self-government, the natural temper is variable by numberless accidents. The man who is full of affection and benevolence this hour, when a cross accident happens to ruffle him, or perhaps when an easterly wind blows, feels a strange revolution in his temper. The kind and benevolent affections give place to the jealous and malignant, which are as readily indulged in their turn, and for the same reason, because he feels a propensity to indulge them.

We may observe, that men who have exercised their rational powers are generally governed in their opinions by fixed principles of belief; and men who have made the greatest advance in self-government are governed, in their practice, by general fixed purposes. Without the former, there would be no steadiness and consistence in our belief; nor without the latter, in our conduct.

When a man is come to years of understanding; from his education, from his company, or from his study, he forms to himself a set of general principles, a creed, which governs his judgment in particular points that occur.

If new evidence be laid before him, which tends to overthrow any of his received principles, it requires in him a great degree of candour and love of truth to give it an impartial examination, and to form a new judgment. Most men, when they are fixed in their principles, upon what they account sufficient evidence, can hardly be drawn into a new and serious examination of them.

They get a habit of believing them, which is strengthened by repeated acts, and remains immoveable, even when the evidence upon which their belief was at first grounded is forgot.

It is this that makes conversions, either from religious or political principles, so difficult.

A mere prejudice of education sticks fast, as a proposition of Euclid does with a man who hath long ago forgot the proof. Both indeed are upon a similar footing. We rest in both, because we have long done so, and think we received them at first upon good evidence, though that evidence be quite forgot.

When we know a man's principles, we judge by them, rather than by the degree of his understanding, how he will determine in any point which is connected with them.

Thus, [the judgment of most men who judge for themselves is

governed by *fixed principles;* and, I apprehend, that the conduct of most men who have any self-government, and any consistency of conduct, is governed by fixed purposes.]

A man of breeding may, in his natural temper, be proud, passionate, revengeful, and in his morals a very bad man; yet, in good company, he can stifle every passion that is inconsistent with good breeding, and be humane, modest, complaisant, even to those whom in his heart he despises or hates. Why is this man, who can command all his passions before company, a slave to them in private? The reason is plain: he has a fixed resolution to be a man of breeding, but hath no such resolution to be a man of virtue. He hath combated his most violent passions a thousand times before he became master of them in company. The same resolution and perseverance would have given him the command of them when alone.

A fixed resolution retains its influence upon the conduct, even when the motives to it are not in view, in the same manner as a fixed principle retains its influence upon the belief, when the evidence of it is forgot. The former may be called a habit of the *will,* the latter a habit of the *understanding.* By such habits chiefly, men are governed in their opinions and in their practice.

A man who has no general fixed purposes may be said, as Pope says of most women (I hope unjustly), to have no character at all. He will be honest or dishonest, benevolent or malicious, compassionate or cruel, as the tide of his passions and affections drives him. This, however, I believe, is the case of but a few in advanced life, and these, with regard to conduct, the weakest and most contemptible of the species.

A man of some constancy may change his general purposes once or twice in life, seldom more. From the pursuit of pleasure in early life, he may change to that of ambition, and from ambition to avarice. But every man who uses his reason in the conduct of life, will have some end, to which he gives a preference above all others. To this he steers his course; his projects and his actions will be regulated by it. Without this, there would be no consistency in his conduct. He would be like a ship in the ocean, which is bound to no port, under no government, but left to the mercy of winds and tides.

We observed before, that [there are moral rules respecting the *attention* we ought to give to objects, and respecting our *deliberations,* which are no less evident than mathematical axioms. The same thing may be observed with respect to our *fixed purposes,* whether particular or general.]

Is it not self-evident, that, after due deliberation, we ought to resolve upon that conduct, or that course of conduct, which, to our sober judgment, appears to be best and most approvable?— that we ought to be firm and steady in adhering to such resolutions, while we are persuaded that they are right; but open to conviction, and ready to change our course, when we have good evidence that it is wrong.

Fickleness, inconstancy, facility, on the one hand; wilfulness, inflexibility, and obstinacy, on the other, are moral qualities, respecting our purposes, which every one sees to be wrong. A manly firmness, grounded upon rational conviction, is the proper mean which every man approves and reveres.

CHAPTER IV.

COROLLARIES.

I. *Of transient and momentary acts of the will.*—From what has been said concerning the will, it appears, [*first*, That, as some acts of the will are *transient* and momentary, so others are *permanent*, and may continue for a long time, or even through the whole course of our rational life.]

When I will to stretch out my hand, that will is at an end as soon as the action is done. It is an act of the will which begins and ends in a moment. But when I will to attend to a mathematical proposition, to examine the demonstration and the consequences that may be drawn from it, this will may continue for hours. It must continue as long as my attention continues; for no man attends to a mathematical proposition longer than he wills.

The same thing may be said of deliberation, with regard, either to any point of conduct, or with regard to any general course of conduct. We will to deliberate as long as we do deliberate; and that may be for days or for weeks.

A purpose or resolution, which we have shown to be an act of the will, may continue for a great part of life, or for the whole, after we are of age to form a resolution.

Thus, a merchant may resolve, that, after he has made such a fortune by traffic, he will give it up, and retire to a country life. He may continue this resolution for thirty or forty years, and execute it at last; but he continues it no longer than he wills, for he may at any time change his resolution.

[There are, therefore, acts of the will which are *not transient and momentary*, which may continue long, and grow into a *habit*.] This deserves the more to be observed, because a very eminent philosopher has advanced a contrary principle, to wit, That all the acts of the will are transient and momentary; and from that principle has drawn very important conclusions with regard to what constitutes the moral character of man.

II. [A *second* corollary is, That nothing in a man, wherein the will is not concerned, can justly be accounted either virtuous or immoral.]

That no blame can be imputed to a man for what is altogether involuntary, is so evident in itself, that no arguments can make it more evident. The practice of all criminal courts, in all enlightened nations, is founded upon it.

If it should be thought an objection to this maxim, that, by the laws of all nations, children often suffer for the crimes of parents, in which they had no hand, the answer is easy.

For, *first*, Such is the connexion between parents and children, that the punishment of a parent must hurt his children whether the law will or not. If a man is fined, or imprisoned; if he loses life, or limb, or estate, or reputation, by the hand of justice, his children suffer by necessary consequence. *Secondly*, When laws intend to appoint any punishment of innocent children for the father's crime, such laws are either unjust, or they are to be considered as acts of police, and not of jurisprudence, and are intended as an expedient to deter parents more effectually from the commission of the crime. The innocent children, in this case, are sacrified to the public good, in like manner as, to prevent the spreading of the plague, the sound are shut up with the infected in a house or ship that has the infection.

☞ By the law of England, if a man is killed by an ox goring him, or a cart running over him, though there be no fault or neglect in the owner, the ox or the cart is a *deodand*, and is confiscated to the church. The legislature surely did not intend to punish the ox as a criminal, far less the cart. The intention evidently was, to inspire the people with a sacred regard to the life of man.

When the parliament of Paris, with a similar intention, ordained the house in which Ravilliac* was born, to be razed to the ground, and never to be rebuilt, it would be great weakness to conclude, that that wise judicature intended to punish the house.

If any judicature should, in any instance, find a man guilty, and an object of punishment, for what they allowed to be altogether involuntary, all the world would condemn them as men who knew nothing of the first and most fundamental rules of justice.

I have endeavoured to show, that, in our attention to objects, in order to form a right judgment of them; in our deliberation about particular actions, or about general rules of conduct; in our purposes and resolutions, as well as in the execution of them, the will has a principal share. If any man could be found, who, in the whole course of his life, had given due attention to

* The assassin of Henri Quatre.

things that concern him, had deliberated duly and impartially about his conduct, had formed his resolutions, and executed them according to his best judgment and capacity, surely such a man might hold up his face before God and man, and plead innocence. He must be acquitted by the impartial Judge, whatever his natural temper was, whatever his passions and affections, as far as they were involuntary.

III. [A *third* corollary, That *all virtuous habits,* when we distinguish them from virtuous actions, *consist in fixed purposes of acting* according to the rules of virtue, as often as we have opportunity.]

We can conceive in a man a greater or a less degree of steadiness to his purposes or resolutions; but that the general tenor of his conduct should be contrary to them, is impossible.

The man who has a determined resolution to do his duty in every instance, and who adheres steadily to his resolution, is a perfect man. The man who has a determined purpose of carrying on a course of action which he knows to be wrong, is a hardened offender. Between these extremes there are many intermediate degrees of virtue and vice.

ESSAY III.

OF THE PRINCIPLES OF ACTION.

PART I.

OF THE MECHANICAL PRINCIPLES OF ACTION.

CHAPTER I.

OF THE PRINCIPLES OF ACTION IN GENERAL.

I. *Actions of men classified.*—In the strict philosophical sense, nothing can be called the action of a man, but what he previously conceived and willed or determined to do. In morals, we commonly employ the word in this sense, and never impute any thing to a man as his doing, in which his will was not interposed. But when moral imputation is not concerned, we call many things actions of the man, which he neither previously conceived nor willed. [Hence the actions of men have been distinguished into three classes, the *voluntary*, the *involuntary*, and the *mixed*. By the last are meant such actions as are under the command of the will, but are commonly performed without any interposition of will.]

We cannot avoid using the word *action* in this popular sense, without deviating too much from the common use of language; and it is in this sense we use it when we inquire into the principles of action in the human mind.

By *principles* of action, I understand every thing that incites us to act.

If there were no incitements to action, active power would be given us in vain. Having no motive to direct our active exertions, the mind would, in all cases, be in a state of perfect indifference, to do this or that, or nothing at all. The active power would either not be exerted at all, or its exertions would be perfectly unmeaning and frivolous, neither wise nor foolish, neither good nor bad. To every action that is of the smallest importance, there must be some incitement, some motive, some reason.

II. *Knowledge of the principles of action important.*—It is therefore a most important part of the philosophy of the human mind, to have a distinct and just view of the various principles of action which the Author of our being hath planted in our nature, to arrange them properly, and to assign to every one its rank.

[By this it is, that we may discover the end of our being, and the part which is assigned us upon the theatre of life.] In this part of the human constitution, the noblest work of God that falls within our notice, we may discern most clearly the character of him who made us, and how he would have us to employ that active power which he hath given us.

I cannot without great diffidence enter upon this subject, observing that almost every author of reputation, who has given attention to it, has a system of his own; and that no man has been so happy as to give general satisfaction to those who came after him.

There is a branch of knowledge much valued, and very justly, which we call knowledge of the world, knowledge of mankind, knowledge of human nature: this, I think, consists in knowing from what principles men generally act; and it is commonly the fruit of natural sagacity joined with experience.

A man of sagacity, who has had occasion to deal in interesting matters, with a great variety of persons of different age, sex, rank, and profession, learns to judge what may be expected from men in given circumstances; and how they may be most effectually induced to act the part which he desires. To know this is of so great importance to men in active life, that it is called knowing men, and knowing human nature.

This knowledge may be of considerable use to a man who would speculate upon the subject we have proposed, but is not, by itself, sufficient for that purpose.

III. *Difficulties attending an investigation of the principles of human actions.*—The man of the world conjectures, perhaps with great probability, how a man will act in certain given circumstances; and this is all he wants to know. [To enter into a detail of the various principles which influence the actions of men, to give them distinct names, to define them, and to ascertain their different provinces, is the business of a philosopher, and not of a man of the world; and, indeed, it is a matter attended with great difficulty from various causes.]

First, On account of the *great number of active principles* that influence the actions of men.

Man has, not without reason, been called an epitome of the universe. His body, by which his mind is greatly affected, being a part of the material system, is subject to all the laws of inanimate matter. During some part of his existence, his state is very like that of a vegetable. He rises, by imperceptible degrees, to the animal, and, at last, to the rational life, and has the principles that belong to all.

Another cause of the difficulty of tracing the various principles of action in man, is, That *the same action,* nay, the same course and train of action, *may proceed from very different principles.*

Men who are fond of a hypothesis, commonly seek no other proof of its truth, but that it serves to account for the appearances which it is brought to explain. This is a very slippery kind of proof in every part of philosophy, and never to be trusted; but least of all, when the appearances to be accounted for are human actions.

Most actions proceed from a variety of principles concurring in their direction; and according as we are disposed to judge favourably or unfavourably of the person, or of human nature in general, we impute them wholly to the best, or wholly to the worst, overlooking others which had no small share in them.

[The principles from which men act can be discovered only in these *two* ways; by *attention* to the conduct of *other men,* or by attention to *our own* conduct, and to what we feel in ourselves. There is much uncertainty in the former, and much difficulty in the latter.]

Men differ much in their characters; and we can observe the conduct of a few only of the species. Men differ not only from other men, but from themselves at different times, and on different occasions; according as they are in the company of their superiors, inferiors, or equals; according as they are in the eye of strangers, or of their familiars only, or in the view of no human eye; according as they are in good or bad fortune, or in good or bad humour. We see but a small part of the actions of our most familiar acquaintance; and what we see may lead us to a probable conjecture, but can give no certain knowledge of the principles from which they act.

A man may, no doubt, know with certainty the principles from which he himself acts, because he is conscious of them. But this knowledge requires an attentive reflection upon the operations of his own mind, which is very rarely to be found. It is perhaps more easy to find a man who has formed a just notion of the character of man in general, or of those of his familiar acquaintance, than one who has a just notion of his own character.

Most men, through pride and self-flattery, are apt to think themselves better than they really are; and some, perhaps from melancholy, or from false principles of religion, are led to think themselves worse than they really are.

IV. *Third cause of the difficulty of tracing the principles of action in man.*—It requires, therefore, a very accurate and impartial examination of a man's own heart, to be able to form a distinct notion of the various principles which influence his conduct. [That this is a matter of great difficulty, we may judge from *the very different and contradictory systems of philosophers* upon this subject, from the earliest ages to this day.]

During the age of Greek philosophy, the Platonist, the Peripatetic, the Stoic, the Epicurean, had each his own system. In the dark ages, the Schoolmen and the Mystics had systems diametrically opposite; and, since the revival of learning, no controversy hath been more keenly agitated, especially among British philosophers, than that about the principles of action in the human constitution.

They have determined, to the satisfaction of the learned, the forces by which the planets and comets traverse the boundless regions of space; but have not been able to determine, with any degree of unanimity, the forces which every man is conscious of in himself, and by which his conduct is directed.

[Some admit no principle but *self-love;* others resolve all into *love of the pleasures of sense*, variously modified by the association of ideas; others admit *disinterested benevolence* along with self-love; others reduce all to *reason* and passion; others to *passion* alone; nor is there less variety about the number and distribution of the passions.]

The names we give to the various principles of action, have so little precision, even in the best and purest writers in every language, that, on this account, there is no small difficulty in giving them names, and arranging them properly.

The words, *appetite, passion, affection, interest, reason,* cannot be said to have one definite signification. They are taken sometimes in a larger, and sometimes in a more limited sense. The same principle is sometimes called by one of those names, sometimes by another; and principles of a very different nature are often called by the same name.

To remedy this confusion of names, it might perhaps seem proper to invent new ones. But there are so few entitled to this privilege, that I shall not lay claim to it; but shall endeavour to class the various principles of human action as distinctly as I am able, and to point out their specific differences; giving them such names as may deviate from the common use of the words as little as possible.

There are some principles of action which require no attention, no deliberation, no will. These, for distinction's sake, we shall call *mechanical.* Another class we may call *animal,* as they seem common to man with other animals. A third class we may call *rational,* being proper to a man as a rational creature.

CHAPTER II.

OF INSTINCT.

I. *Of instinct in man.*—THE *mechanical principles* of action may, I think, be reduced to two species, *instincts* and *habits*.

[By *instinct*, I mean a *natural blind impulse to certain actions*, without having any end in view, without deliberation, and very often without any conception of what we do.]

☞ Thus a man breathes while he is alive, by the alternate contraction and relaxation of certain muscles, by which the chest, and of consequence the lungs, are contracted and dilated. There is no reason to think that an infant new-born knows that breathing is necessary to life in its new state, that he knows how it must be performed, or even that he has any thought or conception of that operation; yet he breathes as soon as he is born, with perfect regularity, as if he had been taught, and got the habit by long practice.

By the same kind of principle, a new-born child, when its stomach is emptied, and nature has brought milk into the mother's breast, sucks and swallows its food as perfectly as if it knew the principles of that operation, and had got the habit of working according to them.

Sucking and swallowing are very complex operations. Anatomists describe about thirty pairs of muscles that must be employed in every draught. Of those muscles, every one must be served by its proper nerve, and can make no exertion but by some influence communicated by the nerve. The exertion of all those muscles and nerves is not simultaneous. They must succeed each other in a certain order, and their order is no less necessary than the exertion itself.

This regular train of operations is carried on according to the nicest rules of art, by the infant, who has neither art, nor science, nor experience, nor habit.

That the infant feels the uneasy sensation of hunger, I admit; and that it sucks no longer than till this sensation be removed. But who informed it that this uneasy sensation might be removed, or by what means? That it knows nothing of this is evident; for it will as readily suck a finger, or a bit of stick, as the nipple.

By a like principle it is, that infants cry when they are pained or hurt; that they are afraid when left alone, especially in the dark; that they start when in danger of falling; that they are terrified by an angry countenance, or an angry tone of voice; and are soothed and comforted by a placid countenance, and by soft and gentle tones of voice.

II. *Of instinct in inferior animals.*—[In the animals we are best acquainted with, and which we look upon as the more perfect of the *brute-creation,* we see much *the same instincts as in the human kind,* or very similar ones, suited to the particular state and manner of life of the animal.]

Besides these, there are in brute-animals instincts peculiar to each tribe, by which they are fitted for defence, for offence, or for providing for themselves, and for their offspring.

It is not more certain, that nature hath furnished various animals with various weapons of offence and defence, than that the same nature hath taught them how to use them;—the bull and the ram to butt, the horse to kick, the dog to bite, the lion to use his paws, the boar his tusks, the serpent his fangs, and the bee and wasp their sting.

The manufactures of animals, if we may call them by that name, present us with a wonderful variety of instincts, belonging to particular species, whether of the social or of the solitary kind;—the nests of birds, so similar in their situation and architecture in the same kind, so various in different kinds ; the webs of spiders, and of other spinning animals; the ball of the silk-worm; the nests of ants and other mining animals; the combs of wasps, hornets, and bees; the dams and houses of beavers.

The instinct of animals is one of the most delightful and instructive parts of a most pleasant study, that of natural history, and deserves to be more cultivated than it has yet been.

Every manufacturing art among men was invented by some man, improved by others, and brought to perfection by time and experience. Men learn to work in it by long practice, which produces a habit. The arts of men vary in every age, and in every nation, and are found only in those who have been taught them.

The manufactures of animals differ from those of men in many striking particulars.

No animal of the species can claim the invention. No animal ever introduced any new improvement, or any variation from the former practice. Every one of the species has equal skill from the beginning, without teaching, without experience or habit. Every one has its art by a kind of inspiration. I do not mean that it is inspired with the principles or rules of the art, but with the ability and inclination of working in it to perfection, without any knowledge of its principles, rules, or end.

The more sagacious animals may be taught to do many things which they do not by instinct. What they are taught to do, they do with more or less skill, according to their sagacity and their training. But, in their own arts, they need no teaching nor training, nor is the art ever improved or lost. Bees gather their honey and their wax, they fabricate their combs and rear their young, at this day, neither better nor worse than they did when Virgil so sweetly sung their works.

The work of every animal is indeed like the works of nature, perfect in its kind, and can bear the most critical examination of the mechanic or the mathematician. One example from the animal last mentioned may serve to illustrate this.

Bees, it is well known, construct their combs with small cells on both sides, fit both for holding their store of honey, and for rearing their young. There are only three possible figures of the cells, which can make them all equal and similar, without any useless interstices. These are the equilateral triangle, the square, and the regular hexagon.

It is well known to mathematicians, that there is not a fourth way possible, in which a plane may be cut into little spaces that shall be equal, similar, and regular, without leaving any interstices. Of the three, the hexagon is the most proper, both for conveniency and strength. Bees, as if they knew this, make their cells regular hexagons.

As the combs have cells on both sides, the cells may either be exactly opposite, having partition against partition, or the bottom of a cell may rest upon the partitions between the cells on the other side, which will serve as a buttress to strengthen it. The last way is best for strength; accordingly, the bottom of each cell rests against the point where three partitions meet on the other side, which gives it all the strength possible.

The bottom of a cell may either be one plane perpendicular to the side-partitions, or it may be composed of several planes, meeting in a solid angle in the middle point. It is only in one of these two ways, that all the cells can be similar without losing room. And, for the same intention, the planes of which the bottom is composed, if there be more than one, must be three in number, and neither more nor fewer.

It has been demonstrated, that, by making the bottoms of the cells to consist of three planes meeting in a point, there is a saving of material and labour no way inconsiderable. The bees, as if acquainted with these principles of solid geometry, follow them most accurately; the bottom of each cell being composed of three planes which make obtuse angles with the side-partitions, and with one another, and meet in a point in the middle of the bottom; the three angles of this bottom being supported by three partitions on the other side of the comb, and the point of it by the common intersection of those three partitions.

One instance more of the mathematical skill displayed in the structure of a honey-comb deserves to be mentioned.

It is a curious mathematical problem, at what precise angle the three planes which compose the bottom of a cell ought to meet, in order to make the greatest possible saving, or the least expense of material and labour.

This is one of those problems, belonging to the higher parts of mathematics, which are called problems of *maxima* and *minima*. It has been resolved by some mathematicians, particularly by the ingenious Mr. Maclarurin, by a fluxionary calculation, which is to be found in the Transactions of the Royal Society of London. He has determined precisely the angle required; and he found, by the most exact mensuration the subject could admit, that it is the very angle in which the three planes in the bottom of the cell of a honeycomb do actually meet.

Shall we ask here, Who taught the bee the properties of solids, and to resolve problems of *maxima* and *minima*? If a honeycomb were a work of human art, every man of common sense would conclude, without hesitation, that he who invented the construction must have understood the principles on which it is constructed.

We need not say, that bees know none of these things. ☞ They work most geometrically, without any knowledge of geometry; somewhat like a child, who, by turning the handle of an organ, makes good music, without any knowledge of music.

The art is not in the child, but in him who made the organ. In like manner, when a bee makes its combs so geometrically, the geometry is not in the bee, but in that great Geometrician who made the bee, and made all things in number, weight, and measure.

III. *Some human instincts transitory, others permanent.*—To return to *instincts in man*. Those are most remarkable which appear in infancy, when we are ignorant of every thing necessary to our preservation, and therefore must perish, if we had not an invisible Guide, who leads us blindfold in the way we should take, if we had eyes to see it.

Besides the instincts which *appear only in infancy,* and are intended to supply the want of understanding in that early period, there are many which *continue through life,* and which supply the defects of our intellectual powers in every period. Of these we may observe three classes.

First. There are many things necessary to be done for our preservation, which, even when we will to do, we *know not the means by which they must be done.*

A man knows that he must swallow his food before it can nourish him. But this action requires the co-operation of many nerves and muscles, of which he knows nothing; and if it were to be directed solely by his understanding and will, he would starve before he learned how to perform it.

Here instinct comes in to his aid. He needs do no more than will to swallow. All the requisite motions of nerves and muscles

L

immediately take place in their proper order, without his knowing or willing any thing about them.

If we ask here, Whose will do these nerves and muscles obey? Not his, surely, to whom they belong. He knows neither their names, nor nature, nor office; he never thought of them. They are moved by some impulse, of which the cause is unknown, without any thought, will, or intention on his part; that is, they are moved instinctively.

This is the case, in some degree, in every voluntary motion of our body. Thus, I will to stretch out my arm. The effect immediately follows. But we know that the arm is stretched out by the contraction of certain muscles; and that the muscles are contracted by the influence of the nerves. I know nothing, I think nothing, either of nerves or muscles, when I stretch out my arm; yet this nervous influence, and this contraction of the muscles, uncalled by me, immediately produce the effect which I willed. This is as if a weight were to be raised, which can be raised only by a complication of levers, pullies, and other mechanical powers, that are behind the curtain, and altogether unknown to me. I will to raise the weight; and no sooner is this volition exerted, than the machinery behind the curtain falls to work, and raises the weight.

If such a case should happen, we would conclude that there was some person behind the curtain, who knew my will, and put the machine in motion to execute it.

The case of my willing to stretch out my arm, or to swallow my food, has evidently a great similarity to this. But who it is that stands behind the curtain, and sets the internal machinery agoing, is hid from us: so strangely and wonderfully are we made. This, however, is evident, that those internal motions are not willed nor intended by us, and therefore are instinctive.

IV. A *second* case in which we have need of instinct, even in advanced life, is, when the action must be so frequently repeated, that to intend *and will* it every time it is done, *would occupy too much of our thought*, and leave no room for other necessary employments of the mind.

We must breathe often every minute, whether awake or asleep. We must often close the eyelids, in order to preserve the lustre of the eye. [If these things required particular attention and volition every time they are done, they would occupy all our thought. Nature, therefore, gives an impulse to do them as often as is necessary, without any thought at all. They *consume no time*, they give not the least interruption to any exercise of the mind; because they are done by instinct.]

V. A *third* case, in which we need the aid of instinct, is, when the action must be done so *suddenly*, that there is no time to think and determine. ☞ When a man loses his balance, either on foot or on horseback, he makes an instantaneous effort to recover it by instinct. The effort would be in vain, if it waited the determination of reason and will.

When any thing threatens our eyes, we wink hard, by instinct, and can hardly avoid doing so, even when we know that the stroke is aimed in jest, and that we are perfectly safe from danger. I have seen this tried upon a wager, which a man was to gain if he could keep his eyes open, while another aimed a stroke at them in jest. The difficulty of doing this shows that there may be a struggle between instinct and will; and that it is not easy to resist the impulse of instinct, even by a strong resolution not to yield to it.

Thus the merciful Author of our nature hath adapted our instincts to the defects and to the weakness of our understanding. In infancy, we are ignorant of every thing; yet many things must be done by us for our preservation: these are done by instinct. When we grow up, there are many motions of our limbs and bodies necessary, which can be performed only by a curious and complex internal machinery—a machinery of which the bulk of mankind are totally ignorant, and which the most skilful anatomist knows but imperfectly. All this machinery is set agoing by instinct. We need only to will the external motion, and all the internal motions previously necessary to the effect take place of themselves, without our will or command.

Some actions must be so often repeated, through the whole of life, that, if they required attention and will, we should be able to do nothing else: these go on regularly by instinct.

Our preservation from danger often requires such *sudden* exertions, that there is no time to think and to determine: accordingly we make such exertions by instinct.

VI. *Fourth case in which instinct, probably, is requisite.*— Another thing in the nature of man, which I take to be partly, though not wholly, instinctive, is his *proneness to imitation*.

Aristotle observed, long ago, that man is an imitative animal. He is so in more respects then one. He is disposed to imitate what he approves. In all arts, men learn more, and more agreeably, by example than by rules. Imitation by the chisel, by the pencil, by description prosaic and poetical, and by action and gesture, have been favourite and elegant entertainments of the whole species. In all these cases, however, the imitation is intended and willed, and therefore cannot be said to be instinctive.

But I apprehend that *human nature disposes us to the imitation* of those among whom we live, when we neither desire nor will it.

☞ Let an Englishman of middle age take up his residence in Edinburgh or Glasgow; although he has not the least intention to use the Scots' dialect, but a firm resolution to preserve his own pure and unmixed, he will find it very difficult to make good his intention. He will, in a course of years, fall, insensibly and without intention, into the tone and accent, and even into the words and phrases, of those he converses with; and nothing can preserve him from this but a strong disgust to every Scotticism, which perhaps may overcome the natural instinct.

It is commonly thought that children often learn to stammer by imitation; yet I believe no person ever desired or willed to learn that quality.

I apprehend that instinctive imitation has no small influence in forming the peculiarities of provincial dialects; the peculiarities of voice, gesture, and manner, which we see in some families; the manners peculiar to different ranks, and different professions; and perhaps even in forming national characters, and the human character in general.

The instances that history furnishes of wild men, brought up from early years without the society of any of their own species, are so few, that we cannot build conclusions upon them with great certainty. But all I have heard of agreed in this, that the wild man gave but very slender indications of the rational faculties; and with regard to his mind, was hardly distinguishable from the more sagacious of the brutes.

There is a considerable part of the lowest rank in every nation, of whom it cannot be said that any pains have been taken by themselves, or by others, to cultivate their understanding, or to form their manners; yet we see an immense difference between them and the wild man.

This difference is wholly the effect of society; and I think it is in a great measure, though not wholly, the effect of undesigned and instinctive imitation.

VII. *Judgment and belief influenced, to a certain extent, by instinct.*—Perhaps, [not only our actions, but even our *judgment* and *belief*, are in some cases guided by instinct, that is, by a natural and blind impulse.]

When we consider man as a rational creature, it may seem right that he should have no belief but what is grounded upon evidence, probable or demonstrative; and it is, I think, commonly taken for granted, that it is always evidence, real or apparent, that determines our belief.

If this be so, the consequence is, that in no case can there be any belief till we find evidence, or at least what, to our judgment, appears to be evidence. I suspect it is not so; but that, on the contrary, before we grow up to the full use of our rational faculties, we do believe, and must believe, many things without any evidence at all.

The faculties which we have in common with brute animals are of earlier growth than reason. We are irrational animals for a considerable time before we can properly be called rational.

The operations of reason spring up by imperceptible degrees; nor is it possible for us to trace accurately the order in which they rise. The power of reflection, by which only we could trace the progress of our growing faculties, comes too late to answer that end. Some operations of brute animals look so like reason, that they are not easily distinguished from it. Whether brutes have any thing that can properly be called belief, I cannot say; but their actions show something that looks very like it.

VIII. If there be any *instinctive belief in man,* it is probably of the same kind with that which we ascribe to brutes, and may be specifically different from that rational belief which is grounded on evidence; but that there is something in man which we call belief, which is not grounded on evidence, I think, must be granted.

We need to be informed of many things before we are capable of discerning the evidence on which they rest. Were our belief to be withheld till we are capable, in any degree, of weighing evidence, we should lose all the benefit of that instruction and information, without which we could never attain the use of our rational faculties.

Man would never acquire the use of reason if he were not brought up in the society of reasonable creatures. The benefit he receives from society is derived partly from imitation of what he sees others do, partly from the instruction and information they communicate to him, without which he could neither be preserved from destruction, nor acquire the use of his rational powers.

Children have a thousand things to learn, and they learn many things every day; more than will be easily believed by those who have never given attention to their progress.

"Oportet discentem credere" is a common adage. Children have every thing to learn, and in order to learn, they must believe their instructors: they need a greater stock of faith from infancy to twelve or fourteen than ever after. But how shall they get this stock, so necessary to them? If their faith depend upon evidence, the stock of evidence, real or apparent, must bear proportion to their faith. But such, in reality, is their situation, that when their faith must be greatest, the evidence is least. They believe a thousand things before they ever spend a thought upon evidence. Nature supplies the want of evidence, and gives the man instinctive kind of faith without evidence.

[(1) *They believe* implicitly *whatever they are told,* and receive with assurance the testimony of every one, *without* ever thinking of *a reason* why they should do so.]

A parent or a master might command them to believe, but in vain, for belief is not in our power; but in the first part of life it is governed by mere testimony in matters of fact, and by mere authority in all other matters, no less than by evidence in riper years.

It is not the words of the testifier, but his belief, that produces this belief in a child; for children soon learn to distinguish what is said in jest, from what is said in good earnest. What appears to them to be said in jest, produces no belief: they glory in showing that they are not to be imposed on. When the signs of belief in the speaker are ambiguous, it is pleasant to observe with what sagacity they pry into his features, to discern whether he really believes what he says, or only counterfeits belief. As soon as this point is determined, their belief is regulated by his. If he be doubtful, they are doubtful; if he be assured, they are also assured.

It is well known what a deep impression religious principles, zealously inculcated, make upon the minds of children. The absurdities of ghosts and hobgoblins, early impressed, have been known to stick so fast, even in enlightened minds, as to baffle all rational conviction.

When we grow up to the use of reason, testimony attended with certain circumstances, or even authority, may afford a rational ground of belief; but with children, without any regard to circumstances, either of them operates like demonstration. And as they seek no reason, nor can give any reason, for this regard to testimony and to authority, it is the effect of a natural impulse, and may be called instinct.

[(2) Another instance of belief which appears to be instinctive, is that which children show even in infancy, that *an event which they have observed in certain circumstances, will happen again in like circumstances*.] A child of half a year old, who has once burned his finger by putting it in the candle, will not put it there again. And if you make a show of putting it in the candle by force, you see the most manifest signs that he believes he shall meet with the same calamity.

IX. Mr. Hume hath shown very clearly, that [*this belief* is *not the effect either of reason or experience*.] He endeavours to account for it by the association of ideas. Though I am not satisfied with his account of this phenomenon, I shall not now examine it; because it is sufficient for the present argument, that this belief is not grounded on evidence, real or apparent, which I think he clearly proves.

A person who has lived so long in the world, as to observe that nature is governed by fixed laws, may have some rational ground to expect similar events in similar circumstances; but this cannot be the case of the child. *His belief*, therefore, is not grounded on evidence. It *is the result of his constitution*.

Nor is it the less so, though it should arise from the association of ideas. For what is called the association of ideas is a law of nature in our constitution; which produces its effects without any operation of reason on our part, and in a manner of which we are entirely ignorant.

CHAPTER III.

OF HABIT.

I. *Vulgar definition of habit.*—HABIT differs from instinct, not in its nature, but in its origin; the latter being natural, the former acquired. Both operate without will or intention, without thought, and therefore may be called *mechanical principles*.

[Habit is commonly defined, *a facility of doing a thing, acquired by having done it frequently*.] This definition is sufficient for habits of art: but the habits which may, with propriety, be called principles of action, must give more than a facility, they must give an inclination or impulse to do the action; and that, in many cases, habits have this force, cannot be doubted.

How many awkward habits, by frequenting improper company, are children apt to learn, in their address, motion, looks, gesture, and pronunciation. They acquire such habits, commonly, from an undesigned and instinctive imitation, before they can judge of what is proper and becoming.

When they are a little advanced in understanding, they may easily be convinced that such a thing is unbecoming, they may resolve to forbear it; but when the habit is formed, such a general resolution is not of itself sufficient; for the habit will operate without intention; and particular attention is necessary, on every occasion, to resist its impulse, until it be undone by the habit of opposing it.

It is owing to the force of habits, early acquired by imitation, that a man who has grown up to manhood in the lowest rank of life, if fortune raise him to a higher rank, very rarely acquires the air and manners of a gentleman.

When to that *instinctive imitation*, which I spoke of before, we join the *force of habit*, it is easy to see, that these mechanical principles have no small share in forming the manners and character of most men.

The difficulty of overcoming vicious habits has, in all ages, been a common topic of theologians and moralists; and we see too many sad examples to permit us to doubt of it.

There are good habits, in a moral sense, as well as bad; and it is certain, that the stated and regular performance of what we approve, not only makes it easy, but makes us uneasy in the omission of it. This is the case, even when the action derives all its goodness from the opinion of the performer. A good illiterate Roman Catholic does not sleep sound if he goes to bed without telling his beads, and repeating prayers which he does not understand.

Aristotle makes wisdom, prudence, good sense, science, and art, as well as the moral virtues and vices, to be *habits.* If he meant no more, by giving this name to all those intellectual and moral qualities, than that they are all strengthened and confirmed by repeated acts, this is undoubtedly true. I take the word in a less extensive sense, when I consider habits as principles of action. I conceive it to be a part of our constitution, that what we have been accustomed to do, we acquire, not only a facility, but a proneness to do on like occasions; so that it requires a particular will and effort to forbear it; but to do it, requires very often no will at all. We are carried by habit as by a stream in swimming, if we make no resistance.

II. *The art of speaking, the strongest illustration of the force of habit.*—[*Every art furnishes examples* both *of the power of habits* and of their utility; no one more than the most common of all arts, the art of speaking.]

Articulate language is spoken, not by nature, but by art. It is no easy matter to children to learn the simple sounds of language; I mean, to learn to pronounce the vowels and consonants. It would be much more difficult, if they were not led by instinct to imitate the sounds they hear; for the difficulty is vastly greater of teaching the deaf to pronounce the letters and words, though experience shows that it can be done.

What is it that makes this pronunciation so easy at last which was so difficult at first? It is habit.

But from what cause does it happen, that a good speaker no sooner conceives what he would express, than the letters, syllables and words arrange themselves according to innumerable rules of speech, while he never thinks of these rules? He means to express certain sentiments. In order to do this properly, a selection must be made of the materials, out of many thousands. He makes this selection without any expense of time or thought. The materials selected must be arranged in a particular order, according to innumerable rules of grammar, logic, and rhetoric, and accompanied with a particular tone and emphasis. He does all this, as it were, by inspiration, without thinking of any of these rules, and without breaking one of them.

This art, if it were not more common, would appear more wonderful than that a man should dance blindfold amidst a thousand burning ploughshares, without being burnt; yet all this may be done by habit.

It appears evident, that as, without instinct, the infant could not live to become a man, so, without habit, man would remain an infant through life, and would be as helpless, as unhandy, as speechless, and as much a child in understanding at threescore as at three.

[I see no reason to think, that we shall ever be able to assign the physical cause, either of *instinct* or of *the power of habit*.]

Both seem to be parts of our original constitution. Their end and use is evident; but we can assign no cause of them, but the will of Him who made us.

III. [With regard to *instinct*, which is *a natural propensity*, this will perhaps be easily granted; but it is no less true with regard to that power and inclination which we acquire by habit.]

No man can show a reason why our doing a thing frequently should produce either facility or inclination to do it.

The fact is so notorious, and so constantly in our eye, that we are apt to think no reason should be sought for it, any more than why the sun shines. But there must be a cause of the sun's shining, and there must be a cause of the power of habit.

We see nothing analogous to it in inanimate matter, or in things made by human art. A clock or a watch, a wagon or a plough, by the custom of going, does not learn to go better, or require less moving force. The earth does not increase in fertility by the custom of bearing crops.

☞ It is said, that trees and other vegetables, by growing long in an unkindly soil or climate, sometimes acquire qualities by which they can bear its inclemency with less hurt. This, in the *vegetable kingdom*, has some resemblance to the power of habit; but, in *inanimate matter*, I know nothing that resembles it.

☞ A stone loses nothing of its weight by being long supported, or made to move upward. A body, by being tossed about ever so long, or ever so violently, loses nothing of its *inertia*, nor acquires the least disposition to change its state.

PART II.

OF ANIMAL PRINCIPLES OF ACTION.

CHAPTER I.

OF APPETITES.

I. *Definition of animal principles of action.*—HAVING discoursed of the *mechanical* principles of action, I proceed to consider those I called *animal.*

They are [such as operate upon the will and intention, but *do not suppose any exercise of judgment or reason;* and are most of them to be found in some brute animals, as well as in man.]

In this class, the first kind I shall call *appetites*, taking that word in a stricter sense than it is sometimes taken, even by good writers.

The word *appetite* is sometimes limited, so as to signify only the desire of food when we hunger; sometimes it is extended so as to signify any strong desire, whatever be its object. Without pretending to censure any use of the word which custom hath authorized, I beg leave to limit it to a particular class of desires, which are distinguished from all others by the following marks.

First. Every appetite is accompanied with an uneasy sensation proper to it, which is strong or weak, in proportion to the desire we have of the object. *Secondly.* Appetites are not constant, but periodical, being sated by their objects for a time, and returning after certain periods. Such is the nature of those principles of action, to which I beg leave, in this essay, to appropriate the name of *appetites.* Those that are chiefly observable in man, as well as in most other animals, are hunger, thirst, and lust.

[If we attend to the appetite of hunger, we shall find in it *two* ingredients, an uneasy *sensation*, and a *desire* to eat.] The desire keeps pace with the sensation, and ceases when it ceases. When a man is sated with eating, both the uneasy sensation and the desire to eat cease for a time, and return after a certain interval. So it is with other appetites.

In infants, for some time after they come into the world, the uneasy sensation of hunger is probably the whole. We cannot suppose in them, before experience, any conception of eating, nor, consequently, any desire of it. They are led by mere instinct to suck when they feel the sensation of hunger. But when experience has connected, in their imagination, the uneasy sensation with the means of removing it, the desire of the last comes to be so associated with the first, that they remain through life inseparable; and we give the name of *hunger* to the principle that is made up of both.

That the appetite of hunger includes the two ingredients I have mentioned, will not, I apprehend, be questioned. I take notice of it the rather because we may, if I mistake not, find a similar composition in other principles of action. They are made up of different ingredients, and may be analyzed into the parts that enter into their composition.

If one philosopher should maintain, that hunger is an uneasy sensation, another, that it is a desire to eat, they seem to differ widely; for a desire and a sensation are very different things, and have no similitude. But they are both in the right; for hunger includes both an uneasy sensation and a desire to eat.

Although there has been no such dispute among philosophers as we have supposed with regard to hunger, yet there have been similar disputes with regard to other principles of action; and it deserves to be considered whether they may not be terminated in a similar manner.

II. [*The ends for which our natural appetites are given* are too evident to escape the observation of any man of the least reflection. Two of those I named are intended *for the preservation of the individual*, and the third for the *continuance of the species*.]

The reason of mankind would be altogether insufficient for these ends, without the direction and call of appetite.

Though a man knew that his life must be supported by eating, reason could not direct him when to eat, or what; how much, or how often. In all these things, appetite is a much better guide than our reason. Were reason only to direct us in this matter, its calm voice would often be drowned in the hurry of business, or the charms of amusement. But the voice of appetite rises gradually, and, at last, becomes loud enough to call off our attention from any other employment.

Every man must be convinced, that, without our appetites, even supposing mankind inspired with all the knowledge requisite for answering their ends, the race of men must have perished long ago; but, by their means, the race is continued from one generation to another, whether men be savage or civilized, knowing or ignorant, virtuous or vicious.

By the same means, every tribe of brute-animals, from the whale that ranges the ocean to the least microscopic insect, has been continued from the beginning of the world to this day; nor has good evidence been found, that any one species which God made has perished.*

Nature has given to every animal, not only an appetite for its food, but taste and smell, by which it distinguishes the food proper for it.

It is pleasant to see a caterpillar, which nature intended to

* This assertion appears to be contradicted by recent geological discoveries.

live upon the leaf of one species of plant, travel over a hundred leaves of other kinds without tasting one, till it comes to that which is its natural food, which it immediately falls on, and devours greedily.

Most caterpillars feed only upon the leaf of one species of plant, and nature suits the season of their production to the food that is intended to nourish them. Many insects and animals have a greater variety of food; but, of all animals, man has the greatest variety, being able to subsist upon almost every kind of vegetable or animal food, from the bark of trees to the oil of whales.

I believe our natural appetites may be made more violent by excessive indulgence, and that, on the other hand, they may be weakened by starving. The first is often the effect of a pernicious luxury, the last may sometimes be the effect of want, sometimes of superstition. I apprehend that nature has given to our appetites that degree of strength which is most proper for us; and that whatever alters their natural tone, either in excess or in defect, does not mend the work of nature, but may mar and pervert it.

A man may eat from appetite only. So the brutes commonly do. He may eat to please his taste, when he has no call of appetite. I believe a brute may do this also. He may eat for the sake of health, when neither appetite nor taste invites. This, as far as I am able to judge, brutes never do.

From so many different principles, and from many more, the same action may be done; and this may be said of most human actions. From this, it appears, that very different and contrary theories may serve to account for the actions of men. The causes assigned may be sufficient to produce the effect, and yet not be the true causes.

To act merely from appetite is neither good nor ill in a moral view. It is neither an object of praise nor of blame. No man claims any praise because he eats when he is hungry, or rests when he is weary. On the other hand, he is no object of blame, if he obeys the call of appetite when there is no reason to hinder him. In this, he acts agreeably to his nature.

III. From this we may observe, that [the definition of virtuous actions, given by the ancient Stoics, and adopted by some modern authors, is imperfect. They defined virtuous actions to be such as are *according to nature*.] What is done according to the animal part of our nature, which is common to us with the brute-animals, is in itself neither virtuous nor vicious, but perfectly indifferent. Then only it becomes vicious, when it is done in opposition to some principle of superior importance and authority. And it may be virtuous, if done for some important or worthy end.

Appetites, considered in themselves, are neither social principles of action, nor selfish. They cannot be called social, because they imply no concern for the good of others. Nor can they justly be called selfish, though they be commonly referred to that class. An appetite draws us to a certain object, without regard to its being good for us, or ill. There is no self-love implied in it any more than benevolence. We see, that, in many cases, appetite may lead a man to what he knows will be to his hurt. To call this acting from self-love, is to pervert the meaning of words. It is evident, that, in every case of this kind, self-love is sacrificed to appetite.

IV. *There are some principles of the human frame very like to our appetites,* though they do not commonly get that name.

Men are made for labour, either of body or mind. Yet excessive labour hurts the powers of both. To prevent this hurt, nature hath given to men, and other animals, an uneasy sensation, which always attends excessive labour, and which we call *fatigue, weariness, lassitude.* This uneasy sensation is conjoined with the desire of rest, or intermission of our labour. And thus nature calls us to rest when we are weary, in the same manner as to eat when we are hungry.

In both cases, there is a desire of a certain object, and an uneasy sensation accompanying that desire. In both cases, the desire is satiated by its object, and returns after certain intervals. In this only they differ, that in the appetites first mentioned, the uneasy sensation arises at intervals without action, and leads to a certain action: in weariness, the uneasy sensation arises from action too long continued, and leads to rest.

But nature intended that we should be active, and we need some principle to incite us to action, when we happen not to be invited by any appetite or passion.

For this end, when strength and spirits are recruited by rest, nature has made total inaction as uneasy as excessive labour.

We may call this the principle of *activity.* It is most conspicuous in children, who cannot be supposed to know how useful and necessary it is for their improvement to be constantly employed. Their constant activity therefore appears not to proceed from their having some end constantly in view, but rather from this, that they desire to be always doing something, and feel uneasiness in total inaction.

V. *The principle of activity belongs to every period of life.*— Nor is this principle confined to childhood; it has great effects in advanced life.

When a man has neither hope, nor fear, nor desire, nor project, nor employment, of body or mind, one might be apt to think him the happiest mortal upon earth, having nothing to do but to enjoy himself: but *we find him,* in fact, *the most unhappy.*

He is more weary of inaction than ever he was of excessive

labour. He is weary of the world, and of his own existence; and is more miserable than the sailor wrestling with a storm, or the soldier mounting a breach.

This dismal state is commonly the lot of the man who has neither exercise of body nor employment of mind. ☞ For the mind, like water, corrupts and putrifies by stagnation, but by running purifies and refines.

Besides the appetites which nature hath given us for useful and necessary purposes, we may create appetites which nature never gave.

The frequent use of things which stimulate the nervous system produces a languor when their effect is gone off, and a desire to repeat them. By this means a desire of a certain object is created, accompanied by an uneasy sensation. Both are removed for a time by the object desired; but they return after a certain interval. This differs from natural appetite, only in being *acquired* by custom. Such are the appetites which some men acquire for the use of tobacco, for opiates, and for intoxicating liquors.

These are commonly called habits, and justly. But there are different kinds of habits, even of the active sort, which ought to be distinguished. Some habits produce only a facility of doing a thing, without any inclination to do it. All arts are habits of this kind; but they cannot be called principles of action. Other habits produce a proneness to do an action, without thought or intention. These we considered before as mechanical principles of action. There are other habits which produce a desire of a certain object, and an uneasy sensation till it is obtained. It is this last kind only that I call acquired appetites.

VI. [As it is best to preserve our natural appetites in that tone and degree of strength which nature gives them, so *we ought to beware of acquiring appetites which nature never gave.* They are always useless, and very often hurtful.]

Although, as was before observed, there be neither virtue nor vice in acting from appetite, there may be much of either in the management of our appetites.

When appetite is opposed by some principle drawing a contrary way, there must be a determination of the will, which shall prevail, and this determination may be, in a moral sense, right or wrong.

Appetite, even in a brute-animal, may be restrained by a stronger principle opposed to it. A dog, when he is hungry, and has meat set before him, may be kept from touching it by the fear of immediate punishment. In this case, his fear operates more strongly than his desire.

Do we attribute any virtue to the dog on this account? I think not. Nor should we ascribe any virtue to a man in a like case. The animal is carried by the strongest moving force. This requires no exertion, no self-government, but passively to yield to the strongest impulse. This, I think, brutes always do; therefore we attribute to them neither virtue nor vice. We consider them as being neither objects of moral approbation nor disapprobation.

VII. *The government of appetites gives a superiority to man over brute animals.*—But it may happen that, when appetite draws one way, it may be opposed, not by any appetite or passion, but by some cool principle of action, which has authority without any impulsive force. For example, by some interest, which is too distant to raise any passion or emotion, or by some consideration of decency or of duty.

In cases of this kind, the man is convinced that he ought not to yield to appetite; yet there is not an equal or a greater impulse to oppose it. There are circumstances, indeed, that convince the judgment; but these are not sufficient to determine the will against a strong appetite, without self-government.

[I apprehend that brute animals have *no power of self-government*. From their constitution, they must be led by the appetite or passion which is strongest for the time.

On this account, they have, in all ages, and among all nations, been thought incapable of being governed by *laws*, though some of them may be subjects of *discipline*.]

The same would be the condition of man, if he had no power to restrain appetite but by a stronger contrary appetite or passion. It would be to no purpose to prescribe laws to him for the government of his actions. You might as well forbid the wind to blow, as forbid him to follow whatever happens to give the strongest present impulse.

Every one knows, that when appetite draws one way, duty, decency, or even interest, may draw the contrary way; and that appetite may give a stronger impulse than any one of these, or even all of them conjoined. Yet it is certain that in every case of this kind, appetite ought to yield to any of these principles when it stands opposed to them. It is in such cases that self-government is necessary.

The man who suffers himself to be led by appetite to do what he knows he ought not to do, has an immediate and natural conviction that he did wrong, and might have done otherwise; and therefore he condemns himself, and confesses that he yielded to an appetite which ought to have been under his command.

[Thus it appears, that though our natural appetites have in themselves neither virtue nor vice; though the acting merely from appetite, when there is no principle of greater authority to oppose it, be a matter indifferent; yet there may be a great deal of *virtue or of vice in the management of our appetites;* and that *the power of self-government is necessary for their regulation.*]

CHAPTER II.

OF DESIRES.

I. *Distinction between appetites and desires twofold.*—Another class of animal principles of action in man, I shall, for want of a better specific name, call *desires*.

[They are distinguished from appetites by this: That (1) there is not an *uneasy sensation* proper to each, and always accompanying it; and that (2) they are not *periodical*, but *constant*, not being sated with their objects for a time, as appetites are.]

The desires I have in view are chiefly these three: the desire of power, the desire of esteem, and the desire of knowledge.

We may, I think, perceive some degree of these principles in brute-animals of the more sagacious kind; but in man they are much more conspicuous, and have a larger sphere.

In a herd of black cattle there is a rank and subordination. When a stranger is introduced into the herd, he must fight every one till his rank is settled. Then he yields to the stronger and assumes authority over the weaker. The case is much the same in the crew of a ship of war.

As soon as men associate together, the desire of superiority discovers itself. In barbarous tribes, as well as among the gregarious kinds of animals, rank is determined by strength, courage, swiftness, or such other qualities. Among civilized nations, many things of a different kind give power and rank—places in government, titles of honour, riches, wisdom, eloquence, virtue, and even the reputation of these. All these are either different species of power, or means of acquiring it; and when they are sought for that end, must be considered as instances of the desire of power.

II. *Of esteem and contempt.*—The desire of *esteem* is not peculiar to man. A dog exults in the approbation and applause of his master, and is humbled by his displeasure. But in man this desire is much more conspicuous, and operates in a thousand different ways.

[Hence it is that so very few are proof against *flattery*, when it is not very gross. We wish to be well in the opinion of others, and therefore are prone to interpret in our own favour the signs of their good opinion, even when they are ambiguous.]

There are few injuries that are not more easy to be borne than *contempt*.

We cannot always avoid seeing, in the conduct of others, things that move contempt; but, in all polite circles, the signs of it must be suppressed, otherwise men could not converse together.

As there is no quality, common to good and bad men, more esteemed than courage, nor any thing in a man more the object of contempt than cowardice; hence every man desires to be thought a man of courage; and the reputation of cowardice is worse than death. How many have died to avoid being thought cowards! How many, for the same reason, have done what made them unhappy to the end of their lives!

I believe many a tragical event, if traced to its source in human nature, might be referred to the desire of esteem, or the dread of contempt.

III. In brute animals there is so little that can be called *knowledge*, that the desire of it can make no considerable figure in them. Yet I have seen a cat, when brought into a new habitation, examine with care every corner of it, and anxious to know every lurking place, and the avenues to it. And I believe the same thing may be observed in many other species, especially in those that are liable to be hunted by man, or by other animals.

But *the desire of knowledge in the human species*, is a principle that *cannot escape* our *observation*.

The curiosity of children is the principle that occupies most of their time while they are awake. What they can handle they examine on all sides, and often break in pieces, in order to discover what is within.

When men grow up, their curiosity does not cease, but is employed upon other objects. Novelty is considered as one great source of the pleasures of taste, and indeed is necessary, in one degree or other, to give a relish to them all.

When we speak of the desire of knowledge as a principle of action in man, we must not confine it to the pursuits of the philosopher, or of the literary man. The desire of knowledge discovers itself, in one person, by an avidity to know the scandal of the village, and who makes love, and to whom; in another, to know the economy of the next family; in another, to know what the post brings; and in another to trace the path of a new comet.

When men show an anxiety, and take pains to know what is of no moment, and can be of no use to themselves or to others, this is trifling, and vain curiosity. It is a culpable weakness and folly; but still it is the wrong direction of a natural principle, and shows the force of that principle, more than when it is directed to matters worthy to be known.

IV. I think it unnecessary to use arguments to show that [the desires of *power*, of *esteem*, and of *knowledge*, are natural principles in the constitution of man.] Those who are not convinced of this by reflecting upon their own feelings and sentiments, will not easily be convinced by arguments.

[Power, esteem and knowledge, are so useful for many purposes, that it is easy to resolve the desire of them into other principles. Those who do so must maintain that we never desire these objects for their own sakes, but as means only of procuring pleasure, or something which is a natural object of desire. This, indeed, was the doctrine of Epicurus; and it had its votaries in modern times. But it has been observed that men desire posthumous fame, which can procure no pleasure.]*

Epicurus himself, though he believed that he should have no existence after death, was so desirous to be remembered with esteem, that, by his last will, he appointed his heirs to commemorate his birth annually, and to give a monthly feast to his disciples, upon the twentieth day of the moon. What pleasure could this give to Epicurus when he had no existence? On this account, Cicero justly observes, that his doctrine was refuted by his own practice.

Innumerable instances occur in life, of men who sacrifice ease, pleasure, and every thing else, to the lust of power, of fame, or even of knowledge. It is absurd to suppose, that men should sacrifice the end to what they desire only as the means of promoting that end.

V. *Such natural desires not selfish principles.*—[The *natural desires* I have mentioned are, in themselves, neither virtuous nor vicious. They are parts of our constitution, and ought to be regulated and restrained, when they stand in competition with more important principles. But to eradicate them, if it were possible (and I believe it is not), would only be like cutting off a leg or an arm, that is, making ourselves other creatures than God has made us.]

They cannot, with propriety, *be called selfish principles*, though they have commonly been accounted such.

When power is desired for its own sake, and not as the means in order to obtain something else, this desire is neither selfish nor social. When a man desires power as the means of doing good to others, this is benevolence. When he desires it only as the means of promoting his own good, this is self-love. But when he desires it for its own sake, this only can properly be called the desire of power; and it implies neither self-love nor benevolence. The same thing may be applied to the desires of esteem and of knowledge.

VI. *Our desires auxiliary to the maintenance of morals.*— The wise intention of nature in giving us these desires, is no less evident than in giving our natural appetites.

[Without the natural appetites, reason, as was before observed, would be insufficient, either for the preservation of the individual, or the continuation of the species; and without the natural desires we have mentioned, *human virtue would*

* The expectation is accompanied by present pleasure.

be insufficient to influence mankind to a tolerable conduct in society.]

To these natural desires, common to good and to bad men, it is owing, that a man, who has little or no regard to virtue, may notwithstanding be a good member of society. It is true, indeed, that perfect virtue, joined with perfect knowledge, would make both our appetites and desires unnecessary incumbrances of our nature; but as human knowledge and human virtue are both very imperfect, these appetites and desires are necessary supplements to our imperfections.

Society among men could not subsist without a certain degree of that regularity of conduct which virtue prescribes. To this regularity of conduct, men who have no virtue are induced by a regard to character, sometimes by a regard to interest.

[Even in those who are *not* destitute of virtue, a regard to character is often an useful auxiliary to it, when both principles concur in their direction.]

VII. The pursuits of power, of fame, and of knowledge, require self-command no less than virtue does. In our behaviour towards our fellow-creatures, they generally lead to that very conduct which virtue requires. I say *generally*, for this, no doubt, admits of exceptions, especially in the case of ambition, or the desire of power.

The evils which *ambition* has produced in the world are a common topic of declamation. But it ought to be observed, that where it has led to one action hurtful to society, it has led to ten thousand that are beneficial to it. And we justly look upon the want of ambition as one of the most unfavourable symptoms in a man's temper.

The desires of esteem and of knowledge are highly useful to society, as well as the desire of power, and, at the same time, are less dangerous in their excesses.

Although actions proceeding merely from the love of power, of reputation, or of knowledge, cannot be accounted virtuous, or be entitled to moral approbation; yet we allow them to be manly, ingenuous, and suited to the dignity of human nature; and therefore they are entitled to a degree of estimation, superior to those which proceed from mere appetite.

Alexander the Great deserved that epithet in the early part of his life, when ease and pleasure, and every appetite, were sacrificed to the love of glory and power. But when we view him conquered by oriental luxury, and using his power to gratify his passions and appetites, he sinks in our esteem, and seems to forfeit the title which he had acquired.

Sardanapalus, who is said to have pursued pleasure as eagerly as Alexander pursued glory, never obtained from mankind the appellation of *the Great*.

Appetite is the principle of most of the actions of brutes, and we account it brutal in a man to employ himself chiefly in the gratification of his appetites. [The desires of power, of esteem, and of knowledge, are *capital parts* in the constitution of man; and the actions proceeding from them, though not properly virtuous, are *human and manly;* and they claim a just superiority over those that proceed from appetite.] This, I think, is the universal and unbiassed judgment of mankind. Upon what ground this judgment is founded, may deserve to be considered in its proper place.

VIII. [The *desires* we have mentioned are not only (1) highly useful in society, and in their nature (2) more noble than our appetites, they are likewise (3) the most proper engines that can be used in the education and *discipline of men.*]

In training brute-animals to such habits as they are capable of, the fear of punishment is the chief instrument to be used. But in training men of ingenuous disposition, ambition to excel, and the love of esteem, are much nobler and more powerful engines, by which they may be led to worthy conduct, and trained to good habits.

To this we may add, that the desires we have mentioned are very friendly to real virtue, and make it more easy to be acquired.

A man that is not quite abandoned must behave so in society as to preserve some degree of reputation. This every man desires to do, and the greater part actually do it. In order to this, he must acquire the habit of restraining his appetites and passions within the bounds which common decency requires, and so as to make himself a tolerable member of society, if not an useful and agreeable one.

It cannot be doubted that many, from a regard to character and to the opinion of others, are led to make themselves both useful and agreeable members of society, in whom a sense of duty has but a small influence.

Thus men, living in society, especially in polished society, are tamed and civilized by the principles that are common to good and bad men. They are taught to bring their appetites and passions under due restraint before the eyes of men, which makes it more easy to bring them under the rein of virtue.

☞ As a horse that is broken is more easily managed than an unbroken colt, so the man who has undergone the discipline of society is more tractable, and is in an excellent state of preparation for the discipline of virtue; and that self-command, which is necessary in the race of ambition and honour, is an attainment of no small importance in the course of virtue.

For this reason, I apprehend, they err very grossly who conceive the life of a hermit to be favourable to a course of virtue.

The hermit, no doubt, is free from some temptations to vice, but he is deprived of many strong inducements to self-government, as well as of every opportunity of exercising the social virtues.

[A very ingenious author has resolved our moral sentiments respecting the virtues of self-government, into *a regard to the opinion of men.* This I think is giving a great deal too much to the love of esteem, and putting the shadow of virtue in place of the substance; but that a regard to the opinion of others is, in most instances of our external behaviour, a great inducement to good conduct, cannot be doubted. For, whatever men may practise themselves, they will always approve of that in others which they think right.]

IX. *Of acquired desires.*—[It was before observed, that, besides the appetites which nature has given us, we may *acquire* appetites which, by indulgence, become as important as the natural. The same thing may be applied to *desires.*]

One of the most remarkable acquired desires is that of money, which, in commercial states, will be found in most men, in one degree or other, and, in some men, swallows up every other desire, appetite and passion.

The desire of money can then only be accounted a principle of action, when it is desired for its own sake, and not merely as the means of procuring something else.

It seems evident, that there is in misers such a desire of money; and, I suppose, no man will say that it is natural, or a part of our original constitution. It seems to be the effect of habit.

In commercial nations, money is an instrument by which almost every thing may be procured that is desired. Being useful for many different purposes as the means, some men lose sight of the end, and terminate their desire upon the means. [Money is also a *species of power,* putting a man in condition to do many things which he could not do without it; and power is a natural object of desire, even when it is not exercised.]

In like manner, a man may acquire the desire of a title of honour, of an equipage, of an estate.

Although our natural desires are highly beneficial to society, and even aiding to virtue, yet acquired desires are not only useless, but hurtful and even disgraceful.

[No man is ashamed to own, that he loves power, that he loves esteem, that he loves knowledge, *for their own sake.* There may be an *excess* in the love of these things, which is a blemish; but there is a *degree* of it, which is natural, and is no blemish.] To love money, titles or equipage, on any other account than as they are useful or ornamental, is allowed by all to be weakness and folly.

The natural desires I have been considering, though they cannot be called *social* principles of action in the common sense that word, since it is not their object to procure any good or benefit to others, yet they have such a relation to society, as to show most evidently the intention of nature to be, that man should live in society.

The desire of knowledge is not more natural than is the desire of communicating our knowledge. Even power would be less valued if there were no opportunity of showing it to others. It derives half its value from that circumstance. And as to the desire of esteem, it can have no possible gratification but in society.

[These parts of our constitution, therefore, are evidently intended for *social life;* and it is not more evident that birds were made for flying and fishes for swimming, than that man, endowed with a natural desire of power, of esteem, and of knowledge, is made, not for the savage and solitary state, but for living in society.]

CHAPTER III.

OF BENEVOLENT AFFECTION IN GENERAL.

I. WE have seen how, by instinct and habit, a kind of mechanical principle, man, without any expense of thought, without deliberation or will, is led to many actions necessary for his preservation and well-being, which, without those principles, all his skill and wisdom would not have been able to accomplish.

It may perhaps be thought that his deliberate and voluntary actions are to be guided by his reason.

[But it ought to be observed, that he is a voluntary agent long *before* he has the use of reason. Reason and virtue, the prerogatives of man, are of the latest growth.] They come to maturity by slow degrees, and are too weak, in the greater part of the species, to secure the preservation of individuals and of communities, and to produce that varied scene of human life, in which they are to be exercised and improved.

Therefore the wise Author of our being hath implanted in human nature many inferior principles of action, which, with little or no aid of reason or virtue, preserve the species, and produce the various exertions, and the various changes and revolutions which we observe upon the theatre of life.

In this busy scene, reason and virtue have access to act their parts, and do often produce great and good effects; but whether they interpose or not, there are actors of an inferior order that will carry on the play, and produce a variety of events, good or bad.

Reason, if it were perfect, would lead men to use the proper means of preserving their own lives, and continuing their kind. But the Author of our being hath not thought fit to leave this task to reason alone, otherwise the race would long ago have been extinct. He hath given us, in common with other animals, appetites, by which those important purposes are secured, whether men be wise or foolish, virtuous or vicious.

Reason, if it were perfect, would lead men neither to lose the benefit of their active powers by inactivity, nor to overstrain them by excessive labour. But nature hath given a powerful assistant to reason, by making inactivity a grievous punishment to itself; and by annexing the pain of lassitude to excessive labour.

Reason, if it were perfect, would lead us to desire power, knowledge, and the esteem and affection of our fellow-men, as means of promoting our own happiness, and of being useful to others. Here, again, Nature, to supply the defects of reason, hath given us a strong natural desire of those objects, which leads us to pursue them without regard to their utility.

II. *Objects of our desires and our affections different.*—[These principles we have already considered; and we may observe, that all of them have *things, not persons*, for their object. They neither imply any good nor ill affections towards any other person, nor even towards ourselves. They cannot, therefore, with propriety, be called either *selfish* or *social*.] But there are various principles of action in man, which have persons for their immediate object, and imply, in their very nature, our being well or ill affected to some person, or at least to some animated being.

Such principles I shall call by the general name of *affections*, whether they dispose to do good or hurt to others.

Perhaps, in giving them this general name, I extend the meaning of the word *affection* beyond its common use in discourse. Indeed, our language seems in this to have departed a little from analogy: for we use the verb *affect*, and the participle *affected*, in an indifferent sense, so that they may be joined either with good or ill. A man may be said to be ill affected towards another man, or well affected. But the word *affection*, which, according to analogy, ought to have the same latitude of signification with that from which it is derived, and therefore ought to be applicable to ill affections as well as to good, seems, by custom, to be limited to good affections. When we speak of having affection for any person, it is always understood to be a benevolent affection.

Malevolent principles, such as anger, resentment, envy, are not commonly called *affections*, but rather *passions*.

I take the reason of this to be, that the malevolent affections are almost always accompanied with that perturbation of mind which we properly call *passion;* and this passion, being the most conspicuous ingredient, gives its name to the whole.

Even love, when it goes beyond a certain degree, is called a *passion*. But it gets not that name when it is so moderate as not to discompose a man's mind, nor deprive him in any measure of the government of himself.

As we give the name of *passion*, even to benevolent affection when it is so vehement as to discompose the mind, so, I think, without trespassing much against propriety of words, we may give the name of *affection* even to malevolent principles, when unattended with that disturbance of mind which commonly, though not always, goes along with them, and which has made them get the name of *passions*.

The principles which lead us immediately to desire the good of others, and those that lead us to desire their hurt, agree in this, that persons, and not things, are their immediate object. Both imply our being some way affected towards the person. They ought therefore to have some common name to express what is common in their nature; and I know no name more proper for this than *affection*.

III. Taking affection, therefore, in this extensive sense, *our affections are* very naturally *divided into benevolent and malevolent*, according as they imply our being well or ill affected towards their object.

There are some things common to all benevolent affections, others wherein they differ.

They differ both in the feeling, or sensation, which is an ingredient in all of them, and in the objects to which they are directed.

They all agree in two things, to wit, That the feeling which accompanies them is agreeable; and that they imply a desire of good and happiness to their object.

The affection we bear to a parent, to a child, to a benefactor, to a person in distress, to a mistress, differ not more in their object than in the feelings they produce in the mind. We have not names to express the differences of these feelings, but every man is conscious of a difference. Yet, with all this difference, they agree in being agreeable feelings.

I know no exception to this rule, if we distinguish, as we ought, the feeling which naturally and necessarily attends the kind affection from those which accidentally, in certain circumstances, it may produce.

The parental affection is an agreeable feeling; but it makes the misfortune or misbehaviour of a child give a deeper wound to the mind. Pity is an agreeable feeling, yet distress, which we are not able to relieve, may give a painful sympathy. Love to one of the other sex is an agreeable feeling; but where it does not meet with a proper return, it may give the most pungent distress.

The joy and comfort of human life consists in the reciprocal exercise of kind affections, and without them life would be undesirable.

It has been observed by Lord Shaftesbury, and by many other judicious moralists, That even the epicure and the debauchee, who are thought to place all their happiness in the gratifications of sense, and to pursue these as their only object, can find no relish in solitary indulgences of this kind, but in those only that are mixed with social intercourse, and a reciprocal exchange of kind affections.

Cicero has observed, that the word convivium, which in Latin signifies a feast, is not borrowed from eating or from drinking, but from that social intercourse which, being the chief part of such an entertainment, gives the name to the whole.

Mutual kind affections are undoubtedly the balm of life, and of all the enjoyments common to good and bad men, are the chief. If a man had no person whom he loved or esteemed, no person who loved or esteemed him, how wretched must his condition be! Surely a man capable of reflection would choose to pass out of existence, rather than to live in such a state.

It has been, by the poets, represented as the state of some bloody and barbarous tyrants; but poets are allowed to paint a little beyond the life. Atreus is represented as saying, Oderint dum metuunt. "I care not for their hatred, providing they dread my power." I believe there never was a man so disposed towards all mankind. The most odious tyrant that ever was, will have his favourites, whose affection he endeavours to deserve or to bribe, and to whom he bears some good will.

[We may therefore lay it down as a principle, that all *benevolent affections* are, in their nature, agreeable; and that, next to a good conscience, to which they are always friendly, and never can be adverse, they *make the capital part of human happiness.*]

[IV. *Another ingredient essential to every benevolent affection, and from which it takes the name, is a desire of the good and happiness of the object.*]

The object of benevolent affection, therefore, must be some being capable of happiness. When we speak of affection to a house, or to any inanimate thing, the word has a different meaning. For that which has no capacity of enjoyment, or of suffering, may be an object of liking or disgust, but cannot possibly be an object either of benevolent or malevolent affection.

A thing may be desired either on its own account, or as the means in order to something else. That only can properly be called an object of desire, which is desired upon its own account; and it is only such desires that I call principles of action. When any thing is desired as the means only, there must be an end for which it is desired; and the desire of the end is, in this case, the principle of action. The means are desired only as they tend to that end; and if different, or even contrary means tended to the same end, they would be equally desired.

On this account I consider those affections only as benevolent, where the good of the object is desired ultimately, and not as the means only, in order to something else.

[To say that we desire the good of others, only in order *to procure some pleasure* or good *to ourselves,* is to say that there is no benevolent affection in human nature.]

This, indeed, has been the opinion of some philosophers, both in ancient and in later times. I intend not to examine this opinion in this place, conceiving it proper to give that view of the principles of action in man, which appears to me to be just, before I examine the systems wherein they have been mistaken or misrepresented.

I observe only at present, that [it appears as unreasonable to resolve all our benevolent affections into self-love, as it would be to resolve hunger and thirst into self-love.]

These appetites are necessary for the preservation of the individual. Benevolent affections are no less necessary for the preservation of society among men, without which man would become an easy prey to the beasts of the field.

We are placed in this world by the Author of our being, surrounded with many objects that are necessary or useful to us, and with many that may hurt us. We are led, not by reason and self-love only, but by many instincts, and appetites, and natural desires, to seek the former and to avoid the latter.

But of all the things of this world, man may be the most useful, or the most hurtful to man. Every man is in the power of every man with whom he lives. Every man has power to do much good to his fellow-men, and to do more hurt.

We cannot live without the society of men; and it would be impossible to live in society, if men were not disposed to do much of that good to men, and but little of that hurt, which it is in their power to do.

But how shall this end, so necessary to the existence of human society, and consequently to the existence of the human species, be accomplished?

[If we judge from *analogy,* we must conclude, that in this, as in other parts of our conduct, our rational principles are *aided by principles of an inferior order,* similar to those by which many brute-animals live in society with their species; and that by means of such principles, that degree of regularity is observed, which we find in all societies of men, whether wise or foolish, virtuous or vicious.]

The benevolent affections planted in human nature, appear therefore no less necessary for the preservation of the human species, than the appetites of hunger and thirst.

CHAPTER IV.

OF THE PARTICULAR BENEVOLENT AFFECTIONS.

I. *Of natural affection.*—HAVING premised these things in general concerning benevolent affections, I shall now attempt some enumeration of them.

1. The *first* I mention is that of parents and children, and other near relations.

This we commonly call *natural* affection. Every language has a name for it. It is common to us with most of the brute-animals; and is variously modified in different animals, according as it is more or less necessary for the preservation of the species.

Many of the insect tribe need no other care of parents, than that the eggs be laid in a proper place, where they shall have neither too little nor too much heat, and where the animal, as soon as it is hatched, shall find its natural food. This care the parent takes, and no more.

In other tribes, the young must be lodged in some secret place, where they cannot be easily discovered by their enemies. They must be cherished by the warmth of the parent's body. They must be suckled, and fed at first with tender food; attended in their excursions, and guarded from danger, till they have learned by experience, and by the example of their parents, to provide for their own subsistence and safety. With what assiduity and tender affection this is done by the parents, in every species that requires it, is well known.

The eggs of the feathered tribe are commonly hatched by incubation of the dam, who leaves off at once her sprightly motions and migrations, and confines herself to her solitary and painful task, cheered by the song of her mate upon a neighbouring bough, and sometimes fed by him, sometimes relieved in her incubation, while she gathers a scanty meal, and with the greatest dispatch returns to her post.

The young birds of many species are so very tender and delicate, that man, with all his wisdom and experience, would not be able to rear one to maturity. But the parents, without any experience, know perfectly how to rear sometimes a dozen or more at one brood, and to give every one its portion in due season. They know the food best suited to their delicate constitution, which is sometimes afforded by nature, sometimes must be cooked and half digested in the stomach of the parent.

In some animals, nature hath furnished the female with a kind of second womb, into which the young retire occasionally, for food, warmth, and the conveniency of being carried about with the mother.

It would be endless to recount all the various ways in which the parental affection is expressed by brute-animals.

[He must, in my apprehension, have a very strange complexion of understanding, who can survey the various ways in which the young of the various species are reared, without wonder, without pious admiration of that manifold Wisdom, which hath so skilfully fitted means to ends, in such an infinite variety of ways.]

In all the brute-animals we are acquainted with, the end of the parental affection is completely answered in a short time; and then it ceases as if it had never been.

II. *Duration of parental affection limited in inferior animals; not so in the human species.*— [The infancy of man is longer and more *helpless* than that of any other animal. The parental affection is necessary for many years; it is highly useful through life; and therefore it terminates only with life. It extends to children's children without any diminution of its force.]

How common is it to see a young woman, in the gayest period of life, who has spent her days in mirth, and her nights in profound sleep, without solicitude or care, all at once transformed into the careful, the solicitous, the watchful nurse of her dear infant: doing nothing by day but gazing upon it, and serving it in the meanest offices; by night, depriving herself of sound sleep for months, that it may lie safe in her arms. Forgetful of herself, her whole care is centred in this little object.

Such a sudden transformation of her whole habits, and occupation, and turn of mind, if we did not see it every day, would appear a more wonderful *metamorphosis* than any that Ovid has described.

This, however, is the work of nature, and not the effect of reason and reflection. For we see it in the good and in the bad, in the most thoughtless, as well as in the thoughtful.

Nature has assigned different departments to the father and mother in rearing their offspring. This may be seen in many brute-animals; and that it is so in the human species, was long ago observed by Socrates, and most beautifully illustrated by him, as we learn from Xenophon's "Œconomics." The parental affection in the different sexes is exactly adapted to the office assigned to each. The father would make an awkward nurse to a new-born child, and the mother too indulgent a guardian. But both act with propriety and grace in their proper sphere.

It is very remarkable, that when the office of rearing a child is transferred from the parent to another person, nature seems to transfer the affection along with the office. A wet nurse, or even a dry nurse, has commonly the same affection for her nursling as if she had borne it. The fact is so well known, that nothing needs be said to confirm it; and it seems to be the work of nature.

III. *Parental affection the effect of our natural constitution.*—Our affections are not immediately in our power, as our outward actions are. Nature has directed them to certain objects. We may do kind offices without affection; but we cannot create an affection which nature has not given.

Reason might teach a man that his children are particularly committed to his care by the providence of God, and, on that account, that he ought to attend to them as his particular charge; but reason could not teach him to love them more than other children of equal merit, or to be more afflicted for their misfortunes or misbehaviour.

[It is evident, therefore, that that peculiar sensibility of affection, with regard to his own children, is not the effect of reasoning or reflection, but the *effect of that constitution* which nature has given him.]

There are some affections which we may call *rational,* because they are grounded upon an opinion of merit in the object. The parental affection is not of this kind. For though a man's affection to his child may be increased by merit, and diminished by demerit, I think no man will say, that it took its rise from an opinion of merit. It is not opinion that creates the affection, but affection often creates opinion. It is apt to pervert the judgment, and create an opinion of merit where there is none.

The absolute necessity of this parental affection, in order to the continuance of the human species, is so apparent, that there is no need of arguments to prove it. The rearing of a child from its birth to maturity requires so much time and care, and such infinite attentions, that, if it were to be done merely from considerations of reason and duty, and were not sweetened by affection in parents, nurses and guardians, there is reason to doubt, whether one child in ten thousand would ever be reared.

IV. *Further uses of parental affection.*—[Beside the absolute *necessity* of this part of the human constitution to the preservation of the species, its *utility* is very great, (1) for tempering the giddiness and impetuosity of youth, and (2) improving its knowledge by the prudence and experience of age, for (3) encouraging industry and frugality in the parents, in order to provide for their children, (4) for the solace and support of parents under the infirmities of old age; not to mention that (5) it probably gave rise to the first civil governments.]

It does not appear that the parental, and other family affections, are, in general, either too strong or too weak for answering their end. If they were too weak, parents would be most apt to err on the side of undue severity; if too strong, of undue indulgence. As they are in fact, I believe no man can say, that the errors are more general on one side than on the other.

When these affections are exerted according to their intention, under the direction of wisdom and prudence, the economy of such a family is a most delightful spectacle, and furnishes the most agreeable and affecting subject to the pencil of the painter, and to the pen of the orator and poet.

V. 2. The next benevolent affection I mention is *gratitude* to benefactors.

That good offices are, by the very constitution of our nature, apt to produce good-will towards the benefactor, in good and bad men, in the savage and in the civilized, cannot surely be denied by any one, in the least acquainted with human nature.

The danger of perverting a man's judgment by good deeds, where he ought to have no bias, is so well known, that it is dishonourable in judges, in witnesses, in electors to offices of trust, to accept of them; and, in all civilized nations, they are, in such cases, prohibited, as the means of corruption.

Those who would corrupt the sentence of a judge, the testimony of a witness, or the vote of an elector, know well, that they must not make a bargain, or stipulate what is to be done in return. This would shock every man who has the least pretension to morals. If the person can only be prevailed upon to accept the good office, as a testimony of pure and disinterested friendship, it is left to work upon his gratitude. He finds himself under a kind of moral obligation to consider the cause of his benefactor and friend in the most favourable light. He finds it easier to justify his conduct to himself, by favouring the interest of his benefactor, than by opposing it.

Thus the principle of gratitude is supposed, even in the nature of a bribe. Bad men know how to make this natural principle the most effectual means of corruption. The very best things may be turned to a bad use. But the natural tendency of this principle, and the intention of nature in planting it in the human breast, are, evidently, to promote good-will among men, and to give to good offices the power of multiplying their kind, like seed sown in the earth, which brings a return, with increase.

Whether there be, or be not, in the more sagacious brutes, something that may be called gratitude, I will not dispute. We must allow this important difference between their gratitude and that of the human kind, that, in the last, the mind of the benefactor is chiefly regarded, in the first, the external action only. A brute-animal will be as kindly affected to him who feeds it in order to kill and eat it, as to him who does it from affection.

A man may be justly entitled to our gratitude, for an office that is useful, though it be, at the same time, disagreeable; and not only for doing, but for forbearing what he had a right to do. Among men, it is not every beneficial office that claims our gratitude, but such only as are not due to us in justice. A favour alone gives a claim to gratitude; and a favour must be something more than justice requires. It does not appear that brutes have any conception of justice. They can neither distinguish hurt from injury, nor a favour from a good office that is due.

VI. 3. A *third* natural benevolent affection is, *pity* and compassion towards the distressed.

Of all persons, those in distress stand most in need of our good offices. And, for that reason, the Author of Nature hath planted in the breast of every human creature a powerful advocate to plead their cause.

In man, and in some other animals, there are signs of distress, which nature hath both taught them to use, and taught all men to understand without any interpreter. These natural signs are more eloquent than language; they move our hearts,-and produce a sympathy, and a desire to give relief.

There are few hearts so hard, but great distress will conquer their anger, their indignation, and every malevolent affection.

We sympathise even with the traitor and with the assassin, when we see him led to execution. It is only self-preservation, and the public good, that makes us reluctantly assent to his being cut off from among men.

The practice of the Canadian nations toward their prisoners would tempt one to think, that they have been able to root out the principle of compassion from their nature. But this, I apprehend, would be a rash conclusion. It is only a part of the prisoners of war that they devote to a cruel death. This gratifies the revenge of the women and children who have lost their husbands and fathers in the war. The other prisoners are kindly used, and adopted as brethren.*

Compassion with bodily pain is no doubt weakened among these savages, because they are trained from their infancy to be superior to death, and to every degree of pain; and he is thought unworthy of the name of a man, who cannot defy his tormentors, and sing his death-song in the midst of the most cruel tortures. He who can do this, is honoured as a brave man, though an enemy. But he must perish in the experiment.

A Canadian has the most perfect contempt for every man who thinks pain an intolerable evil. And nothing is so apt to stifle compassion as contempt, and an apprehension, that the evil suffered is nothing but what ought to be manfully borne.

It must also be observed, that savages set no bounds to their revenge. Those who find no protection in laws and government

* This illustration has lost its propriety by the extension of civilization in Canada.

never think themselves safe, but in the destruction of their enemy. And one of the chief advantages of civil government is, that it tempers the cruel passion of revenge, and opens the heart to compassion with every human woe.

It seems to be false religion only, that is able to check the tear of compassion.

We are told, that, in Portugal and Spain, a man condemned to be burned as an obstinate heretic, meets with no compassion, even from the multitude. It is true, they are taught to look upon him as an enemy to God, and doomed to hell-fire. But should not this very circumstance move compassion? Surely it would, if they were not taught, that, in this case, it is a crime to show compassion, or even to feel it.*

VII. 4. A *fourth* benevolent affection is, esteem of the wise and the good.

The worst men cannot avoid feeling this in some degree. Esteem, veneration, devotion, are different degrees of the same affection. The perfection of wisdom, power and goodness, which belongs only to the Almighty, is the object of the last.

It may be a doubt, whether this principle of esteem, as well as that of gratitude, ought to be ranked in the order of animal principles, or if they ought not rather to be placed in a higher order. They are certainly more allied to the rational nature than the others that have been named; nor is it evident, that there is any thing in brute-animals that deserves the same name.

There is indeed a subordination in a herd of cattle, and in a flock of sheep, which, I believe, is determined by strength and courage, as it is among savage tribes of men. I have been informed, that, in a pack of hounds, a stanch hound acquires a degree of esteem in the pack; so that, when the dogs are wandering in quest of the scent, if he opens, the pack immediately closes in with him, when they would not regard the opening of a dog of no reputation. This is something like a respect to wisdom.

But I have placed esteem of the wise and good in the order of animal principles, not from any persuasion that it is to be found in brute-animals, but because, I think, it appears in the most unimproved and in the most degenerate part of our species, even in those in whom we hardly perceive any exertion, either of reason or virtue.

I will not, however, dispute with any man who thinks that it deserves a more honourable name than that of an animal principle. It is of small importance what name we give it, if we are satisfied that there is such a principle in the human constitution.

VIII. 5. *Friendship* is another benevolent affection.

* The infamous ceremony of the *Auto de fé*, here alluded to, was abolished by Napoleon Buonaparte in 1808.

Of this we have some instances famous in history: few indeed; but sufficient to show, that human nature is susceptible of that extraordinary attachment, sympathy and affection, to one or a few persons, which the ancients thought alone worthy of the name of friendship.

The Epicureans found it very difficult to reconcile the existence of friendship to the principles of their sect. They were not so bold as to deny its existence. They even boasted that there had been more attachments of that kind between Epicureans than in any other sect. But the difficulty was, to account for real friendship upon Epicurean principles. They went into different hypotheses upon this point, three of which are explained by Torquatus the Epicurean, in Cicero's book, " De Finibus."

Cicero, in his reply to Torquatus, examines all the three, and shows them all to be either inconsistent with the nature of true friendship, or inconsistent with the fundamental principles of the Epicurean sect.

[As to the friendship which the Epicureans boasted of among those of their sect, Cicero does not question the fact, but observes, that, as there are many whose practice is worse than their principles, so there are some whose principles are worse than their practice, and that the bad principles of these Epicureans were overcome by the goodness of their nature.]

IX. 6. Among the benevolent affections, *the passion of love* between the sexes cannot be overlooked.

Although it is commonly the theme of poets, it is not unworthy of the pen of the philosopher, as it is a most important part of the human constitution.

It is no doubt made up of various ingredients, as many other principles of action are, but it certainly cannot exist without a very strong benevolent affection toward its object; in whom it finds, or conceives, every thing that is amiable and excellent, and even something more than human. I consider it here, only as a benevolent affection natural to man. And that it is so, no man can doubt who ever felt its force.

It is evidently intended by nature to direct a man in the choice of a mate, with whom he desires to live, and to rear an offspring.

It has effectually secured this end in all ages, and in every state of society.

[The passion of love, and the parental affection, are counterparts to each other; and when they are conducted with prudence, and meet with a proper return, are the source of all domestic felicity, the greatest, next to that of a good conscience, which this world affords.]

As, in the present state of things, pain often dwells near to pleasure, and sorrow to joy, it needs not be thought strange, that a passion, fitted and intended by nature to yield the greatest worldly felicity, should, by being ill-regulated, or wrong directed, prove the occasion of the most pungent distress.

But its joys and its griefs, its different modifications in the different sexes, and its influence upon the character of both, though very important subjects, are fitter to be sung than said; and I leave them to those who have slept upon the two-topped Parnassus.

X. 7. The *last* benevolent affection I shall mention is, what we commonly call *public spirit*, that is, an affection to any community to which we belong.

If there be any man quite destitute of this affection, he must be as great a monster as a man born with two heads. Its effects are manifest in the whole of human life, and in the history of all nations.

The situation of a great part of mankind, indeed, is such, that their thoughts and views must be confined within a very narrow sphere, and be very much engrossed by their private concerns. With regard to an extensive public, such as a state or nation, they are like a drop to the ocean, so that they have rarely an opportunity of acting with a view to it.

In many, whose actions may affect the public, and whose rank and station lead them to think of it, private passions may be an overmatch for public spirit. All that can be inferred from this is, that their public spirit is weak, not that it does not exist.

If a man wishes well to the public, and is ready to do good to it rather than hurt, when it costs him nothing, he has some affection to it, though it may be scandalously weak in degree.

I believe every man has it in one degree or another. What man is there who does not resent satirical reflections upon his country, or upon any community of which he is a member?

Whether the affection be to a college or to a cloister, to a clan or to a profession, to a party or to a nation, it is public spirit. These affections differ, not in kind, but in the extent of their object.

The object extends as our connexions extend; and a sense of the connexion carries the affection along with it to every community to which we can apply the pronouns *we* and *our*.

> Friend, parent, neighbour, first it will embrace,
> His country next, and then all human race.—POPE.

Even in the misanthrope, this affection is not extinguished. It is overpowered by the apprehension he has of the worthlessness, the baseness, and the ingratitude of mankind. Convince him, that there is any amiable quality in the species, and immediately his philanthropy revives, and rejoices to find an object on which it can exert itself.

XI. *Necessity for submitting public spirit to the control of reason and virtue, evident.*—[*Public spirit* has this in common with every subordinate principle of action, that, when it is not under the government of reason and virtue, it may produce much evil as well as good.] Yet, where there is least of reason and virtue to regulate it, its good far overbalances its ill.

[It sometimes kindles or inflames animosities between communities, or contending parties, and makes them treat each other with little regard to justice. It kindles wars between nations, and makes them destroy one another for trifling causes.] But, without it, society could not subsist, and every community would be a rope of sand.

When under the direction of reason and virtue, *it is the very image of God in the soul.* It diffuses its benign influence as far as its power extends, and participates in the happiness of God, and of the whole creation.

These are the benevolent affections which appear to me to be parts of the human constitution.

If any one thinks the enumeration incomplete, and that there are natural benevolent affections, which are not included under any of those that have been named, I shall very readily listen to such a correction, being sensible that such enumerations are very often incomplete.

If others should think that any, or all, the affections I have named are acquired by education, or by habits and associations grounded on self-love, and are not original parts of our constitution; this is a point upon which, indeed, there has been much subtile disputation in ancient and modern times, and which, I believe, must be determined from what a man, by careful reflection, may feel in himself, rather than from what he observes in others. But I decline entering into this dispute, till I shall have explained that principle of action which we commonly call *self-love*.

XII. I shall conclude this subject with some *reflections upon the benevolent affections.*

[The *first* is, that all of them, in as far as they are benevolent, in which view only I consider them, *agree* very much *in the conduct they dispose us to, with regard to their objects.*]

They dispose us to do them good as far as we have power and opportunity; to wish them well, when we can do them no good; to judge favourably, and often partially, of them; to sympathise with them in their afflictions and calamities; and to rejoice with them in their happiness and good fortune.

It is impossible that there can be benevolent affection without sympathy, both with the good and bad fortune of the object; and it appears to be impossible that there can be sympathy without benevolent affection. Men do not sympathise with one whom they hate; nor even with one to whose good or ill they are perfectly indifferent.

We may sympathise with a perfect stranger, or even with an enemy whom we see in distress; but this is the effect of pity; and if we did not pity him, we should not sympathise with him.

I take notice of this the rather, because a very ingenious author* in his "Theory of Moral Sentiments," gives a very different account of the origin of sympathy. It appears to me to be the effect of benevolent affection, and to be inseparable from it.

[A *second* reflection is, that *the constitution of our nature* very powerfully *invites us to cherish* and cultivate in our minds *the benevolent affections.*]

The agreeable feeling which always attends them as a present reward, appears to be intended by nature for this purpose.

Benevolence, from its nature, composes the mind, warms the heart, enlivens the whole frame, and brightens every feature of the countenance. It may justly be said to be medicinal both to soul and body. We are bound to it by duty; we are invited to it by interest; and because both these cords are often feeble, we have natural kind affections to aid them in their operation, and supply their defects; and these affections are joined with a manly pleasure in their exertion.

[A *third* reflection is, that the natural benevolent affections furnish the most irresistible proof, that the Author of our nature intended that *we should live in society*, and *do good to our fellow-men* as we have opportunity; since this great and important part of the human constitution has a manifest relation to society, and can have no exercise nor use in a solitary state.]

[The *last* reflection is, that the *different principles of action* have different *degrees* of dignity, and rise one above another in our estimation, when we make them objects of contemplation.]

We ascribe no dignity to instincts or to habits. They lead us only to admire the wisdom of the Creator, in adapting them so perfectly to the manner of life of the different animals in which they are found. Much the same may be said of appetites. They serve rather for use than ornament.

The desires of knowledge, of power, and of esteem, rise higher in our estimation, and we consider them as giving dignity and ornament to man. The actions proceeding from them, though not properly virtuous, are manly and respectable, and claim a just superiority over those that proceed merely from appetite. This, I think, is the uniform judgment of mankind.

If we apply the same kind of judgment to our benevolent affections, they appear not only manly and respectable, but amiable in a high degree.

They are amiable even in brute-animals. We love the meek-

* Adam Smith.

ness of the lamb, the gentleness of the dove, the affection of a dog to his master. We cannot, without pleasure, observe the timid ewe, who never showed the least degree of courage in her own defence, become valiant and intrepid in defence of her lamb, and boldly assault those enemies, the very sight of whom was wont to put her to flight.

How pleasant is it to see the family economy of a pair of little birds in rearing their tender offspring; the conjugal affection and fidelity of the parents; their cheerful toil and industry in providing food to their family; their sagacity in concealing their habitation; the arts they use, often at the peril of their own lives, to decoy hawks, and other enemies, from their dwelling-place, and the affliction they feel when some unlucky boy has robbed them of the dear pledges of their affection, and frustrated all their hopes of their rising family?

If kind affection be amiable in brutes, it is not less so in our own species. Even the external signs of it have a powerful charm.

☞ Every one knows that a person of accomplished good breeding, charms every one he converses with. And what is this good breeding? If we analyse it, we shall find it to be made up of looks, gestures, and speeches, which are the natural signs of benevolence and good affection. He who has got the habit of using these signs with propriety, and without meanness, is a well-bred and a polite man.

What is that beauty in the features of the face, particularly of the fair sex, which all men love and admire? I believe it consists chiefly in the features which indicate good affections. Every indication of meekness, gentleness, and benignity, is a beauty. On the contrary, every feature that indicates pride, passion, envy, and malignity, is a deformity.

Kind affections, therefore, are amiable in brutes. Even the signs and shadows of them are highly attractive in our own species. Indeed they are the joy and the comfort of human life, not to good men only, but even to the vicious and dissolute.

Without society, and the intercourse of kind affection, man is a gloomy, melancholy and joyless being. His mind oppressed with cares and fears, he cannot enjoy the balm of sound sleep: in constant dread of impending danger, he starts at the rustling of a leaf. His ears are continually upon the stretch, and every zephyr brings some sound that alarms him.

When he enters into society, and feels security in the good affection of friends and neighbours, it is then only that his fear vanishes, and his mind is at ease. His courage is raised, his understanding is enlightened, and his heart dilates with joy.

☞ Human society may be compared to a heap of embers, which when placed asunder, can retain neither their light nor heat, amidst the surrounding elements; but when brought together they mutually give heat and light to each other; the flame breaks forth, and not only defends itself, but subdues every thing around it.

[The security, the happiness, and the strength of human society, spring solely from the *reciprocal benevolent affections* of its members.]

The benevolent affections, though they be all honourable and lovely, are not all equally so. There is a subordination among them; and the honour we pay to them generally corresponds to the extent of their object.

The good husband, the good father, the good friend, the good neighbour, we honour as a good man, worthy of our love and affection. But the man in whom these more private affections are swallowed up in zeal for the good of his country, and of mankind, who goes about doing good, and seeks opportunities of being useful to his species, we revere as more than a good man, as a hero, as a good angel.

CHAPTER V.

OF MALEVOLENT AFFECTION.

I. *Of emulation and resentment.*—ARE there, in the constitution of man, any affections that may be called *malevolent?* What are they? And what is their use and end?

To me there seem to be two, which we may call by that name. [They are *emulation* and *resentment*. These I take to be parts of the human constitution, given us by our Maker for good ends, and, when properly directed and regulated, of excellent use.] But, as their excess or abuse, to which human nature is very prone, is the source and spring of all the malevolence that is to be found among men, it is on that account I call them malevolent.

If any man thinks that they deserve a softer name, since they may be exercised according to the intention of nature, without malevolence, to this I have no objection.

By emulation, I mean, a desire of superiority to our rivals in any pursuit, accompanied with an uneasiness at being surpassed.

Human life has justly been compared to a race. The prize is superiority in one kind or another. But the species or forms (if I may use the expression) of superiority among men are infinitely diversified.

There is no man so contemptible in his own eyes, as to hinder him from entering the lists in one form or another; and he will always find competitors to rival him in his own way.

We see emulation among brute-animals. Dogs and horses contend each with his kind in the race. Many animals of the gregarious kind contend for superiority in their flock or herd, and show manifest signs of jealousy when others pretend to rival them.

The emulation of the brute-animals is mostly confined to swiftness, or strength, or favour with their females. But the emulation of the human kind has a much wider field.

In every profession, and in every accomplishment of body or mind, real or imaginary, there are rivalships. Literary men rival one another in literary abilities. Artists in their several arts. The fair sex in their beauty and attractions, and in the respect paid them by the other sex.

In every political society, from a petty corporation up to the national administration, there is a rivalship for power and influence.

Men have a natural desire of power without respect to the power of others. This we call *ambition*. But the desire of superiority, either in power, or in any thing we think worthy of estimation, has a respect to rivals, and is what we properly call *emulation*.

The stronger the desire is, the more pungent will be the uneasiness of being found behind, and the mind will be the more hurt by this humiliating view.

II. [*Emulation has a* manifest *tendency to improvement.* Without it life would stagnate, and the discoveries of art and genius would be at a stand.] This principle produces a constant fermentation in society, by which, though dregs may be produced, the better part is purified and exalted to a perfection which it could not otherwise attain.

We have not sufficient data for a comparison of the good and bad effects which this principle actually produces in society; but there is ground to think of this, as of other natural principles, that the good overbalances the ill. As far as it is under the dominion of reason and virtue, its effects are always good; when left to be guided by passion and folly, they are often very bad.

Reason directs us to strive for superiority, only in things that have real excellence, otherwise we spend our labour for that which profiteth not. To value ourselves for superiority in things that have no real worth, or none, compared with what they cost, is to be vain of our own folly; and to be uneasy at the superiority of others in such things, is no less ridiculous.

Reason directs us to strive for superiority only in things in our power, and attainable by our exertion, otherwise we shall be like the frog in the fable, who swelled herself till she burst, in order to equal the ox in magnitude.

To check all desire of things not attainable, and every uneasy thought in the want of them, is an obvious dictate of prudence, as well as of virtue and religion.

If emulation be regulated by such maxims of reason, and all undue partiality to ourselves be laid aside, it will be a powerful principle of our improvement, without hurt to any other person. It will give strength to the nerves, and vigour to the mind, in every noble and manly pursuit.

III. [But *dismal are its effects, when it is not under the direction of reason and virtue.* It has often the most malignant influence on men's opinions, on their affections, and on their actions.]

It is an old observation, that affection follows opinion; and it is undoubtedly true in many cases. A man cannot be grateful without the opinion of a favour done him. He cannot have deliberate resentment without the opinion of an injury; nor esteem without the opinion of some estimable quality; nor compassion without the opinion of suffering.

But it is no less true, that opinion sometimes follows affection, not that it ought, but that it actually does so, by giving a false bias to our judgment. We are apt to be partial to our friends, and still more to ourselves.

Hence the desire of superiority leads men to put an undue estimation upon those things wherein they excel, or think they excel. And, by this means, pride may feed itself upon the very dregs of human nature.

The same desire of superiority may lead men to undervalue those things wherein they either despair of excelling, or care not to make the exertion necessary for that end. The grapes are sour, said the fox, when he saw them beyond his reach. The same principle leads men to detract from the merit of others, and to impute their brightest actions to mean or bad motives.

He who runs a race feels uneasiness at seeing another outstrip him. This is uncorrupted nature, and the work of God within him. But this uneasiness may produce either of two very different effects. It may incite him to make more vigorous exertions, and to strain every nerve to get before his rival. This is fair and honest emulation. This is the effect it is intended to produce. [But if he has not fairness and candour of heart, he will look with an evil eye upon his competitor, and will endeavour to trip him, or to throw a stumbling-block in his way. *This is pure envy*, the most malignant passion that can lodge in the human breast; which devours, as its natural food, the fame and the happiness of those who are most deserving of our esteem.]

If there be, in some men, a proneness to detract from the character, even of persons unknown or indifferent, in others an avidity to hear and to propagate scandal, to what principle in human nature must we ascribe these qualities? The failings of others surely add nothing to our worth, nor are they, in themselves, a pleasant subject of thought or of discourse. But they flatter pride, by giving an opinion of our superiority to those from whom we detract.

Is it not possible, that the same desire of superiority may have some secret influence upon those who love to display their eloquence in declaiming upon the corruption of human nature, and the wickedness, fraud and insincerity of mankind in general? It ought always to be taken for granted, that the declaimer is an exception to the general rule, otherwise he would rather choose, even for his own sake, to draw a veil over the nakedness of his species. But hoping that his audience will be so civil as not to include him in the black description, he rises superior by the depression of the species, and stands alone, like Noah in the antediluvian world. *This looks like envy against the human race.*

IV. *Effects of emulation in brute-animals.*—It would be endless, and no ways agreeable, to enumerate all the evils and all the vices which passion and folly beget upon emulation. Here, as in most cases, the corruption of the best things is the worst. [In brute-animals, emulation has little matter to work upon, and its effects, good or bad, are few.] It may produce battles of cocks and battles of bulls, and little else that is observable. But in mankind, it has an infinity of matter to work upon, and its good or bad effects, according as it is well or ill regulated and directed, multiply in proportion.

[The conclusion to be drawn from what has been said upon this principle is, That *emulation,* as far as it is a part of our constitution, is highly *useful and important in society;* that in the wise and good, it produces the best effects without any harm; but in the foolish and vicious, it is *the parent of a great part of the evils of life,* and of the most malignant vices that stain human nature.]

We are next to consider *resentment.*

V. *Definition of resentment.*—[Nature disposes us, when we are hurt, to resist and retaliate. Besides the bodily pain occasioned by the hurt, the mind is ruffled, and *a desire raised to retaliate* upon the author of the hurt or injury. This, in general, is what we call *anger* or *resentment.*]

A very important distinction is made by Bishop Butler between sudden resentment, which is a blind impulse arising from our constitution, and that which is deliberate. The first may be raised by hurt of any kind; but the last can only be raised by injury, real or conceived.

The same distinction is made by Lord Kames, in his "Elements of Criticism." What Butler calls *sudden,* he calls *instinctive.*

We have not, in common language, different names for these

different kinds of resentment; but the distinction is very necessary, in order to our having just notions of this part of the human constitution. It corresponds perfectly with the distinction I have made between the animal and rational principles of action. [For this sudden or instinctive resentment, is *an animal principle common to us with brute-animals.* But that resentment which the authors I have named call *deliberate*, must fall under the class of rational principles.]

It is to be observed, however, that, by referring it to that class, I do not mean, that it is always kept within the bounds that reason prescribes, but only that it is proper to man as a reasonable being, capable, by his rational faculties, of distinguishing between hurt and injury; a distinction which no brute animal can make.

Both these kinds of resentment are raised, whether the hurt or injury be done to ourselves, or to those we are interested in.

Wherever there is any benevolent affection towards others, we resent their wrongs, in proportion to the strength of our affection. Pity and sympathy with the sufferer, produce resentment against the author of the suffering, as naturally as concern for ourselves produces resentment of our own wrongs.

VI. I shall first consider that resentment which I call *animal*, which Butler calls *sudden*, and Lord Kames *instinctive*.

In every animal to which Nature hath given the power of hurting its enemy, we see an endeavour to retaliate the ill that is done to it. Even a mouse will bite when it cannot run away.

Perhaps there may be some animals to whom nature hath given no offensive weapon. To such, anger and resentment would be of no use; and I believe we shall find, that they never show any sign of it. But there are few of this kind.

Some of the more sagacious animals can be provoked to fierce anger, and retain it long. Many of them show great animosity in defending their young, who hardly show any in defending themselves. Others resist every assault made upon the flock or herd to which they belong. Bees defend their hive, wild beasts their den, and birds their nest.

[This sudden resentment operates in a similar manner in men and in brutes, and appears to be given by nature to both for the same end, namely, *for defence*, even in cases *where there is no time for deliberation.*] ☞ It may be compared to that natural instinct, by which a man, who has lost his balance and begins to fall, makes a sudden and violent effort to recover himself, without any intention or deliberation.

In such efforts, men often exert a degree of muscular strength beyond what they are able to exert by a calm determination of the will, and thereby save themselves from many a dangerous fall.

By a like violent and sudden impulse, nature prompts us to

repel hurt upon the cause of it, whether it be man or beast. The instinct before mentioned is solely defensive, and is prompted by fear. This sudden resentment is offensive, and is prompted by anger, but with a view to defence.

[*Man*, in his present state, is surrounded with so many dangers from his own species, from brute-animals, from every thing around him, that he *has need of some defensive armour* that shall always be ready in the moment of danger. *His reason* is of great use for this purpose, when there is time to apply it. But, in many cases, the mischief would be done before reason could think of the means of preventing it.]

[The wisdom of nature hath provided *two* means to supply this defect of our reason. (1) One of these is the *instinct* before mentioned, by which the body, upon the appearance of danger, is instantly, and without thought or intention, put in that posture which is proper for preventing the danger, or lessening it.] Thus, we wink hard when our eyes are threatened; we bend the body to avoid a stroke; we make a sudden effort to recover our balance, when in danger of falling. By such means we are guarded from many dangers which our reason would come too late to prevent.

[(2) But as offensive arms are often the surest means of defence, by deterring the enemy from an assault, nature hath also provided man, and other animals, with this kind of defence, by that *sudden resentment* of which we now speak, which outruns the quickest determinations of reason, and takes fire in an instant, threatening the enemy with retaliation.]

[The first of these principles (*instinct*) operates upon the defender only; but this (*resentment*) operates both upon the defender and the assailant, inspiring the former with courage and animosity, and striking terror into the latter.] It proclaims to all assailants, what our ancient Scottish kings did upon their coins, by the emblem of a thistle, with this motto, "Nemo me impune lacesset." By this, in innumerable cases, men and beasts are deterred from doing hurt, and others thereby secured from suffering it.

But as resentment supposes an object on whom we may retaliate, how comes it to pass, that in brutes very often, and sometimes in our own species, we see it wreaked upon inanimate things, which are incapable of suffering by it?

Perhaps it might be a sufficient answer to this question, That nature acts by general laws, which, in some particular cases may go beyond, or fall short of their intention, though they be ever so well adapted to it in general.

But I confess it seems to me impossible, that there should be resentment against a thing, which at that very moment is considered as inanimate, and consequently incapable either of intending hurt, or of being punished. For what can be more absurd, than to be angry with the knife for cutting me, or with the weight for falling upon my toes? There must therefore, I conceive, be some momentary notion or conception that the object of our resentment is capable of punishment; and if it be natural, before reflection, to be angry with things inanimate, it seems to be a necessary consequence, that it is natural to think that they have life and feeling.

VII. *Children and rude nations generally ascribe life and intelligence to inanimate things.*—[Several phenomena in human nature lead us to conjecture that, in *the earliest period of life, we are apt to think every object about us to be animated.* Judging of them by ourselves, we ascribe to them the feelings we are conscious of in ourselves.] So we see a little girl judges of her doll and of her play-things. And so we see *rude nations* judge of the heavenly bodies, of the elements, and of the sea, rivers, and fountains.*

If this be so, it ought not to be said, that by reason and experience, we learn to ascribe life and intelligence to things which we before considered as inanimate. It ought rather to be said, [That by reason and experience we learn that certain things are inanimate, to which at first we ascribed life and intelligence.]

If this be true, it is less surprising that, before reflection, we should for a moment relapse into this prejudice of our early years, and treat things as if they had life, which we once believed to have it.

It does not much affect our present argument, whether this be, or be not the cause, why a dog pursues and gnashes at the stone that hurt him; and why a man in a passion, for losing at play, sometimes wreaks his vengeance on the cards or dice.

It is not strange that a blind animal impulse should sometimes lose its proper direction. In brutes this has no bad consequence; in men the least ray of reflection corrects it, and shows its absurdity.

[It is sufficiently evident, upon the whole, that this sudden, or *animal resentment, is intended* by nature *for our defence.* It prevents mischief by the fear of punishment.] ☞ It is a kind of penal statute, promulgated by nature, the execution of which is committed to the sufferer.

It may be expected indeed, that one who judges in his own cause, will be disposed to seek more than an equitable redress. But this disposition is checked by the resentment of the other party.

Yet, in the state of nature, injuries once begun, will often be reciprocated between the parties, until mortal enmity is pro-

* Vide sec. 1. chap. iii. Essay IV. seq.

duced, and each party thinks himself safe only in the destruction of his enemy.

This right of redressing and punishing our own wrongs, so apt to be abused, is one of those natural rights, which, in political society, is given up to the laws, and to the civil magistrate; and this indeed is one of the capital advantages we reap from the political union, that the evils arising from ungoverned resentment are in a great degree prevented.

VIII. Although *deliberate resentment* does not properly belong to the class of animal principles; yet, as both have the same name, and are distinguished only by philosophers, and as in real life they are commonly intermixed, I shall here make some remarks upon it.

[A small degree of reason and reflection teaches a man that *injury* only, and *not mere hurt*, is a just object of resentment to a rational creature.] A man may suffer grievously by the hand of another, not only without injury, but with the most friendly intention; as in the case of a painful surgical operation. Every man of common sense sees, that to resent such suffering, is not the part of a man, but of a brute.

Mr. Locke mentions a gentleman who, having been cured of madness by a very harsh and offensive operation, with great sense of gratitude, owned the cure as the greatest obligation he could have received, but could never bear the sight of the operator, because it brought back the idea of that agony which he had endured from his hands.

In this case we see distinctly the operation both of the animal, and of the rational principle. The first produced an aversion to the operator, which reason was not able to overcome; and probably in a weak mind might have produced lasting resentment and hatred. But, in this gentleman, reason so far prevailed, as to make him sensible that gratitude, and not resentment, was due.

Suffering may give a bias to the judgment, and make us apprehend injury where no injury is done. But, I think, without an apprehension of injury, there can be no deliberate resentment.

Hence, among enlightened nations, hostile armies fight without anger or resentment. The vanquished are not treated as offenders, but as brave men who have fought for their country unsuccessfully, and who are entitled to every office of humanity consistent with the safety of the conquerors.

IX. *Agreements and disagreements between deliberate and mere animal resentment.*—[If we analyze that *deliberate resentment* which is proper to rational creatures, we shall find that though it agrees with that which is *merely animal* in some respects, it differs in others. Both are accompanied with an uneasy sensation, which disturbs the peace of the mind. Both prompt us to seek redress of our sufferings, and security from harm. But, in deliberate resentment, there must be an opinion of *injury* done or intended. And an *opinion of injury implies an idea of justice, and consequently a moral faculty.*]

The very notion of an injury is, that it is less than we may justly claim; as, on the contrary, the notion of a favour is that it is more than we can justly claim. Whence it is evident, that justice is the standard, by which both a favour and an injury are to be weighed and estimated. Their very nature and definition consist in their exceeding or falling short of this standard. No man, therefore, can have the idea either of a favour or of an injury, who has not the idea of justice.

That very idea of justice which enters into cool and deliberate resentment, tends to restrain its excesses. For as there is injustice in doing an injury, so there is injustice in punishing it beyond measure.

To a man of candour and reflection, consciousness of the frailty of human nature, and that he has often stood in need of forgiveness himself, the pleasure of renewing good understanding, after it has been interrupted, the inward approbation of a generous and forgiving disposition, and even the irksomeness and uneasiness of a mind ruffled by resentment, plead strongly against its excesses.

Upon the whole, when we consider, That, on the one hand, every benevolent affection is pleasant in its nature, is health to the soul, and a cordial to the spirits; that nature has made even the outward expression of benevolent affections in the countenance, pleasant to every beholder, and the chief ingredient of beauty in the *human face divine;* that, on the other hand, every malevolent affection, not only in its faulty excesses, but in its moderate degrees, is vexation and disquiet to the mind, and even gives deformity to the countenance, it is evident that, by these signals, nature loudly admonishes us to use the former as our daily bread, both for health and pleasure, but to consider the latter as a nauseous medicine, which is never to be taken without necessity; and even then in no greater quantity than the necessity requires.

CHAPTER VI.

OF PASSION.

I. *Passion, Disposition, Opinion.*—BEFORE I proceed to consider the rational principles of action, it is proper to observe, that [there are some things belonging to the mind, which have great influence upon human conduct, by exciting or allaying, inflaming or cooling the animal principles we have mentioned.

Three of this kind deserve particular consideration. I shall call them by the names of *passion, disposition, and opinion.*]

The meaning of the word *passion* is not precisely ascertained, either in common discourse, or in the writings of philosophers.

II. *Definition of passion.*—I think it is commonly put to signify [some agitation of mind, which is opposed to that state of tranquillity and composure, in which a man is most master of himself.]

The word παθος, which answers to it in the Greek language, is, by Cicero, rendered by the word *perturbatio.*

☞ It has always been conceived to bear analogy to a storm at sea, or to a tempest in the air. It does not therefore signify any thing in the mind that is constant and permanent, but something that is occasional, and has a limited duration, like a storm or tempest.

Passion commonly produces sensible effects even upon the body. It changes the voice, the features, and the gesture. The external signs of passion have, in some cases, a great resemblance to those of madness; in others, to those of melancholy. It gives often a degree of muscular force and agility to the body, far beyond what it possesses in calm moments.

The effects of passion upon the mind are not less remarkable. It turns the thoughts involuntarily to the objects related to it, so that a man can hardly think of any thing else. It gives often a strange bias to the judgment, making a man quicksighted in every thing that tends to inflame his passion, and to justify it, but blind to every thing that tends to moderate and allay it.

☞ Like a magic lantern, it raises up spectres and apparitions that have no reality, and throws false colours upon every object. It can turn deformity into beauty, vice into virtue, and virtue into vice.

The sentiments of a man under its influence will appear absurd and ridiculous, not only to other men, but even to himself when the storm is spent and is succeeded by a calm. Passion often gives a violent impulse to the will, and makes a man do what he knows he shall repent as long as he lives.

That such are the effects of passion, I think all men agree. They have been described in lively colours by poets, orators and moralists, in all ages. But men have given more attention to the effects of passion than to its nature; and while they have copiously and elegantly described the former, they have not precisely defined the latter.

III. [*The controversy* between the ancient Peripatetics and the Stoics, with regard to the passions, *was* probably *owing to their affixing different meanings to the word.*] The one sect maintained, that the passions are good, and useful parts of our constitution, while they are held under the government of reason. The other sect, conceiving that nothing is to be called passion which does not, in some degree, cloud and darken the understanding, considered all passion as hostile to reason, and therefore maintained, that in the wise man passion should have no existence, but be utterly exterminated.

If both sects had agreed about the definition of passion, they would probably have had no difference. But while one considered passion only as the cause of those bad effects which it often produces, and the other considered it as fitted by nature to produce good effects, while it is under subjection to reason, it does not appear that what one sect justified was the same thing which the other condemned. Both allowed that no dictate of passion ought to be followed in opposition to reason. Their difference, therefore, was verbal more than real, and was owing to their giving different meanings to the same word.

IV. [The precise *meaning of this word* seems *not* to be *more clearly ascertained among modern philosophers.*]

Mr. Hume gives the name of *passion* to every principle of action in the human mind; and, in consequence of this, maintains, that every man is, and ought to be led by his passions, and that the use of reason is to be subservient to the passions.

Dr. Hutcheson, considering all the principles of action as so many determinations or motions of the will, divides them into the calm and the turbulent. The turbulent, he says, are our appetites and our passions. Of the passions, as well as of the calm determinations, he says, that " some are benevolent, others are selfish; that anger, envy, indignation, and some others, may be either selfish or benevolent, according as they arise from some opposition to our own interests, or to those of our friends, or persons beloved or esteemed."

It appears, therefore, that this excellent author gives the name of *passions*, not to every principle of action, but to some, and to those only when they are turbulent and vehement, not when they are calm and deliberate.

Our natural desires and affections may be so calm as to leave room for reflection, so that we find no difficulty in deliberating coolly, whether, in such a particular instance, they ought to be gratified or not. On other occasions, they may be so importunate as to make deliberation very difficult, urging us, by a kind of violence, to their immediate gratification.

Thus, a man may be sensible of an injury without being inflamed. He judges coolly of the injury, and of the proper means of redress. This is resentment without passion. It leaves to the man the entire command of himself.

On another occasion, the same principle of resentment rises into a flame. His blood boils within him; his looks, his voice, and his gesture are changed; he can think of nothing but immediate revenge, and feels a strong impulse, without regard to consequences, to say and do things which his cool reason cannot justify. This is the passion of resentment.

What has been said of resentment may easily be applied to other natural desires and affections. When they are so calm as neither to produce any sensible effects upon the body, nor to darken the understanding and weaken the power of self-command, they are not called passions. But the same principle, when it becomes so violent as to produce these effects upon the body and upon the mind, is a passion, or, as Cicero very properly calls it, a *perturbation*.

V. *Hume's paradoxes generally reducible to abuses of words.*— It is evident that this meaning of the word *passion* accords much better with its common use in language, than that which Mr. Hume gives it.

[When he says, (1) that men ought to be governed by their passions only, and (2) that the use of reason is to be subservient to the passions, this, at first hearing, appears a shocking paradox, repugnant to good morals and to common sense; but, *like most other paradoxes*, when explained according to his meaning, *it is nothng but an abuse of words.*]

For if we give the name of *passion* to every principle of action, in every degree, and give the name of *reason* solely to the power of discerning the fitness of means to ends, it will be true, that the use of reason is to be subservient to the passions.

[As I wish to use words as agreeably as possible to their common use in language, I shall, by the word *passion*, mean, not any principle of action distinct from those desires and affections before explained, but *such a degree of vehemence* in them, or in any of them, *as is apt to produce those effects* upon the body or upon the mind which have been above described.*]

Our appetites, even when vehement, are not, I think, very commonly called passions, yet they are capable of being inflamed to rage, and in that case their effects are very similar to those of the passions; and what is said of one may be applied to both.

VI. *Common division of the passions.*—Having explained what I mean by passions, I think it unnecessary to enter into any enumeration of them, since *they differ, not in kind*, but rather *in degree*, from the principles already enumerated.

The *common division of the passions* into desire and aversion, hope and fear, joy and grief, has been mentioned almost by every author who has treated of them, and needs no explication. But we may observe, that these are ingredients or modifications, not of the passions only, but of every principle of action, animal and rational.

* Vide Definition of Passion, sec. ii. of this chap.

All of them imply the *desire of some object;* and the desire of an object cannot be without aversion to its contrary; and, according as the object is present or absent, desire and aversion will be variously modified into joy or grief, hope or fear. It is evident, that desire and aversion, joy and grief, hope and fear, may be either calm and sedate, or vehement and passionate.

VII. *Influence of passion.*—Passing these, therefore, as common to all principles of action, whether calm or vehement, I shall only make some observations on *passion in general,* which tend to show *its influence on human conduct.*

[*First, It is passion that makes us liable to strong temptations.* Indeed, if we had no passions, we should hardly be under any temptation to wrong conduct. For, when we view things calmly, and free from any of the false colours which passion throws upon them, we can hardly fail to see the right and the wrong, and to see that the first is more eligible than the last.]

I believe a cool and deliberate preference of ill to good is never the first step into vice.

"When the woman saw that the tree was good for food, and that it was pleasant to the eyes, and a tree to be desired to make one wise, she took of the fruit thereof and did eat, and gave also to her husband with her and he did eat; and the eyes of them both were opened." Inflamed desire had blinded the eyes of their understanding.

> Fix'd on the fruit she gazed, which to behold
> Might tempt alone; and in her ears the sound
> Yet rung of his persuasive words impregn'd
> With reason to her seeming, and with truth.
> —— Fair to the eye, inviting to the taste,
> Of virtue to make wise, what hinders then
> To reach and feed at once both body and mind?—MILTON.

Thus our first parents were tempted to disobey their Maker, and all their posterity are liable to temptation from the same cause. Passion, or violent appetite, first blinds the understanding, and then perverts the will.

[It is *passion, therefore,* and the vehement motions of appetite, that *make us liable,* in our present state, *to strong temptations* to deviate from our duty. This is the lot of human nature in the present period of our existence.]

Human virtue must gather strength by struggle and effort. ☞ As infants, before they can walk without stumbling, must be exposed to many a fall and bruise; as wrestlers acquire their strength and agility by many a combat and violent exertion; so it is in the noblest powers of human nature, as well as the meanest, and even in virtue itself.

It is not only made manifest by temptation and trial, but by these means it acquires its strength and vigour.

Men must acquire patience by suffering, and fortitude by being exposed to danger, and every other virtue by situations that put it to trial and exercise.

This, for any thing we know, may be necessary in the nature of things. It is certainly a law of nature with regard to man.

Whether there may be orders of intelligent and moral creatures who never were subject to any temptation, nor had their virtue put to any trial, we cannot without presumption determine. But it is evident, that this neither is, nor ever was the lot of man, not even in the state of innocence.

Sad, indeed, would be the condition of man, if the temptations to which, by the constitution of his nature, and by his circumstances, he is liable, were irresistible. Such a state would not at all be a state of trial and discipline.

Our condition here is such, that, on the one hand, passion often tempts and solicits us to do wrong; on the other hand, reason and conscience oppose the dictates of passion. The flesh lusteth against the spirit, and the spirit against the flesh. And upon the issue of this conflict, the character of the man and his fate depend.

If reason be victorious, his virtue is strengthened; he has the inward satisfaction of having fought a good fight in behalf of his duty, and the peace of his mind is preserved.

If, on the other hand, passion prevails against the sense of duty, the man is conscious of having done what he ought not, and might not have done. His own heart condemns him, and he is guilty to himself.

This conflict between the passions of our animal nature and the calm dictates of reason and conscience, is not a theory invented to solve the phenomena of human conduct; it is a fact, of which every man who attends to his own conduct is conscious.

☞ In the most ancient philosophy, of which we have any account, I mean that of the Pythagorean school, *the mind of man was compared to* a state or *commonwealth,* in which there are various powers, some that ought to govern, and others that ought to be subordinate.

The good of the whole, which is the supreme law in this, as in every commonwealth, requires that this subordination be preserved, and that the governing powers have always the ascendant over the appetites and the passions. All wise and good conduct consists in this. All folly and vice in the prevalence of passion over the dictates of reason.

[This philosophy was adopted by Plato; and it is so agreeable to what every man feels in himself, that it must always prevail with men who think without bias to a system.]

The governing powers, of which these ancient philosophers speak, are the same which I call the *rational* principles of action and which I shall have occasion to explain. I only mention them here, because, without a regard to them, the influence of the passions, and their rank in our constitution, cannot be distinctly understood.

VIII. [A *second* observation is, that *the impulse of passion is not always to what is bad*, but very often to what is good, and what our reason approves. There are some passions, as Dr. Hutcheson observes, that are benevolent, as well as others that are selfish.]

The affections of resentment and emulation, with those that spring from them, from their very nature, disturb and disquiet the mind, though they be not carried beyond the bounds which reason prescribes; and therefore they are commonly called passions, even in their moderate degrees. From a similar cause, the benevolent affections, which are placid in their nature, and are rarely carried beyond the bounds of reason, are very seldom called passions. We do not give the name of passion to benevolence, gratitude or friendship. Yet [we must *except* from this general rule, *love between the sexes*, which, as it commonly discomposes the mind, and is not easily kept within reasonable bounds, is always called a passion.]

All our natural desires and affections are good and necessary parts of our constitution; and passion, being only a certain degree of vehemence in these, its natural tendency is to good, and it is by accident that it leads us wrong.

Passion is very properly said to be blind. It looks not beyond the present gratification. It belongs to reason to attend to the accidental circumstances which may sometimes make that gratification improper or hurtful. When there is no impropriety in it, much more when it is our duty, passion aids reason, and gives additional force to its dictates.

Sympathy with the distressed may bring them a charitable relief, when a calm sense of duty would be too weak to produce the effect.

Objects, either good or ill, conceived to be very distant, when they are considered coolly, have not that influence upon men which in reason they ought to have. ☞ Imagination, like the eye, diminisheth its objects in proportion to their distance. The passions of hope and fear must be raised, in order to give such objects their due magnitude in the imagination, and their due influence upon our conduct.

The dread of disgrace and of the civil magistrate, and the apprehension of future punishment, prevent many crimes, which bad men, without these restraints, would commit, and contribute greatly to the peace and good order of society.

[There is no bad action which some passion may not prevent; nor is there any external good action, of which some passion may not be the main spring; and, it is very probable, that even *the passions of men,* upon the whole, *do more good to society than hurt.*]

The ill that is done draws our attention more, and is imputed solely to human passions. The good may have better motives, and charity leads us to think that it has; but, as we see not the heart, it is impossible to determine what share men's passions may have in its production.

IX. [The *last* observation is, that if we distinguish, in the effects of our passions, those which are altogether *involuntary*, and without the sphere of our power, from the effects which *may be prevented by an exertion,* perhaps a great exertion, of self-government; we shall find the *first to be good* and highly useful, and *the last only to be bad.*]

Not to speak of the effects of moderate passions upon the health of the body, to which some agitation of this kind seems to be no less useful than storms and tempests to the salubrity of the air; every passion naturally draws our attention to its object, and interests us in it.

The mind of man is naturally desultory, and when it has no interesting object in view, roves from one to another, without fixing its attention upon any one. A transient and careless glance is all that we bestow upon objects in which we take no concern. It requires a strong degree of curiosity, or some more important passion, to give us that interest in an object which is necessary to our giving attention to it. And, without attention, we can form no true and stable judgment of any object.

Take away the passions, and it is not easy to say how great *a part of mankind would resemble* those *frivolous mortals,* who never had a thought that engaged them in good earnest.

It is not mere judgment or intellectual ability that enables a man to excel in any art or science. He must have a love and admiration of it bordering upon enthusiasm, or a passionate desire of the fame, or of some other advantage to be got by that excellence. Without this, he would not undergo the labour and fatigue of his faculties which it requires. So that, I think, we may with justice allow no small merit to the passions, even in the discoveries and improvements of the arts and sciences.

If the passions for fame and distinction were extinguished, it would be difficult to find men ready to undertake the cares and toils of government; and few perhaps would make the exertions necessary to raise themselves above the ignoble vulgar.

The involuntary signs of the passions and dispositions of the mind, in the voice, features, and action, are a part of the human constitution which deserves admiration. The signification of those signs is known to all men by nature, and previous to all experience.

☞ They are so many openings into the souls of our fellow men, by which their sentiments become visible to the eye. They are *a natural language* common to mankind, without which it would have been impossible to have invented any *artificial language.*

X.* [*It is from* the natural signs of *the passions* and dispositions of the mind, that *the human form* derives its beauty; that *painting, poetry,* and *music,* derive their expression; that *eloquence* derives its greatest force, and *conversation* its greatest charm.]

The passions, when kept within their proper bounds, give life and vigour to the whole man. Without them man would be a slug. We see what polish and animation the passion of love, when honourable and not unsuccessful, gives to both sexes.

The passion for military glory raises the brave commander in the day of battle, far above himself, making his countenance to shine, and his eyes to sparkle. The glory of Old England warms the heart even of the British tar, and makes him despise every danger.

As to the bad effects of passion, it must be acknowledged that it often gives a strong impulse to what is bad, and what a man condemns himself for, as soon as it is done. But he must be conscious that the impulse, though strong, was not irresistible, otherwise he could not condemn himself.

We allow that a sudden and violent passion, into which a man is surprised, alleviates a bad action; but if it was irresistible, it would not only alleviate, but totally exculpate, which it never does, either in the judgment of the man himself, or of others.

To sum up all, passion furnishes a very strong instance of the truth of the common maxim, that the corruption of the best things is worst.

CHAPTER VII.

OF DISPOSITION.

I. [By *disposition* I mean *a state of mind which,* while it lasts, *gives a tendency,* or proneness, *to be moved by certain animal principles,* rather than by others; while, at another time, another state of mind, in the same person, may give the ascendant to other animal principles.]

It was before observed, that it is a property of our appetites to be periodical, ceasing for a time, when sated by their objects, and returning regularly after certain periods.

Even those principles which are not periodical, have their ebbs and flows occasionally, according to the present disposition of the mind.

Among some of the principles of action there is a natural affinity, so that one of the tribe naturally disposes to those which are allied to it.

Such an affinity has been observed by many good authors to be among all the benevolent affections. The exercise of one benevolent affection gives a proneness to the exercise of others.

There is a certain placid and agreeable tone of mind which is common to them all, which seems to be the bond of that connexion and affinity they have with one another.

The malevolent affections have also an affinity, and mutually dispose to each other, by means, perhaps, of that disagreeable feeling common to them all, which makes the mind sore and uneasy.

II. [As far as we can trace the *causes of the different dispositions of the mind*, they seem to be in some cases owing (1) to those associating powers of the principles of action, which have a natural affinity, and are prone to keep company with one another; sometimes (2) to accidents of good or bad fortune, and sometimes, no doubt, (3) the state of the body may have influence upon the disposition of the mind.]

At one time the state of the mind, like a serene unclouded sky, shows every thing in the most agreeable light. Then a man is prone to benevolence, compassion, and every kind affection; unsuspicious, not easily provoked.

The poets have observed that men have their *mollia tempora fandi*, when they are averse from saying or doing a harsh thing; and artful men watch these occasions, and know how to improve them to promote their ends.

III. *The excellent consequences of good humour.*—This disposition, I think, we commonly call *good humour*, of which, in the fair sex, Mr. Pope says,

> Good humour only teaches charms to last,
> Still makes new conquests, and maintains the past.

[(1) There is no disposition more comfortable to the person himself, or more agreeable to others, than good humour. (2) *It is to the mind, what good health is to the body*, putting a man in the capacity of enjoying every thing that is agreeable in life, and of using every faculty without clog or impediment. (3) It disposes to contentment with our lot, (4) to benevolence to all men, (5) to sympathy with the distressed. (6) It presents every object in the most favourable light, and (7) disposes us to avoid giving or taking offence.]

[This happy disposition seems to be *the natural fruit of a good conscience*, and a firm belief that the world is under a wise and benevolent administration; and, when it springs from this root, it is an habitual sentiment of piety.

Good humour is likewise apt to be *produced by happy success*, or unexpected good fortune. Joy and hope are favourable to it; vexation and disappointment are unfavourable.]

The only danger of this disposition seems to be, that if we are not upon our guard, it may degenerate into levity, and indispose us to a proper degree of caution, and of attention to the future consequences of our actions.

IV. [There is *a disposition opposite to good humour* which we call *bad humour*, of which the tendency is directly contrary, and therefore its influence is as malignant as that of the other is salutary.]

Bad humour alone is sufficient to make a man unhappy; it tinges every object with its own dismal colour; and, like a part that is galled, is hurt by every thing that touches it. It takes offence where none was meant, and disposes to discontent, jealousy, envy, and, in general, to malevolence.

V. *Elation, magnanimity, a sense of honour and pride.*—Another couple of opposite dispositions are *elation* of mind, on the one hand, and *depression* on the other.

These contrary dispositions are both of *an ambiguous nature;* their influence may be good or bad, according as they are grounded on true or false opinion, and according as they are regulated.

That elation of mind which arises from a just sense of the dignity of our nature, and of the powers and faculties with which God hath endowed us, is *true magnanimity*, and disposes a man to the noblest virtues, and the most heroic actions and enterprises.

There is also an elation of mind which arises from a consciousness of our worth and integrity, such as Job felt, when he said, " Till I die, I will not remove my integrity from me. My righteousness I hold fast, and will not let it go; my heart shall not reproach me while I live." This may be called the pride of virtue; but it is a noble pride. It makes a man disdain to do what is base or mean. This is the true *sense of honour*.

But there is an elation of mind arising from a vain opinion of our having talents, or worth, which we have not; or from putting an undue value upon any of our endowments of mind, body, or fortune. This is *pride*, the parent of many odious vices; such as arrogance, undue contempt of others, self-partiality, and vicious self-love.

VI. *Depression, humility, meanness.*—The opposite disposition to elation of mind, is *depression*, which also has good or bad effects, according as it is grounded upon true or false opinion.

[A just sense of the weakness and imperfections of human nature, and of our own personal faults and defects, is true *humility*. It is *not to think of ourselves above what we ought to think:*] a most salutary and amiable disposition; of great price in the sight of God and man. Nor is it inconsistent with real magnanimity and greatness of soul. They may dwell together with great advantage and ornament to both, and be faithful monitors against the extremes to which each has the greatest tendency.]

But there is a depression of mind which is the opposite to magnanimity, which debilitates the springs of action, and freezes every sentiment that should lead to any noble exertion or enterprise.

Suppose a man to have no belief of a good administration of the world, no conception of the dignity of virtue, no hope of happiness in another state. Suppose him, at the same time, in a state of extreme poverty and dependence, and that he has no higher aim than to supply his bodily wants, or to minister to the pleasure, or flatter the pride, of some being as worthless as himself. Is not the soul of such a man depressed as much as his body or his fortune? And, if fortune should smile upon him while he retains the same sentiments, he is only the slave of fortune. His mind is depressed to the state of a brute, and his human faculties serve only to make him feel that depression.

Depression of mind may be owing to melancholy, a distemper of mind which proceeds from the state of the body, which throws a dismal gloom upon every object of thought, cuts all the sinews of action, and often gives rise to strange and absurd opinions in religion, or in other interesting matters. Yet, where there is real worth at bottom, some rays of it will break forth even in this depressed state of mind.

☞ A remarkable instance of this was exhibited in Mr. Simon Brown, a dissenting clergyman in England, who, by melancholy, was led into the belief that his rational soul had gradually decayed within him, and at last was totally extinct. From this belief he gave up his ministerial function, and would not even join with others in any act of worship, conceiving it to be a profanation to worship God without a soul.

In this dismal state of mind, he wrote an excellent defence of the Christian religion, against Tindal's " Christianity as old as the Creation." To the book he prefixed an epistle dedicatory to Queen Caroline, wherein he mentions, " That he was once a man, but, by the immediate hand of God, for his sins, his very thinking substance has, for more than seven years, been continually wasting away, till it is wholly perished out of him, if it be not utterly come to nothing." And, having heard of her Majesty's eminent piety, he begs the aid of her prayers.

The book was published after his death without the dedication, which, however, having been preserved in manuscript, was afterwards printed in the " Adventurer," No. 88.

Thus this good man, when he believed that he had no soul,

showed a most generous and disinterested concern for those who had souls.

As depression of mind may produce strange opinions, especially in the case of melancholy, so our opinions may have a very considerable influence, either to elevate or to depress the mind, even where there is no melancholy.

Suppose, on the one hand, a man who believes that he is destined to an eternal existence; that he who made, and who governs the world, maketh account of him, and hath furnished him with the means of attaining a high degree of perfection and glory. With this man compare, on the other hand, the man who believes nothing at all, or who believes that his existence is only the play of atoms, and that, after he hath been tossed about by blind fortune for a few years, he shall again return to nothing. Can it be doubted, that the former opinion leads to elevation and greatness of mind, the latter to *meanness* and depression?

CHAPTER VIII.

OF OPINION.

I. *Influence of opinion upon our animal principles.*—WHEN we come to explain the rational principles of action, it will appear that opinion is an essential ingredient in them. Here we are only to consider its *influence upon the animal principles.* Some of those I have ranked in that class cannot, I think, exist in the human mind without it.

Gratitude supposes the opinion of a favour done or intended; resentment the opinion of an injury; esteem the opinion of merit; the passion of love supposes the opinion of uncommon merit and perfection in its object.

Although natural affection to parents, children, and near relations, is not grounded on the opinion of their merit, it is much increased by that consideration. So is every benevolent affection. On the contrary, real malevolence can hardly exist without the opinion of demerit in the object.

There is no natural desire or aversion, which may not be restrained by opinion. Thus, if a man were athirst, and had a strong desire to drink, the opinion that there was poison in the cup would make him forbear.

It is evident that hope and fear, which every natural desire or affection may create, depend upon the opinion of future good or ill.

[Thus it appears that our passions, our dispositions, and *our opinions, have great influence upon our animal principles*, to strengthen or weaken, to excite or restrain them; and, by that means, have great influence upon human actions and characters.]

II. [That brute animals have both passions and dispositions similar, in many respects, to those of men, cannot be doubted. *Whether they have opinions,* is not so clear. *I think they have not,* in the proper sense of the word.] But, waving all dispute upon this point, it will be granted that opinion in men has a much wider field than in brutes. No man will say, that they have systems of theology, morals, jurisprudence or politics; or that they can reason from the laws of nature, in mechanics, medicine, or agriculture.

They feel the evils or enjoyments that are present; probably they imagine those which experience has associated with what they feel. But they can take no large prospect either of the past or of the future, nor see through a train of consequences.

☞ A dog may be deterred from eating what is before him, by the fear of immediate punishment, which he has felt on like occasions; but he is never deterred by the consideration of health, or of any distant good.

☞ I have been credibly informed that a monkey having once been intoxicated with strong drink, in consequence of which it burnt its foot in the fire, and had a severe fit of sickness, could never after be induced to drink any thing but pure water. I believe this is the utmost pitch which the faculties of brutes can reach.

III. [From the *influence of opinion* upon the conduct of mankind, we may learn that it is *one of the chief instruments* to be used *in the* discipline and *government of men.*]

All men, in the early part of life, must be under the discipline and government of parents and tutors. Men who live in society must be under the government of laws and magistrates, through life. The government of men is undoubtedly one of the noblest exertions of human power. And it is of great importance that those who have any share, either in domestic or civil government, should know the nature of man, and how he is to be trained and governed.

Of all instruments of government, opinion is the sweetest, and the most agreeable to the nature of man. Obedience that flows from opinion, is real freedom, which every man desires. That which is extorted by fear of punishment, is slavery; a yoke which is always galling, and which every man will shake off when it is in his power.

The opinions of the bulk of mankind have always been, and will always be, what they are taught by those whom they esteem to be wise and good; and therefore, in a considerable degree, are in the power of those who govern them.

Man, uncorrupted by bad habits and bad opinions, is of all animals the most tractable; corrupted by these, he is of all animals the most untractable.

IV. *Analogy between the discipline of body and mind.*—I apprehend, therefore, that, if ever civil government shall be brought to perfection, it must be the principal care of the state to make good citizens by proper education, and proper instruction and discipline.

☞ The most useful part of *medicine* is that which strengthens the constitution, and prevents diseases by good regimen; the rest is somewhat like propping a ruinous fabric at great expense, and to little purpose. The art of government is the *medicine of the mind*, and the most useful part of it is that which prevents crimes and bad habits, and trains men to virtue and good habits, by proper education and discipline.

The end of government is to make the society happy, which can only be done by making it good and virtuous.

That men in general will be good or bad members of society, according to the education and discipline by which they have been trained, experience may convince us.

The present age has made great advances in the art of training men to military duty. It will not be said that those who enter into that service are more tractable than their fellow-subjects of other professions. And I know not why it should be thought impossible to train men to equal perfection in the other duties of good citizens.

What an immense difference is there, for the purpose of war, between an army properly trained, and a militia hastily drawn out of the multitude? What should hinder us from thinking that, for every purpose of civil government, there may be a like difference between a civil society properly trained to virtue, good habits and right sentiments, and those civil societies which we now behold?—But I fear I shall be thought to digress from my subject into Utopian speculation.

V. *Man actuated by no sense of duty, considered.*—[To make an end of what I have to say upon the animal principles of action, we may take a complex view of their effect in life, by *supposing a being actuated by principles of no higher order, to have no* conscience or *sense of duty*, only let us allow him that superiority of understanding, and that power of self-government which man actually has. Let us speculate a little upon this imaginary being, and consider what conduct and tenor of action might be expected from him.]

It is evident he would be a very different animal from a brute, and perhaps not very different, in appearance, from what a great part of mankind is.

He would be capable of considering the distant consequences of his actions, and of restraining or indulging his appetites, desires, and affections, from the consideration of distant good or evil.

He would be capable of choosing some main end of his life,

and planning such a rule of conduct as appeared most subservient to it. Of this, we have reason to think no brute is capable.

We can, perhaps, conceive such a balance of the animal principles of action, as, with very little self-government, might make a man to be a good member of society, a good companion, and to have many amiable qualities.

The balance of our animal principles, I think, constitutes what we call a man's *natural temper;* which may be good or bad with regard to his virtue.

A man in whom the benevolent affections, the desire of esteem and good humour, are naturally prevalent, who is of a calm and dispassionate nature, who has the good fortune to live with good men, and associate with good companions, may behave properly with little effort.

His natural temper leads him, in most cases, to do what virtue requires. And if he happens not to be exposed to those trying situations, in which virtue crosses the natural bent of his temper, he has no great temptation to act amiss.

But perhaps a happy natural temper, joined with such a happy situation, is more ideal than real, though no doubt some men make nearer approaches to it than others.

The temper and the situation of men is commonly such, that the animal principles alone, without self-government, would never produce any regular and consistent train of conduct.

One principle crosses another. Without self-government, that which is strongest at the time will prevail. And that which is weakest at one time may, from passion, from a change of disposition or of fortune, become strongest at another time.

Every natural appetite, desire, and affection, has its own present gratification only in view. [A man, therefore, who has no other leader than these, would be like a ship in the ocean without hands, which cannot be said to be destined to any port. *He would have no character at all*, but be benevolent or spiteful, pleasant or morose, honest or dishonest, as the present wind of passion or tide of humour moved him.]

VI. [*Every man who pursues an end*, be it good or bad, *must be active* when he is disposed to be indolent; he *must rein every passion* and appetite that would lead him out of his road.]

Mortification and self-denial are found not in the paths of virtue only; they are common to every road that leads to an end, be it ambition, or avarice, or even pleasure itself. Every man who maintains an uniform and consistent character, must sweat and toil, and often struggle with his present inclination.

Yet those who steadily pursue some end in life, though they must often restrain their strongest desires, and practise much self-denial, have, upon the whole, more enjoyment than those who have no end at all, but to gratify the present prevailing inclination.

☞ A dog that is made for the chase, cannot enjoy the happiness of a dog without that exercise. Keep him within doors, feed him with the most delicious fare, give him all the pleasures his nature is capable of, he soon becomes a dull, torpid, unhappy animal. No enjoyment can supply the want of that employment which nature has made his chief good. Let him hunt, and neither pain nor hunger, nor fatigue seem to be evils. Deprived of this exercise, he can relish nothing. Life itself becomes burdensome.

It is no disparagement to the human kind to say, that man, as well as the dog, is made for hunting, and cannot be happy but in some vigorous pursuit. He has indeed nobler game to pursue than the dog, but he must have some pursuit, otherwise life stagnates, all the faculties are benumbed, the spirits flag, and his existence becomes an unsurmountable burden.

Even the mere foxhunter, who has no higher pursuit than his dogs, has more enjoyment than he who has no pursuit at all. *He has an end in view*, and this invigorates his spirits, makes him despise pleasure, and bear cold, hunger, and fatigue, as if they were no evils.

> " Manet sub Jove frigido
> Venator, teneræ conjugis immemor;
> Seu visa est catulis cerva fidelibus
> Seu rupit teretes Marsus aper plagas."

> " The hunter, chill'd by midnight Jove
> Forgets his tender, wedded love,
> Whether his faithful hounds pursue,
> And hold the bounding hind in view:
> Or Marsian boar, fierce-foaming, foils
> The chace, and breaks the spreading toils."

PART III.

OF THE RATIONAL PRINCIPLES OF ACTION.

CHAPTER I.

THERE ARE RATIONAL PRINCIPLES OF ACTION IN MAN.

I. MECHANICAL principles* of action produce their effect without any will or intention on our part. We may, by a voluntary effort, hinder the effect; but if it be not hindered by will and effort, it is produced without them.

Animal principles of action require intention and will in their operation, but not judgment. They are, by ancient moralists, very properly called *cæcæ cupidines*, blind desires.

Having treated of these two classes, [I proceed to the third,

* Vide Essay III. chap. iii., sect. 1, p. 151.

the *rational* principles of action in man; which have that name, because they can have no existence in beings not endowed with reason, and, in all their exertions, require, not only intention and will, but judgment or reason.]

That talent which we call *reason*, by which men that are adult and of a sound mind, are distinguished from brutes, idiots, and infants, has, in all ages, among the learned and unlearned, been conceived to have two offices, to regulate our belief, and to regulate our actions and conduct.

Whatever we believe, we think agreeable to reason, and, on that account, yield our assent to it. Whatever we disbelieve, we think contrary to reason, and, on that account, dissent from it. Reason, therefore, is allowed to be the principle by which our belief and opinions ought to be regulated.

But reason has been no less universally conceived to be a principle, by which our actions ought to be regulated.

To act reasonably, is a phrase no less common in all languages, than to judge reasonably. We immediately approve of a man's conduct, when it appears that he had good reason for what he did. And every action we disapprove, we think unreasonable, or contrary to reason.

A way of speaking so universal among men, common to the learned and the unlearned in all nations, and in all languages, must have a meaning. To suppose it to be words without meaning, is to treat, with undue contempt, the common sense of mankind.

Supposing this phrase to have a meaning, we may consider in what way reason may serve to regulate human conduct, so that some actions of men are to be denominated reasonable, and others unreasonable.

I take it for granted, that there can be no exercise of reason without judgment, nor, on the other hand, any judgment of things abstract and general, without some degree of reason.

If, therefore, there be any principles of action in the human constitution, which, in their nature, necessarily imply such judgment, they are the principles which we may call *rational*, to distinguish them from *animal* principles, which imply desire and will, but not judgment; and from mechanical, which imply neither will nor intention.

II. *Hume's error as to one of the chief offices of reason.*—Every deliberate human action must be done either as the means, or as an end; as the means to some end, to which it is subservient, or as an end, for its own sake, and without regard to any thing beyond it.

That it is a part of the office of reason to determine, what are the proper means to any end which we desire, no man ever denied. But some philosophers, particularly Mr. Hume, *think that it is no part of the office of reason to determine the ends we ought to pursue,* or the preference due to one end above another. This, he thinks, is not the office of reason, but of taste or feeling.

If this be so, reason cannot, with any propriety, be called a principle of action. Its office can only be to minister to the principles of action, by discovering the means of their gratification. Accordingly, Mr. Hume maintains, that reason is no principle of action; but that it is, and ought to be, the servant of the passions.

I shall endeavour to show, that, among the various ends of human actions, there are some, of which, without reason, we could not even form a conception; and that, as soon as they are conceived, a regard to them is, by our constitution, not only a principle of action, but a leading and governing principle, to which all our animal principles are subordinate, and to which they ought to be subject.

These I shall call *rational* principles; because they can exist only in persons endowed with reason, and because, to act from these principles, is what has always been meant by acting according to reason.

The ends of human actions I have in view, are *two*, to wit, what is *good for us* upon the whole, and what appears to be *our duty*. They are very strictly connected, lead to the same course of conduct, and co-operate with each other; and, on that account, have commonly been comprehended under one name, that of *reason*. But as they may be disjoined, and are really distinct principles of action, I shall consider them separately.

CHAPTER II.

OF REGARD TO OUR GOOD ON THE WHOLE.

I. *Chief spring of our early actions.*—It will not be denied that man, when he comes to years of understanding, is led by his rational nature, to form the conception of what is good for him upon the whole.

How early in life this general notion of good enters into the mind, I cannot pretend to determine. It is one of the most general and abstract notions we form.

Whatever makes a man more happy, or more perfect, is good, and is an object of desire as soon as we are capable of forming the conception of it. The contrary is ill, and is an object of aversion.

In the first part of life we have many enjoyments of various kinds; but very similar to those of brute-animals.

They consist in the exercise of our senses and powers of

motion, the gratification of our appetites, and the exertions of our kind affections. These are chequered with many evils of pain, and fear, and disappointment, and sympathy with the suffering of others.

But the goods and evils of this period of life are of short duration, and soon forgot. The mind being regardless of the past, and unconcerned about the future, we have then no other measure of good but the present desire; no other measure of evil but the present aversion.

Every animal desire has some particular and present object, and looks not beyond that object to its consequences, or to the connexions it may have with other things.

The present object, which is most attractive, or excites the strongest desire, determines the choice, whatever be its consequences. The present evil that presses most is avoided, though it should be the road to a greater good to come, or the only way to escape a greater evil. [This is the way in which brutes act, and the way in which men must act, till they come to the use of reason.]

II. *The conception of what is good or ill for us* upon the whole, *the offspring of reason.*—As we grow up to understanding, we extend our view both forward and backward. We reflect upon what is past, and, by the *lamp of experience*, discern what will probably happen in time to come. We find that many things which we eagerly desired, were too dearly purchased, and that things grievous for the present, like nauseous medicines, may be salutary in the issue.

We learn to observe the connexions of things, and the consequences of our actions; and, taking an extended view of our existence, past, present, and future, we correct our first notions of good and ill, and form the conception of what is good or ill upon the whole; which must be estimated, not from the present feeling, or from the present animal desire or aversion, but from a due consideration of its consequences, certain or probable, during the whole of our existence.

That which, taken with all its discoverable connexions and consequences, brings more good than ill, I call *good upon the whole*.

That brute animals have any conception of this good, I see no reason to believe. And it is evident, that man cannot have the conception of it, till reason be so far advanced, that he can seriously reflect upon the past, and take a prospect of the future part of his existence.

[It appears therefore, that the very conception of what is good or ill for us upon the whole, is the offspring of reason, and can be only in beings endowed with reason. And if this conception give rise to any principle of action in man, which he had not before, that principle may very properly be called *a rational principle* of action.]

I pretend not in this to say any thing that is new, but what reason suggested to those who first turned their attention to the philosophy of morals. I beg leave to quote one passage from Cicero, in his first book of "Offices;" wherein, with his usual elegance, he expresses the substance of what I have said. And there is good reason to think that Cicero borrowed it from Panætius, a Greek philosopher, whose books of Offices are lost.

"Sed inter hominem et belluam hoc maxime interest, quod hæc tantum quantum sensu movetur, ad id solum quod adest, quodque præsens est se accommodat, paululum admodum sentiens præteritum aut futurum: homo autem quoniam rationis est particeps, per quam consequentia cernit, causas rerum videt, earumque prægressus et quasi antecessiones non ignorat: similitudines comparat, et rebus præsentibus adjungit atque annectit futuras; facile totius vitæ cursum videt, ad eamque degendam preparat res necessarias."—Lib. I. sect. iv.

"But between man and the lower animals, there is in other respects the greatest difference. The latter, guided by the impulse of their senses alone, are confined to what is present, or near, with a very slight knowledge of the past or the future. Man, however, who partakes of reason, distinguishes the causes and the consequences of events, observes the progress, compares similar circumstances, connects the past with the future, easily surveys the whole course of life, and makes the necessary provision for its well-being."—Book I. sect. iv.

III. [I observe, in the *next* place, that as soon as we have the conception of what is good or ill for us upon the whole, we are led, by *our constitution*, to seek the good and avoid the ill; and this becomes not only a principle of action, but *a leading* or governing *principle, to which all our animal principles ought to be subordinate.*]

I am very apt to think, with Dr. Price, that, in intelligent beings, the desire of what is good, and aversion to what is ill, is necessarily connected with the intelligent nature; and that it is a contradiction to suppose such a being to have the notion of good without the desire of it, or the notion of ill without aversion to it. Perhaps there may be other necessary connexions between understanding and the best principles of action, which our faculties are too weak to discern. That they are necessarily connected in him who is perfect in understanding, we have good reason to believe.

To prefer a greater good, though distant, to a less that is present; to choose a present evil, in order to avoid a greater evil, or to obtain a greater good, is, in the judgment of all men, wise and reasonable conduct; and, when a man acts the contrary part, all men will acknowledge, that he acts foolishly and unreasonably. Nor will it be denied, that, in innumerable cases in common life, our animal principles draw us one way, while a regard to what is good on the whole, draws us the contrary way. Thus the flesh lusteth against the spirit, and the spirit against the flesh, and these two are contrary. That in every conflict of this kind the rational principle ought to prevail, and the animal to be subordinate, is too evident to need, or to admit of proof.

Thus, I think, it appears, that [to pursue what is good upon the whole, and to avoid what is ill upon the whole, is *a rational principle of action*, grounded upon *our constitution* as reasonable creatures.]

It appears that it is not without just cause, that this principle of action has in all ages been called *reason*, in opposition to our animal principles, which in common language are called by the general name of the *passions*.

The first not only operates in a calm and cool manner, like reason, but implies real judgment in all its operations. The second, to wit, the passions, are blind desires, of some particular object, without any judgment or consideration, whether it be good for us upon the whole, or ill.

It appears also, that the fundamental maxim of prudence and of all good morals, That the passions ought, in all cases, to be under the dominion of reason, is not only self-evident, when rightly understood, but is expressed according to the common use and propriety of language.

The contrary maxim maintained by Mr. Hume, can only be defended by a gross and palpable abuse of words. For, in order to defend it, he must include under the *passions*, that very principle which has always, in all languages, been called *reason*, and never was, in any language, called a *passion*. And from the meaning of the word *reason* he must exclude the most important part of it, by which we are able to discern and to pursue what appears to be good upon the whole. And thus, including the most important part of reason under passion, and making the least important part of reason to be the whole, he defends his favourite *paradox, that reason is*, and ought to be, *the servant of the passions*.

IV. *Office of practical reason.*—[To judge of what is true or false in speculative points, is the office of speculative reason; and to judge of what is good or ill for us upon the whole, is the office of practical reason.] Of true and false there are no degrees; but of good and ill there are many degrees, and many kinds; and men are very apt to form erroneous opinions concerning them; misled by their passions, by the authority of the multitude, and by other causes.

Wise men, in all ages, have reckoned it a chief point of wisdom, to make a right estimate of the goods and evils of life. They have laboured to discover the errors of the multitude on this important point, and to warn others against them.

The ancient moralists, though divided into sects, all agreed in this, that *opinion* has a mighty influence upon what we commonly account the goods and ills of life, to alleviate or to aggravate them.

The Stoics carried this so far, as to conclude that they all depend on opinion. Πάντα Ὑπόληψις was a favourite maxim with them.

We see, indeed, that the same station or condition of life which makes one man happy, makes another miserable, and to a third is perfectly indifferent. We see men miserable through life, from vain fears, and anxious desires, grounded solely upon wrong opinions. We see men wear themselves out with toilsome days, and sleepless nights, in pursuit of some object which they never attain; or which, when attained, gives little satisfaction, perhaps real disgust.

The evils of life, which every man must feel, have a very different effect upon different men. What sinks one into despair and absolute misery, rouses the virtue and magnanimity of another, who bears it as the lot of humanity, and as the discipline of a wise and merciful Father in heaven. He rises superior to adversity, and is made wiser and better by it, and consequently happier.

It is therefore of the last importance, in the conduct of life, to have just opinions with respect to good and evil; and surely it is the province of reason to correct wrong opinions, and to lead us into those that are just and true.

It is true indeed, that men's passions and appetites too often draw them to act contrary to their cool judgment and opinion of what is best for them. " Video meliora proboque, deteriora sequor,"—(I perceive and approve of better things, I follow worse,) is the case in every wilful deviation from our true interest and our duty.

When this is the case, the man is self-condemned, he sees that he acted the part of a brute, when he ought to have acted the part of a man. He is convinced that reason ought to have restrained his passion, and not to have given the rein to it.

When he feels the bad effects of his conduct, he imputes them to himself, and would be stung with remorse for his folly, though he had no account to make to a superior Being. He has sinned against himself, and brought upon his own head the punishment which his folly deserved.

From this we may see, that this rational principle of a regard to our good upon the whole, gives us the conception of a *right* and a *wrong* in human conduct, at least of a *wise* and a *foolish*.

It produces a kind of self-approbation, when the passions and appetites are kept in their due subjection to it; and a kind of remorse and compunction, when it yields to them.

In these respects, this principle is so similar to the moral principle, or conscience, and so interwoven with it, that both are commonly comprehended under the name of *reason*. [This similarity led many of the ancient philosophers, and some among the moderns, to resolve conscience, or *a sense of duty*, entirely into a regard to what is good for us upon the whole.]

That they are distinct principles of action, though both lead to the same conduct in life, I shall have occasion to show, when I come to treat of *conscience*.

CHAPTER III.

THE TENDENCY OF THIS PRINCIPLE.

I. *Question of the ancient moralists, " What is the greatest good ?"*—It has been the opinion of the wisest men, in all ages, that this principle, of a regard to our good upon the whole, in a man duly enlightened, leads to the practice of every virtue.

This was acknowledged, even by Epicurus; and the best moralists among the ancients derived all the virtues from this principle. For, among them, the whole of morals was reduced to this question, *what is the greatest good?* Or what course of conduct is best for us upon the whole?

In order to resolve this question, they divided goods into three classes, the goods of the body; the goods of fortune, or external goods; and the goods of the mind; meaning, by the last, wisdom and virtue.

Comparing these different classes of goods, they showed, with convincing evidence, that the goods of the mind are, in many respects, superior to those of the body and of fortune, not only as they have more dignity, are more durable, and less exposed to the strokes of fortune, but chiefly as they are the only goods in our power, and which depend wholly on our conduct.

II. *Fallacy of the Epicurean doctrine.*—Epicurus himself maintained, that the wise man may be happy in the tranquillity of his mind, even when racked with pain, and struggling with adversity.

They observed very justly, that the goods of fortune, and even those of the body, depend much on opinion; and that, when our opinion of them is duly corrected by reason, we shall find them of small value in themselves.

[*How can he be happy who places his happiness in things which it is not in his power to attain,* or in things from which, when attained, a fit of sickness, or a stroke of fortune, may tear him asunder?]

The value we put upon things, and our uneasiness in the want of them, depend upon the strength of our desires; correct the desire, and the uneasiness ceases.

The fear of the evils of body and of fortune, is often a greater evil than the things we fear. As the wise man moderates his desires by temperance, so to real or imaginary dangers he opposes the shield of fortitude and magnanimity, which raises him above himself, and makes him happy and triumphant in those moments wherein others are most miserable.

III. *Doctrine of the Stoics not original.*—These oracles of reason led the Stoics so far as to maintain, that all desires and fears, with regard to things not in our power, ought to be totally eradicated; *that virtue is the only good;* that what we call the goods of the body and of fortune, are really things indifferent, which may, according to circumstances, prove good or ill, and therefore have no intrinsic goodness in themselves; that our sole business ought to be, to act our part well, and to do what is right, without the least concern about things not in our power, which we ought, with perfect acquiescence, to leave to the care of Him who governs the world.

[This noble and elevated conception of human wisdom and duty was taught by Socrates, free from the extravagances which the Stoics afterwards joined with it.] We see it in the Alcibiades of Plato; from which Juvenal hath taken it in his tenth satire, and adorned it with the graces of poetry.

> Omnibus in terris quæ sunt a gadibus usque
> Auroram et Gangen, pauci dignoscere possunt
> Vera bona, atque illis multum diversa, remotâ
> Erroris nebulâ. Quid enim ratione timemus?
> Aut cupimus? Quid tam dextrâ pede concupis ut te
> *Conatus non* pœniteat, votique peracti?
> Nil ergo optabunt homines? Si consilium vis,
> Permittes ipsis expendere numinibus, quid
> Conveniat nobis, rebusque sit utile nostris.
> Nam pro jucundis aptissima quæque dabunt Dii.
> Charior est illis homo quam sibi. Nos animorum
> Impulsu, et cæca magnaque cupidine ducti,
> Conjugium petimus, partumque uxoris; at illis
> *Notum qui pueri,* qualisque futura sit uxor.
> Fortem posce animum, et mortis terrore carentem,
> Qui spatium vitæ extremum inter munera ponat
> Naturæ; qui ferre queat quoscunque labores,
> Nesciat irasci, cupiat nihil, et potiores
> Herculis ærumnas credat, sævosque labores
> Et venere, et cœnis, et plumis, Sardanapali.
> Monstro quid ipse tibi possis dare. Semita certe
> Tranquillæ per virtutem patet unica vitæ.
> Nullum numen abest si sit prudentia; sed te
> Nos facimus fortuna Deam, cœloque locamus.

"In all lands that extend from Gades to the east and the Ganges, few can distinguish true good things, and those greatly different from them, the cloud of error being removed: for what, with reason, do we fear or desire? What do you contrive so prosperously, that you may not repent of your endeavours and of your accomplished wish? Shall men, therefore, wish for nothing? If you wish for advice, permit the gods themselves to consider what may suit us and be useful to our affairs. For instead of what are pleasant, the gods will give things that are fittest. Man is dearer to them than to himself. Led by the impulse of our minds, and by a blind and great desire, we ask marriage and fruitfulness in a wife; but the gods alone know what sort those children and that wife may prove to be. Ask for a mind firm and free from the fear of death, which counts the last stage of life amongst the gifts of nature,—which can endure any troubles whatsoever,—is unconscious of anger,—covets nothing,—and which thinks the sufferings of Hercules and his cruel labours preferable to the lasciviousness, luxury, and plumes of Sardanapalus. I point out what you yourself may give to yourself,—undoubtedly the only path to a tranquil life lies open through virtue. You would have no divinity, O Fortune, if we had prudence; but we make you a goddess, and place you in heaven."

Even Horace, in his serious moments, falls into this system.

> Nil admirari, prope res est una Numici,
> Solaque quæ possit facere et servare beatum.
> "Not to admire, is of all means the best,
> The only means, to make, and keep us blest."

We cannot but admire the Stoical system of morals, even when we think that, in some points, it went beyond the pitch of human nature. The virtue, the temperance, the fortitude, and magnanimity of some who sincerely embraced it, amidst all the flattery of sovereign power and the luxury of a court, will be everlasting monuments to the honour of that system, and to the honour of human nature.

That a due regard to what is best for us upon the whole, in an enlightened mind, leads to the practice of every virtue, may be argued from considering what we think best for those for whom we have the strongest affection, and whose good we tender as our own. In judging for ourselves, our passions and appetites are apt to bias our judgment; but when we judge for others, this bias is removed, and we judge impartially.

What is it then that a wise man would wish as the greatest good to a brother, a son, or a friend?

Is it that he may spend his life in a constant round of the pleasures of sense, and fare sumptuously every day?

No, surely: we wish him to be a man of real virtue and worth. We may wish for him an honourable station in life; but only with this condition, that he acquit himself honourably in it, and acquire just reputation, by being useful to his country and to mankind. We would a thousand times rather wish him honourably to undergo the labours of Hercules, than to dissolve in pleasure with Sardanapalus.

Such would be the wish of every man of understanding for

the friend whom he loves as his own soul. Such things, therefore, he judges to be best for him upon the whole; and if he judges otherwise for himself, it is only because his judgment is perverted by animal passions and desires.

IV. *Recapitulation of what has been advanced relative to the rational principles of action.*—The sum of what has been said in these three chapters amounts to this:

[(1) *There is a principle of action* in men that are adult and of a sound mind, which, in all ages, has been called *reason,* and set in opposition to the animal principles which we call the *passions.*] [(2) The *ultimate object* of this principle is what we judge to be good upon the whole.] This is not the object of any of our animal principles, they being all directed to particular objects, without any comparison with others, or any consideration of their being good or ill upon the whole.

[(3) *What is good* upon the whole *cannot even be conceived without* the exercise of *reason,* and therefore cannot be an object to beings that have not some degree of reason.]

[(4) As soon as we have the conception of this object, we are led, *by our constitution,* to desire and pursue it.] It justly claims a preference to all objects of pursuit that can come in competition with it. In preferring it to any gratification that opposes it, or in submitting to any pain or mortification which it requires, we act according to reason; and every such action is accompanied with self-approbation and the approbation of mankind. The contrary actions are accompanied with shame and self-condemnation in the agent, and with contempt in the spectator, as foolish and unreasonable.

[(5) The *right application* of this principle to our conduct requires an extensive prospect of human life, and a correct judgment and estimate of its goods and evils, with respect to their intrinsic worth and dignity, their constancy and duration, and their attainableness.] He must be a wise man, indeed, if any such man there be, who can perceive, in every instance, or even in every important instance, what is best for him upon the whole, if he have no other rule to direct his conduct.

However, [(6) according to the best judgment which wise men have been able to form, *this principle leads to the practice of every virtue.*] It leads directly to the virtues of prudence, temperance, and fortitude. And, when we consider ourselves as social creatures, whose happiness or misery is very much connected with that of our fellow-men; when we consider, that there are many benevolent affections planted in our constitution, whose exertions make a capital part of our good and enjoyment; from these considerations, this principle leads us also, though more indirectly, to the practice of justice, humanity, and all the social virtues.

It is true, that a regard to our own good cannot, of itself, produce any benevolent affection. But, if such affections be a part of our constitution, and if the exercise of them make a capital part of our happiness, a regard to our own good ought to lead us to cultivate and exercise them, as every benevolent affection makes the good of others to be our own.

CHAPTER IV.

DEFECTS OF THIS PRINCIPLE.

I. *The rational principle of action not the only regulator of human conduct.*—HAVING explained the nature of this principle of action, and shown in general the tenor of conduct to which it leads, I shall conclude what relates to it, by pointing out some of its defects, if it be supposed, as it has been by some philosophers, to be the *only* regulating principle of human conduct.

[Upon that supposition, it would (1) neither be a sufficiently plain rule of conduct, (2) nor would it raise the human character to that degree of perfection of which it is capable, (3) nor would it yield so much real happiness as when it is joined with another rational principle of action, to wit, a disinterested regard to duty.]

First, I apprehend the greater part of mankind can never attain such extensive views of human life, and so correct a judgment of good and ill, as the right application of this principle requires.

The authority of the poet before quoted is of weight in this point. "Pauci dignoscere possunt vera bona, remota erroris nebula."* The ignorance of the bulk of mankind concurs with the strength of their passions to lead them into error in this most important point.

Every man, in his calm moments, wishes to know what is best for him on the whole, and to do it. But the difficulty of discovering it clearly, amid such variety of opinions, and the importunity of present desires, tempt men to give over the search, and to yield to the present inclination.

Though philosophers and moralists have taken much laudable pains to correct the errors of mankind in this great point, their instructions are known to few; they have little influence upon the greater part of those to whom they are known, and sometimes little even upon the philosopher himself.

[Speculative discoveries gradually spread from the knowing to the ignorant, and diffuse themselves over all, so that, with

* Page 214.

regard to them, the world, it may be hoped, will still be growing wiser. But *the errors of men, with regard to what is truly good or ill,* after being discovered and refuted in every age, *are still prevalent.*]

Men stand in need of a sharper monitor to their duty than a dubious view of distant good. There is reason to believe, that a present sense of duty has, in many cases, a stronger influence than the apprehension of distant good would have of itself. And it cannot be doubted, that a sense of guilt and demerit is a more pungent reprover than the bare apprehension of having mistaken our true interest.

☞ The brave soldier, in exposing himself to danger and death, is animated, not by a cold computation of the good and the ill, but by a noble and elevated sense of military duty.

A philosopher shows, by a copious and just induction, what is our real good and what our ill. But this kind of reasoning is not easily apprehended by the bulk of men. It has too little force upon their minds to resist the sophistry of the passions. They are apt to think, that if such rules be good in the general, they may admit of particular exceptions, and that what is good for the greater part, may, to some persons, on account of particular circumstances, be ill.

Thus, I apprehend, that, [if we had no plainer rule to direct our conduct in life than *a regard to our greatest good,* the greatest part of mankind would be fatally misled, even by *ignorance* of the road to it.]

II. [*Secondly,* Though *a steady pursuit of our own real good* may, in an enlightened mind, produce a kind of virtue which is entitled to some degree of approbation, yet it *can never produce the noblest kind of virtue,* which claims our highest love and esteem.]

We account him a wise man who is wise for himself; and if he prosecutes this end through difficulties and temptations that lie in his way, his character is far superior to that of the man who, having the same end in view, is continually starting out of the road to it, from an attachment to his appetites and passions, and doing every day what he knows he shall heartily repent.

Yet, after all, this wise man, whose thoughts and cares are all centred ultimately in himself, who indulges even his social affections only with a view to his own good, is not the man whom we cordially love and esteem.

☞ Like a cunning merchant, he carries his goods to the best market, and watches every opportunity of putting them off to the best account. He does well and wisely. But it is for himself. We owe him nothing upon this account. Even when he does good to others, he means only to serve himself; and therefore has no just claim to their gratitude or affection.

This surely, if it be virtue, is not the noblest kind, but *a low and mercenary species of it.* It can neither give a noble elevation to the mind that possesses it, nor attract the esteem and love of others.

Our cordial love and esteem is due only to the man whose soul is not contracted within itself, but embraces a more extensive object: who loves virtue, not for her dowry only, but for her own sake: whose benevolence is not selfish, but generous and disinterested: who, forgetful of himself, has the common good at heart, not as the means only, but as the end: who abhors what is base, though he were to be a gainer by it, and loves that which is right, although he should suffer by it.

Such a man we esteem the perfect man, compared with whom he who has no other aim but good to himself, is a mean and despicable character.

Disinterested goodness and rectitude is the glory of the Divine Nature, without which he might be an object of fear or hope, but not of true devotion. And it is the image of this divine attribute, in the human character, that is the glory of man.

To serve God, and be useful to mankind, without any concern about our own good and happiness, is, I believe, beyond the pitch of human nature. But to serve God, and be useful to men, merely to obtain good to ourselves, or to avoid ill, is servility, and not that liberal service which true devotion and real virtue require.

III. *Thirdly,* Though one might be apt to think that he has the best chance for happiness, who has no other end of his deliberate actions but his own good; yet a little consideration may satisfy us of the contrary.

[A concern for our own good is *not* a principle that, of itself, gives any enjoyment. On the contrary, it is apt to fill the mind with fear, and care, and anxiety. And these concomitants of this principle, often give *pain and uneasiness, that overbalance the good they have in view.*]

[☞ We may here compare, in point of present happiness, two imaginary characters; the first, of the man who has no other ultimate end of his deliberate actions but *his own good;* and who has no regard to virtue or duty, but as the means to that end. The second character is that of the man who is not indifferent with regard to his own good, but has another ultimate end perfectly consistent with it, to wit, *a disinterested love of virtue,* for its own sake, or a regard to duty as an end.]

Comparing these two characters in point of happiness, that we may give all possible advantage to the *selfish principle,* we shall suppose the man who is actuated solely by it, to be so far enlightened as to see it his interest to live soberly, righteously, and godly in the world, and that he follows the same course of conduct from the motive of his own good only, which the other does, in a great measure, from a sense of duty and rectitude.

We put the case so as that the difference between these two persons may be, not in what they do, but in the *motive* from which they do it : and, I think, there can be no doubt that he who acts from the noblest and most generous motive, will have most happiness in his conduct.

The one labours only for hire, without any love to the work. The other loves the work, and thinks it the noblest and most honourable he can be employed in. To the first, the mortification and self-denial which the course of virtue requires, is a grievous task, which he submits to only through necessity. To the other it is victory and triumph in the most honourable warfare.

It ought further to be considered, That although wise men have concluded that virtue is the only road to happiness, this conclusion is founded chiefly upon the natural respect men have for virtue, and the good or happiness that is intrinsic to it and arises from the love of it. If we suppose a man, as we now do, altogether destitute of this principle, who considered virtue only as the means to another end, there is no reason to think that he would ever take it to be the road to happiness, but would wander for ever, seeking this object where it is not to be found.

[IV. *Do the roads of duty and happiness coincide?—The road of duty is so plain*, that the man who seeks it, with an upright heart, cannot greatly err from it. But *the road to happiness*, if that be supposed the only end our nature leads us to pursue, would be found dark and intricate, *full of snares and dangers*, and therefore not to be trodden without fear, and care, and perplexity.]

The happy man, therefore, is not he whose happiness is his only care, but he who, with perfect resignation, *leaves the care of his happiness to Him who made him*, while he pursues with ardour the road of his duty.

This gives an elevation to his mind, which is real happiness. Instead of care, and fear, and anxiety, and disappointment, it brings joy and triumph. It gives a relish to every good we enjoy, and brings good out of evil.

And as no man can be indifferent about his happiness, the good man has the consolation to know that he consults his happiness most effectually, when, without any painful anxiety about future events, he does his duty.

Thus, I think, it appears, That although a regard to our good, upon the whole, be a rational principle in man, yet, if it be supposed the *only* regulating principle of our conduct, it would be a more uncertain rule, it would give far less perfection to the human character, and far less happiness, than when joined with another rational principle, to wit, a regard to duty.

CHAPTER V.

OF THE NOTION OF DUTY, RECTITUDE, MORAL OBLIGATION.

I. *A sense of interest or a sense of duty, or both, necessary to the social state.*—A BEING endowed with the animal principles of action only, may be capable of being trained to certain purposes by discipline, as we see many brute animals are, but would be altogether incapable of being governed by law.

The subject of law must have the conception of a general rule of conduct, which, without some degree of reason, he cannot have. He must likewise have a sufficient inducement to obey the law, even when his strongest animal desires draw him the contrary way.

This inducement may be *a sense of interest, or a sense of duty*, or both concurring.

These are the only principles I am able to conceive, which can reasonably induce a man to regulate all his actions according to a certain general rule or law. They may therefore be justly called the *rational* principles of action, since they can have no place but in a being endowed with reason, and since it is by them only, that man is capable either of political or of moral government.

☞ Without them, human life would be like a ship at sea without hands, left to be carried by winds and tides as they happen. It belongs to the rational part of our nature to intend a certain port, as the end of the voyage of life; to take the advantage of winds and tides when they are favourable, and to bear up against them when they are unfavourable.

A sense of interest may induce us to do this, when a suitable reward is set before us. But there is a nobler principle in the constitution of man, which, in many cases, gives a clearer and more certain rule of conduct, than a regard merely to interest would give, and a principle, without which man would not be a moral agent.

A man is prudent when he consults his real interest, but he cannot be virtuous, if he has no regard to duty.

II. *Of a sense of duty only.*—I proceed now to consider this *regard to duty* as *a rational principle of action in man*, and as that principle *alone* by which he is capable of virtue or vice.

I shall first offer some observations with regard to the general notion of duty, and its contrary, or of right and wrong in human conduct, and then consider how we come to judge and determine certain things in human conduct to be right, and others to be wrong.

With regard to the notion or conception of duty, I take it to be too simple to admit of a logical definition.

We can define it only by synonymous words or phrases, or by its properties and necessary concomitants, as when we say that [it is what we ought to do, what is fair and honest, what is approvable, what every man professes to be the rule of his conduct, what all men praise, and what is in itself laudable, though no man should praise it.]

I observe, in the *next* place, That *the notion of duty cannot be resolved into that of interest*, or what is most for our happiness.

Every man may be satisfied of this who attends to his own conceptions, and the language of all mankind shows it. When I say, this is my interest, I mean one thing; when I say, it is my duty, I mean another thing. And though the same course of action, when rightly understood, may be both my duty and my interest, the conceptions are very different. Both are reasonable motives to action, but quite distinct in their nature.

I presume it will be granted, that in every man of real worth, there is a principle of honour, a regard to what is honourable or dishonourable, very distinct from a regard to his interest. It is folly in a man to disregard his interest, but to do what is dishonourable is baseness. The first may move our pity, or, in some cases, our contempt, but the last provokes our indignation.

[As these two principles are different in their nature, and not resolvable into one, so *the principle of honour is* evidently *superior in dignity to that of interest*.]

No man would allow him to be a man of honour, who should plead his interest to justify what he acknowledged to be dishonourable: but to sacrifice interest to honour never costs a blush.

It likewise will be allowed by every man of honour, that this principle is not to be resolved into a regard to our reputation among men, otherwise the man of honour would not deserve to be trusted in the dark. He would have no aversion to lie, or cheat, or play the coward, when he had no dread of being discovered.

I take it for granted, therefore, that every man of real honour feels an abhorrence of certain actions, because they are in themselves base, and feels an obligation to certain other actions, because they are in themselves what honour requires, and this independently of any consideration of interest or reputation.

[*This is an immediate moral obligation.*—This principle of honour, which is acknowledged by all men who pretend to character, is only another name for what we call a regard to duty, to rectitude, to propriety of conduct. It is a moral obligation which obliges a man to do certain things because they are right, and not to do other things because they are wrong.]

Ask the man of honour, why he thinks himself obliged to pay a debt of honour? The very question shocks him. To suppose that he needs any other inducement to do it but the principle of honour, is to suppose that he has no honour, no worth, and deserves no esteem.

There is, therefore, a principle in man, which, when he acts according to it, gives him a consciousness of worth, and when he acts contrary to it, a sense of demerit.

[III. *The notion of this principle invariable, its extent not so.* —From the varieties of education, of fashion, of prejudices, and of habits, men may differ much in opinion with regard to the *extent* of this principle, and of what it commands and forbids; but *the notion of it*, as far as it is carried, *is the same in all*. It is that which gives a man real worth, and is the object of moral approbation.]

Men of rank call it *honour*, and too often confine it to certain virtues that are thought most essential to their rank. The vulgar call it *honesty, probity, virtue, conscience*. Philosophers have given it the names of *the moral sense, the moral faculty, rectitude*.

The universality of this principle in men that are grown up to years of understanding and reflection, is evident. The words that express it, the names of the virtues which it commands, and of the vices which it forbids, the *ought* and *ought not* which express its dictates, make an essential part of every language. The natural affections of respect to worthy characters, of resentment of injuries, of gratitude for favours, of indignation against the worthless, are parts of the human constitution which suppose a right and a wrong in conduct. Many transactions that are found necessary in the rudest societies go upon the same supposition. In all testimony, in all promises, and in all contracts, there is necessarily implied a moral obligation on one party, and a trust in the other, grounded upon this obligation.

IV. *Reality of moral distinctions.*—The variety of opinions among men in points of morality, is not greater, but, as I apprehend, much less than in speculative points; and this variety is as easily accounted for from the common causes of error, in the one case as in the other; so that it is not more evident, that there is a real distinction between true and false, in matters of speculation, than that there is a real distinction between right and wrong in human conduct.

Mr. Hume's authority, if there were any need of it, is of weight in this matter, because he was not wont to go rashly into vulgar opinions.

"Those," says he, "who have denied the reality of moral distinctions, may be ranked among the disingenuous disputants (who really do not believe the opinions they defend, but engage in the controversy, from affectation, from a spirit of opposition, or from a desire of showing wit and ingenuity superior to the rest of mankind); nor is it conceivable that any human creature could ever seriously believe that all characters and actions were alike entitled to the regard and affection of every one.

"Let a man's insensibility be ever so great, he must often be touched with the images of right and wrong; and let his prejudices be ever so obstinate, he must observe that others are susceptible of like impressions. The only way, therefore, of convincing an antagonist of this kind is to leave him to himself. For, finding that nobody keeps up the controversy with him, it is probable he will at last, of himself, from mere weariness, come over to the side of common sense and reason."

What we call *right* and *honourable* in human conduct, was, by the ancients, called *honestum*, τὸ καλὸν; of which Tully says, "Quod vere dicimus, etiamsi a nullo laudetur, natura esse laudabile." De Officiis, lib. i. sect. 3.

All the ancient sects, except the Epicureans, distinguished the *honestum* from the *utile*, as we distinguish what is a man's duty from what is his interest.

The word *officium* (καθῆκον) extended both to the *honestum* and the *utile:* so that every reasonable action, proceeding either from a sense of duty or a sense of interest, was called *officium*. It is defined by Cicero to be, "Id quod cur factum sit ratio probabilis reddi potest."—Such a one as a fair and reasonable account may be given for the doing of it. We commonly render it by the word *duty*, but it is more extensive; for the word *duty*, in the English language, I think, is commonly applied only to what the ancients called *honestum*. Cicero, and Pannætius before him, treating of offices, first point out those that are grounded upon the *honestum*, and next those that are grounded upon the *utile*.

V. *The most ancient philosophical system concerning the principles of action in the human mind*, and, I think, the most agreeable to Nature, is that which we find in some fragments of the ancient Pythagoreans, and which is adopted by Plato, and explained in some of his dialogues.

According to this system, there is a leading principle in the soul, which, like the supreme power in a commonwealth, has authority and right to govern. This leading principle they called *reason*. It is that which distinguishes men that are adult from brutes, idiots, and infants. The inferior principles, which are under the authority of the leading principle, are our passions and appetites, which we have in common with the brutes.

Cicero adopts this system, and expresses it well in few words. " Duplex enim est vis animorum atque naturæ. Una pars in appetitu posita est, quæ hominem huc et illuc rapit, quæ est ὁρμὴ græce, altera in ratione, quæ docet, et explanat quid faciendum fugiendumve sit. Ita sit ut ratio præsit appetitus obtemperet."—" For the impulse of our minds and nature is twofold; one part consists in appetite, which hurries man hither and thither, which is ὁρμὴ in Greek; the other in reason, which teaches and explains what is to be done, what to be avoided. Whence it is that reason should guide, appetite obey."

This division of our active principles can hardly indeed be accounted a discovery of philosophy, because it has been common to the unlearned in all ages of the world, and seems to be dictated by the common sense of mankind.

What I would now observe concerning this common division of our active powers, is, that the leading principle, which is called *reason*, comprehends both a regard to what is *right* and honourable, and a regard to our *happiness* upon the whole.

Although these be really two distinct principles of action, it is very natural to comprehend them under one name, because both are leading principles, both suppose the use of reason, and, when rightly understood, both lead to the same course of life. ☞ They are like two fountains whose streams unite and run in the same channel.

When a man, on one occasion, consults his real happiness in things not inconsistent with his duty, though in opposition to the solicitation of appetite or passion; and when, on another occasion, without any selfish consideration, he does what is right and honourable, because it is so; in both these cases, he acts reasonably; every man approves of his conduct, and calls it reasonable, or according to reason.

So that, when we speak of reason as a principle of action in man, it includes a regard both to the honestum and to the utile. Both are combined under one name; and accordingly the dictates of both, in the Latin tongue, were combined under the name officium, and in the Greek under καθῆκον.

VI. *Moral obligation a relation.*—[If we examine *the abstract notion of duty*, or *moral obligation*, it appears to be neither any real quality of the action considered by itself, nor of the agent considered without respect to the action, but *a certain relation* between the one and the other.]

When we say a man ought to do such a thing, the *ought*, which expresses the moral obligation, has a respect, on the one hand, to the person who ought, and, on the other, to the action which he ought to do. Those two correlates are essential to every moral obligation; take away either, and it has no existence. So that, if we seek the place of moral obligation among the categories, it belongs to the category of *relation*.

[There are many relations of things, of which we have the most distinct conception, without being able to define them logically. *Equality and proportion* are relations between quantities, which every man understands, but *no man can define*.]

Moral obligation is *a relation* of its own kind, which every man understands, but is perhaps too simple to admit of logical definition. Like all other relations, it may be changed or annihilated by a change in any of the two related things, I mean the agent or the action.

VII. Perhaps it may not be improper to point out briefly *the circumstances*, both in the action and in the agent, *which are necessary to constitute moral obligation*. The universal agreement of men in these, shows that they have one and the same notion of it.

With regard to the action, it must be a voluntary action, or prestation of the person obliged, and not of another. There can be no moral obligation upon a man to be six feet high. Nor can I be under a moral obligation that another person should do such a thing. His actions must be imputed to himself, and mine only to me, either for praise or blame.

I need hardly mention, that a person can be under a moral obligation only to things within the sphere of his natural power.

As to the party obliged, it is evident, there can be *no moral obligation upon an inanimate thing*. To speak of moral obligation upon a stone or a tree is ridiculous, because it contradicts every man's notion of moral obligation.

The person obliged must have understanding and will, and some degree of active power. He must not only have the natural faculty of understanding, but the means of knowing his obligation. An invincible ignorance of this destroys all moral obligation.

The opinion of the agent in doing the action gives it its moral denomination. If he does a materially good action, without any belief of its being good, but from some other principle, it is no good action in him. And if he does it with the belief of its being ill, it is ill in him.

Thus, if a man should give to his neighbour a potion which he really believes will poison him, but which, in the event, proves salutary, and does much good; in moral estimation, he is a poisoner, and not a benefactor.

These qualifications of the action and of the agent, in moral obligation, are self-evident; and the agreement of all men in them shows, that all men have the same notion and a distinct notion of moral obligation.

CHAPTER VI.

OF THE SENSE OF DUTY.

I. *The moral sense,—the moral faculty,—conscience.*—WE are next to consider, how we learn to judge and determine, that this is right, and that is wrong.

The abstract notion of moral good and ill would be of no use to direct our life, if we had not the power of applying it to particular actions, and determining what is morally good, and what is morally ill.

Some philosophers, with whom I agree, ascribe this to an original power or faculty in man, which they call the *moral sense*, the *moral faculty, conscience.* Others think, that our moral sentiments may be accounted for without supposing any original sense or faculty appropriated to that purpose, and go into very different systems to account for them.

I am not, at present, to take any notice of those systems, because the opinion first mentioned seems to me to be the truth, to wit, that, by an original power of the mind, when we come to years of understanding and reflection, we not only have the notions of right and wrong in conduct, but perceive certain things to be right, and others to be wrong.

The name of the *moral sense*, though more frequently given to conscience since Lord Shaftesbury and Dr. Hutcheson wrote, is not new. The " sensus recti et honesti," is a phrase not unfrequent among the ancients, neither is the *sense of duty* among us.

II. *This analogy excusable.*—[It has got this name of *sense*, no doubt, from some *analogy* which it is conceived to bear to the external senses. And if we have just notions of the office of the external senses, the analogy is very evident, and I see no reason to take offence, as some have done, at the name of the *moral sense.*]

The offence taken at this name seems to be owing to this, that philosophers have degraded the senses too much, and deprived them of the most important part of their office.

We are taught, that, by the senses, we have only certain ideas which we could not have otherwise. They are represented as powers by which we have sensations and ideas, not as powers by which we judge.

This notion of the senses I take to be very lame, and to contradict what nature and accurate reflection teach concerning them.

A man who has totally lost the sense of seeing, may retain very distinct notions of the various colours; but he cannot judge of colours, because he has lost the sense by which alone he could judge. By my eyes I not only have the ideas of a square and a circle, but I perceive this surface to be a square, that to be a circle.

By my ear, I not only have the idea of sounds, loud and soft, acute and grave, but I immediately perceive and judge this sound to be loud, that to be soft, this to be acute, that to be grave. Two or more synchronous sounds I perceive to be concordant, others to be discordant.

These are judgments of the senses. They have always been called and accounted such, by those whose minds are not tinctured by *philosophical theories.* They are the immediate testimony of nature by our senses; and we are so constituted by nature, that we must receive their testimony, for no other reason but because it is given by our senses.

In vain do sceptics endeavour to overturn this evidence by metaphysical reasoning. Though we should not be able to answer their arguments, we believe our senses still, and rest our most important concerns upon their testimony.

If this be a just notion of our external senses, as I conceive it is, our moral faculty may, I think, without impropriety, be called the *moral sense.*

III. *Further shown.*—In its dignity it is, without doubt, far superior to every other power of the mind; but [there is this analogy between it and the external senses, that, as by them we have not only the original conceptions of the various qualities of bodies, but the original judgments that this body has such a quality, that such another; so by our moral faculty, we have both the original *conceptions* of right and wrong in conduct, of merit and demerit, and the original *judgments* that this conduct is right, that is wrong; that this character has worth, that, demerit.]

The testimony of our moral faculty, like that of the external senses, is the testimony of nature, and we have the same reason to rely upon it.

The truths *immediately* testified by the external senses are the first principles from which we reason, with regard to the material world, and from which all our knowledge of it is deduced.

The truths *immediately* testified by our moral faculty, are the first principles of all moral reasoning, from which all our knowledge of our duty must be deduced.

IV. [By *moral reasoning*, I understand all reasoning that *is brought to prove that such conduct is right*, and deserving of moral approbation, *or that it is wrong*, or that it is *indifferent*, and, in itself, neither morally good nor ill.]

I think all we can properly call moral judgments are reducible to one or other of these, as all human actions, considered in a moral view, are either good, or bad, or indifferent.

I know the term *moral reasoning* is often used by good writers in a more extensive sense; but as the reasoning I now speak of is of a peculiar kind, distinct from all others, and therefore ought to have a distinct name, I take the liberty to limit the name of *moral reasoning* to this kind.

Let it be understood, therefore, that [in the reasoning I call *moral*, the conclusion always is, that something in the conduct of moral agents is *good* or *bad,* in a greater or a less degree, *or indifferent.*]

[All reasoning must be grounded on first principles. This holds in moral reasoning, as in all other kinds. There must, therefore, be in morals, as in all other sciences, *first* or self-evident *principles,* on which all moral reasoning is grounded, and on which it ultimately rests.] From such self-evident principles, conclusions may be drawn synthetically with regard to the moral conduct of life; and particular duties or virtues may be traced back to such principles, analytically. But, without such principles, we can no more establish any conclusion in morals, than we can build a castle in the air, without any foundation.

An example or two will serve to illustrate this.

[It is *a first principle in morals,* that we ought not to do to another what we should think wrong to be done to us in like circumstances.] If a man is not capable of perceiving this in his cool moments, when he reflects seriously, he is not a moral agent, nor is he capable of being convinced of it by reasoning.

From what topic can you reason with such a man? You may possibly convince him by reasoning, that it is his interest to observe this rule; but this is not to convince him that it is his duty. To reason about justice with a man who sees nothing to be just or unjust; or about benevolence with a man who sees nothing in benevolence preferable to malice, is like reasoning with a blind man about colour, or with a deaf man about sound.

☞ It is a question in morals that admits of reasoning, whether, by the law of nature, a man ought to have only one wife?

We reason upon this question, by balancing the advantages and disadvantages to the family, and to society in general, that are naturally consequent both upon monogamy and polygamy. And if it can be shown that the advantages are greatly upon the side of monogamy, we think the point is determined.

But if a man does not perceive that he ought to regard the good of society, and the good of his wife and children, the reasoning can have no effect upon him, because he denies the first principle upon which it is grounded.

Suppose again, that we reason for monogamy from the intention of nature, discovered by the proportion of males and of females that are born; a proportion which corresponds perfectly with monogamy, but by no means with polygamy. This argument can have no weight with a man who does not perceive that he ought to have a regard to the intention of nature.

Thus we shall find that all moral reasonings rest upon one or more first principles of morals, whose truth is immediately perceived without reasoning, by all men come to years of understanding.

V. *Universality of first principles.*—And [this indeed is common to every branch of human knowledge that deserves the name of science. There must be first principles proper to that science, by which the whole superstructure is supported.]

The first principles of all the sciences must be the immediate dictates of our natural faculties; nor is it possible that we should have any other evidence of their truth. And in different sciences, the faculties which dictate their first principles are very different.

☞ Thus, in astronomy and in optics, in which such wonderful discoveries have been made, that the unlearned can hardly believe them to be within the reach of human capacity, *the first principles are phenomena attested solely by* that little organ, *the human eye.* If we disbelieve its report, the whole of those two noble fabrics of science falls to pieces like the visions of the night.

The principles of music all depend upon the testimony of *the ear.* The principles of natural philosophy, upon the facts attested *by the senses.* The principles of *mathematics,* upon the *necessary relations of quantities* considered abstractly, such as, that equal quantities added to equal quantities make equal sums, and the like; which necessary relations are immediately perceived by the understanding.

The science of politics borrows its principles from what we know by experience of the character and conduct of man. We consider not what he ought to be, but what he is, and thence conclude what part he will act in different situations and circumstances. From such principles we reason concerning the causes and effects of different forms of government, laws, customs, and manners. If man were either a more perfect or a more imperfect, a better or a worse creature than he is, politics would be a different science from what it is.

VI. *The first principles of morals are the immediate dictates of the moral faculty.* They show us, not what man is, but what he ought to be. Whatever is immediately perceived to be just, honest, and honourable, in human conduct, carries moral obligation along with it, and the contrary carries demerit and blame; and, from those moral obligations that are immediately perceived, all other moral obligations must be deduced by reasoning.

He that will judge of the colour of an object, must consult his eyes, in a good light, when there is no medium or contiguous objects that may give it a false tinge. But in vain will he consult every other faculty in this matter.

In like manner, he that will judge of the first principles of morals, must consult his *conscience* or *moral faculty* when he is calm and dispassionate, unbiassed by interest, affection, or fashion.

As we rely upon the clear and distinct testimony of our eyes, concerning the colours and figures of the bodies about us, we have the same reason to rely with security upon the clear and unbiassed testimony of our conscience, with regard to what we ought and ought not to do. In many cases, moral worth and demerit are discerned no less clearly by the last of those natural faculties, than figure and colour by the first.

The faculties which nature hath given us, are the only engines we can use to find out the truth. We cannot indeed prove, that those faculties are not fallacious, unless God should give us new faculties to sit in judgment upon the old. But we are born under a necessity of trusting them.*

Every man in his senses believes his eyes, his ears, and his other senses. He believes his consciousness, with respect to his own thoughts and purposes; his memory, with regard to what is past; his understanding, with regard to abstract relations of things; and his taste, with regard to what is elegant and beautiful. And he has the same reason, and, indeed, is under the same necessity of believing the clear and unbiassed dictates of his conscience, with regard to what is honourable and what is base.

VII. *Recapitulation.*—[The *sum of what has been said* in this chapter is, (1) that, by an original power of the mind, which we call *conscience*, or the *moral faculty*, we have the conceptions of right and wrong in human conduct, of merit and demerit, of duty and moral obligation, and our other moral conceptions; and that, (2) by the same faculty, we perceive some things in human conduct to be right, and others to be wrong; (3) that the first principles of morals are the dictates of this faculty; and (4) that we have the same reason to rely upon those dictates, as upon the determinations of our senses, or of our other natural faculties.]

CHAPTER VII.

OF MORAL APPROBATION AND DISAPPROBATION.

I. *Of affections and feelings included in our moral judgments.*—Our moral judgments are not like those we form in speculative matters, dry and unaffecting, but, from their nature, are

* Vide Essay IV. chap. vi. sect. 1.

necessarily accompanied with affections and feelings; which we are now to consider.

It was before observed, that every human action, considered in a moral view, appears to us *good, or bad, or indifferent.* When we judge the action to be indifferent, neither good nor bad, though this be a moral judgment, it produces no affection nor feeling, any more than our judgments in speculative matters.

But we approve of good actions, and disapprove of bad; and this approbation and disapprobation, when we analyse it, appears to include, not only a moral judgment of the action, but some *affection,* favourable or unfavourable, towards the agent, and some *feeling* in ourselves.

Nothing is more evident than this, that moral worth, even in a stranger, with whom we have not the least connexion, never fails to produce some degree of *esteem* mixed with *good will.*

The esteem which we have for a man on account of his moral worth, is different from that which is grounded upon his intellectual accomplishments, his birth, fortune, and connexion with us.

☞ Moral worth, when it is not set off by eminent abilities, and external advantages, *is like a diamond in the mine,* which is rough and unpolished, and perhaps crusted over with some baser material that takes away its lustre.

But, when it is attended with these advantages, it is like a diamond cut, polished, and set. Then its lustre attracts every eye. Yet these things which add so much to its appearance, add but little to its real value.

II. [We must further observe, that *esteem and benevolent regard,* not only *accompany real worth* by the constitution of our nature, but are perceived to be really and properly due to it; and that, on the contrary, unworthy conduct really merits dislike and indignation.]

There is no judgment of the heart of man more clear or more irresistible than this,—that esteem and regard are really due to good conduct, and the contrary to base and unworthy conduct. Nor can we conceive a greater depravity in the heart of man, than it would be to see and acknowledge worth without feeling any respect to it; or to see and acknowledge the highest worthlessness without any degree of dislike and indignation.

The esteem that is due to worthy conduct is not lessened when a man is conscious of it in himself. Nor can he help having some esteem for himself, when he is conscious of those qualities for which he most highly esteems others.

Self-esteem, grounded upon external advantages, or the gifts of fortune, is pride. When it is grounded upon a vain conceit of inward worth which we do not possess, it is arrogance and self-deceit. [But when a man, without thinking of himself more highly than he ought to think, is conscious of that integrity of heart and uprightness of conduct, which he most highly esteems in others, and values himself duly upon this account; this perhaps may be called *the pride of virtue,* but it is not a vicious pride. It is a noble and magnanimous disposition, without which there can be no steady virtue.]

A man who has a character with himself which he values, will disdain to act in a manner unworthy of it. The language of his heart will be like that of Job, " My righteousness I hold fast, and will not let it go; my heart shall not reproach me while I live."

A good man owes much to his character with the world, and will be concerned to vindicate it from unjust imputations. But he owes much more to his character with himself. For if his heart condemns him not, he has confidence towards God; and he can more easily bear the lash of tongues than the reproach of his own mind.

The sense of honour, so much spoken of, and so often misapplied, is nothing else, when rightly understood, but the disdain which a man of worth feels to do a dishonourable action, though it should never be known nor suspected.

A good man will have a much greater abhorrence against doing a bad action, than even against having it unjustly imputed to him. The last may give a wound to his reputation, but the first gives a wound to his conscience, which is more difficult to heal, and more painful to endure.

III. *Moral disapprobation.*—[Let us, on the other hand, consider how we are affected by *disapprobation,* either of the conduct of others or of our own.]

Every thing we disapprove in the conduct of a man, lessens him in our esteem. There are indeed brilliant faults, which, having a mixture of good and ill in them, may have a very different aspect, according to the side on which we view them.

In such faults of our friends, and much more of ourselves, we are disposed to view them on the best side, and on the contrary side in those to whom we are ill affected.

This partiality, in taking things by the best or by the worst handle, is the chief cause of wrong judgment with regard to the character of others, and of self-deceit with regard to our own.

But when we take complex actions to pieces, and view every part by itself, ill conduct of every kind lessens our esteem of a man, as much as good conduct increases it. It is apt to turn love into indifference, indifference into contempt, and contempt into aversion and abhorrence.

When a man is conscious of immoral conduct in himself, it lessens his self-esteem. It depresses and humbles his spirit, and makes his countenance to fall. He could even punish himself for his misbehaviour, if that could wipe out the stain. There is a sense of dishonour and worthlessness arising from guilt, as well as a sense of honour and worth arising from worthy conduct. And this is the case, even if a man could conceal his guilt from all the world.

IV. We are next to consider the *agreeable or uneasy feelings*, in the breast of the spectator or judge, which naturally accompany moral approbation and disapprobation.

There is no affection that is not accompanied with some agreeable or uneasy emotion. It has often been observed, that all the benevolent affections give pleasure, and the contrary ones pain, in one degree or another.

☞ When we contemplate a noble character, though but in ancient history, or even in fiction; like a beautiful object, it gives a lively and pleasant emotion to the spirits. It warms the heart, and invigorates the whole frame. Like the beams of the sun, it enlivens the face of nature, and diffuses heat and light all around.

We feel a *sympathy* with every noble and worthy character that is represented to us. We rejoice in his prosperity, we are afflicted in his distress. We even catch some sparks of that celestial fire that animated his conduct, and feel the glow of his virtue and magnanimity.

[This *sympathy* is the necessary effect of our judgment of his conduct, and of the *approbation* and esteem *due to it;* for real sympathy is always the effect of some benevolent affection, such as esteem, love, pity, or humanity.]

When the person whom we approve is connected with us by acquaintance, friendship, or blood, the pleasure we derive from his conduct is greatly increased. We claim some property in his worth, and are apt to value ourselves on account of it. This shows a stronger degree of sympathy, which gathers strength from every social tie.

V. But the highest pleasure of all is, when we are *conscious of good conduct in ourselves*. This, in sacred scripture, is called the *testimony of a good conscience;* and it is represented, not only in the sacred writings, but in the writings of all moralists, of every age and sect, as the purest, the most noble and valuable of all human enjoyments.

Surely, were we to place the chief happiness of this life (a thing that has been so much sought after) in any one kind of enjoyment, that which arises from the consciousness of integrity, and a uniform endeavour to act the best part in our station, would most justly claim the preference to all other enjoyments the human mind is capable of, on account of its dignity, the intenseness of the happiness it affords, its stability and duration, its being in our power, and its being proof against all accidents of time and fortune.

☞ On the other hand, the view of a vicious character, like that of an ugly and deformed object, is disagreeable. It gives disgust and abhorrence.

If the unworthy person be nearly connected with us, we have a very painful sympathy indeed. We blush even for the smaller faults of those we are connected with, and feel ourselves, as it were, dishonoured by their ill conduct.

But, when there is a high degree of depravity in any person connected with us, we are deeply humbled and depressed by it. The sympathetic feeling has some resemblance to that of guilt, though it be free from all guilt. We are ashamed to see our acquaintance; we would, if possible, disclaim all connexion with the guilty person. We wish to tear him from our hearts, and to blot him out of our remembrance.

Time, however, alleviates those sympathetic sorrows which arise from bad behaviour in our friends and connexions, if we are conscious that we had no share in their guilt.

VI. *Social ties auxiliary to virtue, unfavourable to vice.*— [The wisdom of God, in the constitution of our nature, hath intended, that this sympathetic distress should interest us the more deeply in the good behaviour, as well as in the good fortune, of our friends; and that thereby friendship, relation, and every social tie, should be aiding to virtue and unfavourable to vice.]

How common is it, even in vicious parents, to be deeply afflicted when their children go into these courses in which perhaps they have gone before them, and, by their example, shown them the way.

If bad conduct in those in whom we are interested, be uneasy and painful, it is so much more when we are conscious of it in ourselves. This uneasy feeling has a name in all languages. We call it *remorse*.

It has been described in such frightful colours by writers sacred and profane, by writers of every age and of every persuasion, even by Epicureans, that I will not attempt the description of it.

VII. *Consequences of remorse.*—It is on account of the uneasiness of this feeling, that bad men take so much pains to get rid of it, and to hide, even from their own eyes, as much as possible, the pravity of their conduct. [Hence arise (1) all the arts of self-deceit, by which men varnish their crimes, or endeavour to wash out the stain of guilt. Hence (2) the various methods of expiation which superstition has invented, to solace the conscience of the criminal, and give some cooling to his parched breast. Hence also arise, very often, (3) the efforts of men of bad hearts to excel in some amiable quality, which may be a kind of counterpoise to their vices, both in the opinion of others and in their own.]

For no man can bear the thought of being absolutely destitute of all worth. The consciousness of this would make him detest himself, hate the light of the sun, and fly, if possible, out of existence.

VIII. *Operations of the faculty called moral sense.*—I have now endeavoured to delineate the natural operations of that principle of action in man, which we call the *moral sense,* the *moral faculty, conscience.* We know nothing of our natural faculties, but by their operations within us. Of their operations in our own minds, we are conscious, and we see the signs of their operations in the minds of others. [Of this faculty the operations appear to be, the judging ultimately of what is right, what is wrong, and what is indifferent, in the conduct of moral agents; the approbation of good conduct and disapprobation of bad in consequence of that judgment, and the agreeable emotions which attend obedience, and disagreeable which attend disobedience to its dictates.]

The Supreme Being, who has given us eyes to discern what may be useful and what hurtful to our natural life, hath also given us this light within to direct our moral conduct.

Moral conduct is the business of every man; and therefore the knowledge of it ought to be within the reach of all.

Epicurus reasoned acutely and justly to show, that a regard to our present happiness should induce us to the practice of temperance, justice, and humanity. But the bulk of mankind cannot follow long trains of reasoning. The loud voice of the passions drowns the calm and still voice of reasoning.

Conscience commands and forbids with more authority, and, in the most common and most important points of conduct, without the labour of reasoning. Its voice is heard by every man, and cannot be disregarded with impunity.

The sense of guilt makes a man at variance with himself. He sees that he is what he ought not to be. He has fallen from the dignity of his nature, and has sold his real worth for a thing of no value. He is conscious of demerit, and cannot avoid the dread of meeting with its reward.

On the other hand, he who pays a sacred regard to the dictates of his conscience, cannot fail of a present reward, and a reward proportioned to the exertion required in doing his duty.

The man who, in opposition to strong temptation, by a noble effort maintains his integrity, is the happiest man on earth. The more severe his conflict has been, the greater is his triumph. The consciousness of inward worth gives strength to his heart, and makes his countenance to shine. Tempests may beat and floods roar; but he stands firm as a rock, in the joy of a good conscience, and confidence of Divine approbation.

[To this I shall only add, what every man's conscience dictates, that he who does his duty, *from* the *conviction* that it is right and honourable, and what he ought to do, *acts from a nobler principle*, and with more inward satisfaction, than he who is *bribed* to do it, merely from the consideration of a reward present or future.]

CHAPTER VIII.

OBSERVATIONS CONCERNING CONSCIENCE.

I. *Our judgment of moral conduct advances from infancy by insensible degrees.*—I SHALL now conclude this Essay with some observations concerning this power of the mind which we call *conscience*, by which its nature may be better understood.

The *first* is, that, like all our other powers, it comes to maturity by insensible degrees, and may be much aided in its strength and vigour by proper culture.

All the human faculties have their infancy and their state of maturity.

The faculties which we have in common with the brutes appear first, and have the quickest growth. In the first period of life, children are not capable of distinguishing right from wrong in human conduct; neither are they capable of abstract reasoning in matters of science. Their judgment of moral conduct, as well as their judgment of truth, advances by insensible degrees, like the corn and the grass.

☞ In vegetables, first the blade or the leaf appears, then the flower, and last of all the fruit, the noblest production of the three, and that for which the others were produced. These succeed one another in a regular order. They require moisture and heat and air and shelter to bring them to maturity, and may be much improved by culture. According to the variations of soil, season, and culture, some plants are brought to much greater perfection than others of the same species. But no variation of culture or season or soil can make grapes grow from thorns, or figs from thistles.

We may observe a similar progress in the faculties of the mind: for there is a wonderful *analogy among all the works of God,* from the least even to the greatest.

The faculties of man unfold themselves in a certain order, appointed by the great Creator. In their gradual progress, they may be greatly assisted or retarded, improved or corrupted, by education, instruction, example, exercise, and by the society and conversation of men, which, like soil and culture in plants, may produce great changes to the better or to the worse.

II. [But *these means can never produce any new faculties,* nor any other than were originally planted in the mind by the

Author of nature. And what is common to the whole species, in all the varieties of instruction and education, of improvement and degeneracy, is the work of God, and *not the operation of second causes.*]

Such we may justly account *conscience*, or the faculty of distinguishing right conduct from wrong; since it appears, and in all nations and ages has appeared, in men that are come to maturity.

The seeds, as it were, of moral discernment are planted in the mind by Him that made us: they grow up in their proper season, and are at first tender and delicate, and easily warped. Their progress depends very much upon their being duly cultivated and properly exercised.

It is so with the power of reasoning, which all acknowledge to be one of the most eminent natural faculties of man. It appears not in infancy. It springs up, by insensible degrees, as we grow to maturity. But its strength and vigour depend so much upon its being duly cultivated and exercised, that we see many individuals, nay, many nations, in which it is hardly to be perceived.

Our intellectual discernment is not so strong and vigorous by nature, as to secure us from errors in speculation. On the contrary, we see a great part of mankind, in every age, sunk in gross ignorance of things that are obvious to the more enlightened, and fettered by errors and false notions, which the human understanding, duly improved, easily throws off.

III. *Scepticism twofold.*—[It would be extremely absurd, from the errors and ignorance of mankind, to conclude (1) *that there is no such thing as truth;* or (2) *that man has not a natural faculty of discerning it*, and distinguishing it from error.]*

In like manner, our moral discernment of what we ought, and what we ought not to do, is not so strong and vigorous by nature, as to secure us from very gross mistakes with regard to our duty.

In matters of conduct, as well as in matters of speculation, we are liable to be misled by prejudices of education, or by wrong instruction. But, in matters of conduct, we are also very liable to have our judgment warped by our appetites and passions, by fashion, and by the contagion of evil example.

We must not therefore think, because man has the natural power of discerning what is right and what is wrong, that he has no need of instruction; that this power has no need of cultivation and improvement; that he may safely rely upon the suggestions of his mind, or upon opinions he has got, he knows not how.

☞ What should we think of a man who, because he has by nature the power of moving all his limbs, should therefore con-

* Vide Locke's Essays, book I. sect. 2. Introduction.

clude that he needs not be taught to dance, or to fence, to ride, or to swim? All these exercises are performed by that power of moving our limbs, which we have by nature; but they will be performed very awkwardly and imperfectly by those who have not been trained to them, and practised in them.

What should we think of the man who, because he has the power by nature of distinguishing what is true from what is false, should conclude that he has no need to be taught mathematics, or natural philosophy, or other sciences? It is by the natural power of human understanding that every thing in those sciences has been discovered, and that the truths they contain are discerned. But the understanding, left to itself, without the aid of instruction, training, habit, and exercise, would make very small progress, as every one sees, in persons uninstructed in those matters.

IV. [*Our natural power of discerning between right and wrong needs the aid of instruction,* education, exercise, and habit, as well as our other natural powers.]

There are persons who, as the scripture speaks, have, by reason of use, their senses exercised to discern both good and evil; by that means, they have a much quicker, clearer, and more certain judgment in morals than others.

The man who neglects the means of improvement in the knowledge of his duty, may do very bad things, while he follows the light of his mind. And though he be not culpable for acting according to his judgment, he may be very culpable for not using the means of having his judgment better informed.

V. It may be observed, That *there are truths, both speculative and moral, which a man left to himself would never discover;* yet, when they are fairly laid before him, he owns and adopts them, not barely upon the authority of his teacher, but upon their own intrinsic evidence, and perhaps wonders that he could be so blind as not to see them before.

☞ Like a man whose son has been long abroad, and supposed dead. After many years the son returns, and is not known by his father. He would never find that this is his son. But, when he discovers himself, the father soon finds, by many circumstances, that this is his son who was lost, and can be no other person.

[Truth has an affinity with the human understanding, which error has not. And right principles of conduct have an affinity with a candid mind, which wrong principles have not.] When they are set before it in a just light, a well disposed mind recognises this affinity, feels their authority, and perceives them to be genuine. It was this, I apprehend, that led Plato to conceive that the knowledge we acquire in the present state, is only reminiscence of what, in a former state, we were acquainted with.

A man born and brought up in a savage nation, may be taught to pursue injury with unrelenting malice, to the destruction of his enemy. Perhaps when he does so, his heart does not condemn him.

Yet, if he be fair and candid, and, when the tumult of passion is over, have the virtues of clemency, generosity, and forgiveness, laid before him, as they were taught and exemplified by the Divine Author of our religion, he will see, that it is more noble to overcome himself, and subdue a savage passion, than to destroy his enemy. He will see, that to make a friend of an enemy, and to overcome evil with good, is the greatest of all victories, and gives a manly and a rational delight, with which the brutish passion of revenge deserves not to be compared. He will see, that hitherto he acted like a man to his friends, but like a brute to his enemies: now he knows how to make his whole character consistent, and one part of it to harmonize with another.

He must indeed be a great stranger to his own heart, and to the state of human nature, who does not see that he has need of all the aid which his situation affords him, in order to know how he ought to act in many cases that occur.

VI. [A *second* observation is, That *conscience is peculiar to man*. We see not a vestige of it in brute-animals. It is one of those prerogatives by which we are raised above them.]

Brute-animals have many faculties in common with us. They see, and hear, and taste, and smell, and feel. They have their pleasures and pains. They have various instincts and appetites. They have an affection for their offspring, and some of them for their herd or flock. Dogs have a wonderful attachment to their masters, and give manifest signs of sympathy with them.

We see, in brute-animals, *anger and emulation, pride and shame*. Some of them are capable of being trained by habit, and by rewards and punishments, to many things useful to man.

All this must be granted; and if our perception of what we ought, and what we ought not to do, could be resolved into any of these principles, or into any combination of them, it would follow, that some brutes are moral agents, and accountable for their conduct.

But common sense revolts against this conclusion. A man who seriously charged a brute with a crime, would be laughed at. They may do actions hurtful to themselves, or to man. They may have qualities, or acquire habits, that lead to such actions; and this is all we mean when we call them vicious. But they cannot be immoral; nor can they be virtuous. They are not capable of self-government; and, when they act according to the passion or habit which is strongest at the time, they act according to the nature that God has given them, and no more can be required of them.

They cannot lay down a rule to themselves, which they are not to transgress, though prompted by appetite, or ruffled by passion. We see no reason to think that they can form the conception of a general rule, or of obligation to adhere to it.

They have no conception of a promise or contract; nor can you enter into any treaty with them. They can neither affirm nor deny, nor resolve, nor plight their faith. If nature had made them capable of these operations, we should see the signs of them in their motions and gestures.

[The most sagacious brutes *never invented a language*, nor learned the use of one before invented. They *never formed a plan of government*, nor transmitted inventions to their posterity.]

These things, and many others that are obvious to common observation, show, that there is just reason why mankind have always considered the brute-creation as destitute of the noblest faculties with which God hath endowed man, and particularly of that faculty which makes us moral and accountable beings.

VII. [The *next* observation is, That *conscience is* evidently *intended by nature to be the immediate guide* and director *of our conduct*, after we arrive at the years of understanding.]

There are many things which, from their nature and structure, show intuitively the end for which they were made.

☞ A man who knows the structure of a watch or clock, can have no doubt in concluding that it was made to measure time. And he that knows the structure of the eye, and the properties of light, can have as little doubt whether it was made that we might see by it.

In the fabric of the body, the intention of the several parts is, in many instances, so evident, as to leave no possibility of doubt. Who can doubt whether the muscles were intended to move the parts in which they were inserted? Whether the bones were intended to give strength and support to the body; and some of them to guard the parts which they inclose?

When we attend to the structure of the mind, the intention of its various original powers is no less evident. Is it not evident, that the *external senses* are given, that we may discern those qualities of bodies which may be useful or hurtful to us? *Memory*, that we may retain the knowledge we have acquired: *judgment* and *understanding*, that we may distinguish what is true from what is false?

VIII. *The intention or end of our active powers obvious.*—The natural appetites of hunger and thirst, the natural affections of parents to their offspring, and of relations to each other, the natural docility and credulity of children, the affections of pity and sympathy with the distressed, the attachment we feel to neighbours, to acquaintance, and to the laws and constitution of our country; these are parts of our constitution, which plainly point out their end, so that he must be blind, or very inattentive, who does not perceive it. [Even the passions of anger and resentment, appear very plainly to be a kind of *defensive* armour, given by our Maker to guard us against injuries, and to deter the injurious.]

Thus it holds generally with regard both to the *intellectual and active powers of man,* that the intention for which they are given is written in legible characters upon the face of them.

IX. *Office of conscience.*—[Nor is this the case of any of them more evidently than of *conscience.* Its intention is manifestly implied in its office; which is, to show us what is good, what bad, and what indifferent in human conduct.]

It judges of every action before it is done. For we can rarely act so precipitately, but we have the consciousness that what we are about to do is right, or wrong, or indifferent. Like the bodily eye, it naturally looks forward, though its attention may be turned back to the past.

To conceive, as some seem to have done, that its office is only to reflect on past actions, and to approve or disapprove, is, as if a man should conceive, that the office of his eyes is only to look back upon the road he has travelled, and to see whether it be clean or dirty; a mistake which no man can make who has made the proper use of his eyes.

Conscience prescribes measures to every appetite, affection, and passion, and says to every other principle of action, so far thou mayest go, but no farther.

We may indeed transgress its dictates, but we cannot transgress them with innocence, nor even with impunity.

[We condemn ourselves, or, in the language of Scripture, *our heart condemns us,* whenever we go beyond the rules of right and wrong which conscience prescribes.

Other principles of action may have more strength, but this only has *authority.*] Its sentence makes us guilty to ourselves, and guilty in the eyes of our Maker, whatever other principle may be set in opposition to it.

It is evident therefore, that this principle has, from its nature, an authority to direct and determine with regard to our conduct; to judge, to acquit, or to condemn, and even to punish; an authority which belongs to no other principle of the human mind.

☞ It is the candle of the Lord set up within us, to guide our steps. Other principles may urge and impel, but this only authorises. Other principles ought to be controlled by this; this may be, but never ought to be, controlled by any other, and never can be with innocence.

The authority of conscience over the other active principles of the mind, I do not consider as a point that requires proof by argument, but as self-evident. For it implies no more than this, That in all cases a man ought to do his duty. He only who does in all cases what he ought to do, is the perfect man.

X. *Stoical perfection ideal.*—[Of this perfection in the human nature, the Stoics formed the idea, and held it forth in their writings as the goal to which the race of life ought to be directed. Their *wise man* was one in whom a regard to the *honestum* swallowed up every other principle of action.]

The *wise man* of the Stoics, like the *perfect orator* of the rhetoricians, was *an ideal character*, and was, in some respects, carried beyond nature; yet it was perhaps the most perfect model of virtue, that ever was exhibited to the heathen world; and some of those who copied after it, were ornaments to human nature.

XI. [The *last* observation is, That *the moral faculty* or conscience *is both an active and an intellectual power* of the mind.]

It is an active power, as every truly virtuous action must be more or less influenced by it. Other principles may concur with it, and lead the same way; but no action can be called morally good, in which a regard to what is right has not some influence. Thus a man who has no regard to justice, may pay his just debt, from no other motive, but that he may not be thrown into prison. In this action there is no virtue at all.

The moral principle, in particular cases, may be opposed by any of our animal principles. Passion or appetite may urge to what we know to be wrong. In every instance of this kind, the moral principle ought to prevail, and the more difficult its conquest is, it is the more glorious.

[In some cases, a regard to what is right may be the sole motive, without the concurrence or opposition of any other principle of action; as when a judge or an arbiter determines a plea between two indifferent persons, solely from a regard to justice.

Thus we see, that conscience, as an active principle, sometimes concurs with other active principles, sometimes opposes them, and sometimes is the sole principle of action.]

I endeavoured before to show, that a regard to our own good upon the whole is not only a rational principle of action, but a leading principle, to which all our animal principles are subordinate. As there are, therefore, two regulating or leading principles in the constitution of man, a regard to what is best for us upon the whole, and a regard to duty, it may be asked, Which of these ought to yield if they happen to interfere?

XII. *Extravagance of Mysticism.*—Some well meaning persons have maintained, [That all regard to ourselves and to our own happiness ought to be extinguished; that we should love virtue for its own sake only, even though it were to be accompanied with eternal misery.]

This seems to have been the extravagance of some Mystics, which perhaps they were led into, in opposition to a contrary extreme of the schoolmen of the middle ages, who made the desire of good to ourselves to be the *sole* motive to action, and virtue to be approvable only on account of its present or future reward.

Juster views of human nature will teach us to avoid both these extremes.

On the one hand, the disinterested love of virtue is undoubtedly the noblest principle in human nature, and ought never to stoop to any other.

On the other hand, there is no active principle which God hath planted in our nature that is vicious in itself, or that ought to be eradicated, even if it were in our power.

They are all useful and necessary in our present state. The perfection of human nature consists, not in extinguishing, but in restraining them within their proper bounds, and keeping them in due subordination to the governing principles.

XIII. [As to *the supposition of an opposition between the two governing principles*, that is, between a regard to our happiness upon the whole, and a regard to duty, this supposition *is merely imaginary*. There can be no such opposition.]

While the world is under a wise and benevolent administration, it is impossible that any man should, in the issue, be a loser by doing his duty. Every man, therefore, who believes in God, while he is careful to do his duty, may safely leave the care of his happiness to Him who made him. He is conscious that he consults the last most effectually, by attending to the first.

Indeed, if we suppose a man to be an atheist in his belief, and, at the same time, by wrong judgment, to believe that virtue is contrary to his happiness upon the whole, this case, as Lord Shaftesbury justly observes, is without remedy. It will be impossible for the man to act so as not to contradict a leading principle of his nature. He must either sacrifice his happiness to virtue, or virtue to happiness; and is reduced to this miserable dilemma, whether it be best to be a fool or a knave.

[This shows the *strong connexion between morality and the principles of natural religion;* as the last only can secure a man from the possibility of an apprehension, that he may play the fool by doing his duty.]

Hence even Lord Shaftesbury, in his gravest work, concludes, *That virtue without piety is incomplete.* Without piety it loses its brightest example, its noblest object, and its firmest support.

XIV. [I conclude with observing, That *conscience,* or the moral faculty, *is likewise an intellectual power.*]

By it solely we have the original conceptions or ideas of right and wrong in human conduct. And of right and wrong, there are not only many different degrees, but many different species. Justice and injustice, gratitude and ingratitude, benevolence and malice, prudence and folly, magnanimity and meanness, decency and indecency, are various moral forms, all comprehended under the general notion of right and wrong in conduct, all of them objects of moral approbation or disapprobation, in a greater or a less degree.

The conception of these, as moral qualities, we have by our moral faculty; and by the same faculty, when we compare them together, we perceive various moral relations among them. Thus we perceive that justice is entitled to a small degree of praise, but injustice to a high degree of blame; and the same may be said of gratitude and its contrary. When justice and gratitude interfere, gratitude must give place to justice, and unmerited beneficence must give place to both.

Many such relations between the various moral qualities compared together, are immediately discerned by our moral faculty. A man needs only to consult his own heart to be convinced of them.

All our reasonings in morals, in natural jurisprudence, in the law of nations, as well as our reasonings about the duties of natural religion, and about the moral government of the Deity, must be grounded upon the dictates of our moral faculty, as first principles.

As this faculty, therefore, furnishes the human mind with many of its original conceptions or ideas, as well as with the first principles of many important branches of human knowledge, it may justly be accounted an intellectual, as well as an active power of the mind.

ESSAY IV.

OF THE LIBERTY OF MORAL AGENTS.

CHAPTER I.

THE NOTIONS OF MORAL LIBERTY AND NECESSITY STATED.

I. *Moral liberty.*—By the *liberty* of a moral agent, I understand, *a power over the determinations of his own will.*

If, in any action, he had power to will what he did, or not to will it, in that action he is free. But if, in every voluntary action, the determination of his will be the necessary consequence of something involuntary in the state of his mind, or of something in his external circumstances, he is not free; he has not what I call the liberty of a moral agent, but is subject to necessity.

This liberty supposes the agent to have understanding and will; for the determinations of the will are the sole object about which this power is employed; and there can be no will without, at least, such a degree of understanding as gives the conception of that which we will.

[The liberty of a moral agent implies, not only a *conception* of what he wills, but some degree of practical *judgment* or reason.]

For if he has not the judgment to discern one determination to be preferable to another, either in itself, or for some purpose which he intends, what can be the use of a power to determine? His determinations must be made perfectly in the dark, without reason, motive, or end. They can neither be right nor wrong, wise nor foolish. Whatever the consequences may be, they cannot be imputed to the agent, who had not the capacity of foreseeing them, or of perceiving any reason for acting otherwise than he did.

We may perhaps be able to conceive a being endowed with power over the determinations of his will, without any light in his mind to direct that power to some end. But such power would be given in vain. No exercise of it could be either blamed or approved. As nature gives no power in vain, I see no ground to ascribe a power over the determinations of the will to any being who has no judgment to apply it to the direction of his conduct, no discernment of what he ought or ought not to do.

For that reason, in this Essay, I speak only of the liberty of moral agents, who are capable of acting well or ill, wisely or foolishly, and this, for distinction's sake, I shall call *moral liberty*.

II. *The voluntary actions of brutes determined by the present predominant passion.*—What kind, or what degree of liberty belongs to brute animals, or to our own species, before any use of reason, I do not know. We acknowledge that they have not the power of self-government. [Such of their actions as may be called *voluntary*, seem to be invariably determined by the passion or appetite, or affection or habit, which is strongest at the time.]

This seems to be the law of their constitution, to which they yield, as the inanimate creation does, without any conception of the law, or any intention of obedience.

But of civil or moral government, which are addressed to the rational powers, and require a conception of the law and an intentional obedience, they are, in the judgment of all mankind, incapable. Nor do I see what end could be served by giving them a power over the determinations of their own will, unless to make them intractable by discipline, which we see they are not.

III. [The *effect of moral liberty* is, That it is in the power of the agent to do well or ill.] This power, like every other gift of God, may be abused. The right use of this gift of God is to do well and wisely, as far as his best judgment can direct him, and thereby merit esteem and approbation. The abuse of it is to act contrary to what he knows or suspects to be his duty and his wisdom, and thereby justly merit disapprobation and blame.

IV. [By *necessity*, I understand *the want of that moral liberty* which I have above defined.]

If there can be a better and a worse in actions on the system of necessity, let us suppose a man necessarily determined in all cases to will and to do what is best to be done, he would surely be innocent and inculpable. But, as far as I am able to judge, he would not be entitled to the esteem and moral approbation of those who knew and believed this necessity. What was, by an ancient author, said of Cato, might indeed be said of him. *He was good because he could not be otherwise.* But this saying, if understood literally and strictly, is not the praise of Cato, but of his constitution, which was no more the work of Cato, than his existence.

On the other hand, if a man be necessarily determined to do ill, this case seems to me to move pity, but not disapprobation. He was ill, because he could not be otherwise. Who can blame him? Necessity has no law.

If he *knows* that he acted under this necessity, has he not just ground to exculpate himself? The blame, if there be any, is not in him, but in his constitution. If he be charged by his Maker with doing wrong, may he not expostulate with him, and say, Why hast thou made me thus? I may be sacrificed at thy pleasure for the common good, like a man that has the plague, but not for ill desert; for thou knowest that what I am charged with is thy work, and not mine.

V. [Such are my notions of *moral liberty and necessity*, and of the consequences inseparably connected with both the one and the other.]

This moral liberty a man may have, though it do not extend to all his actions, or even to all his voluntary actions. He does many things by instinct, many things by the force of habit without any thought at all, and consequently without will. In the first part of life, he has not the power of self-government any more than the brutes. That power over the determinations of his own will, which belongs to him in ripe years, is limited, as all his powers are; and it is perhaps beyond the reach of his understanding to define its limits with precision. We can only say, in general, that it extends to every action for which he is accountable.

This power is given by his Maker, and at his pleasure, whose gift it is: it may be enlarged or diminished, continued or withdrawn. No power in the creature can be independent of the Creator. His hook is in its nose; he can give it line as far as he sees fit, and when he pleases, can restrain it, or turn it whithersoever he will. Let this be always understood, when we ascribe liberty to man, or to any created being.

VI. [Supposing it therefore to be true, *That man is a free agent*, it may be true, at the same time, that his liberty may be impaired or lost, (1) by disorder of body or mind, as in melancholy, or in madness; it may be impaired or lost (2) by vicious habits; it may, in particular cases, (3) be restrained by Divine interposition.]

We call a man a free agent in the same way as we call him a reasonable agent. In many things he is not guided by reason, but by principles similar to those of the brutes. His reason is weak at best. It is liable to be impaired or lost, by his own fault, or by other means. In like manner, he may be a free agent, though his freedom of action may have many similar limitations.

The liberty I have described has been represented by some philosophers as inconceivable, and as involving an absurdity.

" Liberty, they say, consists only in a power to act as we will; and it is impossible to conceive in any being a greater liberty than this. Hence it follows, that liberty does not extend to the determinations of the will, but only to the actions consequent to its determination, and depending upon the will. To say that we have power to will such an action, is to say, that we may will it, if we will. This supposes the will to be determined by a prior will; and, for the same reason, that will must be determined by a will prior to it, and so on in an infinite series of wills, which is absurd. To act freely, therefore, can mean nothing more than to act voluntarily; and this is all the liberty that can be conceived in man, or in any being."

This reasoning, first, I think, advanced by Hobbes, has been very generally adopted by the defenders of necessity. It is grounded upon a definition of liberty totally different from that which I have given, and therefore does not apply to moral liberty,* as above defined.

VII. *Three additional meanings of the word liberty.*—[But it is said that this is the *only* liberty that is possible, that is conceivable, that does not involve an absurdity.]

It is strange, indeed! if the word *liberty* has no meaning but this one. I shall mention *three*, all very common. The objection applies to one of them, but to neither of the other two.

[Liberty is sometimes opposed to external force or confinement of the body. Sometimes it is opposed to obligation by law, or by lawful authority. Sometimes it is opposed to necessity.]

1. It is opposed to *confinement of the body* by superior force. So we say a prisoner is set at liberty when his fetters are knocked off, and he is discharged from confinement. This is the liberty defined in the objection; and I grant that this liberty extends not to the will, neither does the confinement, because the will cannot be confined by external force.

2. Liberty is opposed to *obligation by law*, or lawful authority. This liberty is a right to act one way or another, in things which the law has neither commanded nor forbidden; and this liberty is meant when we speak of a man's natural liberty, his civil liberty, his Christian liberty. It is evident that this liberty, as well as the obligation opposed to it, extends to the will: for it is the will to obey that makes obedience; the will to transgress that makes a transgression of the law. Without will there can be neither obedience nor transgression. Law supposes a power to obey or to transgress; it does not take away this power, but proposes the motives of duty and of interest, leaving the power to yield to them, or to take the consequence of transgression.

3. Liberty is opposed *to necessity*, and in this sense it extends to the determinations of the will only, and not to what is consequent to the will.

In every voluntary action, the determination of the will is the first part of the action, upon which alone the moral estimation of

* Vide sect. i. and ii. of this chapter.

it depends. It has been made a question among philosophers, Whether, in every instance, this determination be the necessary consequence of the constitution of the person, and the circumstances in which he is placed; or whether he had not power in many cases, to determine this way or that?

This has, by some, been called the *philosophical* notion of liberty and necessity; but it is by no means peculiar to philosophers. The lowest of the vulgar have, in all ages, been prone to have recourse to this necessity, to exculpate themselves or their friends in what they do wrong, though, in the general tenor of their conduct, they act upon the contrary principle.

VIII. Whether this notion of moral liberty be conceivable or not, every man must judge for himself. To me there appears no difficulty in conceiving it. I consider the determination of the will as an effect. This effect must have a cause which had power to produce it; and the cause must be either the person himself, whose will it is, or some other being. The first is as easily conceived as the last. If the person was the cause of that determination of his own will, he was free in that action, and it is justly imputed to him, whether it be good or bad. But, if another being was the cause of this determination, either by producing it immediately, or by means and instruments under his direction, then the determination is the act and deed of that being, and is solely imputable to him.

But it is said, "That nothing is in our power but what depends upon the will, and therefore the will itself cannot be in our power."

I answer, That this is *a fallacy arising from taking a common saying in a sense which it never was intended to convey*, and in a sense contrary to what it necessarily implies.

In common life, when men speak of what is, or is not, in a man's power, they attend only to the external and visible effects, which only can be perceived, and which only can affect them. Of these, it is true, that nothing is in a man's power, but what depends upon his will, and this is all that is meant by this common saying.

But this is so far from excluding his will from being in his power, that it necessarily implies it. For to say that what depends upon the will is in a man's power, but the will is not in his power, is to say that the end is in his power, but the means necessary to that end are not in his power, which is a contradiction.

[In many propositions which we express universally, there is *an exception* necessarily implied, and therefore always understood. Thus when we say, that all things depend upon God, God himself is necessarily excepted. In like manner, when we say, that all that is in our power depends upon the will, the will itself is necessarily excepted: [for if the will be not, nothing else can be in our power.] Every effect must be in the power of its cause. The determination of the will is an effect, and therefore must be in the power of its cause, whether that cause be the agent himself, or some other being.

From what has been said in this chapter, I hope the notion of moral liberty will be distinctly understood, and that it appears that this notion is neither inconceivable, nor involves any absurdity or contradiction.

CHAPTER II.

OF THE WORDS CAUSE AND EFFECT, ACTION, AND ACTIVE POWER.

I. *The use of ambiguous terms has impeded our reasonings about moral liberty.*—THE writings upon liberty and necessity have been much darkened, by the ambiguity of the words used in reasoning upon that subject. The words *cause* and *effect, action* and *active power, liberty and necessity,* are related to each other. The meaning of one determines the meaning of the rest. When we attempt to define them, we can only do it by synonymous words which need definition as much. There is a strict sense in which those words must be used, if we speak and reason clearly about moral liberty; but to keep to this strict sense is difficult, because in all languages they have, by custom, got a great latitude of signification.

As we cannot reason about moral liberty, without using those ambiguous words, it is proper to point out, as distinctly as possible, their proper and original meaning, in which they ought to be understood in treating of this subject, and to show from what causes they have become so ambiguous in all languages, as to darken and embarrass our reasonings upon it.

[Every thing that *begins to exist,* must have a cause of its existence, which had power to give it existence.] [And every thing that *undergoes any change,* must have some cause of that change.]

That neither existence, nor any mode of existence, can begin without an efficient cause, is a principle that appears very early in the mind of man; and it is so universal, and so firmly rooted in human nature, that the most determined scepticism cannot eradicate it.

It is upon this principle that we ground the rational belief of a Deity. But that is not the only use to which we apply it. Every man's conduct is governed by it every day, and almost every hour of his life. And if it were possible for any man to root out this principle from his mind, he must give up every thing that is called common prudence, and be fit only to be confined as insane.

From this principle it follows, that every thing which undergoes any change, must either be the efficient cause of that change in itself, or it must be changed by some other being.

In the *first* case it is said to have *active power*, and to *act* in producing that change. In the *second* case it is merely *passive*, or is *acted upon*, and the active power is in that being only which produces the change.

II. *Active power.*—The name of a *cause* and of an *agent*, is properly given to that being only, which, by its active power, produces some change in itself, or in some other being. The change, whether it be of thought, of will, or of motion, is the *effect*. *Active power, therefore, is a quality in the cause, which enables it to produce the effect*. And the exertion of that active power in producing the effect, is called *action, agency, efficiency*.

[In order to the production of any effect, there must be in the cause not only *power*, but the *exertion* of that power: for power that is not exerted produces no effect.]

All that is necessary to the production of any effect, is power, is an efficient cause to produce the effect, and the exertion of that power: for it is a contradiction to say, that the cause has power to produce the effect, and exerts that power, and yet the effect is not produced. The effect cannot be in his power, unless all the means necessary to its production be in his power.

It is no less a contradiction to say, that a cause has power to produce a certain effect, but that he cannot exert that power: for power which cannot be exerted is no power, and is a contradiction in terms.

To prevent mistake, it is proper to observe, that a being may have a power at one time which it has not at another. It may commonly have a power, which, at a particular time, it has not. Thus, a man may commonly have power to walk or to run; but he has not this power when asleep, or when he is confined by superior force. In common language, he may be said to have a power which he cannot then exert. But this popular expression means only that he commonly has this power, and will have it when the cause is removed which at present deprives him of it: for when we speak strictly and philosophically, it is a contradiction to say that he has this power, at that moment when he is deprived of it.

[These, I think, are necessary consequences from the principle first mentioned, that every change which happens in nature must have *an efficient cause* which had power to produce it.]

III. [Another principle, which appears very early in the mind of man, is, That *we are efficient causes in our deliberate and voluntary actions.*]

We are conscious of making an exertion, sometimes with difficulty, in order to produce certain effects. An exertion made deliberately and voluntarily, in order to produce an effect, implies a conviction that the effect is in our power. No man can deliberately attempt what he does not believe to be in his power. The language of all mankind, and their ordinary conduct in life, demonstrate, that they have a conviction of some active power in themselves to produce certain motions in their own and in other bodies, and to regulate and direct their own thoughts. This conviction we have so early in life, that we have no remembrance when, or in what way, we acquired it.

That such a conviction is at first the necessary result of our constitution, and that it can never be entirely obliterated, is, I think, acknowledged by one of the most zealous defenders of necessity.—" Free Discussion," &c. p. 298. " Such are the influences to which all mankind, without distinction, are exposed, that they necessarily refer actions (I mean refer them ultimately) first of all to themselves and others; and it is a long time before they begin to consider themselves and others as instruments in the hand of a superior agent. Consequently, the associations which refer actions to themselves, get so confirmed, that they are never entirely obliterated; and therefore the common language, and the common feelings of mankind, will be adapted to the first, the limited and imperfect, or rather erroneous, view of things."

It is very probable that the very conception or idea of active power, and of efficient causes, is derived from our voluntary exertions in producing effects; and that, if we were not conscious of such exertions, we should have no conception at all of a cause, or of active power, and consequently no conviction of the necessity of a cause of every change which we observe in nature.

IV. [It is certain that *we can conceive no kind of active power but what is similar or analogous to that which we attribute to ourselves;* that is, a power which is exerted by will and with understanding. Our notion, even of Almighty power, is derived from the notion of human power, by removing from the former those imperfections and limitations to which the latter is subjected.]

It may be difficult to explain the origin of our conceptions and belief concerning efficient causes and active power. [The common theory, that all our ideas are ideas of sensation or reflection, and that all our belief is a perception of the agreement or the disagreement of those ideas, appears to be repugnant, both to the idea of an efficient cause, and to the belief of its necessity.]

An attachment to that theory has led some philosophers to deny that we have any conception of an efficient cause, or of active power, because efficiency and active power are not ideas, either of sensation or reflection. They maintain, therefore, that *a cause* is only something *prior to the effect*, and constantly conjoined with it. This is Mr. Hume's notion of a cause, and seems to be adopted by Dr. Priestley, who says, " That a cause cannot be defined to be any thing, but *such previous circumstances as are constantly followed by a certain effect*, the constancy of the result making us conclude, that there must be a *sufficient reason*, in the nature of the things, why it should be produced in those circumstances."

But theory ought to stoop to fact, and not fact to theory. Every man who understands the language knows, that neither priority, nor constant conjunction, nor both taken together, imply efficiency. Every man, free from prejudice, must assent to what Cicero has said: " Itaque non sic causa intelligi debet, ut quod cuique antecedat, id et causa sit, sed quod cuique efficienter antecedit."—" That which precedes any thing is not to be considered as its cause, but that which precedes it *efficiently*."

[*The very dispute*, whether we have the *conception* of an efficient cause, *shows that we have*. For though men may dispute about things which have no existence, they cannot dispute about things of which they have no conception.]

V. *Recapitulation.*—What has been said in this chapter is intended to show, That the *conception* of causes, of action and of active power, in the strict and proper sense of these words, *is found in the minds of all men very early*, even in the dawn of their rational life. *It is* therefore *probable*, that, in all languages, *the words* by which these conceptions were expressed *were at first distinct and unambiguous;* yet it is certain, that, among the most enlightened nations, these words are applied to so many things of different natures, and used in so vague a manner, that it is very difficult to reason about them distinctly.

This phenomenon, at first view, seems very unaccountable. But a little reflection may satisfy us, that it is a natural consequence of the slow and gradual progress of human knowledge.

And since the ambiguity of these words has so great influence upon our reasoning about moral liberty, and furnishes the strongest objections against it, it is not foreign to our subject to show whence it arises. [When we know the *causes* that have produced this *ambiguity*, we shall be less in danger of being misled by it, and the proper and strict meaning of the words will more evidently appear.]

CHAPTER III.

CAUSES OF THE AMBIGUITY OF THOSE WORDS.

I. *Premature conclusion as to objects indued with motion.*—When we turn our attention to external objects, and begin to exercise our rational faculties about them, we find, that there are some motions and changes in them, which we have power to produce, and that they have many which must have some other cause. Either the objects must have life and active power, as we have, or they must be moved or changed by something that has life and active power, as external objects are moved by us.

[Our first thoughts seem to be, That *the objects* in which we perceive such motion *have understanding and active power* as we have.]

"Savages," says the Abbé Raynal, "wherever they see motion which they cannot account for, there they suppose a soul."*

All men may be considered as savages in this respect, until they are capable of instruction, and of using their faculties in a more perfect manner than savages do.

The rational conversations of birds and beasts in Æsop's Fables do not shock the belief of children. To them they have that probability which we require in an epic poem. Poets give us a great deal of pleasure, by clothing every object with intellectual and moral attributes in metaphor and in other figures. May not the pleasure which we take in this poetical language, arise, in part, from its correspondence with our earliest sentiments?

II. However this may be, the [Abbé Raynal's observation is sufficiently confirmed, both from *fact*, and from *the structure of all languages.*]

Rude nations do really believe sun, moon and stars, earth, sea and air, fountains and lakes, to have understanding and active power. To pay homage to them, and implore their favour, is a kind of idolatry natural to savages.

All languages carry in their structure the marks of their being formed when this belief prevailed. [The distinction of verbs and participles into *active and passive*, which is found in all languages, must have been originally intended to distinguish what is really active from what is merely passive; and, in all languages, we find *active verbs applied to those objects, in which*, according to the Abbé Raynal's observation, *savages suppose a soul.*]

Thus we say the sun rises and sets, and comes to the meridian, the moon changes, the sea ebbs and flows, the winds blow.

* Vide sect. vii. chap. 5, Essay III.

Languages were formed by men who believed these objects to have life and active power in themselves. It was therefore proper and natural to express their motions and changes by active verbs.

III. [*There is no surer way of tracing the sentiments of nations before they have records than by the structure of their language*, which, notwithstanding the changes produced in it by time, will always retain some signatures of the thoughts of those by whom it was invented. When we find the same sentiments indicated in the structure of all languages, those sentiments must have been common to the human species when languages were invented.]

When a few of superior intellectual abilities find leisure for speculation, they begin to philosophize, and soon discover, that many of those objects which, at first, they believed to be intelligent and active, are really lifeless and passive. This is a very important discovery. It elevates the mind, emancipates from many vulgar superstitions, and invites to farther discoveries of the same kind.

As philosophy advances, life and activity in natural objects retire, and leave them dead and inactive. Instead of moving voluntarily, we find them to be moved necessarily; instead of acting, we find them to be acted upon; and nature appears as one great machine, where one wheel is turned by another, that by a third; and how far this necessary succession may reach, the philosopher does not know.

IV. [*The weakness of human reason makes men prone, when they leave one extreme, to rush into the opposite;** and thus philosophy, even in its infancy, may lead men from idolatry and polytheism into atheism, and from ascribing active power to inanimate beings, to conclude all things to be carried on by necessity.]

Whatever origin we ascribe to the doctrines of atheism and of fatal necessity, it is certain, that both may be traced almost as far back as philosophy; and both appear to be the opposites of the earliest sentiments of men.

It must have been by the observation and reasoning of the speculative *few*, that those objects were discovered to be inanimate and inactive, to which the *many* ascribed life and activity. But while the *few* are convinced of this, they must speak the language of the *many* in order to be understood. ☞ So we see, that when the *Ptolemaic system of astronomy*, which agrees with vulgar prejudice and with vulgar language, *has been universally rejected* by philosophers, *they continue to use the phraseology* that is grounded upon it, not only in speaking to the vulgar, but in speaking to one another. They say, The sun rises

* As, from dogmatism to scepticism.

and sets, and moves annually through all the signs of the zodiac, while they believe that he never leaves his place.

[In like manner, those *active verbs* and participles, which were applied to the inanimate objects of nature, when they were believed to be really active, *continue to be applied to them after they are discovered to be passive.*]

V. [*The forms of language, once established by custom, are not so easily changed as the notions on which they were originally founded.* While the sounds remain, their signification is gradually enlarged or altered.] This is sometimes found, even in those sciences in which the signification of words is the most accurate and precise. Thus, in arithmetic, the word *number,* among the ancients, always signified so many units, and it would have been absurd to apply it either to unity or to any part of an unit; but now we call unity, or any part of unity, a *number.* With them, multiplication always increased a number, and division diminished it; but we speak of multiplying by a fraction, which diminishes, and of dividing by a fraction, which increases the number. We speak of dividing or multiplying by unity, which neither diminishes nor increases a number. These forms of expression, in the ancient language, would have been absurd.

VI. *A chief cause of the imperfection of language.*—[By such changes, in the meaning of words, ☞ the language of every civilized nation resembles *old furniture new modelled,* in which many things are put to uses *for which they were not originally intended,* and for which they are not perfectly fitted.]

This is *one great cause of the imperfection of language,* and it appears very remarkably in those verbs and participles which are active in their form, but are frequently used so as to have nothing active in their signification.

Hence we are authorised by custom to ascribe action and active power to things which we believe to be passive. The proper and original signification of every word, which at first signified action and causation, is buried and lost under that vague meaning which custom has affixed to it.

That there is a real distinction, and perfect opposition, between acting and being acted upon, every man may be satisfied who is capable of reflection. And that this distinction is perceived by all men as soon as they begin to reason, appears by the distinction between active and passive verbs, which is original in all languages, though, from the causes that have been mentioned, they come to be confounded in the progress of human improvement.

VII. [*Another way in which philosophy has contributed* very much *to the ambiguity of the words* under our consideration, deserves to be mentioned.]

The first step into natural philosophy, and what hath commonly been considered as its ultimate end, is *the investigation of the causes of the phenomena of nature;* that is, the causes of those appearances in nature which are not the effects of human power. "Felix qui potuit rerum cognoscere causas," is the sentiment of every mind that has a turn to speculation.

The knowledge of the causes of things promises no less the enlargement of human power than the gratification of human curiosity; and therefore, among the enlightened part of mankind, this knowledge has been pursued in all ages with an avidity proportioned to its importance.

In nothing does the difference between the intellectual powers of man and those of brutes appear more conspicuous than in this. For in them we perceive no desire to investigate the causes of things, nor indeed any sign that they have the proper notion of a cause.

[There is reason, however, to apprehend, that, in this investigation, men have wandered much in the dark, and that their success has by no means been equal to their desire and expectation.]

We easily discover an established order and connexion in the phenomena of nature. We learn, in many cases, from what has happened, to know what will happen. The discoveries of this kind, made by common observation, are many, and are the foundation of common prudence in the conduct of life. Philosophers, by more accurate observation and experiment, have made many more; by which arts are improved, and human power, as well as human knowledge, is enlarged.

But, as to the real causes of the phenomena of nature, how little do we know! [all our knowledge of things external, must be grounded upon the *information of our senses;* but *causation* and *active power are not objects of sense;* nor is that always the cause of a phenomenon which is prior to it, and constantly conjoined with it; otherwise night would be the cause of day, and day the cause of the following night.]

It is to this day problematical, whether all the phenomena of the material system be produced by the immediate operation of the First Cause, according to the laws which his wisdom determined, or whether subordinate causes are employed by him in the operations of nature; and, if they be, what their nature, their number, and their different offices are? And whether, in all cases, they act by commission, or, in some, according to their discretion?

When we are so much in the dark with regard to the real causes of the phenomena of nature, and have a strong desire to know them, it is not strange, that ingenious men should form numberless conjectures and theories, by which the soul, hungering for knowledge, is fed with chaff instead of wheat.

VIII. *Absurd theories of philosophers to explain causation.*—In a very ancient system, love and strife were made the causes of things. In the Pythagorean and Platonic system, matter, ideas, and an intelligent mind. By Aristotle, matter, form, and privation. Des Cartes thought, that matter, and a certain quantity of motion given at first by the Almighty, are sufficient to account for all the phenomena of the natural world. Leibnitz, that the universe is made up of monades, active and percipient, which, by their active power received at first, produce all the changes they undergo.

While men thus wandered in the dark in search of causes, unwilling to confess their disappointment, they vainly conceived every thing they stumbled upon to be a cause, and the proper notion of a cause is lost, by giving the name to numberless things which neither are nor can be causes.

IX. *Not mischievous.*—[This *confusion of various things under the name of causes*, is the more easily tolerated, because however hurtful it may be to sound philosophy, it *has little influence upon the concerns of life.*] A constant antecedent, or concomitant, of the phenomenon whose cause is sought, may answer the purpose of the inquirer, as well as if the real cause were known. ☞ Thus a sailor desires to know the cause of the tides, that he may know when to expect high water: he is told that it is high water when the moon is so many hours past the meridian: and now he thinks he knows the cause of the tides. What he takes for the cause answers his purpose, and his mistake does him no harm.

Those philosophers seem to have had the justest views of nature, as well as of the weakness of human understanding, who, giving up the pretence of discovering the causes of the operations of nature, have applied themselves to discover, by observation and experiment, the rules, or laws of nature according to which the phenomena of nature are produced.

In compliance with custom, or perhaps, to gratify the avidity of knowing the causes of things, we call the laws of nature causes and active powers. So we speak of the powers of gravitation, of magnetism, of electricity.

We call them causes of many of the phenomena of nature; and such they are esteemed by the ignorant, and by the half learned.

[But those of juster discernment see, that *laws* of nature *are not agents.* They are not endowed with active power, and therefore *cannot be causes* in the proper sense. They are only the rules according to which the unknown cause acts.]

Thus it appears, that our natural desire to know the causes of the phenomena of nature, our inability to discover them, and the vain theories of philosophers employed in this search, have made the word *cause* and *the related words so ambiguous,* and to signify so many things of different natures, that they have in a manner lost their proper and original meaning, and yet we have no other words to express it.

Every thing joined with the effect, and prior to it, is called its cause. An instrument, an occasion, a reason, a motive, an end, are called causes. And the related words *effect, agent, power,* are extended in the same vague manner.

[Were it not that the terms *cause* and *agent* have lost their proper meaning in the crowd of meanings that have been given them, we should immediately perceive a contradiction in the terms *necessary cause* and *necessary agent.*] And although the loose meaning of those words is authorised by custom, the arbiter of language, and therefore cannot be censured, perhaps cannot always be avoided, yet we ought to be upon our guard, that we be not misled by it to conceive things to be the same which are essentially different.

To say that man is a free agent, is no more than to say that, in some instances, he is truly an agent and a cause, and is not merely acted upon as a passive instrument. On the contrary, to say that he acts from necessity, is to say that he does not act at all, that he is no agent, and that, for any thing we know, there is only one agent in the universe, who does every thing that is done, whether it be good or ill.

If this necessity be attributed even to the Deity, the consequence must be, that *there neither is nor can be a cause at all;* that nothing acts, but every thing is acted upon; nothing moves, but every thing is moved; all is passion without action; all instrument without an agent; and that every thing that is, or was, or shall be, has that necessary existence in its season which we commonly consider as the prerogative of the First Cause.

This I take to be the genuine and the most tenable system of necessity. It was the system of Spinoza, though he was not the first that advanced it; for it is very ancient. And if this system be true, our reasoning to prove the existence of a first cause of every thing that begins to exist, must be given up as fallacious.

X. *Proof of a Deity on these principles presents no difficulty.*—If it be evident to the human understanding, as I take it to be, that what begins to exist must have an efficient cause, which had power to give or not to give it existence; and if it be true, that effects well and wisely fitted for the best purposes, demonstrate intelligence, wisdom, and goodness, in the efficient cause, as well as power, the proof of a Deity from these principles is very easy and obvious to all men that can reason.

If, on the other hand, our belief that every thing that begins to exist has a cause, be got only by experience; and if, as Mr. Hume maintains, the only notion of a cause be something prior to the effect, which experience has shown to be constantly conjoined with such an effect, *I see not how, from these principles, it is possible to prove the existence of an intelligent cause of the universe.*

Mr. Hume seems to me to reason justly from his definition of a cause, when, in the person of an Epicurean, he maintains, that with regard to a cause of the universe, we can conclude nothing; because it is a singular effect. We have no experience that such effects are always conjoined with such a cause. Nay, the cause which we assign to this effect, is a cause which no man hath seen, nor can see, and therefore experience cannot inform us that it has ever been conjoined with any effect. He seems to me to reason justly from his definition of a cause, when he maintains, that *any thing* may be the cause of any thing; since priority and constant conjunction is all that can be conceived in the notion of a cause.

Another zealous defender of the doctrine of necessity says, that " a cause cannot be defined to be any thing but *such previous circumstances as are constantly followed by a certain effect,* the *constancy* of the result making us conclude, that there must be a *sufficient reason,* in the nature of things, why it should be produced in those circumstances."

This seems to me to be Mr. Hume's definition of a cause in other words, and neither more nor less; but I am far from thinking that the author of it will admit the consequences which Mr. Hume draws from it, however necessary they may appear to others.

CHAPTER IV.

OF THE INFLUENCE OF MOTIVES.

I. THE modern advocates for the doctrine of necessity lay the stress of their cause upon *the influence of motives.*

" Every deliberate action," they say, " must have a motive. When there is no motive on the other side, this motive must determine the agent: when there are contrary motives, the strongest must prevail: we reason from men's motives to their actions, as we do from other causes to their effects: if man be a free agent, and be not governed by motives, all his actions must be mere caprice, rewards and punishments can have no effect, and such a being must be absolutely ungovernable."

In order therefore to understand distinctly, in what sense we ascribe moral liberty to man, it is necessary to understand *what influence we allow to motives.* To prevent misunderstanding, which has been very common upon this point, I offer the following observations:

1. I grant that all rational beings are influenced, and ought to be influenced by motives. But *the influence of motives is of a very different nature from that of efficient causes.* They are neither causes nor agents. They suppose an efficient cause, and can do nothing without it. We cannot, without absurdity, suppose a motive, either to act, or to be acted upon; it is equally incapable of action and of passion; because it is not a thing that exists, but a thing that is conceived; it is what the schoolmen called an *ens rationis.* Motives, therefore, may *influence* to action, but they do not act. They may be compared to advice, or exhortation, which leaves a man still at liberty. For in vain is advice given when there is not a power either to do, or to forbear, what it recommends. In like manner, motives suppose liberty in the agent, otherwise they have no influence at all.

It is a law of nature, with respect to matter, that every motion and change of motion is proportional to the force impressed, and in the direction of that force. The scheme of necessity supposes a similar law to obtain in all the actions of intelligent beings; which, with little alteration, may be expressed thus: every action, or change of action, in an intelligent being, is proportional to the force of motives impressed, and in the direction of that force.

The law of nature respecting matter is grounded upon this principle—that matter is an inert, inactive substance, which does not act, but is acted upon; and the law of necessity must be grounded upon the supposition, that an intelligent being is an inert, inactive substance, which does not act, but is acted upon.

II. [2. Rational beings, in proportion as they are wise and good, will act according to the best *motives;* and every rational being, who does otherwise, abuses his liberty.] The most perfect being, in every thing where there is a right and a wrong, a better and a worse, always infallibly acts according to the best motives. This indeed is little else than an identical proposition; for it is a contradiction to say, that a perfect being does what is wrong or unreasonable. But to say, that he does not act freely, because he always does what is best, is to say, that the proper use of liberty destroys liberty, and that liberty consists only in its abuse.

The moral perfection of the Deity consists, not in having no power to do ill, otherwise, as Dr. Clarke justly observes, there would be no ground to thank him for his goodness to us any more than for his eternity or immensity; but his moral perfection consists in this, that, when he has power to do every thing, a power which cannot be resisted, he exerts that power only in doing what is wisest and best. *To be subject to necessity is to have no power at all; for power and necessity are opposites.* We grant, therefore, that motives have influence, similar to that of advice or persuasion; but this influence is perfectly consistent with liberty, and indeed supposes liberty.

III. [3. Whether every deliberate action *must have a motive*, depends on the meaning we put upon the word *deliberate*.] If, by a deliberate action, we mean an action wherein motives are weighed, which seems to be the original meaning of the word, surely there must be motives, and contrary motives, otherwise they could not be weighed. But if a deliberate action means only, as it commonly does, an action done by a cool and calm determination of the mind, with forethought and will, I believe there are innumerable such actions done *without a motive*.

This must be appealed to every man's consciousness. I do many trifling actions every day, in which, upon the most careful reflection, I am conscious of no motive; and to say that I may be influenced by a motive of which I am not conscious, is, in the first place, an arbitrary supposition without any evidence, and then, it is to say, that I may be convinced by an argument which never entered into my thought.

Cases frequently occur, in which an end that is of some importance may be answered equally well by any one of several different means. In such cases, a man who intends the end finds not the least difficulty in taking one of these means, though he be firmly persuaded, that it has no title to be preferred to any of the others.

To say that this is a case that cannot happen, is to contradict the experience of mankind; for surely a man who has occasion to lay out a shilling, or a guinea, may have two hundred that are of equal value, both to the giver and to the receiver, any one of which will answer his purpose equally well. To say, that, if such a case should happen, the man could not execute his purpose, is still more ridiculous, though it have the authority of some of the schoolmen, who determined, that the ass, between two equal bundles of hay, would stand still till it died of hunger.

IV. [If *a man could not act without a motive, he would have no power at all;* for motives are not in our power; and he that has not power over a necessary mean, has not power over the end.]

That an action done without any motive can neither have merit nor demerit, is much insisted on by the writers for necessity, and triumphantly, as if it were the very hinge of the controversy. I grant it to be a self-evident proposition, and I know no author that ever denied it.

How insignificant soever, in moral estimation, the actions may be which are done without any motive, they are of moment in the question concerning moral liberty. For, if there ever was any action of this kind, motives are not the *sole* causes of human actions. And if we have the power of acting without a motive, that power, joined to a weaker motive, may counterbalance a stronger.

V. [4. It can never be proved, that when there is a motive *on one side only*, that motive must determine the action.]

According to the laws of reasoning, the proof is incumbent on those who hold the affirmative; and I have never seen a shadow of argument which does not take for granted the thing in question, to wit, *that motives are the sole causes of actions.*

Is there no such thing as wilfulness, caprice, or obstinacy among mankind? If there be not, it is wonderful that they should have names in all languages. If there be such things, a single motive, or even *many motives, may be resisted.*

VI. *Motives of the same kind may be compared.*—[5. When it is said, that *of contrary motives the strongest always prevails*, this can neither be affirmed nor denied with understanding, until we know distinctly what is meant by the *strongest* motive.]

I do not find, that those who have advanced this as a self-evident axiom, have ever attempted to explain what they mean by the strongest motive, or have given any rule by which we may judge which of two motives is the strongest.

How shall we know whether the strongest motive always prevails, if we know not which is strongest? *There must be some test* by which their strength is to be tried, some balance in which they may be weighed, otherwise, to say that the strongest motive always prevails, is to speak without any meaning. We must therefore search for this test or balance, since they who have laid so much stress upon this axiom, have left us wholly in the dark as to its meaning. I grant, that when the contrary motives are of *the same kind*, and differ only in quantity, it may be easy to say which is the strongest. Thus a bribe of a thousand pounds is a stronger motive than a bribe of a hundred pounds. But when the motives are of *different kinds*, as money and fame, duty and worldly interest, health and strength, riches and honour, by what rule shall we judge which is the strongest motive?

Either we measure the strength of motives, merely by their prevalence, or by some other standard distinct from their prevalence.

If we measure their strength merely by their prevalence, and by the strongest motive mean only the motive that prevails, it will be true indeed that the strongest motive prevails; but the proposition will be identical, and mean no more than that the strongest motive is the strongest motive. From this surely no conclusion can be drawn.

[If it should be said, that by the strength of a motive is not meant its prevalence, but *the cause* of its prevalence; that we measure the cause by the effect, and from the superiority of the effect conclude the superiority of the cause, as we conclude that to be the heaviest weight which bears down the scale: I answer, that, according to this explication of the axiom, it takes for granted that *motives are the causes*, and the *sole* causes of actions.] Nothing is left to the agent, but to be acted upon by the motives, as the balance is by the weights. The axiom supposes, that the agent does not act, but is acted upon; and, from this supposition, it is concluded that he does not act. This is to reason in a circle, or rather it is not reasoning but begging the question.

☞ Contrary motives may very properly be compared to advocates pleading the opposite sides of a cause at the bar. It would be very weak reasoning to say, that such an advocate is the most powerful pleader, because sentence was given on his side. The sentence is in the power of the judge, not of the advocate. It is equally weak reasoning, in proof of necessity, to say, such a motive prevailed, therefore it is the strongest; since the defenders of liberty maintain that the determination was made by the man, and not by the motive.

VII. [We are therefore brought to this issue, that unless some measure of the strength of motives can be found distinct from their prevalence, it cannot be determined, whether the strongest motive always prevails or not. If such a measure can be found and applied, we may be able to judge of the truth of this maxim, but not otherwise.]

Every thing that can be called a motive is addressed either to the animal or to the rational part of our nature. Motives of the former kind are common to us with the brutes; those of the latter are peculiar to rational beings. We shall beg leave, for distinction's sake, to call the former, *animal* motives, and the latter, *rational*.

Hunger is a motive in a dog to eat; so is it in a man. According to the strength of the appetite, it gives a stronger or a weaker impulse to eat. And the same thing may be said of every other appetite and passion. Such animal motives give an impulse to the agent, to which he yields with ease; and, if the impulse be strong, it cannot be resisted without an effort which requires a greater or a less degree of self-command. *Such motives are not addressed to the rational powers.* Their influence is immediately upon the will. We feel their influence, and judge of their strength, by the conscious effort which is necessary to resist them.

VIII. *Animal test of the strength of motives.*—When a man is acted upon by contrary motives of this kind, he finds it easy to yield to the strongest. They are like two forces pushing him in contrary directions. To yield to the strongest, he needs only to be passive. By exerting his own force, he may resist; but this requires an effort of which he is conscious. [The strength of motives of this kind is perceived, not by our judgment, but by our *feeling;* and that is the strongest of contrary motives to which he can yield with ease, or which it requires an effort of self-command to resist; and this we may call the *animal test* of the strength of motives.]

If it be asked, whether, in motives of this kind, the strongest always prevails? I answer, That *in brute-animals I believe it does.* They do not appear to have any self-command; an appetite or passion in them is overcome only by a stronger contrary one. On this account, they are not accountable for their actions, nor can they be the subjects of law.

But *in men* who are able to exercise their rational powers, and have any degree of self-command, *the strongest animal motive does not always prevail.* The flesh does not always prevail against the spirit, though too often it does. And if men were necessarily determined by the strongest animal motive, they could no more be accountable, or capable of being governed by law, than brutes are.

IX. *Rational motives defined.*—Let us next consider *rational motives,* to which the name of *motive* is more commonly and more properly given. Their influence is upon the judgment, by *convincing* us that such an action ought to be done, that it is our duty, or conducive to our real good, or to some end which we have determined to pursue.

They do not give a blind impulse to the will as animal motives do. They convince, but they do not impel, unless, as may often happen, they excite some passion of hope, or fear, or desire. Such passions may be excited by conviction, and may operate in its aid as other animal motives do. But there may be conviction without passion; and [the conviction of what we ought to do, in order to some end which we have judged fit to be pursued, is what I call a *rational motive.*]

Brutes, I think, cannot be influenced by such motives. They have not the conception of *ought* and *ought not.* Children acquire these conceptions as their rational powers advance; and they are found in all of ripe age, who have the human faculties.

X. *Rational test of the strength of motives.*—[If there be any *competition* between rational motives, it is evident that the strongest, in the eye of reason, is that which it is most our duty and our real happiness to follow.] Our duty and our real happiness are ends which are inseparable; and they are the ends which every man, endowed with reason, is conscious he ought to pursue in preference to all others. [This we may call the *rational test* of the strength of motives. A motive which is the strongest, according to the *animal test,* may be, and very often is, the weakest according to the *rational.*]

[The grand and the important competition of contrary motives is between the animal, on the one hand, and the rational on the other. This is the *conflict between the flesh and the spirit*, upon the event of which the character of men depends.]

If it be asked, which of these is the strongest motive? The answer is, That the first is commonly strongest, when they are tried by the animal test. If they were not so, human life would be no state of trial. It would not be a warfare, nor would virtue require any effort or self-command. No man would have any temptation to do wrong. But when we try the contrary motives by the rational test, it is evident that the rational motive is always the strongest.

And now, I think, it appears that the *strongest motive*, according to either of the tests I have mentioned, *does not always prevail.*

[*In every wise* and *virtuous action*, the motive that prevails is the strongest, according to the rational test, but commonly the weakest according to the animal. *In every foolish, and* in every *vicious action*, the motive that prevails is commonly the strongest according to the animal test, but always the weakest according to the rational.]

XI. [6. It is true, that *we reason from men's motives to their actions*, and in many cases with great probability, but *never with absolute certainty.* And to infer from this, that men are necessarily determined by motives, is very weak reasoning.]

For, let us suppose, for a moment, that men have moral liberty, I would ask, what use may they be expected to make of this liberty? It may surely be expected that, of the various actions within the sphere of their power, they will choose what pleases them most for the present, or what appears to be most for their real, though distant good. When there is a competition between these motives, the foolish will prefer present gratification; the wise, the greater and more distant good.

Now, is not this the very way in which we see men act? Is it not from the presumption that they act in this way, that we reason from their motives to their actions? Surely it is. Is it not weak reasoning, therefore, to argue, that men have not liberty, because they act in that very way in which they would act if they had liberty? It would surely be more like reasoning, to draw the contrary conclusion from the same premises.

XII. [7. Nor is it better reasoning to conclude, that *if men are not necessarily determined by motives, all their actions must be capricious.*]

To resist the strongest animal motives when duty requires, is so far from being capricious, that it is, in the highest degree, wise and virtuous. And we hope this is often done by good men.

To act against rational motives, must always be foolish, vicious, or capricious. And it cannot be denied that there are too many such actions done. But is it reasonable to conclude, that because liberty may be abused by the foolish and the vicious, therefore it can never be put to its proper use, which is to act wisely and virtuously?

XIII. [8. It is equally unreasonable to conclude, that *if men are not necessarily determined by motives, rewards and punishments would have no effect.* With wise men they will have their due effect; but not always with the foolish and the vicious.]

Let us consider what effect rewards and punishments do really, and in fact, produce, and what may be inferred from that effect, upon each of the opposite systems of liberty and of necessity.

I take it for granted that, in fact, the best and wisest laws, both human and divine, are often transgressed, notwithstanding the rewards and punishments that are annexed to them. If any man should deny this fact, I know not how to reason with him.

From this fact, it may be inferred with certainty, upon the supposition of necessity, that, in every instance of transgression, the motive of reward or punishment was not of sufficient strength to produce obedience to the law. This implies a fault in the lawgiver; but there can be no fault in the transgressor who acts mechanically by the force of motives. ☞ We might as well impute a fault to the balance, when it does not raise a weight of two pounds by the force of one pound.

XIV. *The supposition of necessity precludes rewards and punishments—liberty gives efficacy to both.*—[Upon the supposition of necessity, there can be neither reward nor punishment, in the proper sense, as those words imply good and ill desert.] Reward and punishment are only tools employed to produce a mechanical effect. When the effect is not produced, the tool must be unfit or wrong applied.

Upon the supposition of liberty, rewards and punishments will have a proper effect upon the wise and the good; but not so upon the foolish and the vicious, when opposed by their animal passions or bad habits; and this is just what we see to be the fact. Upon this supposition, the transgression of the law implies no defect in the law, no fault in the lawgiver; the fault is solely in the transgressor. And it is upon this supposition only that there can be either reward or punishment, in the proper sense of the words, because it is only on this supposition that there can be good or ill desert.

CHAPTER V.

LIBERTY CONSISTENT WITH GOVERNMENT.

I. *Mechanical and moral government.*—WHEN it is said that liberty would make us absolutely ungovernable by God or man; to understand the strength of this conclusion, it is necessary to know distinctly what is meant by *government*. There are *two kinds of government,* very different in their nature. The one we may, for distinction's sake, call **mechanical** government, the other *moral.* The first is the government of beings which have no active power, but are merely passive and acted upon; the second, of intelligent and active beings.

☞ An instance of mechanical government may be, That of a master or *commander of a ship* at sea. Supposing her skilfully built, and furnished with every thing proper for the destined voyage, to govern her properly for this purpose requires much art and attention: and, as every art has its rules, or laws, so has this. But by whom are those laws to be obeyed, or those rules observed? not by the ship, surely, for she is an inactive being, but by the governor. A sailor may say that she does not obey the rudder; and he has a distinct meaning when he says so, and is perfectly understood. But he means not obedience in the proper, but in a metaphorical sense: [for, in the proper sense, the ship can no more obey the rudder, than she can give a command. Every motion, both of the ship and rudder, is exactly proportioned to the force impressed, and in the direction of that force. The ship never disobeys the laws of motion, even in the metaphorical sense; and they are the only laws she can be subject to.]

The sailor, perhaps, curses her for not obeying the rudder; but this is not the voice of reason, but of passion, like that of the losing gamester, when he curses the dice. The ship is as innocent as the dice.

Whatever may happen during the voyage, whatever may be its issue, the ship, in the eye of reason, is neither an object of approbation nor of blame; because she does not act, but is acted upon. If the material, in any part, be faulty; Who put it to that use? If the form; Who made it? If the rules of navigation were not observed; Who transgressed them? If a storm occasioned any disaster, it was no more in the power of the ship than of the master.

Another instance to illustrate the nature of mechanical government may be, That of the *man who* makes and *exhibits a puppet-show.* The puppets, in all their diverting gesticulations, do not move, but are moved by an impulse secretly conveyed, which they cannot resist. If they do not play their parts properly, the fault is only in the maker or manager of the machinery. Too much or too little force was applied, or it was wrong directed. No reasonable man imputes either praise or blame to the puppets, but solely to their maker or their governor.

If we suppose for a moment, the puppets to be endowed with understanding and will, but without any degree of active power, this will make no change in the nature of their government: for understanding and will, without some degree of active power, can produce no effect. They might, upon this supposition, be called *intelligent machines;* but they would be machines still, and as much subject to the laws of motion as inanimate matter, and therefore incapable of any other than mechanical government.

II. *Let us next consider the nature of moral government.* This is the government of persons who have reason and active power, and have laws prescribed to them for their conduct, by a legislator. Their obedience is obedience in the proper sense; it must therefore be their own act and deed, and consequently they must have power to obey or to disobey. To prescribe laws to them which they have not power to obey, or to require a service beyond their power, would be tyranny and injustice in the highest degree.

When the laws are equitable, and prescribed by just authority, they produce moral obligation in those that are subject to them, and disobedience is a crime deserving punishment. [But if the obedience be impossible; if the transgression be necessary; it is self-evident, that there can be no moral obligation to what is impossible, that there can be no crime in yielding to necessity, and that there can be no justice in punishing a person for what it was not in his power to avoid. *These are first principles in morals,* and, to every unprejudiced mind, as self-evident as the axioms of mathematics. The whole science of morals must stand or fall with them.]

III. Having thus explained the nature both of mechanical and of moral government, the only kinds of government I am able to conceive, it is easy to see *how far liberty or necessity agrees with either.*

On the one hand, I acknowledge that necessity agrees perfectly with mechanical government. *This kind of government is most perfect when the governor is the sole agent;* every thing done is the doing of the governor only. The praise of every thing well done is his solely; and his is the blame if there be any thing ill done, because he is the sole agent.

It is true that, in common language, praise or dispraise is often metaphorically given to the work; but, in propriety, it belongs solely to the author. Every workman understands this perfectly, and takes to himself very justly the praise or dispraise of his own work.

On the other hand, it is no less evident, that, on the supposition of necessity in the governed, there can be no moral government. There can be neither wisdom nor equity in prescribing laws that cannot be obeyed. There can be no moral obligation upon beings that have no active power. There can be no crime in not doing what it was impossible to do; nor can there be justice in punishing such omission.

[If we apply these *theoretical principles* to the kinds of government which do actually exist, whether human or divine, we shall find that, among men, *even mechanical government is imperfect.*]

Men do not make the matter they work upon. Its various kinds, and the qualities belonging to each kind, are the work of God. The laws of nature, to which it is subject, are the work of God. The motions of the atmosphere and of the sea, the heat and cold of the air, the rain and wind, which are useful instruments in most human operations, are not in our power. So that, in all the mechanical productions of men, the work is more to be ascribed to God than to man.

IV. *Civil government among men is a species of moral government,* but imperfect, as its lawgivers and its judges are. [Human laws may be unwise or unjust; human judges may be partial or unskilful. But in all equitable civil governments, the maxims of moral government above mentioned, are acknowledged as rules which ought never to be violated.] Indeed, the rules of justice are so evident to all men, that the most tyrannical governments profess to be guided by them, and endeavour to palliate what is contrary to them by the plea of necessity.

That a man cannot be under an obligation to what is impossible; that he cannot be criminal in yielding to necessity, nor justly punished for what he could not avoid, are maxims admitted, in all criminal courts, as fundamental rules of justice.

[In opposition to this, it has been said by some of the most able defenders of necessity, That *human laws require no more to constitute a crime,* but that it be *voluntary;* whence it is inferred, that the criminality consists in the determination of the will, whether that determination be free or necessary.] This, I think indeed, is the only possible plea by which criminality can be made consistent with necessity; and therefore it deserves to be considered.

I acknowledge that a crime must be voluntary; for, if it be not voluntary, it is no deed of the man, nor can be justly imputed to him; but it is no less necessary that the criminal have moral liberty. In men that are adult, and of a sound mind, this liberty is presumed. But in every case where it cannot be presumed, no criminality is imputed, even to voluntary actions.

This is evident from the following instances: *First*, The actions of brutes appear to be voluntary; yet they are never conceived to be criminal, though they may be noxious. *Secondly*, Children in nonage act voluntarily, but they are not chargeable with crimes. *Thirdly*, Madmen have both understanding and will, but they have not moral liberty, and therefore are not chargeable with crimes. *Fourthly*, Even in men that are adult, and of a sound mind, a motive that is thought irresistible by any ordinary degree of self-command, such as the rack, or the dread of present death, either exculpates, or very much alleviates a voluntary action, which, in other circumstances, would be highly criminal; whence it is evident, that if the motive were absolutely irresistible, the exculpation would be complete. *So far is it from being true in itself, or agreeable to the common sense of mankind, that the criminality of an action depends solely upon its being voluntary.*

V. [*The government of brutes, so far as they are subject to man, is a species of mechanical government, or something very like to it, and has no resemblance to moral government.*] As inanimate matter is governed by our knowledge of the qualities which God hath given to the various productions of nature, and our knowledge of the laws of nature which he hath established; so brute-animals are governed by our knowledge of the natural instincts, appetites, affections and passions, which God hath given them. By a skilful application of these springs of their actions, they may be trained to many habits useful to man. After all, we find that, from causes unknown to us, not only some species, but some individuals of the same species, are more tractable than others.

Children under age are governed much in the same way as the most sagacious brutes. The opening of their intellectual and moral powers, which may be much aided by proper instruction and example, is that which makes them, by degrees, capable of moral government.

Reason teaches us to ascribe to the Supreme Being a government of the inanimate and inactive part of his creation, analogous to that mechanical government which men exercise, but infinitely more perfect. This, I think, is what we call God's *natural* government of the universe. [In this part of the Divine government, whatever is done is God's doing. He is the *sole cause*, and the *sole agent*, whether he act immediately, or by instruments subordinate to him; and his will is always done: for instruments are not causes, they are not agents, though we sometimes improperly call them so.]

It is therefore no less agreeable to reason, than to the language of Holy Writ, to impute to the Deity whatever is done in the natural world. When we say of anything, that it is the work of nature, this is saying that it is the work of God, and can have no other meaning.

VI. [The natural world is a grand machine, *contrived, made,* and *governed* by the wisdom and power of the Almighty: and if there be in this natural world, beings that have life, intelligence, and will, without any degree of active power, they can only be subject to the same kind of mechanical government.] Their determinations, whether we call them good or ill, must be the actions of the Supreme Being, as much as the productions of the earth: for, life, intelligence, and will, without active power, can do nothing, and therefore nothing can justly be imputed to it.

This grand machine of the natural world, displays the power and wisdom of the artificer. But in it, there can be no display of moral attributes, which have a relation to moral conduct in his creatures, such as justice and equity in rewarding or punishing, the love of virtue and abhorrence of wickedness: for, as every thing in it is God's doing, there can be no vice to be punished or abhorred, no virtue in his creatures to be rewarded.

[*According to the system of necessity,* the whole universe of creatures in this natural world; and of every thing done in it, God is the sole agent. There can be no moral government, *nor moral obligation.* Laws, rewards, and punishments, are only mechanical engines, and the will of the lawgiver is obeyed as much when his laws are transgressed, as when they are observed.] Such must be our notions of the government of the world, upon the supposition of necessity. It must be purely mechanical, and there can be no moral government upon that hypothesis.

VII. *The moral government of God consistent with liberty.*—Let us consider, on the other hand, what notion of the Divine government we are naturally led into *by the supposition of liberty.*

They who adopt this system conceive, that in that small portion of the universe which falls under our view, as a great part has no active power, but moves, as it is moved, by necessity, and therefore must be subject to a mechanical government, so it has pleased the Almighty to bestow upon some of his creatures, particularly upon man, some degree of active power, and of reason, to direct him to the right use of his power.

What connexion there may be, in the nature of things, between reason and active power, we know not. But we see evidently, that, as reason without active power can do nothing, so active power without reason has no guide to direct it to any end.

These two conjoined make moral liberty, which, in how small a degree soever it is possessed, raises man to a superior rank in the creation of God. He is not merely a tool in the hand of the master, but a servant, in the proper sense, who has a certain trust, and is accountable for the discharge of it. Within the sphere of his power, he has a subordinate dominion or government, and therefore may be said to be made after *the* image of God, the Supreme Governor. But [as his dominion is subordinate, he is under a moral obligation to make a right use of it, as far as the reason which God hath given him can direct him.] When he does so, he is a just object of moral approbation; and no less an object of disapprobation and just punishment when he abuses the power with which he is intrusted. And he must finally render an account of the talent committed to him, to the Supreme Governor and righteous Judge.

[This is the moral government of God, which, far from being inconsistent with liberty, *supposes liberty* in those that are subject to it, and can extend no farther than that liberty extends; for accountableness can no more agree with necessity than light with darkness.]

VIII. [It ought likewise to be observed, that as *active power in man*, and in every created being, *is the gift of God*, it depends entirely on his pleasure for its existence, its degree and its continuance, and *therefore can do nothing which he does not see fit to permit.*]

Our power to act does not exempt us from being acted upon, and restrained or compelled by a superior power; and the power of God is always superior to that of man.

It would be great folly and presumption in us to pretend to know all the ways in which the government of the Supreme Being is carried on, and his purposes accomplished by men, acting freely and having different or opposite purposes in their view. For, as the heavens are high above the earth, so are his thoughts above our thoughts, and his ways above our ways.

That a man may have great influence upon the voluntary determinations of other men, by means of education, example, and persuasion, is a fact which must be granted, whether we adopt the system of liberty or necessity. How far such determinations ought to be imputed to the person who applied those means, how far to the person influenced by them, we know not, but God knows, and will judge righteously.

But what I would here observe, is, that if a man of superior talents may have so great influence over the actions of his fellow-creatures, without taking away their liberty, it is surely reasonable to allow a much greater influence of the same kind to him who made man. Nor can it ever be proved, that the wisdom and power of the Almighty are insufficient for governing free agents, so as to answer his purposes.

[He who *made* man may have *ways of governing* his determinations, consistent with moral liberty, *of which we have no con-*

ception. And he who gave this liberty *freely*, may lay any restraint upon it that is necessary for answering his wise and benevolent purposes.] The justice of his government requires that his creatures should be accountable only for what they have received, and not for what was never intrusted to them. And we are sure that the Judge of all the earth will do what is right.

[Thus, I think, it appears that, *upon the supposition of necessity, there can be no moral government of the universe.* Its government must be perfectly mechanical, and every thing done in it, whether good or ill, must be God's doing; and that, *upon the supposition of liberty, there may be a perfect moral government of the universe,* consistent with his accomplishing all his purposes, in its creation and government.]

The arguments to prove that man is endowed with moral liberty, which have the greatest weight with me, are three: *First,* Because he has a natural conviction or belief, that, in many cases, he acts freely; *secondly,* Because he is accountable; and, *thirdly,* Because he is able to prosecute an end by a long series of means adapted to it.

CHAPTER VI.

FIRST ARGUMENT.

I. *We have,* by our constitution, *a natural conviction or belief that we act freely:* a conviction so early, so universal, and so necessary in most of our rational operations, that it must be the result of our constitution, and the work of Him that made us.

Some of the most strenuous advocates for the doctrine of necessity acknowledge that it is impossible to act upon it. They say that we have a natural sense or conviction that we act freely, but that this is a fallacious sense.

[This doctrine is dishonourable to our Maker, and lays a foundation for universal scepticism. It supposes the Author of our being to have given us one faculty on purpose to deceive us, and another by which we may detect the fallacy, and find that he imposed upon us.]*

If any one of our natural faculties be fallacious, there can be no reason to trust to any of them; for he that made one made all.

The genuine dictate of our natural faculties is the voice of God, no less than what he reveals from heaven; and to say that it is fallacious, is to impute a lie to the God of truth.

* Vide Essay III. chap. vi. sect. 5; "The Intellectual Powers," Essay II. chap. xxii. sect. 3; and Essay VII. chap. xxii. sect. 11.

If candour and veracity be not an essential part of moral excellence, there is no such thing as moral excellence, nor any reason to rely on the declarations and promises of the Almighty. A man may be tempted to lie, but not without being conscious of guilt and of meanness. Shall we impute to the Almighty what we cannot impute to a man without a heinous affront?

II. Passing this opinion, therefore, as shocking to an ingenuous mind, and, in its consequences, subversive of all religion, all morals and all knowledge, let us proceed to consider *the evidence of our having a natural conviction that we have some degree of active power*.

The very conception or idea of active power must be derived from something in our own constitution. It is impossible to account for it otherwise. We see events, but we see not the power that produces them. We perceive one event to follow another, but we perceive not the chain that binds them together. The notion of power and causation, therefore, cannot be got from external objects.

Yet the notion of causes, and the belief that every event must have a cause which had power to produce it, is found in every human mind so firmly established, that it cannot be rooted out.

This notion and this belief must have its origin from something in our constitution; and that it is natural to man, appears from the following observations.

[1. We are conscious of many *voluntary* exertions, some easy, others more difficult, some requiring a great effort. *These are exertions of power*.] And though a man may be unconscious of his power when he does not exert it, he must have both the conception and the belief of it, when he knowingly and willingly exerts it, with intention to produce some effect.

[2. *Deliberation* about an action of moment, whether we shall do it or not, *implies a conviction that it is in our power*.] To deliberate about an end, we must be convinced that the means are in our power; and to deliberate about the means, we must be convinced that we have power to choose the most proper.

[3. *Suppose* our deliberation brought to an issue, and that *we resolve to do what appeared proper*, can we form such a resolution or purpose, *without any conviction of power* to execute it? No; it is impossible.] A man cannot resolve to lay out a sum of money, which he neither has, nor hopes ever to have.

[4. Again, when I plight my faith in any promise or contract, *I must believe that I shall have power to perform what I promise*.] Without this persuasion, a promise would be downright fraud.

There is a condition implied in every promise, *if we live*, and *if* God *continue with us the power which he hath given us*. Our conviction, therefore, of this power, derogates not in the least from our dependence upon God. The rudest savage is taught by nature to admit this condition in all promises, whether it be expressed or not. For it is a dictate of common sense, that we can be under no obligation to do what it is impossible for us to do.

If we act upon the *system of necessity*, there must be another condition implied in all deliberation, in every resolution, and in every promise, and that is, *if we shall be willing*. But the will not being in our power, we cannot engage for it.

If this condition be understood, as it must be understood if we act upon the system of necessity, there can be no deliberation or resolution, nor any obligation in a promise. A man might as well deliberate, resolve, and promise, upon the actions of other men as upon his own.

It is no less evident, that we have a conviction of power in other men, when we advise, or persuade, or command, or conceive them to be under obligation by their promises.

[5. *Is it possible for any man to blame himself for yielding to necessity?* Then he may blame himself for dying, or for being a man.] Blame supposes a wrong use of power; and when a man does as well as it was possible for him to do, wherein is he to be blamed? Therefore all conviction of wrong conduct, all remorse and self-condemnation, imply *a conviction of our power* to have done better. Take away this conviction, and there may be a sense of misery, or a dread of evil to come, but there can be no sense of guilt, or resolution to do better.

Many who hold the doctrine of necessity, disown these consequences of it, and think to evade them. To such they ought not to be imputed; but their inseparable connexion with that doctrine appears self-evident: and therefore some late patrons of it have had the boldness to avow them. " They cannot accuse themselves of having done anything wrong in the ultimate sense of the words. In a strict sense, they have nothing to do with repentance, confession, and pardon, these being adapted to a fallacious view of things."

Those who can adopt these sentiments, may indeed celebrate, with high encomiums, *the great and glorious doctrine of necessity*. It restores them, in their own conceit, to the state of innocence. It delivers them from all the pangs of guilt and remorse, and from all fear about their future conduct, though not about their fate. They may be as secure that they shall do nothing wrong, as those who have finished their course. A doctrine so flattering to the mind of a sinner, is very apt to give strength to weak arguments.

After all, it is acknowledged by those who boast of this glorious doctrine, "That every man, let him use what efforts he can, will necessarily feel the sentiments of shame, remorse, and repentance, and, oppressed with a sense of guilt, will have recourse to that mercy of which he stands in need."

The meaning of this seems to me to be, that although the doctrine of necessity be supported by invincible arguments, and though it be the most *consolatory* doctrine in the world; yet no man, in his most serious moments, when he sifts himself before the throne of his Maker, can possibly believe it, but must then necessarily lay aside this glorious doctrine, and all its flattering consequences, and return to the humiliating conviction of his having made a bad use of the power which God had given him.

III. [*The belief of acting freely is coeval with our reason, universal, and necessary.*—If the belief of our having active power be necessarily implied in those rational operations we have mentioned, it must be *coeval with our reason;* it must be as *universal* among men, and as *necessary* in the conduct of life as those operations are.]

We cannot recollect by memory when it began. It cannot be a prejudice of education, or of false philosophy. It must be a part of our constitution, or the necessary result of our constitution, and therefore the work of God.

It resembles, in this respect, our belief of the existence of a material world; our belief that those we converse with are living and intelligent beings; our belief that those things did really happen which we distinctly remember, and our belief that we continue the same identical persons.

We find difficulty in accounting for our belief of these things; and some philosophers think that they have discovered good reasons for throwing it off. But it sticks fast, and the greatest sceptic finds, that he must yield to it in his practice, while he wages war with it in speculation.

IV. [If it be *objected to this argument*, that the belief of our acting freely cannot be implied in the operations we have mentioned, because *those operations are performed by them who believe that we are*, in all our actions, *governed by necessity*. The answer to this objection is, that men in their *practice* may be governed by a belief which in speculation they reject.]

However strange and unaccountable this may appear, there are many well known instances of it.

☞ I knew a man who was as much convinced as any man of the folly of the popular belief of apparitions in the dark, yet he could not sleep in a room alone, nor go alone into a room in the dark. Can it be said, that his fear did not imply a belief of danger? This is impossible. Yet his philosophy convinced him, that he was in no more danger in the dark when alone, than with company.

Here an unreasonable belief, which was merely a prejudice of the nursery, stuck so fast as to govern his conduct, in opposition to his speculative belief as a philosopher and a man of sense.

There are few persons who can look down from the battlement of a very high tower without fear, while their reason convinces them that they are in no more danger than when standing upon the ground.

There have been persons who professed to believe that there is no distinction between virtue and vice, yet in their practice they resented injuries, and esteemed noble and virtuous actions.

There have been sceptics who professed to disbelieve their senses, and every human faculty; but no sceptic was ever known, who did not, in practice, pay a regard to his senses and to his other faculties.*

There are some points of belief so necessary, that, without them, a man would not be the being which God made him. These may be opposed in speculation, but it is impossible to root them out. In a speculative hour they seem to vanish, but in practice they resume their authority. This seems to be the case of those who hold the doctrine of necessity, and yet act as if they were free.

[This natural conviction of some degree of power in ourselves and in other men, respects *voluntary actions only*. For, as all our power is directed by our will, we can form no conception of power, properly so called, that is not under the direction of will. And therefore our exertions, our deliberations, our purposes, our promises, are only in things that depend upon our will.] Our advices, exhortations, and commands, are only in things that depend upon the will of those to whom they are addressed. We impute no guilt to ourselves, nor to others, in things where the will is not concerned.

V. *Exceptions.*—But it deserves our notice, that we do not conceive every thing, without exception, to be in a man's power which depends upon his will. There are *many exceptions* to this general rule. The most obvious of these I shall mention, because they both serve to illustrate the rule, and are of importance in the question concerning the liberty of man.

[(1) In the rage of *madness*, men are absolutely deprived of the power of self-government. They act voluntarily, but their will is driven as by a tempest, which, in lucid intervals, they resolve to oppose with all their might, but are overcome when the fit of madness returns.]

[(2) *Idiots* are like men walking in the dark, who cannot be said to have the power of choosing their way, because they cannot distinguish the good road from the bad.] Having no light in their understanding, they must either sit still, or be carried on by some blind impulse.

* Vide "The Intellectual Powers of Man," Essay VII. chap. iv. sec. 12.

[(3) Between the *darkness of infancy*, which is equal to that of idiots, and the maturity of reason, there is a long twilight, which, by insensible degrees, advances to the perfect day.

In this period of life, man has but little of the power of self-government.] His actions, by nature, as well as by the laws of society, are in the power of others more than in his own. His folly and indiscretion, his levity and inconstancy, are considered as the fault of youth, rather than of the man. We consider him as half a man and half a child, and expect that each by turns should play its part. He would be thought a severe and unequitable censor of manners, who required the same cool deliberation, the same steady conduct, and the same mastery over himself in a boy of thirteen, as in a man of thirty.

[(4) It is an old adage, that *violent anger is a short fit of madness*. If this be literally true in any case, a man, in such a fit of passion, cannot be said to have the command of himself.] If real madness could be proved, it must have the effect of madness while it lasts, whether it be for an hour or for life. But the madness of a short fit of passion, if it be really madness, is incapable of proof; and therefore is not admitted in human tribunals as an exculpation. And, I believe, there is no case where a man can satisfy his own mind that his passion, both in its beginning and in its progress, was irresistible. The Searcher of hearts alone knows infallibly what allowance is due in cases of this kind.

[But *a violent passion*, though it may not be irresistible, is difficult to be resisted: and a man, surely, has not the same power over himself in passion as when he is cool. On this account it *is allowed* by all men *to alleviate*, when it cannot exculpate; and has its weight in criminal courts, as well as in private judgment.]

It ought likewise to be observed, that he who has accustomed himself to restrain his passions, enlarges by habit his power over them, and consequently over himself. When we consider that a Canadian savage can acquire the power of defying death, in its most dreadful forms, and of braving the most exquisite torment for many long hours, without losing the command of himself;* we may learn from this, that, in the constitution of human nature, there is ample scope for the enlargement of that power of self-command, without which there can be no virtue nor magnanimity.

[(5) There are cases, however, in which a man's voluntary actions are thought to be very little, if at all, in his power, on account of the violence of the motive that impels him. The magnanimity of *a hero*, or of *a martyr*, is not expected in every man, and on all occasions.]

* Vide note to page 175.

☞ If a man trusted by the government with a secret, which it is high treason to disclose, be prevailed upon by a bribe, we have no mercy for him, and hardly allow the greatest bribe to be any alleviation of his crime.

But, on the other hand, if the secret be extorted by the rack, or by the dread of present death, we pity him more than we blame him, and would think it severe and unequitable to condemn him as a traitor.

What is the reason that all men agree in condemning this man as a traitor in the first case, and in the last, either exculpate him, or think his fault greatly alleviated? If he acted necessarily in both cases, compelled by an irresistible motive, I can see no reason why we should not pass the same judgment on both.

But the reason of these different judgments is evidently this, that the love of money, and of what is called a man's interest, is a cool motive, which leaves to a man the entire power over himself: but the torment of the rack, or the dread of present death, are so violent motives, that men, who have not uncommon strength of mind, are not masters of themselves in such a situation, and therefore what they do is not imputed, or is thought less criminal.

If a man resist such motives, we admire his fortitude, and think his conduct heroical rather than human. If he yields, we impute it to human frailty, and think him rather to be pitied than severely censured.

[(6) *Inveterate habits* are acknowledged to diminish very considerably the power a man has over himself. Although we may think him highly blameable in acquiring them, yet, when they are confirmed to a certain degree, we consider him as *no longer master of himself*, and hardly reclaimable without a miracle.]

VI. [Thus we see, that *the power which we* are led, by common sense, to *ascribe to man, respects his voluntary actions only*, and that it has various limitations even with regard to them.] Some actions that depend upon our will are easy, others very difficult, and some, perhaps, beyond our power. In different men, the power of self-government is different, and in the same man at different times. It may be diminished, or perhaps lost, by bad habits; it may be greatly increased by good habits.

These are facts attested by experience, and supported by the common judgment of mankind. Upon the system of liberty, they are perfectly intelligible; but, I think, irreconcilable to that of necessity; for, how can there be an easy and a difficult in actions equally subject to necessity? or, how can power be greater or less, increased or diminished, in those who have no power?

This natural conviction of our acting freely, which is acknowledged by many who hold the doctrine of necessity, ought to throw the whole burden of proof upon that side: for, by this, the side of liberty has what lawyers call a *jus quæsitum*, or a right of ancient possession, which ought to stand good till it be overturned. If it cannot be proved that we always act from necessity, there is no need of arguments on the other side, to convince us that we are free agents.

To illustrate this by a similar case: If a philosopher would persuade me, that my fellow-men with whom I converse, are not thinking intelligent beings, but mere machines, though I might be at a loss to find arguments against this strange opinion, I should think it reasonable to hold the belief which nature gave me before I was capable of weighing evidence, until convincing proof is brought against it.

CHAPTER VII.

SECOND ARGUMENT.

1. *Certain first principles universally conceded.*—THAT there is a real and essential distinction between right and wrong conduct, between just and unjust; that the most perfect moral rectitude is to be ascribed to the Deity; that man is a moral and accountable being, capable of acting right and wrong, and answerable for his conduct to him who made him, and assigned him a part to act upon the stage of life; are principles proclaimed by every man's conscience; principles upon which the systems of morality and natural religion, as well as the system of revelation, are grounded, and which have been generally acknowledged by those who hold contrary opinions on the subject of human liberty. I shall therefore here take them for granted.

These principles afford an obvious, and, I think, an invincible argument, that man is endowed with moral liberty.

[Two things are implied in the notion of a moral and accountable being; *understanding* and *active power*.]

First. He must understand the law to which he is bound, and his obligation to obey it. Moral obedience must be voluntary, and must regard the authority of the law. I may command my horse to eat when he hungers, and drink when he thirsts. He does so; but his doing it is no moral obedience. He does not understand my command, and therefore can have no will to obey it. He has not the conception of moral obligation, and therefore cannot act from the conviction of it. In eating and drinking he is moved by his own appetite only, and not by my authority.

Brute animals are incapable of moral obligation, because they have not that degree of understanding which it implies. They have not the conception of a rule of conduct, and of obligation to obey it, and therefore, though they may be noxious, they cannot be criminal.

Man, by his rational nature, is capable both of understanding the law that is prescribed to him, and of perceiving its obligation. He knows what it is to be just and honest, to injure no man, and to obey his Maker. From his constitution, he has an immediate conviction of his obligation to these things. He has the approbation of his conscience when he acts by these rules; and he is conscious of guilt and demerit when he transgresses them. And, without this knowledge of his duty and his obligation, he would not be a moral and accountable being.

Secondly. Another thing implied in the notion of a moral and accountable being, is *power to do what he is accountable for*.

That no man can be under a moral obligation to do what it is impossible for him to do, or to forbear what is impossible for him to forbear, is an axiom as self-evident as any in mathematics. It cannot be contradicted without overturning all notion of moral obligation; nor can there be any exception to it, when it is rightly understood.

Some moralists have mentioned what they conceive to be an *exception* to this maxim. The exception is this: [When a man, by his own fault, has disabled himself from doing his duty, his obligation, they say, remains, though he is now unable to discharge it. Thus, if a man by sumptuous living has become *bankrupt*, his inability to pay his debt does not take away his obligation.]

To judge whether, in this and similar cases, there be any exception to the axiom above mentioned, they must be stated accurately.

No doubt a man is highly criminal in living above his fortune, and his crime is greatly aggravated by the circumstance of his being thereby unable to pay his just debt. Let us suppose, therefore, that he is punished for this crime as much as it deserves; that his goods are fairly distributed among his creditors, and that one half remains unpaid: let us suppose also, that he adds no new crime to what is past, that he becomes a new man, and not only supports himself by honest industry, but does all in his power to pay what he still owes.

I would now ask, Is he further punishable and really guilty for not paying more than he is able? Let every man consult his conscience, and say whether he can blame this man for not doing more than he is able to do. His guilt before his bankruptcy is out of the question, as he has received the punishment due for it. But that his subsequent conduct is unblameable, every man must allow; and that, in his present state, he is accountable for no more than he is able to do. *His obligation is not cancelled, it returns with his ability,* and can go no farther.

☞ Suppose *a sailor,* employed in the navy of his country, and longing for the ease of a public hospital as an invalid, to cut off his fingers, so as to disable him from doing the duty of a sailor; he is guilty of a great crime; but, after he has been punished according to the demerit of his crime, will his captain insist that he shall still do the duty of a sailor? Will he command him to go aloft when it is impossible for him to do it, and punish him as guilty of disobedience? Surely if there be any such thing as justice and injustice, this would be unjust and wanton cruelty.

☞ Suppose *a servant,* through negligence and inattention, mistakes the orders given him by his master, and, from this mistake, does what he was ordered not to do. It is commonly said that culpable ignorance does not excuse a fault: this decision is inaccurate, because it does not show where the fault lies: the fault was solely in that inattention, or negligence, which was the occasion of his mistake: there was no subsequent fault.

This becomes evident, when we vary the case so far as to suppose that he was unavoidably led into the mistake without any fault on his part. His mistake is now invincible, and, in the opinion of all moralists, takes away all blame; yet this new case supposes no change, but in the cause of his mistake. His subsequent conduct was the same in both cases. The fault, therefore, lay solely in the negligence and inattention which was the cause of his mistake.

[The axiom, that "Invincible ignorance takes away all blame," is only a particular case of the general axiom, "That there can be no moral obligation to what is impossible;" the former is grounded upon the latter, and can have no other foundation.]

☞ I shall put only one case more. Suppose that *a man,* by excess and intemperance, *has entirely destroyed his rational faculties,* so as to have become perfectly mad or idiotical; suppose him forewarned of his danger, and that though he foresaw that this must be the consequence, he went on still in his criminal indulgence. A greater crime can hardly be supposed, or more deserving of severe punishment. Suppose him punished as he deserves; will it be said, that the duty of a man is incumbent upon him now, when he has not the faculties of a man, or that he incurs new guilt when he is not a moral agent? Surely we may as well suppose a plant, or a clod of earth, to be a subject of moral duty.

The decisions I have given of these cases, are grounded upon the fundamental principles of morals, the most immediate dictates of conscience. If these principles are given up, all moral reasoning is at an end, and no distinction is left between what is just and what is unjust. And it is evident, that [none of these cases* furnishes any exception to the axiom above mentioned. No moral obligation can be consistent with impossibility in the performance.]

II. [*Active power*, therefore, *is necessarily implied in the very notion of a moral accountable being.* And if man be such a being, he must have a degree of active power proportioned to the account he is to make.] He may have a model of perfection set before him which he is unable to reach; but, if he does to the utmost of his power, this is all he can be answerable for. To incur guilt by not going beyond his power is impossible.

What was said, in the first argument,† of the limitation of our power, adds much strength to the present argument. A man's power, it was observed, extends only to his voluntary actions, and has many limitations, even with respect to them.

His accountableness has the same extent and the same limitations.

In the rage of madness he has no power over himself, neither is he accountable, or capable of moral obligation. In ripe age man is accountable, in a greater degree than in non-age, because his power over himself is greater. Violent passions, and violent motives alleviate what is done through their influence, in the same proportion as they diminish the power of resistance.

There is, therefore, a perfect correspondence between power, on the one hand, and moral obligation and accountableness, on the other. They not only correspond in general, as they respect voluntary actions only, but every limitation of the first produces a corresponding limitation of the two last. This, indeed, amounts to nothing more than that maxim of common sense confirmed by Divine authority, That to whom much is given, of him much will be required.

III. [*The sum of this argument* is, (1) That a certain degree of active power is the talent which God hath given to every rational accountable creature, and of which he will require an account. (2) If man had no power, he would have nothing to account for. (3) All wise and all foolish conduct, all virtue and vice, consist in the right use or in the abuse of that power which God hath given us. If man had no power, he could neither be wise nor foolish, virtuous nor vicious.]

If we adopt the system of necessity, the terms *moral obligation* and *accountableness*, *praise* and *blame*, *merit* and *demerit*, *justice* and *injustice*, *reward* and *punishment*, *wisdom* and *folly*, *virtue*

* The bankrupt, sailor, servant, and spendthrift.
† Vide preceding chapter, sec. 5, et seq.

and *vice*, ought to be disused, or to have new meanings given to them when they are used in religion, in morals, or in civil government; for upon that system, there can be no such things as they have been always used to signify.

CHAPTER VIII.

THIRD ARGUMENT.

I. THAT *man has power over his own actions and volitions* appears, because he is capable of carrying on, wisely and prudently, a system of conduct, which he has before conceived in his mind, and resolved to prosecute.

I take it for granted, that, among the various characters of men, there have been some, who, after they came to years of understanding, deliberately laid down a plan of conduct, which they resolved to pursue through life; and that of these, some have steadily pursued the end they had in view, by the proper means.

It is of no consequence in this argument, whether one has made the best choice of his main end or not; whether his end be riches, or power, or fame, or the approbation of his Maker. I suppose only, that he has prudently and steadily pursued it; that, in a long course of deliberate actions, he has taken the means that appeared most conducive to his end, and avoided whatever might cross it.

That such conduct in a man demonstrates a certain degree of wisdom and understanding, no man ever doubted; and, I say, it demonstrates, with equal force, a certain degree of power over his voluntary determinations.

This will appear evident, if we consider, that [understanding without power may project, but can execute nothing. A regular plan of conduct, as it cannot be contrived without understanding, so it cannot be carried into execution without power; and, therefore, the *execution*, as an effect, *demonstrates*, with equal force, *both power and understanding* in the cause.] Every indication of wisdom, taken from the effect, is equally an indication of power to execute what wisdom planned. And, if we have any evidence, that the wisdom which formed the plan is in the man, we have the very same evidence, that the power which executed it is in him also.

II. *Argument from analogy.*—In this argument, we reason from the same principles, as in demonstrating the being and perfections of the First Cause of all things.

The effects we observe in the course of nature require a cause.

Effects wisely adapted to an end, require a wise cause. Every indication of the wisdom of the Creator is equally an indication of his power. His wisdom appears only in the works done by his power; for wisdom without power may speculate, but it cannot act: it may plan, but it cannot execute its plans.

The same reasoning we apply to the works of men. ☞ In a stately palace we see the wisdom of the architect. His wisdom contrived it, and wisdom could do no more. The execution required, both a distinct conception of the plan, and power to operate according to that plan.

III. *Its application.*—Let us apply these principles to the supposition we have made, That a man, in a long course of conduct, has determined and acted prudently in the prosecution of a certain end. If the man had both the wisdom to plan this course of conduct, and that power over his own actions that was necessary to carry it into execution, he is a free agent, and used his liberty, in this instance, with understanding.

But if all his particular determinations, which concurred in the execution of this plan, were produced, not by himself, but by some cause acting necessarily upon him, then there is no evidence left that he contrived this plan, or that he ever spent a thought about it.

[The cause that directed all these determinations so wisely, whatever it was, must be *a wise and intelligent cause;* it must have understood the plan, and have intended the execution of it.]

IV. *Objection and answer.*—[If it be said, that all *this course of determinations was produced by motives;* motives surely have not understanding to conceive a plan, and intend its execution. We must therefore go back beyond motives to some intelligent being who had the power of arranging those motives, and applying them, in their proper order and season, so as to bring about the end.]

This intelligent being must have understood the plan, and intended to execute it. If this be so, as the man had no hand in the execution, we have not any evidence left, that he had any hand in the contrivance, or even that he is a thinking being.

If we can believe, that an extensive series of means may conspire to promote an end without a cause that intended the end, and had power to choose and apply those means for the purpose, we may as well believe, that this world was made by a fortuitous concourse of atoms, without an intelligent and powerful cause.

☞ If a lucky concourse of motives could produce the conduct of an Alexander or a Julius Cæsar, no reason can be given why a lucky concourse of atoms might not produce the planetary system.

If, therefore, wise conduct in a man demonstrates that he has *some degree of wisdom*, it demonstrates, with equal force and evidence, that he has *some degree of power* over his own determinations.

All the reason we can assign for believing that our fellow-men think and reason, is grounded upon their actions and speeches. If they are not the cause of these, there is no reason left to conclude that they think and reason.

Des Cartes thought that the human body is merely a mechanical engine, and that all its motions and actions are produced by mechanism. If such a machine could be made to speak and to act rationally, we might indeed conclude with certainty, that the maker of it had both reason and active power; but if we once knew, that all the motions of the machine were purely mechanical, we should have no reason to conclude that the man had reason or thought.

[The conclusion of this argument is, That, if the actions and speeches of other men give us sufficient evidence that they are reasonable beings, they give us *the same evidence*, and the same degree of evidence, *that they are free agents.*]

V. There is *another conclusion* that *may be drawn from this reasoning*, which it is proper to mention.

Suppose *a fatalist*, rather than give up the scheme of necessity, should acknowledge that he has no evidence that there is thought and reason in any of his fellow-men, and that they may be mechanical engines for all that he knows; he will be forced to acknowledge, that there must be active power, as well as understanding, in the maker of those engines, and that the First Cause is a free agent. We have the same reason to believe this, as to believe his existence and his wisdom. [And *if the Deity acts freely*, every argument brought to prove that freedom of action is impossible, must fall to the ground.]

The First Cause gives us evidence of his power by every effect that gives us evidence of his wisdom. And, if he is pleased to communicate to the work of his hands some degree of his wisdom, no reason can be assigned why he may not communicate some degree of his power, as the talent which wisdom is to employ.

That the first motion, or the first effect, whatever it be, cannot be produced necessarily, and, consequently, that the First Cause must be a free agent, has been demonstrated so clearly and unanswerably by Dr. Clarke, both in his "Demonstration of the Being and Attributes of God," and in the end of his Remarks on Collins's "Philosophical Inquiry concerning Human Liberty," that I can add nothing to what he has said; nor have I found any objection made to his reasoning, by any of the defenders of necessity.

CHAPTER IX.

OF ARGUMENTS FOR NECESSITY.

I. *Three classes of arguments against human liberty.*—SOME of the arguments that have been offered for necessity were already considered in this Essay.

It has been said, That human liberty respects only the actions that are subsequent to volition; and that power over the determinations of the will is inconceivable, and involves a contradiction. This argument was considered in the first chapter.

It has been said, That liberty is inconsistent with the influence of motives, that it would make human actions capricious, and man ungovernable by God or man. These arguments were considered in the fourth and fifth chapters.

[I am now to make some remarks upon other arguments that have been urged in this cause. They may, I think, be reduced to three classes. They are intended to prove, either (1) that liberty of determination is impossible, or (2) that it would be hurtful, or (3) that, in fact, man has no such liberty.]

To prove that liberty of determination is impossible, it has been said, That there must be a sufficient reason for every thing. *For every existence, for every event, for every truth, there must be a sufficient reason.*

II. *Boast of Leibnitz.*—The famous German Philosopher Leibnitz boasted much of having first applied this principle to philosophy, and of having, by that means, *changed metaphysics from being a play of unmeaning words, to be a rational and demonstrative science.* On this account it deserves to be considered.

A very obvious objection to this principle was, That two or more means may be equally fit for the same end; and that, in such a case, there may be a sufficient reason for taking one of the number, though there be no reason for preferring one to another, of means equally fit.

To obviate this objection, Leibnitz maintained, that the case supposed could not happen; or, if it did, that none of the means could be used, for want of a sufficient reason to prefer one to the rest. Therefore he determined, with some of the schoolmen, That if an ass could be placed between two bundles of hay, or two fields of grass, equally inviting, the poor beast would certainly stand still and starve; but the case, he says, could not happen without a miracle.

When it was objected to this principle, That there could be no reason but the will of God why the material world was placed in one part of unlimited space rather than another, or created at one point of unlimited duration rather than another, or why the planets should move from west to east, rather than in a contrary direction; these objections Leibnitz obviated by maintaining, That there is no such thing as unoccupied space or duration; that space is nothing but the order of things co-existing, and duration is nothing but the order of things successive; that all motion is relative, so that if there were only one body in the universe, it would be immoveable; that it is inconsistent with the perfection of the Deity, that there should be any part of space unoccupied by body; and, I suppose, he understood the same of every part of duration. So that, according to this system, the world, like its Author, must be infinite, eternal, and immoveable; or, at least, as great in extent and duration as it is possible for it to be.

III. *Identity of indiscernibles.*—When it was objected to the principle of a sufficient reason, *That of two particles of matter perfectly similar*, there can be no reason but the will of God for placing *this* here and *that* there; this objection Leibnitz obviated by maintaining, That it is impossible that there can be two particles of matter, or any two things, perfectly similar. And this seems to have led him to another of his grand principles, which he calls, *The identity of indiscernibles.*

When the principle of a sufficient reason had produced so many surprising discoveries in philosophy, it is no wonder that it should determine the long disputed question about human liberty. This it does in a moment. [The determination of the will is an event for which there must be a sufficient reason, that is, something previous, which was necessarily followed by that determination, and could not be followed by any other determination; therefore it was necessary.]

Thus we see, that this principle of the necessity of a sufficient reason for every thing, is very fruitful of consequences; and by its fruits we may judge of it. Those who will adopt it, must adopt all the consequences that hang upon it. To fix them all beyond dispute, no more is necessary but to prove the truth of the principle on which they depend.

IV. *Leibnitz' proof of the truth of his principle only a petitio principii.*—I know of no argument offered by Leibnitz in proof of this principle, but the authority of Archimedes, who, he says, makes use of it to prove, that a balance loaded with equal weights on both ends will continue at rest.

I grant it to be good reasoning with regard to a balance, or with regard to any machine, That, when there is no external cause of its motion, it must remain at rest, because the machine has no power of moving itself. But to apply this reasoning to a man, is to take for granted that the man is a machine, which is *the very point in question.*

Leibnitz, and his followers, would have us to take this principle of the necessity of a sufficient reason for every existence, for every event, for every truth, *as a first principle*, without proof, without explanation; though it be evidently a vague proposition, capable of various meanings, as the word *reason* is. It must have different meanings when applied to things of so different nature as an event and a truth; and it may have different meanings when applied to the same thing. We cannot therefore form a distinct judgment of it in the gross, but only by taking it to pieces, and applying it to different things, in a precise and distinct meaning.

V. *Three meanings of the principle of "a sufficient reason" applied to the determinations of the will.*—It can have no connexion with the dispute about liberty, except when it is applied to the determinations of the will. Let us therefore suppose a voluntary action of a man; and that the question is put, Whether was there a sufficient reason for this action or not?

The natural and obvious meaning of this question is, (1) *Was there a motive to the action* sufficient to justify it to be wise and good, or, at least, innocent? Surely, in this sense, there is not a sufficient reason for every human action, because there are many that are foolish, unreasonable and unjustifiable.

If the meaning of the question be, (2) *Was there a cause of the action?* Undoubtedly there was: of every event there must be a cause, that had power sufficient to produce it, and that exerted that power for the purpose. In the present case, either the man was the cause of the action, and then it was a free action, and is justly imputed to him; or it must have had another cause, and cannot justly be imputed to the man. In this sense, therefore, it is granted that there was a sufficient reason for the action; but the question about liberty is not in the least affected by this concession.

If, again, the meaning of the question be, (3) *Was there something previous to the action*, which made it to be necessarily produced? Every man, who believes that the action was free, will answer to this question in the negative.

[I know no other meaning that can be put upon the principle of a sufficient reason, when applied to the determinations of the human will, besides the three I have mentioned. In the first, it is evidently *false;* in the second, it is true, but *does not affect the question* about liberty; in the third, it is *a mere assertion* of necessity without proof.]

VI. *The principle further examined.*—Before we leave this boasted principle, we may see how it applies to events of another kind. When we say that a philosopher has assigned *a sufficient reason for such a phenomenon*, What is the meaning of this? The meaning surely is, That he has accounted for it from the known laws of nature. The sufficient reason of a phenomenon of nature must therefore be some law or laws of nature, of which the phenomenon is a necessary consequence. But are we sure that, in this sense, there is a sufficient reason for every phenomenon of nature? I think we are not.

For, not to speak of miraculous events, in which the laws of nature are suspended, or counteracted, we know not but that, in the ordinary course of God's providence, there may be particular acts of his administration, that do not come under any general law of nature.

Established laws of nature are necessary for enabling intelligent creatures to conduct their affairs with wisdom and prudence, and prosecute their ends by proper means; but still it may be fit, that some particular events should not be fixed by general laws, but be directed by particular acts of the Divine government, that so his reasonable creatures may have sufficient inducement to supplicate his aid, his protection and direction, and to depend upon him for the success of their honest designs.

We see that, in human governments, even those that are most legal, it is impossible that every act of the administration should be directed by established laws. Some things must be left to the direction of the executive power, and particularly acts of clemency and bounty to petitioning subjects. That there is nothing analogous to this in the Divine government of the world, no man is able to prove.

We have no authority to pray that God would counteract or suspend the laws of nature in our behalf. Prayer, therefore, supposes that he may lend an ear to our prayers, without transgressing the laws of nature. Some have thought, that the only use of prayer and devotion is, to produce a proper temper and disposition in ourselves, and that it has no efficacy with the Deity. But this is a hypothesis without proof. It contradicts our most natural sentiments, as well as the plain doctrine of Scripture, and tends to damp the fervour of every act of devotion.

It was indeed an article of the system of Leibnitz, That the Deity, since the creation of the world, never did any thing, excepting in the case of *miracles;* his work being made so perfect at first, as never to need his interposition. But, in this, he was opposed by Sir Isaac Newton, and others of the ablest philosophers, nor was he ever able to give any proof of this tenet.

[There is no evidence, therefore, that there is a sufficient reason for every natural event; if, by a sufficient reason, we understand some fixed law or laws of nature, of which that event is a necessary consequence.]

VII. [But *what*, shall we say, *is the sufficient reason for a truth?* For our belief of a truth, I think, the sufficient reason is our having good evidence; but what may be meant by a sufficient reason for its being a truth, I am not able to guess, unless the sufficient reason of a contingent truth be, That it *is* true; and, of a necessary truth, that it *must be* true. This makes a man little wiser.]

From what has been said, I think it appears, That this principle of the necessity of a sufficient reason for every thing, is very *indefinite in its signification*. If it mean, That of every event there must be a cause that had sufficient power to produce it, this is true, and has always been admitted as a first principle in philosophy, and in common life. If it mean that every event must be necessarily consequent upon something (called a sufficient reason) that went before it; this is a direct assertion of universal fatality, and has many strange, not to say absurd, consequences: but, in this sense, it is neither self-evident, nor has any proof of it been offered. [And, in general, in every sense in which it has evidence, it gives no new information; and, in every sense in which it would give new information, it wants evidence.]

VIII. *Another argument* that has been used *to prove liberty of action to be impossible* is, That it implies "an effect without a cause."*

To this it may be briefly answered, [That a free action is an effect produced by *a being who had power and will* to produce it; therefore it is not an effect without a cause.]

To suppose any other cause necessary to the production of an effect, than a being who had the power and the will to produce it, is a contradiction; for it is to suppose that being to have power to produce the effect, and not to have power to produce it.

But as great stress is laid upon this argument by a late zealous advocate for necessity, we shall consider the light in which he puts it.

He introduces this argument with an observation to which I entirely agree: it is, [That to establish this doctrine of necessity, nothing is necessary but that, throughout all nature, the same consequences should invariably result from the same circumstances.]

I know nothing more that can be desired to establish universal fatality throughout the universe. When it is proved that, through all nature, the same consequences invariably result from the same circumstances, the doctrine of liberty must be given up.

To prevent all ambiguity, I grant, that, in reasoning, the same consequences, throughout all nature, will invariably follow from the same premises: because good reasoning must be good rea-

* Vide sect. 1. of this chapter, p. 289.

soning in all times and places. But this has nothing to do with the doctrine of necessity. [The thing to be proved, therefore, in order to establish that doctrine, is, That, through all nature, the *same events* invariably result from the *same circumstances*.]

Of this capital point, the proof offered by that author is, That an event not preceded by any circumstances that determined it to be what it was, would be *an effect without a cause*. Why so? "For," says he, "a *cause* cannot be defined to be any thing but *such previous circumstances as are constantly followed by a certain effect;* the constancy of the result making us conclude, that there must be a *sufficient reason,* in the nature of things, why it should be produced in those circumstances."

I acknowledge that, if this be the only definition that can be given of a cause, it will follow, That an event not preceded by circumstances that determined it to be what it was, would be, not an *effect* without a cause, which is a contradiction in terms, but an *event* without a cause, which I hold to be impossible. [The matter therefore is brought to this issue, Whether this be the only definition that can be given of a cause?]

IX. *Four consequences of this definition of a cause.*—With regard to this point, we may observe, *first,* That this definition of a cause, bating the phraseology of putting a *cause* under the category of *circumstances,* which I take to be new, is the same, in other words, with that which Mr. Hume gave, of which he ought to be acknowledged the inventor.* For I know of no author before Mr. Hume, who maintained, that we have no other notion of a cause, but that it is something prior to the effect, which has been found by experience to be constantly followed by the effect. This is a main pillar of his system; and he has drawn very important consequences from this definition, which I am far from thinking this author will adopt.

Without repeating what I have before said of causes in the first of these Essays, and in the second and third chapters of this, I shall here mention some of the *consequences* that may be justly *deduced from this definition* of a cause, that we may judge of it by its fruits.

First, It follows from this definition of a cause, that *night is the cause of day,* and day the cause of night. For no two things have more constantly followed each other since the beginning of the world.

Secondly, It follows from this definition of a cause, that, for what we know, *any thing may be the cause of any thing,* since nothing is essential to a cause but its being constantly followed by the effect. If this be so, what is unintelligent may be the cause of what is intelligent; folly may be the cause of wisdom, and evil of good; all reasoning from the nature of the effect to

* Essay I. chap. iv. sect. 2.

the nature of the cause, and all reasoning from final causes, must be given up as fallacious.

Thirdly, From this definition of a cause, it follows, that we have *no reason to conclude, that every event must have a cause:* for innumerable events happen, when it cannot be shown that there were certain previous circumstances that have constantly been followed by such an event. And though it were certain, that every event we have had access to observe had a cause, it would not follow, that every event must have a cause: for it is contrary to the rules of logic to conclude, that, because a thing has always been, therefore it must be; to reason from what is contingent, to what is necessary.

Fourthly, From this definition of a cause, it would follow, that we have *no reason to conclude that there was any cause of the creation of this world:* for there were no previous circumstances that had been constantly followed by such an effect. And, for the same reason, it would follow from the definition, that whatever was singular in its nature, or the first thing of its kind, could have no cause.

Several of *these consequences* were fondly embraced by Mr. Hume, as necessarily following from his definition of a cause, and as *favourable to* his system of *absolute scepticism*. Those who adopt the definition of a cause, from which they follow, may choose whether they will adopt its consequences, or show that they do not follow from the definition.

X. A *second* observation with regard to this argument* is, that a definition of a cause may be given, which is not burdened with such untoward consequences.

Why may not an efficient cause be defined to be a being that had power and will to produce the effect? The production of an effect requires active power, and active power, being a quality, must be in a being endowed with that power. Power, without will, produces no effect; but, where these are conjoined, the effect must be produced.

This, I think, is the proper meaning of the word *cause*, when it is used in metaphysics; and particularly when we affirm that every thing that begins to exist must have a cause; and when, by reasoning, we prove that there must be an eternal First Cause of all things.

Was the world produced by previous circumstances which are constantly followed by such an effect? or, Was it produced by a Being that had power to produce it, and willed its production?

In natural philosophy, the word *cause* is often used in a very different sense. When an event is produced according to a known law of nature, the law of nature is called the cause of

---

* *i. e.* That a cause is " such previous circumstances as are constantly followed by a certain effect."

that event. But a law of nature is not the efficient cause of any event. It is only the rule, according to which the efficient cause acts. A law is a thing conceived in the mind of a rational being, not a thing that has a real existence; and, therefore, like a motive, it can neither act nor be acted upon, and consequently cannot be an efficient cause. If there be no being that acts according to the law, it produces no effect.

This author *takes it for granted*, that every voluntary action of man was determined to be what it was by the laws of nature, in the same sense as mechanical motions are determined by the laws of motion; and that every choice, not thus determined, " is just as impossible, as that a mechanical motion should depend upon no certain law or rule, or that any other effect should exist without a cause."

[It ought here to be observed, that there are two kinds of laws, both very properly called *laws of nature*, which ought not to be confounded. There are moral laws of nature, and physical laws of nature.] *The first* are the rules which God has prescribed to his rational creatures for their conduct. They *respect voluntary and free actions only;* for no other actions can be subject to moral rules. These laws of nature ought to be always obeyed, but they are often transgressed by men. There is therefore no impossibility in the violation of the moral laws of nature, nor is such a violation an effect without a cause. The transgressor is the cause, and is justly accountable for it.

The physical laws of nature are the rules according to which the Deity commonly acts in his natural government of the world; and, whatever is done according to them, is not done by man, but by God, either immediately, or by instruments under his direction. These laws of nature neither restrain the power of the Author of nature, nor bring him under any obligation to do nothing beyond their sphere. He has sometimes acted contrary to them, *in the case of miracles*, and perhaps often acts without regard to them, in the ordinary course of his providence. Neither miraculous events, which are contrary to the physical laws of nature, nor such ordinary acts of the Divine administration as are without their sphere, are impossible, nor are they *effects without a cause*. God is the cause of them, and to him only they are to be imputed.

That the moral laws of nature are often transgressed by man, is undeniable. If the physical laws of nature make his obedience to the moral laws to be impossible, then he is, in the literal sense, *born under one law, bound unto another*, which contradicts every notion of a righteous government of the world.

But though this supposition were attended with no such shocking consequence, it is merely a supposition; and until it be proved that every choice or voluntary action of man is determined by the physical laws of nature, this argument for necessity is only the taking for granted the point to be proved.

Of the same kind is the argument for the impossibility of liberty, taken from a balance, which cannot move but as it is moved by the weights put into it. This argument, though urged by almost every writer in defence of necessity, is so pitiful, and has been so often answered, that it scarce deserves to be mentioned.

Every argument in a dispute, which is not grounded on principles granted by both parties, is that kind of sophism which logicians call *petitio principii;* and such, in my apprehension, are all the arguments offered to prove that liberty of action is impossible.

It may farther be observed, that every argument of this class if it were really conclusive, must *extend to the Deity*, as well as to all created beings; and necessary existence, which has always been considered as the prerogative of the Supreme Being, must belong equally to every creature and to every event even the most trifling.

This I take to be the system of Spinosa, and of those among the ancients who carried fatality to the highest pitch.

I before referred the reader to Dr. Clarke's argument, which professes to demonstrate that the First Cause is a free agent. Until that argument shall be shown to be fallacious, a thing which I have not seen attempted, such weak arguments as have been brought to prove the contrary, ought to have little weight.

CHAPTER X.

THE SAME SUBJECT.

I. With regard to the *second* class of arguments for necessity, which are intended to prove that *liberty of action would be hurtful to man*,* I have only to observe, that it is a fact too evident to be denied, whether we adopt the system of liberty or that of necessity, that men actually receive hurt from their own voluntary actions, and from the voluntary actions of other men; nor can it be pretended that this fact is inconsistent with the doctrine of liberty, or that it is more unaccountable upon this system than upon that of necessity.

In order, therefore, to draw any solid argument against liberty, from its hurtfulness, it ought to be proved, that if man were a free agent, he would do more hurt to himself, or to others, than he actually does.

To this purpose it has been said, that liberty would make

* Chap. ix. sect. I.

"For," says he, "as certainly as nothing can be known to exist, but what does exist, so certainly can nothing be known to *arise from what does exist,* but what does arise from it or depend upon it. But, according to the definition of the terms, a contingent event does not depend upon any previous known circumstances, since some other event might have arisen in the same circumstances."

This argument, when stripped of incidental and explanatory clauses, and affected variations of expression, amounts to this: nothing can be known to arise from what does exist, but what does arise from it: but a contingent event does not arise from what does exist. [The conclusion, which is left to be drawn by the reader, must, according to the rules of reasoning, be: therefore a contingent event cannot be known to arise from what does exist.]

It is here very obvious, that a thing may arise from what does exist, two ways, freely or necessarily. A contingent event arises from its cause, not necessarily but freely, and so, that another event might have arisen from the same cause, in the same circumstances.

The second proposition of the argument is, that a contingent event does not depend upon any previous known circumstances, which I take to be only a variation of the term of *not arising from what does exist.* Therefore, in order to make the two propositions to correspond, we must understand by *arising from what does exist,* arising necessarily from what does exist. When this ambiguity is removed, the argument stands thus: nothing can be known to arise necessarily from what does exist, but what does necessarily arise from it: but a contingent event does not arise necessarily from what does exist; therefore a contingent event cannot be known to arise necessarily from what does exist.

I grant the whole; but the conclusion of this argument is not what he undertook to prove, and therefore the argument is that kind of sophism which logicians call *ignoratio elenchi.*

The thing to be proved is not, that a contingent event cannot be known to arise necessarily from what exists; but that a contingent future event cannot be the object of knowledge.

To draw the argument to this conclusion, it must be put thus: nothing can be known to arise from what does exist, but what arises necessarily from it: but a contingent event does not arise necessarily from what does exist; therefore a contingent event cannot be known to arise from what does exist.

The conclusion here is what it ought to be; but the first proposition assumes the thing to be proved, and therefore the argument is what logicians call *petitio principii.*

To the same purpose he says, "That nothing can be known at present, except itself or its necessary cause exist at present."

This is affirmed, but I find no proof of it.

Again he says, " That knowledge supposes an object, which, in this case, does not exist." It is true that knowledge supposes an object, and every thing that is known is an object of knowledge, whether past, present, or future, whether contingent or necessary.

Upon the whole, the arguments I can find upon this point, bear no proportion to the confidence of the assertion, that there cannot be a greater absurdity or contradiction, than that a contingent event should be the object of knowledge.

IV. To those who, without pretending to show a manifest absurdity or contradiction in the knowledge of future contingent events, are still of opinion, that it is impossible that the future free actions of man, a being of imperfect wisdom and virtue, should be certainly foreknown, I would humbly offer the following considerations.

[1. I grant that there is *no knowledge of this kind in man;* and this is the cause that we find it so difficult to conceive it in any other being.]

All our knowledge of future events is drawn either from their necessary connexion with the present course of nature, or from their connexion with the character of the agent that produces them. Our knowledge, even of those future events that necessarily result from the established laws of nature, is hypothetical. It supposes the continuance of those laws with which they are connected. And how long those laws may be continued, we have no certain knowledge. God only knows when the present course of nature shall be changed, and therefore he only has certain knowledge even of events of this kind.

The character of perfect wisdom and perfect rectitude in the Deity, gives us certain knowledge that he will always be true in all his declarations, faithful in all his promises, and just in all his dispensations. But [when we reason from the character of *men* to their future actions, though, in many cases, we have such probability as we rest upon in our most important worldly concerns, yet we have no certainty, because *men are imperfect in wisdom and in virtue.*] If we had even the most perfect knowledge of the character and situation of a man, this would not be sufficient to give certainty to our knowledge of his future actions; because, in some actions, both good and bad men deviate from their general character.

The *prescience of the Deity*, therefore, must be *different not only in degree, but in kind*, from any knowledge we can attain of futurity.

[2. Though we can have *no conception how the future free actions of men may be known by the Deity*, this is not a sufficient reason to conclude that they cannot be known.] Do we know, or can we conceive, how God knows the secrets of men's hearts? Can we conceive how God made this world without any preexistent matter? All the ancient philosophers believed this to be impossible: and for what reason but this, that they could not conceive how it could be done. Can we give any better reason for believing that the actions of men cannot be certainly foreseen?

[3. *Can we conceive how we ourselves have certain knowledge by those faculties with which God has endowed us?* If any man thinks that he understands distinctly how he is conscious of his own thoughts; how he perceives external objects by his senses; how he remembers past events, I am afraid that he is not yet so wise as to understand his own ignorance.]

[4. There seems to me to be a great *analogy* between the *prescience* of future contingents, and the *memory* of past contingents. We possess the last in some degree, and therefore find no difficulty in believing that it may be perfect in the Deity. But the first we have in no degree, and therefore are apt to think it impossible.]

[In both, the object of knowledge is neither what presently exists, nor has any necessary connexion with what presently exists. Every argument brought to prove the impossibility of *prescience*, proves, with equal force, the impossibility of *memory*.] If it be true that nothing can be known to arise from what does exist, but what necessarily arises from it, it must be equally true, that nothing can be known to have gone before what does exist, but what must necessarily have gone before it. If it be true that nothing future can be known unless its necessary cause exist at present, it must be equally true that nothing past can be known unless something consequent, with which it is necessarily connected, exist at present. If the fatalist should say, that past events are indeed necessarily connected with the present, he will not surely venture to say that it is by tracing this necessary connexion that we remember the past.

Why, then, should we think prescience impossible in the Almighty, when he has given us a faculty which bears a strong analogy to it, and which is no less unaccountable to the human understanding than prescience is. It is more reasonable, as well as more agreeable to the sacred writings, to conclude with a pious father of the church, "Quocirca nullo modo cogimur, aut retentâ præscientia Dei tollere voluntatis arbitrium, aut retento voluntatis arbitrio, Deum, quod nefas est, negare præscium futurorum: sed utrumque amplectimur, utrumque fideliter et veraciter confitemur: illud ut bene credamus; hoc ut bene vivamus."—Aug. "Wherefore we are under no necessity of rejecting the freedom of the will, in case we admit the prescience of the Deity, or in case we admit the freedom of the will to fall into the impiety of denying such prescience: on the contrary, we acknowledge both points—one as essential to the soundness of our faith, the other to righteousness of life."

CHAPTER XI.

OF THE PERMISSION OF EVIL.

I. ANOTHER use has been made of Divine prescience by the advocates for necessity, which it is proper to consider before we leave this subject.

It has been said, "that all those consequences follow from the Divine prescience which are thought most alarming in the scheme of necessity; and particularly God's being the proper cause of moral evil. For, to suppose God to foresee and permit what it was in his power to have prevented, is the very same thing as to suppose him to will, and directly to cause it. He distinctly foresees all the actions of a man's life, and all the consequences of them. If, therefore, he did not think any particular man and his conduct proper for his plan of creation and providence, he certainly would not have introduced him into being at all."

In this reasoning we may observe, that a supposition is made which seems to contradict itself.

That all the actions of a particular man should be distinctly foreseen, and, at the same time, that that man should never be brought into existence, seems to me to be a contradiction: and the same contradiction there is, in supposing any action to be distinctly foreseen, and yet prevented. For, if it be foreseen, it shall happen; and, if it be prevented, it shall not happen; and therefore could not be foreseen.

II. [*Scientia media.*—The knowledge here supposed is *neither prescience nor science*, but something very different from both. It is a kind of knowledge which some metaphysical divines, in their controversies about the order of the Divine decrees, a subject far beyond the limits of human understanding, attributed to the Deity, and of which other divines denied the possibility, while they firmly maintained the Divine prescience.]

It was called *scientia media*, to distinguish it from prescience; and by this *scientia media* was meant, not the knowing from eternity all things that shall exist, which is prescience, [nor the knowing all the connexions and relations of things that exist or may be conceived, which is science;] but a knowledge of things contingent, that never did nor shall exist. For instance, the knowing every action that would be done by a man who is barely conceived, and shall never be brought into existence.

Against the possibility of the *scientia media* arguments may be urged, which cannot be applied to prescience. Thus it may be said, *that nothing can be known but what is true*. It is true force, prove other moral attributes to be so; or what objections can be brought against the latter, which have not equal strength against the former, unless it be admitted to be an objection against other moral attributes, that they do not accord with the doctrine of necessity.

If other moral evils may be attributed to the Deity as the means of promoting general good, why may not false declarations and false promises? And then what ground have we left to believe the truth of what he reveals, or to rely upon what he promises?

Supposing this strange view of the Divine nature were to be adopted in favour of the doctrine of necessity, there is still a great difficulty to be resolved.

Since it is supposed that the Supreme Being had no other end in making and governing the universe, but to produce the greatest degree of happiness to his creatures in general, how comes it to pass that there is so much misery in a system made and governed by infinite wisdom and power for a contrary purpose?

IV. The *solution of this difficulty leads us necessarily to another hypothesis*, That all the misery and vice that is in the world is a necessary ingredient in that system which produces the greatest sum of happiness upon the whole. This connexion betwixt the greatest sum of happiness and all the misery that is in the universe, must be fatal and necessary in the nature of things, so that even Almighty power cannot break it : for benevolence can never lead to inflict misery without necessity.

This necessary connexion between the greatest sum of happiness upon the whole, and all the natural and moral evil that is, or has been, or shall be, being once established, it is impossible for mortal eyes to discern how far this evil may extend, or on whom it may happen to fall; whether this fatal connexion may be temporary or eternal, or what proportion of the happiness may be balanced by it.

A world made by perfect wisdom and almighty power, for no other end but to make it happy, presents the most pleasing prospect that can be imagined. We expect nothing but uninterrupted happiness to prevail for ever. But, alas! when we consider that in this happiest system, there must be necessarily all the misery and vice we see, and how much more we know not, how is the prospect darkened!

[These two hypotheses, the one limiting the *moral* character of the Deity, the other limiting his *power*, seem to me to be the necessary *consequences of necessity*, when it is joined with Theism; and they have accordingly been adopted by the ablest defenders of that doctrine.]

If some defenders of liberty, by limiting too rashly the Divine prescience, in order to defend that system, have raised high indignation in their opponents; have they not equal ground of indignation against those who, to defend necessity, limit the moral perfection of the Deity, and his almighty power?

V. [Let us consider, on the other hand, what consequences may be fairly drawn from God's permitting the *abuse of liberty in agents on whom he has bestowed it.*]

If it be asked, Why does God permit so much sin in his creation? I confess I cannot answer the question, but must lay my hand upon my mouth. He giveth no account of his conduct to the children of men. It is our part to obey his commands, and not to say unto him, Why dost thou thus?

Hypotheses might be framed; but while we have ground to be satisfied that he does nothing but what is right, it is more becoming us to acknowledge that the ends and reasons of his universal government are beyond our knowledge, and perhaps beyond the comprehension of human understanding. We cannot penetrate so far into the counsel of the Almighty, as to know all the reasons why it became him, of whom are all things, and to whom are all things, to create, not only machines, which are solely moved by his hand, but servants and children, who, by obeying his commands, and imitating his moral perfections, might rise to a high degree of glory and happiness in his favour, or, by perverse disobedience, might incur guilt and just punishment. In this he appears to us awful in his justice, as well as amiable in his goodness.

But, as he disdains not to appeal to men for the equity of his proceedings towards them when his character is impeached, we may, with humble reverence, plead for God, and vindicate that moral excellence which is the glory of his nature, and of which the image is the glory and the perfection of man.

Let us observe, first of all, that *to permit* hath two meanings. It signifies, not to forbid; and it signifies, not to hinder by superior power. In the first of these senses, *God never permits sin.* His law forbids every moral evil. By his laws and by his government, he gives every encouragement to good conduct, and every discouragement to bad. But *he does not always,* by his superior power, *hinder it from being committed.* This is the ground of the accusation; and this, it is said, is the very same thing as directly to will and to cause it.

As this is asserted without proof, and is far from being self-evident, it might be sufficient to deny it until it be proved. But, without resting barely on the defensive, we may observe, that the only moral attributes that can be supposed inconsistent with the permission of sin, are either goodness or justice.

The defenders of necessity, with whom we have to do in this point, as they maintain that goodness is the only essential moral attribute of the Deity, and the motive of all his actions, must, if they will be consistent, maintain, That to will, and directly to cause sin, much more not to hinder it, is consistent with perfect goodness, nay, that goodness is a sufficient motive to justify the willing and directly causing it.

With regard to them, therefore, it is surely unnecessary to attempt to reconcile the permission of sin with the goodness of God; since an inconsistency between that attribute and the causing of sin would overturn their whole system.

If the causing of moral evil, and being the real author of it, be consistent with perfect goodness, what pretence can there be to say, that not to hinder it is inconsistent with perfect goodness?

[What is incumbent upon them, therefore, to prove is, "That the permission of sin is inconsistent with justice;" and, upon this point, we are ready to join issue with them.]

But what pretence can there be to say, that the permission of sin is perfectly consistent with goodness in the Deity, but inconsistent with justice?

Is it not as easy to conceive, that he should permit sin, though virtue be his delight, as that he inflicts misery, when his sole delight is to bestow happiness? Should it appear incredible, that the permission of sin may tend to promote virtue, to them who believe that the infliction of misery is necessary to promote happiness?

The justice, as well as the goodness of God's moral government of mankind, appears in this: That his laws are not arbitrary nor grievous, as it is only by the obedience of them that our nature can be perfected and qualified for future happiness; that he is ready to aid our weakness, to help our infirmities, and not to suffer us to be tempted above what we are able to bear; that he is not strict to mark iniquity, or to execute judgment speedily against an evil work, but is long-suffering, and waits to be gracious; that he is ready to receive the humble penitent to his favour; that he is no respecter of persons, but in every nation he that fears God and works righteousness is accepted of him; that of every man he will require an account, proportioned to the talents he hath received; that he delights in mercy, but hath no pleasure in the death of the wicked; and therefore in punishing will never go beyond the demerit of the criminal, nor beyond what the rules of his universal government require.

There were, in ancient ages, some who said, "The way of the Lord is not equal;" to whom the prophet, in the name of God, makes this reply, which, in all ages, is sufficient to repel this accusation: "Hear now, O house of Israel, Is not my way equal? are not your ways unequal? When a righteous man turneth away from his righteousness, and committeth iniquity, for his iniquity which he hath done, shall he die." Again, when the wicked man turneth away from his wickedness that he hath committed, and doeth that which is lawful and right, he shall save his soul alive. O house of Israel, are not my ways equal? are not your ways unequal? Repent, and turn from all your transgressions; so iniquity shall not be your ruin. Cast away from you all your transgressions, whereby ye have transgressed, and make you a new heart, and a new spirit: for why will ye die, O house of Israel? For I have no pleasure in the death of him that dieth, saith the Lord God."

VI. *Another argument for necessity* has been lately offered, which we shall very briefly consider.

[It has been maintained, that *the power of thinking is* the *result of a certain modification of matter*, and that a certain configuration of brain makes a soul; and, if man be wholly a material being, it is said that it will not be denied that he must be a mechanical being; that the doctrine of necessity is a direct inference from that of materialism, and its undoubted consequence.]

As this argument can have no weight with those who do not see reason to embrace this system of materialism; so, even with those who do, it seems to me to be a mere sophism.

Philosophers have been wont to conceive matter to be an inert passive being, and to have certain properties inconsistent with the power of thinking or of acting. But a philosopher arises, who proves, we shall suppose, that we were quite mistaken in our notion of matter; that it has not the properties we supposed, and, in fact, has no properties but those of attraction and repulsion; but still he thinks that, being matter, it will not be denied that it is a mechanical being, and that the doctrine of necessity is a direct inference from that of materialism.

Herein, however, he deceives himself. If matter be what we conceived it to be, it is equally incapable of thinking and of acting freely. But if the properties, from which we drew this conclusion, have no reality, as he thinks he has proved; if it have the powers of attraction and repulsion, and require only a certain configuration to make it think rationally, it will be impossible to show any good reason why the same configuration may not make it act rationally and freely. If its reproach of solidity, inertness, and sluggishness, be wiped off; and if it be raised in our esteem to a nearer approach to the nature of what we call spiritual and immaterial beings, why should it still be nothing but a mechanical being? Is its solidity, inertness, and sluggishness, to be first removed to make it capable of thinking, and then restored in order to make it incapable of acting?

[Those, therefore, who reason justly from this system of materialism will easily perceive that the *doctrine of necessity* is so far from being a direct inference, that it *can receive no support from it.*]

VII. To conclude this Essay: Extremes of all kinds ought to be avoided; yet men are prone to run into them; and, to shun one extreme, we often run into the contrary.

Of all extremes of opinion, none are more dangerous than those that exalt the powers of man too high, on the one hand, or sink them too low, on the other.

By raising them too high, we feed pride and vainglory, we lose the sense of our dependence upon God and engage in attempts beyond our abilities. By depressing them too low, we cut the sinews of action and of obligation, and are tempted to think that, as we can do nothing, we have nothing to do but to be carried passively along by the stream of necessity.

Some good men, apprehending that, to kill pride and vainglory, our active powers cannot be too much depressed, have been led, by zeal for religion, to deprive us of all active power.

Other good men, by a like zeal, have been led to depreciate the human understanding, and to put out the light of nature and reason, in order to exalt that of revelation.

Those weapons which were taken up in support of religion, are now employed to overturn it; and what was, by some, accounted the bulwark of orthodoxy, is become the stronghold of atheism and infidelity.

[Atheists join hands with theologians, (1) in depriving man of all active power, *that they may destroy all moral obligation*, and all sense of right and wrong. They join hands with theologians, (2) in depreciating the human understanding, *that they may lead us into absolute scepticism.*]

God, in mercy to the human race, has made us of such a frame, that no speculative opinion whatsoever can root out the sense of guilt and demerit when we do wrong, nor the peace and joy of a good conscience when we do what is right. No speculative opinion can root out a regard to the testimony of our senses, of our memory, and of our rational faculties. But we have reason to be jealous of opinions which run counter to those natural sentiments of the human mind, and tend to shake, though they never can eradicate them.

There is little reason to fear, that the conduct of men, with regard to the concerns of the present life, will ever be much affected, either by the doctrine of necessity, or by scepticism. It were to be wished that men's conduct, with regard to the concerns of another life, were in as little danger from those opinions.

In the present state, we see some who zealously maintain the doctrine of necessity, others who as zealously maintain that of liberty. One would be apt to think that a practical belief of these contrary systems should produce very different conduct in them that hold them; yet we see no such difference in the affairs of common life.

The fatalist deliberates, and resolves, and plights his faith. He lays down a plan of conduct, and prosecutes it with vigour and industry. He exhorts and commands, and holds those to be answerable for their conduct to whom he hath committed any charge. He blames those that are false or unfaithful to him, as other men do. He perceives dignity and worth in some characters and actions, and in others demerit and turpitude. He resents injuries, and is grateful for good offices.

If any man should plead the doctrine of necessity to exculpate murder, theft, or robbery, or even wilful negligence in the discharge of his duty, his judge, though a fatalist, if he had common sense, would laugh at such a plea, and would not allow it even to alleviate the crime.

In all such cases, he sees that it would be absurd not to act and to judge as those ought to do who believe themselves and other men to be free agents—just as the sceptic, to avoid absurdity, must, when he goes into the world, act and judge like other men who are not sceptics.

If the fatalist be as little influenced by the opinion of necessity *in his moral and religious concerns,* and in his expectations concerning another world, as he is in *the common affairs of life,* his speculative opinion will probably do him little hurt. But, if he trust so far to the doctrine of necessity, as to indulge sloth and inactivity in his duty, and hope to exculpate himself to his Maker by that doctrine, let him consider whether he sustains this excuse from his servants and dependants, when they are negligent or unfaithful in what is committed to their charge.

Bishop Butler, in his "Analogy," has an excellent chapter upon *the opinion of necessity considered as influencing practice,* which I think highly deserving the consideration of those who are inclined to that opinion.*

* "Analogy of Religion, Natural and Revealed, to the Constitution and Course of Nature," Part I. chap. vi.

ESSAY V.

OF MORALS.

CHAPTER I.

OF THE FIRST PRINCIPLES OF MORALS.

I. MORALS, like all other sciences, must have *first principles*, on which all moral reasoning is grounded.

In every branch of knowledge where disputes have been raised, it is useful to distinguish the first principles from the superstructure. They are the foundation on which the whole fabric of the science leans; and whatever is not supported by this foundation can have no stability.

[In all rational belief, the thing believed is (1) either itself a first principle, or (2) it is by just reasoning deduced from first principles.] When men differ about deductions of reasoning, the appeal must be made to the rules of reasoning, which have been very unanimously fixed from the days of Aristotle. But when they differ about a first principle, the appeal is made to another tribunal; to that of common sense.

How the genuine decisions of common sense may be distinguished from the counterfeit, has been considered in Essay VI. on "The Intellectual Powers of Man," chapter fourth, to which the reader is referred. What I would here observe is, that as first principles differ from deductions of reasoning in the nature of their evidence, and must be tried by a different standard when they are called in question, it is of importance to know to which of these two classes a truth, which we would examine, belongs. When they are not distinguished, men are apt to demand proof for every thing they think fit to deny: and when we attempt to prove by direct argument, what is really self-evident, the reasoning will always be inconclusive: for it will either take for granted the thing to be proved, or something not more evident; and so, instead of giving strength to the conclusion, will rather tempt those to doubt of it, who never did so before.

II. I propose, therefore, in this chapter, to point out some of the first principles of morals, without pretending to a complete enumeration.

The principles I am to mention, relate either to virtue in general, or to the different particular branches of virtue, or to the comparison of virtues where they seem to interfere.

1. There are some things in human conduct, that merit approbation and praise, others that merit blame and punishment; and different degrees either of approbation or of blame, are due to different actions.

2. What is in no degree *voluntary*, can neither deserve moral approbation nor blame.

3. What is done from *unavoidable necessity* may be agreeable or disagreeable, useful or hurtful, but cannot be the object either of blame or of moral approbation.

4. Men may be highly culpable in *omitting* what they ought to have done, as well as in *doing* what they ought not.

5. We ought to use the best means we can to be *well informed of our duty*, by serious attention to moral instruction; by observing what we approve, and what we disapprove, in other men, whether our acquaintance, or those whose actions are recorded in history; by reflecting often, in a calm and dispassionate hour, on our own past conduct, that we may discern what was wrong, what was right, and what might have been better; by deliberating coolly and impartially upon our future conduct, as far as we can foresee the opportunities we may have of doing good, or the temptations to do wrong; and by having this principle deeply fixed in our minds, that as moral excellence is the true worth and glory of a man, so the knowledge of our duty is to every man, in every station of life, the most important of all knowledge.

6. It ought to be our most serious concern *to do our duty* as far as we know it, and to *fortify our minds* against every temptation to deviate from it; by maintaining a lively sense of the beauty of right conduct, and of its present and future reward, of the turpitude of vice, and of its bad consequences here and hereafter; by having always in our eye the noblest examples; by the habit of subjecting our passions to the government of reason; by firm purposes and resolutions with regard to our conduct; by avoiding occasions of temptation when we can; and by imploring the aid of Him who made us, in every hour of temptation.

III. These principles concerning virtue and vice in general, must appear self-evident to every man who hath a conscience, and who hath taken pains to exercise this natural power of his mind. I proceed to *others that are more particular*.

1. We ought to prefer a greater good, though more distant, to a less; and a less evil to a greater.

A regard to our own good, though we had no conscience, dictates this principle; and we cannot help disapproving the man that acts contrary to it, as deserving to lose the good which he wantonly threw away, and to suffer the evil which he knowingly brought upon his own head.

We observed before, that the ancient moralists, and many among the modern, have deduced the whole of morals from this principle, and that when we make a right estimate of goods and evils according to their degree, their dignity, their duration, and according as they are more or less in our power, it leads to the practice of every virtue : more directly, indeed, to the virtues of self-government, to prudence, to temperance, and to fortitude ; and, though more indirectly, even to justice, humanity, and all the social virtues, when their influence upon our happiness is well understood.

Though it be not the noblest principle of conduct, it has this peculiar advantage, that its force is felt by the most ignorant, and even by the most abandoned.

Let a man's moral judgment be ever so little improved by exercise, or ever so much corrupted by bad habits, he cannot be indifferent to his own happiness or misery. When he is become insensible to every nobler motive to right conduct, he cannot be insensible to this. And though to act from this motive solely may be called *prudence* rather than *virtue*, yet this prudence deserves some regard upon its own account, and much more as it is the friend and ally of virtue, and the enemy of all vice ; and as it gives a favourable testimony of virtue to those who are deaf to every other recommendation.

[If a man can be induced to do his duty even from a regard to *his own happiness*, he will soon find reason to love virtue for her own sake, and to *act from motives less mercenary*.]

I cannot therefore approve of those moralists who would banish all persuasives to virtue taken from the consideration of private good. In the present state of human nature these are not useless to the best, and they are the only means left of reclaiming the abandoned.

2. As far as the *intention of nature* appears in the constitution of man, we ought to comply with that intention, and to act agreeably to it.

The Author of our being hath given us not only the power of acting within a limited sphere, but various principles or springs of action, of different nature and dignity, to direct us in the exercise of our active power.

From the constitution of every species of the inferior animals, and especially from the active principles which nature has given them, we easily perceive the manner of life for which nature intended them ; and they uniformly act the part to which they are led by their constitution, without any reflection upon it, or intention of obeying its dictates. Man only, of the inhabitants of this world, is made capable of observing his own constitution, what kind of life it is made for, and of acting according to that intention, or contrary to it. He only is capable of yielding an intentional obedience to the dictates of his nature, or of rebelling against them.

In treating of the principles of action in man, it has been shown, that as his natural instincts and bodily appetites are well adapted to the preservation of his natural life, and to the continuance of the species; so his natural desires, affections, and passions, when uncorrupted by vicious habits, and under the government of the leading principles of reason and conscience, are excellently fitted for the rational and social life. Every vicious action shows an excess, or defect, or wrong direction of some natural spring of action, and therefore may, very justly, be said to be unnatural. Every virtuous action agrees with the uncorrupted principles of human nature.

The Stoics defined virtue to be a life according to nature. Some of them, more accurately, a life according to the nature of man, in so far as it is superior to that of brutes. The life of a brute is according to the nature of the brute; but it is neither virtuous nor vicious. The life of a moral agent cannot be according to his nature, unless it be virtuous. That conscience, which is in every man's breast, is the law of God written in his heart, which he cannot disobey without acting unnaturally, and being self-condemned.

The intention of nature, in the various active principles of man, in the desires of power, of knowledge, and of esteem, in the affection to children, to near relations, and to the communities to which we belong, in gratitude, in compassion, and even in resentment and emulation, is very obvious, and has been pointed out in treating of those principles. Nor is it less evident, that reason and conscience are given us to regulate the inferior principles, so that they may conspire, in a regular and consistent plan of life, in pursuit of some worthy end.

3. *No man is born for himself only.* Every man, therefore, ought to consider himself as a member of the common society of mankind, and of those subordinate societies to which he belongs, such as family, friends, neighbourhood, country, and to do as much good as he can, and as little hurt to the societies of which he is a part.

[This axiom leads directly to the practice of every *social virtue*, and indirectly to the virtues of self-government, by which only we can be qualified for discharging the duty we owe to society.]

4. In every case, we ought to act that part towards another, which we would judge to be right in him to act towards us, if we were in his circumstances and he in ours; or, more generally,

what we approve in others, that we ought to practise in like circumstances; and what we condemn in others, we ought not to do.

If there be any such thing as right and wrong in the conduct of moral agents, it must be the same to all in the same circumstances.

We stand all in the same relation to Him who made us, and will call us to account for our conduct; for with Him there is no respect of persons. We stand in the same relation to one another as members of the great community of mankind. The duties consequent upon the different ranks and offices and relations of men are the same to all in the same circumstances.

[It is not want of judgment, but want of *candour* and impartiality, that hinders men from discerning what they owe to others.] They are quicksighted enough in discerning what is due to themselves. When they are injured, or ill treated, they see it, and feel resentment. It is the want of candour that makes men use one measure for the duty they owe to others, and another measure for the duty that others owe to them in like circumstances. That men ought to judge with candour, as in all other cases, so especially in what concerns their moral conduct, is surely self-evident to every intelligent being. The man who takes offence when he is injured in his person, in his property, in his good name, pronounces judgment against himself if he act so toward his neighbour.

[As the equity and obligation of this rule of conduct is self-evident to every man who hath a conscience; so it is, *of all the rules of morality, the most comprehensive*, and truly deserves the encomium given it by the highest authority, that *it is the law and the prophets*.]

It comprehends every rule of justice without exception. It comprehends all the relative duties, arising either from the more permanent relations of parent and child, of master and servant, of magistrate and subject, of husband and wife, or from the more transient relations of rich and poor, of buyer and seller, of debtor and creditor, of benefactor and beneficiary, of friend and enemy. It comprehends every duty of charity and humanity, and even of courtesy and good manners.

Nay, I think that, without any force or straining, it extends even to the duties of self-government. For, as every man approves in others the virtues of prudence, temperance, self-command, and fortitude, he must perceive, that what is right in others must be right in himself in like circumstances.

To sum up all, he who acts invariably by this rule will never deviate from the path of his duty but from an error of judgment. And, as he feels the obligation that he and all men are under to use the best means in his power to have his judgment well informed in matters of duty, his errors will only be such as are invincible.

[It may be observed, that this axiom supposes (1) a faculty in man by which he can distinguish right conduct from wrong. It supposes also, (2) that, by this faculty, we easily perceive the right and the wrong in other men that are indifferent to us; but are very apt to be blinded by the partiality of selfish passions when the case concerns ourselves.] Every claim we have against others is apt to be magnified by self-love, when viewed directly. A change of persons removes this prejudice, and brings the claim to appear in its just magnitude.

5. To every man who believes the existence, the perfections, and the providence of God, the veneration and submission we owe to him is self-evident. Right sentiments of the Deity and of his works, not only make the duty we owe to him obvious to every intelligent being, but likewise add the *authority* of a divine law to every rule of right conduct.

IV. [There is *another class of axioms in morals*, by which, when there seems to be an opposition between the actions that different virtues lead to, we determine to which the preference is due.]

Between the several virtues, as they are dispositions of mind, or determinations of will to act according to a certain general rule, there can be no opposition. They dwell together most amicably, and give mutual aid and ornament, without the possibility of hostility or opposition, and, taken altogether, make one uniform and consistent rule of conduct. But, between particular external actions, which different virtues would lead to, there may be an opposition. Thus, the same man may be in his heart generous, grateful, and just. These dispositions strengthen, but never can weaken one another. Yet it may happen that an external action which generosity or gratitude solicits, justice may forbid.

That in all such cases, unmerited generosity should yield to gratitude, and both to justice, is self-evident. Nor is it less so, that unmerited beneficence to those who are at ease should yield to compassion to the miserable, and external acts of piety to works of mercy, because God loves mercy more than sacrifice.

At the same time, we perceive, that [those acts of virtue which ought to yield in the case of a *competition*, have most intrinsic worth when there is no competition. Thus, it is evident that there is more worth in pure and unmerited benevolence than in compassion, more in compassion than in gratitude, and more in gratitude than in justice.]

I call these *first principles*, because they appear to me to have in themselves an intuitive evidence which I cannot resist. I find I can express them in other words. I can illustrate them by examples and authorities, and perhaps can deduce one of them from another; but I am not able to deduce them from other principles that are more evident. And I find the best moral reasonings of authors I am acquainted with, ancient and modern, heathen and Christian, to be grounded upon one or more of them.

The evidence of mathematical axioms is not discerned till men come to a certain degree of maturity of understanding. A boy must have formed the general conception of *quantity*, and of *more* and *less* and *equal*, of *sum* and *difference;* and he must have been accustomed to judge of these relations in matters of common life, before he can perceive the evidence of the mathematical axiom, that equal quantities, added to equal quantities, make equal sums.

In like manner, our moral judgment, or conscience, grows to maturity from an imperceptible seed, planted by our Creator. When we are capable of contemplating the actions of other men, or of reflecting upon our own calmly and dispassionately, we begin to perceive in them the qualities of honest and dishonest, of honourable and base, of right and wrong, and to feel the sentiments of moral approbation and disapprobation.

These sentiments are at first feeble, easily warped by passions and prejudices, and apt to yield to authority. By use and time, the judgment, in morals, as in other matters, gathers strength, and feels more vigour. We begin to distinguish the dictates of passion from those of cool reason, and to perceive that it is not always safe to rely upon the judgment of others. By an impulse of nature we venture to judge for ourselves, as we venture to walk by ourselves.

☞ There is a strong analogy between the progress of the body from infancy to maturity, and the progress of all the powers of the mind. This progression in both is the work of nature, and in both may be greatly aided or hurt by proper education. It is natural to a man to be able to walk or run or leap; but if his limbs had been kept in fetters from his birth, he would have none of those powers. It is no less natural to a man trained in society, and accustomed to judge of his own actions and those of other men, to perceive a right and a wrong, an honourable and a base, in human conduct; and to such a man, I think, the principles of morals I have above mentioned will appear self-evident. Yet there may be individuals of the human species so little accustomed to think or judge of any thing but of gratifying their animal appetites, as to have hardly any conception of right or wrong in conduct, or any moral judgment; as there certainly are some who have not the conceptions and the judgment necessary to understand the axioms of geometry.

V. *Conclusion.*—From the principles above mentioned, the whole system of moral conduct follows so easily, and with so little aid of reasoning, that every man of common understanding who wishes to know his duty may know it. The path of duty is a plain path, which the upright in heart can rarely mistake. Such it must be, since every man is bound to walk in it. There are some intricate cases in morals which admit of disputation; but these seldom occur in practice; and when they do, the learned disputant has no great advantage: for the unlearned man, who uses the best means in his power to know his duty, and acts according to his knowledge, is inculpable in the sight of God and man. He may err, but he is not guilty of immorality.

CHAPTER II.

OF SYSTEMS OF MORALS.

I. *Instruction in morals necessary.*—If the knowledge of our duty be so level to the apprehension of all men, as has been represented in the last chapter, it may seem hardly to deserve the name of a science. It may seem that there is no need for instruction in morals.

From what cause then has it happened, that we have many large and learned systems of moral philosophy, and systems of natural jurisprudence, or the law of nature and nations; and that, in modern times, public professions have been instituted in most places of education for instructing youth in these branches of knowledge?

This event, I think, may be accounted for, and the utility of such systems and professions justified, without supposing any difficulty or intricacy in the knowledge of our duty.

[I am far from thinking instruction in morals unnecessary. Men may, to the end of life, be ignorant of self-evident truths. They may, to the end of life, entertain gross absurdities. Experience shows that this happens often in matters that are indifferent. Much more may it happen in matters where interest, passion, prejudice, and fashion, are so apt to pervert the judgment.]

The most obvious truths are not perceived without some ripeness of judgment. For we see that children may be made to believe any thing, though ever so absurd. Our judgment of things is ripened, not by time only, but chiefly by being exercised about things of the same or of a similar kind.

Judgment, even in things self-evident, requires a clear, distinct, and steady conception of the things about which we judge.

Our conceptions are at first obscure and wavering. The habit of attending to them is necessary to make them distinct and steady; and this habit requires an exertion of mind to which many of our animal principles are unfriendly. The love of truth calls for it; but its still voice is often drowned by the louder call of some passion, or we are hindered from listening to it by laziness and desultoriness. Thus men often remain through life ignorant of things which they needed but to open their eyes to see, and which they would have seen if their attention had been turned to them.

[*The most knowing derive the greatest part of their knowledge*, even in things obvious, *from instruction* and information, and from being taught to exercise their natural faculties, which, without instruction, would lie dormant.]

[I am very apt to think, that, if a man could be reared from infancy without any society of his fellow-creatures, he would hardly ever show any sign, either of moral judgment, or of the power of reasoning. His own actions would be directed by his animal appetites and passions, without cool reflection, and he would have no access to improve by observing the conduct of other beings like himself.]

The power of vegetation in the seed of a plant, without heat and moisture, would for ever lie dormant. The rational and moral powers of man would perhaps lie dormant without instruction and example. Yet these powers are a part, and the noblest part, of his constitution; as the power of vegetation is of the seed.

Our first moral conceptions are probably got by attending coolly to the conduct of others, and observing what moves our approbation, what our indignation. These sentiments spring from our moral faculty as naturally as the sensations of sweet and bitter from the faculty of taste. They have their natural objects. But most human actions are of a mixed nature, and have various colours, according as they are viewed on different sides. Prejudice against, or in favour of the person, is apt to warp our opinion. It requires attention and candour to distinguish the good from the ill, and, without favour or prejudice, to form a clear and impartial judgment. In this we may be greatly aided by instruction.

He must be very ignorant of human nature, who does not perceive that the seed of virtue in the mind of man, like that of a tender plant in an unkindly soil, requires care and culture in the first period of life, as well as our own exertion when we come to maturity.

If the irregularities of passion and appetite be timely checked, and good habits planted; if we be excited by good examples, and bad examples be shown in their proper colour; if the attention be prudently directed to the precepts of wisdom and virtue, as the mind is capable of receiving them; a man thus trained will rarely be at a loss to distinguish good from ill in his own conduct, without the labour of reasoning.

II. [*The bulk of mankind have but little of this culture in the proper season;* and what they have is often unskilfully applied; by which means bad habits gather strength, and false notions of pleasure, of honour, and of interest, occupy the mind.] They give little attention to what is right and honest. Conscience is seldom consulted, and so little exercised, that its decisions are weak and wavering. Although, therefore, to a ripe understanding, free from prejudice, and accustomed to judge of the morality of actions, most truths in morals will appear self-evident, it does not follow that moral instruction is unnecessary in the first part of life, or that it may not be very profitable in its more advanced period.

III. *Necessity of instruction in morals shown from the evidence of history.*—The history of past ages shows that nations, highly civilized and greatly enlightened in many arts and sciences, may, for ages, not only hold the grossest absurdities with regard to the Deity and his worship, but with regard to the duty we owe to our fellow-men, particularly to children, to servants, to strangers, to enemies, and to those who differ from us in religious opinions.

Such corruptions in religion, and in morals, had spread so wide among mankind, and were so confirmed by custom, as to require a light from heaven to correct them. *Revelation was* not *intended* to supersede, but *to aid the use of our natural faculties;* and I doubt not, but the attention given to moral truths, in such systems as we have mentioned, has contributed much to correct the errors and prejudices of former ages, and may continue to have the same good effect in time to come.

IV. It needs not seem strange, that *systems of morals may swell to great magnitude*, if we consider that, although the general principles be few and simple, their application extends to every part of human conduct, in every condition, every relation, and every transaction of life. [They are *the rule of life* to the magistrate and to the subject, to the master and to the servant, to the parent and to the child, to the fellow-citizen and to the alien, to the friend and to the enemy, to the buyer and to the seller, to the borrower and to the lender. Every human creature is subject to their authority in his actions and words, and even in his thoughts.] They may, in this respect, be compared to the laws of motion in the natural world, which, though few and simple, serve to regulate an infinite variety of operations throughout the universe.

And as the beauty of the laws of motion is displayed in the

most striking manner, when we trace them through all the variety of their effects; so the divine beauty and sanctity of the principles of morals, appear most august when we take a comprehensive view of their application to every condition and relation, and to every transaction of human society.

This is, or ought to be, the design of systems of morals. They may be made more or less extensive, having no limits fixed by nature, but the wide circle of human transactions. When the principles are applied to these in detail, the detail is pleasant and profitable. It requires no profound reasoning, (excepting, perhaps, in a few disputable points.) It admits of the most agreeable illustration from examples and authorities; it serves to exercise, and thereby to strengthen moral judgment. And one who has given much attention to the duty of man, in all the various relations and circumstances of life, will probably be more enlightened in his own duty, and more able to enlighten others.

V. *The first writers in morals,* we are acquainted with, delivered their moral instructions, not in systems, but in short unconnected sentences, or aphorisms. They saw no need for deductions of reasoning, because the truths they delivered could not but be admitted by the candid and attentive.

Subsequent writers, to improve the way of treating this subject, gave method and arrangement to moral truths, by reducing them under certain divisions and subdivisions, as parts of one whole. By this means the whole is more easily comprehended and remembered, and from this arrangement gets the name of a system and of a science.

A system of morals is not like a system of geometry, where the subsequent parts derive their evidence from the preceding, and one chain of reasoning is carried on from the beginning; so that, if the arrangement is changed, the chain is broken, and the evidence is lost. It resembles more a system of botany, or mineralogy, where the subsequent parts depend not for their evidence upon the preceding, and the arrangement is made to facilitate apprehension and memory, and not to give evidence.

VI. [*Morals have been methodized* in different ways. The ancients commonly arranged them under the *four cardinal virtues* of prudence, temperance, fortitude, and justice. Christian writers, I think more properly, under the *three heads* of the duty we owe to God, to ourselves, and to our neighbour. One division may be more comprehensive, or more natural, than another; but the truths arranged are the same, and their evidence the same in all.]

I shall only further observe, with regard to systems of morals, that they have been made more voluminous, and more intricate, partly by mixing political questions with morals, which I think improper, because they belong to a different science, and are grounded on different principles; partly by making what is commonly, but I think improperly, called the "theory of morals," a part of the system.

VII. By *the theory of morals is* meant *a just account of the structure of our moral powers;* that is, of those powers of the mind by which we have our moral conceptions, and distinguish right from wrong in human actions. This, indeed, is an intricate subject, and there have been various theories and much controversy about it in ancient and in modern times. But it has little connexion with the knowledge of our duty; and those who differ most in the theory of our moral powers, agree in the practical rules of morals which they dictate.

As a man may be a good judge of colours, and of the other visible qualities of objects, without any knowledge of the anatomy of the eye, and of the theory of vision; so a man may have a very clear and comprehensive knowledge of what is right and what is wrong in human conduct, who never studied the structure of our moral powers.

A good ear in music may be much improved by attention and practice in that art; but very little by studying the anatomy of the ear, and the theory of sound. In order to acquire a good eye or a good ear in the arts that require them, the theory of vision and the theory of sound are by no means necessary, and indeed of very little use. Of as little necessity or use is what we call the theory of morals, in order to improve our moral judgment.

I mean not to depreciate this branch of knowledge. It is a very important part of the philosophy of the human mind, and ought to be considered as such, but not as any part of morals. By the name we give to it, and by the custom of making it a part of every system of morals, men may be led into this gross mistake, which I wish to obviate, That in order to understand his duty, a man must needs be a philosopher and a metaphysician.

CHAPTER III.

OF SYSTEMS OF NATURAL JURISPRUDENCE.

I. *Jurisprudence and morals closely related.*—SYSTEMS of natural jurisprudence, of the rights of peace and war, or of the law of nature and nations, are a modern invention, which soon acquired such reputation, as gave occasion to many public establishments for teaching it along with the other sciences. It has so close a relation to morals, that it may answer the purpose of a system of morals, and is commonly put in the place of it, as far, at least, as concerns our duty to our fellow-men. *They differ in the name and form, but agree in substance.* This will appear from a slight attention to the nature of both.

[The direct intention of morals is to teach the *duty* of men: that of natural jurisprudence, to teach the *rights* of men.] Right and duty are things very different, and have even a kind of opposition; yet they are so related, that the one cannot even be conceived without the other; and he that understands the one must understand the other.

They have the same relation which credit has to debt. As all credit supposes an equivalent debt; so all right supposes a corresponding duty. There can be no credit in one party without an equivalent debt in another party; and there can be no right in one party, without a corresponding duty in another party. The sum of credit shows the sum of debt; and the sum of men's rights shows, in like manner, the sum of their duty to one another.

II. [The word *right* has a very different meaning, according as it is applied to *actions or to persons*. A right action is an action agreeable to our duty. But when we speak of the rights of men, the word has a very different and a more artificial meaning. It is a term of art in law, and signifies all that a man may lawfully do, all that he may lawfully possess and use, and all that he may lawfully claim of any other person.]

This comprehensive meaning of the word *right*, and of the Latin word *jus*, which corresponds to it, though long adopted into common language, is too artificial to be the birth of common language. It is a term of art, contrived by civilians when the civil law became a profession.

The whole end and object of law is to protect the subjects in all that they may lawfully do, or possess, or demand. This threefold object of law, civilians have comprehended under the word *jus* or *right*, which they define, "Facultas aliquid agendi, vel possidendi, vel ab alio consequendi:" a lawful claim to do any thing, to possess any thing, or to demand some prestation from some other person. The first of these may be called the right of *liberty*, the second that of *property*, which is also called a *real right*, the third is called *personal right*, because it respects some particular person or persons of whom the prestation may be demanded.

We can be at no loss to perceive the duties corresponding to the several kinds of rights. What I have a right to do, it is the duty of all men not to hinder me from doing. What is my property or real right, no man ought to take from me; or to molest me in the use and enjoyment of it. And what I have a right to demand of any man, it is his duty to perform. Between the right, on the one hand, and the duty, on the other, there is not only a necessary connexion, but, in reality, they are only different expressions of the same meaning; just as it is the same thing to say I am your debtor, and to say you are my creditor; or as it is the same thing to say I am your father, and to say you are my son.

[Thus we see, that there is such *a correspondence between the rights of men and the duties of men,* that the one points out the other; and a system of the one may be substituted for a system of the other.]

III. [But here an objection occurs. It may be said, That although every right implies a duty, yet every duty does not imply a right.] Thus, it may be my duty to do a humane or kind office to a man who has no claim of right to it; and therefore a system of the rights of men, though it teach all the duties of strict justice, yet it leaves out all the duties of charity and humanity, without which the system of morals must be very lame.

[In *answer* to this objection, it may be observed, That, as there is a strict notion of justice, in which it is distinguished from humanity and charity, so there is a more extensive signification of it, in which it includes those virtues.] The ancient moralists, both Greek and Roman, under the cardinal virtue of justice, included beneficence; and, in this extensive sense, it is often used in common language. The like may be said of right, which, in a sense not uncommon, is extended to every proper claim of humanity and charity, as well as to the claims of strict justice. But, as it is proper to distinguish these two kinds of claims by different names, writers in natural jurisprudence have given the name of *perfect* rights to the claims of strict justice, and that of *imperfect* rights to the claims of charity and humanity. Thus, all the duties of humanity have imperfect rights corresponding to them, as those of strict justice have perfect rights.

IV. [*Another objection* may be, That there is still a class of duties to which no right, perfect or imperfect, corresponds.]

We are bound in duty to pay due respect, not only to what is truly the right of another, but to what, through ignorance or mistake, we believe to be his right. Thus, if my neighbour is possessed of a horse which he stole, and to which he has no right; while I believe the horse to be really his, and am ignorant of the theft, it is my duty to pay the same respect to this conceived right as if it were real. Here, then, is a moral obligation on one party, without any corresponding right on the other.

To supply this defect in the system of rights, so as to make right and duty correspond in every instance, writers in jurisprudence have had recourse to something like what is called *a fiction of law.* [They give the name of *right* to the claim which even the thief hath to the goods he has stolen, while the theft is unknown, and to all similar claims grounded on the ignorance or mistake of the parties concerned. And to distinguish this kind of right from genuine rights, perfect or imperfect, they call it an *external* right.]

Thus it appears, That although a system of the perfect rights of men, or the rights of strict justice, would be a lame substitute for a system of human duty; yet when we add to it the imperfect and the external rights, it comprehends the whole duty we owe to our fellow-men.

But it may be asked, Why should men be taught their duty in this indirect way, by reflection, as it were, from the rights of other men?

Perhaps it may be thought, that this indirect way may be more agreeable to the pride of man, as we see that men of rank like better to hear of obligations of honour than of obligations of duty (although the dictates of true honour and of duty be the same) for this reason, that honour puts a man in mind of what he owes to himself, whereas duty is a more humiliating idea. For a like reason, men may attend more willingly to their rights, which put them in mind of their dignity, than to their duties, which suggest their dependence. And we see that men may give great attention to their rights who give but little to their duty.

V. *True origin of systems of natural jurisprudence.*—Whatever truth there may be in this, I believe better reasons can be given *why systems of natural jurisprudence have been contrived* and put in the place of systems of morals.

Systems of *civil law* were invented many ages before we had any system of natural jurisprudence; and the former seem to have suggested the idea of the latter.

Such is the weakness of human understanding, that no large body of knowledge can be easily apprehended and remembered, unless it be arranged and methodized, that is, reduced into a system. When the laws of the Roman people were multiplied to a great degree, and the study of them became an honourable and lucrative profession, it became necessary that they should be methodized into a system. And the most natural and obvious way of methodizing law was found to be according to the divisions and subdivisions of men's rights, which it is the intention of law to protect.

The study of law produced not only systems of law, but a language proper for expressing them. Every art has its terms of art, for expressing the conceptions that belong to it; and the civilian must have terms for expressing accurately the divisions and subdivisions of rights, and the various ways whereby they may be acquired, transferred, or extinguished, in the various transactions of civil society. He must have terms accurately defined, for the various crimes by which men's rights are violated, not to speak of the terms which express the different forms of actions at law, and the various steps of the procedure of judicatories.

[Those who have been bred to any profession are very *prone to use the terms of their profession* in speaking or writing on subjects that have any analogy to it. And they may do so with advantage, as terms of art are commonly more precise in their signification, and better defined, than the words of common language.] To such persons it is also very natural to model and arrange other subjects, as far as their nature admits, into a method similar to that of the system which fills their minds.

It might, therefore, be expected, that a civilian, intending to give a detailed system of morals, would use many of the terms of civil law, and mould it, as far as it can be done, into the form of a system of law, or of the rights of mankind.

The necessary and close relation of right to duty, which we before observed, justified this: and moral duty had long been considered as a *law of nature;* a law, not wrote on tables of stone or brass, but on the heart of man; a law of greater antiquity and higher authority than the laws of particular states; a law which is binding upon all men of all nations, and therefore is called by Cicero *the law of nature and of nations.*

VI. The idea of a system of this law was worthy of the genius of the immortal Hugo Grotius, and he was the first who executed it in such a manner, as to draw the attention of the learned in all the European nations; and to give occasion to several princes and states to establish public professions for the teaching of this law.

The multitude of commentators and annotators upon this work of Grotius, and the public establishments to which it gave occasion, are sufficient vouchers of its merit.

It is, indeed, a work so well designed, and so skilfully executed; so free from the scholastic jargon which infected the learned at that time, so much addressed to the common sense and moral judgment of mankind, and so agreeably illustrated by examples from ancient history, and authorities from the sentiments of ancient authors, Heathen and Christian, that it must always be esteemed as the capital work of a great genius upon a most important subject.

VII. *The utility of a just system of natural jurisprudence appears,* 1. As it is a system of the moral duty we owe to men, which, by the aid they have taken from the terms and divisions of the civil law, has been given more in detail and more systematically by writers in natural jurisprudence than it was formerly. 2. As it is the best preparation for the study of law, being, as it were, cast in the mould, and using and explaining many of the terms of the civil law, on which the law of most of the European nations is grounded. 3. It is of use to lawyers, who ought to make their laws as agreeable as possible to the laws of nature. And as laws made by men, like all human works, must be imperfect, it points out the errors and imperfections of human laws. 4. To judges and interpreters of the law it is of use, because that interpretation ought to be preferred which is founded in the law of nature. 5. It is of use in civil controversies between states, or between individuals who have no common superior. In such controversies, the appeal must be made to the law of nature; and the standard systems of it, particularly that of Grotius, have great authority. And, 6. to say no more upon this point, it is of great use to sovereigns and states who are above all human laws, to be solemnly admonished of the conduct they are bound to observe to their own subjects, to the subjects of other states, and to one another, in peace and in war. The better and the more generally the law of nature is understood, the greater dishonour, in public estimation, will follow every violation of it.

VIII. Some authors have imagined, that systems of natural jurisprudence ought to be confined to the *perfect rights of men*, because the duties which correspond to the imperfect rights, the duties of charity and humanity, cannot be enforced by human laws, but must be left to the judgment and conscience of men, free from compulsion. But the systems which have had the greatest applause of the public, have not followed this plan, and, I conceive, for good reasons. *First*, because a system of perfect rights could by no means serve the purpose of a system of morals, which surely is an important purpose. *Secondly*, because, in many cases, it is hardly possible to fix the precise limit between justice and humanity, between perfect and imperfect right. Like the colours in a prismatic image, they run into each other, so that the best eye cannot fix the precise boundary between them. *Thirdly*, as wise legislators and magistrates ought to have it as their end to make the citizens good, as well as just, we find, in all civilized nations, laws that are intended to encourage the duties of humanity. Where human laws cannot enforce them by punishments, they may encourage them by rewards. Of this the wisest legislators have given examples; and how far this branch of legislation may be carried, no man can foresee.

The substance of the four following chapters was written long ago, and read in a literary society, with a view to justify some points of morals from metaphysical objections urged against them in the writings of David Hume, Esq. If they answer that end, and, at the same time, serve to illustrate the account I have given of our moral powers, it is hoped that the reader will not think them improperly placed here; and that he will forgive some repetitions, and perhaps anachronisms, occasioned by their being wrote at different times, and on different occasions.

CHAPTER IV.

WHETHER AN ACTION DESERVING MORAL APPROBATION, MUST BE DONE WITH THE BELIEF OF ITS BEING MORALLY GOOD.

I. THERE is no part of philosophy more subtile and intricate than that which is called " the theory of morals." Nor is there any more plain and level to the apprehension of man than the *practical part of morals.*

In the former, the Epicurean, the Peripatetic and the Stoic, had each his different system of old; and almost every modern author of reputation has a system of his own. At the same time, there is no branch of human knowledge in which there is so general an agreement among ancients and moderns, learned and unlearned, as in the practical rules of morals.

From this discord in the theory, and harmony in the practical part, we may judge, that the rules of morality stand upon another and a firmer foundation than the theory. And of this it is easy to perceive the reason.

For, in order to know what is right and what is wrong in human conduct, we need only listen to the dictates of our conscience, when the mind is calm and unruffled, or attend to the judgment we form of others in like circumstances. But, to judge of the various theories of morals, we must be able to analyze and dissect, as it were, the active powers of the human mind, and especially to analyze accurately that conscience or moral power by which we discern right from wrong.

☞ The conscience may be compared to the eye in this, as in many other respects. The learned and the unlearned see objects with equal distinctness. The former have no title to dictate to the latter, as far as the eye is judge, nor is there any disagreement about such matters. But, to dissect the eye, and to explain the theory of vision, is a difficult point, wherein the most skilful have differed.

From this remarkable disparity between our decisions in the theory of morals and in the rules of morality, we may, I think, draw this conclusion, that wherever we find any disagreement between the practical rules of morality, which have been received in all ages, and the principles of any of the theories advanced upon this subject, the practical rules ought to be the standard by which the theory is to be corrected, and that it is both unsafe and unphilosophical to warp the practical rules, in order to make them tally with a favourite theory.

II. The question to be considered in this chapter belongs to *the practical part* of morals, and therefore is capable of a more easy and more certain determination. And, if it be determined in the affirmative, I conceive that it may serve as a touchstone to try some celebrated theories which are inconsistent with that determination, and which have led the theorists to oppose it by very subtile metaphysical arguments.

Every question about what is or is not the proper object of moral approbation, belongs to practical morals, and such is the question now under consideration: whether actions deserving moral approbation must be done with the belief of their being morally good? Or, whether an action, done without any regard to duty or to the dictates of conscience, can be entitled to moral approbation?

In every action of a moral agent, his conscience is either altogether silent, or it pronounces the action to be good, or bad, or indifferent. This, I think, is a complete enumeration. If it be perfectly silent, the action must be very trifling, or appear so. For conscience, in those who have exercised it, is a very pragmatical faculty, and meddles with every part of our conduct, whether we desire its counsel or not. And what a man does in perfect simplicity, without the least suspicion of its being bad, his heart cannot condemn him for, nor will he that knows the heart condemn him. If there was any previous culpable negligence or inattention which led him to a wrong judgment, or hindered his forming a right one, that I do not exculpate. I only consider the action done, and the disposition with which it was done, without its previous circumstances. And in this there appears nothing that merits disapprobation. As little can it merit any degree of moral approbation, because there was neither good nor ill intended. And the same may be said when conscience pronounces the action to be indifferent.

If, in the *second* place, I do what my conscience pronounces to be bad or dubious, I am guilty to myself, and justly deserve the disapprobation of others. Nor am I less guilty in this case, though what I judged to be bad should happen to be good or indifferent. I did it believing it to be bad, and this is an immorality.

Lastly, if I do what my conscience pronounces to be right and my duty, either I have some regard to duty, or I have none. The last is not supposable; for I believe there is no man so abandoned, but that he does what he believes to be his duty, with more assurance and alacrity upon that account. The more weight the rectitude of the action has in determining me to do it, the more I approve of my own conduct. And if my worldly interest, my appetites or inclinations, draw me strongly the contrary way, my following the dictates of my conscience, in opposition to these motives, adds to the moral worth of the action.

When a man acts from an erroneous judgment, if his error be invincible, all agree that he is inculpable: but if his error be owing to some previous negligence or inattention, there seems to be some difference among moralists. This difference, however, is only seeming, and not real. For wherein lies the fault in this case? It must be granted by all, that the fault lies in this, and solely in this, that he was not at due pains to have his judgment well informed. Those moralists, therefore, who consider the action and the previous conduct that led to it as one whole, find something to blame in the whole; and they do so most justly. But those who take this whole to pieces, and consider what is blameable and what is right in each part, find all that is blameable in what preceded this wrong judgment, and nothing but what is approvable in what followed it.

☞ Let us suppose, for instance, that a man believes that God has indispensably required him to observe a very rigorous fast in Lent; and that, from a regard to this supposed Divine command, he fasts in such a manner as is not only a great mortification to his appetite, but even hurtful to his health.

His superstitious opinion may be the effect of a culpable negligence, for which he can by no means be justified. Let him, therefore, bear all the blame upon this account that he deserves. But now, having this opinion fixed in his mind, shall he act according to it or against it? Surely we cannot hesitate a moment in this case. It is evident, that in following the light of his judgment, he acts the part of a good and pious man; whereas, in acting contrary to his judgment, he would be guilty of wilful disobedience to his Maker.

☞ If my servant, by mistaking my orders, does the contrary of what I commanded, believing, at the same time, that he obeys my orders, there may be some fault in his mistake, but to charge him with the crime of disobedience, would be inhuman and unjust.

These determinations appear to me to have intuitive evidence, no less than that of mathematical axioms. A man who is come to years of understanding, and who has exercised his faculties in judging of right and wrong, sees their truth as he sees daylight. Metaphysical arguments brought against them have the same effect as when brought against the evidence of sense; they may puzzle and confound, but they do not convince. It appears evident, therefore, that those actions only can truly be called virtuous, or deserving of moral approbation, which the agent believed to be right, and to which he was influenced, more or less, by that belief.

III. If it should be *objected*, [that this principle makes it to be of no consequence to a man's morals, what his opinions may be, providing he acts agreeably to them, the answer is easy.]

[Morality requires, not only that a man should act according to his judgment, but that he should use the best means in his power that his judgment be according to truth.] If he fail in either of these points, he is worthy of blame; but, if he fail in neither, I see not wherein he can be blamed.

When a man must act, and has no longer time to deliberate, he ought to act according to the light of his conscience, even when he is in an error. But, when he has time to deliberate, he ought surely to use all the means in his power to be rightly informed. When he has done so, he may still be in an error; but it is an invincible error, and cannot justly be imputed to him as a fault.

IV. A *second* objection is, that we immediately approve of benevolence, gratitude, and other primary virtues, without inquiring whether they are practised from a persuasion that they are our duty. And the laws of God place the sum of virtue in loving God and our neighbour, without any provision that we do it from a persuasion that we ought to do so.]

The answer to this objection is, [that the love of God, the love of our neighbour, justice, gratitude, and other primary virtues, are, by the constitution of human nature, necessarily accompanied with a conviction of their being morally good. We may therefore safely presume, that these things are never disjoined, and that every man who practises these virtues does it with a good conscience.] In judging of men's conduct, we do not suppose things which cannot happen, nor do the laws of God give decisions upon impossible cases, as they must have done, if they supposed the case of a man who thought it contrary to his duty to love God or to love mankind.

But if we wish to know how the laws of God determine the point in question, we ought to observe their decision with regard to such actions as may appear good to one man and ill to another. And here the decisions of Scripture are clear: *Let every man be persuaded in his own mind. He that doubteth is condemned if he eat, because he eateth not of faith, for whatsoever is not of faith is sin. To him that esteemeth any thing to be unclean, it is unclean.* The Scripture often placeth the sum of virtue in *living in all good conscience*, in acting so *that our hearts condemn us not.*

V. *The last objection* I shall mention *is a metaphysical one* urged by Mr. Hume.

It is a favourite point in his system of morals, that justice is not a natural but an artificial virtue. To prove this, he has exerted the whole strength of his reason and eloquence. And as the principle we are considering stood in his way, he takes pains to refute it.

"Suppose," says he, "a person to have lent me a sum of money, on condition that it be restored in a few days. After the expiration of the term he demands the sum. I ask, what reason or motive have I to restore the money? It will perhaps be said, that my regard to justice, and abhorrence of villany and knavery, are sufficient reasons for me." And this, he acknowledges, would be a satisfactory answer to a man in a civilized state, and when trained up according to a certain discipline and education. "But in his rude and more natural condition," says he, "if you are pleased to call such a condition natural, this answer would be rejected as perfectly unintelligible and sophistical.

"For wherein consists this honesty and justice? Not surely in the external action. It must, therefore, consist in the motive from which the external act is derived. This motive can never be a regard to the honesty of the action. For it is a plain fallacy to say, that a virtuous motive is requisite to render an action honest, and, at the same time, that a regard to the honesty is the motive to the action. We can never have a regard to the virtue of an action, unless the action be antecedently virtuous."

And, in another place, "To suppose that the mere regard to the virtue of the action is that which rendered it virtuous, is to reason in a circle. An action must be virtuous, before we can have a regard to its virtue. Some virtuous motive, therefore, must be antecedent to that regard. Nor is this merely a metaphysical subtilty," &c.—Treatise of Human Nature, book iii. part 2, sect. 1.

VI. *I am not to consider* at this time, how this reasoning is applied to support the author's opinion, *that justice is not a natural but an artificial virtue.* I consider it only as far as it opposes the principle I have been endeavouring to establish, " That, to render an action truly virtuous, the agent must have some regard to its rectitude." And I conceive the whole force of the reasoning amounts to this:

When we judge an action to be good or bad, it must have been so in its own nature antecedent to that judgment, otherwise the judgment is erroneous. If, therefore, the action be good in its nature, the judgment of the agent cannot make it bad; nor can his judgment make it good, if, in its nature, it be bad. For this would be to ascribe to our judgment a strange magical power to transform the nature of things, and to say, that my judging a thing to be what it is not, makes it really to be what I erroneously judge it to be. This, I think, is the objection in its full strength. And, in answer to it,

First, If we could not loose this metaphysical knot, I think we might fairly and honestly cut it, because it fixes an absurdity upon the clearest and most indisputable principles of morals and of common sense. For I appeal to any man whether there be any principle of morality, or any principle of common sense, more clear and indisputable than that which we just now quoted from the Apostle Paul, that although a thing be not unclean in itself, yet to him that esteemeth it to be unclean, to him it is unclean. But the metaphysical argument makes this absurd. For, says the metaphysician, if the thing was not unclean in itself, you judged wrong in esteeming it to be unclean; and what can be more absurd, than that your esteeming a thing to be what it is not, should make it what you erroneously esteem it to be?

Let us try the edge of this argument in another instance. Nothing is more evident than that an action does not merit the name of benevolent, unless it be done from a belief that it tends to promote the good of our neighbour. But this is absurd, says the metaphysician. For, if it be not a benevolent action in itself, your belief of its tendency cannot change its nature. It is absurd, that your erroneous belief should make the action to be what you believe it be. Nothing is more evident, than that a man who tells the truth, believing it to be a lie, is guilty of falsehood; but the metaphysician would make this to be absurd.

In a word, if there be any strength in this argument, it would follow, that a man might be, in the highest degree, virtuous, without the least regard to virtue; that he might be very benevolent, without ever intending to do a good office; very malicious, without ever intending any hurt; very revengeful, without ever intending to retaliate an injury; very grateful, without ever intending to return a benefit; and a man of strict veracity, with an intention to lie. We might, therefore, reject this reasoning, as repugnant to self-evident truths, though we were not able to point out the fallacy of it.

2. But let us try, in the *second* place, whether the fallacy of this argument may not be discovered.

We ascribe moral goodness to actions considered abstractly, without any relation to the agent. We likewise ascribe moral goodness to an agent on account of an action he has done; we call it a good action, though, in this case, the goodness is properly in the man, and is only by a figure ascribed to the action.

Now, it is to be considered, whether *moral goodness*, when applied to an action considered abstractly, has the same meaning as when we apply it to a man on account of that action; or whether we do not unawares change the meaning of the word, according as we apply it to the one or to the other.

[The *action*, considered abstractly, has neither understanding nor will; it is not accountable, nor can it be under any moral obligation.] But all these things are essential to that moral goodness which belongs to a man: for if a man had not understanding and will, he could have no moral goodness. Hence it follows necessarily, that the moral goodness which we ascribe to an action considered abstractly, and that which we ascribe to a person for doing that action, are not the same. The meaning of the word is changed when it is applied to these different subjects.

This will be more evident, when we consider what is meant by the moral goodness which we ascribe to a man for doing an action, and what by the goodness which belongs to the action considered abstractly. A good action in a man is that in which he applied his intellectual powers properly, in order to judge what he ought to do, and acted according to his best judgment. This is all that can be required of a moral agent; and in this his moral goodness, in any good action, consists. But is this the goodness which we ascribe to an action considered abstractly? No, surely. For the action, considered abstractly, is neither endowed with judgment nor with active power; and, therefore, can have none of that goodness which we ascribe to the man for doing it.

But what do we mean by goodness in an action considered abstractly? To me it appears to lie in this, and in this only, that it is an action which ought to be done by those who have the power and opportunity, and the capacity of perceiving their obligation to do it. I would gladly know of any man what other moral goodness can be in an action considered abstractly. And this goodness is inherent in its nature, and inseparable from it. No opinion or judgment of an agent can in the least alter its nature.

☞ Suppose the action to be that of relieving an innocent person out of great distress. This surely has all the moral goodness that an action considered abstractly can have. Yet it is evident, that an agent, in relieving a person in distress, may have no moral goodness, may have great merit, or may have great demerit.

Suppose, *first*, that mice cut the cords which bound the distressed person, and so bring him relief. Is there moral goodness in this act of the mice?

Suppose, *secondly*, that a man maliciously relieves the distressed person, in order to plunge him into greater distress. In this action there is surely no moral goodness, but much malice and inhumanity.

If, in the *last* place, we suppose a person, from real sympathy and humanity, to bring relief to the distressed person, with considerable expense or danger to himself; here is an action of real worth, which every heart approves and every tongue praises. [But wherein lies the worth? *Not in the action* considered by itself, which was common to all the three, *but in the man* who, on this occasion, acted the part which became a good man. He did what his heart approved, and therefore he is approved by God and man.]

VII. Upon the whole, if we distinguish between that goodness which may be ascribed to an action considered by itself, and that goodness which we ascribe to a man when he puts it in execution, we shall find a key to this metaphysical lock. We admit that the goodness of an action, considered abstractly, can have no dependence upon the opinion or belief of an agent, any more than the truth of a proposition depends upon our believing it to be true. But when a man exerts his active power well, or ill, there is a moral goodness or turpitude which we figuratively impute to the action, but which is truly and properly imputable to the man only; and this *goodness or turpitude depends* very much *upon the intention* of the agent, and the opinion he had of his action.

This distinction has been understood in all ages by those who gave any attention to morals, though it has been variously expressed. The Greek moralists gave the name of καθῆκον to an action good in itself; such an action might be done by the most worthless. But an action done with a right intention, which implies real worth in the agent, they called κατόρθωμα. The distinction is explained by Cicero in his "Offices." He calls the first *officium medium*, and the second *officium perfectum*, or *rectum*. In the scholastic ages, an action good in itself was said to be *materially* good, and an action done with a right intention was called *formally* good. This last way of expressing the distinction is still familiar among theologians; but Mr. Hume seems not to have attended to it, or to have thought it to be words without any meaning.

Mr. Hume, in the section already quoted, tells us with great assurance, "In short, it may be established as an undoubted maxim, that no action can be virtuous or morally good, unless there be in human nature some motive to produce it distinct from the sense of its morality." And upon this maxim he founds many of his reasonings on the subject of morals.

Whether it be consistent with Mr. Hume's own system, that an action may be produced merely from the sense of its morality, without any motive of agreeableness or utility, I shall not now inquire. But, if it be true, and I think it evident to every man of common understanding, that a judge or an arbiter acts the most virtuous part when his sentence is produced by no other motive but a regard to justice and a good conscience, nay, when all other motives distinct from this are on the other side: if this, I say, be true, then that undoubted maxim of Mr. Hume must be false, and all the conclusions built upon it must fall to the ground.

VIII. From the principle I have endeavoured to establish, I think some *consequences* may be drawn *with regard to the theory of morals.*

First, If there be no virtue without the belief that what we do is right, it follows, that a moral faculty, that is, a power of discerning moral goodness and turpitude in human conduct, is essential to every being capable of virtue or vice. A being who has no more conception of moral goodness and baseness, of right and wrong, than a blind man hath of colours, can have no regard to it in his conduct, and therefore can neither be virtuous nor vicious.

He may have qualities that are agreeable or disagreeable, useful or hurtful, so may a plant or a machine. And we sometimes use the word *virtue* in such a latitude, as to signify any agreeable or useful quality, as when we speak of the virtues of plants. But we are now speaking of virtue in the strict and proper sense, as it signifies that quality in a man which is the object of moral approbation.

This virtue a man could not have, if he had not a power of discerning a right and a wrong in human conduct, and of being influenced by that discernment. For in so far only he is virtuous as he is guided in his conduct by that part of his constitution. Brutes do not appear to have any such power, and therefore are not moral or accountable agents. They are capable of culture and discipline, but not of virtuous or criminal conduct. Even human creatures, in infancy and non-age, are not moral agents, because their moral faculty is not yet unfolded. These sentiments are supported by the common sense of mankind, which has always determined, that neither brutes nor infants can be indicted for crimes.

IX. *Conscience, or moral sense.*—[It is of small consequence what name we give to this moral power of the human mind; but it is so important a part of our constitution, as to deserve an appropriated name. The name of *conscience,* as it is the most common, seems to me as proper as any that has been given it. I find no fault with the name *moral sense,* although I conceive this name has given occasion to some mistakes concerning the nature of our moral power.] Modern philosophers have conceived of the external senses as having no other office but to give us certain sensations, or simple conceptions, which we could not have without them. And this notion has been applied to the moral sense. But it seems to me a mistaken notion in both. By the sense of seeing, I not only have the conception of the different colours, but I perceive one body to be of this colour, another of that. In like manner, by my moral sense, I not only have the conceptions of right and wrong in conduct, but I perceive *this* conduct to be right, *that* to be wrong, and *that* indifferent. All our senses are judging faculties, so also is conscience. Nor is this power only a judge of our own actions and those of others, it is likewise a principle of action in all good men; and so far only can our conduct be denominated virtuous, as it is influenced by this principle.

X. [A *second* consequence from the principle laid down in this chapter is, That the formal nature and *essence of that virtue which is the object of moral approbation consists* neither in a prudent prosecution of our private interest, nor in benevolent affections towards others, nor in qualities useful or agreeable to ourselves or to others, nor in sympathizing with the passions and affections of others, and in attuning our own conduct to the tone of other men's passions; but it consists *in living in all good conscience*, that is, in using the best means in our power to know our duty, and acting accordingly.]

Prudence is a virtue, benevolence is a virtue, fortitude is a virtue; but the essence and formal nature of virtue must lie in something that is common to all these, and to every other virtue. And this I conceive can be nothing else but the rectitude of such conduct, and turpitude of the contrary, which is discerned by a good man. And so far only he is virtuous as he pursues the former, and avoids the latter.

CHAPTER V.

WHETHER JUSTICE BE A NATURAL OR AN ARTIFICIAL VIRTUE.

I. *Hume consistent as a writer on morals.*—Mr. Hume's philosophy concerning morals was first presented to the world in the third volume of his "Treatise of Human Nature," in the year 1740; afterwards in his "Enquiry concerning the Principles of Morals," which was first published by itself, and then in several editions of his "Essays and Treatises."

In these two works on morals the system is the same. A more popular arrangement, great embellishment, and the omission of some metaphysical reasonings, have given a preference in the public esteem to the last; but I find neither any new principles in it, nor any new arguments in support of the system common to both.

In this system, the proper object of moral approbation is not actions or any voluntary exertion, but qualities of mind; that is, natural affections or passions, which are involuntary, a part of the constitution of the man, and common to us with many brute animals. When we praise or blame any voluntary action, it is only considered as a sign of the natural affection from which it flows, and from which all its merit or demerit is derived.

Moral approbation or disapprobation is not an act of the judgment, which, like all acts of judgment, must be true or false, it is only a certain feeling, which, from the constitution of human nature, arises upon contemplating certain characters or qualities of mind coolly and impartially.

This feeling, when agreeable, is moral approbation; when disagreeable, disapprobation. The qualities of mind which produce this agreeable feeling are the moral virtues, and those that produce the disagreeable, the vices.

II. These preliminaries being granted, the question about the foundation of morals is reduced to a simple question of fact, viz. [What are the qualities of mind which produce, in the disinterested observer, the feeling of approbation, or the contrary feeling?]

In answer to this question, the author endeavours to prove, by a very copious induction, that all personal merit, all virtue, all that is the object of moral approbation, consists in the qualities of mind which are *agreeable* or *useful* to the person who possesses them, or to others.

The *dulce* and the *utile* is the whole sum of merit in every character, in every quality of mind, and in every action of life. There is no room left for that *honestum* which Cicero thus defines, " Honestum igitur id intelligimus, quod tale est, ut detracta omni utilitate, sine ullis premiis fructibusve, per se ipsum possit jure laudari."—" Moral worth is of such a character, that, setting aside all idea of utility, without rewards or fruits of any kind, it may justly be praised on its own account solely."

III. *Hume agrees with the Epicureans in one respect.*—[Among the ancient moralists, the Epicureans were the only sect who denied that there is any such thing as *honestum*, or moral worth, distinct from pleasure. In this Mr. Hume's system agrees with theirs. For the addition of *utility to pleasure*, as a foundation of morals, makes only a verbal, but no real difference.] What is useful only has no value in itself, but derives all its merit from the end for which it is useful. That end, in this system, is agreeableness or pleasure. So that, in both systems, pleasure is the only end, the only thing that is good in itself, and desirable for its own sake; and virtue derives all its merit from its tendency to produce pleasure.

Agreeableness and utility are not moral conceptions, nor have they any connexion with morality. What a man does, merely because it is agreeable, or useful to procure what is agreeable, is not virtue. Therefore the Epicurean system was justly thought by Cicero, and the best moralists among the ancients, to subvert morality, and to substitute another principle in its room; and this system is liable to the same censure.

IV. *Disagrees in another.*—[In one thing, however, it differs remarkably from that of Epicurus. It allows, that there are *disinterested affections* in human nature; that the love of children and relations, friendship, gratitude, compassion, and humanity, are not, as Epicurus maintained, different modifications of self-love, but simple and original parts of the human constitution; that when interest, or envy, or revenge, pervert not our disposition, we are inclined, from natural philanthropy, to desire, and to be pleased with the happiness of the human kind.]

All this, in opposition to the Epicurean system, Mr. Hume maintains with great strength of reason and eloquence, and, in this respect, his system is more liberal and disinterested than that of the Greek philosopher. According to Epicurus, virtue is whatever is agreeable to ourselves. According to Mr. Hume, every quality of mind that is agreeable or useful to ourselves or to others.

V. *Effect of this doctrine.*—[This theory of the nature of virtue, it must be acknowledged, *enlarges* greatly *the catalogue of moral virtues*, by bringing into that catalogue every quality of mind that is useful or agreeable.] Nor does there appear any good reason why the useful and agreeable qualities of body and of fortune, as well as those of the mind, should not have a place among moral virtues in this system. They have the essence of virtue; that is, agreeableness and utility, why then should they not have the name?

But, to compensate this addition to the moral virtues, one class of them seems to be greatly degraded and deprived of all intrinsic merit. The useful virtues, as was above observed, are only ministering servants of the agreeable, and purveyors for them; they must, therefore, be so far inferior in dignity, as hardly to deserve the same name.

VI. *Natural and artificial virtues.*—[Mr. Hume, however, gives the name of *virtue* to both; and to distinguish them, calls the agreeable qualities *natural* virtues, and the useful *artificial*.]

[The *natural virtues* are those natural affections of the human constitution which give immediate pleasure in their exercise. Such are all the benevolent affections.] Nature disposes to them, and from their own nature they are agreeable, both when we exercise them ourselves, and when we contemplate their exercise in others.

[The *artificial virtues* are such as are esteemed solely on account of their utility, either (1) to promote the good of society, as justice, fidelity, honour, veracity, allegiance, chastity; or (2) on account of their utility to the possessor, as industry, discretion, frugality, secrecy, order, perseverance, forethought, judgment, and others,] of which, he says, many pages could not contain the catalogue.

This general view of Mr. Hume's system concerning the foundation of morals, seemed necessary, in order to understand distinctly the meaning of that principle of his, which is to be the subject of this chapter, and on which he has bestowed much labour, to wit, "that justice is not a natural but an artificial virtue."

VII. [*This system* of the foundation of virtue is so *contradictory* in many of its essential points to the account we have before given of the active powers of human nature, that, if the one be true, the other must be false.]

If God has given to man a power which we call *conscience*, the *moral faculty*, the *sense of duty*, by which, when he comes to years of understanding, he perceives certain things that depend on his will to be his duty, and other things to be base and unworthy; if the notion of duty be a simple conception, of its own kind, and of a different nature from the conceptions of utility and agreeableness, of interest or reputation; if this moral faculty be the prerogative of man, and no vestige of it be found in brute animals; if it be given us by God to regulate all our animal affections and passions; if to be governed by it be the glory of man and the image of God in his soul, and to disregard its dictates be his dishonour and depravity: I say, if these things be so, to seek the foundation of morality in the affections which we have in common with the brutes, is to seek the living among the dead, and to change the glory of man, and the image of God in his soul, into the similitude of an ox that eateth grass.

If virtue and vice be a matter of choice, they must consist in voluntary actions, or in fixed purposes of acting according to a certain rule when there is opportunity, and not in qualities of mind which are involuntary.

It is true, that every virtue is both agreeable and useful in the highest degree; and that every quality that is agreeable or useful, has a merit upon that account. But virtue has a merit peculiar to itself, a merit which does not arise from its being useful or agreeable, but from its being virtue. This merit is discerned by the same faculty by which we discern it to be virtue, and by no other.

VIII. *Esteem.*—[We give the name of *esteem* both to *the regard* we have *for things useful and agreeable*, and to *the regard* we have *for virtue;* but these are different kinds of esteem.] I esteem a man for his ingenuity and learning. I esteem him for his moral worth. The sound of *esteem* in both these speeches is the same, but its meaning is very different.

Good breeding is a very amiable quality; and even if I knew that the man had no motive to it but its pleasure and utility to himself and others, I should like it still, but I would not in that case call it a moral virtue.

A dog has a tender concern for her puppies; so has a man for his children. The natural affection is the same in both, and is amiable in both. But why do we impute moral virtue to the man on account of this concern, and not to the dog? The reason surely is, that, in the man, the natural affection is accompanied with a sense of duty, but, in the dog, it is not. The same thing may be said of all the kind affections common to us with the brutes. They are amiable qualities, but they are not moral virtues.

IX. *The merit of justice, according to Hume.*—What has been said relates to Mr. Hume's system in general. We are now to consider his notion of the particular virtue of justice, that its *merit consists* wholly *in its utility to society.*

That justice is highly useful and necessary in society, and on that account, ought to be loved and esteemed by all that love mankind, will readily be granted. And as justice is a social virtue, it is true also that there could be no exercise of it, and perhaps we should have no conception of it without society. But this is equally true of the natural affections of benevolence, gratitude, friendship, and compassion, which Mr. Hume makes to be the natural virtues.

It may be granted to Mr. Hume, that men have no conception of the virtue of justice till they have lived some time in society. It is purely a moral conception, and our moral conceptions and moral judgments are not born with us. They grow up by degrees, as our reason does. Nor do I pretend to know how early, or in what order, we acquire the conception of the several virtues. The conception of justice supposes some exercise of the moral faculty, which, being the noblest part of the human constitution, and that to which all its other parts are subservient, appears latest.

It may likewise be granted, that there is no animal affection in human nature that prompts us immediately to acts of justice, as such. We have natural affections of the animal kind, which immediately prompt us to acts of kindness; but none, that I know, that has the same relation to justice. The very conception of justice supposes a moral faculty; but our natural kind affections do not; otherwise we must allow that brutes have this faculty.

X. What I maintain is, *first,* That when men come to the

exercise of their moral faculty, *they perceive* a turpitude in injustice, as they do in other crimes, and consequently *an obligation to justice,* abstracting from the consideration of its utility. And, *secondly*, That as soon as men have any rational conception of a favour, and of an injury, *they must have the conception of justice*, and perceive its obligation distinct from its utility.

The first of these points hardly admits of any other proof, but an appeal to the sentiments of every honest man, and every man of honour, whether his indignation is not immediately inflamed against an atrocious act of villany, without the cool consideration of its distant consequences upon the good of society?

We might appeal even to robbers and pirates, Whether they have not had great struggles with their conscience, when they first resolved to break through all the rules of justice? And whether, in a solitary and serious hour, they have not frequently felt the pangs of guilt? They have very often confessed this at a time when all disguise is laid aside.

The common good of society, though a pleasing object to all men, when presented to their view, hardly ever enters into the thoughts of the far greatest part of mankind; and if a regard to it were the sole motive to justice, the number of honest men must be small indeed. It would be confined to the higher ranks, who, by their education, or by their office, are led to make the public good an object; but that it is so confined, I believe no man will venture to affirm.

The temptations to injustice are strongest in the lowest class of men; and if nature had provided no motive to oppose those temptations but a sense of public good, there would not be found an honest man in that class.

To all men that are not greatly corrupted, injustice, as well as cruelty and ingratitude, is an object of disapprobation on its own account. There is a voice within us that proclaims it to be base, unworthy, and deserving of punishment.

That there is, in all ingenuous natures, an antipathy to roguery and treachery, a reluctance to the thoughts of villany and baseness, we have the testimony of Mr. Hume himself; who, as I doubt not but he felt it, has expressed it very strongly in the conclusion to his "Enquiry," and acknowledged that, in some cases, without this reluctance and antipathy to dishonesty, a sensible knave would find no sufficient motive from public good to be honest.

I shall give the passage at large from the "Enquiry concerning the Principles of Morals," sec. 9, near the end.

" Treating vice with the greatest candour, and making it all possible concessions, we must acknowledge that there is not, in any instance, the smallest pretext for giving it the preference above virtue, with a view to self-interest; except, perhaps, in the case of justice, where a man, taking things in a certain light, may often seem to be a loser by his integrity. And though it is allowed that, without a regard to property, no society could subsist; yet, according to the imperfect way in which human affairs are conducted, a sensible knave, in particular incidents, may think, that an act of iniquity or infidelity will make a considerable addition to his fortune, without causing any considerable breach in the social union and confederacy. That *honesty is the best policy*, may be a good general rule, but it is liable to many exceptions: and he, it may perhaps be thought, conducts himself with most wisdom who observes the general rule, and takes advantage of all the exceptions.

" I must confess that, if a man think that this reasoning much requires an answer, it will be a little difficult to find any which will to him appear satisfactory and convincing. If his heart rebel not against such pernicious maxims, if he feel no reluctance to the thoughts of villany and baseness, he has indeed lost a considerable motive to virtue, and we may expect that his practice will be answerable to his speculation. But in all ingenuous natures, the antipathy to treachery and roguery is too strong to be counterbalanced by any views of profit or pecuniary advantage. Inward peace of mind, consciousness of integrity, a satisfactory review of our own conduct; these are circumstances very requisite to happiness, and will be cherished and cultivated by every honest man who feels the importance of them."

The reasoning of the *sensible knave* in this passage, seems to me to be justly founded upon the principles of the " Enquiry," and of the " Treatise of Human Nature," and therefore it is no wonder that the author should find it a little difficult to give any answer which would appear satisfactory and convincing to such a man. To counterbalance this reasoning, he puts in the other scale a reluctance, an antipathy, a rebellion of the heart against such pernicious maxims, which is felt by ingenuous natures.

XI. [Let us consider a little the force of *Mr. Hume's answer to this sensible knave*, who reasons upon his own principles.] I think it is either an acknowledgment, that there is a natural judgment of conscience in man, that injustice and treachery is a base and unworthy practice, which is the point I would establish; or it has no force to convince either the knave or an honest man.

A clear and intuitive judgment, resulting from the constitution of human nature, is sufficient to overbalance a train of subtile reasoning on the other side. Thus, the testimony of our senses is sufficient to overbalance all the subtile arguments brought against their testimony. And, if there be a like testimony of conscience in favour of honesty, all the subtile reasoning of the knave against it ought to be rejected without examination, as fallacious and sophistical, because it concludes against a self-evident principle; just as we reject the subtile reasoning of the metaphysician against the evidence of sense.

If, therefore, the *reluctance*, the *antipathy*, the *rebellion of the heart* against injustice, which Mr. Hume sets against the reasoning of the knave, *include* in their meaning *a natural* intuitive *judgment of conscience*, that injustice is base and unworthy, the reasoning of the knave is convincingly answered; but the principle, *That justice is an artificial virtue, approved solely for its utility*, is given up.

If, on the other hand, the antipathy, reluctance, and rebellion of heart, *imply no judgment*, but barely an uneasy feeling, and that not natural, but acquired and artificial, the answer is indeed very agreeable to the principles of the "Enquiry," but has no force to convince the knave or any other man.

The knave is here supposed by Mr. Hume to have no such feelings, and therefore the answer does not touch his case in the least, but leaves him in the full possession of his reasoning. And *ingenuous natures*, who have these feelings, are left to deliberate whether they will yield to acquired and artificial feelings, in opposition to rules of conduct, which, to their best judgment, appear wise and prudent.

XII. [The *second* thing I proposed to show was, That as soon as men have any rational conception of a *favour* and of an *injury*, they *must have the conception of justice*, and perceive its obligation.]*

The power with which the Author of nature hath endowed us, may be employed either to do good to our fellow men, or to hurt them. When we employ our power to promote the good and happiness of others, this is a benefit or favour; when we employ it to hurt them, it is an injury. Justice fills up the middle between these two. It is such a conduct as does no injury to others; but it does not imply the doing them any favour.

The notions of a *favour* and of an *injury*, appear as early in the mind of man as any rational notion whatever. They are discovered not by language only, but by certain affections of mind, of which they are the natural objects. A favour naturally produces gratitude. An injury done to ourselves produces resentment; and even when done to another, it produces indignation.

I take it for granted that gratitude and resentment are no less natural to the human mind than hunger and thirst; and that those affections are no less naturally excited by their proper objects and occasions than these appetites.

* Vide p. 343, sect. 10.

It is no less evident, that the proper and formal object of gratitude is a person who has done us a favour; that of resentment, a person who has done us an injury.

Before the use of reason, the distinction between a favour and an agreeable office is not perceived. Every action of another person which gives present pleasure produces love and good will towards the agent. Every action that gives pain or uneasiness produces resentment. This is common to man before the use of reason, and to the more sagacious brutes; and it shows no conception of justice in either.

But as we grow up to the use of reason, the notion, both of a favour and of an injury, grows more distinct and better defined. It is not enough that a good office be done; it must be done from good-will, and with a good intention, otherwise it is no favour, nor does it produce gratitude.

☞ I have heard of a physician who gave spiders in a medicine to a dropsical patient, with an intention to poison him, and that this medicine cured the patient, contrary to the intention of the physician. Surely no gratitude, but resentment, was due by the patient, when he knew the real state of the case. It is evident to every man, that a benefit arising from the action of another, either without or against his intention, is not a motive to gratitude; that is, is no favour.

Another thing implied in the nature of a favour is, that it be not due. A man may save my credit by paying what he owes me. In this case, what he does tends to my benefit, and perhaps is done with that intention; but it is not a favour, it is no more than he was bound to do.

☞ If a servant do his work, and receive his wages, there is no favour done on either part, nor any object of gratitude; because, though each party has benefited the other, yet neither has done more than he was bound to do.

What I infer from this is, That the conception of a favour in every man come to years of understanding, implies the conception of things not due, and consequently the conception of things that are due.

A negative cannot be conceived by one who has no conception of the correspondent positive. Not to be due is the negative of being due; and he who conceives one of them must conceive both. The conception of things due and not due must therefore be found in every mind which has any rational conception of a favour, or any rational sentiment of gratitude.

XIII. [If we consider, on the other hand, *what an injury is* which is the object of the natural passion of resentment, every man, capable of reflection, perceives, that *an injury implies more than being hurt.*] If I be hurt by a stone falling out of the wall, or by a flash of lightning, or by a convulsive and involuntary motion of another man's arm, no injury is done, no resentment raised in a man that has reason. In this, as in all moral actions, there must be the will and intention of the agent to do the hurt.

Nor is this sufficient to constitute an injury. The man who breaks my fences, or treads down my corn, when he cannot otherwise preserve himself from destruction, who has no injurious intention, and is willing to indemnify me for the hurt which necessity, and not ill-will, led him to do, is not injurious, nor is an object of resentment.

The executioner who does his duty, in cutting off the head of a condemned criminal, is not an object of resentment. He does nothing unjust, and therefore nothing injurious.

From this it is evident, that an injury, the object of the natural passion of resentment, implies in it the notion of injustice. And it is no less evident, that no man can have a notion of injustice without having the notion of justice.

XIV. [*To sum up* what has been said upon this point: *a favour*, an *act of justice*, and *an injury*, are so related to one another, that he who conceives one must conceive the other two. They lie, as it were, in one line, and resemble the relations of greater, less and equal.] If one understands what is meant by one line being greater or less than another, he can be at no loss to understand what is meant by its being equal to the other; for, if it be neither greater nor less, it must be equal.

In like manner, of those actions by which we profit or hurt other men, a favour is more than justice, an injury is less; and that which is neither a favour nor an injury is a just action.

As soon, therefore, as men come to have any proper notion of a favour and of an injury; as soon as they have any rational exercise of gratitude and of resentment; so soon they must have the conception of justice and of injustice; and if gratitude and resentment be natural to man, which Mr. Hume allows, the notion of justice must be no less natural.

The notion of justice carries inseparably along with it, a perception of its moral obligation. For to say that such an action is an act of justice, that it is due, that it ought to be done, that we are under a moral obligation to do it, are only different ways of expressing the same thing. It is true, that we perceive no high degree of moral worth in a merely just action, when it is not opposed by interest or passion; but we perceive a high degree of turpitude and demerit in unjust actions, or in the omission of what justice requires.

[Indeed, if there were no other argument to prove, that the obligation of justice is not solely derived from its utility to procure what is agreeable either to ourselves or to society, this would be sufficient, That *the very conception of justice implies its obligation.* The morality of justice is included in the very idea of it:] nor is it possible that the conception of justice can enter into the human mind, without carrying along with it the conception of duty and moral obligation. Its obligation, therefore, is inseparable from its nature, and is not derived solely from its utility, either to ourselves or to society.

XV. We may further observe, That as in all moral estimation, *every action takes its denomination from the motive that produces it;* so no action can properly be denominated an act of justice, unless it be done from a regard to justice.

☞ If a man pays his debt, only that he may not be cast into prison, he is not a just man, because prudence, and not justice, is his motive. And if a man, from benevolence and charity, gives to another what is really due to him, but what he believes not to be due, this is not an act of justice in him, but of charity or benevolence, because it is not done from a motive of justice. These are self-evident truths; nor is it less evident, that what a man does, merely to procure something agreeable, either to himself or to others, is not an act of justice, nor has the merit of justice.

Good music and good cookery have the merit of utility, in procuring what is agreeable both to ourselves and to society, but they never obtained among mankind the denomination of moral virtues. Indeed, if this author's system be well founded, great injustice has been done them on that account.

XVI. I shall now make some observations upon the reasoning of this author, in proof of his favourite principle, *That justice is not a natural but an artificial virtue;* or, as it is expressed in the "Enquiry," That public utility is the sole origin of justice, and that reflections on the beneficial consequences of this virtue are the sole foundation of its merit.

1. It must be acknowledged, that *this principle has a necessary connexion with his system* concerning the foundation of all virtue; and therefore it is no wonder that he hath taken so much pains to support it; for the whole system must stand or fall with it.

If the *dulce* and the *utile,* that is, pleasure, and what is useful to procure pleasure, be the whole merit of virtue, justice can have no merit beyond its utility to procure pleasure. If, on the other hand, an intrinsic worth in justice, and demerit in injustice, be discerned by every man that hath a conscience; if there be a natural principle in the constitution of man, by which justice is approved, and injustice disapproved and condemned, then the whole of this laboured system must fall to the ground.

2. We may observe, That as justice is directly opposed to injury, and as there are various ways in which a man may be injured, so *there must be various branches of justice opposed to the different kinds of injury.*

XVII. *Six branches of justice.*—A man may be injured, *first*, in his person, by wounding, maiming or killing him; *secondly*, in his family, by robbing him of his children, or any way injuring those he is bound to protect; *thirdly*, in his liberty, by confinement; *fourthly*, in his reputation; *fifthly*, in his goods or property; and, *lastly*, in the violation of contracts or engagements made with him. This enumeration, whether complete or not, is sufficient for the present purpose.

The different branches of justice, opposed to these different kinds of injury, are commonly expressed by saying, that an innocent man has a right to the safety of his person and family, a right to his liberty and reputation, a right to his goods, and to fidelity to engagements made with him. To say that he has a right to these things, has precisely the same meaning as to say, that justice requires that he should be permitted to enjoy them, or that it is unjust to violate them. For injustice is the violation of right, and justice is, to yield to every man what is his right.

XVIII. [These things being understood as the simplest and most common ways of expressing the various branches of justice, we are to consider *how* far Mr. Hume's *reasoning proves any or all of them to be artificial*, or grounded solely upon public utility.] The last of them, fidelity to engagements, is to be the subject of the next chapter, and therefore I shall say nothing of it in this.

The four first named, to wit, the right of an innocent man to the safety of his (1) person and (2) family, to his (3) liberty and (4) reputation, are, by the writers on jurisprudence, called *natural* rights of man, because they are grounded in the nature of man as a rational and moral agent, and are, by his Creator, committed to his care and keeping. By being called *natural* or *innate*, they are distinguished from *acquired* rights, which suppose some previous act or deed of man by which they are acquired, whereas natural rights suppose nothing of this kind.

When a man's natural rights are violated, he perceives *intuitively*, and he feels, that he is injured. The feeling of his heart arises from the judgment of his understanding; for if he did not believe that the hurt was intended, and unjustly intended, he would not have that feeling. He perceives that injury is done to himself, and that he has a right to redress. The natural principle of resentment is roused by the view of its proper object, and excites him to defend his right. Even the injurious person is conscious of his doing injury; he dreads a just retaliation; and if it be in the power of the injured person, he expects it as due and deserved.

[That these sentiments spring up in the mind of man as *naturally* as his body grows to its proper stature; that they are not the birth of instruction, either of parents, priests, philosophers or politicians, but the pure growth of nature, cannot, I think, without effrontery, be denied.] We find them equally strong in the most savage and in the most civilized tribes of mankind; and nothing can weaken them but an inveterate habit of rapine and bloodshed, which benumbs the conscience, and turns men into wild beasts.

The public good is very properly considered by the judge who punishes a private injury, but seldom enters into the thought of the injured person. In all criminal law, the redress due to the private sufferer is distinguished from that which is due to the public; a distinction which could have no foundation, if the demerit of injustice arose solely from its hurting the public. And every man is conscious of a specific difference between the resentment he feels for an injury done to himself, and his indignation against a wrong done to the public.

I think, therefore, it is evident, that, of the *six branches of justice* we mentioned, four are natural, in the strictest sense, being founded upon the constitution of man, and antecedent to all deeds and conventions of society; so that, if there were but two men upon the earth, one might be unjust and injurious, and the other injured.

XIX. But does Mr. Hume maintain the contrary?

To this question I answer, That *his doctrine seems to imply it*, but I hope he meant it not.

He affirms in general, that justice is not a natural virtue; that it derives its origin solely from public utility, and that reflections on the beneficial consequences of this virtue are the sole foundation of its merit. He mentions no particular branch of justice as an exception to this general rule; yet justice, in common language, and in all the writers on jurisprudence I am acquainted with, comprehends the four branches above mentioned. His doctrine, therefore, according to the common construction of words, extends to these four, as well as to the two other branches of justice.

On the other hand, if we attend to his long and laboured proof of this doctrine, it appears evident, that he had in his eye only two particular branches of justice. No part of his reasoning applies to the other four. He seems, I know not why, to have taken up a confined notion of justice, and to have restricted it to a regard to property and fidelity and contracts. As to other branches he is silent. He nowhere says, that it is not naturally criminal to rob an innocent man of his life, of his children, of his liberty, or of his reputation; and I am apt to think he never meant it.

XX. *Mr. Hobbes' system.*—[The only philosopher I know who has had the assurance to maintain this, is Mr. Hobbes, who makes the *state of nature to be a state of war*, of every man against every man; and of such a war in which every man has a right to do and to acquire whatever his power can, by any means, accomplish; that is, a state wherein neither right nor injury, justice nor injustice, can possibly exist.]

Mr. Hume mentions this system of Hobbes, but without adopting it, though he allows it the authority of Cicero in its favour.

He says in a note, " This fiction of a state of nature as a state of war was not first started by Mr. Hobbes, as is commonly imagined. Plato endeavours to refute an hypothesis very like it, in the second, third and fourth books, 'De Republica.' Cicero, on the contrary, supposes it certain and universally acknowledged, in the following passage, &c.: 'Pro Sextio,' l. 42."

The passage, which he quotes at large, from one of Cicero's "Orations," seems to me to require some straining to make it tally with the system of Mr. Hobbes. Be this as it may, Mr. Hume might have added, That Cicero, in his "Orations," *like many other pleaders*, sometimes says, not what he believed, but what was fit to support the cause of his client. That Cicero's opinion, with regard to the natural obligation of justice, was very different from that of Mr. Hobbes, and even from Mr. Hume's, is very well known.

XXI. 3. As Mr. Hume, therefore, has said nothing to prove the four branches of justice which relate to the innate rights of men, to be artificial, or to derive their origin solely from public utility, I proceed to the *fifth branch*, which requires us not to invade another man's *property*.

The right of property is not innate, but acquired. It is not grounded upon the constitution of man, but upon his actions. Writers on jurisprudence have explained its origin in a manner that may satisfy every man of common understanding.

The earth is given to men in common for the purposes of life, by the bounty of Heaven. But, to divide it, and appropriate one part of its produce to one, another part to another, must be the work of men who have power and understanding given them, by which every man may accommodate himself without hurt to any other.

☞ This common right of every man to what the earth produces, before it be occupied and appropriated by others, was, by ancient moralists, very properly compared to the right which every citizen had to the *public theatre*, where every man that came might occupy an empty seat, and thereby acquire a right to it while the entertainment lasted; but no man had a right to dispossess another.

The earth is a great theatre, furnished by the Almighty, with perfect wisdom and goodness, for the entertainment and employment of all mankind. Here every man has a right to accommodate himself as a spectator, and to perform his part as an actor, but without hurt to others.

He who does so is a just man, and thereby entitled to some degree of moral approbation; and he who not only does no hurt, but employs his power to do good, is a good man, and is thereby entitled to a higher degree of moral approbation. But he who jostles and molests his neighbour, who deprives him of any accommodation which his industry has provided without hurt to others, is unjust, and a proper object of resentment.

It is true, therefore, that property has a beginning from the actions of men, occupying, and perhaps improving, by their industry, what was common by nature. It is true also, that before property exists, that branch of justice and injustice which regards property cannot exist. But it is also true, that where there are men, there will very soon be property of one kind or another, and consequently there will be that branch of justice which attends property as its guardian.

XXII. There are *two kinds of property* which we may distinguish.

The *first*, is what must presently be consumed to sustain life; the *second*, which is more permanent, is what may be laid up and stored for the supply of future wants.

Some of the gifts of nature must be used and consumed by individuals for the daily support of life; but they cannot be used till they be occupied and appropriated. If another person may, without injustice, rob me of what I have innocently occupied for present subsistence, the necessary consequence must be, that he may, without injustice, take away my life.

A right to life implies a right to the necessary means of life. And that justice which forbids the taking away the life of an innocent man, forbids no less the taking from him the necessary means of life. He has the same right to defend the one as the other; and nature inspires him with the same just resentment of the one injury as of the other.

The natural right of liberty implies a right to such innocent labour as a man chooses, and to the fruit of that labour. To hinder another man's innocent labour, or to deprive him of the fruit of it, is an injustice of the same kind, and has the same effect as to put him in fetters or in prison, and is equally a just object of resentment.

Thus, it appears, that some kind, or some degree, of property must exist wherever men exist, and that the right to such property is the necessary consequence of the natural right of men to life and liberty.

It has been further observed, that God has made man a sagacious and provident animal, led by his constitution not only to occupy and use what nature has provided for the supply of his present wants and necessities, but to foresee future wants, and to provide for them; and that not only for himself, but for his family, his friends, and connexions.

He therefore acts in perfect conformity to his nature, when he stores, of the fruit of his labour, what may afterwards be useful to himself or to others; when he invents and fabricates utensils or machines by which his labour may be facilitated, and its produce increased; and when, by exchanging with his fellow-men commodities or labour, he accommodates both himself and them. These are the natural and innocent exertions of that understanding wherewith his Maker has endowed him. He has therefore a right to exercise them, and to enjoy the fruit of them. Every man who impedes him in making such exertions, or deprives him of the fruit of them, is injurious and unjust, and an object of just resentment.

☞ Many brute-animals are led by instinct to provide for futurity, and to defend their store and their store-house against all invaders. There seems to be in man, before the use of reason, an instinct of the same kind. When reason and conscience grow up, they approve and justify this provident care, and condemn, as unjust, every invasion of others, that may frustrate it.

XXIII. [Two *instances of* this *provident sagacity* seem to be peculiar to man. I mean (1) the invention of utensils and machines for facilitating labour, and (2) the making exchanges with his fellow-men for mutual benefit.] No tribe of men has been found so rude as not to practise these things in some degree. And I know no tribe of brutes that was ever observed to practise them. They neither invent nor use utensils or machines, nor do they traffic by exchanges.

[From these observations, I think it evident, that *man, even in the state of nature*, by his powers of body and mind, *may acquire permanent property*, or what we call *riches*, by which his own and his family's wants are more liberally supplied, and his power enlarged to requite his benefactors, to relieve objects of compassion, to make friends, and to defend his property against unjust invaders.] And we know from history, that men, who had no superior on earth, no connexion with any public beyond their own family, have acquired property, and had distinct notions of that justice and injustice, of which it is the object.

Every man, as a reasonable creature, has a right to gratify his natural and innocent desires without hurt to others. No desire is more natural, or more reasonable, than that of supplying his wants. When this is done without hurt to any man, to hinder or frustrate his innocent labour, is an unjust violation of his natural liberty. Private utility leads a man to desire property, and to labour for it; and his right to it is only a right to labour for his own benefit.

XXIV. [*That public utility is the sole origin*, even of that branch of justice which regards property, is *so far from being true*, that when men confederate and constitute a public, under laws and government, *the right of each individual* to his property *is*, by that confederation, *abridged and limited.*] In the state of nature, every man's property was solely at his own disposal, because he had no superior. In civil society, it must be subject to the laws of the society. He gives up to the public part of that right which he had in the state of nature, as the price of that protection and security which he receives from civil society. In the state of nature, he was sole judge in his own cause, and had a right to defend his property, his liberty, and life, as far as his power reached. In the state of civil society, he must submit to the judgment of the society, and acquiesce in its sentence, though he should conceive it to be unjust.

What was said above, of the natural right every man has to acquire permanent property, and to dispose of it, must be understood with this condition, that no other man be thereby deprived of the necessary means of life. The right of an innocent man to the necessaries of life, is, in its nature, superior to that which the rich man has to his riches, even though they be honestly acquired. The use of riches, or permanent property, is to supply future and casual wants, which ought to yield to present and certain necessity.

☞ As, in a family, justice requires that the children who are unable to labour, and those who, by sickness, are disabled, should have their necessities supplied out of the common stock, so, in the great family of God, of which all mankind are the children, justice, I think, as well as charity, requires, that the necessities of those who, by the providence of God, are disabled from supplying themselves, should be supplied from what might otherwise be stored for future wants.

From this it appears, that the right of acquiring and that of disposing of property, may be subject to limitations and restrictions, even in the state of nature, and much more in the state of civil society, in which the public has what writers in jurisprudence call an *eminent dominion* over the property, as well as over the lives of the subjects, as far as the public good requires.

XXV. [If these principles be well founded, Mr. Hume's arguments to prove *that justice is an artificial virtue*, or that its *public utility is the sole foundation of its merit*, may be *easily answered.*]

He supposes, *first*, a state in which nature has bestowed on the human race such abundance of external goods, that every man, without care or industry, finds himself provided of whatever he can wish or desire. It is evident, says he, that in such a state, the cautious, jealous virtue of justice would never once have been dreamed of.

It may be observed, *first*, that this argument applies only to *one* of the six branches of justice before mentioned. The other five are not in the least affected by it; and the reader will easily perceive that this observation applies to almost all his arguments, so that it needs not be repeated.

Secondly, all that this argument proves is, that *a state* of the human race *may be conceived wherein no property exists*, and where, of consequence, there can be no exercise of that branch of justice which respects property. But does it follow from this, that where property exists, and must exist, that no regard ought to be had to it?

He *next* supposes that the necessities of the human race continuing the same as at present, the mind is so enlarged with friendship and generosity, that every man feels as much tenderness and concern for the interest of every man, as for his own. It seems evident, he says, that the use of justice would be suspended by such an extensive benevolence, nor would the divisions and barriers of property and obligation have ever been thought of.

I answer, the conduct which this extensive benevolence leads to, is either perfectly consistent with justice, or it is not. *First*, if there be any case where this benevolence would lead us to do injustice, the use of justice is not suspended. Its obligation is superior to that of benevolence; and, to show benevolence to one, at the expense of injustice to another, is immoral. *Secondly*, supposing no such case could happen, the use of justice would not be suspended, because by it we must distinguish good offices to which we had a right, from those to which we had no right, and which therefore require a return of gratitude. *Thirdly*, supposing the use of justice to be suspended, as it must be in every case where it cannot be exercised, will it follow, that its obligation is suspended, where there is access to exercise it?

A *third* supposition is, the reverse of the first, that a society falls into extreme want of the necessaries of life : the question is put, whether, in such a case, an equal partition of bread, without regard to private property, though effected by power, and even by violence, would be regarded as criminal and injurious? And the author conceives, that this would be a suspension of the strict laws of justice.

I answer, that such an equal partition as Mr. Hume mentions, is so far from being criminal or injurious, that justice requires it; and surely that cannot be a suspension of the laws of justice, which is an act of justice. [All that the strictest justice requires in such a case, is, that the man whose life is preserved at the expense of another, and without his consent, should indemnify him when he is able. His case is similar to that of a debtor who is insolvent, without any fault on his part. Justice requires that he should be forborn till he is able to pay.] It is strange that Mr. Hume should think that an action, neither criminal nor injurious, should be a suspension of the laws of justice. This seems to me a contradiction, for *justice* and *injury* are contradictory terms.

The *next* argument is thus expressed : " When any man, even in political society, renders himself, by crimes, obnoxious to the public, he is punished in his goods and person; that is, the ordinary rules of justice are, with regard to him, suspended for a moment, and it becomes equitable to inflict on him, what otherwise he could not suffer without wrong or injury."

This argument, like the former, refutes itself. For that an action should be a *suspension* of the rules of justice, and at the same time equitable, seems to me a contradiction. It is possible that equity may interfere with the letter of human laws, because all the cases that may fall under them cannot be foreseen; but that equity should interfere with justice is impossible. It is strange that Mr. Hume should think, that justice requires that a criminal should be treated in the same way as an innocent man.

Another argument is taken from *public war*. What is it, says he, but *a suspension of justice* among the warring parties? The laws of war, which then succeed to those of equity and justice, are rules calculated for the advantage and utility of that particular state in which men are now placed.

I answer, when war is undertaken for self-defence, or for reparation of intolerable injuries, justice authorises it. The laws of war, which have been described by many judicious moralists, are all drawn from the fountain of justice and equity; and every thing contrary to justice, is contrary to the laws of war. That justice, which prescribes one rule of conduct to a master, another to a servant; one to a parent, another to a child; prescribes also one rule of conduct towards a friend, another towards an enemy. I do not understand what Mr. Hume means by the *advantage* and *utility* of a state of war, for which he says the laws of war are calculated, and succeed to those of justice and equity. I know no laws of war that are not calculated for justice and equity.

The *next* argument is this, Were there *a species of creatures* intermingled with men, which, though rational, were possessed *of such inferior strength,* both of body and mind, that they were *incapable of all resistance,* and could never, upon the highest provocation, make us feel the effects of their resentment; the necessary consequence, I think, is, that we should be bound, by the laws of humanity, to give gentle usage to these creatures, but should not, properly speaking, lie under any restraint of justice with regard to them, nor could they possess any right or property, exclusive of such arbitrary lords.

If Mr. Hume had not owned this sentiment as a consequence of his " Theory of Morals," I should have thought it very uncharitable to impute it to him. However, we may judge of the Theory by its avowed consequence. For there cannot be better evidence, that a theory of morals, or of any particular virtue, is false, than when it subverts the practical rules of morals. [This defenceless species of rational creatures is doomed by Mr. Hume to have no rights. Why? Because they have no power to defend themselves. Is not this to say, *that right has its origin from power;* which, indeed, was the doctrine of Mr. Hobbes.] And to illustrate this doctrine, Mr. Hume adds, that as no inconvenience ever results from the exercise of a power, so firmly established in nature, the restraints of justice and property being totally useless, could never have place in so unequal a confederacy; and, to the same purpose, he says, that the female part of our own species, owe the share they have in the rights of society, to the power which their address and their charms give them. If this be sound morals, Mr. Hume's " Theory of Justice " may be true.

We may here observe, that though, in other places, Mr. Hume founds the obligation of justice upon its utility to *ourselves*, or to *others*, it is here founded solely upon utility to *ourselves*. For surely to be treated with justice would be highly useful to the defenceless species he here supposes to exist. But as no inconvenience to ourselves can ever result from our treatment of them, he concludes that justice would be useless, and therefore can have no place. Mr. Hobbes could have said no more.

XXVI. *This argument would prove all social virtues to be artificial, as well as justice.*—[He supposes, in the *last* place, a state of human nature, wherein *all society and intercourse is cut off between man and man.* It is evident, he says, that so solitary a being would be as much incapable of justice as of social discourse and conversation.]

And would not so solitary a being be as incapable of friendship, generosity, and compassion, as of justice? If this argument prove justice to be an artificial virtue, it will, with equal force, prove every social virtue to be artificial.

These are the arguments which Mr. Hume has advanced in his *Enquiry,* in the first part of a long section upon justice.

XXVII. In the *second* part, the arguments are not so clearly distinguished, nor can they be easily collected. I shall offer some remarks upon what seems most specious in this second part.

He begins with observing, " That, if we examine the particular laws by which justice is directed and property determined, they present us with the same conclusion. The good of mankind is the only object of all those laws and regulations."

It is not easy to perceive where the stress of this argument lies. *The good of mankind is the object of all the laws and regulations by which justice is directed and property determined; therefore justice is not a natural virtue, but has its origin solely from public utility, and its beneficial consequences are the sole foundation of its merit.*

Some step seems to be wanting to connect the antecedent proposition with the conclusion, which, I think, must be one or other of these two propositions; first, *All the rules of justice tend to public utility;* or, secondly, *Public utility is the only standard of justice, from which alone all its rules must be deduced.*

If the argument be, That justice must have its origin solely from public utility, because all its rules tend to public utility, I cannot admit the consequence; nor can Mr. Hume admit it without overturning his own system. For the rules of benevolence and humanity do all tend to the public utility, and yet in his system they have another foundation in human nature; so likewise may the rules of justice.

I am apt to think, therefore, that the argument is to be taken in the last sense, That public utility is the only standard of justice, from which all its rules must be deduced; and therefore justice has its origin solely from public utility.

This seems to be Mr. Hume's meaning, because, in what follows, he observes, That, in order to establish laws for the regulation of *property*, we must be acquainted with the nature and situation of man; must reject appearances which may be false, though specious; and must search for those rules which are, on the whole, most useful and beneficial; and endeavours to show, that the established rules which regard property are more for the public good than the system, either of those religious fanatics of the last age, who held that saints only should inherit the earth; or of those political fanatics who claimed an equal division of property.

XXVIII. *Obvious defect in Mr. Hume's reasoning as to the standard of justice generally.*—We see here, as before, that though Mr. Hume's conclusion respects justice in general, his argument is confined to one branch of justice, to wit, *the right of property;* and it is well known that to conclude from a part to the whole is not good reasoning.

Besides, the proposition from which his conclusion is drawn cannot be granted, either with regard to property, or with regard to the other branches of justice.

[We endeavoured before to show that property, though not an innate but an *acquired* right, *may be acquired in the state of nature*, and agreeably to the laws of nature; and that this right has not its origin from human laws, made for the public good, though, when men enter into political society, it may and ought to be regulated by those laws.]

If there were but two men upon the face of the earth, of ripe faculties, each might have his own property, and might know his right to defend it, and his obligation not to invade the property of the other. He would have no need to have recourse to reasoning from public good, in order to know when he was injured, either in his property, or in any of his natural rights, or to know what rules of justice he ought to observe towards his neighbour.

The simple rule of not doing to his neighbour what he would think wrong to be done to himself, would lead him to the knowledge of every branch of justice, without the consideration of public good, or of laws and statutes made to promote it.

It is not true, therefore, that public utility is the only standard of justice, and that the rules of justice can be deduced only from their public utility.

XXIX. *Standard of justice among the ancients.*—Aristides, and the people of Athens, had surely another notion of justice, when he pronounced the counsel of Themistocles, which was communicated to him only, to be highly useful, but unjust; and the assembly, upon this authority, rejected the proposal unheard. These honest citizens, though subject to no laws but of their own making, *far from making utility the standard of justice, made justice to be the standard of utility.*

"*What is a man's property?* Anything which it is lawful for him, and for him alone, to use. *But what rule have we by which we can distinguish these objects?* Here we must have recourse to statutes, customs, precedents, analogies, &c."

Does not this imply that, in the state of nature, there can be no distinction of property? If so, Mr. Hume's state of nature is the same with that of Mr. Hobbes.

It is true, that when men become members of a political society, they subject their property, as well as themselves, to the laws, and must either acquiesce in what the laws determine, or leave the society. But justice, and even that particular branch of it which our author always supposes to be the whole, is antecedent to political societies and to their laws; and the intention of these laws is, to be the guardians of justice, and to redress injuries.

As all the works of men are imperfect, human laws may be unjust; which could never be, if justice had its origin from law, as the author seems here to insinuate.

Justice requires that a member of a state should submit to the laws of the state when they require nothing unjust or impious. There may, therefore, be statutory rights and statutory crimes. A statute may create a right which did not before exist, or make that to be criminal which was not so before. But this could never be, if there were not an antecedent obligation upon the subject to obey the statutes. In like manner, the command of a master may make that to be the servant's duty which, before, was not his duty, and the servant may be chargeable with injustice if he disobeys, because he was under an antecedent obligation to obey his master in lawful things.

We grant, therefore, that particular laws may direct justice and determine property, and sometimes even upon very slight reasons and analogies, or even for no other reason but that it is better that such a point should be determined by law than that it should be left a dubious subject of contention. But this, far from presenting us with the conclusion which the author would establish, presents us with a contrary conclusion. For all these particular laws and statutes derive their whole obligation and force from a general rule of justice antecedent to them, to wit, that subjects ought to obey the laws of their country.

XXX. The author compares the rules of justice with the most *frivolous superstitions,* and can find no foundation for moral sentiment in the one more than in the other, excepting that justice is requisite to the well-being and existence of society.

It is very true, that, if we examine *mine* and *thine* by the *senses of sight, smell, or touch, or scrutinize them by the sciences of medicine, chemistry, or physics,* we perceive no difference. But the reason is, that none of these senses or sciences are the judges of right or wrong, or can give any conception of them, any more than the ear of colour, or the eye of sound. Every man of common understanding, and every savage, when he applies his moral faculty to those objects, perceives a difference as clearly as he perceives daylight. When that sense or faculty is not consulted, in vain do we consult every other, in a question of right and wrong.

To perceive that justice tends to the good of mankind, would lay no moral obligation upon us to be just, unless we be conscious of a moral obligation to do what tends to the good of mankind. If such a moral obligation be admitted, why may we not admit a stronger obligation to do injury to no man? The last obligation is as easily conceived as the first, and there is as clear evidence of its existence in human nature.

XXXI. The last argument is *a dilemma,* and is thus expressed: " The dilemma seems obvious. As justice evidently tends to promote public utility, and to support civil society, the sentiment of justice is either *derived from our reflecting* on that tendency, or, like hunger, thirst, and other appetites, resentment, love of life, attachment to offspring, and other passions, *arises from a simple original instinct* in the human breast, which nature has implanted for like salutary purposes. If the latter be the case, it follows, that property, which is the object of justice, is also distinguished by a simple original instinct, and is not ascertained by any argument or reflection. But who is there that ever heard of such an instinct," &c.

I doubt not but Mr. Hume has heard of a principle called *conscience*, which nature has implanted in the human breast. Whether he will call it a simple original instinct, I know not, as he gives that name to all our appetites and to all our passions. From this principle, I think, we derive the sentiment of justice.

☞ As the eye not only gives us the conception of colours, but makes us perceive one body to have one colour, and another body another; and as our reason not only gives us the conception of true and false, but makes us perceive one proposition to be true and another to be false; so our conscience, or moral faculty, not only gives us the conception of honest and dishonest, but makes us perceive one kind of conduct to be honest, another to be dishonest. By this faculty we perceive a merit in honest conduct, and a demerit in dishonest, without regard to public utility.

That these sentiments are not the effect of education or of acquired habits, we have the same reason to conclude, as that our perception of what is true and what false, is not the effect of education or of acquired habits. There have been men who professed to believe, that there is no ground to assent to any one proposition rather than its contrary; but I never yet heard of a man who had the effrontery to profess himself to be under no obligation of honour or honesty, of truth or justice, in his dealings with men.

Nor does this faculty of conscience require *innate ideas of property, and of the various ways of acquiring and transferring it, or innate ideas of kings and senators, of pretors and chancellors, and juries,* any more than the faculty of seeing requires innate ideas of colours, or than the faculty of reasoning requires innate ideas of cones, cylinders, and spheres.

CHAPTER VI.

OF THE NATURE AND OBLIGATION OF A CONTRACT.

I. *Promise and contract different.*—THE obligation of contracts and promises is a matter so sacred, and of such consequence to human society, that speculations which have a tendency to weaken that obligation, and to perplex men's notions on a subject so plain and so important, ought to meet with the disapprobation of all honest men.

Some such speculations, I think, we have in the third volume of Mr. Hume's " Treatise of Human Nature," and in his " Enquiry into the Principles of Morals;" and my design in this chapter is, to offer some observations on the nature of a contract or promise, and on two passages of that author on this subject.

I am far from saying or thinking, that Mr. Hume meant to weaken men's obligations to honesty and fair dealing, or that he had not a sense of these obligations himself. It is not the man I impeach, but his writings. Let us think of the first as charitably as we can, while we freely examine the import and tendency of the last.

Although the nature of a contract and of a promise is perfectly understood by all men of common understanding, yet, by attention to the operations of mind signified by these words, we shall be better enabled to judge of the metaphysical subtleties which have been raised about them. A promise and a contract differ so little in what concerns the present disquisition, that the same reasoning (as Mr. Hume justly observes) extends to both. [In a promise, *one party* only comes under the obligation, the other acquires a right to the prestation promised. But we give the name of a contract to a transaction in which *each party* comes under an obligation to the other, and each *reciprocally* acquires a right to what is promised by the other.]

II. *Definition of a contract.*—The Latin word pactum seems to extend to both; and the definition given of it in the civil law, and borrowed from Ulpian, is, "Duorum pluriumve in idem placitum consensus." Titius, a modern civilian, has endeavoured to make this definition more complete, by adding the words, "Obligationis licitè constituendæ vel tollendæ causa datus." With this addition, the definition is, That [a contract is the consent of *two or more* persons in the same thing, given with the intention of constituting or dissolving lawfully some obligation.]

This definition is perhaps as good as any other that can be given; yet, I believe, every man will acknowledge, that it gives him no clearer or more distinct notion of a contract than he had before. If it is considered as a strictly logical definition, I believe some objections might be made to it; but I forbear to mention them, because I believe that similar objections might be made to any definition of a contract that can be given.

Nor can it be inferred from this, that the notion of a contract is not perfectly clear in every man come to years of understanding. For this is common to many operations of the mind, that although we understand them perfectly, and are in no danger of confounding them with any thing else; yet we cannot define them according to the rules of logic, by a genus and a specific difference. And when we attempt it, we rather darken than give light to them.

Is there any thing more distinctly understood by all men, than what it is to see, to hear, to remember, to judge? Yet it is the most difficult thing in the world to define these operations according to the rules of logical definition. But it is not more difficult than it is useless.

Sometimes philosophers attempt to define them; but, if we examine their definitions, we shall find, that they amount to no more than giving one synonymous word for another, and commonly a worse for a better. So when we define a contract, by calling it a consent, a convention, an agreement, what is this but giving a synonymous word for it, and a word that is neither more expressive nor better understood?

☞ One boy has a top, another a scourge; says the first to the other, "If you will lend me your scourge as long as I can keep up my top with it, you shall next have the top as long as you can keep it up." "Agreed," says the other. This is a contract perfectly understood by both parties, though they never heard of the definition given by Ulpian or by Titius. And each of them knows, that he is injured if the other breaks the bargain, and that he does wrong if he breaks it himself.

III. [The *operations of the human mind may be divided into two classes*, the *solitary* and the *social*. As promises and contracts belong to the last class, it may be proper to explain this division.]*

I call those operations *solitary*, which may be performed by a man in solitude, without intercourse with any other intelligent being.

I call those operations *social*, which necessarily imply social intercourse with some other intelligent being who bears a part in them.

A man may see, and hear, and remember, and judge, and reason; he may deliberate and form purposes, and execute them, without the intervention of any other intelligent being. They are solitary acts. But when he asks a question for information, when he testifies a fact, when he gives a command to his servant, when he makes a promise, or enters into a contract, these are social acts of mind, and can have no existence without the intervention of some other intelligent being, who acts a part in them. Between the operations of the mind which, for want of a more proper name, I have called *solitary*, and those I have called *social*, there is this very remarkable distinction, that, in the solitary, the expression of them by words, or any other sensible sign, is

---

* Vide "Essays on the Intellectual Powers," Essay I. chap. viii., where the arguments used in this section are given more at length.

accidental. They may exist, and be complete, without being expressed, without being known to any other person. But, in the social operations, the expression is essential. They cannot exist without being expressed by words or signs, and known to the other party.

If nature had not made man capable of such social operations of mind, and furnished him with a language to express them, he might think, and reason, and deliberate, and will; he might have desires and aversions, joy and sorrow; in a word, he might exert all those operations of mind which the writers in logic and pneumatology have so copiously described; but, at the same time, he would still be a solitary being, even when in a crowd; it would be impossible for him to put a question, or give a command, to ask a favour, or testify a fact, to make a promise or a bargain.

I take it to be the common opinion of philosophers, that the social operations of the human mind are not specifically different from the solitary, and that they are only various modifications or compositions of our solitary operations, and may be resolved into them.

It is for this reason, probably, that, in enumerating the operations of the mind, the solitary only are mentioned, and no notice at all taken of the social, though they are familiar to every man, and have names in all languages.

I apprehend, however, it will be found extremely difficult, if not impossible, to resolve our social operations into any modification or composition of the solitary: and that an attempt to do this would prove as ineffectual as the attempts that have been made to resolve all our social affections into the selfish. The social operations appear to be as simple in their nature as the solitary. They are found in every individual of the species, even before the use of reason.

The power which man has of holding social intercourse with his kind, by asking and refusing, threatening and supplicating, commanding and obeying, testifying and promising, must either be a distinct faculty given by our Maker, and a part of our constitution, like the powers of seeing, and hearing, or it must be a human invention. If men have invented this art of social intercourse, it must follow, that every individual of the species must have invented it for himself. It cannot be taught, for though when once carried to a certain pitch, it may be improved by teaching; yet it is impossible it can begin in that way, because all teaching supposes a social intercourse and language already established between the teacher and the learner. This intercourse must, from the very first, be carried on by sensible signs; for the thoughts of other men can be discovered in no other way. I think it is likewise evident, that this intercourse, in its beginning, at least, must be carried on by natural signs, whose meaning is understood by both parties, previous to all compact or agreement. For there can be no compact without signs, nor without social intercourse.

I apprehend, therefore, that the social intercourse of mankind, consisting of those social operations which I have mentioned, is the exercise of a faculty appropriated to that purpose, which is the gift of God, no less than the powers of seeing and hearing. And that, in order to carry on this intercourse, God has given to man a natural language, by which his social operations are expressed, and, without which, the artificial languages of articulate sounds, and of writing, could never have been invented by human art.

The signs in this natural language are looks, changes of the features, modulations of the voice, and gestures of the body. All men understand this language without instruction, and all men can use it in some degree. But they are most expert in it who use it most. It makes a great part of the language of savages, and therefore they are more expert in the use of natural signs than the civilized.

☞ The language of *dumb persons* is mostly formed of natural signs; and they are all great adepts in this language of nature. All that we call action and pronunciation, in the most perfect orator, and the most admired actor, is nothing else but superadding the language of nature to the language of articulate sounds. The *pantomimes* among the Romans carried it to the highest pitch of perfection. For they could act part of comedies and tragedies in dumb-show, so as to be understood, not only by those who were accustomed to this entertainment, but by all the strangers that came to Rome, from all the corners of the earth.

For it may be observed of this natural language, (and nothing more clearly demonstrates it to be a part of the human constitution,) that although it require practice and study to enable a man to express his sentiments by it in the most perfect manner; yet it requires neither study nor practice in the spectator to understand it. The knowledge of it was before latent in the mind, and we no sooner see it, than we immediately recognise it, as we do an acquaintance whom we had long forgot, and could not have described; but no sooner do we see him, than we know for certain that he is the very man.

This knowledge, in all mankind, of the natural signs of men's thoughts and sentiments, is indeed so like to reminiscence, that it seems to have led Plato to conceive all human knowledge to be of that kind.

It is not by reasoning, that all mankind know, that an open countenance, and a placid eye, is a sign of amity; that a contracted brow, and a fierce look, is the sign of anger. It is not from reason that we learn to know the natural signs of consenting and refusing, of affirming and denying, of threatening and supplicating.

No man can perceive any necessary connexion between the signs of such operations, and the things signified by them. But we are so formed by the Author of our nature, that the operations themselves become visible, as it were, by their natural signs. This knowledge resembles reminiscence, in this respect, that it is immediate. We form the conclusion with great assurance, without knowing any premises from which it may be drawn by reasoning.

[It would lead us too far from the intention of the present inquiry, to consider more particularly, *in what degree the social intercourse is natural,* and a part of our constitution; how far it is of human invention.]

It is sufficient to observe, that this intercourse of human minds, by which their thoughts and sentiments are exchanged, and their souls mingle together as it were, is common to the whole species from infancy.

Like our other powers, its first beginnings are weak, and scarcely perceptible. But it is a certain fact, that we can perceive some communication of sentiments between the nurse and her nursling, before it is a month old. And I doubt not, but that, if both had grown out of the earth, and had never seen another human face, they would be able in a few years to converse together.

There appears indeed to be some degree of social intercourse among brute-animals, and between some of them and man. A dog exults in the caresses of his master, and is humbled at his displeasure. [But there are two operations of the social kind, of which the brute-animals seem to be altogether incapable. They can neither plight their veracity by testimony, nor their fidelity by any engagement or promise.] If nature had made them capable of these operations, they would have had a language to express them by, as man has: but of this we see no appearance.

A fox is said to use stratagems, but he cannot lie; because he cannot give his testimony, or plight his veracity. A dog is said to be faithful to his master; but no more is meant but that he is affectionate, for he never came under any engagement. I see no evidence that any brute-animal is capable of either giving testimony, or making a promise.

A dumb man cannot speak any more than a fox or a dog; but he can give his testimony by signs as early in life as other men can do by words. He knows what a lie is as early as other men, and hates it as much. He can plight his faith, and is sensible of the obligation of a promise or contract.

[It is, therefore, *a prerogative of man,* that he can communicate his knowledge of facts by testimony, and enter into engagements by *promise or contract*.] God has given him these powers by a part of his constitution, which distinguishes him from all brute-animals. And whether they are original powers, or resolvable into other original powers, it is evident that they spring up in the human mind at an early period of life, and are found in every individual of the species, whether savage or civilized.

IV. *These prerogative powers of man*, like all his other powers, *must be given for some end*, and for a good end. And if we consider a little farther the economy of nature, in relation to this part of the human constitution, we shall perceive the wisdom of nature in the structure of it, and discover clearly our duty in consequence of it.

It is evident, in the *first* place, that if no credit was given to testimony, if there was no reliance upon promises, they would answer no end at all, not even that of deceiving.

Secondly, supposing men disposed by some principle in their nature to rely on declarations and promises; yet if men found in experience, that there was no fidelity on the other part in making and in keeping them, no man of common understanding would trust to them, and so they would become useless.

Hence it appears, *thirdly*, that this power of giving testimony, and of promising, can answer no end in society, unless there be a considerable degree, both of fidelity on the one part, and of trust on the other. These two must stand or fall together, and one of them cannot possibly subsist without the other.

Fourthly, it may be observed, that fidelity in declarations and promises, and its counter-part, trust and reliance upon them, form a system of social intercourse, the most amiable, the most useful, that can be among men. Without fidelity and trust, there can be no human society. There never was a society, even of savages, nay, even of robbers or pirates, in which there was not a great degree of veracity and of fidelity among themselves. Without it man would be the most dissocial animal that God has made. His state would be in reality what Hobbes conceived the state of nature to be, a state of war of every man against every man; nor could this war ever terminate in peace.

It may be observed, in the *fifth* place, that man is evidently made for living in society. His social affections show this as evidently as that the eye was made for seeing. His social operations, particularly those of testifying and promising, make it no less evident.

V. *Contracts and promises have a foundation in nature.*— [From these observations it follows, that if no provision were made by nature, to engage men to fidelity in declarations and promises, human nature would be a contradiction to itself, made for an end, yet without the necessary means of attaining it.] As if the species had been furnished with good eyes, but without the power of opening their eye-lids. There are no blunders of this kind in the works of God. Wherever there is an end intended, the means are admirably fitted for the attainment of it; and so we find it to be in the case before us.

For we see that children, as soon as they are capable of understanding declarations and promises, are led by their constitution to rely upon them. They are no less led by constitution to veracity and candour, on their own part. Nor do they ever deviate from this road of truth and sincerity, until corrupted by bad example and bad company. This disposition to sincerity in themselves, and to give credit to others, whether we call it *instinct*, or whatever name we give it, must be considered as the effect of their constitution.

[So that the things essential to human society, I mean *good faith* on the one part, and *trust* on the other, *are formed by nature* in the minds of children, before they are capable of knowing their utility, or being influenced by considerations either of duty or interest.]

When we grow up so far as to have the conception of a right and a wrong in conduct, the turpitude of lying, falsehood, and dishonesty, is discerned, not by any train of reasoning, but by an immediate perception. For we see that every man disapproves it in others, even those who are conscious of it in themselves.

Every man thinks himself injured and ill used, and feels resentment when he is imposed upon by it. Every man takes it as a reproach when falsehood is imputed to him. These are the clearest evidences that all men disapprove of falsehood, when their judgment is not biassed.

I know of no evidence that has been given of any nation so rude as not to have these sentiments. It is certain that dumb people have them, and discover them about the same period of life in which they appear in those who speak. And it may reasonably be thought that dumb persons, at that time of life, have had as little advantage, with regard to morals, from their education, as the greatest savages.

Every man come to years of reflection, when he pledges his veracity or fidelity, thinks he has a right to be credited, and is affronted if he is not. But there cannot be a shadow of right to be credited, unless there be an obligation to good faith. For right on one hand, necessarily implies obligation on the other.

When we see that in the most savage state that ever was known of the human race, men have always lived in societies greater or less, this of itself is a proof from fact, that they have had that sense of their obligation to fidelity, without which no human society can subsist.

From these observations, I think, it appears very evident, that as fidelity on one part, and trust on the other, are essential to that intercourse of men, which we call human society; so the Author of our nature has made wise provision for perpetuating them among men, in that degree that is necessary to human society in all the different periods of human life, and in all the stages of human improvement and degeneracy.

In early years we have an innate disposition to them. In riper years we feel our obligation to fidelity as much as to any moral duty whatsoever.

VI. [Nor is it necessary to mention the *collateral inducements* to this virtue, from considerations of prudence, which are obvious to every man that reflects.] Such as, that it creates trust, the most effectual engine of human power; that it requires no artifice or concealment; dreads no detection; that it inspires courage and magnanimity, and is the natural ally of every virtue; so that there is no virtue whatsoever to which our natural obligation appears more strong or more apparent.

An observation or two with regard to the nature of a contract, will be sufficient for the present purpose.

It is obvious that *the prestation promised must be understood by both parties.* One party engages to do such a thing, another accepts of this engagement. An engagement to do, one does not know what, can neither be made nor accepted. It is no less obvious that a contract is a voluntary transaction.

But it ought to be observed that the will, which is essential to a contract, is only a will to engage, or to become bound. We must beware of confounding this will, with a will to perform what we have engaged. The last can signify nothing else than an intention and fixed purpose to do what we have engaged to do. The will to become bound, and to confer a right upon the other party, is indeed the very essence of a contract; but the purpose of fulfilling our engagement is no part of the contract at all.

A purpose is a solitary act of mind, which lays no obligation on the person, nor confers any right on another. A fraudulent person may contract with a fixed purpose of not performing his engagement. But this purpose makes no change with regard to his obligation. He is as much bound as the honest man, who contracts with a fixed purpose of performing.

As the contract is binding without any regard to the purpose, so there may be a purpose without any contract. A purpose is no contract, even when it is declared to the person for whose benefit it is intended. I may say to a man, I intend to do such a thing for your benefit, but I come under no engagement. Every man understands the meaning of this speech, and sees no contradiction in it: whereas, if a purpose declared were the same thing with a contract, such a speech would be a contradiction, and would be the same as if one should say, I promise to do such a thing, but I do not promise.

All this is so plain to every man of common sense, that it would have been unnecessary to be mentioned, had not so acute a man as Mr. Hume grounded some of the contradictions he finds in a contract, upon confounding a will to engage in a contract with a will or purpose to perform the engagement.

VII. *Natural tendency of Mr. Hume's principles.*—I come now to consider *the speculations of that author with regard to contracts.*

[In order to support a favourite notion of his own, That justice is not a natural but an artificial virtue, and that it derives its whole merit from its utility, he has laid down some principles which, I think, have a tendency to *subvert all faith and fair-dealing* among mankind.]

In the third volume of the " Treatise of Human Nature," p. 40, he lays it down as an undoubted maxim, [That no action can be virtuous or morally good, unless there be, in human nature, some motive to produce it, *distinct* from its morality.] Let us apply this undoubted maxim in an instance or two. If a man keeps his word, from this sole motive, that he ought to do so, this is no virtuous or morally good action. If a man pays his debt, from this motive, that justice requires this of him, this is no virtuous or morally good action. If a judge or an arbiter gives a sentence in a cause, from no other motive but regard to justice, this is no virtuous or morally good action. These appear to me to be shocking absurdities, which no metaphysical subtilty can ever justify.

Nothing is more evident than that every human action takes its denomination and its moral nature from the motive from which it is performed. That is a benevolent action, which is done from benevolence. That is an act of gratitude, which is done from a sentiment of gratitude. That is an act of obedience to God, which is done from a regard to his command. And, in general, that is an act of virtue, which is done from a regard to virtue.

Virtuous actions are so far from needing other motives, besides their being virtuous, to give them merit, that their merit is then greatest and most conspicuous, when every motive that can be put in the opposite scale is outweighed by the sole consideration of their being our duty.

This maxim, therefore, of Mr. Hume, That no action can be virtuous or morally good, unless there be some motive to produce it *distinct* from its morality, is so far from being undoubtedly true, that it is undoubtedly false. It was never, so far as I know, maintained by any moralist, but by the Epicureans; and it savours of the very dregs of that sect. It agrees well with the principles of those who maintained, that virtue is an empty name, and that it is entitled to no regard, but in as far as it ministers to pleasure or profit.

VIII. *Mr. Hume's practice probably contradicted his principles.*—I believe the author of this maxim acted upon better moral principles than he wrote; and that what Cicero says of Epicurus, may be applied to him: " Redarguitur ipse a sese, vincunturque scripta ejus probitate ipsius et moribus, et ut alii existimantur dicere melius quam facere, sic ille mihi videtur facere melius quam dicere."—" He is refuted by himself, and his writings defeated by his probity and moral worth; and as some imagine that he spoke better than he acted, so to me he appears to have acted better than he spoke."

But let us see how he applies this maxim to contracts. I give you his words from the place formerly cited. " I suppose," says he, " a person to have lent me a sum of money, on condition that it be restored in a few days; and, after the expiration of the term agreed on, he demands the sum. I ask, what reason or motive have I to restore the money? It will, perhaps, be said, that my regard to justice, and abhorrence of villany and knavery, are sufficient reasons for me, if I have the least grain of honesty, or sense of duty and obligation. And this answer, no doubt, is just and satisfactory to man in his civilized state, and when trained up according to a certain discipline and education. But, in his rude and more natural condition, if you are pleased to call such a condition natural, this answer would be rejected as perfectly unintelligible and sophistical."

The doctrine we are taught in this passage is this—that though a man, in a civilized state, and when trained up according to a certain discipline and education, may have a regard to justice, and an abhorrence of villany and knavery, and some sense of duty and obligation; yet, to a man in his rude and more natural condition, the considerations of honesty, justice, duty, and obligation, will be perfectly unintelligible and sophistical. And this is brought as an argument to show, that *justice is not a natural*, but an *artificial virtue*.

IX. I shall offer some observations on this argument.

1. Although it may be true, that what is unintelligible to man in his rude state may be intelligible to him in his civilized state, I cannot conceive, that what is sophistical in the rude state should change its nature, and become just reasoning, when man is more improved. What is a sophism, will always be so; nor can any change in the state of the person who judges, make that to be just reasoning which before was sophistical. Mr. Hume's argument requires, that to man in his rude state, the motives to justice and honesty should not only appear to be sophistical, but should really be so. If the motives were just in themselves,

then justice would be a natural virtue, although the rude man, by an error of his judgment, thought otherwise. But if justice be not a natural virtue, which is the point Mr. Hume intends to prove, then every argument, by which man in his natural state may be urged to it, must be a sophism in reality, and not in appearance only; and the effect of discipline and education in the civilized state can only be to make those motives to justice appear just and satisfactory, which, in their own nature, are sophistical.

2. It were to be wished, that this ingenious author had shown us, why that state of man, in which the obligation to honesty, and an abhorrence of villany, appear perfectly unintelligible and sophistical, should be his *more natural state.*

It is the nature of human society to be progressive, as much as it is the nature of the individual. In the individual, the state of infancy leads to that of childhood, childhood to youth, youth to manhood, and manhood to old age. If one should say, that the state of infancy is a more natural state than that of manhood or of old age, I am apt to think, that this would be words without any meaning. In like manner, in human society, there is a natural progress from rudeness to civilization, from ignorance to knowledge. What period of this progress shall we call man's natural state? To me they appear all equally natural. Every state of society is equally natural, wherein men have access to exert their natural powers about their proper objects, and to improve those powers by the means which their situation affords.

Mr. Hume, indeed, shows some timidity in affirming the rude state to be the more natural state of man; and, therefore, adds this qualifying parenthesis, *If you are pleased to call such a condition natural.*

But it ought to be observed, that if the premises of his argument be weakened by this clause, the same weakness must be communicated to the conclusion; and the conclusion, according to the rules of good reasoning, ought to be—that justice is an artificial virtue, if you be *pleased* to call it artificial.

3. It were likewise to be wished, that Mr. Hume had shown from fact, that there *ever did exist such a state of man as that which he calls his more natural state.* It is a state wherein a man borrows a sum of money, on the condition that he is to restore it in a few days; yet when the time of payment comes, his obligation to repay what he borrowed is perfectly unintelligible and sophistical. It would have been proper to have given at least a single instance of some tribe of the human race that was found to be in this natural state. If no such instance can be given, it is probably a state merely imaginary; like that state which some have imagined, wherein men were *ouran outangs,* or wherein they were fishes with tails.

Indeed, such a state seems impossible. That a man should

lend without any conception of his having a right to be repaid; or that a man should borrow on the condition of paying in a few days, and yet have no conception of his obligation, seems to me to involve a contradiction.

I grant, that a humane man may lend without any expectation of being repaid; but that he should lend without any conception of a right to be repaid, is a contradiction. In like manner, a fraudulent man may borrow without an intention of paying back; but that he should borrow, while an obligation to repay is perfectly unintelligible to him: this is a contradiction.

The same author, in his "Enquiry into the Principles of Morals," sect. iii., treating of the same subject, has the following note:—

" 'Tis evident, that the will or consent alone never transfers property, nor causes the obligation of a promise, (for the same reasoning extends to both,) but the will must be expressed by words or signs, in order to impose a tie upon any man. The expression being once brought in as subservient to the will, soon becomes the principal part of the promise; nor will a man be less bound by his word, though he secretly give a different direction to his intention, and withhold the assent of his mind. But though the expression makes, on most occasions, the whole of the promise, yet it does not always so; and one who should make use of any expression, of which he knows not the meaning, and which he uses without any sense of the consequences, would not certainly be bound by it. Nay, though he know its meaning; yet if he uses it in jest only, and with such signs as show evidently he has no serious intention of binding himself, he would not be under any obligation of performance; but it is necessary that the words be a perfect expression of the will, without any contrary signs. Nay, even this we must not carry so far as to imagine, that one whom, from our quickness of understanding, we conjecture to have an intention of deceiving us, is not bound by his expression or verbal promise, if we accept of it, but must limit this conclusion to those cases where the signs are of a different nature from those of deceit. All these contradictions are easily accounted for, if justice arises entirely from its usefulness to society, but will never be explained on any other hypothesis."

[Here we have the opinion of this grave moralist and acute metaphysician, that the principles of *honesty and fidelity* are at bottom a *bundle of contradictions.*] This is one part of his moral system which, I cannot help thinking, borders upon licentiousness. It surely tends to give a very unfavourable notion of that cardinal virtue, without which no man has a title to be called an honest man. What regard can a man pay to the virtue of fidelity, who believes that its essential rules contradict each other? Can a man be bound by contradictory rules of conduct? No more, surely, than he can be bound to believe contradictory principles.

He tells us, " That all these contradictions are easily accounted for, if justice arises entirely from its usefulness to society, but will never be explained upon any other hypothesis."

I know not indeed what is meant by accounting for contradictions, or explaining them. I apprehend, that no hypothesis can make that which is a contradiction to be no contradiction. However, without attempting to account for these contradictions upon his own hypothesis, he pronounces, in a decisive tone, that they will never be explained upon any other hypothesis.

X. *Origin of the contradictions in Mr. Hume's arguments.*—What if it shall appear, that the contradictions mentioned in this paragraph, do all take their rise from *two capital mistakes* the author has made with regard to the nature of promises and contracts; and if, when these are corrected, there shall not appear a shadow of contradiction in the cases put by him?

The *first* mistake is, That a promise is some kind of will, consent, or intention, which may be expressed, or may not be expressed. This is to mistake the nature of a promise: for no will, no consent or intention that is not expressed, is a promise. A promise, being a *social* transaction between two parties, without being expressed, can have no existence.

Another capital mistake that runs through the passage cited is, That this will, consent or intention, which makes a promise, is a will or intention to perform what we promise. Every man knows that there may be a fraudulent promise, made without intention of performing. But the intention to perform the promise, or not to perform it, whether the intention be known to the other party or not, makes no part of the promise, it is a solitary act of the mind, and can neither constitute nor dissolve an obligation. What makes a promise is, that it be expressed to the other party with understanding, and with an intention to become bound, and that it be accepted by him.

XI. Carrying these remarks along with us, let us review the passage cited.

First, He observes, that the will or consent alone does not cause the obligation of a promise, but it must be expressed.

I answer: The will *not expressed* is not a promise; and is it a contradiction that that which is not a promise should not cause the obligation of a promise? He goes on: The expression being once brought in as subservient to the will, soon *becomes* a principal part of the promise. Here it is supposed, that the expression was not originally a constituent part of the promise, but it soon *becomes* such. It is brought in to aid and be subservient to the promise which was made before by the will. If Mr. Hume had considered, that it is the expression accompanied with understanding and will to become bound, that constitutes a promise, he would never have said, that the expression soon becomes a part, and is brought in as subservient.

He adds, Nor will a man be less bound by his word, though he secretly gives a different direction to his intention, and withholds the assent of his mind.

The case here put needs some explication. Either it means, that the man knowingly and voluntarily gives his word, without any intention of giving his word, or that he gives it without the intention of keeping it, and performing what he promises. The last of these is indeed a possible case, and is, I apprehend, what Mr. Hume means. But the intention of keeping his promise is no part of the promise, nor does it in the least affect the obligation of it, as we have often observed.

If the author meant that the man may knowingly and voluntarily give his word, without the intention of giving his word, this is impossible : For such is the nature of all social acts of the mind, that, as they cannot be without being expressed, so they cannot be expressed knowingly and willingly, but they must be. If a man puts a question knowingly and willingly, it is impossible that he should at the same time will not to put it. If he gives a command knowingly and willingly, it is impossible that he should at the same time will not to give it. We cannot have contrary wills at the same time. And, in like manner, if a man knowingly and willingly becomes bound by a promise, it is impossible that he should at the same time will not to be bound.

To suppose, therefore, that when a man knowingly and willingly gives his word, he withholds that will and intention which makes a promise, is indeed a contradiction ; but the contradiction is not in the nature of the promise, but in the case supposed by Mr. Hume.

He adds, though *the expression*, for the most part, makes the whole of the promise, it *does not always so*.

I answer, That *the expression, if it is not accompanied with understanding, and will to engage, never makes a promise*. The author here assumes a postulate, which nobody ever granted, and which can only be grounded on the impossible supposition made in the former sentence. And as there can be no promise without knowledge, and will to engage, is it marvellous that words which are not understood, or words spoken in jest, and without any intention to become bound, should not have the effect of a promise ?

XII. [*The last case* put by Mr. Hume, is that of *a man who promises fraudulently with an intention not to perform*, and whose fraudulent intention is discovered by the other party, who, notwithstanding, accepts the promise. He is bound, says Mr. Hume, by his verbal promise.] Undoubtedly he is bound, because an intention not to perform the promise, whether known to the other party or not, makes no part of the promise, nor affects its obligation, as has been repeatedly observed.

From what has been said, I think it evident, that to one who attends to the nature of a promise or contract, there is not the least appearance of contradiction in the principles of morality relating to contracts.

It would indeed appear wonderful, that such a man as Mr. Hume should have imposed upon himself in so plain a matter, if we did not see frequent instances of ingenious men, whose zeal in supporting a favourite hypothesis, darkens their understanding, and hinders them from seeing what is before their eyes.

CHAPTER VII.

THAT MORAL APPROBATION IMPLIES A REAL JUDGMENT.

I. THE approbation of good actions, and disapprobation of bad, are so familiar to every man come to years of understanding, that it seems strange there should be any dispute about their nature.

Whether we reflect upon our own conduct, or attend to the conduct of others with whom we live, or of whom we hear or read, we cannot help approving of some things, disapproving of others, and regarding many with perfect indifference.

These operations of our minds we are conscious of every day, and almost every hour we live. Men of ripe understanding are capable of reflecting upon them, and of attending to what passes in their own thoughts on such occasions; yet, for half a century, it has been a serious dispute among philosophers, what this approbation and disapprobation is, Whether there be a real judgment included in it, which, like all other judgments, must be true or false; or, Whether it include no more but some agreeable or uneasy feeling in the person who approves or disapproves.

II. [Mr. Hume observes very justly, that this is a controversy *started of late*. Before the modern system of ideas and impressions was introduced, nothing would have appeared more absurd than to say, That when I condemn a man for what he has done, I pass no judgment at all about the man, but only express some uneasy feeling in myself.]

Nor did the new system produce this discovery at once, but gradually, by several steps, according as its consequences were more accurately traced, and its spirit more thoroughly imbibed by successive philosophers.

Des Cartes and Mr. Locke went no farther than to maintain, that the *secondary qualities* of body, heat and cold, sound, colour, taste and smell, which we perceive and judge to be in the external object, *are mere feelings or sensations* in our minds, there being nothing in bodies themselves to which these names can be applied; and that *the office of the external senses is not to judge* of external things, but only to give us ideas or sensations, from which we are by reasoning to deduce the existence of a material world without us, as well as we can.

Arthur Collier and Bishop Berkeley discovered, from the same principles, that the *primary, as well as the secondary, qualities* of bodies, such as extension, figure, solidity, motion, *are only sensations* in our minds; and therefore, that there is no material world without us at all.

The same philosophy, when it came to be applied to matters of taste, discovered that beauty and deformity are not anything in the objects to which men, from the beginning of the world, ascribed them, but certain feelings in the mind of the spectator.

III. [*The next step was an easy consequence from all the preceding*, that moral approbation and disapprobation are not judgments, which must be true or false, but barely, agreeable and uneasy feelings or sensations.]

Mr. Hume made the last step in this progress, and crowned the system by what he calls his *hypothesis*, to wit, That belief is more properly an act of the sensitive, than of the cogitative part of our nature.

Beyond this I think no man can go in this track; sensation or feeling is all, and what is left to the cogitative part of our nature, I am not able to comprehend.

I have had occasion to consider each of these paradoxes, excepting that which relates to morals, in Essays on the Intellectual Powers of Man; and, though they be strictly connected with each other, and with the system which has produced them, I have attempted to show, that they are inconsistent with just notions of our intellectual powers, no less than they are with the common sense and common language of mankind. And this, I think, will likewise appear with regard to the conclusion relating to morals, to wit, That moral approbation is only an agreeable feeling, and not a real judgment.

IV. [*Of feeling and judgment.*—To prevent ambiguity as much as possible, let us attend to the meaning of *feeling* and of *judgment*. These operations of the mind, perhaps, cannot be logically defined; but they are well understood, and *easily distinguished, by their properties and adjuncts.*]

Feeling or sensation seems to be the lowest degree of animation we can conceive. We give the name of *animal* to every being that feels pain or pleasure; and this seems to be the boundary between the inanimate and animal creation.

We know no being of so low a rank in the creation of God, as to possess this animal power only without any other.

We commonly distinguish *feeling* from *thinking*, because it hardly deserves the name; and though it be, in a more general sense, a species of thought, is least removed from the passive and inert state of things inanimate.

A feeling must be agreeable, or uneasy, or indifferent. It may be weak or strong. It is expressed in language either by a single word, or by such a contexture of words as may be the subject or predicate of a proposition, but such as cannot by themselves make a proposition. For it implies neither affirmation nor negation; and therefore cannot have the qualities of true or false, which distinguish propositions from all other forms of speech, and judgments from all other acts of the mind.

That I have such a feeling, is indeed an affirmative proposition, and expresses testimony grounded upon an intuitive judgment. But the feeling is only one term of this proposition; and it can only make a proposition when joined with another term, by a verb affirming or denying.

[*As feeling distinguishes the animal nature from the inanimate;* so judging seems to distinguish the rational nature from the merely animal.]

Though judgment in general is expressed by one word in language, as the most complex operations of the mind may be; yet a particular judgment can only be expressed by a sentence, and by that kind of sentence which logicians call a *proposition*, in which there must necessarily be a verb in the indicative mood, either expressed or understood.

Every judgment must necessarily be true or false, and the same may be said of the proposition which expresses it. It is a determination of the understanding, with regard to what is true, or false, or dubious.*

In judgment, we can distinguish the object about which we judge, from the act of the mind in judging of that object. In mere feeling there is no such distinction. The object of judgment must be expressed by a proposition; and belief, disbelief, or doubt, always accompanies the judgment we form. If we judge the proposition to be true, we must believe it; if we judge it to be false, we must disbelieve it; and if we be uncertain whether it be true or false, we must doubt.

The *toothache*, the *headache*, are words which express uneasy feelings; but to say that they express a judgment would be ridiculous.

That the sun is greater than the earth, is a proposition, and therefore the object of judgment; and when affirmed or denied,

* Vide Essays on the Intellectual Powers of Man, Essay VI. chap. i.

believed or disbelieved, or doubted, it expresses judgment; but to say that it expresses only a feeling in the mind of him that believes it, would be ridiculous.

These two operations of mind, when we consider them separately, are very different, and easily distinguished. When we feel without judging, or judge without feeling, it is impossible, without very gross inattention, to mistake the one for the other.

But in many operations of the mind, both are inseparably conjoined under one name; and when we are not aware that the operation is complex, we may take one ingredient to be the whole, and overlook the other.

In former ages, that moral power, by which human actions ought to be regulated, was called *reason*, and considered, both by philosophers, and by the vulgar, as the power of judging what we ought, and what we ought not to do.

This is very fully expressed by Mr. Hume, in his "Treatise of Human Nature," Book ii. Part iii. sec. 3: "Nothing is more usual in philosophy, and even in common life, than to talk of the combat of passion and reason, to give the preference to reason, and assert that men are only so far virtuous as they conform themselves to its dictates. Every rational creature, 'tis said, is obliged to regulate his actions by reason; and if any other motive or principle challenge the direction of his conduct, he ought to oppose it, till it be entirely subdued, or, at least, brought to a conformity to that superior principle. On this method of thinking, the greatest part of moral philosophy, ancient and modern, seems to be founded."

That those philosophers attended chiefly to the judging power of our moral faculty, appears from the names they gave to its operations, and from the whole of their language concerning it.

V. [The *modern philosophy has led men to attend* chiefly *to their sensations and feelings*, and thereby to resolve into mere feeling, complex acts of the mind, of which feeling is only *one* ingredient.]

I had occasion, in the preceding Essays, to observe, That several operations of the mind, to which we give one name, and consider as one act, are compounded of more simple acts, inseparably united in our constitution, and that in these, sensation or feeling often makes one ingredient.

Thus the appetites of hunger and thirst are compounded of an uneasy sensation, and the desire of food or drink. In our benevolent affections, there is both an agreeable feeling, and a desire of happiness to the object of our affection; and malevolent affections have ingredients of a contrary nature.

In these instances, sensation or feeling is inseparably conjoined with desire. In other instances, we find sensation inseparably conjoined with judgment or belief, and that in two different ways. In some instances, the judgment or belief seems to be the consequence of the sensation, and to be regulated by it. In other instances, the sensation is the consequence of the judgment.

When we perceive an external object by our senses, we have a sensation conjoined with a firm belief of the existence and sensible qualities of the external object. Nor has all the subtilty of metaphysics been able to disjoin what nature has conjoined in our constitution. Des Cartes and Locke endeavoured, by reasoning, to deduce the existence of external objects from our sensation, but in vain. Subsequent philosophers, finding no reason for this connexion, endeavoured to throw off the belief of external objects as being unreasonable; but this attempt is no less vain. Nature has doomed us to believe the testimony of our senses, whether we can give a good reason for doing so or not.

In this instance, the belief or judgment is the consequence of the sensation, as the sensation is the consequence of the impression made on the organ of sense.

But in most of the operations of mind in which judgment or belief is combined with feeling, the feeling is the consequence of the judgment, and is regulated by it.

Thus, an account of the good conduct of a friend at a distance gives me a very agreeable feeling, and a contrary account would give me a very uneasy feeling; but these feelings depend entirely upon my belief of the report.

In *hope*, there is an agreeable feeling, depending upon the belief or expectation of good to come: fear is made up of contrary ingredients; in both, the feeling is regulated by the degree of belief.

In the *respect* we bear to the worthy, and in our contempt of the worthless, there is both judgment and feeling, and the last depends entirely upon the first.

The same may be said of *gratitude* for good offices, and *resentment* of injuries.

VI. Let me now consider how I am affected when I see a man exerting himself nobly in a good cause. I am conscious that the effect of his conduct on my mind is *complex*, though it may be called by *one name*. I look up to his virtue, I approve, I admire it. In doing so, I have pleasure indeed, or an agreeable feeling; this is granted. But I find myself interested in his success and in his fame. This is affection; it is love and esteem, which is more than mere feeling. The man is the object of this esteem; but in mere feeling there is no object.

I am likewise conscious that this agreeable feeling in me, and this esteem of him, depend entirely upon *the judgment I form of his conduct*. I judge that this conduct merits esteem; and, while I thus judge, I cannot but esteem him, and contemplate his conduct with pleasure. Persuade me that he was bribed, or that he acted from some mercenary or bad motive, immediately my esteem and my agreeable feeling vanish.

[In the approbation of a good action, therefore, there is *feeling* indeed, but there is also *esteem* of the agent; and both the feeling and the esteem depend upon the *judgment* we form of his conduct.]

When I exercise my moral faculty about my own actions or those of other men, I am conscious that I judge as well as feel. I accuse and excuse, I acquit and condemn, I assent and dissent, I believe and disbelieve, and doubt. These are acts of judgment, and not feelings.

Every determination of the understanding, with regard to what is true or false, is judgment. That I ought not to steal, or to kill, or to bear false witness, are propositions, of the truth of which I am as well convinced as of any proposition in Euclid. I am conscious that I judge them to be true propositions; and my consciousness makes all other arguments unnecessary, with regard to the operations of my own mind.

That other men judge, as well as feel, in such cases, I am convinced, because they understand me when I express my moral judgment, and express theirs by the same terms and phrases.

Suppose that, in a case well known to both, my friend says, *Such a man did well and worthily; his conduct is highly approvable*. This speech, according to all rules of interpretation, expresses my friend's judgment of the man's conduct. This judgment may be true or false, and I may agree in opinion with him, or I may dissent from him without offence, as we may differ in other matters of judgment.

Suppose again, that, in relation to the same case, my friend says, *The man's conduct gave me a very agreeable feeling*.

This speech, if approbation be nothing but an agreeable feeling, must have the very same meaning with the first, and express neither more nor less. But this cannot be, for two reasons.

First, Because there is no rule in grammar or rhetoric, nor any usage in language, by which these two speeches can be construed, so as to have the same meaning. The *first* expresses plainly an opinion or judgment of the conduct of the man, but says nothing of the speaker. The *second* only testifies a fact concerning the speaker, to wit, that he had such a feeling.

Another reason why these two speeches cannot mean the same thing is, that the first may be contradicted without any ground of offence, such contradiction being only a difference of opinion, which, to a reasonable man, gives no offence. But the second speech cannot be contradicted without an affront; for, as every man must know his own feelings, to deny that a man had a feeling which he affirms he had, is to charge him with falsehood.

If moral approbation be a real judgment, which produces an agreeable feeling in the mind of him who judges, both speeches are perfectly intelligible, in the most obvious and literal sense. Their meaning is different, but they are related, so that the one may be inferred from the other, as we infer the effect from the cause, or the cause from the effect. I know, that what a man judges to be a very worthy action, he contemplates with pleasure; and what he contemplates with pleasure must, in his judgment, have worth. But the judgment and the feeling are different acts of his mind, though connected as cause and effect. He can express either the one or the other with perfect propriety; but the speech which expresses his feeling is altogether improper and inept to express his judgment, for this evident reason, that judgment and feeling, though in some cases connected, are things in their nature different.

If we suppose, on the other hand, that moral approbation is nothing more than an agreeable feeling, occasioned by the contemplation of an action, the second speech above mentioned has a distinct meaning, and expresses all that is meant by moral approbation. But the first speech either means the very same thing, (which cannot be, for the reasons already mentioned,) or it has no meaning.

Now, we may appeal to the reader, whether, in conversation upon human characters, such speeches as the first are not as frequent, as familiar, and as well understood, as anything in language; and whether they have not been common in all ages that we can trace, and in all languages?

[This doctrine, therefore, That moral approbation is merely a feeling without judgment, necessarily carries along with it this consequence, *that a form of speech*, upon one of the most common topics of discourse, *which* either *has no meaning*, or a meaning irreconcilable to all rules of grammar or rhetoric, *is found to be common and familiar in all languages,* and in all ages of the world, while every man knows how to express the meaning, if it have any, in plain and proper language.]

Such a consequence I think sufficient to sink any philosophical opinion on which it hangs.

A particular language may have some oddity, or even absurdity, introduced by some man of eminence, from caprice or wrong judgment, and followed by servile imitators, for a time, till it be detected, and, of consequence, discountenanced and dropt; but that the same absurdity should pervade all languages, through all ages, and that, after being detected and exposed, it should still keep its countenance and its place in language as much as before, this can never be while men have understanding.

VII. [It may be observed by the way, that *the same argument may be applied*, with equal force, *against those other paradoxical opinions of modern philosophy* which we before mentioned as connected with this, such as, that beauty and deformity are not at all in the objects to which language universally ascribes them, but are merely feelings in the mind of the spectator; that the secondary qualities are not in external objects, but are merely feelings or sensations in him that perceives them; and, in general, that our external and internal senses are faculties by which we have sensations or feelings only, but by which we do not judge.]

That every form of speech which language affords to express our judgments, should, in all ages, and in all languages, be used to express what is no judgment; and that feelings, which are easily expressed in proper language, should as universally be expressed by language altogether improper and absurd, I cannot believe; and therefore must conclude, that if language be the expression of thought, men *judge* of the primary and secondary qualities of body by their external senses, of beauty and deformity by their taste, and of virtue and vice by their moral faculty.

A truth so evident as this is, can hardly be obscured and brought into doubt, but by the abuse of words. And much abuse of words there has been upon this subject. To avoid this, as much as possible, I have used the word *judgment*, on one side, and *sensation* or *feeling*, upon the other; because these words have been least liable to abuse or ambiguity. But it may be proper to make some observations upon other words that have been used in this controversy.

Mr. Hume, in his "Treatise of Human Nature," has employed two sections upon it, the titles of which are, *Moral Distinctions not derived from Reason*, and *Moral Distinctions derived from a Moral Sense*.

When he is not, by custom, led unawares to speak of reason like other men, he limits that word to signify only the power of judging in matters merely speculative. Hence he concludes, "That reason of itself is inactive and perfectly inert." That "actions may be laudable or blameable, but cannot be reasonable or unreasonable." That "it is not contrary to reason, to prefer the destruction of the whole world to the scratching of my finger." That "it is not contrary to reason, for me to choose my total ruin to prevent the least uneasiness of an Indian, or of a person wholly unknown to me." That "reason is, and ought only to be, the slave of the passions, and can never pretend to any other office, than to serve and obey them."

If we take the word *reason* to mean what common use, both of philosophers and of the vulgar, hath made it to mean, these maxims are not only false, but licentious. It is only his abuse of the words *reason* and *passion*, that can justify them from this censure.

The meaning of a common word is not to be ascertained by philosophical theory, but by common usage; and if a man will take the liberty of limiting or extending the meaning of common words at his pleasure, he may, like Mandeville, insinuate the most licentious paradoxes with the appearance of plausibility. I have before made some observations upon the meaning of this word, Essay II. chap. 2, and Essay III. Part iii. chap. 1, to which the reader is referred.

When Mr. Hume derives moral difficulties from a moral sense, I agree with him in words, but we differ about the meaning of the word *sense*. Every power to which the name of a sense has been given, is a power of judging of the objects of that sense, and has been accounted such in all ages; the moral sense therefore is the power of judging in morals. But Mr. Hume will have the moral sense to be only a power of feeling, without judging: This I take to be an abuse of the word.

[Authors who place moral approbation in feeling only, very often use the word *sentiment*, to express *feeling without judgment*. This I take likewise to be an abuse of the word.] Our moral determinations may, with propriety, be called *moral sentiments*. For the word *sentiment*, in the English language, never, as I conceive, signifies mere feeling, but judgment accompanied with feeling. It was wont to signify opinion or judgment of any kind, but, of late, is appropriated to signify an opinion or judgment, that strikes, and produces some agreeable or uneasy emotion. So we speak of sentiments of respect, of esteem, of gratitude. But I never heard the pain of the gout, or any other mere feeling, called a sentiment.

Even the word *judgment* has been used by Mr. Hume to express what he maintains to be only a feeling. "Treatise of Human Nature," Part iii. p. 3. "The term *perception* is no less applicable to those *judgments* by which we distinguish moral good and evil, than to every other operation of the mind." Perhaps he used this word inadvertently; for I think there cannot be a greater abuse of words, than to put judgment for what he held to be mere feeling.

VIII. [*Improper use of words has impeded the study of moral philosophy.*—All the words most commonly used, both by philosophers and the vulgar, to express the operations of our moral faculty, such as *decision, determination, sentence, approbation, disapprobation, applause, censure, praise, blame*, necessarily imply judgment in their meaning. When, therefore, they are used by Mr. Hume, and others who hold his opinion, to signify *feelings only*, this is an abuse of words.] If these philosophers wish to speak plainly and properly, they must, in discoursing of morals, discard these words altogether, because their established signification in the language, is contrary to what they would express by them.

They must likewise discard from morals the words *ought* and *ought not*, which very properly express judgment, but cannot be applied to mere feelings. Upon these words Mr. Hume has made a particular observation in the conclusion of his first section above mentioned. I shall give it in his own words, and make some remarks upon it.

" I cannot forbear adding to these reasonings, an observation which may, perhaps, be found of some importance. In every system of morality which I have hitherto met with, I have always remarked, that the author proceeds for some time in the ordinary way of reasoning, and establishes the being of a God, or makes observations concerning human affairs; when, of a sudden, I am surprised to find, that, instead of the usual copulations of propositions, *is*, and *is not*, I meet with no proposition that is not connected with an *ought*, or an *ought not*. This change is imperceptible, but is, however, of the last consequence. For as this *ought* or *ought not* expresses some new relation or affirmation, it is necessary that it should be observed and explained: and, at the same time, that a reason should be given for what seems altogether inconceivable; how this new relation can be a deduction from others which are entirely different from it. But as authors do not commonly use this precaution, I shall presume to recommend it to the readers; and am persuaded, that this small attention would subvert all the vulgar systems of morality, and let us see, that the distinction of vice and virtue, is not founded merely on the relations of objects, nor is perceived by reason."

We may here observe, that it is acknowledged, that the words *ought* and *ought not* express some relation and affirmation; but a relation or affirmation which Mr. Hume thought inexplicable, or, at least, inconsistent with his system of morals. He must, therefore, have thought, that they ought not to be used in treating of that subject.

He likewise makes two demands, and, taking it for granted that they cannot be satisfied, is persuaded, that an attention to this is sufficient to subvert all the vulgar systems of morals.

The *first* demand is, that *ought* and *ought not* be explained.

To a man that understands English, there are surely no words that require explanation less. Are not all men taught, from their early years, that they ought not to lie, nor steal, nor swear falsely? But Mr. Hume thinks, that men never understood what these precepts mean, or rather that they are unintelligible. If this be so, I think indeed it will follow, that all the vulgar systems of morals are subverted.

Dr. Johnson, in his Dictionary, explains the word *ought* to signify, being obliged by duty; and I know no better explication that can be given of it. The reader will see what I thought necessary to say concerning the moral relation expressed by this word, in Essay III. part iii. chap. 5.

The *second* demand is, that a reason should be given why this relation should be a deduction from others which are entirely different from it.

This is to demand a reason for what does not exist. The first principles of morals are not deductions. They are self-evident; and their truth, like that of other axioms, is perceived without reasoning or deduction. And moral truths, that are not self-evident, are deduced, not from relations quite different from them, but from the first principles of morals.

In a matter so interesting to mankind, and so frequently the subject of conversation among the learned and the unlearned as morals is, it may surely be expected, that men will express both their judgments and their feelings with propriety, and consistently with the rules of language. An opinion, therefore, which makes the language of all nations, upon this subject, to be improper, contrary to all rules of language, and fit to be discarded, needs no other refutation.

As mankind have, in all ages, understood *reason* to mean the power by which not only our speculative opinions, but our actions, ought to be regulated, we may say, with perfect propriety, that all vice is contrary to reason; that, by reason, we are to judge of what we ought to do, as well as of what we ought to believe.

But though all vice be contrary to reason, I conceive that it would not be a proper definition of vice to say, that it is a conduct contrary to reason, because this definition would apply equally to folly, which all men distinguish from vice.

IX. [There are *other phrases* which have been used on the same side of the question, *which I see no reason for adopting*, such as, *acting contrary to the relations of things*, contrary *to the reason of things, to the fitness of things, to the truth of things, to absolute fitness.*] These phrases have not the authority of common use, which in matters of language, is great. They seem to have been invented by some authors, with a view to explain the nature of vice; but I do not think they answer that end. If intended as definitions of vice, they are improper: because, in the most favourable sense they can bear, they extend to every kind of foolish and absurd conduct, as well as to that which is vicious.

I shall conclude this chapter with some observations upon the five arguments which Mr. Hume has offered upon this point in his Inquiry.

The *first* is, that it is impossible that the hypothesis he opposes can, in any particular instance, be so much as rendered intelligible, whatever specious figure it may make in general discourse. "Examine," says he, "the crime of ingratitude, anatomise all its circumstances, and examine, by your reason alone, in what consists the demerit or blame, you will never come to any issue or conclusion."

I think it unnecessary to follow him through all the accounts of ingratitude which he conceives may be given by those whom he opposes, because I agree with him in that which he himself adopts, to wit, "That this crime arises from a complication of circumstances, which, being presented to the spectator, excites the sentiment of blame by the particular structure and fabric of his mind."

This he thought a true and intelligible account of the criminality of ingratitude. So do I. And therefore I think the hypothesis he opposes is intelligible, when applied to a particular instance.

Mr. Hume, no doubt, thought, that the account he gives of ingratitude is inconsistent with the hypothesis he opposes, and could not be adopted by those who hold that hypothesis. He could be led to think so, only by taking for granted one of these two things. Either, *first*, That the *sentiment of blame* means a feeling only, without judgment; or *secondly*, That whatever is excited by the particular fabric and structure of the mind must be feeling only, and not judgment. But I cannot grant either the one or the other.

For, as to the *first*, it seems evident to me, that both *sentiment* and *blame* imply judgment; and, therefore, that the *sentiment of blame* means a judgment accompanied with feeling, and not mere feeling without judgment.

The *second* can as little be granted; for no operation of mind, whether judgment or feeling, can be excited but by that particular structure and fabric of the mind which makes us capable of that operation.

By that part of our fabric which we call *the faculty of seeing*, we judge of visible objects; by *taste*, another part of our fabric, we judge of beauty and deformity; by that part of our fabric, which enables us to form abstract conceptions, to compare them, and perceive their relations, we judge of abstract truths; and by that part of our fabric which we call the *moral faculty*, we judge of virtue and vice. If we suppose a being without any moral faculty in his fabric, I grant that he could not have the sentiments of blame and moral approbation.

[There are, therefore, *judgments*, as well as *feelings*, that are excited by the particular structure and fabric of the mind. But there is this *remarkable difference between them*, That *every judgment is,* in its own nature, *true or false;* and though it depends upon the fabric of a mind, whether it have such a judgment or not, it depends not upon that fabric whether the judgment be true or not. A true judgment will be true, whatever be the fabric of the mind; but a particular structure and fabric is necessary, in order to our perceiving that truth. *Nothing like this can be said of mere feelings,* because the attributes of true or false do not belong to them.]

Thus I think it appears, that the hypothesis which Mr. Hume opposes is not unintelligible, when applied to the particular instance of ingratitude; because the account of ingratitude which he himself thinks true and intelligible, is perfectly agreeable to it.

The *second* argument amounts to this: That in moral deliberation, we must be acquainted beforehand with all the objects and all their relations. After these things are known, the understanding has no further room to operate. Nothing remains but to feel, on our part, some sentiment of blame or approbation.

Let us apply this reasoning to the office of a judge. In a cause that comes before him, he must be made acquainted with all the objects, and all their relations. After this, his understanding has no further room to operate. Nothing remains, on his part, but to feel the right or the wrong; and mankind have, very absurdly, called him a *judge;* he ought to be called a *feeler.*

To answer this argument more directly: the man who deliberates, after all the objects and relations mentioned by Mr. Hume are known to him, has a point to determine; and that is, whether the action under his deliberation ought to be done or ought not. In most cases, this point will appear self-evident to a man who has been accustomed to exercise his moral judgment; in some cases it may require reasoning.

In like manner, the judge, after all the circumstances of the cause are known, has to judge, whether the plaintiff has a just plea or not.

The *third* argument is taken from the analogy between moral beauty and natural, between moral sentiment and taste. As beauty is not a quality of the object, but a certain feeling of the spectator, so virtue and vice are not qualities in the persons to whom language ascribes them, but feelings of the spectator.

But is it certain beauty is not any quality of the object? This is indeed a paradox of modern philosophy, built upon a philosophical theory; but a paradox so contrary to the common language and common sense of mankind, that it ought rather to overturn the theory on which it stands, than receive any support from it. And if beauty be really a quality of the object, and not merely a feeling of the spectator, the whole force of this argument goes over to the other side of the question.

"Euclid," he says, "has fully explained all the qualities of the circle, but has not, in any proposition, said a word of its beauty. The reason is evident. The beauty is not a quality of the circle."

By the *qualities of the circle*, he must mean its properties; and there are here two mistakes.

First, Euclid has not fully explained all the properties of the circle. Many have been discovered and demonstrated which he never dreamt of.

Secondly, The reason why Euclid has not said a word of the beauty of the circle, is not, *that beauty is not a quality of the circle;* the reason is, that Euclid never digresses from his subject. His purpose was to demonstrate the mathematical properties of the circle. Beauty is a quality of the circle, not demonstrable by mathematical reasoning, but immediately perceived by a good taste. To speak of it would have been a digression from his subject; and that is a fault he is never guilty of.

The *fourth* argument is, That inanimate objects may bear to each other all the same relations which we observe in moral agents.

If this were true, it would be very much to the purpose; but it seems to be thrown out rashly, without any attention to its evidence. Had Mr. Hume reflected but a very little upon this dogmatical assertion, a thousand instances would have occurred to him in direct contradiction to it.

May not one animal be more tame, or more docile, or more cunning, or more fierce, or more ravenous, than another? Are these relations to be found in inanimate objects? May not one man be a better painter, or sculptor, or shipbuilder, or tailor, or shoemaker, than another? Are these relations to be found in inanimate objects, or even in brute-animals? May not one moral agent be more just, more pious, more attentive to any moral duty, or more eminent in any moral virtue, than another? Are not these relations peculiar to moral agents? But to come to the relations most essential to morality.

When I say that *I ought to do such an action*, that *it is my duty*, do not these words express a relation between me and a certain action in my power; a relation which cannot be between inanimate objects, or between any other objects but a moral agent and his moral actions; a relation which is well understood by all men come to years of understanding, and expressed in all languages?

Again, when in deliberating about two actions in my power, which cannot both be done, I say *this* ought to be preferred to the other; that justice, for instance, ought to be preferred to generosity; I express a moral relation between two actions of a moral agent, which is well understood, and which cannot exist between objects of any other kind.

[There are, therefore, *moral relations* which can have no existence but between moral agents and their voluntary actions. To determine these relations is the object of morals; and to determine relations, is the province of *judgment*, and *not of mere feeling*.]

The *last* argument is a chain of several propositions, which deserve distinct consideration. They may, I think, be summed up in these four: 1. There must be ultimate ends of action, beyond which it is absurd to ask a reason of acting. 2. The ultimate ends of human actions can never be accounted for by reason; 3. but recommend themselves entirely to the sentiments and affections of mankind, without any dependence on the intellectual faculties. 4. As virtue is an end, and is desirable on its own account, without fee or reward, merely for the immediate satisfaction it conveys; it is requisite, that there should be some sentiment which it touches, some internal taste or feeling, or whatever you please to call it, which distinguishes moral good and evil, and which embraces the one and rejects the other.

To the *first* of these propositions I entirely agree. The ultimate ends of action are what I have called *the principles of action*, which I have endeavoured, in the third Essay, to enumerate, and to class under three heads of mechanical, animal and rational.

The *second* proposition needs some explication. I take its meaning to be, That there cannot be another end for the sake of which an ultimate end is pursued: for the reason of an action means nothing but the end for which the action is done; and the reason of an end of action can mean nothing but another end, for the sake of which that end is pursued, and to which it is the means.

That this is the author's meaning is evident from his reasoning in confirmation of it. " Ask a man, *why he uses exercise?* he will answer, *because he desires to keep his health.* If you then inquire, *why he desires health?* he will readily reply, *because sickness is painful.* If you push your inquiries further, and desire a reason why he hates pain, it is impossible he can ever give any. This is an ultimate end, and is never referred to any other object." To account by reason for an end, therefore, is to show another end, for the sake of which that end is desired and pursued. And that, in this sense, an ultimate end can never be accounted for by reason, is certain, because that cannot be an ultimate end which is pursued only for the sake of another end.

I agree therefore with Mr. Hume in this second proposition, which indeed is implied in the first.

The *third* proposition is, That ultimate ends recommend themselves entirely to the sentiments and affections of mankind, without any dependence on the intellectual faculties.

By *sentiments* he must here mean feelings without judgment, and by *affections*, such affections as imply no judgment. For surely any operation that implies judgment, cannot be independent of the intellectual faculties.

This being understood, I cannot assent to this proposition.

The Author seems to think it implied in the preceding, or a necessary consequence from it, that because an ultimate end cannot be accounted for by reason; that is, cannot be pursued merely for the sake of another end; therefore it can have no dependence on the intellectual faculties. I deny this consequence, and can see no force in it.

I think it not only does not follow from the preceding proposition, but that it is contrary to truth.

A man may act from gratitude as an ultimate end; but gratitude implies a judgment and belief of favours received, and therefore is dependent on the intellectual faculties. A man may act from respect to a worthy character as an ultimate end; but this respect necessarily implies a judgment of worth in the person, and therefore is dependent on the intellectual faculties.

I have endeavoured in the third Essay before mentioned, to show that, beside the animal principles of our nature, which require will and intention, but not judgment, there are also in human nature rational principles of action, or ultimate ends, which have, in all ages, been called rational, and have a just title to that name, not only from the authority of language, but because they can have no existence but in beings endowed with reason, and because, in all their exertions, they require not only intention and will, but judgment or reason.

Therefore, until it can be proved that an ultimate end cannot be dependent on the intellectual faculties, this third proposition, and all that hangs upon it, must fall to the ground.

The *last* proposition assumes, with very good reason, that virtue is an ultimate end, and desirable on its own account. From which, if the third proposition were true, the conclusion would undoubtedly follow, that virtue has no dependence on the intellectual faculties. But as that proposition is not granted, nor proved, this conclusion is left without any support from the whole of the argument.

I should not have thought it worth while to insist so long upon this controversy, if I did not conceive that the consequences which the contrary opinions draw after them are important.

If what we call *moral judgment* be no real judgment, but merely a feeling, it follows, that the principles of morals which we have been taught to consider as an immutable law to all intelligent beings, have no other foundation but an arbitrary structure and fabric in the constitution of the human mind: so that, by a change in our structure, what is immoral might become moral, virtue might be turned into vice, and vice into virtue. And beings of a different structure, according to the variety of their feelings, may have different, nay opposite measures of moral good and evil.

It follows, that, from our notions of morals, we can conclude nothing concerning a moral character in the Deity, which is the foundation of all religion, and the strongest support of virtue.

X. *Impiety of the assertion, that moral judgment is merely a feeling.*—Nay, this opinion seems to conclude strongly against a moral character in the Deity, since nothing arbitrary or mutable can be conceived to enter into the description of a nature eternal, immutable, and necessarily existent. Mr. Hume seems perfectly consistent with himself, in allowing of no evidence for the moral attributes of the Supreme Being, whatever there may be for his natural attributes.

On the other hand, if moral judgment be a true and real judgment, the principles of morals stand upon the immutable foundation of truth, and can undergo no change by any difference of fabric or structure of those who judge of them. There may be, and there are beings, who have not the faculty of conceiving moral truths, or perceiving the excellence of moral worth, as there are beings incapable of perceiving mathematical truths; but no defect, no error of understanding, can make what is true to be false.

If it be true that piety, justice, benevolence, wisdom, temperance, fortitude, are in their own nature the most excellent and most amiable qualities of a human creature; that vice has an inherent turpitude which merits disapprobation and dislike; these truths cannot be hid from Him whose understanding is infinite, whose judgment is always according to truth, and who must esteem every thing according to its real value.

[The Judge of all the earth, we are sure, will do right. He has given to men the faculty of perceiving the right and the wrong in conduct, *as far as is necessary to our present state,* and of perceiving the dignity of the one, and the demerit of the other; and surely there can be no real knowledge or real excellence in man, which is not in his Maker.]

We may, therefore, justly conclude, that what we know in part, and see in part, of right and wrong, He sees perfectly; that the moral excellence which we see and admire in some of our fellow-creatures, is a faint but true copy of that moral excellence which is essential to His nature; and that to tread the path of virtue is the true dignity of our nature, an imitation of God, and the way to obtain his favour.

AN INQUIRY

INTO

THE HUMAN MIND,

ON THE

PRINCIPLES OF COMMON SENSE.

"The inspiration of the Almighty giveth them understanding."—JOB.

TO
THE RIGHT HONOURABLE
JAMES LORD DESKFOORD,
CHANCELLOR OF THE UNIVERSITY OF OLD ABERDEEN.

MY LORD,

Though I apprehend that there are things new, and of some importance in the following Inquiry, it is not without timidity that I have consented to the publication of it. The subject has been canvassed by men of very great penetration and genius: for who does not acknowledge Des Cartes, Malebranche, Locke, Berkeley, and Hume, to be such? A view of the human understanding so different from that which they have exhibited, will, no doubt, be condemned by many without examination, as proceeding from temerity and vanity.

But I hope the candid and discerning few, who are capable of attending to the operations of their own minds, will weigh deliberately what is here advanced, before they pass sentence upon it. To such I appeal, as the only competent judges. If they disapprove, I am probably in the wrong, and shall be ready to change my opinion upon conviction. If they approve, the many will at last yield to their authority, as they always do.

However contrary my notions are to those of the writers I have mentioned, their speculations have been of great use to me, and seem even to point out the road which I have taken; and your lordship knows that the merit of useful discoveries is sometimes not more justly due to those that have hit upon them, than to others who have ripened them, and brought them to the birth.

I acknowledge, my lord, that I never thought of calling in question the principles commonly received with regard to the human understanding, until the "Treatise of Human Nature" was published in the year 1739. The ingenious author of that treatise, upon the principles of Locke, who was no sceptic, hath built a system of scepticism, which leaves no ground to believe any one thing rather than its contrary. His reasoning appeared to me to be just: there was therefore a necessity to call in question the principles upon which it was founded, or to admit the conclusion.

But can any ingenuous mind admit this sceptical system without reluctance? I truly could not, my lord: for I am persuaded that absolute scepticism is not more destructive of the faith of a Christian than of the science of a philosopher, and of the prudence of a man of common understanding. I am persuaded that the unjust *live by faith* as well as the *just;* that if all belief could be laid aside, piety, patriotism, friendship, parental affection, and private virtue, would appear as ridiculous as knight-errantry; and that the pursuits of pleasure, of ambition, and of avarice, must be grounded upon belief, as well as those that are honourable and virtuous.

The day-labourer toils at his work, in the belief that he shall receive his wages at night; and if he had not this belief, he would not toil. We may venture to say, that even the author of this sceptical system wrote it in the belief that it should be read and regarded. I hope he wrote it in the belief also that it would be useful to mankind: and perhaps it may prove so at last. For I conceive the sceptical writers to be a set of men whose business it is to pick holes in the fabric of knowledge wherever it is weak and faulty; and when these places are properly repaired, the whole building becomes more firm and solid than it was formerly.

For my own satisfaction, I entered into a serious examination of the principles upon which this sceptical system is built; and was not a little surprised to find that it leans with its whole weight upon a hypothesis, which is ancient indeed, and hath been very generally received by philosophers, but of which I could find no solid proof. The hypothesis I mean is, that nothing is perceived but what is in the mind which perceives it; that we do not really perceive things that are external, but only certain images and pictures of them imprinted upon the mind, which are called *impressions* and *ideas.*

If this be true; supposing certain impressions and ideas to exist presently in my mind, I cannot, from their existence, infer the existence of any thing else; my impressions and ideas are the only existences of which I can have any knowledge or conception: and they are such fleeting and transitory beings, that they can have no existence at all, any longer than I am conscious of them. So that, upon this hypothesis, the whole universe about me, bodies and spirits, sun, moon, stars, and earth, friends and relations, all things without exception, which I imagined to have a permanent existence whether I thought of them or not, vanish at once;

> " And like the baseless fabric of a vision,
> Leave not a track behind."

I thought it unreasonable, my lord, upon the authority of philosophers, to admit a hypothesis which, in my opinion, overturns all philosophy, all religion and virtue, and all common sense: and finding that all the systems concerning the human understanding which I was acquainted with, were built upon this hypothesis, I resolved to inquire into this subject anew, without regard to any hypothesis.

What I now humbly present to your lordship, is the fruit of this inquiry, so far only as it regards the five senses. In which I claim no other merit, than that of having given great attention to the operations of my own mind, and of having expressed, with all the perspicuity I was able, what, I conceive, every man who gives the same attention, will feel and perceive. The productions of imagination require a genius which soars above the common rank; but the treasures of knowledge are commonly buried deep, and may be reached by those drudges who can dig with labour and patience, though they have not wings to fly. The experiments that were to be made in this investigation suited me, as they required no other expense, but that of time and attention, which I could bestow. The leisure of an academical life, disengaged from the pursuits of interest and ambition; the duty of my profession, which obliged me to give prelections on these subjects to the youth; and an early inclination to speculations of this kind, have enabled me, as I flatter myself, to give a more minute attention to the subject of this inquiry, than has been given before.

My thoughts upon this subject were, a good many years ago, put together in another form, for the use of my pupils; and afterwards were submitted to the judgment of a private philosophical society, of which I have the honour to be a member. A great part of this inquiry was honoured even by your lordship's perusal. And the encouragement which you, my lord, and others, whose friendship is my boast, and whose judgment I reverence, were pleased to give me, counterbalanced my timidity and diffidence, and determined me to offer it to the public.

If it appears to your lordship to justify the common sense and reason of mankind, against the sceptical subtilties which, in this age, have endeavoured to put them out of countenance; if it appears to throw any new light upon one of the noblest parts of the Divine workmanship; the respect which your lordship puts upon the arts and sciences, and your attention to every thing which tends to the improvement of them, as well as to every thing else that contributes to the felicity of your country, leaves me no room to doubt of your favourable acceptance of this Essay, as the fruit of my industry in a profession wherein I am accountable to your lordship; and as a testimony of the great esteem and respect wherewith I have the honour to be,

My lord,

Your lordship's most obliged, and most devoted servant,

THOMAS REID.

King's College, November 9, 1763.

AN INQUIRY

INTO

THE HUMAN MIND.

CHAPTER I.

INTRODUCTION.

I. *The importance of the subject, and the means of prosecuting it.*—The fabric of the human mind is curious and wonderful, as well as that of the human body. The faculties of the one are with no less wisdom adapted to their several ends, than the organs of the other. Nay, it is reasonable to think, that as the mind is a *nobler* work, and of a higher order than the body, even more of the wisdom and skill of the Divine Architect hath been employed in its structure. [It is, therefore, a subject highly worthy of inquiry (1) *on its own account*, but still more worthy (2) on account of the extensive influence which the knowledge of it hath over every other branch of science.]

In the arts and sciences which have least connexion with the mind, its faculties are the engines which we must employ; and the better we understand their nature and use, their defects and disorders, the more skilfully we shall apply them, and with the greater success. But in the noblest arts, the mind is also the subject upon which we operate. The painter, the poet, the actor, the orator, the moralist, and the statesman, attempt to operate upon the mind in different ways, and for different ends; and they succeed, according as they touch properly the strings of the human frame. Nor can their several arts ever stand on a solid foundation, or rise to the dignity of science, until they are built on the principles of the human constitution.

[Wise men now agree, or ought to agree in this—that there is but one way to the knowledge of nature's works—the way of observation and *experiment*.] By our constitution, we have a strong propensity to trace particular facts and observations to general rules, and to apply such general rules to account for other effects, or to direct us in the production of them. This procedure of the understanding is familiar to every human creature in the common affairs of life, and it is the only one by which any real discovery in philosophy can be made.

☞ The man who first discovered that cold freezes water, and that heat turns it into vapour, proceeded on the same general principles, and in the same method, by which Newton discovered the law of gravitation and the properties of light. His *regulæ philosophandi* are maxims of common sense, and are practised every day in common life; and he who philosophizes by other rules, either concerning the material system or concerning the mind, mistakes his aim.

Conjectures and theories are the creatures of men, and will always be found very unlike the creatures of God. If we would know the works of God, we must consult themselves with attention and humility, without daring to add anything of ours to what they declare. A just interpretation of nature is the only sound and orthodox philosophy: whatever we add of our own, is apocryphal, and of no authority.

All our curious theories of the formation of the earth, of the generation of animals, of the origin of natural and moral evil, so far as they go beyond a just induction from facts, are vanity and folly, no less than the vortices of Des Cartes, or the Archæus of Paracelsus. Perhaps the philosophy of the mind hath been no less adulterated by theories than that of the material system. The theory of ideas is indeed very ancient, and hath been very universally received; but as neither of these titles can give it authenticity, they ought not to screen it from a free and candid examination; especially in this age, when it hath produced a system of scepticism, that seems to triumph over all science, and even over the dictates of common sense.

[All that we know of the body, is owing to anatomical *dissection* and observation, and it must be by an *anatomy of the mind* that we can discover its powers and principles.]

II. *The impediments to our knowledge of the mind.*—But it must be acknowledged, that this kind of anatomy is much more difficult than the other; and therefore it needs not seem strange, that mankind have made less progress in it. To attend accurately to the operations of our minds, and make them an object of thought, is *no easy matter* even to the contemplative, and to the bulk of mankind is next to *impossible*.

An anatomist who hath happy opportunities, may have access to examine with his own eyes, and with equal accuracy, bodies of all different ages, sexes, and conditions; so that what is defective, obscure, or preternatural in one, may be discerned clearly, and in its most perfect state in another. But the anatomist of the mind cannot have the same advantage. It is his own mind only that he can examine with any degree of accuracy and distinctness. This is the only subject he can look into. He may, from outward signs, collect the operations of other minds; but these signs are for the most part ambiguous, and must be interpreted by what he perceives within himself.

So that if a philosopher could delineate to us distinctly and methodically all the operations of the thinking principle within him, which no man was ever able to do, this would be only the anatomy of one particular subject; which would be both deficient and erroneous, if applied to human nature in general. For a little reflection may satisfy us, that the difference of minds is greater than that of any other beings, which we consider as of the same species.

Of the various powers and faculties we possess, there are some which *nature seems* both *to have planted* and reared, so as to have left nothing to human industry. Such are the powers which we have in common with the brutes, and which are necessary to the preservation of the individual, or the continuance of the kind. There are other powers, of which nature hath only planted the seeds in our minds, but hath left the rearing of them to human culture. It is by the proper culture of these, that we are capable of all those improvements in intellectuals, in taste, and in morals, which exalt and dignify human nature; while, on the other hand, the neglect or perversion of them makes its degeneracy and corruption.

☞ The two-legged animal that eats of nature's dainties what his taste or appetite craves, and satisfies his thirst at the crystal fountain, who propagates his kind as occasion and lust prompt, repels injuries, and takes alternate labour and repose, is, like a tree in the forest, purely of nature's growth. But this same savage hath within him the seeds of the logician, the man of taste and breeding, the orator, the statesman, the man of virtue, and the saint; which seeds, though planted in his mind by nature, yet through want of culture and exercise, must lie for ever buried, and be hardly perceivable by himself or by others.

The lowest degree of social life will bring to light some of those principles which lay hid in the savage state; and according to his training, and company, and manner of life, some of them, either by their native vigour, or by the force of culture, will thrive and grow up to great perfection, others will be strangely perverted from their natural form, and others checked, or perhaps quite eradicated.

This makes human nature so various and multiform in the individuals that partake of it, that in point of morals, and intellectual endowments, it fills up all that gap which we conceive to be between brutes and devils below, and the celestial orders above; and such a prodigious diversity of minds must make it extremely difficult to discover the common principles of the species.

The language of philosophers with regard to the *original faculties* of the mind, is so adapted to the prevailing system, that it cannot fit any other; ☞ like a coat that fits the man for whom it was made, and shows him to advantage, which yet will sit very awkward upon one of a different make, although perhaps as handsome and as well proportioned. It is hardly possible to make any innovation in our philosophy concerning the mind and its operations, without using new words and phrases, or giving a different meaning to those that are received; a liberty which, even when necessary, creates prejudice and misconstruction, and which must wait the sanction of time to authorize it. For innovations in language, like those in religion and government, are always suspected and disliked by the many, till use hath made them familiar, and prescription hath given them a title.

If the original perceptions and notions of the mind were to make their appearance single and unmixed, as we first received them from the hand of nature, one accustomed to reflection would have less difficulty in tracing them; but before we are capable of reflection, they are so mixed, compounded, and decompounded, by *habits, associations,* and *abstractions,* that it is hard to know what they were originally. ☞ The mind may in this respect be compared to an apothecary or chemist; whose materials indeed are furnished by nature; but for the purposes of his art, he mixes, compounds, dissolves, evaporates, and sublimes them, till they put on a quite different appearance; so that it is very difficult to know what they were at first, and much more to bring them back to their original and natural form. And this work of the mind is not carried on by deliberate acts of mature reason, which we might recollect, but by means of *instincts, habits, associations,* and other principles, which operate before we come to the use of reason; so that it is extremely difficult for the mind to return upon its own footsteps, and trace back those operations which have employed it since it first began to think and to act.

Could we obtain a distinct and full history of all that hath passed in the mind of a child from the beginning of life and sensation, till it grows up to the use of reason; how its infant faculties began to work, and how they brought forth and ripened all the various notions, opinions, and sentiments, which we find in ourselves when we come to be capable of reflection; this would be a treasure of natural history, which would probably give more light into the human faculties, than all the systems of philosophers about them since the beginning of the world. But it is in vain to wish for what nature has not put within the reach of our power. [*Reflection, the only instrument by which we can discern the powers of the mind,* comes too late to observe the progress of nature in raising them from their infancy to perfection.]

It must therefore require great caution, and great application of mind, for a man that is grown up in all the prejudices of education, fashion, and philosophy, to unravel his notions and opinions, till he finds out the simple and original principles of his constitution, of which no account can be given but the will of our Maker. This may be truly called an *analysis* of the human faculties; and till this is performed, it is in vain we expect any just system of the mind; that is, an enumeration of the original powers and laws of our constitution, and an explication from them of the various phenomena of human nature.

Success, in an inquiry of this kind, it is not in human power to command; but perhaps it is possible, by caution and humility, to avoid error and delusion. The labyrinth may be too intricate, and the thread too fine, to be traced through all its windings; but if we stop where we can trace it no farther, and secure the ground we have gained, there is no harm done; a quicker eye may in time trace it farther.

It is genius, and not the want of it, that adulterates philosophy, and fills it with error and false theory. A creative imagination disdains the mean offices of digging for a foundation, of removing rubbish, and carrying materials: leaving these servile employments to the drudges in science, it plans a design, and raises a fabric. Invention supplies materials where they are wanting, and fancy adds colouring, and every befitting ornament. The work pleases the eye, and wants nothing but solidity and a good foundation. It seems even to vie with the works of nature, till the envious blast of some succeeding architect blows it into rubbish, and builds as goodly a fabric of his own in its place. Happily for the present age, the castle-builders employ themselves more in romance than in philosophy. That is undoubtedly their province, and in those regions the offspring of fancy is legitimate, but in philosophy it is all spurious.

III. *The present state of this part of philosophy. Of Des Cartes, Malebranche, and Locke.*—That our philosophy concerning the mind and its faculties is but in a very low state, may be reasonably conjectured, even by those who never have narrowly examined it. Are there any principles with regard to the mind, settled with that perspicuity and evidence, which attends the principles of mechanics, astronomy, and optics? These are really sciences, built upon laws of nature which universally obtain. What is discovered in them, is no longer matter of dispute: future ages may add to it, but till the course of nature be changed, what is already established can never be overturned. But when we turn our attention inward, and consider the phenomena of human thoughts, opinions, and perceptions, and endeavour to trace them to the general laws and the first principles of our constitution, we are immediately involved in darkness and perplexity. And if *common sense,* or the principles of education, happen not to be stubborn, it is odds but we end in absolute scepticism.

(1) [Des Cartes finding nothing established in this part of philosophy, in order to lay the foundation of it deep, resolved *not to believe his own existence* till he should be able to give a good reason for it.] He was, perhaps, the first that took up such a resolution: but if he could indeed have effected his purpose, and really become diffident of his existence, his case would have been deplorable, and without any remedy from reason or philosophy. A man that disbelieves his own existence, is surely as unfit to be reasoned with, as a man that believes he is made of glass. There may be disorders in the human frame that may produce such extravagances, but they will never be cured by reasoning. Des Cartes, indeed, would make us believe, that he got out of this delirium by this logical argument, " Cogito, ergo sum." But it is evident he was in his senses all the time, and never seriously doubted of his existence. For he takes it for granted in this argument, and proves nothing at all. I am thinking, says he, therefore I am: and is it not as good reasoning to say, I am sleeping, therefore I am? or, I am doing nothing, therefore I am? If a body moves, it must exist, no doubt; but if it is at rest, it must exist likewise.*

Perhaps Des Cartes meant not to assume his own existence in this *enthymeme,* but the existence of thought; and to infer from that the existence of a mind, or subject of thought. But why did he not prove the existence of his thought? Consciousness, it may be said, vouches that. But who is voucher for consciousness? Can any man prove that his consciousness may not deceive him? No man can: nor can we give a better reason for trusting to it, than that every man, while his mind is sound, is determined, by *the constitution of his nature,* to give implicit belief to it, and to laugh at or pity the man who doubts its testimony. And is not every man in his wits, as much determined to take his existence upon trust as his consciousness?

(2) [The other proposition assumed in this argument, That *thought cannot be without a mind or subject,* is liable to the same objection: not that it wants evidence; but that its evidence is no clearer, nor more immediate, than that of the proposition to be proved by it.] And taking all these propositions together,— I think,—I am conscious,—every thing that thinks exists,—I exist,—would not every sober man form the same opinion of the man who seriously doubted any one of them? And if he was his friend, would he not hope for his cure from physic and good regimen, rather than from metaphysics and logic?

But supposing it proved that my thought and my conscious-

* Vide Essays on the Intellectual Powers, Essay II., chap. viii., sect. 7.

ness must have a subject, and consequently that I exist, how do I know that all that train and succession of thoughts which I remember, belong to one subject, and that the I of this moment is the very individual I of yesterday, and of times past?

Des Cartes did not think proper to start this doubt: but Mr. Locke has done it; and in order to resolve it, gravely determines, that "*personal identity consists in consciousness;*" that is, if you are conscious that you did such a thing a twelvemonth ago, this consciousness makes you to be the very person that did it. Now, consciousness of what is past, can signify nothing else but the remembrance that I did it. So that Mr. Locke's principle must be, that *identity consists in remembrance;* and consequently a man must lose his personal identity with regard to every thing he forgets.*

Nor are these the only instances whereby our philosophy concerning the mind appears to be very fruitful in creating doubts, but very unhappy in resolving them.

Des Cartes, Malebranche, and Locke, have all employed their genius and skill to prove the existence of a material world; and with very bad success. Poor untaught mortals believe, undoubtedly, that there is a sun, moon, and stars; an earth, which we inhabit; country, friends, and relations, which we enjoy; land, houses, and moveables, which we possess. But philosophers, pitying the credulity of the vulgar, resolve to have no faith but what is founded on reason. They apply to philosophy to furnish them with reasons for the belief of those things which all mankind have believed, without being able to give any reason for it. And surely one would expect that in matters of such importance the proof would not be difficult: but it is the most difficult thing in the world. For [these three great men, with the best good will, have not been able, from all the treasures of philosophy, to draw one argument that is fit to convince a man that can reason, of the existence of any one thing without him.] Admired philosophy! daughter of light! parent of wisdom and knowledge! if thou art she! surely thou hast not yet risen upon the human mind, nor blessed us with more of thy rays than are sufficient to shed a darkness visible upon the human faculties, and to disturb that repose and security which happier mortals enjoy, who never approached thine altar, nor felt thine influence! But if, indeed, thou hast not power to dispel these clouds and phantoms which thou hast discovered or created, withdraw this penurious and malignant ray: I despise philosophy, and renounce its guidance: let my soul dwell with common sense.

IV. *Apology for these philosophers.*—But instead of despising the dawn of light, we ought rather to hope for its in-

* Vide Essay on the Intellectual Powers, &c., Essay III., chap. vi., sect. 1, et seq.

crease; instead of blaming the philosophers I have mentioned, for the defects and blemishes of their system, we ought rather to honour their memories, as the first discoverers of a region in philosophy formerly unknown; and however lame and imperfect the system may be, they have opened the way to future discoveries, and are justly entitled to a great share in the merit of them. They have removed an infinite deal of dust and rubbish collected in the ages of scholastic sophistry, which had obstructed the way. They have put us in the right road, that of experience and accurate reflection. They have taught us to avoid the snares of ambiguous and ill-defined words, and have spoken and thought upon this subject with a distinctness and perspicuity formerly unknown. They have made many openings that may lead to the discovery of truths which they did not reach, or to the detection of errors in which they were involuntarily entangled.

It may be observed, that the defects and blemishes in the received philosophy concerning the mind, which have most exposed it to the contempt and ridicule of sensible men, have chiefly been owing to this: [That the votaries of this philosophy, from a natural prejudice in her favour, have endeavoured to extend her jurisdiction beyond its just limits, and to call to her bar the dictates of common sense.] But these decline this jurisdiction; they disdain the trial of reasoning, and disown its authority; they neither claim its aid, nor dread its attacks.

In this unequal contest betwixt common sense and philosophy, the latter will always come off both with dishonour and loss; nor can she ever thrive till this rivalship is dropped, these encroachments given up, and a cordial friendship restored: for in reality [common sense holds nothing of philosophy, nor needs her aid. But, on the other hand, philosophy (if I may be permitted to change the metaphor) has no other root but the *principles of common sense;* it grows out of them, and draws its nourishment from them: severed from this root, its honours wither, its sap is dried up, it dies and rots.]

The philosophers of the last age, whom I have mentioned, did not attend to the preserving this union and subordination so carefully as the honour and interest of philosophy required: but those of the present have waged open war with common sense, and hope to make a complete conquest of it by the subtleties of philosophy; an attempt no less audacious and vain, than that of the giants to dethrone almighty Jove.

V. *Of Bishop Berkeley; the Treatise of Human Nature; and of scepticism.*—The present age, I apprehend, has not produced two more acute or more practised in this part of philosophy, than the Bishop of Cloyne, and the author of the "Treatise of Human Nature." The first was no friend to scepticism, but had that warm concern for religious and moral principles which became his order: yet [the result of his inquiry was, a serious conviction, that there is no such thing as a material world; nothing in nature but spirits and ideas; and that the belief of material substances, and of abstract ideas, are the chief causes of all our errors in philosophy, and of all infidelity and heresy in religion.] His arguments are founded upon the principles which were formerly laid down by Des Cartes, Malebranche, and Locke, and which have been very generally received.

[And the opinion of the ablest judges seems to be, that they neither have been, nor can be confuted; and *that he hath proved by unanswerable arguments what no man in his senses can believe.*]

The second proceeds upon the same principles, but carries them to their full length; and as the bishop undid the whole material world, this author, upon the same grounds, undoes the world of spirits, and *leaves nothing in nature but ideas and impressions,* without any subject on which they may be impressed.

It seems to be a peculiar strain of humour in this author, to set out in his introduction, by promising, with a grave face, no less than a complete system of the sciences, upon a foundation entirely new, to wit, that of human nature; when the intention of the whole work is to show that there is neither human nature nor science in the world. It may perhaps be unreasonable to complain of this conduct in an author who neither believes his own existence nor that of his reader; and therefore could not mean to disappoint him, or to laugh at his credulity. Yet I cannot imagine that the author of the " Treatise of Human Nature" is so sceptical as to plead this apology. He believed, against his principles, that he should be read, and that he should retain his personal identity, till he reaped the honour and reputation justly due to his metaphysical *acumen.* Indeed [he ingenuously acknowledges, that it was *only in solitude* and retirement that he could yield any assent to his own philosophy; society, like daylight, dispelled the darkness and fogs of scepticism, and made him yield to the dominion of common sense.] Nor did I ever hear him charged with doing anything, even in solitude, that argued such a degree of scepticism as his principles maintain. Surely if his friends apprehended this, they would have had the charity never to leave him alone.

Pyrrho the Elean, the father of this philosophy, seems to have carried it to greater perfection than any of his successors: for if we may believe Antigonus the Carystian, quoted by Diogenes Laertius, his life corresponded to his doctrine. And therefore, if a cart run against him, or a dog attacked him, or if he came upon a precipice, he would not stir a foot to avoid the danger, giving no credit to his senses. But his attendants, who, happily for him, were not so great sceptics, took care to keep him out of harm's way; so that he lived till he was ninety years of age.

Nor is it to be doubted but this author's friends would have been equally careful to keep him from harm, if ever his principles had taken too strong a hold of him.

It is probable the " Treatise of Human Nature" was not written in company; yet it contains manifest indications that the author every now and then relapsed into the faith of the vulgar, and could hardly, for half a dozen pages, keep up the sceptical character.

In like manner the great *Pyrrho* himself *forgot his principles* on some ocasions; and is said once to have been in such a passion with his cook, who probably had not roasted his dinner to his mind, that with the spit in his hand, and the meat upon it, he pursued him even into the market-place.

It is a bold philosophy that rejects, without ceremony, principles which irresistibly govern the belief and the conduct of all mankind in the common concerns of life; and to which the philosopher himself must yield, after he imagines he hath confuted them. Such principles are older, and of more authority, than philosophy: *she rests upon them as her basis, not they upon her.*[*] If she could overturn them, she must be buried in their ruins; but all the engines of philosophical subtlety are too weak for this purpose; and the attempt is no less ridiculous than if a mechanic should contrive an *axis in peritrochio* to remove the earth out of its place; or if a mathematician should pretend to demonstrate that things equal to the same thing are not equal to one another.

Zeno endeavoured to demonstrate the impossibility of motion; Hobbes, that there was no difference between right and wrong; and this author, that no credit is to be given to our senses, to our memory, or even to demonstration. Such philosophy is justly ridiculous, even to those who cannot detect the fallacy of it. It can have no other tendency than to show the acuteness of the sophist, at the expense of disgracing reason and human nature, and making mankind yahoos.

VI. *Of the " Treatise of Human Nature."*—There are other prejudices against this system of human nature, which even upon a general view, may make one diffident of it.

Des Cartes, Hobbes, and this author, have each of them given us a system of human nature; an undertaking *too vast for any one man*, how great soever his genius and abilities may be. There must surely be reason to apprehend, that many parts of human nature never came under their observation; and that others have been stretched and distorted, to fill up blanks, and complete the system. Christopher Columbus, or Sebastian Cabot, might almost as reasonably have undertaken to give us a complete map of America.

* Vide p. 406.

There is a certain character and style in nature's works, which is never attained in the most perfect imitation of them. This seems to be wanting in the systems of human nature I have mentioned, and particularly in the last. One may see a puppet make a variety of motions and gesticulations, which strike much at first view; but when it is accurately observed, and taken to pieces, our admiration ceases; we comprehend the whole art of the maker. How unlike is it to that which it represents! what a poor piece of work compared with the body of a man, whose structure the more we know the more wonders we discover in it, and the more sensible we are of our ignorance! Is the mechanism of the mind so easily comprehended, when that of the body is so difficult? Yet by this system, three laws of association, joined to a few original feelings, explain the whole mechanism of sense, imagination, memory, belief, and of all the actions and passions of the mind. Is this the man that nature made? I suspect it is not so easy to look behind the scenes in nature's work. This is a puppet surely, contrived by too bold an apprentice of nature to mimic her work. It shows tolerably by candlelight, but brought into clear day, and taken to pieces, it will appear to be a man made with mortar and a trowel. The more we know of other parts of nature, the more we like and approve them. The little I know of the planetary system; of the earth which we inhabit; of minerals, vegetables, and animals; of my own body, and of the laws which obtain in these parts of nature, opens to my mind grand and beautiful scenes, and contributes equally to my happiness and power. But when I look within, and consider the mind itself, which makes me capable of all these prospects and enjoyments; if it is indeed what the "Treatise of Human Nature" makes it, I find I have been only in an enchanted castle, imposed upon by spectres and apparitions. I blush inwardly to think how I have been deluded; I am ashamed of my frame, and can hardly forbear expostulating with my destiny: Is this thy pastime, O Nature, to put such tricks upon a silly creature, and then to take off the mask, and show him how he hath been befooled? If this is the philosophy of human nature, my soul enter thou not into her secrets. It is surely the forbidden tree of knowledge; I no sooner taste of it, than I perceive myself naked, and stripped of all things, yea even of my very self. I see myself, and the whole frame of nature, shrink into fleeting ideas, which, like Epicurus's atoms, dance about in emptiness.

VII. *The system of all these authors is the same, and leads to scepticism.*—But what if these profound disquisitions into the first principles of human nature, do naturally and necessarily plunge a man into this abyss of scepticism? May we not reasonably judge so from what hath happened? Des Cartes no sooner began to dig in this mine, than scepticism was ready to break in upon him. He did what he could to shut it out. Malebranche and Locke, who dug deeper, found the difficulty of keeping out this enemy still to increase: but they laboured honestly in the design. Then Berkeley, who carried on the work, despairing of securing all, bethought himself of an expedient: *by giving up the material world,* which he thought might be spared without loss, and even with advantage, he hoped by an impregnable partition to secure the world of spirits. But, alas! the "Treatise of Human Nature" wantonly sapped the foundation of this partition, and drowned all in one universal deluge. These facts, which are undeniable, do indeed give reason to apprehend, that Des Cartes's system of the human understanding, which I shall beg leave to call *the ideal system,* and which, with some improvements made by later writers, is now generally received, hath some original defect; that this *scepticism is inlaid in it,* and reared along with it; and, therefore, that we must lay it open to the foundation, and examine the materials before we can expect to raise any solid and useful fabric of knowledge on this subject.

VIII. *We ought not to despair of a better.*—But is this to be despaired of, because Des Cartes and his followers have failed? By no means. This pusillanimity would be injurious to ourselves, and injurious to truth. Useful discoveries are sometimes indeed the effect of superior genius, but more frequently they are the birth of time and of accidents. ☞ A traveller of good judgment may mistake his way, and be unawares led into a wrong track; and while the road is fair before him, he may go on without suspicion, and be followed by others; but when it ends in a coal-pit, it requires no great judgment to know that he hath gone wrong, nor perhaps to find out what misled him.

In the mean time the unprosperous state of this part of philosophy hath produced an effect, somewhat discouraging indeed to any attempt of this nature, but an effect which might be expected, and which time only and better success can remedy. Sensible men, who never will be sceptics in matters of common life, are apt to treat with sovereign contempt every thing that hath been said, or is to be said, upon this subject. It is metaphysic, say they: who minds it? Let scholastic sophisters entangle themselves in their own cobwebs; I am resolved to take my own existence, and the existence of other things, upon trust; and to believe that snow is cold, and honey sweet, whatever they may say to the contrary. He must either be a fool, or want to make a fool of me, that would reason me out of my reason and senses.

I confess I know not what a sceptic can answer to this, nor by what good argument he can plead even for a hearing; for either his reasoning is sophistry, and so deserves contempt; or there is no truth in the human faculties, and then why should we reason?

If, therefore, a man find himself entangled in these metaphysical toils, and can find no other way to escape, let him bravely cut the knot which he cannot loose, curse metaphysic, and dissuade every man from meddling with it. For if I have been led into bogs and quagmires by following an ignis fatuus, what can I do better than to warn others to beware of it? If philosophy contradicts herself, befools her votaries, and deprives them of every object worthy to be pursued or enjoyed, let her be sent back to the infernal regions from which she must have had her original.

But is it absolutely certain that this fair lady is of the party? Is it not possible she may have been misrepresented? Have not men of genius in former ages often made their own dreams to pass for her oracles? Ought she then to be condemned without any further hearing? This would be unreasonable. [I have found her in all other matters an agreeable companion, a faithful counsellor, *a friend to common sense*, and to the happiness of mankind. This justly entitles her to my correspondence and confidence, till I find infallible proofs of her infidelity.]

CHAPTER II.

OF SMELLING.

I. *The order of proceeding. Of the medium and organ of smell.*—It is so difficult to unravel the operations of the human understanding, and to reduce them to their first principles, that we cannot expect to succeed in the attempt, but by beginning with the simplest, and proceeding by very cautious steps to the more complex. The five external senses may for this reason claim to be first considered in an analysis of the human faculties. And the same reason ought to determine us to make a choice even among the senses, and to give the precedence, not to the noblest, or most useful, but to the simplest, and that whose objects are least in danger of being mistaken for other things.

In this view, an analysis of our sensations may be carried on perhaps with most ease and distinctness, by taking them in this order: Smelling, Tasting, Hearing, Touch, and, last of all, Seeing.

Natural philosophy informs us, that all animal and vegetable bodies, and probably all or most other bodies, while exposed to the air, are continually sending forth effluvia of vast subtlety, not only in their state of life and growth, but in the states of fermentation and putrefaction. These volatile particles do probably repel each other, and so scatter themselves in the air, until they meet with other bodies to which they have some chemical affinity, and with which they unite, and form new concretes. All the smell of plants, and of other bodies, is caused by these volatile parts, and is smelled wherever they are scattered in the air: and the acuteness of smell in some animals, shows us that these effluvia spread far, and must be inconceivably subtile.

Whether, as some chemists conceive, every species of bodies hath a spiritus rector, a kind of soul, which causes the smell, and all the specific virtues of that body, and which, being extremely volatile, flies about in the air in quest of a proper receptacle, I do not inquire. This, like most other theories, is perhaps rather the product of imagination than of just induction. But that all bodies are smelled by means of effluvia which they emit, and which are drawn into the nostrils along with the air, there is no reason to doubt. So that there is manifest appearance of design in placing the organ of smell in the inside of that canal, through which the air is continually passing in inspiration and expiration.

Anatomy informs us, that the membrana pituitaria, and the olfactory nerves, which are distributed to the villous parts of this membrane, are the organs destined by the wisdom of nature to this sense: so that when a body emits no effluvia, or when they do not enter into the nose, or when the pituitary membrane or olfactory nerves are rendered unfit to perform their office, it cannot be smelled.

[Yet, notwithstanding this, it is evident, that *neither the organ of smell, nor the medium, nor any motions* we can conceive excited in the membrane above mentioned, or in the nerve or animal spirits, do in the least *resemble the sensation of smelling:* nor could that sensation of itself ever have led us to think of nerves, animal spirits, or effluvia.]

II. *The sensation considered abstractly.*—Having premised these things, with regard to the medium and organ of this sense, let us now attend carefully to what the mind is conscious of when we smell a rose or a lily; and since our language affords no other name for this sensation, we shall call it a *smell* or *odour*, carefully excluding from the meaning of those names every thing but the sensation itself, at least till we have examined it.

Suppose a person who never had this sense before, to receive it all at once, and to smell a rose; can he perceive any similitude or agreement between the smell and the rose? or indeed between it and any other object whatsoever? Certainly he cannot. He finds himself affected in a new way, he knows not why, or from what cause. Like a man that feels some pain or pleasure formerly unknown to him, he is conscious that he is not the cause of it himself; but cannot, from the nature of the thing, determine whether it is caused by body or spirit, by something near, or by something at a distance. It has no similitude to anything else, so as to admit of a comparison; and therefore he can conclude nothing from it, unless perhaps that there must be some unknown cause of it.

It is evidently ridiculous, to ascribe to it figure, colour, extension, or any other quality of bodies. He cannot give it a place, any more than he can give a place to melancholy or joy: nor can he conceive it to have any existence, but when it is smelled. So that it appears to be a simple and *original affection* or feeling of the mind, altogether inexplicable and unaccountable. It is indeed impossible that it can be in any body: it is a sensation, and a sensation can only be in a sentient thing.

The various odours have each their different degrees of strength or weakness. Most of them are agreeable or disagreeable; and frequently those that are agreeable when weak, are disagreeable when stronger. When we compare different smells together, we can perceive very few resemblances or contrarieties, or indeed relations of any kind between them: they are all so simple in themselves, and so different from each other, that it is hardly possible to divide them into *genera* and *species*. Most of the names we give them are particular; as the smell of a *rose*, of a *jessamine*, and the like. Yet there are some general names; as *sweet, stinking, musty, putrid, cadaverous, aromatic*. Some of them seem to refresh and animate the mind, others to deaden and depress it.

III. *Sensation and its remembrance natural principles of belief.*—So far we have considered this sensation abstractly. Let us next compare it with other things to which it bears some relation. And first I shall compare this sensation with the remembrance and the imagination of it.

I can think of the smell of a rose when I do not smell it; and it is possible that when I think of it, there is neither rose nor smell any where existing. But when I smell it, I am necessarily determined to believe that the sensation really exists. This is common to all sensations, that as they cannot exist but in being perceived, so they cannot be perceived but they must exist. I could as easily doubt of my own existence, as of the existence of my sensations. Even those profound philosophers who have endeavoured to disprove their own existence, have yet left their sensations to stand upon their own bottom, stript of a subject, rather than call in question the reality of their existence.

Here then a sensation, a smell for instance, may be presented to the mind three different ways; it may be smelled, it may be remembered, it may be imagined or thought of. In the first case, it is necessarily accompanied with a belief of its present existence; in the second, it is necessarily accompanied with a belief of its past existence; and in the last, it is not accompanied with belief at all, but is what the logicians call *a simple apprehension*.

Why sensation should compel our belief of the present existence of the thing, memory a belief of its past existence, and imagination no belief at all, is what I believe no philosopher can give a shadow of reason for, but that such is the nature of these operations: they are all simple and *original*, and therefore inexplicable *acts of the mind*.

Suppose that once, and only once, I smelled a tuberose in a certain room where it grew in a pot, and gave a very grateful perfume. Next day I relate what I saw and smelled. When I attend as carefully as I can to what passes in my mind in this case, it appears evident, that the very thing I saw yesterday, and the fragrance I smelled, are now the immediate objects of my mind when I remember it. Further, I can imagine this pot and flower transported to the room where I now sit, and yielding the same perfume. Here likewise it appears, that the individual thing which I saw and smelled, is the object of my imagination.

[Philosophers indeed tell me, that the immediate object of my memory and imagination in this case, is not the past sensation, but an idea of it, an image, phantasm, or species of the odour I smelled: that this idea presently exists in my mind, or in my sensorium; and the mind contemplating this present idea, finds it a representation of what is past, or of what may exist; and accordingly calls it memory, or imagination.] This is the doctrine of the ideal philosophy; which we shall not now examine, that we may not interrupt the thread of the present investigation. Upon the strictest attention, memory appears to me to have things that are past, and not present ideas, for its object. [We shall afterwards examine this system of ideas, and endeavour to make it appear, that *no solid proof has ever been advanced of the existence of ideas;* that they are a mere fiction and hypothesis, contrived to solve the phenomena of the human understanding; that they do not at all answer this end; and that this hypothesis of ideas or images of things in the mind, or in the sensorium, is the parent of those many paradoxes so shocking to common sense, and of that scepticism, which disgrace our philosophy of the mind, and have brought upon it the ridicule and contempt of sensible men.]

In the mean time, I beg leave to think with the vulgar, that when I remember the smell of the tuberose, that very sensation which I had yesterday, and which has now no more any existence, is the immediate object of my memory; and when I imagine it present, the sensation itself, and not any idea of it, is the object of my imagination. But though the object of my sensation, memory, and imagination, be in this case the same, yet these acts or operations of the mind are as different, and as easily distinguishable, as smell, taste, and sound. I am conscious of a difference in kind between sensation and memory, and between both and imagination. I find this also, that the sensation compels my belief of the present existence of the smell, and memory my belief of its past existence. There is a smell, is the immediate testimony of sense; there was a smell, is the immediate testimony of memory. If you ask me why I believe that the smell exists, I can give no other reason, nor will ever be able to give any other, than that I smell it. If you ask why I believe that it existed yesterday, I can give no other reason but that I remember it.

Sensation and memory, therefore, are simple, *original*, and perfectly distinct *operations of the mind*, and both of them are original principles of belief. Imagination is distinct from both, but is no principle of belief. Sensation implies the present existence of its object; memory its past existence; but imagination views its object naked, and without any belief of its existence or non-existence, and is therefore what the schools call *simple apprehension*.

IV. *Judgment and belief in some cases precede simple apprehension.*—But here again the ideal system comes in our way: it teaches us, that the first operation of the mind about its ideas, is *simple apprehension;* that is, *the bare conception of a thing without any belief about it;* and that after we have got simple apprehensions, by comparing them together, we perceive agreements or disagreements between them; and that this perception of the agreement or disagreement of ideas is all that we call belief, judgment, or knowledge. Now, this appears to me to be all fiction, without any foundation in nature : for it is acknowledged by all, that sensation must go before memory and imagination; and hence it necessarily follows that apprehension, accompanied with belief and knowledge, must go before simple apprehension, at least in the matters we are now speaking of. So that here, [instead of saying, that the belief or knowledge is got by putting together and comparing the simple apprehensions, we ought rather to say, that the simple apprehension is performed by resolving and analyzing a natural and original judgment.] And it is with the operations of the mind, in this case, as with natural bodies, which are indeed compounded of simple principles or elements. Nature does not exhibit these elements separate, to be compounded by us; she exhibits them mixed and compounded in concrete bodies, and it is only by art and chemical analysis that they can be separated.

V. *Two theories of the nature of belief refuted. Conclu-*

sions from what hath been said.—But what is this belief or knowledge which accompanies sensation and memory? Every man knows what it is, but no man can define it. Does any man pretend to define sensation, or to define consciousness? It is happy, indeed, that no man does. And if no philosopher had endeavoured to define and explain belief, we had wanted some of those paradoxes of the ideal philosophy, which will always to sensible men appear as incredible as anything that ever enthusiasm dreamed or superstition swallowed. Of this kind surely is that modern discovery of the ideal philosophy, that sensation, memory, belief, and imagination, where they have the same object, are only different degrees of strength and vivacity in the idea. Suppose the idea to be that of a future state after death; one man believes it firmly; this means no more than that he hath a strong and lively idea of it: another neither believes nor disbelieves, that is, he has a weak and faint idea. Suppose now a third person believes firmly that there is no such thing; I am at a loss to know whether his idea be faint or lively: if it is faint, then there may be a firm belief where the idea is faint; if the idea is lively, then the belief of a future state and the belief of no future state must be one and the same. The same arguments that are used to prove that belief implies only a stronger idea of the object than simple apprehension, might as well be used to prove that love implies only a stronger idea of the object than indifference. And then what shall we say of hatred, which must upon this hypothesis be a degree of love, or a degree of indifference? If it should be said, that in love there is something more than an idea, to wit, an affection of the mind; may it not be said with equal reason, that in belief there is something more than an idea, to wit, an assent or persuasion of the mind?

But perhaps it may be thought as ridiculous to argue against this strange opinion, as to maintain it. Indeed, if a man should maintain that a circle, a square, and a triangle, differ only in magnitude, and not in figure, I believe he would find nobody disposed either to believe him or to argue against him; and yet I do not think it less shocking to common sense to maintain that sensation, memory, and imagination, differ only in degree, and not in kind. I know it is said, that in a delirium, or in dreaming, men are apt to mistake one for the other. But does it follow from this, that men who are neither dreaming, nor in a delirium, cannot distinguish them? [But how does a man know, that he is not in a delirium? *I cannot tell;* neither can I tell how a man knows that he exists: but if any man seriously doubts whether he is in a delirium, I think it highly probable that he is, and that it is time to seek for a cure,] which I am persuaded he will not find in the whole system of logic.

I mentioned before Mr. Locke's notion of belief or knowledge: he holds that it consists in *a perception of the agreement or disagreement of ideas;* and this he values himself upon as a very important discovery.

[We shall have occasion afterwards to examine more particularly *this* grand *principle* of Mr. Locke's philosophy, and to show that it *is one of the main pillars of modern scepticism,* although Mr. Locke had no intention to make that use of it.] At present, let us only consider how it agrees with the instances of belief now under consideration; and whether it gives any light to them. I believe that the sensation I have, exists; and that the sensation I remember, does not now exist, but did exist yesterday. Here, according to Mr. Locke's system, I compare the idea of a sensation with the ideas of past and present existence: at one time I perceive that this idea agrees with that of present existence, but disagrees with that of past existence; but at another time it agrees with the idea of past existence, and disagrees with that of present existence. Truly these ideas seem to be very capricious in their agreements and disagreements. Besides, I cannot for my heart conceive what is meant by either. I say a sensation exists, and I think I understand clearly what I mean. But you want to make the thing clearer, and for that end tell me, that there is an agreement between the idea of that sensation and the idea of existence. To speak freely, this conveys to me no light, but darkness; I can conceive no otherwise of it, than as an odd and obscure circumlocution. I conclude, then, that the belief which accompanies sensation and memory, is a simple act of the mind, which cannot be defined. It is in this respect like seeing and hearing, which can never be so defined as to be understood by those who have not these faculties; and to such as have them, no definition can make these operations more clear than they are already. In like manner, every man that has any belief, (and he must be a curiosity that has none,) knows perfectly what belief is, but can never define or explain it. I conclude also, that sensation, memory, and imagination, even where they have the same object, are operations of a quite different nature, and perfectly distinguishable by those who are sound and sober. A man that is in danger of confounding them, is indeed to be pitied; but whatever relief he may find from another art, he can find none from logic or metaphysics. I conclude further, that it is no less a part of the human constitution, to believe the present existence of our sensations, and to believe the past existence of what we remember, than it is to believe that twice two make four. [The evidence of (1) sense, the evidence of (2) memory, and the evidence of the (3) necessary relations of things, are all distinct and *original* kinds of evidence, equally grounded on our constitution: none of them is dependent upon or resolvable into any of the rest.] To reason against any of these kinds of evidence is absurd; nay, to reason for them is absurd. They are first principles; and such fall not within the province of reason, but of common sense.

VI. *Apology for metaphysical absurdities. Sensation without a sentient, a consequence of the theory of ideas. Consequences of this strange opinion.*—Having considered the relation which the sensation of smelling bears to the remembrance and imagination of it, I proceed to consider, what relation it bears to a mind, or sentient principle. It is certain, no man can conceive or believe smelling to exist of itself, without a mind, or something that has the power of smelling, of which it is called a sensation, an operation, or feeling. Yet if any man should demand a proof, that sensation cannot be without a mind, or sentient being, I confess that I can give none; and that to pretend to prove it, seems to me almost as absurd as to deny it.

This might have been said without any apology before the "Treatise of Human Nature" appeared in the world. For till that time no man, as far as I know, ever thought either of calling in question that principle, or of giving a reason for his belief of it. Whether thinking beings were of an ethereal or igneous nature, whether material or immaterial, was variously disputed; but that thinking is an operation of some kind of being or other, was always taken for granted, as a principle that could not possibly admit of doubt.

However, since the author above mentioned, who is undoubtedly one of the most acute metaphysicians that this or any age hath produced, hath treated it as a vulgar prejudice, and maintained, that the mind is only a succession of ideas and impressions, without any subject; his opinion, however contrary to the common apprehensions of mankind, deserves respect. I beg, therefore, once for all, that no offence may be taken at charging this or other metaphysical notions with absurdity, or with being contrary to the common sense of mankind. No disparagement is meant to the understandings of the authors or maintainers of such opinions. [Indeed they commonly proceed not from defect of understanding, but *from an excess of refinement:* the reasoning that leads to them, often gives new light to the subject, and shows real genius and deep penetration in the author; and the premises do more than atone for the conclusion.]

[If there are certain *principles,* as I think there are, *which the constitution of our nature leads us to believe,* and which we are under a necessity to take for granted in the common concerns of life, without being able to give a reason for them; *these are what we call the principles of common sense;* and what is manifestly contrary to them, is what we call absurd.]

Indeed, if it is true, and to be received as a principle of philosophy, "That sensation and thought may be without a thinking being;" it must be acknowledged to be the most wonderful discovery that this or any other age hath produced. The received doctrine of ideas is the principle from which it is deduced, and of which indeed it seems to be a just and natural consequence. And it is probable, that it would not have been so late a discovery, but that it is so shocking and repugnant to the common apprehensions of mankind, that it required an uncommon degree of philosophical intrepidity to usher it into the world. It is a fundamental principle of the ideal system, that every object of thought must be an impression, or an idea, that is, a faint copy of some preceding impression. This is a principle so commonly received, that the author above mentioned, although his whole system is built upon it, never offers the least proof of it. It is upon this principle, as a fixed point, that he erects his metaphysical engines, to overturn heaven and earth, body and spirit. And indeed, in my apprehension, it is altogether sufficient for the purpose. For if impressions and ideas are the only objects of thought, then heaven and earth, and body and spirit, and every thing you please, must signify only impressions and ideas, or they must be words without any meaning. It seems, therefore, that this notion, however strange, is closely connected with the received doctrine of ideas, and we must either admit the conclusion, or call in question the premises.

Ideas seem to have something in their nature unfriendly to other existences. They were first introduced into philosophy, in the humble character of images or representatives of things; and in this character they seemed not only to be inoffensive, but to serve admirably well for explaining the operations of the human understanding. But since men began to reason clearly and distinctly about them, they have by degrees supplanted their constituents, and undermined the existence of every thing but themselves. First they discarded all secondary qualities of bodies; and it was found out by their means, that fire is not hot, nor snow cold, nor honey sweet; and, in a word, that heat and cold, sound, colour, taste, and smell, are nothing but ideas or impressions. Bishop Berkeley advanced them a step higher, and found out, by just reasoning, from the same principles, that extension, solidity, space, figure, and body, are ideas, and that there is nothing in nature but ideas and spirits. But the triumph of ideas was completed by the "Treatise of Human Nature," which discards spirits also, and leaves ideas and impressions as the sole existences in the universe. What if at last, having nothing else to contend with, they should fall foul of one another, and leave no existence in nature at all? This would surely bring philosophy into danger; for what should we have left to talk or to dispute about?

[However, hitherto these philosophers acknowledge the existence of impressions and ideas; they acknowledge certain laws of attraction, or rules of precedence, according to which ideas and impressions range themselves in various forms, and succeed one another: but that they should belong to a mind, as its proper goods and chattels, this they have found to be a vulgar error.] These ideas are as free and independent as the birds of the air, or as Epicurus's atoms when they pursued their journey in the vast inane. Shall we conceive them like the films of things in the Epicurean system?

" Principio hoc dico, rerum simulacra vagari,
Multa modis multis, in cunctas undique parteis
Tenuia, quæ facile inter se junguntur in auris,
Obvia cum veniunt."—Lucr.

" I assert that many images of things wander freely, attenuated forms, into every part of the universe, which, when they meet, are readily united in the atmosphere."

Or do they rather resemble Aristotle's intelligible species after they are shot forth from the object, and before they have yet struck upon the passive intellect? But why should we seek to compare them with any thing, since there is nothing in nature but themselves? They make the whole furniture of the universe; starting into existence, or out of it, without any cause; combining into parcels, which the vulgar call *minds;* and succeeding one another by fixed laws, without time, place, or author of those laws.

Yet after all, these self-existent and independent ideas look pitifully naked and destitute, when left thus alone in the universe, and seem, upon the whole, to be in a worse condition than they were before. Des Cartes, Malebranche, and Locke, as they made much use of ideas, treated them handsomely, and provided them in decent accommodation; lodging them either in the pineal gland, or in the pure intellect, or even in the Divine mind. They moreover clothed them with a commission, and made them representatives of things, which gave them some dignity and character. But the " Treatise of Human Nature," though no less indebted to them, seems to have made but a bad return, by bestowing upon them this independent existence; since thereby they are turned out of house and home, and set adrift in the world, without friend or connexion, without a rag to cover their nakedness: and who knows but the whole system of ideas may perish by the indiscreet zeal of their friends to exalt them?

However this may be, [it is certainly a most amazing discovery, *that thought* and ideas *may be without any thinking being.* A discovery big with consequences which cannot easily be traced by those deluded mortals who think and reason in the common track.] We were always apt to imagine, that thought supposed a thinker, and love a lover, and treason a traitor: but this, it seems, was all a mistake; and it is found out, that there may be treason without a traitor, and love without a lover, laws without a legislator, and punishment without a sufferer, succession without time, and motion without any thing moved, or space in which it may move: or if, in these cases, ideas are the lover, the sufferer, the traitor, it were to be wished that the author of this discovery had further condescended to acquaint us, whether ideas can converse together, and be under obligations of duty or gratitude to each other; whether they can make promises and enter into leagues and covenants, and fulfil or break them, and be punished for the breach. If one set of ideas makes a covenant, another breaks it, and a third is punished for it, there is reason to think that justice is no natural virtue in this system.

It seemed very natural to think, that the " Treatise of Human Nature" required an author, and a very ingenious one too; but now we learn, that it is only a set of ideas which came together, and arranged themselves by certain associations and attractions.

After all, this curious system appears not to be fitted to the present state of human nature. How far it may suit some choice spirits, who are refined from the dregs of common sense, I cannot say. It is acknowledged, I think, that even these can enter into this system only in their most speculative hours, when they soar so high in pursuit of those self-existent ideas, as to lose sight of all other things. But when they condescend to mingle again with the human race, and to converse with a friend, a companion, or a fellow-citizen, the ideal system vanishes; [common sense, like an irresistible torrent, carries them along; and, in spite of all their reasoning and philosophy, they believe their *own existence*, and the *existence of other things.*]

Indeed, it is happy they do so; for if they should carry their closet-belief into the world, the rest of mankind would consider them as diseased, and send them to an infirmary. Therefore, as Plato required certain previous qualifications of those who entered his school, I think it would be prudent for the doctors of this ideal philosophy to do the same, and to refuse admittance to every man who is so weak as to imagine that he ought to have the same belief in solitude and in company, or that his principles ought to have any influence upon his practice: for this philosophy is like a hobby horse, which a man in bad health may ride in his closet without hurting his reputation; but if he should take him abroad with him to church, or to the exchange, or to the playhouse, his heir would immediately call a jury, and seize his estate.

VII. *The conception and belief of a sentient being or mind, is suggested by our constitution. The notion of relations not always got by comparing the related ideas.*—Leaving this philosophy, therefore, to those who have occasion for it, and can use it discreetly as a chamber-exercise, we may still inquire how the rest of mankind, and even the adepts themselves, except in some solitary moments, have got so strong and irresistible a belief, that thought must have a subject, and be the act of some thinking being: [how every man believes himself to be something distinct from his ideas and impressions; something which continues the same identical self when all his ideas and impressions are changed.] It is impossible to trace the origin of this opinion in history: for all languages have it interwoven in their original construction. All nations have always believed it. The constitution of all laws and governments, as well as the common transactions of life, suppose it.

It is no less impossible for any man to recollect *when* he himself came by this notion: for, as far back as we can remember, we were already in possession of it, and as fully persuaded of our own existence, and the existence of other things, as that one and one make two. It seems, therefore, that this opinion preceded all reasoning, and experience, and instruction; and this is the more probable, because we could not get it by any of these means. It appears, then, to be an undeniable fact, that from thought or sensation, all mankind, constantly and invariably, from the first dawning of reflection, do infer a power or faculty of thinking, and a permanent being or mind to which that faculty belongs; and that we as invariably ascribe all the various kinds of sensation and thought we are conscious of, to one individual mind or self.

But by what rules of logic we make these inferences, it is impossible to show; nay, it is impossible to show how our sensations and thoughts can give us the very notion and conception either of a mind or of a faculty. The faculty of smelling is something very different from the actual sensation of smelling; for the faculty may remain when we have no sensation. And the mind is no less different from the faculty; for it continues the same individual being when that faculty is lost. Yet this sensation suggests to us both a faculty and a mind; and not only suggests the notion of them, but creates a belief of their existence; although it is impossible to discover, by reason, any tie or connexion between one and the other.

What shall we say then? Either those inferences which we draw from our sensations, namely, the existence of a mind, and of powers or faculties belonging to it, are *prejudices of philosophy* or education, mere fictions of the mind, which a wise man should throw off as he does the belief of fairies; *or* they are *judgments of nature*, judgments not got by comparing ideas, and perceiving agreements and disagreements, but immediately *inspired by our constitution.*

If this last is the case, as I apprehend it is, it will be impossible to shake off those opinions, and we must yield to them at last, though we struggle hard to get rid of them. And if we could, by a determined obstinacy, shake off the principles of our nature, this is not to act the philosopher, but the fool or the madman. It is incumbent upon those who think that these are not natural principles, to show, in the first place, how we can otherwise get the notion of a mind and its faculties; and then to show how we come to deceive ourselves into the opinion that sensation cannot be without a sentient being.

It is the received doctrine of philosophers, that our notions of relations can only be got by comparing the related ideas: but in the present case, there seems to be an instance to the contrary. It is not by having first the notions of mind and sensation, and then comparing them together, that we perceive the one to have the relation of a subject or substratum, and the other that of an act or operation: on the contrary, one of the related things, to wit, sensation, suggests to us both the correlate and the relation.

I beg leave to make use of the word *suggestion,* because I know not one more proper, to express a power of the mind, which seems entirely to have escaped the notice of philosophers, and to which we owe many of our simple notions which are neither impressions nor ideas, as well as many original principles of belief. I shall endeavour to illustrate, by an example, what I understand by this word. [We all know that a certain kind of sound suggests immediately to the mind a coach passing in the street; and not only produces the imagination, but the belief, that a coach is passing. Yet there is here no comparing of ideas, no perception of agreements or disagreements, to produce this belief; nor is there the least similitude between the sound we hear, and the coach we imagine and believe to be passing.]

It is true that this suggestion is not natural and original; it is the *result of experience* and habit. But I think it appears from what hath been said, that there are *natural suggestions;* particularly, that sensation suggests the notion of present existence, and the belief that what we perceive or feel, does presently exist; that memory suggests the notion of past existence, and the belief that what we remember did exist in time past; and that our sensations and thoughts do also suggest the notion of a mind, and the belief of its existence, and relation to our thoughts.

By a like natural principle it is, that a beginning of existence, or any change in nature, suggests to us the notion of a cause, and compels our belief of its existence. And in like manner, as shall be shown when we come to the sense of touch, certain sensations of touch, by the constitution of our nature, suggest to us extension, solidity, and motion, which are nowise like to sensations, although they have been hitherto confounded with them.

VIII. *There is a quality or virtue in bodies, which we call their smell. How this is connected in the imagination with the sensation.*—We have considered smell as signifying a sensation, feeling, or impression upon the mind; and in this sense, it can only be in a mind, or sentient being: but it is evident that mankind give the name of *smell* much more frequently to something which they conceive to be external, and to be a quality of body: they understand something by it which does not at all infer a mind; and have not the least difficulty in conceiving odoriferous plants spreading their fragrance in the deserts of Arabia, or in some uninhabited island where the human foot never trod. Every sensible day-labourer hath as clear a notion of this, and as full a conviction of the possibility of it, as he hath of his own existence; and can no more doubt of the one than of the other.

Suppose that such a man meets with a modern philosopher, and wants to be informed what smell in plants is. The philosopher tells him that there is no smell in plants, nor in any thing, but in the mind; that it is impossible there can be smell but in a mind; and that all this hath been demonstrated by modern philosophy. The plain man will, no doubt, be apt to think him merry: but if he finds that he is serious, his next conclusion will be that he is mad; or that philosophy, like magic, puts men into a new world, and gives them different faculties from common men. And thus philosophy and common sense are set at variance. But who is to blame for it? In my opinion the philosopher is to blame. For if he means by smell, what the rest of mankind most commonly mean, he is certainly mad. But if he puts a different meaning upon the word, without observing it himself, or giving warning to others, he abuses language, and disgraces philosophy, without doing any service to truth: as if a man should exchange the meaning of the words *daughter* and *cow*, and then endeavour to prove to his plain neighbour, that his cow is his daughter, and his daughter his cow.

I believe there is not much more wisdom in many of those paradoxes of the ideal philosophy, which to plain sensible men appear to be palpable absurdities, but with the adepts pass for profound discoveries. I resolve, for my own part, always to pay a great regard to the dictates of common sense, and not to depart from them without absolute necessity: and therefore I am apt to think that there is really something in the rose or lily, which is by the vulgar called *smell*, and which continues to exist when it is not smelled: and shall proceed to inquire what this is; how we come by the notion of it; and what relation this quality or virtue of smell hath to the sensation, which we have been obliged to call by the same name, for want of another.

Let us therefore suppose, as before, a person *beginning* exercise the sense of smelling: a little experience will discover to him that the nose is the organ of this sense, and that the air, or something in the air, is a medium of it. And finding, by further experience, that when a rose is near, he has a certain sensation; when it is removed, the sensation is gone; he finds a connexion in nature betwixt the rose and this sensation. The rose is considered as a cause, occasion, or antecedent, of the sensation; the sensation as an effect or consequent of the presence of the rose: they are associated in the mind, and constantly found conjoined in the imagination.

But here it deserves our notice, that although the sensation may seem more closely related to the mind its subject, or to the nose its organ; yet neither of these connexions operate so powerfully upon the imagination, as its connexion with the rose its concomitant. The reason of this seems to be, that its connexion with the mind is more general, and nowise distinguisheth it from other smells, or even from tastes, sounds, and other kinds of sensations. The relation it hath to the organ is likewise general, and doth not distinguish it from other smells: but [the connexion it hath with the rose is special and constant; by which means they become almost inseparable in the imagination, in like manner as thunder and lightning, freezing and cold.]

IX. *That there is a principle in human nature, from which the notion of this, as well as all other natural virtues or causes, is derived.*—In order to illustrate further how we come to conceive a *quality* or *virtue* in the rose which we call *smell*, and what this smell is, it is proper to observe, that the mind begins very early to thirst after principles, which may direct it in the exertion of its powers. The smell of a rose is a certain affection or feeling of the mind; and as it is not constant, but comes and goes, we want to know when and where we may expect it, and are uneasy till we find something, which being present, brings this feeling along with it, and being removed, removes it. This, when found, we call the *cause* of it; not in a strict and philosophical sense, as if the feeling were really effected or produced by that cause, but in a popular sense; for the mind is satisfied, if there is a constant conjunction between them; and such causes are in reality nothing else but laws of nature. Having found the smell thus constantly conjoined with the rose, the mind is at rest, without inquiring whether this conjunction is owing to a real efficiency or not; that being a philosophical inquiry, which does not concern human life. But every discovery of such a constant conjunction is of real importance in life, and makes a strong impression upon the mind.

[So ardently do we desire to find every thing that happens within our observation, thus connected with something else, as its *cause* or *occasion*, that we are apt to fancy connexions upon the slightest grounds: and *this weakness is most remarkable in the ignorant*, who know least of the real connexions established in nature.] A man meets with an unlucky accident on a certain day of the year; and knowing no other cause of his misfortune, he is apt to conceive something unlucky in that day of the calendar: and if he find the same connexion hold a second time, is strongly confirmed in his superstition. I remember, many years ago, a white ox was brought into the country, of so enormous a size that people came many miles to see him. There happened, some months after, an uncommon fatality among women in child-bearing. Two such uncommon events following one another, gave a suspicion of their connexion, and occasioned a common opinion among the country-people, that the white ox was the cause of this fatality.

However silly and ridiculous this opinion was, it sprung from the same root in human nature, on which all natural philosophy grows; namely, an eager desire to find out connexions in things, and a natural, original, and unaccountable propensity to believe, that the connexions which we have observed in time past, will continue in time to come. Omens, portents, good and bad luck, palmistry, astrology, all the numerous arts of divination, and of interpreting dreams, false hypotheses and systems, and true principles in the philosophy of nature, are all built upon the same foundation in the human constitution; and are distinguished only according as we conclude rashly from too few instances, or cautiously from a sufficient induction.

As it is *experience* only that *discovers these connexions* between natural causes and their effects, without inquiring further, we attribute to the cause some vague and indistinct notion of power or virtue to produce the effect. And in many cases, the purposes of life do not make it necessary to give distinct names to the cause and the effect. Whence it happens, that being closely connected in the imagination, although very unlike to each other, one name serves for both; and, in common discourse, is most frequently applied to that which, of the two, is most the object of our attention. This occasions an ambiguity in many words, which is common to all languages, having the same causes, and which is apt to be overlooked even by philosophers. Some instances will serve both to illustrate and confirm what we have said.

Magnetism signifies both the tendency of the iron towards the magnet, and the power of the magnet to produce that tendency: and if it was asked, whether it is a quality of the iron or of the magnet, one would perhaps be puzzled at first, [but a little attention would discover, that we conceive a power or virtue in the magnet as the cause, and a motion in the iron as the effect;] and although these are things quite unlike, they are so united in the imagination, that we give the common name of *magnetism* to both. The same thing may be said of *gravitation*, which sometimes signifies the tendency of bodies towards the earth, sometimes the attractive power of the earth, which we conceive as the cause of that tendency. We may observe the same ambiguity in some of Sir Isaac Newton's definitions; and that even in words of his own making. In three of his definitions, he explains very distinctly what he understands by the *absolute* quantity, what by the *accelerative* quantity, and what by the *motive* quantity, of a centripetal force. In the first of these three definitions, centripetal force is put for the cause, which we conceive to be some power or virtue in the centre or central body: in the two last, the same word is put for the effect of this cause, in producing velocity, or in producing motion towards that centre.

[*Heat* signifies a *sensation*, and *cold* a contrary one. But *heat* likewise signifies a *quality* or state of bodies, which hath no contrary, but different degrees.] When a man feels the same water hot to one hand and cold to the other, this gives him occasion to distinguish between the feeling and the heat of the body; and although he knows that the sensations are contrary, he does not imagine that the body can have contrary qualities at the same time.* And when he finds a different taste in the same body in sickness and in health, he is easily convinced, that the quality in the body called *taste* is the same as before, although the sensations he has from it are perhaps opposite.

The vulgar are commonly charged by philosophers with the absurdity of imagining the smell in the rose to be something like to the sensation of smelling: but I think, unjustly; for they neither give the same epithets to both, nor do they reason in the same manner from them. [What is *smell in the rose?* It is a *quality* or virtue of the rose, or of something proceeding from it, which we perceive by the sense of smelling; and this is all we know of the matter.] [But what is *smelling?* It is *an act of the mind*, but is never imagined to be a quality of the mind.] Again, the sensation of smelling is conceived to infer necessarily a mind or sentient being; but smell in the rose infers no such

* Vide Locke's Essay, Book II. chap. viii. sect. 21.

thing. We say, This body smells sweet, that stinks; but we do not say, This mind smells sweet, and that stinks. Therefore, smell in the rose, and the sensation which it causes, are not conceived, even by the vulgar, to be things of the same kind, although they have the same name.

[From what hath been said, we may learn, that the smell of a rose signifies two things. *First*, a *sensation*, which can have no existence but when it is perceived, and can only be in a sentient being or mind. *Secondly*, it signifies some power, *quality*, or virtue in the rose, or in effluvia proceeding from it, which hath a permanent existence, independent of the mind, and which, by the constitution of nature, produces the sensation in us.] By the original constitution of our nature, we are both led to believe, that there is a permanent cause of the sensation, and prompted to seek after it; and experience determines us to place it in the rose. The names of all smells, tastes, sounds, as well as heat and cold, have a like ambiguity in all languages: but it deserves our attention, that these names are but rarely, in common language, used to signify the sensations; for the most part, they signify the external qualities which are indicated by the sensations. The cause of which phenomenon I take to be this. Our sensations have very different degrees of strength. Some of them are so quick and lively, as to give us a great deal either of pleasure or of uneasiness. When this is the case, we are compelled to attend to the sensation itself, and to make it an object of thought and discourse; we give it a name, which signifies nothing but the sensation; and in this case we immediately and readily acknowledge, that the thing meant by that name is in the mind only, and not in any thing external. Such are the various kinds of pain, sickness, and the sensations of hunger and other appetites. But where the sensation is not so interesting as to require to be made an object of thought, our constitution leads us to consider it as a sign of something external, which hath a constant conjunction with it; and having found what it indicates, we give a name to that: the sensation, having no proper name, falls in as an accessory to the thing signified by it, and is confounded under the same name. So that the name may indeed be applied to the sensation, but most properly and commonly is applied to the thing indicated by that sensation. The sensations of smell, taste, sound, and colour, are of infinitely more importance as signs or indications, than they are upon their own account; like the words of a language, wherein we do not attend to the sound, but to the sense.

X. *Whether in sensations the mind is active or passive.*—There is one inquiry remains—Whether in smelling, and in other sensations, the mind is active or passive? This possibly may seem to be a question about words, or at least of very small importance; however, if it leads us to attend more accurately to the operations of our minds, than we are accustomed to do, it is upon that very account not altogether unprofitable. I think the opinion of modern philosophers is, that in sensation the mind is altogether passive. And this undoubtedly is so far true, that we cannot raise any sensation in our minds by willing it; and, on the other hand, it seems hardly possible to avoid having the sensation when the object is presented. Yet it seems likewise to be true, that in proportion as the attention is more or less turned to a sensation, or diverted from it, that sensation is more or less perceived and remembered. Every one knows, that very intense pain may be diverted by surprise, or by any thing that entirely occupies the mind. When we are engaged in earnest conversation, the clock may strike by us without being heard; at least we remember not the next moment that we did hear it. The noise and tumult of a great trading city is not heard by them who have lived in it all their days; but it stuns those strangers who have lived in the peaceful retirement of the country. [Whether, therefore, there can be any sensation where the mind is purely passive, I will not say; but I think we are conscious of having given some attention to every sensation which we remember, though ever so recent.]

No doubt, where the impulse is strong and uncommon, it is as difficult to withhold attention, as it is to forbear crying out in racking pain, or starting in a sudden fright: but how far both might be attained by strong resolution and practice, is not easy to determine. So that, although the Peripatetics had no good reason to suppose an active and a passive intellect, since attention may be well enough accounted an act of the will; yet I think they came nearer to the truth, in holding the mind to be in sensation partly passive and partly active, than the moderns, in affirming it to be purely passive. Sensation, imagination, memory, and judgment, have, by the vulgar, in all ages, been considered as acts of the mind. The manner in which they are expressed in all languages, shows this. When the mind is much employed in them, we say it is very active; whereas, if they were impressions only, as the ideal philosophy would lead us to conceive, we ought in such a case rather to say, that the mind is very passive; for I suppose no man would attribute great activity to the paper I write upon, because it receives variety of characters.

The relation which the sensation of smell bears to the memory and imagination of it, and to a mind or subject, is common to all our sensations, and indeed to all the operations of the mind: the relation it bears to the will, is common to it with all the powers of understanding: and the relation it bears to that quality or virtue of bodies which it indicates, is common to it with the sensations of taste, hearing, colour, heat, and cold: so that what hath been said of this sense, may easily be applied to several of our senses, and to other operations of the mind; and this, I hope, will apologize for our insisting so long upon it.

CHAPTER III.

OF TASTING.

I. A GREAT part of what hath been said of the sense of smelling is so easily applied to those of tasting and hearing, that we shall leave the application entirely to the reader's judgment, and save ourselves the trouble of a tedious repetition.

It is probable that every thing that affects the taste, is in some degree soluble in the saliva. It is not conceivable how any thing should enter readily and of its own accord, as it were, into the pores of the tongue, palate, and fauces, unless it had some chemical affinity to that liquor with which these pores are always replete. It is therefore an admirable contrivance of nature, that the organs of taste should always be moist with a liquor which is so universal a menstruum, and which deserves to be examined more than it hath been hitherto, both in that capacity, and as a medical unguent. Nature teaches dogs and other animals to use it in this last way; and its subserviency both to taste and digestion shows its efficacy in the former.

It is with manifest design and propriety, that the organ of this sense guards the entrance of the alimentary canal, as that of smell, the entrance of the canal for respiration. And from these organs being placed in such manner, that every thing that enters into the stomach must undergo the scrutiny of both senses, it is plain that they were intended by nature to distinguish wholesome food from that which is noxious. The brutes have no other means of choosing their food; nor would mankind in the savage state. And it is very probable that the smell and taste, nowise vitiated by luxury or bad habits, would rarely, if ever, lead us to a wrong choice of food among the productions of nature; although the artificial compositions of a refined and luxurious cookery, or of chemistry and pharmacy, may often impose upon both, and produce things agreeable to the taste and smell, which are noxious to health. And it is probable, that both smell and taste are vitiated, and rendered less fit to perform their natural offices, by the unnatural kind of life men commonly lead in society.

These senses are likewise of great use to distinguish bodies that cannot be distinguished by our other senses, and to discern the changes which the same body undergoes, which in many cases are sooner perceived by taste and smell than by any other means. How many things are there in the market, the eating-house, and the tavern, as well as in the apothecary and chemist's shops, which are known to be what they are given out to be, and are perceived to be good or bad in their kind, only by taste or smell! And how far our judgment of things, by means of our senses, might be improved by accurate attention to the small differences of taste and smell, and other sensible qualities, is not easy to determine. Sir Isaac Newton, by a noble effort of his great genius, attempted, from the colour of opaque bodies, to discover the magnitude of the minute pellucid parts of which they are compounded: and who knows what new lights natural philosophy may yet receive from other secondary qualities duly examined?

Some tastes and smells stimulate the nerves and raise the spirits: but such an artificial elevation of the spirits is, by the laws of nature, followed by a depression, which can only be relieved by time, or by the repeated use of the like stimulus. [By the use of such things we create an appetite for them, which very much resembles, and hath all the force of a natural one. It is in this manner that men acquire an appetite for snuff, tobacco, strong liquors, laudanum, and the like.]

Nature indeed seems studiously to have set bounds to the pleasures and pains we have by these two senses, and to have confined them within very narrow limits, that we might not place any part of our happiness in them; there being hardly any smell or taste so disagreeable that use will not make it tolerable, and at last perhaps agreeable; nor any so agreeable as not to lose its relish by constant use. Neither is there any pleasure or pain of these senses which is not introduced, or followed, by some degree of its contrary, which nearly balances it. [So that we may here apply the beautiful allegory of the divine Socrates; ☞ That although pleasure and pain are contrary in their nature, and their faces look different ways, yet Jupiter hath tied them so together, that he that lays hold of the one, draws the other along with it.]

II. As there is a great variety of smells, seemingly simple and uncompounded, not only altogether unlike, but some of them contrary to others; and as the same thing may be said of tastes; it would seem that one taste is not less different from another than it is from a smell: and therefore it may be a question, How all smells come to be considered as one genus, and all tastes as another? What is the generical distinction? Is it only that the nose is the organ of the one, and the palate of the other? or, abstracting from the organ, is there not in the sensations themselves something common to smells, and something else common to tastes, whereby the one is distinguished from the other? It seems most probable that the latter is the case; and that, under the appearance of the greatest simplicity, there is still in these sensations something of composition.

If one considers the matter abstractedly, it would seem that a number of sensations, or indeed of any other individual things, which are perfectly simple and uncompounded, are incapable of being reduced into genera and species; because individuals which belong to a species, must have something peculiar to each, by which they are distinguished, and something common to the whole species. And the same may be said of species which belong to one genus. And whether this does not imply some kind of composition, we shall leave to metaphysicians to determine.

The sensations both of smell and taste do undoubtedly admit of an immense variety of modifications, which no language can express. If a man was to examine five hundred different wines, he would hardly find two of them that had precisely the same taste: the same thing holds in cheese, and in many other things. Yet of five hundred different tastes in cheese or wine, we can hardly describe twenty, so as to give a distinct notion of them to one who had not tasted them.

Dr. Nehemiah Grew, a most judicious and laborious naturalist, in a discourse read before the Royal Society, anno 1675, hath endeavoured to show that there are at least sixteen different simple tastes, which he enumerates. How many compounded ones may be made out of all the various combinations of two, three, four, or more of these simple ones, they who are acquainted with the theory of combinations will easily perceive. All these have various degrees of intenseness and weakness. Many of them have other varieties: in some the taste is more quickly perceived upon the application of the sapid body, in others more slowly; in some the sensation is more permanent, in others more transient; in some it seems to undulate or return after certain intervals, in others it is constant: the various parts of the organ, as the lips, the tip of the tongue, the root of the tongue, the fauces, the uvula, and the throat, are some of them chiefly affected by one sapid body, and others by another. All these, and other varieties of tastes, that accurate writer illustrates by a number of examples. Nor is it to be doubted, but smells, if examined with the same accuracy, would appear to have as great variety.

CHAPTER IV.

OF HEARING.

I. *Variety of sounds. Their place and distance learned by custom, without reasoning.*—SOUNDS have probably no less variety of modifications, than either tastes or odours. For, first, sounds differ in tone. The ear is capable of perceiving four or five hundred variations of tone in sound, and probably as many different degrees of strength; by combining these, we have above twenty thousand simple sounds that differ either in tone or strength, supposing every tone to be perfect. But it is to be observed, that to make a perfect tone, a great many undulations of elastic air are required, which must all be of equal duration and extent, and follow one another with perfect regularity; and each undulation must be made up of the advance and recoil of innumerable particles of elastic air, whose motions are all uniform in direction, force, and time. Hence we may easily conceive a prodigious variety in the same tone, arising from irregularities of it, occasioned by the constitution, figure, situation, or manner of striking the sonorous body; from the constitution of the elastic medium, or its being disturbed by other motions; and from the constitution of the ear itself upon which the impression is made.

A flute, a violin, a hautboy, and a French horn, may all sound the same tone, and be easily distinguishable. Nay, if twenty human voices sound the same note, and with equal strength, there will still be some difference. The same voice, while it retains its proper distinctions, may yet be varied many ways, by sickness or health, youth or age, leanness or fatness, good or bad humour. The same words spoken by foreigners and natives, nay, by persons of different provinces of the same nation, may be distinguished. Such an immense variety of sensations of smell, taste, and sound, surely was not given us in vain. They are signs, by which we know and distinguish things without us; and it was fit that the variety of the signs should in some degree correspond with the variety of the things signified by them.

[It seems to be by *custom*, that we learn to distinguish both the place of things, and their nature, by means of their sound.] That such a noise is in the street, such another in the room above me; that this is a knock at my door; that, a person walking up stairs; is probably learnt by experience. I remember, that once lying a-bed, and having been put into a fright, I heard my own heart beat; but I took it to be one knocking at the door, and arose and opened the door oftener than once, before I discovered that the sound was in my own breast. It is probable, that previous to all experience, we should as little know whether a sound came from the right or left, from above or below, from a great or a small distance, as we should know whether it was the sound of a drum, or a bell, or a cart. Nature is frugal in her operations, and will not be at the expense of a particular instinct, to give us that knowledge which experience will soon produce, by means of a general principle of human nature.

[For a little *experience, by the constitution of human nature*, ties together, not only in our imagination, but in our belief, those things which were in their nature unconnected.] When I hear a certain sound, immediately, without reasoning, I conclude that a coach passes by. There are no premises from which this conclusion is inferred by any rules of logic. It is the effect of a principle of our nature, common to us with the brutes.

Although it is by hearing that we are capable of the perceptions of harmony and melody, and of all the charms of music; yet it would seem that these require a higher faculty, which we call *a musical ear*. This seems to be in very different degrees, in those who have the bare faculty of hearing equally perfect; and therefore ought not to be classed with the external senses, but in a higher order.

II. *Of natural language.*—One of the noblest purposes of sound undoubtedly is language; without which mankind would hardly be able to attain any degree of improvement above the brutes. Language is commonly considered as purely an invention of men, who by nature are no less mute than the brutes, but having a superior degree of invention and reason, have been able to contrive artificial signs of their thoughts and purposes, and to establish them by common consent. But the origin of language deserves to be more carefully inquired into, not only as this inquiry may be of importance for the improvement of language, but as it is related to the present subject, and tends to lay open some of the first principles of human nature. I shall therefore offer some thoughts upon this subject.

[By language I understand all those *signs* which mankind use in order to communicate to others their thoughts and intentions, their purposes and desires.] And such signs may be conceived to be of two kinds: first, such as have no meaning but what is affixed to them by compact or agreement among those who use them; these are artificial signs: secondly, such as, previous to all compact or agreement, have a meaning which every man understands by the principles of his nature. Language, so far as it consists of artificial signs, may be called *artificial;* so far as it consists of natural signs, I call it *natural.*

Having premised these definitions, I think it is demonstrable, that if mankind had not a natural language, they could never have invented an artificial one by their reason and ingenuity. For all artificial language supposes some compact or agreement to affix a certain meaning to certain signs; therefore there must be compacts or agreements before the use of artificial signs: but there can be no compact or agreement without signs, nor without language; and therefore *there must be a natural language before any artificial language can be invented:* which was to be demonstrated.

Had language in general been a human invention, as much as writing or printing, we should find whole nations as mute as the brutes. Indeed even the brutes have some natural signs by which they express their own thoughts, and affections, and desires, and understand those of others. A chick, as soon as hatched, understands the different sounds whereby its dam calls it to food, or gives the alarm of danger. A dog or a horse understands, by nature, when the human voice caresses, and when it threatens him. But brutes, as far as we know, have no notion of contracts or covenants, or of moral obligation to perform them. If nature had given them these notions, she would probably have given them natural signs to express them. And where nature has denied these notions, it is as impossible to acquire them by art, as it is for a blind man to acquire the notion of colours. Some brutes are sensible of honour or disgrace; they have resentment and gratitude: but none of them, as far as we know, can make a promise, or plight their faith, having no such notions from their constitution. And if mankind had not these notions by nature, and natural signs to express them by, with all their wit and ingenuity they could never have invented language.

The elements of this natural language of mankind, or the signs that are naturally expressive of our thoughts, may, I think, be reduced to these three kinds: modulations of the voice, gestures, and features. By means of these, two savages who have no common artificial language, can converse together; can communicate their thoughts in some tolerable manner; can ask and refuse, affirm and deny, threaten and supplicate; can traffic, enter into covenants, and plight their faith. This might be confirmed by historical facts of undoubted credit, if it were necessary.

Mankind having thus a common language by nature, though a scanty one, adapted only to the necessities of nature, there is no great ingenuity required in improving it by the addition of artificial signs, to supply the deficiency of the natural. These artificial signs must multiply with the arts of life, and the improvements of knowledge. The articulations of the voice seem to be, of all signs, the most proper for artificial language; and as mankind have universally used them for that purpose, we may reasonably judge that nature intended them for it. But nature probably does not intend that we should lay aside the use of the natural signs; it is enough that we supply their defects by artificial ones. A man that rides always in a chariot, by degrees loses the use of his legs; and one who uses artificial signs only, loses both the knowledge and use of the natural. Dumb people retain much more of the natural language than others, because necessity obliges them to use it. And for the same reason, savages have much more of it than civilized nations. It is by natural signs chiefly that we give force and energy to language; and the less language has of them, it is the less expressive and persuasive. Thus writing is less expressive than reading, and reading less expressive than speaking without book; speaking without the proper and natural modulations, force, and variations of the voice, is a frigid and dead language, compared with that which is attended with them; it is still more expressive when we add the language of the eyes and features; and is then only in its perfect and natural state, and attended with its proper energy, when to all these we superadd the force of action.

Where speech is natural, it will be an exercise, not of the voice and lungs only, but of all the muscles of the body; like that of dumb people and savages, whose language, as it has more of nature, is more expressive, and is more easily learned.

Is it not pity that the refinements of a civilized life, instead of supplying the defects of natural language, should root it out, and plant in its stead dull and lifeless articulations of unmeaning sounds, or the scrawling of insignificant characters? The perfection of language is commonly thought to be, to express human thoughts and sentiments distinctly by these dull signs; but if this is the perfection of artificial language, it is surely the corruption of the natural.

Artificial signs signify, but they do not express; they speak to the understanding, as algebraical characters may do, but the passions, the affections, and the will, hear them not: these continue dormant and inactive, till we speak to them in the language of nature, to which they are all attention and obedience.

It were easy to show, that the fine arts of the musician, the painter, the actor, and the orator, so far as they are expressive—although the knowledge of them requires in us a delicate taste, a nice judgment, and much study and practice—yet they are nothing else but the language of nature, which we brought into the world with us, but have unlearned by disuse, and so find the greatest difficulty in recovering it.

Abolish the use of articulate sounds and writing among mankind for a century, and every man would be a painter, an actor, and an orator. We mean not to affirm that such an expedient is practicable; or if it were, that the advantage would counterbalance the loss; but that, as men are led by nature and necessity to converse together, they will use every mean in their power to make themselves understood; and where they cannot do this by artificial signs, they will do it as far as possible by natural ones: and he that understands perfectly the use of natural signs, must be the best judge in all the expressive arts.

CHAPTER V.

OF TOUCH.

I. *Of heat and cold.*—The senses which we have hitherto considered, are very simple and uniform, each of them exhibiting only one kind of sensation, and thereby indicating only one quality of bodies. By the ear we perceive sounds, and nothing else; by the palate, tastes; and by the nose, odours: these qualities are all likewise of one order, being all secondary qualities: whereas by touch we perceive not one quality only, but many, and those of very different kinds. The chief of them are heat and cold, hardness and softness, roughness and smoothness, figure, solidity, motion, and extension. We shall consider these in order.

As to heat and cold, it will easily be allowed that they are secondary qualities, of the same order with smell, taste, and sound. And, therefore, what hath been already said of smell, is easily applicable to them; that is, that the words *heat* and *cold* have each of them two significations; they sometimes signify certain sensations of the mind, which can have no existence when they are not felt, nor can exist anywhere but in a mind or sentient being; but more frequently they signify a quality in bodies, which, by the laws of nature, occasions the sensations of heat and cold in us: a quality which, though connected by custom so closely with the sensations, that we cannot without difficulty separate them; yet hath not the least resemblance to it, and may continue to exist when there is no sensation at all.

The sensations of heat and cold are perfectly known; for they neither are, nor can be, anything else than what we feel them to be; but the qualities in bodies which we call *heat* and *cold*, are unknown. They are only conceived by us, as unknown causes or occasions of the sensations to which we give the same names. But though common sense says nothing of the nature of these qualities, it plainly dictates the existence of them; and to deny that there can be heat and cold when they are not felt, is an absurdity too gross to merit confutation. ☞ For what could be more absurd, than to say, that the thermometer cannot rise or fall unless some person be present, or that the coast of Guinea would be as cold as Nova Zembla, if it had no inhabitants?

It is the business of philosophers to investigate, by proper experiments, and induction, what heat and cold are in bodies. And whether they make heat a particular element diffused through nature, and accumulated in the heated body, or whether they make it a certain vibration of the parts of the heated body; whether they determine that heat and cold are contrary qualities, as the sensations undoubtedly are contrary, or that heat only is a quality, and cold its privation; these questions are within the province of philosophy; for common sense says nothing on the one side or the other.

But whatever be the nature of that quality in bodies which we call *heat*, we certainly know this, that it cannot in the least resemble the sensation of heat. It is no less absurd to suppose a likeness between the sensation and the quality, than it would be to suppose, that the pain of the gout resembles a square or a triangle. The simplest man that hath common sense, does not imagine the sensation of heat, or any thing that resembles that sensation, to be in the fire. He only imagines, that there is something in the fire, which makes him and other sentient beings feel heat. Yet as the name of *heat*, in common language, more frequently and more properly signifies this unknown something in the fire, than the sensation occasioned by it, he justly laughs at the philosopher who denies that there is any heat in the fire, and thinks that he speaks contrary to common sense.

II. *Of hardness and softness.*—Let us next consider hardness and softness; by which words we always understand real properties or qualities of bodies, of which we have a distinct conception.

When the parts of a body adhere so firmly, that it cannot easily be made to change its figure, we call it *hard;* when its parts are easily displaced, we call it *soft*. This is the notion which all mankind have of hardness and softness: they are neither sensations, nor like any sensation; they were real qualities before they were perceived by touch, and continue to be so when they are not perceived: for if any man will affirm that diamonds were not hard till they were handled, who would reason with him?

There is, no doubt, a sensation by which we perceive a body to be hard or soft. This sensation of hardness may easily be had, by pressing one's hand against the table, and attending to the feeling that ensues, setting aside, as much as possible, all thought of the table and its qualities, or of any external thing. [But it is one thing to have the sensation, and another to attend to it, and *make it a distinct object of reflection*. The first is very easy; the last, in most cases, extremely difficult.]

We are so accustomed to use the sensation as a sign, and to pass immediately to the hardness signified, that, as far as appears, it was never made an object of thought, either by the vulgar or philosophers; nor has it a name in any language. There is no sensation more distinct, or more frequent; yet it is never attended to, but passes through the mind instantaneously, and serves only to introduce that quality in bodies which, by a law of our constitution, it suggests.

There are indeed some cases wherein it is no difficult matter to attend to the sensation occasioned by the hardness of a body; for instance, when it is so violent as to occasion considerable pain: then nature calls upon us to attend to it, and then we acknowledge that it is a mere sensation, and can only be in a sentient being. If a man runs his head with violence against a pillar, I appeal to him, whether the pain he feels resembles the hardness of the stone; or if he can conceive any thing like what he feels to be in an inanimate piece of matter.

The attention of the mind is here entirely turned towards the painful feeling; and, to speak in the common language of mankind, he feels nothing in the stone, but feels a violent pain in his head. It is quite otherwise when he leans his head gently against the pillar; for then he will tell you that he feels nothing in his head, but feels hardness in the stone. Hath he not a sensation in this case as well as in the other? Undoubtedly he hath: but it is a sensation which nature intended only as a sign of something in the stone; and, accordingly, he instantly fixes his attention upon the thing signified; and cannot, without great difficulty, attend so much to the sensation as to be persuaded that there is any such thing, distinct from the hardness it signifies.

But however difficult it may be to attend to this *fugitive* sensation, to stop its rapid progress, and to disjoin it from the external quality of hardness, in whose shadow it is apt immediately to hide itself; this is what a philosopher by pains and practice must attain, otherwise it will be impossible for him to reason justly upon this subject, or even to understand what is here advanced. For the last appeal, in subjects of this nature, must be to what a man feels and perceives in his own mind.

It is indeed strange, that a sensation which we have every time that we feel a body hard, and which, consequently, we can command as often, and continue as long as we please, a sensation as distinct and determinate as any other, should yet be so much unknown, as never to have been made an object of thought and reflection, nor to have been honoured with a name in any language; that philosophers, as well as the vulgar, should have entirely overlooked it, or confounded it with that quality of bodies which we call *hardness*, to which it hath not the least similitude. May we not hence conclude, that the knowledge of the human faculties is but in its infancy? That we have not yet learned to attend to those operations of the mind of which we are conscious every hour of our lives? That there are habits of inattention acquired very early, which are as hard to be overcome as other habits? For I think it is probable, that the novelty of this sensation will procure some attention to it in children at first; but being nowise interesting in itself, as soon as it becomes familiar, it is overlooked, and the attention turned solely to that which it signifies. Thus, when one is learning a language, he attends to the sounds; but when he is master of it, he attends only to the sense of what he would express. If this is the case, we must become as little children again, if we will be philosophers: we must overcome this habit of inattention which has been gathering strength ever since we began to think; a habit, the usefulness of which, in common life, atones for the difficulty it creates to the philosopher in discovering the first principles of the human mind.

The firm cohesion of the parts of a body, is no more like that sensation by which I perceive it to be hard, than the vibration of a sonorous body is like the sound I hear: nor can I possibly perceive, by my reason, any connexion between the one and the other. No man can give a reason, why the vibration of a body might not have given the sensation of smelling, and the effluvia of bodies affected our hearing, if it had so pleased our Maker. In like manner, no man can give a reason why the sensations of smell, or taste, or sound, might not have indicated hardness, as well as that sensation which, by our constitution, does indicate it. [Indeed (1) no man can conceive any sensation to *resemble* any known quality of bodies. Nor (2) can any man show, by any good argument, that all *our sensations might not have been as they are*, though no body, nor quality of body, had ever existed.]

Here then is a phenomenon of human nature, which comes to be resolved. Hardness of bodies is a thing that we conceive as distinctly, and believe as firmly, as anything in nature. We have no way of coming at this conception and belief, but by means of a certain sensation of touch, to which hardness hath not the least similitude; nor can we, by any rules of reasoning, infer the one from the other. The question is, how we come by this (1) conception and (2) belief?

First, as to the *conception:* shall we call it an idea of sensation, or of reflection? The last will not be affirmed; and as little can the first, unless we will call that an idea of sensation which hath no resemblance to any sensation. So that the origin of this idea of hardness, one of the most common and most distinct we have, is not to be found in all our systems of the mind: not even in those which have so copiously endeavoured to deduce all our notions from sensation and reflection.

But, *secondly*, supposing we have got the conception of hardness, how come we by the *belief* of it? Is it self-evident, from comparing the ideas, that such a sensation could not be felt, unless such a quality of bodies existed? No. Can it be proved by probable or certain arguments? No, it cannot. Have we got this belief then by tradition, by education, or by experience? No, it is not got in any of these ways. Shall we then throw off this belief, as having no foundation in reason? Alas! it is not in our power; it triumphs over reason, and laughs at all the arguments of a philosopher. Even the author of the " Treatise of Human Nature," though he saw no reason for this belief, but many against it, could hardly conquer it in his speculative and solitary moments; at other times he fairly yielded to it, and confesses that he found himself under a necessity to do so.

[What shall we say then of this *conception*, and this *belief*, which are so unaccountable and untractable? I see nothing left, but to conclude, that, by an *original principle of our constitution*, a certain sensation of touch both suggests to the mind the conception of hardness, and creates the belief of it: or, in other words, that this sensation is a natural sign of hardness.] And this I shall endeavour more fully to explain.

III. *Of natural signs.*—As in artificial signs there is often neither similitude between the sign and thing signified, nor any connexion that arises necessarily from the nature of the things; so it is also in natural signs. The word *gold* has no similitude to the substance signified by it; nor is it in its own nature more fit to signify this than any other substance: yet, by habit and custom, it suggests this and no other. In like manner, a sensation of touch suggests hardness, although it hath neither similitude to hardness, nor, as far as we can perceive, any necessary connexion with it. The difference betwixt these two signs lies only in this, that, in the first, the suggestion is the effect of *habit* and custom; in the second, it is not the effect of habit, but of the *original constitution* of our minds.

It appears evident from what hath been said on the subject of language, that there are natural signs, as well as artificial; and particularly, that the thoughts, purposes, and dispositions of the mind, have their natural signs in the features of the face, the modulation of the voice, and the motion and attitude of the body: that without a natural knowledge of the connexion between these signs, and the things signified by them, language could never have been invented, and established among men: and that the fine arts are all founded upon this connexion, which we may call *the natural language of mankind.* It is now proper to observe, that there are different orders of natural signs, and to point out the different classes into which they may be distinguished, that we may more distinctly conceive the relation between our sensations and the things they suggest, and what we mean by calling sensations signs of external things.

[The *first class of natural signs* comprehends those whose connexion with the thing signified is established by nature, but discovered only by experience.] The whole of genuine philosophy consists in discovering such connexions, and reducing them to general rules. The great Lord Verulam had a perfect comprehension of this, when he called it *an interpretation of nature.* No man ever more distinctly understood or happily expressed the nature and foundation of the philosophic art. What is all we know of mechanics, astronomy, and optics, but connexions established by nature, and discovered by experience or observation, and consequences deduced from them? All the knowledge we have in agriculture, gardening, chemistry, and medicine, is built upon the same foundation. And if ever our philosophy concerning the human mind is carried so far as to deserve the name of science, which ought never to be despaired of, it must be by observing facts, reducing them to general rules, and drawing just conclusions from them. What we commonly call natural *causes* might, with more propriety, be called natural *signs*, and what we call *effects*, the things signified. The causes have no proper efficiency or causality, as far as we know; and all we can certainly affirm is, that nature hath established a constant conjunction between them and the things called their effects; and hath given to mankind a disposition to observe those connexions; to confide in their continuance, and to make use of them for the improvement of our knowledge, and increase of our power.

[A *second class is* that wherein the connexion between the sign and thing signified is not only established by nature, but *discovered to us by a natural principle, without reasoning or experience.*] Of this kind are the natural signs of human thoughts, purposes, and desires, which have been already mentioned as the natural language of mankind. An infant may be put into a fright by an angry countenance, and soothed again by smiles and blandishments. A child that has a good musical ear, may be put to sleep or to dance, may be made merry or sorrowful, by the modulation of musical sounds. The principles of all the fine arts, and of what we call *a fine taste*, may be resolved into connexions of this kind. A fine taste may be improved by reasoning and experience; but if the first principles of it were not planted in our minds by nature, it could never be acquired. Nay, we have already made it appear, that a great part of this knowledge, which we have by nature, is lost by the disuse of natural signs, and the substitution of artificial in their place.

[*A third class of natural signs* comprehends those which, though we never before had any notion or conception of the thing signified, do suggest it, or conjure it up, as it were, by a natural kind of magic, and at once give us a conception, and create a belief of it.] I showed formerly, that our sensations suggest to us a sentient being or mind to which they belong: a being which hath a permanent existence, although the sensations are transient and of short duration: a being which is still the same, while its sensations and other operations are varied ten thousand ways: a being which hath the same relation to all that infinite variety of thoughts, purposes, actions, affections, enjoyments, and sufferings, which we are conscious of, or can remember. The conception of a mind is neither an idea of sensation nor of reflection; for it is neither like any of our sensations, nor like any thing we are conscious of. The first conception of it, as well as the belief of it, and of the common relation it bears to all that we are conscious of, or remember, is suggested to every thinking being, we do not know how.

The notion of hardness in bodies, as well as the belief of it, are got in a similar manner; being by an original principle of our nature annexed to that sensation which we have when we feel a hard body. And so naturally and necessarily does the sensation convey the notion and belief of hardness, that hitherto they have been confounded by the most acute inquirers into the principles of human nature, although they appear, upon accurate reflection, not only to be different things, but as unlike as pain is to the point of a sword.

[It may be observed, that as the first class of natural signs I have mentioned, is the foundation of true philosophy, and the second, the foundation of the fine arts, or of taste; so the last is the foundation of *common sense;* a part of human nature which hath never been explained.]

I take it for granted, that the notion of hardness, and the belief of it, is first got by means of that particular sensation, which, as far back as we can remember, does invariably suggest it; and that if we had never had such a feeling, we should never have had any notion of hardness. [I think it is evident, that we cannot, by reasoning from our sensations, collect the existence of bodies at all, far less any of their qualities. This hath been proved by *unanswerable arguments* by the Bishop of Cloyne, and by the author of the " Treatise of Human Nature."] It appears as evident, that this connexion between our sensations and the conception and belief of external existences cannot be produced by habit, experience, education, or any principle of human nature that hath been admitted by philosophers. At the same time it is a fact, that such sensations are invariably connected with the conception and belief of external existences. Hence, by all rules of just reasoning, we must conclude, that this connexion is the effect of our constitution, and ought to be considered as an original principle of human nature, till we find some more general principle into which it may be resolved.

IV. *Of hardness, and other primary qualities.*—Further I observe, that hardness is a quality, of which we have as clear and distinct a conception as of any thing whatsoever. The cohesion of the parts of a body with more or less force, is perfectly understood, though its cause is not : we know what it is, as well as how it affects the touch. It is therefore a quality of a quite different order from those secondary qualities we have already taken notice of, whereof we know no more naturally, than that they are adapted to raise certain sensations in us. If hardness were a quality of the same kind, it would be a proper inquiry for philosophers, what hardness in bodies is? and we should have had various hypotheses about it, as well as about colour and heat. But it is evident that any such hypothesis would be ridiculous. If any man should say, that hardness in bodies is a certain vibration of their parts, or that it is certain effluvia emitted by them which affect our touch in the manner we feel; such hypotheses would shock common sense; because we all know, that if the parts of a body adhere strongly, it is hard, although it should neither emit effluvia, nor vibrate. Yet at the same time, no man can say, but that effluvia, or the vibration of the parts of a body, might have affected our touch in the same manner that hardness now does, if it had so pleased the Author of our nature : and if either of these hypotheses is applied to explain a secondary quality, such as smell, or taste, or sound, or colour, or heat, there appears no manifest absurdity in the supposition.

V. *The distinction betwixt primary and secondary qualities hath had several revolutions.* Democritus and Epicurus, and their followers, maintained it. Aristotle and the Peripatetics abolished it. Des Cartes, Malebranche, and *Locke, revived it,* and were thought to have put it in a very clear light. But Bishop Berkeley again discarded this distinction, by such proofs as must be convincing to those that hold the received doctrine of ideas. Yet, after all, *there appears to be a real foundation for it* in the principles of our nature.

What hath been said of hardness, is so easily applicable, not only to its opposite, softness, but likewise to roughness and smoothness, to figure and motion, that we may be excused from making the application, which would only be a repetition of what hath been said. All these, by means of certain corresponding sensations of touch, are presented to the mind as real external qualities; the conception and the belief of them are invariably connected with the corresponding sensations, by an original principle of human nature. Their sensations have no name in any language; they have not only been overlooked by the vulgar, but by philosophers; or if they have been at all taken notice of, they have been confounded with the external qualities which they suggest.

VI. *Of extension.*—It is further to be observed, that hardness and softness, roughness and smoothness, figure and motion, do all suppose extension, and cannot be conceived without it; yet I think it must, on the other hand, be allowed, that if we had never felt any thing hard or soft, rough or smooth, figured or moved, we should never have had a conception of extension: so that there is good ground to believe, that the notion of extension could not be prior to that of other primary qualities; so it is certain that it could not be posterior to the notion of any of them, being necessarily implied in them all.

[*Extension*, therefore, seems to be a quality *suggested* to us, by the very same suggestions which suggest the other qualities above mentioned.] ☞ When I grasp a ball in my hand, I perceive it at once hard, figured, and extended. The feeling is very simple, and hath not the least resemblance to any quality of body. Yet it suggests to us three primary qualities perfectly distinct from one another, as well as from the sensation which indicates them. When I move my hand along the table, the feeling is so simple, that I find it difficult to distinguish it into things of different natures; yet it immediately suggests hardness, smoothness, extension, and motion, things of very different natures, and all of them as distinctly understood as the feeling which suggests them.

We are commonly told by philosophers, that we get the idea of extension by feeling along the extremities of a body, as if there was no manner of difficulty in the matter. I have sought, with great pains I confess, to find out how this idea can be got by feeling, but I have sought in vain. Yet it is one of the clearest and most distinct notions we have; nor is there any thing whatsoever, about which the human understanding can carry on so many long and demonstrative trains of reasoning.

The notion of extension is so familiar to us from infancy, and so constantly obtruded by every thing we see and feel, that we are apt to think it obvious how it comes into the mind; but upon a narrower examination, we shall find it utterly inexplicable. [It is true we have feelings of touch, which every moment *present extension to the mind;* but how they come to do so is the question; for *those feelings do no more resemble extension*, than they resemble justice or courage: nor can the existence of extended things be inferred from those feelings by any rules of reasoning; so that the feelings we have by touch, can neither explain how we get the notion, nor how we come by the belief of extended things.]

What hath imposed upon philosophers in this matter is, that

the feelings of touch, which *suggest primary qualities, have no names*, nor are they ever reflected upon. They pass through the mind instantaneously, and serve only to introduce the notion and belief of external things, which by our constitution are connected with them. They are natural signs, and the mind immediately passes to the thing signified, without making the least reflection upon the sign, or observing that there was any such thing. Hence it hath always been taken for granted, that the ideas of extension, figure, and motion, are ideas of sensation, which enter into the mind by the sense of touch, in the same manner as the sensations of sound and smell do by the ear and nose. The sensations of touch are so connected by our constitution with the notions of extension, figure, and motion, that philosophers have mistaken the one for the other, and never have been able to discern that they were not only distinct things, but altogether unlike. However, if we will reason distinctly upon this subject, we ought to give names to those feelings of touch; we must accustom ourselves to attend to them, and to reflect upon them, that we may be able to disjoin them from, and to compare them with the qualities signified or suggested by them.

[The habit of doing this is *not to be attained without pains and practice;* and till a man hath acquired this habit, it will be impossible for him to think distinctly, or to judge right upon this subject.]

Let a man press his hand against the table; *he feels it hard*. But what is the meaning of this? The meaning undoubtedly is, that he hath a certain feeling of touch, from which he concludes, without any reasoning, or comparing ideas, that there is something external really existing, whose parts stick so firmly together, that they cannot be displaced without considerable force.

There is here a feeling, and a conclusion drawn from it, or some way suggested by it. In order to compare these, we must view them separately, and then consider by what tie they are connected, and wherein they resemble one another. The hardness of the table is the conclusion, the feeling is the medium by which we are led to that conclusion. Let a man attend distinctly to this medium, and to the conclusion, and he will perceive them to be as unlike as any two things in nature. The one is a sensation of the mind, which can have no existence but in a sentient being; nor can it exist one moment longer than it is felt: the other is in the table, and we conclude, without any difficulty, that it was in the table before it was felt, and continues after the feeling is over. The one implies no kind of extension, nor parts, nor cohesion; the other implies all these. Both indeed admit of degrees, and the feeling, beyond a certain degree, is a species of pain; but adamantine hardness does not imply the least pain.

And as the feeling hath no similitude to hardness, so neither can our reason perceive the least tie or connexion between them; nor will the logician ever be able to show a reason why we should conclude hardness from this feeling, rather than softness, or any other quality whatsoever. But in reality all mankind are led by their constitution to conclude hardness from this feeling.

[The sensation of heat, and the sensation we have by pressing a hard body, are equally feelings; nor can we by reasoning draw any conclusion from the one, but what may be drawn from the other: but *by our constitution* we conclude from the first *an* obscure or *occult quality*, of which we have only this relative conception, that it is something adapted to raise in us the sensation of heat; from the second, we conclude a quality of which we have a *clear* and distinct *conception*, to wit, the hardness of the body.]

VII. *Of extension.*—To put this matter in another light, it may be proper to try whether from sensation alone we can collect any notion of extension, figure, motion, and space. I take it for granted, that a blind man hath the same notion of extension, figure, and motion, as a man that sees; that Dr. Saunderson had the same notion of a cone, a cylinder, and a sphere, and of the motions and distances of the heavenly bodies, as Sir Isaac Newton.

As sight, therefore, is not necessary for our acquiring those notions, we shall leave it out altogether in our inquiry into the first origin of them: and shall suppose a blind man, by some strange distemper, to have lost all the experience, and habits, and notions he had got by touch; not to have the least conception of the existence, figure, dimensions, or extension, either of his own body, or of any other; but to have all his knowledge of external things to acquire anew, by means of sensation and the power of reason, which we suppose to remain entire.

☞ We shall *first* suppose his body fixed immoveably in one place, and that he can only have the feelings of touch, by the application of other bodies to it. Suppose him first to be pricked with a pin: this will, no doubt, give a smart sensation: he feels pain; but what can he infer from it? Nothing, surely, with regard to the existence or figure of a pin. He can infer nothing from this species of pain, which he might not as well infer from the gout or sciatica. Common sense might lead him to think that this pain had a cause; but whether this cause was body or spirit, extended or unextended, figured or not figured, he could not possibly, from any principles he is supposed to have, form the least conjecture. Having had formerly no notion of body or of extension, the prick of a pin could give him none.

Suppose *next* a body not pointed, but blunt, is applied to his body with a force gradually increased until it bruises him. What has he got by this, but another sensation, or train of sensations, from which he will be able to conclude as little as from the former? A schirrous tumor in any inward part of the body, by pressing upon the adjacent parts, may give the same kind of sensation as the pressure of an external body, without conveying any notion but that of pain, which surely hath no resemblance to extension.

Suppose, *thirdly,* that the body applied to him touched a larger or a lesser part of his body. Could this give him any idea of its extension or dimensions? To me it seems impossible that it should, unless he had some previous notion of the dimensions and figure of his own body, to serve him as a measure. When my two hands touch the extremities of a body, if I know them to be a foot asunder, I easily collect that the body is a foot long; and if I know them to be five feet asunder, that it is five feet long: but if I know not what the distance of my hands is, I cannot know the length of the object they grasp; and if I have no previous notion of hands at all, or of distance between them, I can never get that notion by their being touched.

Suppose, *again,* (4) that a body is drawn along his hands or face while they are at rest. Can this give him any notion of space or motion? It no doubt gives a new feeling; but how it should convey a notion of space or motion to one who had none before, I cannot conceive. The blood moves along the arteries and veins, and this motion, when violent, is felt; but I imagine no man, by this feeling, could get the conception of space or motion, if he had it not before. Such a motion may give a certain succession of feelings, as the cholic may do; but no feelings, nor any combination of feelings, can ever resemble space or motion.

Let us *next* (5) suppose that he makes some instinctive effort to move his head or his hand; but that no motion follows, either on account of external resistance or of palsy. Can this effort convey the notion of space and motion to one who never had it before? Surely it cannot.

Last of all, (6) let us suppose that he moves a limb by instinct, without having had any previous notion of space or motion. He has here a new sensation, which accompanies the flexure of joints, and the swelling of muscles. But how this sensation can convey into his mind the idea of space and motion, is still altogether mysterious and unintelligible. The motions of the heart and lungs are all performed by the contraction of muscles, yet give no conception of space or motion. An embryo in the womb has many such motions, and probably the feelings that accompany them, without any idea of space or motion.

Upon the whole, it appears that our philosophers have imposed upon themselves and upon us, in pretending *to deduce from sensation* the first origin of our notions of *external existences*, of space, motion, and extension, and all the primary qualities of body, that is, the qualities whereof we have the most clear and distinct conception. These qualities do not at all tally with any system of the human faculties that hath been advanced. They have no resemblance to any sensation, or to any operation of our minds; and therefore *they cannot be ideas either of sensation or of reflection.* The very conception of them is irreconcilable to the principles of all our philosophic systems of the understanding. The belief of them is no less so.

VIII. *Of the existence of a material world.*—It is beyond our power to say, when or in what order we came by our notions of these qualities. When we trace the operations of our minds as far back as memory and reflection can carry us, we find them already in possession of our imagination and belief, and quite familiar to the mind: but how they came first into its acquaintance, or what has given them so strong a hold of our belief, and what regard they deserve, are no doubt very important questions in the philosophy of human nature.

Shall we, with the Bishop of Cloyne, serve them with a quo warranto, and have them tried at the bar of philosophy, upon the statute of the ideal system? Indeed, in this trial they seem to have come off very pitifully. For although they had very able counsel, learned in the law, *viz.*, Des Cartes, Malebranche, and Locke, who said every thing they could for their clients, the Bishop of Cloyne, believing them to be aiders and abettors of heresy and schism, prosecuted them with great vigour, fully answered all that had been pleaded in their defence, and silenced their ablest advocates, who seem, for half a century past, to decline the argument, and to trust to the favour of the jury rather than to the strength of their pleadings.

Thus, the wisdom of *philosophy* is set in opposition to the *common sense* of mankind. The first pretends to demonstrate *à priori*, that there can be no such thing as a material world; that sun, moon, stars, and earth, vegetable and animal bodies, are and can be nothing else but sensations in the mind, or images of those sensations in the memory and imagination; that, like pain and joy, they can have no existence when they are not thought of. The last can conceive no otherwise of this opinion, than as a kind of metaphysical lunacy; and concludes that too much learning is apt to make men mad; and that the man who seriously entertains this belief, though in other respects he may be a very good man, as a man may be who believes that he is made of glass, yet surely he hath a soft place in his understanding, and hath been hurt by much thinking.

This opposition betwixt philosophy and common sense is apt

to have a very unhappy influence upon the philosopher himself. He sees human nature in an odd, unamiable, and mortifying light. He considers himself, and the rest of his species, as born under a necessity of believing ten thousand absurdities and contradictions, and endowed with such a pittance of reason as is just sufficient to make this unhappy discovery : and this is all the fruit of his profound speculations. Such notions of human nature tend to slacken every nerve of the soul, to put every noble purpose and sentiment out of countenance, and spread a melancholy gloom over the whole face of things.

If this is wisdom, let me be deluded with the vulgar. I find something within me that recoils against it, and inspires more reverent sentiments of the human kind, and of the universal administration. Common sense and reason have both one Author, —that Almighty Author, in all whose other works we observe a consistency, uniformity, and beauty, which charm and delight the understanding : there must therefore be some order and consistency in the human faculties, as well as in other parts of his workmanship. A man that thinks reverently of his own kind, and esteems true wisdom and philosophy, will not be fond, nay, will be very suspicious, of such strange and paradoxical opinions. If they are false, they disgrace philosophy; and if they are true, they degrade the human species, and make us justly ashamed of our frame.

To what purpose is it for philosophy to decide against common sense in this or any other matter? The belief of a material world is older, and of more authority, than any principles of philosophy. It declines the tribunal of reason, and laughs at all the artillery of the logician. It retains its sovereign authority in spite of all the edicts of philosophy, and reason itself must stoop to its orders. Even those philosophers who have disowned the authority of our notions of an external material world, confess that they find themselves under a necessity of submitting to their power.

Methinks, therefore, it were better to make a virtue of necessity; and since we cannot get rid of the vulgar notion and belief of an external world, to reconcile our reason to it as well as we can : for if reason should stomach and fret ever so much at this yoke, she cannot throw it off; if she will not be the servant of common sense, she must be her slave.

In order, therefore, to reconcile reason to common sense in this matter, I beg leave to offer to the consideration of philosophers these two observations. [*First.* That in all this debate about the existence of a material world, it hath been taken for granted on both sides, that this same *material world*, if any such there be, must be *the express image of our sensations;* that we can have no conception of any material thing which is not like some sensation in our minds; and particularly that the sensations of touch are images of extension, hardness, figure, and motion.] Every argument brought against the existence of a material world, either by the Bishop of Cloyne, or by the author of the "Treatise of Human Nature," supposeth this. If this is true, their arguments are conclusive and unanswerable: but, on the other hand, if it is not true, there is no shadow of argument left. Have those philosophers, then, given any solid proof of this hypothesis, upon which the whole weight of so strange a system rests? No. They have not so much as attempted to do it. But because ancient and modern philosophers have agreed in this opinion, they have taken it for granted. But let us, as becomes philosophers, lay aside authority; we need not surely consult Aristotle or Locke, to know whether pain be like the point of a sword. I have as clear a conception of extension hardness, and motion, as I have of the point of a sword; and, with some pains and practice, I can form as clear a notion of the other sensations of touch, as I have of pain. When I do so, and compare them together, it appears to me clear as daylight, that the former are not of kin to the latter, nor resemble them in any one feature. They are as unlike, yea, as certainly and manifestly unlike, as pain is to the point of a sword. It may be true that those sensations first introduced the material world to our acquaintance; it may be true that it seldom or never appears without their company: but for all that, they are as unlike as the passion of anger is to those features of the countenance which attend it.

So that, in the sentence those philosophers have passed against the material world, there is an error personæ. Their proof touches not matter, or any of its qualities, but strikes directly against an idol of their own imagination, a material world made of ideas and sensations, which never had nor can have an existence.

[*Secondly*. The very *existence of our conceptions of extension*, figure, and motion, since they are neither ideas of sensation or reflection, *overturns the whole ideal system* by which the material world hath been tried and condemned: so that there hath been likewise in this sentence an error juris.]

It is a very fine and a just observation of Locke, that as no human art can create a single particle of matter, and the whole extent of our power over the material world consists in compounding, combining, and disjoining the matter made to our hands; so in the world of thought, the materials are all made by nature, and can only be variously combined and disjoined by us. So that it is impossible for reason or prejudice, true or false philosophy, to produce one simple notion or conception, which is not the work of nature and the result of our constitution.

The conception of extension, motion, and the other attributes of matter, cannot be the effect of error or prejudice; it must be the work of nature. And the power or faculty by which we acquire those conceptions must be something different from any power of the human mind that hath been explained, since it is neither sensation nor reflection.

This I would therefore humbly propose as an experimentum crucis, by which the ideal system must stand or fall; and it brings the matter to a short issue: extension, figure, motion, may, any one or all of them, be taken for the subject of this experiment. Either they are ideas of sensation, or they are not. If any one of them can be shown to be an idea of sensation, or to have the least resemblance to any sensation, I lay my hand upon my mouth, and give up all pretence to reconcile reason to common sense in this matter, and must suffer the ideal scepticism to triumph. But if, on the other hand, they are not ideas of sensation, nor like to any sensation, then the ideal system is a rope of sand, and all the laboured arguments of the sceptical philosophy against a material world, and against the existence of every thing but impressions and ideas, proceed upon a false hypothesis.

If our philosophy concerning the mind be so lame with regard to the origin of our notions of the clearest, most simple, and most familiar objects of thought, and the powers from which they are derived, can we expect that it should be more perfect in the account it gives of the origin of our opinions and belief? We have seen already some instances of its imperfection in this respect: and perhaps that same nature which hath given us the power to conceive things altogether unlike to any of our sensations, or to any operation of our minds, hath likewise provided for our belief of them, by some part of our constitution hitherto not explained.

Bishop Berkeley hath proved, beyond the possibility of reply, that we cannot by reasoning infer the existence of matter from our sensations: and the author of the "Treatise of Human Nature" hath proved no less clearly that we cannot by reasoning infer the existence of our own or other minds from our sensations. But are we to admit nothing but what can be proved by reasoning? Then we must be sceptics indeed, and believe nothing at all. The author of the "Treatise of Human Nature" appears to me to be but a half-sceptic. He hath not followed his principles so far as they lead him: but after having, with unparalleled intrepidity and success, combated vulgar prejudices, when he had but one blow to strike, his courage fails him, he fairly lays down his arms, and yields himself a captive to the most common of all vulgar prejudices, I mean the belief of the existence of his own impressions and ideas.

I beg therefore to have the honour of making an addition to

the sceptical system, without which I conceive it cannot hang together. I affirm that [the belief of the existence of impressions and ideas is as little supported by reason as that of the existence of minds and bodies.] No man ever did or could offer any reason for this belief. Des Cartes took it for granted, that he thought, and had sensations and ideas: so have all his followers done. Even the hero of scepticism hath yielded this point, I crave leave to say, weakly and imprudently. I say so, because I am persuaded that there is no principle of his philosophy that obliged him to make this concession. And what is there in impressions and ideas so formidable, that this all-conquering philosophy, after triumphing over every other existence, should pay homage to them? Besides, the concession is dangerous: for belief is of such a nature, that if you leave any root, it will spread; and you may more easily pull it up altogether than say, Hitherto shalt thou go, and no further; the existence of impressions and ideas I give up to thee: but see thou pretend to nothing more. A thorough and consistent sceptic will never, therefore, yield this point; and while he holds it, you can never oblige him to yield any thing else.

To such a sceptic I have nothing to say; but of the semi-sceptics I should beg to know why they believe the existence of their impressions and ideas. The true reason I take to be, because they cannot help it; and the same reason will lead them to believe many other things.

[*All reasoning must be from first principles*, and for first principles no other reason can be given but this, that, by the *constitution of our nature*, we are under a necessity of assenting to them.] Such principles are parts of our constitution, no less than the power of thinking: reason can neither make nor destroy them; nor can it do any thing without them: it is like a telescope, which may help a man to see further, who hath eyes; but without eyes a telescope shows nothing at all. A mathematician cannot prove the truth of his axioms, nor can he prove any thing, unless he takes them for granted. We cannot prove the existence of our minds, nor even of our thoughts and sensations. A historian, or a witness, can prove nothing, unless it is taken for granted that the memory and senses may be trusted. A natural philosopher can prove nothing, unless it is taken for granted that the course of nature is steady and uniform.

How or when I got such first principles, upon which I build all my reasoning, I know not; for I had them before I can remember: but I am sure they are parts of my constitution, and that I cannot throw them off. That our thoughts and sensations must have a subject, which we call *ourself*, is not therefore an opinion got by reasoning, but a natural principle. That our sensations of touch indicate something external, extended, figured, hard or soft, is not a deduction of reason, but a natural principle. The belief of it, and the very conception of it, are equally parts of our constitution. If we are deceived in it, we are deceived by Him that made us, and there is no remedy.

I do not mean to affirm, that the sensations of touch do from the very first suggest the same notions of body and its qualities, which they do when we are grown up. Perhaps nature is frugal in this, as in her other operations. The passion of love, with all its concomitant sentiments and desires, is naturally suggested by the perception of beauty in the other sex. Yet the same perception does not suggest the tender passion, till a certain period of life. A blow given to an infant, raises grief and lamentation; but when he grows up, it as naturally stirs resentment, and prompts him to resistance. Perhaps a child in the womb, or for some short period of its existence, is merely a sentient being: the faculties, by which it perceives an external world, by which it reflects on its own thoughts, and existence, and relation to other things, as well as its reasoning and moral faculties, do possibly unfold themselves by degrees; so that it is inspired with the various principles of common sense, as with the passions of love and resentment, when it has occasion for them.

IX. *Of the systems of philosophers concerning the senses.*—[All the systems of philosophers about our senses and their objects have split upon this rock, of *not distinguishing* properly *sensations*, which can have no existence but when they are felt, *from the things suggested by them.*] Aristotle, with as distinguishing a head as ever applied to philosophical disquisitions, confounds these two; and makes every sensation to be the form, without the matter, of the thing perceived by it. ☞ As the impression of a seal upon wax has the form of the seal, but nothing of the matter of it; so he conceived our sensations to be impressions upon the mind, which bear the image, likeness, or form of the external thing perceived, without the matter of it. Colour, sound, and smell, as well as extension, figure, and hardness, are, according to him, various forms of matter: our sensations are the same forms imprinted on the mind, and perceived in its own intellect. It is evident from this, that Aristotle made no distinction between primary and secondary qualities of bodies, although that distinction was made by Democritus, Epicurus, and others of the ancients.

Des Cartes, Malebranche, and Locke, revived the distinction between primary and secondary qualities. But they made the *secondary qualities* mere *sensations*, and the *primary* ones *resemblances* of our sensations. They maintained, that colour, sound, and heat, are not any thing in bodies, but sensations of the mind: at the same time, they acknowledged some particular texture or modification of the body, to be the cause or occasion of those sensations; but to this modification they gave no name. Whereas, by the vulgar, the names of colour, heat, and sound, are but rarely applied to the sensations, and most commonly to those unknown causes of them; as hath been already explained. The constitution of our nature leads us rather to attend to the things signified by the sensation, than to the sensation itself, and to give a name to the former rather than to the latter. Thus we see, that with regard to secondary qualities, these philosophers thought with the vulgar, and with common sense. Their paradoxes were only an abuse of words. For when they maintain as an important modern discovery, that there is no heat in the fire, they mean no more, than that the fire does not feel heat, which every one knew before.

With regard to primary qualities, these philosophers erred more grossly: they indeed believed the existence of those qualities; but they did not at all attend to the sensations that *suggest* them, which having no names, have been as little considered as if they had no existence. They were aware, that figure, extension, and hardness, are perceived by means of sensations of touch; whence they rashly concluded, that these sensations must be images and resemblances of figure, extension, and hardness.

The received *hypothesis of ideas* naturally led them to this conclusion; and indeed could not consist with any other; for according to that hypothesis, external things must be perceived by means of images of them in the mind; and what can those images of external things in the mind be, but the sensations by which we perceive them?

This however was to draw a conclusion from a hypothesis against fact. We need not have recourse to any hypothesis to know what our sensations are, or what they are like. By a proper degree of reflection and attention we may understand them perfectly, and be as certain that they are not like any quality of body, as we can be, that the toothache is not like a triangle. How a sensation should instantly make us conceive and believe the existence of an external thing altogether unlike to it, I do not pretend to know; and when I say that the one suggests the other, I mean not to explain the manner of their connexion, but to express a fact, which every one may be conscious of; namely, that, by a law of our nature, such a conception and belief constantly and immediately follow the sensation.

[Bishop Berkeley gave new light to this subject, by showing, that the qualities of an inanimate thing, such as matter is conceived to be, cannot resemble any sensation; that it is *impossible to conceive any thing like the sensations of our minds, but the sensations of other minds.*] Every one that attends properly to his sensations must assent to this; yet it had escaped all the philosophers that came before Berkeley: it had escaped even the ingenious Locke, who had so much practised reflection on the operations of his own mind. So difficult it is to attend properly even to our own feelings. They are so accustomed to pass through the mind unobserved, and instantly to make way for that which nature intended them to signify, that it is extremely difficult to stop, and survey them; and when we think we have acquired this power, perhaps the mind still fluctuates between the sensation and its associated quality, so that they mix together, and present something to the imagination that is compounded of both. ☞ Thus in a globe or cylinder, whose opposite sides are quite unlike in colour, if you turn it slowly, the colours are perfectly distinguishable, and their dissimilitude is manifest; but if it is turned fast, they lose their distinction, and seem to be of one and the same colour.

No succession can be more quick than that of tangible qualities to the sensations with which nature has associated them: but when one has once acquired the art of making them separate and distinct objects of thought, he will then clearly perceive, that the maxim of Bishop Berkeley above mentioned is self-evident; and that the features of the face are not more unlike to a passion of the mind which they indicate, than the sensations of touch are to the primary qualities of body.

But let us observe what use the Bishop makes of this important discovery: why, he concludes, that we can have no conception of an inanimate substance, such as matter is conceived to be, or of any of its qualities; and that there is the strongest ground to believe that there is no existence in nature but minds, sensations, and ideas: if there is any other kind of existences, it must be what we neither have nor can have any conception of. But how does this follow? Why thus: we can have no conception of any thing but what resembles some sensation or idea in our minds; but the sensations and ideas in our minds can resemble nothing but the sensations and ideas in other minds; therefore, the conclusion is evident. This argument, we see, leans upon two propositions. The last of them the ingenious author hath indeed made evident to all that understand his reasoning, and can attend to their own sensations: but the first proposition he never attempts to prove; it is taken from the doctrine of ideas, which hath been so universally received by philosophers, that it was thought to need no proof.

We may here again observe, that this acute writer argues from a *hypothesis* against *fact*, and against the common sense of mankind. That we can have no conception of any thing, unless there is some impression, sensation, or idea, in our minds which resembles it, is indeed an opinion which hath been very generally received among philosophers; but it is neither self-evident, nor hath it been clearly proved: and therefore it had been more reasonable to call in question this doctrine of philosophers, than to discard the material world, and by that means expose philosophy to the ridicule of all men who will not offer up common sense as a sacrifice to metaphysics.

We ought, however, to do this justice both to the Bishop of Cloyne and to the author of the " Treatise of Human Nature," to acknowledge, that their conclusions are justly drawn from the doctrine of ideas, which has been so universally received. On the other hand, from the character of Bishop Berkeley, and of his predecessors Des Cartes, Locke, and Malebranche, we may venture to say, that if they had seen all the consequences of this doctrine, as clearly as the author before mentioned did, they would have suspected it vehemently, and examined it more carefully than they appear to have done.

The theory of ideas, like the Trojan horse, had a specious appearance both of innocence and beauty; but if those philosophers had known that it carried in its belly death and destruction to all science and common sense, they would not have broken down their walls to give it admittance.

That we have clear and distinct conceptions of extension, figure, motion, and other attributes of body, which are neither sensations, nor like any sensation, is a fact of which we may be as certain, as that we have sensations. And that all mankind have a fixed belief of an external material world, a belief which is neither got by reasoning nor education, and a belief which we cannot shake off, even when we seem to have strong arguments against it, and no shadow of argument for it, is likewise a fact, for which we have all the evidence that the nature of the thing admits. These facts are phenomena of human nature, from which we may justly argue against any hypothesis, however generally received. But to argue from a hypothesis against facts, is contrary to the rules of true philosophy.

CHAPTER VI.

OF SEEING.

I. *The excellence and dignity of this faculty.*—THE advances made in the knowledge of optics in the last age, and in the present, and chiefly the discoveries of Sir Isaac Newton, do honour, not to philosophy only, but to human nature. Such discoveries ought for ever to put to shame the ignoble attempts of our modern sceptics to depreciate the human understanding, and to dispirit men in the search of truth, by representing the human faculties as fit for nothing, but to lead us into absurdities and contradictions.

Of the faculties called *the five senses*, sight is without doubt the noblest. The rays of light, which minister to this sense, and of which, without it, we could never have had the least conception, are the most wonderful and astonishing part of the inanimate creation. We must be satisfied of this, if we consider their extreme minuteness, their inconceivable velocity, the regular variety of colours which they exhibit, the invariable laws according to which they are acted upon by other bodies, in their reflections, inflections, and refractions, without the least change of their original properties, and the facility with which they pervade bodies of great density, and of the closest texture, without resistance, without crowding or disturbing one another, without giving the least sensible impulse to the lightest bodies.

The structure of the eye, and of all its appurtenances, the admirable contrivances of nature for performing all its various external and internal motions, and the variety in the eyes of different animals, suited to their several natures and ways of life, do clearly demonstrate this organ to be a masterpiece of nature's work. And he must be very ignorant of what hath been discovered about it, or have a very strange cast of understanding, who can seriously doubt whether or not the rays of light and the eye were made for one another, with consummate wisdom, and perfect skill in optics.

If we should suppose an order of beings, endued with every human faculty but that of sight, how incredible would it appear to such beings, accustomed only to the slow informations of touch, that by the addition of an organ, consisting of a ball and socket of an inch diameter, they might be enabled in an instant of time, without changing their place, to perceive the disposition of a whole army, or the order of a battle, the figure of a magnificent palace, or all the variety of a landscape? If a man were by feeling to find out the figure of the Peak of Teneriffe, or even of St. Peter's church at Rome, it would be the work of a lifetime.

It would appear still more incredible to such beings as we have supposed, if they were informed of the discoveries which may be made by this little organ in things far beyond the reach of any other sense: that by means of it we can find our way in the pathless ocean; that we can traverse the globe of the earth, determine its figure and dimensions, and delineate every region of it: yea, that we can measure the planetary orbs, and make discoveries in the sphere of the fixed stars.

Would it not appear still more astonishing to such beings, if they should be further informed, that, by means of this same organ, we can perceive the tempers and dispositions, the passions and affections of our fellow-creatures, even when they want most to conceal them? That when the tongue is taught most artfully to lie and dissemble, the hypocrisy should appear in the countenance to a discerning eye? And that by this organ, we can often perceive what is straight and what is crooked in the mind as well as in the body? How many mysterious things must a blind man believe, if he will give credit to the relations of those that see? Surely he needs as strong a faith as is required of a good Christian.

It is not, therefore, without reason, that the faculty of seeing is looked upon, not only as more noble than the other senses, but as having something in it of a nature superior to sensation. The evidence of reason is called *seeing*, not *feeling*, *smelling*, or *tasting*. Yea, we are wont to express the manner of the Divine knowledge by *seeing*, as that kind of knowledge which is most perfect in us.

II. *Sight discovers almost nothing which the blind may not comprehend. The reason of this.*—Notwithstanding what hath been said of the dignity and superior nature of this faculty, it is worthy of our observation, that there is very little of the knowledge acquired by sight, that may not be communicated to a man born blind. One who never saw the light, may be learned and knowing in every science, even in optics; and may make discoveries in every branch of philosophy. He may understand as much as another man, not only of the order, distances, and motions of the heavenly bodies; but of the nature of light, and of the laws of the reflection and refraction of its rays. He may understand distinctly, how those laws produce the phenomena of the rainbow, the prism, the camera obscura, and the magic lantern, and all the powers of the microscope and telescope. This is a fact sufficiently attested by experience.

[In order to perceive the reason of it, we must distinguish the appearance that objects make to the eye, from the things *suggested* by that appearance: and again, in the visible appearance of objects, we must distinguish the appearance of colour from the appearance of extension, figure, and motion. *First*, then, as to the visible *appearance of the figure*, and motion, and extension of bodies, I conceive that a man born blind may have a distinct notion, if not of the very things, at least of something extremely like to them. May not a blind man be made to conceive, that a body moving directly from the eye, or directly towards it, may appear to be at rest? and that the same motion may appear quicker or slower, according as it is nearer to the eye or further off, more direct or more oblique? May he not be made to conceive, that a plain surface, in a certain position, may appear as a straight line, and vary its visible figure, as its position, or the position of the eye, is varied? That a circle seen obliquely will appear an ellipse; and a square, a rhombus or an oblong rectangle? Dr. Saunderson understood the projection of the sphere, and the common rules of perspective; and if he did, he must have understood all that I have mentioned. If there were any doubt of Dr. Saunderson's understanding these things, I could mention my having heard him say in conversation, that he found great difficulty in understanding Dr. Halley's demonstration of that proposition, That the angles made by the circles of the sphere, are equal to the angles made by their representatives in the stereographic projection: but, said he, when I laid aside that demonstration, and considered the proposition in my own way, I saw clearly that it must be true. Another gentleman, of undoubted credit, and judgment in these matters, who had part in this conversation, remembers it distinctly.

Secondly. As to the *appearance of colour*, a blind man must be more at a loss; because he hath no perception that resembles it. Yet he may, by a kind of analogy, in part supply this defect. To those who see, a scarlet colour signifies an unknown quality in bodies, that makes to the eye an appearance which they are well acquainted with, and have often observed: to a blind man, it signifies an unknown quality that makes to the eye an appearance which he is unacquainted with. But he can conceive the eye to be variously affected by different colours, as the nose is by different smells, or the ear by different sounds. Thus he can conceive scarlet to differ from blue, as the sound of a trumpet does from that of a drum; or as the smell of an orange differs from that of an apple. It is impossible to know whether a scarlet colour has the same appearance to me which it hath to another man; and if the appearances of it to different persons differed as much as colour does from sound, they might never be able to discover this difference. Hence it appears obvious, that a blind man might talk long about colours distinctly and pertinently: and if you were to examine him in the dark about the nature, composition, and beauty of them, he might be able to answer so as not to betray his defect.

We have seen how far a blind man may go in the knowledge of the appearances which things make to the eye. As to the things which are suggested by them, or inferred from them; although he could never discover them of himself, yet he may understand them perfectly by the information of others. And every thing of this kind that enters into our minds by the eye, may enter into his by the ear. Thus, for instance, he would never, if left to the direction of his own faculties, have dreamed of any such thing as light: but he can be informed of every thing we know about it. He can conceive, as distinctly as we, the minuteness and velocity of its rays, their various degrees of refrangibility and reflexibility, and all the magical powers and virtues of that wonderful element. He would never of himself have found out that there are such bodies as the sun, moon, and stars; but he may be informed of all the noble discoveries of astronomers about their motions, and the laws of nature by which they are regulated. Thus it appears that there is very little knowledge got by the eye which may not be communicated by language to those who have no eyes.

If we should suppose that it were as uncommon for men to see as it is to be born blind, would not the few who had this rare gift appear as prophets and inspired teachers to the many? We conceive inspiration to give a man no new faculty, but to communicate to him in a new way, and by extraordinary means, what the faculties common to mankind can apprehend, and what he can communicate to others by ordinary means. On the supposition we have made, sight would appear to the blind very similar to this: for the few who had this gift could communicate the knowledge acquired by it to those who had it not. They could not indeed convey to the blind any distinct notion of the manner in which they acquired this knowledge. A ball and socket would seem, to a blind man, in this case, as improper an instrument for acquiring such a variety and extent of knowledge, as a dream or a vision. The manner in which a man who sees discerns so many things by means of the eye, is as unintelligible to the blind, as the manner in which a man may be inspired with knowledge by the Almighty is to us. Ought the blind man therefore, without examination, to treat all pretences to the gift of seeing as imposture? Would he not, if he were candid and tractable, find reasonable evidence of the reality of this gift in others, and draw great advantages from it to himself?

The distinction we have made between the visible appearances of the objects of sight, and things suggested by them, is necessary to give us a just notion of the intention of nature in giving us eyes. [If we attend duly to the operation of our mind in the use of this faculty, we shall perceive that the visible appearance of objects is hardly ever regarded by us. It is not at all made an object of thought or reflection, but serves only as *a sign* to introduce to the mind something else, which may be distinctly conceived by those who never saw.]

Thus the visible appearance of things in my room varies almost every hour, according as the day is clear or cloudy, as the sun is in the east, or south, or west, and as my eye is in one part of the room or in another: but I never think of these variations otherwise than as signs of morning, noon, or night, of a clear or cloudy sky. A book or a chair has a different appearance to the eye in every different distance and position; yet we conceive it to be still the same; and, overlooking the appearance, we immediately conceive the real figure, distance, and position of the body, of which its visible or perspective appearance is a sign and indication.

When I see a man at the distance of ten yards, and afterwards see him at the distance of a hundred yards, his visible appearance, in its length, breadth, and all its linear proportions, is ten times less in the last case than it is in the first: yet I do not conceive him one inch diminished by this diminution of his visible figure. Nay, I do not in the least attend to this diminution, even when I draw from it the conclusion of his being at a greater distance. For such is the subtilty of the mind's operation in this case, that we draw the conclusion without perceiving that ever the premises entered into the mind. A thousand such instances might be produced, in order to show that the visible appearances of objects are intended by nature only as signs or indications; and that the mind passes instantly to the thing signified, without making the least reflection upon the sign, or even perceiving that there is any such thing. It is in a way somewhat similar, that the sounds of a language, after it is become familiar, are overlooked, and we attend only to the things signified by them.

It is therefore a just and important observation of the Bishop of Cloyne, that the visible appearance of objects is a kind of language used by nature to inform us of their distance, magnitude, and figure. And this observation hath been very happily applied by that ingenious writer, to the solution of some phenomena in optics, which had before perplexed the greatest masters in that science. The same observation is further improved by the judicious Dr. Smith, in his Optics, for explaining the apparent figure of the heavens, and the apparent distances and magnitudes of objects seen with glasses, or by the naked eye.

Avoiding as much as possible the repetition of what hath been said by these excellent writers, we shall avail ourselves of the distinction between the signs that nature useth in this visual language, and the things signified by them; and in what remains to be said of sight, shall first make some observations upon the signs.

III. *Of the visible appearances of objects.*—In this section we must speak of things which are never made the object of reflection, though almost every moment presented to the mind. Nature intended them only for *signs;* and in the whole course of life they are put to no other use. The mind has acquired a confirmed and inveterate habit of inattention to them: for they no sooner appear, than quick as lightning the thing signified succeeds, and engrosses all our regard. They have *no name in language;* and although we are conscious of them when they pass through the mind, yet their passage is so quick, and so familiar, that it is absolutely unheeded; nor do they leave any footsteps of themselves either in the memory or imagination. That this is the case with regard to the sensations of touch, hath been shown in the last chapter; and it holds no less with regard to the visible appearances of objects.

I cannot, therefore, entertain the hope of being intelligible to those readers who have not, by pains and practice, acquired the habit of distinguishing the appearance of objects to the eye, from the judgment which we form by sight of their colour, distance, magnitude, and figure. The only profession in life wherein it is necessary to make this distinction, is that of painting. The painter hath occasion for an abstraction, with regard to visible objects, somewhat similar to that which we here require; and this indeed is the most difficult part of his art. For it is evident, that if he could fix in his imagination the visible appearance of objects, without confounding it with the things signified by that appearance, it would be as easy for him to paint from the life, and to give every figure its proper shading and relief, and its perspective proportions, as it is to paint from a copy. Perspective, shading, giving relief, and colouring, are nothing else but copying the appearance which things make to the eye. We may therefore borrow some light on the subject of visible appearance from this art.

☞ Let one look upon any familiar object, such as a book, at different distances and in different positions, is he not able to affirm, upon the testimony of his sight, that it is the same book, the same object, whether seen at the distance of one foot or of ten, whether in one position or another; that the colour is the same, the dimensions the same, and the figure the same, as far as the eye can judge? This surely must be acknowledged. The same individual object is presented to the mind, only placed at different distances, and in different positions. Let me ask, in the next place, whether this object has the same appearance to the eye in these different distances? Infallibly it hath not. For,

First. However certain our judgment may be that the colour is the same, it is as certain that it hath not the *same appearance at different distances.* There is a certain degradation of the colour, and a certain confusion and indistinctness of the minute parts, which is the natural consequence of the removal of the object to a greater distance. Those that are not painters, or critics in painting, overlook this; and cannot easily be persuaded that the colour of the same object hath a different appearance at the distance of one foot and of ten, in the shade and in the light. But the masters in painting know how, by the degradation of the colour, and the confusion of the minute parts, figures, which are upon the same canvass, and at the same distance from the eye, may be made to represent objects which are at the most unequal distances. They know how to make the objects appear to be of the same colour, by making their pictures really of different colours according to their distances or shades.

Secondly. Every one who is acquainted with the rules of perspective knows, that the *appearance* of the figure of the book *must vary* in every different position; yet if you ask a man that has no notion of perspective, whether the figure of it does not appear to his eye to be the same in all its different positions, he can, with a good conscience, affirm that it does. He hath learned to make allowance for the variety of visible figure arising from the difference of position, and to draw the proper conclusions from it. But he draws these conclusions so readily and habitually, as to lose sight of the premises; and therefore, where he hath made the same conclusion, he conceives the visible appearance must have been the same.

Thirdly. Let us consider the *apparent magnitude* or dimensions of the book. Whether I view it at the distance of one foot or of ten feet, it seems to be about seven inches long, five broad, and one thick. I can judge of these dimensions very nearly by the eye, and I judge them to be the same at both distances. But yet it is certain, that at the distance of one foot its visible length and breadth is about ten times as great as at the distance of ten feet; and consequently its surface is about a hundred times as great. This great change of apparent magnitude is altogether overlooked, and every man is apt to imagine, that it appears to the eye of the same size at both distances. Further, when I look at the book, it seems plainly to have three dimensions, of length, breadth, and thickness; but it is certain that the visible appearance hath no more than two, and can be exactly represented upon a canvass which hath only length and breadth.

In the *last place*, does not every man, by sight, perceive the distance of the book from his eye? Can he not affirm with certainty, that in one case it is not above one foot distant, that in another it is ten? Nevertheless, it appears certain, that *distance from the eye* is no *immediate* object of sight. There are certain things in the visible appearance which are signs of distance from the eye, and from which, as we shall afterwards show, we learn by experience to judge of that distance within certain limits; but it seems beyond doubt, that a man born blind, and suddenly made to see, could form no judgment at first of the distance of the objects which he saw. The young man couched by Cheselden thought, at first, that every thing he saw touched his eye, and learned only by experience to judge of the distance of visible objects.

[I have entered into this long detail, in order to show, that the *visible appearance* of an object is extremely *different from* the notion of it which *experience* teaches us to form by sight; and to enable the reader to attend to the visible appearance of colour, figure, and extension in visible things, which is no common object of thought, but must be carefully attended to by those who would enter into the philosophy of this sense, or would comprehend what shall be said upon it.] ☞ To a man newly made to see, the visible appearance of objects would be the same as to us; but he would see nothing at all of their real dimensions, as we do. He could form no conjecture, by means of his sight only, how many inches or feet they were in length, breadth, or thickness. He could perceive little or nothing of their real figure; nor could he discern, that this was a cube, that a sphere; that this was a cone, and that a cylinder. His eye could not inform him, that this object was near, and that more remote. The habit of a man or of a woman, which appeared to us of one uniform colour, variously folded and shaded, would present to his eye neither fold nor shade, but variety of colour. In a word, his eyes, though ever so perfect, would at first give him almost no information of things without him. They would indeed present the same appearances to him as they do to us, and speak the same language; but to him it is an unknown language, and therefore he would attend only to the signs, without knowing the signification of them: whereas to us it is a language perfectly familiar; and therefore we take no notice of the signs, but attend only to the things signified by them.

IV. *That colour is a quality of bodies, not a sensation of the mind.*—[By colour, all men, who have not been tutored by modern philosophy, understand, not a sensation of the mind, which can have no existence when it is not perceived, but *a quality* or modification *of bodies, which continues to be the same, whether it is seen or not.*] The scarlet rose, which is before me, is still a scarlet rose when I shut my eyes, and was so at midnight, when no eye saw it. The colour remains, when the appearance ceases: it remains the same when the appearance changes. For when I view this scarlet rose through a pair of green spectacles, the appearance is changed, but I do not conceive the colour of the rose changed. To a person in the jaundice, it has still another appearance; but he is easily convinced, that the change is in his eye, and not in the colour of the object. Every different degree of light makes it have a different appearance, and total darkness takes away all appearance, but makes not the least change in the colour of the body. We may, by a variety of optical experiments, change the appearance of figure and magnitude in a body, as well as that of colour; we may make one body appear to be ten. But all men believe, that as a multiplying glass does not really produce ten guineas out of one, nor a microscope turn a guinea into a ten pound piece; so neither does a coloured glass change the real colour of the object seen through it, when it changes the appearance of that colour.

The common language of mankind shows evidently, that we ought to distinguish between the *colour of a body*, which is conceived to be a fixed and *permanent quality* in the body, and the *appearance of that colour* to the eye, *which may be varied* a thousand ways, by a variation of the light, of the medium, of the eye itself. The permanent colour of the body is the cause, which, by the mediation of various kinds or degrees of light, and of various transparent bodies interposed, produces all this variety of appearances. When a coloured body is presented, there is a certain apparition to the eye, or to the mind, which we have called *the appearance of colour.* Mr. Locke calls it *an idea;* and indeed it may be called so with the greatest propriety. This idea can have no existence but when it is perceived. It is a kind of thought, and can only be the act of a percipient or thinking being. By the constitution of our nature, we are led to conceive this idea as a sign of something external, and are impatient till we learn its meaning. ☞ A thousand experiments for this purpose are made every day by children, even before they come to the use of reason. They look at things, they handle them, they put them in various positions, at different distances, and in different lights. The ideas of sight, by these means, come to be associated with, and readily to suggest, things external, and altogether unlike them. In particular, that idea which we have called *the appearance of colour*, suggests the conception and belief of some unknown quality in the body, which occasions the idea; and it is to this quality, and not to the idea, that we give the name of *colour.* The various colours, although in their nature equally unknown, are easily distinguished when we think or speak of them, by being associated with the ideas which they excite. In like manner, gravity, magnetism, and electricity, although all unknown qualities, are distinguished by their different effects. As we grow up, the mind acquires a habit of passing so rapidly from the ideas of sight to the external things suggested by them, that the ideas are not in the least attended to, nor have they names given them in common language.

When we think or speak of any particular colour, however simple the notion may seem to be which is presented to the imagination, it is really in some sort compounded. It involves an unknown cause, and a known effect. The name of *colour* belongs indeed to the cause only, and not to the effect. But as the cause is unknown, we can form no distinct conception of it, but by its relation to the known effect. And therefore both go together in the imagination, and are so closely united, that they are mistaken for one simple object of thought. When I would conceive those colours of bodies which we call *scarlet* and *blue;* if I conceived them only as *unknown qualities,* I could perceive no distinction between the one and the other. I must, therefore, for the sake of distinction, join to each of them in my imagination some effect or some relation that is peculiar. And the most obvious distinction is, the appearance which one and the other makes to the eye. [Hence the appearance is, in the imagination, so closely united with the quality called *a scarlet colour*, that they are apt to be mistaken for one and the same thing, although they are in reality so different and so unlike, that one is an *idea in the mind*, the other is *a quality of body*.]

[I conclude, then, that colour is not a sensation, but a *secondary quality of bodies*, in the sense we have already explained; that it is a certain power or virtue in bodies, that in fair daylight exhibits to the eye an appearance which is very familiar to us, although it *hath no name*.] Colour differs from other secondary qualities in this, that whereas the name of the quality is sometimes given to the sensation which indicates it, and is occasioned by it, we never, as far as I can judge, give the name of *colour* to the sensation, but to the quality only. Perhaps the reason of this may be, that the appearances of the same colour are so various, and changeable, according to the different modifications of the light, of the medium, and of the eye, that language could not afford names for them. And, indeed, they are so little interesting, that they are never attended to, but serve only as signs to introduce the things signified by them. Nor ought it to appear incredible, that appearances so frequent and so familiar should have no names, nor be made objects of thought; since we have before shown, that this is true of many sensations of touch, which are no less frequent, nor less familiar.

V. *First inference from the preceding.*—From what hath been said about colour, we may infer two things. The *first* is, that one of the most remarkable paradoxes of modern philosophy, which hath been universally esteemed as a great discovery, is, in reality, when examined to the bottom, nothing else but *an abuse of words*. The paradox I mean is, that colour is not a quality of bodies, but only an idea in the mind. We have shown, that the word *colour*, as used by the vulgar, cannot signify an idea in the mind, but a permanent quality of body. We have shown, that there is really a permanent quality of body, to which the common use of this word exactly agrees. Can any stronger proof be desired, that this quality is that to which the vulgar give the name of *colour?* If it should be said, that this quality to which we give the name of *colour*, is unknown to the vulgar, and therefore can have no name among them; I answer, it is indeed known, only by its effects; that is, by its exciting a certain idea in us: but are there not numberless qualities of bodies which are known only by their effects, to which, notwithstanding, we find it necessary to give names? Medicine alone might furnish us with a hundred instances of this kind. Do not the words *astringent, narcotic, epispastic, caustic,* and innumerable others, signify qualities of bodies which are known only by their effects upon animal bodies? Why, then, should not the vulgar give a name to a quality whose effects are every moment perceived by their eyes? We have all the reason, therefore, that the nature of the thing admits, to think that the vulgar apply the name of *colour* to that quality of bodies which excites in us what the philosophers call the *idea of colour*. And that there is such a quality in bodies, all philosophers allow, who allow that there is any such thing as body. Philosophers have thought fit to leave that quality of bodies which the vulgar call *colour* without a name, and to give the name of *colour* to the idea or appearance, to which, as we have shown, the vulgar give no name, because they never make it an object of thought or reflection. [Hence it appears, that when philosophers affirm that colour is not in bodies, but in the mind, and the vulgar affirm, that colour is not in the mind, but is a quality of bodies, there is no difference between them about things, but only about the *meaning of a word*.]

The vulgar have undoubted right to give names to things which they are daily conversant about; and philosophers seem justly chargeable with an abuse of language, when they change the meaning of a common word without giving warning.

If it is a good rule to think with philosophers and speak with the vulgar, it must be right to speak with the vulgar when we think with them, and not to shock them by philosophical paradoxes, which, when put into common language, express only the common sense of mankind.

If you ask a man that is no philosopher, what colour is? or, what makes one body appear white, another scarlet? he cannot tell. He leaves that inquiry to philosophers, and can embrace any hypothesis about it, except that of our modern philosophers, who affirm, that colour is not in body, but only in the mind.

Nothing appears more shocking to his apprehension, than that visible objects should have no colour, and that colour should be in that which he conceives to be invisible. Yet this strange paradox is not only universally received, but considered as one of the noblest discoveries of modern philosophy. The ingenious Mr. Addison, in the " Spectator," No. 413, speaks thus of it. " I have here supposed that my reader is acquainted with that great modern discovery, which is at present universally acknowledged by all the inquirers into natural philosophy, namely, that light and colours, as apprehended by the imagination, are only *ideas* in the mind, and *not qualities* that have any existence in matter. As this is a truth which has been proved incontestably by many modern philosophers, and is indeed one of the finest speculations in that science, if the English reader would see the notion explained at large, he may find it in the eighth chapter of the second book of Mr. Locke's ' Essay on Human Understanding.' "

Mr. Locke and Mr. Addison are writers who have deserved so well of mankind, that one must feel some uneasiness in differing from them, and would wish to ascribe all the merit that is due to a discovery upon which they put so high a value. And indeed it is just to acknowledge, that Mr. Locke, and other modern philosophers, on the subject of secondary qualities, have the merit of distinguishing more accurately than those that went before them, between the sensation in the mind, and that constitution or quality of bodies which gives occasion to the sensation. They have shown clearly, that these two things are not only distinct, but altogether unlike: that there is no similitude between the effluvia of an odorous body, and the sensation of smell which they occasion; nor between the vibrations of a sounding body, and the sensation of sound: that there can be no resemblance between the feeling of heat, and the constitution of the heated body which occasions it; nor between the appearance which a coloured body makes to the eye, and the texture of the body which causes that appearance.

Nor was the merit small of distinguishing these things accurately; because, however different and unlike in their nature, they have been always so associated in the imagination, as to coalesce as it were into one two-faced form, which, from its amphibious nature, could not justly be appropriated either to body or mind; and until it was properly distinguished into its different constituent parts, it was impossible to assign to either their just shares in it. None of the ancient philosophers had made this distinction. The followers of Democritus and Epicurus conceived the forms of heat, and sound, and colour, to be in the mind only, but that our senses fallaciously represented them as being in bodies. The Peripatetics imagined, that those forms were really in bodies; and that the images of them were conveyed to the mind by our senses.

The one system made the senses naturally fallacious and deceitful; the other made the qualities of body to resemble the sensations of the mind. Nor was it possible to find a third, without making the distinction we have mentioned; by which indeed the errors of both these ancient systems are avoided, and we are not left under the hard necessity of believing, either, on the one hand, that our sensations are like to the qualities of body, or, on the other, that God hath given us one faculty to deceive us, and another to detect the cheat.

We desire, therefore, with pleasure, *to do justice to the doctrine* of Mr. Locke, and other modern philosophers, with regard to colour, and other secondary qualities, and to ascribe to it its due merit, while we beg leave *to censure the language* in which they have expressed their doctrine. When they had explained and established the distinction between the appearance which colour makes to the eye, and the modification of the coloured body, which, by the laws of nature, causes that appearance; the question was, whether to give the name of *colour* to the cause, or to the effect? By giving it, as they have done, to the effect, they set philosophy apparently in opposition to common sense, and expose it to the ridicule of the vulgar. But had they given the name of *colour* to the cause, as they ought to have done, they must then have affirmed, with the vulgar, that colour is a quality of bodies; and that there is neither colour, nor any thing like it, in the mind. Their language, as well as their sentiments, would have been perfectly agreeable to the common apprehensions of mankind, and true philosophy would have joined hands with common sense. As Mr. Locke was no enemy to common sense, it may be presumed that in this instance, as in some others, he was seduced by some received hypothesis: and that this was actually the case, will appear in the following section.

VI. *Second. That none of our sensations are resemblances of any of the qualities of bodies.*—A *second* inference is, that although colour is really a quality of body, yet it is *not represented* to the mind by an idea or sensation that resembles it; on the contrary, *it is suggested* by an idea which does not in the least resemble it. And this inference is applicable, not to colour only, but to all the qualities of body which we have examined.

It deserves to be remarked, that in the analysis we have hitherto given of the operations of the five senses, and of the qualities of bodies discovered by them, no instance hath occurred, either of any sensation which resembles any quality of body, or of any quality of body whose image or resemblance is conveyed to the mind by means of the senses.

There is no phenomenon in nature more unaccountable, than the intercourse that is carried on between the mind and the external material world: there is no phenomenon which philosophical spirits have shown greater avidity to pry into, and to resolve. It is agreed by all, that this intercourse is carried on by means of the senses: and this satisfies the vulgar curiosity, but not the philosophic. Philosophers must have some system, some hypothesis, that shows the manner in which our senses make us acquainted with external things. All the fertility of human invention seems to have produced only one hypothesis for this purpose; which therefore hath been universally received; and that is, that the mind, like a mirror, receives the images of things from without, by means of the senses; so that their use must be to convey these images into the mind.

Whether to these images of external things in the mind we give the name of *sensible forms*, or *sensible species*, with the Peripatetics, or the name *of ideas of sensation*, with Mr. Locke; or whether, with later philosophers, we distinguish *sensations,* which are immediately conveyed by the senses, from *ideas of sensation*, which are faint copies of our sensations retained in the memory and imagination; these are only differences about words. The hypothesis I have mentioned is common to all these different systems.

The necessary and allowed consequence of this hypothesis is, that no material thing, nor any quality of material things, can be conceived by us, or made an object of thought, until its image is conveyed to the mind by means of the senses. We shall examine this hypothesis particularly afterwards, and at this time only observe, that in consequence of it one would naturally expect, that to every quality and attribute of body we know or can conceive, there should be a sensation corresponding, which is the image and resemblance of that quality; and that the sensations which have no similitude or resemblance to body, or to any of its qualities, should give us no conception of a material world, or of any thing belonging to it. These things might be expected as the natural consequences of the hypothesis we have mentioned.

Now, we have considered, in this and the preceding chapters, extension, figure, solidity, motion, hardness, roughness, as well as colour, heat and cold, sound, taste, and smell. We have endeavoured to show, that our nature and constitution lead us to conceive these as qualities of body, as all mankind have always conceived them to be. We have likewise examined, with great attention, the various sensations we have by means of the five senses, and are not able to find among them all one single image of body, or of any of its qualities. From whence then come those images of body and of its qualities into the mind? Let philosophers resolve this question. All I can say is, that they come not by the senses. I am sure, that by proper attention and care I may know my sensations, and be able to affirm with certainty what they resemble, and what they do not resemble. I have examined them one by one, and compared them with matter and its qualities; and I cannot find one of them that confesses a resembling feature.

A truth so evident as this, that our sensations are not images of matter, or of any of its qualities, ought not to yield to an hypothesis such as that above mentioned, however ancient, or however universally received by philosophers; nor can there be any amicable union between the two. This will appear by some reflections upon the spirit of the ancient and modern philosophy concerning sensation.

[During the reign of the Peripatetic philosophy, our sensations were not minutely or accurately examined. The *attention of philosophers*, as well as of the vulgar, was turned to the things signified by them: therefore, in consequence of the common hypothesis, it was taken for granted, that all the sensations we have from external things, were the forms or images of these external things. And thus the truth we have mentioned, yielded entirely to the hypothesis, and was altogether suppressed by it.]

Des Cartes gave a noble example of turning our attention inward, and scrutinizing our sensations; and this example hath been very worthily followed by modern philosophers, particularly by Malebranche, Locke, Berkeley, and Hume. [The effect of this scrutiny hath been, a gradual discovery of the truth above mentioned, to wit, the *dissimilitude* between the *sensations* of our minds and the *qualities* or attributes of an insentient, inert substance, such as we conceive matter to be.] But this valuable and useful discovery, in its different stages, hath still been unhappily united to the ancient hypothesis: and from this inauspicious match of opinions, so unfriendly and discordant in their natures, have arisen those monsters of paradox and scepticism with which the modern philosophy is too justly chargeable.

Mr. Locke saw clearly, and proved incontestably, that the sensations we have by taste, smell, and hearing, as well as the sensations of colour, heat, and cold, are *not resemblances* of any thing in bodies; and in this he agrees with Des Cartes and Malebranche. Joining this opinion with the hypothesis, it follows necessarily, that three senses of the five are cut off from giving us any intelligence of the material world, as being altogether inept for that office. Smell, and taste, and sound, as well as colour and heat, can have no more relation to body, than anger or gratitude; nor ought the former to be called qualities of body, whether primary or secondary, any more than the latter. For it was natural and obvious to argue thus from that hypothesis: if heat, and colour, and sound, are real qualities of body, the sensations by which we perceive them, must be resemblances of those qualities: but these sensations are not resemblances; therefore those are not real qualities of body.

We see, then, that Mr. Locke having found, that the ideas of secondary qualities are no resemblances, was compelled, *by an hypothesis* common to all philosophers, to deny that they are real qualities of body. It is more difficult to assign a reason, why, after this, he should call them *secondary qualities;* for this name, if I mistake not, was of his invention. Surely he did not mean that they were secondary qualities of the mind; and I do not see with what propriety, or even by what tolerable license, he could call them secondary qualities of body, after finding that they were no qualities of body at all. In this, Mr. Locke seems to have sacrificed to common sense, and to have been led by her authority even in opposition to his hypothesis. The same sovereign mistress of our opinions that led Mr. Locke to call those things secondary qualities of body, which, according to his principles and reasonings, were no qualities of body at all, hath led, not the vulgar of all ages only, but philosophers also, and even the disciples of Mr. Locke, to believe them to be real qualities of body: she hath led them to investigate, by experiments, the nature of colour, and sound, and heat, in bodies. Nor hath this investigation been fruitless, as it must have been, if there had been no such thing in bodies: on the contrary, it hath produced very noble and useful discoveries, which make a very considerable part of natural philosophy. If then natural philosophy be not a dream, there is something in bodies which we call *colour*, and *heat*, and *sound*. And if this be so, the hypothesis from which the contrary is concluded, must be false: for the argument, leading to a false conclusion, recoils against the hypothesis from which it was drawn, and thus directs its force backward. If the qualities of body were known to us only by sensations that resemble them, then colour, and sound, and heat, could be no qualities of body: but these are real qualities of body; and therefore the qualities of body are not known only by means of sensations that resemble them.

But to proceed: what Mr. Locke had proved with regard to the sensations we have by smell, taste, and hearing, Bishop Berkeley proved no less unanswerably with regard to all our other sensations; to wit, that none of them can in the least resemble the qualities of a lifeless and insentient being, such as matter is conceived to be. Mr. Hume hath confirmed this by his authority and reasoning. This opinion surely looks with a very malign aspect upon the old hypothesis; yet that hypothesis hath still been retained, and conjoined with it. And what a brood of monsters hath this produced!

The first-born of this union, and perhaps the most harmless, was, that the secondary qualities of body were mere sensations of the mind. To pass by Malebranche's notion of seeing all things in the ideas of the Divine Mind, as a foreigner never naturalized in this island; the next was Berkeley's system, That extension, and figure, and hardness, and motion; that land, and sea, and houses, and our own bodies, as well as those of our wives, and children, and friends, are nothing but ideas in the mind; and that there is nothing existing in nature but minds and ideas.

The progeny that followed is still more frightful; so that it is surprising that one could be found who had the courage to act the midwife, to rear it up, and to usher it into the world. No causes nor effects; no substances, material or spiritual; no evidence even in mathematical demonstration; no liberty nor active power; nothing existing in nature, but impressions and ideas, following each other, without time, place, or subject. Surely no age ever produced such a system of opinions, justly deduced with great acuteness, perspicuity, and elegance, from a principle universally received. The hypothesis we have mentioned is the father of them all. The dissimilitude of our sensations and feelings to external things is the innocent mother of most of them.

As it happens sometimes in an arithmetical operation, that two errors balance one another, so that the conclusion is little or nothing affected by them; but when one of them is corrected, and the other left, we are led further from the truth than by both together; so it seems to have happened in the Peripatetic philosophy of sensation, compared with the modern. The Peripatetics adopted two errors, but the last served as a corrective to the first, and rendered it mild and gentle; so that their system had no tendency to scepticism. The moderns have retained the first of those errors, but have gradually detected and corrected the last. The consequence hath been, that the light we have struck out hath created darkness, and scepticism hath advanced hand in hand with knowledge, spreading its melancholy gloom, first over the material world, and at last over the whole face of nature. Such a phenomenon as this is apt to stagger even the lovers of light and knowledge, while its cause is latent; but when that is detected, it may give hopes that this darkness shall not be everlasting, but that it shall be succeeded by a more permanent light.

VII. *Of visible figure and extension.*—Although there is no resemblance, nor, as far as we know, any necessary connexion, between that quality in a body which we call its *colour,* and the appearance which that colour makes to the eye; it is quite otherwise with regard to its figure and magnitude. There is certainly a resemblance, and a necessary connexion between the visible figure and magnitude of a body, and its real figure and magnitude. No man can give a reason why a scarlet colour affects the eye in the manner it does: no man can be sure that it affects his eye in the same manner as it affects the eye of another, and that it has the same appearance to him as it has to another man: but we can assign a reason why a circle placed obliquely to the eye should appear in the form of an ellipse. The visible figure, magnitude, and position, may, by mathematical reasoning, be deduced from the real; and it may be demonstrated that every eye that sees distinctly and perfectly must, in the same situation, see it under this form, and no other. Nay, we may venture to affirm, that a man born blind, if he were instructed in mathematics, would be able to determine the visible figure of a body, when its real figure, distance, and position, are given. Dr. Saunderson understood the projection of a sphere, and perspective. Now, I require no more knowledge in a blind man, in order to his being able to determine the visible figure of bodies, than that he can project the outline of a given body, upon the surface of a hollow sphere, whose centre is in the eye. This projection is the visible figure he wants; for it is the same figure with that which is projected upon the *tunica retina* in vision.

A blind man can conceive lines drawn from every point of the object to the centre of the eye, making angles. He can conceive that the length of the object will appear greater or less, in proportion to the angle which it subtends at the eye; and that, in like manner, the breadth, and in general the distance of any one point of the object from any other point, will appear greater or less, in proportion to the angles which those distances subtend. He can easily be made to conceive that the visible appearance has no thickness, any more than a projection of the sphere, or a perfect draught. He may be informed that the eye, until it is aided by experience, does not represent one object as nearer or more remote than another. Indeed, he would probably conjecture this of himself, and be apt to think that the rays of light must make the same impression upon the eye, whether they come from a greater or a less distance.

These are all the principles which we suppose our blind mathematician to have; and these he may certainly acquire by information and reflection. It is no less certain that from these principles, having given the real figure and magnitude of a body, and its position and distance with regard to the eye, he can find out its visible figure and magnitude. He can demonstrate in general, from these principles, that the visible figure of all bodies will be the same with that of their projection upon the surface of a hollow sphere, when the eye is placed in the centre. And he can demonstrate that their visible magnitude will be greater or less, according as their projection occupies a greater or less part of the surface of this sphere.

To set this matter in another light, let us distinguish betwixt the *position* of objects with regard to the eye, and their *distance* from it. Objects that lie in the same right line drawn from the centre of the eye, have the same position, however different their distances from the eye may be: but objects which lie in different right lines drawn from the eye's centre, have a different position; and this difference of position is greater or less in proportion to the angle made at the eye by the right lines mentioned. Having thus defined what we mean by the position of objects with regard to the eye, it is evident that as the real figure of a body consists in the situation of its several parts with regard to one another, so its visible figure consists in the position of its several parts with regard to the eye; and as he that hath a distinct conception of the situation of the parts of the body with regard to one another, must have a distinct conception of its real figure; so he that conceives distinctly the position of its several parts with regard to the eye, must have a distinct conception of its visible figure. Now, there is nothing surely to hinder a blind man from conceiving the position of the several parts of a body with regard to the eye, any more than to conceive their situation with regard to one another; and therefore I conclude that a blind man may attain a distinct conception of the visible figure of bodies.

Although we think the arguments that have been offered are sufficient to prove that a blind man may conceive the visible extension and figure of bodies; yet, in order to remove some prejudices against this truth, it will be of use to compare the notion which a blind mathematician might form to himself of visible figure, with that which is presented to the eye in vision, and to observe wherein they differ.

[*First. Visible figure is never presented to the eye but in conjunction with colour:* and although there be no connexion between them from the nature of the things, yet having so invariably kept company together, we are hardly able to disjoin them even in our imagination.] What mightily increases this difficulty is, that we have never been accustomed to make visible figure an object of thought. It is only used as a sign, and having served this purpose, passes away, without leaving a trace behind. The drawer or designer, whose business it is to hunt this fugitive form, and to take a copy of it, finds how difficult his task is, after many years' labour and practice. Happy! if at last he can acquire the art of arresting it in his imagination, until he can delineate it. For then it is evident that he must be able to draw as accurately from the life as from a copy. But how few of the professed masters of designing are ever able to arrive at this degree of perfection? It is no wonder, then, that we should find so great difficulty in conceiving this form apart from its constant associate, when it is so difficult to conceive it at all. But our blind man's notion of visible figure will not be associated with colour, of which he hath no conception: but it will perhaps be associated with hardness or smoothness, with which he is acquainted by touch. These different associations are apt to impose upon us, and to make things seem different, which in reality are the same.

[*Secondly,* The blind man forms the notion of *visible figure* to himself, *by thought*, and by mathematical *reasoning* from principles; whereas the man that sees, has it presented to his eye at once, without any labour, *without any reasoning*, by a kind of inspiration.] A man may form to himself the notion of a parabola, or a cycloid, from the mathematical definition of those figures, although he had never seen them drawn or delineated. Another, who knows nothing of the mathematical definition of the figures, may see them delineated on paper, or feel them cut out in wood. Each may have a distinct conception of the figures, one by mathematical reasoning, the other by sense. Now, the blind man forms his notion of visible figure in the same manner as the first of these formed his notion of a parabola or a cycloid, which he never saw.

[*Thirdly*, *Visible figure* leads the man that sees, directly to *the conception of the real figure*, of which it is *a sign*. But the blind man's thoughts move in a *contrary* direction. For he must first know the real figure, distance, and situation, of the body, and from thence he slowly traces out the visible figure by mathematical reasoning. Nor does his nature lead him to conceive this visible figure as a sign; it is a creature of his own reason and imagination.]

VIII. *Some queries concerning visible figure answered.*—It may be asked, What kind of thing is this visible figure? Is it a sensation, or an idea? If it is an idea, from what sensation is it copied? These questions may seem trivial or impertinent to one who does not know, that there is a tribunal of inquisition erected by certain modern philosophers, before which every thing in nature must answer. The articles of inquisition are few indeed, but very dreadful in their consequences. They are only these: is the prisoner an impression, or an idea? If an idea, from what impression copied? Now, if it appears that the prisoner is neither an impression, nor an idea copied from some impression, immediately, without being allowed to offer any thing in arrest of judgment, he is sentenced to pass out of existence, and to be, in all time to come, an empty unmeaning sound, or the ghost of a departed entity.

Before this dreadful tribunal, cause and effect, time and place, matter and spirit, have been tried and cast: how then shall such a poor flimsy form as visible figure stand before it? It must even plead guilty, and confess that it is neither an impression, nor an idea. For, alas! it is notorious, that it is extended in length and breadth; it may be long or short, broad or narrow, triangular, quadrangular, or circular: and therefore unless ideas and impressions are extended and figured, it cannot belong to that category.

If it should still be asked, To what category of beings does *visible figure* then belong? I can only in answer give some tokens, by which those who are better acquainted with the categories, may chance to find its place. [It is, as we have said, the position of the several parts of a figured body, with regard to the eye.] The different positions of the several parts of the body, with regard to the eye, when put together, make a real figure, which is truly extended in length and breadth, and which represents a figure that is extended in length, breadth, and thickness. In like manner, a projection of the sphere is a real figure, and hath length and breadth, but represents the sphere, which hath three dimensions. A projection of the sphere, or a perspective view of a palace, is a representative in the very same sense as visible figure is, and wherever they have their lodgings in the categories, this will be found to dwell next door to them.

It may further be asked, Whether there be *any sensation proper to visible figure,* by which it is suggested in vision? Or by what means it is presented to the mind? This is a question of some importance, in order to our having a distinct notion of the faculty of seeing: and to give all the light to it we can, it is necessary to compare this sense with other senses, and to make some suppositions, by which we may be enabled to distinguish things that are apt to be confounded, although they are totally different.

There are three of our senses which give us intelligence of things at a distance; smell, hearing, and sight. In smelling, and in hearing, we have a sensation or impression upon the mind, which, by our constitution, we conceive to be a sign of something external: but the position of this external thing, with regard to the organ of sense, is not presented to the mind along with the sensation. ☞ When I hear the sound of a coach, I could not, previous to experience, determine whether the sounding body was above or below, to the right hand or to the left. So that the sensation suggests to me some external object as the cause or occasion of it; but it suggests not the position of that object, whether it lies in this direction or in that. The same thing may be said with regard to smelling. But the case is quite different with regard to seeing. When I see an object, the appearance which the colour of it makes, may be called *the sensation,* which suggests to me some external thing as its cause; but it suggests likewise the individual direction and position of this cause with regard to the eye. I know it is precisely in such a direction, and in no other. At the same time I am not conscious of any thing that can be called *sensation,* but the sensation of colour. The position of the coloured thing is no sensation, but it is by the laws of my constitution presented to the mind along with the colour, without any additional sensation.

Let us suppose, that the eye were so constituted, that the rays coming from any one point of the object were not, as they are in our eyes, collected in one point of the *retina*, but diffused over the whole: it is evident to those who understand the structure of the eye, that such an eye as we have supposed, would show the colour of a body as our eyes do, but that it would neither show figure nor position. The operation of such an eye would be precisely similar to that of hearing and smell; it would give no perception of figure or extension, but merely of colour. Nor is the supposition we have made altogether imaginary: for it is nearly the case of most people who have cataracts, whose crystalline, as Mr. Cheselden observes, does not altogether exclude the rays of light, but diffuses them over the *retina,* so that such persons see things as one does through a glass of broken jelly: they perceive the colour, but nothing of the figure or magnitude of objects.

Again, if we should suppose, that smell and sound were conveyed in right lines from the objects, and that every sensation of hearing and smell suggested the precise direction or position of its object; in this case the operations of hearing and smelling would be similar to that of seeing; we should smell and hear the figure of objects, in the same sense as now we see; and every smell and sound would be associated with some figure in the imagination, as colour is in our present state.

We have reason to believe, that the rays of light make some impression upon the *retina;* but we are not conscious of this impression; nor have anatomists or philosophers been able to discover the nature and effects of it; whether it produces a vibration in the nerve, or the motion of some subtile fluid contained in the nerve, or something different from either, to which we cannot give a name. Whatever it is, we shall call it the *material impression;* remembering carefully, that it is not an impression upon the mind, but upon the body; and that it is no sensation, nor can resemble sensation, any more than figure or motion can resemble thought. Now, this material impression, made upon a particular point of the *retina,* by the laws of our constitution suggests two things to the mind, namely, the colour, and the position of some external object. No man can give a reason, why the same material impression might not have suggested sound, or smell, or any of these along with the position of the object. That it should suggest colour and position, and nothing else, we can resolve only into our constitution, or the will of our Maker. And since there is no necessary connexion between these two things suggested by this material impression, it might, if it had so pleased our Creator, have suggested one of them without the other. Let us suppose, therefore, since it plainly appears to be possible, that our eyes had been so framed, as to suggest to us the position of the object, without suggesting colour, or any other quality. What is the consequence of this supposition? It is evidently this, that the person endued with such an eye, would perceive the visible figure of bodies, without having any sensation or impression made upon his mind. The figure he perceives is altogether external; and therefore cannot be called an impression upon the mind, without the grossest abuse of language. If it should be said, that it is impossible to perceive a figure, unless there be some impression of it upon the mind; I beg leave not to admit the impossibility of this without some proof; and I can find none. [Neither can I conceive what is meant by *an impression of figure upon the mind.* I can conceive an impression of figure upon wax, or upon any body that is fit to receive it; but an impression of it upon the mind is to me quite unintelligible; and although I form the most distinct conception of the figure, I cannot, upon the strictest examination, find any impression of it upon my mind.]

If we suppose, last of all, that the eye hath the power restored of perceiving colour, I apprehend that it will be allowed, that now it perceives figure in the very same manner as before, with this difference only, that colour is always joined with it.

[In answer therefore to the question proposed, there seems to be *no sensation* that *is appropriated to visible figure*, or whose office it is to suggest it. It seems to be suggested immediately by the material impression upon the organ, of which we are not conscious:] and why may not a material impression upon the *retina* suggest visible figure, as well as the material impression made upon the hand, when we grasp a ball, suggests real figure? One and the same material impression, in one case, suggests both colour and visible figure; and in the other case, one and the same material impression suggests hardness, heat, or cold, and real figure, all at the same time.

We shall conclude this section with another question upon this subject. Since the visible figure of bodies is a real and external object to the eye, as their tangible figure is to the touch; it may be asked, *whence* arises *the difficulty of attending to the first, and the facility of attending to the last?** It is certain that the first is more frequently presented to the eye, than the last is to the touch; the first is as distinct and determinate an object as the last, and seems in its own nature as proper for speculation. Yet so little hath it been attended to, that it never had a name in any language, until Bishop Berkeley gave it that which we have used after his example, to distinguish it from the figure which is the object of touch.

The difficulty of attending to the visible figure of bodies, and making it an object of thought, appears so similar to that which we find in attending to our sensations, that both have probably like causes. Nature intended the visible figure as a sign of the tangible figure and situation of bodies, and hath taught us by a kind of instinct to put it always to this use. Hence it happens, that the mind passes over it with a rapid motion, to attend to the things signified by it. It is as unnatural to the mind to stop at the visible figure, and attend to it, as it is to a spherical body to stop upon an inclined plane. There is an inward principle, which constantly carries it forward, and which cannot be overcome but by a contrary force.

There are other external things which nature intended for signs; and we find this common to them all, that the mind is disposed to overlook them, and to attend only to the things sig-

* Vide p. 481.

nified by them. Thus there are certain modifications of the human face, which are natural signs of the present disposition of the mind. Every man understands the meaning of these signs, but not one of a hundred ever attended to the signs themselves, or knows any thing about them. Hence you may find many an excellent practical physiognomist, who knows nothing of the proportions of a face, nor can delineate or describe the expression of any one passion.

☞ An excellent painter or statuary can tell, not only what are the proportions of a good face, but what changes every passion makes in it. This, however, is one of the chief mysteries of his art, to the acquisition of which, infinite labour and attention, as well as a happy genius, are required. But when he puts his art in practice, and happily expresses a passion by its proper signs, every one understands the meaning of these signs, without art, and without reflection.

What has been said of painting, might easily be applied to all the fine arts. The difficulty in them all consists in knowing and attending to those natural signs, whereof every man understands the meaning.

[We pass *from the sign to the thing signified*, with ease and by natural impulse; but to go backward *from the thing signified to the sign*, is a work of labour and difficulty. So visible figure being intended by nature to be a sign, we pass on immediately to the thing signified, and cannot easily return to give any attention to the sign.]

Nothing shows more clearly our indisposition to attend to visible figure and visible extension than this, that although mathematical reasoning is no less applicable to them than to tangible figure and extension, yet they have entirely escaped the notice of mathematicians. While that figure and that extension which are objects of touch, have been tortured ten thousand ways for twenty centuries, and a very noble system of science drawn out of them; not a single proposition do we find with regard to the figure and extension which are the immediate objects of sight!

When the geometrician draws a diagram with the most perfect accuracy; when he keeps his eye fixed upon it, while he goes through a long process of reasoning, and demonstrates the relations of the several parts of his figure; he does not consider that the visible figure presented to his eye, is only the representative of a tangible figure, upon which all his attention is fixed; he does not consider that these two figures have really different properties; and that what he demonstrates to be true of the one, is not true of the other.

This perhaps will seem so great a paradox, even to mathematicians, as to require demonstration before it can be believed.

Nor is the demonstration at all difficult, if the reader will have patience to enter but a little into the mathematical consideration of visible figure, which we shall call *the geometry of visibles*.

IX. *Of the geometry of visibles.*—In this geometry, the definitions of a point; of a line, whether straight or curve; of an angle, whether acute, or right, or obtuse; and of a circle, are the same as in common geometry. The mathematical reader will easily enter into the whole mystery of this geometry, if he attends duly to these few evident principles.

1. Supposing the eye placed in the centre of a sphere, every great circle of the sphere will have the same appearance to the eye as if it was a straight line. For the curvature of the circle being turned directly toward the eye, is not perceived by it. And for the same reason, any line which is drawn in the plane of a great circle of the sphere, whether it be in reality straight or curve, will appear straight to the eye.

2. Every visible right line will appear to coincide with some great circle of the sphere; and the circumference of that great circle, even when it is produced, until it returns into itself, will appear to be a continuation of the same visible right line, all the parts of it being visibly in directum. For the eye, perceiving only the position of objects with regard to itself, and not their distance, will see those points in the same visible place which have the same position with regard to the eye, how different soever their distances from it may be. Now, since a plane passing through the eye and a given visible right line, will be the plane of some great circle of the sphere, every point of the visible right line will have the same position as some point of the great circle; therefore they will both have the same visible place, and coincide to the eye; and the whole circumference of the great circle continued even until it returns into itself, will appear to be a continuation of the same visible right line.

Hence it follows,

3. That every visible right line, when it is continued in directum, as far as it may be continued, will be represented by a great circle of a sphere, in whose centre the eye is placed. It follows,

4. That the visible angle comprehended under two visible right lines, is equal to the spherical angle comprehended under the two great circles which are the representatives of these visible lines. For since the visible lines appear to coincide with the great circles, the visible angle comprehended under the former, must be equal to the visible angle comprehended under the latter. But the visible angle comprehended under the two great circles, when seen from the centre, is of the same magnitude with the spherical angle which they really comprehend, as

mathematicians know; therefore the visible angle made by any two visible lines, is equal to the spherical angle made by the two great circles of the sphere which are their representatives.

5. Hence it is evident, that every visible right-lined triangle will coincide in all its parts with some spherical triangle. The sides of the one will appear equal to the sides of the other, and the angles of the one to the angles of the other, each to each; and therefore the whole of the one triangle will appear equal to the whole of the other. In a word, to the eye they will be one and the same, and have the same mathematical properties. The properties therefore of visible right-lined triangles, are not the same with the properties of plain triangles, but are the same with those of spherical triangles.

6. Every lesser circle of the sphere, will appear a circle to the eye placed, as we have supposed all along, in the centre of the sphere. And, on the other hand, every visible circle will appear to coincide with some lesser circle of the sphere.

7. Moreover, the whole surface of the sphere will represent the whole of visible space: for since every visible point coincides with some point of the surface of the sphere, and has the same visible place, it follows, that all the parts of the spherical surface taken together, will represent all possible visible places, that is, the whole of visible space. And from this it follows, in the last place,

8. That every visible figure will be represented by that part of the surface of the sphere, on which it might be projected, the eye being in the centre. And every such visible figure will bear the same ratio to the whole of visible space, as the part of the spherical surface which represents it, bears to the whole spherical surface.

The mathematical reader, I hope, will enter into these principles with perfect facility, and will as easily perceive, that the following propositions with regard to visible figure and space, which we offer only as a specimen, may be mathematically demonstrated from them, and are not less true nor less evident than the propositions of Euclid, with regard to tangible figures.

Prop. 1. Every right line being produced, will at last return into itself.

2. A right line returning into itself, is the longest possible right line; and all other right lines bear a finite ratio to it.

3. A right line returning into itself, divides the whole of visible space into two equal parts, which will both be comprehended under this right line.

4. The whole of visible space bears a finite ratio to any part of it.

5. Any two right lines being produced, will meet in two points, and mutually bisect each other.

6. If two lines be parallel, that is, every where equally distant from each other, they cannot both be straight.

7. Any right line being given, a point may be found, which is at the same distance from all the points of the given right line.

8. A circle may be parallel to a right line, that is, may be equally distant from it in all its parts.

9. Right-lined triangles that are similar, are also equal.

10. Of every right-lined triangle, the three angles taken together, are greater than two right angles.

11. The angles of a right-lined triangle may all be right angles, or all obtuse angles.

12. Unequal circles are not as the squares of their diameters, nor are their circumferences, in the ratio of their diameters.

This small specimen of the geometry of visibles is intended to lead the reader to a clear and distinct conception of the figure and extension which is presented to the mind by *vision;* and to demonstrate the truth of what we have affirmed above, namely, That those figures and that extension which are the immediate objects of sight, are not the figures and the extension about which common geometry is employed; that the geometrician, while he looks at his diagram, and demonstrates a proposition, hath a figure presented to his eye, which is only a sign and representative of a tangible figure; that he gives not the least attention to the first, but attends only to the last; and that these two figures have different properties, so that what he demonstrates of the one, is not true of the other.

It deserves, however, to be remarked, that as a small part of a spherical surface differs not sensibly from a plain surface; so a small part of visible extension differs very little from that extension in length and breadth, which is the object of touch. And it is likewise to be observed, that the human eye is so formed, that an object which is seen distinctly and at one view, can occupy but a small part of visible space: for we never see distinctly what is at a considerable distance from the axis of the eye; and therefore, when we would see a large object at one view, the eye must be at so great distance, that the object occupies but a small part of visible space. From these two observations it follows, that plain figures which are seen at one view, when their planes are not oblique, but direct to the eye, differ little from the visible figures which they present to the eye. The several lines in the tangible figure, have very nearly the same proportion to each other as in the visible; and the angles of the one are very nearly, although not strictly and mathematically, equal to those of the other. Although, therefore, we have found many instances of natural signs which have no similitude to the things signified, this is not the case with regard to visible figure. It hath in all cases such a similitude to the thing signified by it, as a plan or profile hath to that which it represents; and in some cases the sign and thing signified have to all sense the same figure and the same proportions. If we could find a being endued with sight only, without any other external sense, and capable of reflecting and reasoning upon what he sees, the notions and philosophical speculations of such a being, might assist us in the difficult task of distinguishing the perceptions which we have purely by sight, from those which derive their origin from other senses. Let us suppose such a being, and conceive, as well as we can, what notion he would have of visible objects, and what conclusions he would deduce from them. We must not conceive him disposed by his constitution, as we are, to consider the visible appearance as a sign of something else: it is no sign to him, because there is nothing signified by it; and therefore we must suppose him as much disposed to attend to the visible figure and extension of bodies, as we are disposed to attend to their tangible figure and extension.

If various figures were presented to his sense, he might without doubt, as they grow familiar, compare them together, and perceive wherein they agree, and wherein they differ. He might perceive visible objects to have length and breadth, but could have no notion of a third dimension, any more than we can have of a fourth. All visible objects would appear to be terminated by lines, straight or curve; and objects terminated by the same visible lines, would occupy the same place, and fill the same part of visible space. It would not be possible for him to conceive one object to be behind another, or one to be nearer, another more distant.

To us, who conceive *three* dimensions, a line may be conceived straight; or it may be conceived incurvated in one dimension, and straight in another; or, lastly, it may be incurvated in two dimensions. Suppose a line to be drawn upwards and downwards, its length makes one dimension, which we shall call *upwards and downwards;* and there are two dimensions remaining, according to which it may be straight or curve. It may be bent to the right or to the left; and if it has no bending either to right or left, it is straight in this dimension. But supposing it straight in this dimension of right and left, there is still another dimension remaining, in which it may be curve; for it may be bent backwards or forwards. When we conceive a tangible straight line, we exclude curvature in either of these two dimensions: and as what is conceived to be excluded, must be conceived, as well as what is conceived to be included, it follows, that all the three dimensions enter into our conception of a straight line. Its length is one dimension, its straightness in two other dimensions is included, or curvature in these two dimensions excluded, in the conception of it.

The being we have supposed, having no conception of more than two dimensions, of which the length of a line is one, cannot possibly conceive it either straight or curve in more than one dimension: so that in his conception of a right line, curvature to the right hand or left is excluded; but curvature backwards or forwards cannot be excluded, because he hath not, nor can have any conception of such curvature. Hence we see the reason that a line which is straight to the eye, may return into itself: for its being straight to the eye, implies only straightness in one dimension; and a line which is straight in one dimension, may notwithstanding be curve in another dimension, and so may return into itself.

To us, who conceive three dimensions, a surface is that which hath length and breadth, excluding thickness: and a surface may be either plain in this third dimension, or it may be incurvated: so that the notion of a third dimension enters into our conception of a surface; for it is only by means of this third dimension that we can distinguish surfaces into plain and curve surfaces; and neither one nor the other can be conceived without conceiving a third dimension.

The being we have supposed having no conception of a third dimension, his visible figures have length and breadth indeed; but thickness is neither included nor excluded, being a thing of which he has no conception. And therefore visible figures, although they have length and breadth, as surfaces have, yet they are neither plain surfaces, nor curve surfaces. For a curve surface implies curvature in a third dimension, and a plain surface implies the want of curvature in a third dimension; and such a being can conceive neither of these, because he has no conception of a third dimension. Moreover, although he hath a distinct conception of the inclination of two lines which makes an angle, yet he can neither conceive a plain angle nor a spherical angle. Even his notion of a point is somewhat less determined than ours. In the notion of a point we exclude length, breadth, and thickness; he excludes length and breadth, but cannot either exclude or include thickness, because he hath no conception of it.

Having thus settled the notions which such a being as we have supposed might form of mathematical points, lines, angles, and figures, it is easy to see, that by comparing these together, and reasoning about them, he might discover their relations, and form geometrical conclusions built upon self-evident principles. He might likewise without doubt have the same notions of numbers as we have, and form a system of arithmetic. It is not material to say in what order he might proceed in such discoveries, or how much time and pains he might employ about them; but what such a being, by reason and ingenuity, without any materials of sensation but those of sight only, might discover.

As it is more difficult to attend to a detail of possibilities, than of facts even of slender authority, I shall beg leave to give an extract from the travels of Johannes Rudolphus Anepigraphus, a Rosicrucian philosopher, who having by deep study of the occult sciences, acquired the art of transporting himself to various sublunary regions, and of conversing with various orders of intelligences, in the course of his adventures became acquainted with an order of beings exactly such as I have supposed.

How they communicate their sentiments to one another, and by what means he became acquainted with their language, and was initiated into their philosophy, as well as of many other particulars, which might have gratified the curiosity of his readers, and perhaps added credibility to his relation, he hath not thought fit to inform us; these being matters proper for adepts only to know.

His account of their philosophy is as follows.

"The Idomenians," saith he, "are many of them very ingenious, and much given to contemplation. In arithmetic, geometry, metaphysics, and physics, they have most elaborate systems. In the two latter indeed they have had many disputes carried on with great subtilty, and are divided into various sects; yet in the two former there hath been no less unanimity than among the human species. Their principles relating to numbers and arithmetic, making allowance for their notation, differ in nothing from ours: but their geometry differs very considerably."

As our author's account of the geometry of the Idomenians agrees in every thing with the geometry of visibles, of which we have already given a specimen, we shall pass over it. He goes on thus: "Colour, extension, and figure, are conceived to be the essential properties of body. A very considerable sect maintains, that colour is the essence of body. If there had been no colour, say they, there had been no perception or sensation. Colour is all that we perceive, or can conceive, that is peculiar to body; extension and figure being modes common to body and to empty space. And if we should suppose a body to be annihilated, colour is the only thing in it that can be annihilated; for its place, and consequently the figure and extension of that place must remain, and cannot be imagined not to exist. These philosophers hold space to be the place of all bodies, immoveable and indestructible, without figure, and similar in all its parts, incapable of increase or diminution, yet not unmeasurable: for every the least part of space bears a finite ratio to the whole. So that with them the whole extent of space is the common and natural measure of every thing that hath length and breadth, and the magnitude of every body and of every figure is expressed by its being such a part of the universe. In like manner, the common and natural measure of length is an infinite right line, which, as hath been before observed, returns into itself, and hath no limits, but bears a finite ratio to every other line.

"As to their natural philosophy, it is now acknowledged by the wisest of them to have been for many ages in a very low state. The philosophers observing, that one body can differ from another only in colour, figure, or magnitude, it was taken for granted, that all their particular qualities must arise from the various combinations of these their essential attributes. And therefore it was looked upon as the end of natural philosophy, to show how the various combinations of these three qualities in different bodies produced all the phenomena of nature. It were endless to enumerate the various systems that were invented with this view, and the disputes that were carried on for ages; the followers of every system exposing the weak sides of other systems, and palliating those of their own with great art.

"At last, some free and facetious spirits, wearied with eternal disputation, and the labour of patching and propping weak systems, began to complain of the subtilty of nature; of the infinite changes that bodies undergo in figure, colour, and magnitude; and of the difficulty of accounting for these appearances, making this a pretence for giving up all inquiries into the causes of things, as vain and fruitless.

"These wits had ample matter of mirth and ridicule in the systems of philosophers, and finding it an easier task to pull down than to build or support, and that every sect furnished them with arms and auxiliaries to destroy another, they began to spread mightily, and went on with great success. Thus philosophy gave way to scepticism and irony, and those systems which had been the work of ages, and the admiration of the learned, became the jest of the vulgar: for even the vulgar readily took part in the triumph over a kind of learning which they had long suspected, because it produced nothing but wrangling and altercation. The wits having now acquired great reputation, and being flushed with success, began to think their triumph incomplete, until every pretence to knowledge was overturned; and accordingly began their attacks upon arithmetic, geometry, and even upon the common notions of untaught Idomenians. So difficult it hath always been (says our author) for great conquerors to know where to stop.

"In the mean time, natural philosophy began to rise from its ashes, under the direction of a person of great genius, who is looked upon as having had something in him above Idomenian nature. He observed, that the Idomenian faculties were certainly intended for contemplation, and that the works of nature were a nobler subject to exercise them upon than the follies of systems or the errors of the learned; and being sensible of the difficulty of finding out the causes of natural things, he proposed, by accurate observation of the phenomena of nature, to find out the rules according to which they happen, without inquiring into the causes of those rules. In this he made considerable progress himself, and planned out much work for his followers, who call themselves *inductive philosophers*. The sceptics look with envy upon this rising sect, as eclipsing their reputation, and threatening to limit their empire; but they are at a loss on what hand to attack it. The vulgar begin to reverence it, as producing useful discoveries.

"It is to be observed, that every Idomenian firmly believes, that two or more bodies may exist in the same place. For this they have the testimony of sense, and they can no more doubt of it, than they can doubt whether they have any perception at all. They often see two bodies meet, and coincide in the same place, and separate again, without having undergone any change in their sensible qualities by this penetration. When two bodies meet, and occupy the same place, commonly one only appears in that place, and the other disappears. That which continues to appear, is said to overcome, the other to be overcome."

To this quality of bodies they give a name, which our author tells us hath no word answering to it in any human language. And therefore, after making a long apology, which I omit, he begs leave to call it *the overcoming quality of bodies*. He assures us, that "the speculations which had been raised about this single quality of bodies, and the hypotheses contrived to account for it, were sufficient to fill many volumes. Nor have there been fewer hypotheses invented by their philosophers, to account for the changes of magnitude and figure; which, in most bodies that move, they perceive to be in a continual fluctuation. The founder of the inductive sect, believing it to be above the reach of Idomenian faculties, to discover the real causes of these phenomena, applied himself to find from observation, by what laws they are connected together; and discovered many mathematical ratios and relations concerning the motions, magnitudes, figures, and overcoming quality of bodies, which constant experience confirms. But the opposers of this sect choose rather to content themselves with feigned causes of these phenomena, than to acknowledge the real laws whereby they are governed, which humble their pride, by being confessedly unaccountable."

Thus far Johannes Rudolphus Anepigraphus. Whether this Anepigraphus be the same who is recorded among the Greek alchemistical writers not yet published, by Borrichius, Fabricius, and others, I do not pretend to determine. The identity of their name, and the similitude of their studies, although no slight arguments, yet are not absolutely conclusive. Nor will I take upon me to judge of the narrative of this learned traveller by the *external* marks of his credibility; I shall confine myself to those which the critics call *internal*. It would even be of small importance to inquire, whether the Idomenians have a real, or only an ideal existence; since this is disputed among the learned with regard to things with which we are more nearly connected. The important question is, Whether the account above given is a just account of their geometry and philosophy? We have all the faculties which they have, with the addition of others which they have not: we may, therefore, form some judgment of their philosophy and geometry, by separating from all others, the perceptions, we have by sight, and reasoning upon them. As far as I am able to judge in this way after a careful examination, their geometry must be such as Anepigraphus hath described. Nor does his account of their philosophy appear to contain any evident marks of imposture; although here, no doubt, proper allowance is to be made for liberties which travellers take, as well as for involuntary mistakes which they are apt to fall into.

X. *Of the parallel motion of the eyes.*—Having explained as distinctly as we can visible figure, and shown its connexion with the things signified by it, it will be proper next to consider some phenomena of the eyes and of vision, which have commonly been referred to custom, to anatomical or to mechanical causes; but which, as I conceive, must be resolved into original powers and principles of the human mind; and therefore belong properly to the subject of this inquiry.

The first is, the parallel motion of the eyes, by which, when one eye is turned to the right or to the left, upwards or downwards, or straight forwards, the other always goes along with it in the same direction. We see plainly, when both eyes are open, that they are always turned the same way, as if both were acted upon by the same motive force; and if one eye is shut, and the hand laid upon it, while the other turns various ways, we feel the eye that is shut turn at the same time, and that whether we will or not. What makes this phenomenon surprising is, that it is acknowledged by all anatomists, that the muscles which move the two eyes, and the nerves which serve these muscles, are entirely distinct and unconnected. It would be thought very surprising and unaccountable, to see a man who, from his birth, never moved one arm without moving the other precisely in the same manner, so as to keep them always parallel: yet it would not be more difficult to find the physical cause of such a motion of the arms, than it is to find the cause of the parallel motion of the eyes, which is perfectly similar.

[The only cause that hath been assigned of this parallel motion of the eyes, is *custom*. We find by experience, it is said, when we begin to look at objects, that in order to have distinct vision, it is necessary to turn both eyes the same way; therefore we soon acquire the habit of doing it constantly, and by degrees lose the power of doing otherwise.]

This account of the matter seems to be insufficient; because habits are not got at once; it takes time to acquire and to confirm them; and if this motion of the eyes were got by habit, we should see children, when they are born, turn their eyes different ways, and move one without the other, as they do their hands or legs. I know some have affirmed that they are apt to do so. But I have never found it true from my own observation, although I have taken pains to make observations of this kind, and have had good opportunities. I have likewise consulted experienced midwives, mothers, and nurses, and found them agree, that they had never observed distortions of this kind in the eyes of children, but when they had reason to suspect convulsions, or some preternatural cause.

[It seems, therefore, to be extremely probable, that, previous to custom, there is something in the *constitution*, some *natural instinct*, which directs us to move both eyes always the same way.]

We know not how the mind acts upon the body, nor by what power the muscles are contracted and relaxed; but we see, that in some of the voluntary, as well as in some of the involuntary motions, this power is so directed, that many muscles which have no material tie or connexion, act in concert, each of them being taught to play its part in exact time and measure. Nor doth a company of expert players in a theatrical performance, or of excellent musicians in a concert, or of good dancers in a country-dance, with more regularity and order, conspire and contribute their several parts, to produce one uniform effect, than a number of muscles do, in many of the animal functions, and in many voluntary actions. Yet we see such actions no less skilfully and regularly performed in children, and in those who know not that they have such muscles, than in the most skilful anatomist and physiologist.

Who taught all the muscles that are concerned in sucking, in swallowing our food, in breathing, and in the several natural expulsions, to act their part in such regular order and exact measure? It was not custom, surely. It was that same powerful and wise Being who made the fabric of the human body, and fixed the laws by which the mind operates upon every part of it, so that they may answer the purposes intended by them. And when we see, in so many other instances, a system of unconnected muscles conspiring so wonderfully in their several functions, without the aid of habit, it needs not be thought strange, that the muscles of the eyes should, without this aid, conspire to give that direction to the eyes, without which they could not answer their end.

We see a like conspiring action in the muscles which contract the pupils of the two eyes; and in those muscles, whatever they be, by which the conformation of the eyes is varied according to the distance of objects.

[It ought, however, to be observed, that although it appears to be by natural instinct that both eyes are always turned the same way, there is still *some latitude left for custom*.]

What we have said of the parallel motion of the eyes, is not to be understood so strictly as if nature directed us to keep their axes always precisely and mathematically parallel to each other. Indeed, although they are always nearly parallel, they hardly ever are exactly so. When we look at an object, the axes of the eyes meet in that object; and therefore make an angle, which is always small, but will be greater or less, according as the object is nearer or more remote. Nature hath very wisely left us the power of varying the parallelism of our eyes a little, so that we can direct them to the same point, whether remote or near. This, no doubt, is learned by custom; and accordingly we see, that it is a long time before children get this habit in perfection.

This power of varying the parallelism of the eyes is naturally no more than is sufficient for the purpose intended by it, but by much practice and straining it may be increased. Accordingly we see, that some have acquired the power of distorting their eyes into unnatural directions, as others have acquired the power of distorting their bodies into unnatural postures.

[Those who have lost the sight of an eye, commonly *lose what they had got by custom*, in the direction of their eyes, but *retain what they had by nature;* that is, although their eyes turn and move always together; yet, when they look upon an object, the blind eye will often have a very small deviation from it;] which is not perceived by a slight observer, but may be discerned by one accustomed to make exact observations in these matters.

XI. *Of our seeing objects erect by inverted images.*—Another phenomenon which hath perplexed philosophers, is our seeing objects *erect*, when it is well known that *their images* or pictures upon the tunica retina of the eye *are inverted*.

The sagacious Kepler first made the noble discovery, that distinct but inverted pictures of visible objects, are formed upon the retina by the rays of light coming from the object. The same great philosopher demonstrated, from the principles of optics, how these pictures are formed, to wit, that the rays coming from any one point of the object, and falling upon the various parts of the pupil, are, by the cornea and crystalline, refracted so as to meet again in one point of the retina, and there paint the colour of that point of the object from which they come. As the rays from different points of the object cross each other before they come to the retina, the picture they form must be inverted; the upper part of the object being painted upon the lower part of the retina, the right side of the object upon the left of the retina, and so of the other parts.

[This philosopher thought that we see objects erect by means of these inverted pictures, for this reason, that as the rays from different points of the object cross each other, before they fall upon the retina, we conclude that the impulse which we feel upon the lower part of the retina, comes from above; and that the impulse which we feel upon the higher part, comes from below.]

Des Cartes afterwards gave the same solution of this phenomenon, and illustrated it by the judgment which we form of the position of objects which we feel with our arms crossed, or with two sticks that cross each other.

But we cannot acquiesce in this solution. *First*, Because it supposes our seeing things erect, to be a deduction of reason, drawn from certain premises; whereas it seems to be an immediate perception. And, *secondly*, Because the premises from which all mankind are supposed to draw this conclusion, never entered into the minds of the far greater part, but are absolutely unknown to them. We have no feeling or perception of the pictures upon the retina, and as little surely of the position of them. In order to see objects erect, according to the principles of Kepler or Des Cartes, we must previously know, that the rays of light come from the object to the eye in straight lines; we must know, that the rays from different points of the object cross one another, before they form the pictures upon the retina; and lastly, we must know that these pictures are really inverted. Now, although all these things are true, and known to philosophers, yet they are absolutely unknown to the far greatest part of mankind: nor is it possible that they who are absolutely ignorant of them, should reason from them, and build conclusions upon them. Since therefore visible objects appear erect to the ignorant as well as to the learned, this cannot be a conclusion drawn from premises which never entered into the minds of the ignorant. We have indeed had occasion to observe many instances of conclusions drawn, either by means of original principles, or by habit, from premises which pass through the mind very quickly, and which are never made the objects of reflection; but surely no man will conceive it possible to draw conclusions from premises which never entered into the mind at all.

Bishop Berkeley having justly *rejected this solution*, gives one founded upon his own principles; wherein he is followed by the judicious Mr. Smith in his " Optics;" and this we shall next explain and examine.

That ingenious writer conceives the ideas of sight to be altogether unlike those of touch. And since the notions we have of an object by these different senses have no similitude, we can learn only by *experience* how one sense will be affected, by what, in a certain manner, affects the other. Figure, position, and even number, in tangible objects, are ideas of touch; and although there is no similitude between these and the ideas of sight, yet we learn by experience, that a triangle affects the sight in such a manner, and that a square affects it in such another manner: hence we judge that which affects it in the first manner, to be a triangle, and that which affects it in the second, to be a square. [In the same way, finding from *experience*, that an object in an erect position, affects the eye in one manner, and the same object in an inverted position, affects it in another, we learn to *judge*, by the manner in which the eye is affected, whether the object is erect or inverted.] In a word, visible ideas, according to this author, are signs of the tangible; and the mind passeth from the sign to the thing signified, not by means of any similitude between the one and the other, nor by any natural principle; but by having found them constantly conjoined in experience, as the sounds of a language are with the things they signify. So that if the images upon the retina had been always erect, they would have shown the objects erect, in the same manner as they do now that they are inverted: nay, if the visible idea which we now have from an inverted object, had been associated from the beginning with the erect position of that object, it would have signified an erect position, as readily as it now signifies an inverted one. And if the visible appearance of two shillings had been found connected from the beginning with the tangible idea of one shilling, that appearance would as naturally and readily have signified the unity of the object, as now it signifies its duplicity.

This opinion is undoubtedly very ingenious; and if it is just, serves to resolve, not only the phenomenon now under consideration, but likewise that which we shall next consider, our *seeing objects single with two eyes.*

It is evident, that in this solution it is supposed, that we do not originally, and previous to acquired habits, see things either erect or inverted, of one figure or another, single or double, but *learn from experience* to *judge* of their tangible position, figure, and number, by certain visible signs.

Indeed it must be acknowledged to be extremely difficult to distinguish the immediate and natural objects of sight, from the conclusions which we have been accustomed from infancy to draw from them. Bishop Berkeley was the first that attempted to distinguish the one from the other, and to trace out the boundary that divides them. And if, in doing so, he hath gone a little to the right hand or to the left, this might be expected in a subject altogether new, and of the greatest subtilty. The nature of vision hath received great light from this distinction; and many phenomena in optics, which before appeared altogether unaccountable, have been clearly and distinctly resolved by it. It is natural, and almost unavoidable, to one who hath made an important discovery in philosophy, to carry it a little beyond its sphere, and to apply it to the resolution of phenomena which do not fall within its province. Even the great Newton, when he had discovered the universal law of gravitation, and observed how many of the phenomena of nature depend upon this, and other laws of attraction and repulsion, could not help expressing his conjecture, that all the phenomena of the material world depend upon attracting and repelling forces in the particles of matter. And I suspect that the ingenious Bishop of Cloyne having found so many phenomena of vision reducible to the constant association of the ideas of sight and touch, carried this principle a little beyond its just limits.

In order to judge as well as we can, whether it is so, let us suppose such a blind man as Dr. Saunderson, having all the knowledge and abilities which a blind man may have, suddenly made to see perfectly. Let us suppose him kept from all opportunities of associating his ideas of sight with those of touch, until the former become a little familiar; and the first surprise occasioned by objects so new being abated, he has time to canvass them, and to compare them in his mind, with the notions which he formerly had by touch; and in particular to compare in his mind that visible extension which his eyes present, with the extension in length and breadth with which he was before acquainted.

We have endeavoured to prove, that a blind man may form a notion of the visible extension and figure of bodies, from the relation which it bears to their tangible extension and figure. Much more, when this visible extension and figure are presented to his eye, will he be able to compare them with tangible extension and figure, and to perceive, that the one has length and breadth as well as the other; that one may be bounded by lines, either straight or curve, as well as the other. And therefore he will perceive, that there may be visible, as well as tangible circles, triangles, quadrilateral and multilateral figures. And although the visible figure is coloured, and the tangible is not, they may, notwithstanding, have the same figure; as two objects of touch may have the same figure, although one is hot and the other cold.

We have shown above, that the properties of visible figures

differ from those of the plain figures which they represent: but it was observed at the same time, that when the object is so small as to be seen distinctly at one view, and is placed directly before the eye, the difference between the visible and the tangible figure is too small to be perceived by the senses. Thus it is true, that of every visible triangle, the three angles are greater than two right angles; whereas in a plain triangle, the three angles are equal to two right angles: but when the visible triangle is small, its three angles will be so nearly equal to two right angles, that the sense cannot discern the difference. In like manner, the circumferences of unequal visible circles are not, but those of plain circles are, in the ratio of their diameters; yet in small visible circles, the circumferences are very nearly in the ratio of their diameters; and the diameter bears the same ratio to the circumference, as in a plain circle, very nearly.

Hence it appears, that small visible figures (and such only can be seen distinctly at one view) have not only a resemblance to the plain tangible figures which have the same name, but are to all sense the same. So that if Dr. Saunderson had been made to see, and had attentively viewed the figures of the first book of Euclid, he might, by thought and consideration, without touching them, have found out that they were the very figures he was before so well acquainted with by touch.

When plain figures are seen obliquely, their visible figure differs more from the tangible; and the representation which is made to the eye, of solid figures, is still more imperfect; because visible extension hath not three, but two dimensions only. Yet as it cannot be said that an exact picture of a man hath no resemblance of the man, or that a perspective view of a house hath no resemblance of the house; so it cannot be said, with any propriety, that the visible figure of a man, or of a house, hath no resemblance of the objects which they represent.

Bishop Berkeley therefore proceeds upon a capital mistake, in supposing that there is no resemblance betwixt the extension, figure, and position which we see, and that which we perceive by touch.

We may further observe, that Bishop Berkeley's system with regard to material things, must have made him see this question, of the erect appearance of objects, in a very different light from that in which it appears to those who do not adopt his system.

In his theory of vision, he seems indeed to allow, that there is an external material world: but he believed that this external world is tangible only, and not visible; and that the visible world, the proper object of sight, is not external, but in the mind. If this is supposed, he that affirms that he sees things erect and not inverted, affirms that there is a top and a bottom, a right and a left in the mind. Now, I confess I am not so well acquainted with the topography of the mind, as to be able to affix a meaning to these words when applied to it.

We shall therefore allow, that if visible objects were not external, but existed only in the mind, they could have no figure, or position, or extension; and that it would be absurd to affirm, that they are seen either erect or inverted; or that there is any resemblance between them and the objects of touch. But when we propose the question, Why objects are seen erect, and not inverted? we take it for granted, that we are not in Bishop Berkeley's ideal world, but in that world which men who yield to the dictates of common sense believe themselves to inhabit. We take it for granted, that the objects both of sight and of touch are external, and have a certain figure, and a certain position with regard to one another, and with regard to our bodies, whether we perceive it or not.

When I hold my walking-cane upright in my hand, and look at it, I take it for granted, that I see and handle the same individual object. When I say that I feel it erect, my meaning is, that I feel the head directed from the horizon, and the point directed towards it: and when I say that I see it erect, I mean that I see it with the head directed from the horizon, and the point towards it. I conceive the horizon as a fixed object both of sight and touch, with relation to which, objects are said to be high or low, erect or inverted: and when the question is asked, Why I see the object erect, and not inverted? it is the same as if you should ask, why I see it in that position which it really hath? or why the eye shows the real position of objects, and doth not show them in an inverted position, as they are seen by a common astronomical telescope, or as their pictures are seen upon the retina of an eye when it is dissected?

XII. *The same subject continued.*—It is impossible to give a satisfactory answer to this question, otherwise than by pointing out the laws of nature which take place in vision; for by these the phenomena of vision must be regulated.

Therefore I answer, first, That, by a law of nature, the rays of light proceed from every point of the object to the pupil of the eye in straight lines. Secondly, That, by the laws of nature, the rays coming from any one point of the object to the various parts of the pupil, are so refracted, as to meet again in one point of the retina; and the rays from different points of the object, first crossing each other, and then proceeding to as many different points of the retina, form an inverted picture of the object.

[So far the principles of optics carry us; and *experience* further assures us, that if there is no such picture upon the retina, there is no vision; and that such as the picture on the retina is, such is the appearance of the object, in colour and figure, distinctness or indistinctness, brightness or faintness.]

It is evident, therefore, that the pictures upon the retina are, by the laws of nature, a mean of vision; but in what way they accomplish their end, we are totally ignorant. Philosophers conceive that the impression made on the retina by the rays of light is communicated to the optic nerve, and by the optic nerve conveyed to some part of the brain, by them called the sensorium; and that the impression thus conveyed to the sensorium is immediately perceived by the mind, which is supposed to reside there. But we know nothing of the seat of the soul: and we are so far from perceiving *immediately* what is transacted in the brain, that of all parts of the human body we know least about it. It is indeed very probable that the optic nerve is an instrument of vision no less necessary than the retina; and that some impression is made upon it, by means of the pictures on the retina. But of what kind this impression is, we know nothing.

There is not the least probability that there is any picture or image of the object either in the optic nerve or brain. The pictures on the retina are formed by the rays of light; and whether we suppose, with some, that their impulse upon the retina causes some vibration of the fibres of the optic nerve; or, with others, that it gives motion to some subtile fluid contained in the nerve; neither that vibration, nor this motion, can resemble the visible object which is presented to the mind. [Nor is there any probability that the mind perceives the pictures upon the retina. These pictures are no more objects of our perception than the brain is, or the optic nerve. No man ever saw the pictures in his own eye, nor indeed the pictures in the eye of another, until it was taken out of the head, and duly prepared.]

It is very strange that philosophers of all ages should have agreed in this notion, " That the *images* of external objects are conveyed by the organs of sense to the *brain*, and are there perceived by the mind." Nothing can be more unphilosophical. [For, *first*, This notion hath no foundation in fact and observation.] Of all the organs of sense, the eye only, as far as we can discover, forms any kind of image of its object; and the images formed by the eye are not in the brain, but only in the bottom of the eye; nor are they at all perceived or felt by the mind. [*Secondly*, It is as difficult to conceive *how* the mind perceives images in the brain, as how it perceives things more distant.] If any man will show how the mind may perceive images in the brain, I will undertake to show how it may perceive the most distant objects: for if we give eyes to the mind, to perceive what is transacted at home in its dark chamber, why may we not make these eyes a little longer sighted? and then we shall have no occasion for that unphilosophical fiction of images in the brain. In a word, the manner and mechanism of the mind's perception is quite beyond our comprehension: and this way of explaining it by images in the brain, seems to be founded upon very gross notions of the mind and its operations; as if the supposed images in the brain, by a kind of contact, formed similar impressions or images of objects upon the mind, of which impressions it is supposed to be conscious.

We have endeavoured to show, throughout the course of this inquiry, that the impressions made upon the mind by means of the five senses, have not the least resemblance to the objects of sense: and therefore, as we see no shadow of evidence, that there are any such images in the brain, so we see no purpose, in philosophy, that the supposition of them can answer. Since the picture upon the retina, therefore, is neither itself seen by the mind, nor produces any impression upon the brain or sensorium, which is seen by the mind, nor makes any impression upon the mind that resembles the object, it may still be asked, *How* this picture upon the retina causes vision?

Before we answer this question, it is proper to observe, that in the operations of the mind, as well as in those of bodies, we must often be satisfied with knowing that certain things are *connected, and invariably follow one another*, without being able to discover the chain that goes between them. It is to such connexions that we give the name of *laws of nature;* and when we say that one thing produces another by a law of nature, this signifies no more, but that one thing, which we call in popular language *the cause*, is constantly and invariably followed by another, which we call *the effect;* and that we know not how they are connected. Thus we see it is a fact, that bodies gravitate towards bodies; and that this gravitation is regulated by certain mathematical proportions, according to the distances of the bodies from each other, and their quantities of matter. Being unable to discover the cause of this gravitation, and presuming that it is the immediate operation, either of the Author of nature, or of some subordinate cause, which we have not hitherto been able to reach, we call it *a law of nature*. If any philosopher should hereafter be so happy as to discover the cause of gravitation, this can only be done by discovering some more general law of nature, of which the gravitation of bodies is a necessary consequence. In every chain of natural causes, the highest link is a primary law of nature; and the highest link which we can trace, by just induction, is either this primary law of nature, or a necessary consequence of it. To trace out the laws of nature, by induction, from the phenomena of nature, is all that true philosophy aims at, and all that it can ever reach.

There are laws of nature, by which the operations of the mind are regulated; there are also laws of nature that govern the material system: and as the latter are the ultimate conclusions which the human faculties can reach in the philosophy of bodies, so the former are the ultimate conclusions we can reach in the philosophy of minds.

To return, therefore, to the question above proposed,* we may see, from what hath been just now observed, that it amounts to this: " By what law of nature is a picture upon the retina, the mean or occasion of my seeing an external object of the same figure and colour, in a contrary position, and in a certain direction from the eye ?"

It will, without doubt, be allowed, that I see the whole object in the same manner and by the same law by which I see any one point of it. Now, I know it to be a fact, that, in direct vision, I see every point of the object in the direction of the right line that passeth from the centre of the eye to that point of the object; and I know, likewise, from optics, that the ray of light that comes to the centre of my eye, passes on to the retina in the same direction. Hence it appears to be a fact, that every point of the object is seen in the direction of a right line passing from the picture of that point on the retina through the centre of the eye. As this is a fact that holds universally and invariably, it must either be a law of nature, or the necessary consequence of some more general law of nature. And according to the just rules of philosophizing, we may hold it for a law of nature, until some more general law be discovered, whereof it is a necessary consequence, which I suspect can never be done.

Thus we see, that the phenomena of vision lead us by the hand to a law of nature, or a law of our constitution, of which law our seeing objects erect by inverted images is a necessary consequence. For it necessarily follows, from the law we have mentioned, that the object whose picture is lowest on the retina, must be seen in the highest direction from the eye; and that the object whose picture is on the right of the retina, must be seen on the left; so that if the pictures had been erect in the retina, we should have seen the object inverted. My chief intention in handling this question, was to point out this law of nature; which, as it is a part of the constitution of the human mind, belongs properly to the subject of this inquiry. For this reason I shall make some further remarks upon it, after doing justice to the ingenious Dr. Porterfield, who, long ago in the " Medical Essays," and more lately in his " Treatise of the Eye," pointed out, as a primary law of our nature, " That a visible object appears in the direction of a right line perpendicular to the retina at that point where its image is painted." If lines drawn from the centre of the eye to all parts of the retina be perpendicular to it, as they must be very nearly, this coincides with the law we have mentioned, and is the same in other words. In

* Vide preceding page.

order, therefore, that we may have a more distinct notion of this law of our constitution, we may observe,

1. That we can give no reason why the retina is, of all parts of the body, the only one on which pictures made by the rays of light cause vision : and therefore we must resolve this solely into a law of our constitution. We may form such pictures, by means of optical glasses, upon the hand, or upon any other part of the body; but they are not felt, nor do they produce any thing like vision. A picture upon the retina is as little felt as one upon the hand; but it produces vision; for no other reason, that we know, but because it is destined by the wisdom of nature to this purpose. The vibrations of the air strike upon the eye, the palate, and the olfactory membrane, with the same force as upon the membrana tympani of the ear: the impression they make upon the last produces the sensation of sound; but their impression upon any of the former produces no sensation at all. This may be extended to all the senses, whereof each hath its peculiar laws, according to which, the impressions made upon the organ of that sense produce sensations or perceptions in the mind that cannot be produced by impressions made upon any other organ.

2. We may observe, that the laws of perception, by the different senses, are very different, not only in respect of the nature of the objects perceived by them, but likewise in respect of the notices they give us of the distance and situation of the object. In all of them the object is conceived to be external, and to have real existence, independent of our perception: but in one, the distance, figure, and situation of the object, are all presented to the mind; in another, the figure and situation, but not the distance; and in others, neither figure, situation, nor distance. In vain do we attempt to account for these varieties in the manner of perception by the different senses, from principles of anatomy or natural philosophy. They must at last be resolved into the will of our Maker, who intended that our powers of perception should have certain limits, and adapted the organs of perception, and the laws of nature by which they operate, to his wise purposes.

When we hear an unusual sound, the sensation indeed is in the mind, but we know that there is something external that produced this sound. At the same time our hearing does not inform us, whether the sounding body is near or at a distance, in this direction or that: and therefore we look round to discover it.

If any new phenomenon appears in the heavens, we see exactly its colour, its apparent place, magnitude, and figure; but we see not its distance. It may be in the atmosphere, it may be among the planets, or it may be in the sphere of the fixed stars, for any thing the eye can determine.

The testimony of the sense of touch reaches only to objects that are contiguous to the organ, but with regard to them is more precise and determinate. When we feel a body with our hand, we know the figure, distance, and position of it, as well as whether it is rough or smooth, hard or soft, hot or cold.

The sensations of touch, of seeing, and hearing, are all in the mind, and can have no existence but when they are perceived. How do they all constantly and invariably suggest the conception and belief of external objects, which exist whether they are perceived or not? No philosopher can give any other answer to this, but that such is the constitution of our nature. How do we know that the object of touch is at the finger's end, and no where else? that the object of sight is in such a direction from the eye, and in no other, but may be at any distance? and that the object of hearing may be at any distance, and in any direction? Not by custom, surely; not by reasoning, or comparing ideas; but by the constitution of our nature. How do we perceive visible objects in the direction of right lines perpendicular to that part of the retina on which their rays strike, while we do not perceive the objects of hearing in lines perpendicular to the membrana tympani, upon which the vibrations of the air strike? Because such are the laws of our nature. How do we know the parts of our bodies affected by particular pains? Not by experience or reasoning, but by the constitution of nature. The sensation of pain is, no doubt, in the mind, and cannot be said to have any relation from its own nature to any part of the body; but this sensation, by our constitution, gives a perception of some particular part of the body, whose disorder causes the uneasy sensation. If it were not so, a man who never before felt either the gout or the tooth-ache, when he is first seized with the gout in his toe, might mistake it for the tooth-ache.

Every sense, therefore, hath its peculiar laws and limits, by the constitution of our nature; and one of the laws of sight is, that we always see an object in the direction of a right line passing from its image on the retina through the centre of the eye.

3. Perhaps some readers will imagine that it is easier, and will answer the purpose as well, to conceive a law of nature, by which we shall always see objects in the place in which they are, and in their true position, without having recourse to images on the retina, or to the optical centre of the eye.

To this I answer, That nothing can be a law of nature which is contrary to fact. The laws of nature are the most general facts we can discover in the operations of nature. Like other facts, they are not to be hit upon by a happy conjecture, but justly deduced from observation: like other general facts, they are not to be drawn from a few particulars, but from a copious, patient, and cautious induction. That we see things always in their true place and position, is not fact; and therefore it can be no law of nature. In a plain mirror, I see myself, and other things, in places very different from those they really occupy. And so it happens in every instance, wherein the rays coming from the object are either reflected or refracted before falling upon the eye. Those who know any thing of optics, know that, in all such cases, the object is seen in the direction of a line passing from the centre of the eye to the point where the rays were last reflected or refracted; and that upon this all the powers of the telescope and microscope depend.

Shall we say, then, that it is a law of nature that the object is seen in the direction which the rays have when they fall on the eye, or rather in the direction contrary to that of the rays when they fall upon the eye? No. This is not true; and therefore it is no law of nature. For the rays, from any one point of the object, come to all parts of the pupil; and therefore must have different directions: but we see the object only in one of these directions, to wit, in the direction of the rays that come to the centre of the eye. And this holds true, even when the rays that should pass through the centre are stopped, and the object is seen by rays that pass at a distance from the centre.

Perhaps it may still be imagined, that although we are not made so as to see objects always in their *true place*, nor so as to see them precisely in the direction of the rays when they fall upon the cornea; yet we may be so made as to see the object in the direction which the rays have when they fall upon the retina, after they have undergone all their refractions in the eye, that is, in the direction in which the rays pass from the crystalline to the retina. But neither is this true; and consequently it is no law of our constitution. In order to see that it is not true, we must conceive all the rays that pass from the crystalline to one point of the retina, as forming a small cone, whose base is upon the back of the crystalline, and whose vertex is a point of the retina. It is evident that the rays which form the picture in this point, have various directions, even after they pass the crystalline; yet the object is seen only in one of these directions, to wit, in the direction of the rays that come from the centre of the eye. Nor is this owing to any particular virtue in the central rays, or in the centre itself; for the central rays may be stopped. When they are stopped, the image will be formed upon the same point of the retina as before, by rays that are not central, nor have the same direction which the central rays had: and in this case the object is seen in the same direction as before, although there are now no rays coming in that direction.

From this induction we conclude, that our seeing an object in that particular direction in which we do see it, is not owing to any law of nature by which we are made to see it in the direction of the rays, either before their refractions in the eye, or after, but " to a law of our nature, by which we see the object in the direction of the right line that passeth from the picture of the object upon the retina to the centre of the eye."

The facts upon which I ground this induction, are taken from some curious experiments of Scheiner, in his "Fundament. Optic." quoted by Dr. Porterfield, and confirmed by his experience. I have also repeated these experiments, and found them to answer. As they are easily made, and tend to illustrate and confirm the law of nature I have mentioned, I shall recite them as briefly and distinctly as I can.

Experiment 1. Let a very small object, such as the head of a pin, well illuminated, be fixed at such a distance from the eye, as to be beyond the nearest limit and within the farthest limit of distinct vision. For a young eye, not near-sighted, the object may be placed at the distance of eighteen inches. Let the eye be kept steadily in one place, and take a distinct view of the object. We know from the principles of optics, that the rays from any one point of this object, whether they pass through the centre of the eye, or at any distance from the centre which the breadth of the pupil will permit, do all unite again in one point of the retina. We know, also, that these rays have different directions, both before they fall upon the eye, and after they pass through the crystalline.

Now we can see the object by any one small parcel of these rays, excluding the rest, by looking through a small pin-hole in a card. Moving this pin-hole over the various parts of the pupil, we can see the object, first by the rays that pass above the centre of the eye, then by the central rays, then by the rays that pass below the centre, and in like manner by the rays that pass on the right and left of the centre. Thus we view this object, successively, by rays that are central, and by rays that are not central; by rays that have different directions, and are variously inclined to each other, both when they fall upon the cornea, and when they fall upon the retina; but always by rays which fall upon the same point of the retina. And what is the event? It is this, that the object is seen in the same individual direction, whether seen by all these rays together, or by any one parcel of them.

Experiment 2. Let the object above mentioned be now placed within the nearest limit of distinct vision, that is, for an eye that is not near-sighted, at the distance of four or five inches. We know that, in this case, the rays coming from one point of the object, do not meet in one point of the retina, but spread over a small circular spot of it: the central rays occupying the centre of this circle, the rays that pass above the centre occupying the upper part of the circular spot, and so of the rest. And we know that the object is in this case seen confused, every point of it being seen, not in one, but in various directions. To remedy this confusion, we look at the object through the pin-hole, and while we move the pin-hole over the various parts of the pupil, the object does not keep its place, but seems to move in a contrary direction.

It is here to be observed, that when the pin-hole is carried upwards over the pupil, the picture of the object is carried upwards upon the retina, and the object at the same time seems to move downwards, so as to be always in the right line passing from the picture through the centre of the eye. It is likewise to be observed, that the rays which form the upper and the lower pictures upon the retina do not cross each other as in ordinary vision; yet still the higher picture shows the object lower, and the lower picture shows the object higher, in the same manner as when the rays cross each other. Whence we may observe, by the way, that this phenomenon of our seeing objects in a position contrary to that of their pictures upon the retina, does not depend upon the crossing of the rays, as Kepler and Des Cartes conceived.

Experiment 3. Other things remaining as in the last experiment, make three pin-holes in a straight line, so near, that the rays coming from the object through all the holes, may enter the pupil at the same time. In this case we have a very curious phenomenon; for the object is seen triple with one eye. And if you make more holes within the breadth of the pupil, you will see as many objects as there are holes. However, we shall suppose them only three; one on the right, one in the middle, and one on the left; in which case you see three objects standing in a line from right to left.

It is here to be observed, that there are three pictures on the retina; that on the left being formed by the rays which pass on the left of the eye's centre; the middle picture being formed by the central rays; and the right-hand picture by the rays which pass on the right of the eye's centre. It is further to be observed, that the object which appears on the right is not that which is seen through the hole on the right, but that which is seen through the hole on the left; and in like manner, the left-hand object is seen through the hole on the right, as is easily proved by covering the holes successively. So that, whatever is the direction of the rays which form the right-hand and left-hand pictures, still the right-hand picture shows a left-hand object, and the left-hand picture shows a right-hand object.

Experiment 4. It is easy to see how the two last experiments may be varied, by placing the object beyond the furthest limit of distinct vision. In order to make this experiment, I looked at a candle at the distance of ten feet, and put the eye of my spectacles behind the card, that the rays from the same point of the object might meet, and cross each other, before they reached the retina. In this case, as in the former, the candle was seen triple through the three pin-holes; but the candle on the right was seen through the hole on the right; and, on the contrary, the left-hand candle was seen through the hole on the left. In this experiment it is evident from the principles of optics, that the rays forming the several pictures on the retina cross each other a little before they reach the retina; and therefore the left-hand picture is formed by the rays which pass through the hole on the right : so that the position of the pictures is contrary to that of the holes by which they are formed; and therefore is also contrary to that of their objects, as we have found it to be in the former experiments.

These experiments exhibit several uncommon phenomena, that regard the apparent place, and the direction of visible objects from the eye; phenomena that seem to be most contrary to the common rules of vision. When we look at the same time through three holes that are in a right line, and at certain distances from each other, we expect that the objects seen through them should really be, and should appear to be, at a distance from each other: yet, by the first experiment, we may, through three such holes, see the same object, and the same point of that object; and through all the three it appears in the same individual place and direction.

When the rays of light come from the object in right lines to the eye, without any reflection, inflection, or refraction, we expect that the object should appear in its real and proper direction from the eye ; and so it commonly does : but in the second, third, and fourth experiments we see the object in a direction which is not its true and real direction from the eye, although the rays come from the object to the eye, without any inflection, reflection, or refraction.

When both the object and the eye are fixed without the least motion, and the medium unchanged, we expect that the object should appear to rest, and keep the same place. Yet in the second and fourth experiments, when both the eye and the object are at rest, and the medium unchanged, we make the object appear to move upwards or downwards, or in any direction we please.

When we look at the same time, and with the same eye, through holes that stand in a line from right to left, we expect, that the object seen through the left-hand hole should appear on the left, and the object seen through the right-hand hole should appear on the right. Yet in the third experiment, we find the direct contrary. Although many instances occur of seeing the same object double with two eyes, we always expect that it should appear single when seen only by one eye. Yet in the second and fourth experiments, we have instances wherein the same object may appear double, triple, or quadruple to one eye, without the help of a polyhedron or multiplying glass.

All these extraordinary phenomena, regarding the direction of visible objects from the eye, as well as those that are common and ordinary, lead us to that law of nature which I have mentioned, and are the necessary consequences of it. [And, as there is no probability that we shall ever be able to give a reason why pictures upon the retina should make us see external objects, any more than pictures upon the hand or upon the cheek; or that we shall ever be able to give a reason why we should see the object in the direction of a line passing from its picture through the centre of the eye, rather than in any other direction; I am therefore apt to look upon this law *as a primary law of our constitution.*]

To prevent being misunderstood, I beg the reader to observe, that I do not mean to affirm, that the picture upon the retina will make us see an object in the direction mentioned, or in any direction, unless the optic nerve, and the other more immediate instruments of vision, be sound, and perform their function. We know not well what is the office of the optic nerve, nor in what manner it performs that office; but that it hath some part in the faculty of seeing, seems to be certain; because, in an amaurosis, which is believed to be a disorder of the optic nerve, the pictures on the retina are clear and distinct, and yet there is no vision.

We know still less of the use and function of the choroid membrane; but it seems likewise to be necessary to vision: for it is well known, that pictures upon that part of the retina where it is not covered by the choroid, I mean at the entrance of the optic nerve, produce no vision, any more than a picture upon the hand. We acknowledge, therefore, that the retina is not the last and most immediate instrument of the mind in vision. There are other material organs, whose operation is necessary to seeing, even after the pictures upon the retina are formed. If ever we come to know the structure and use of the choroid membrane, the optic nerve, and the brain, and what impressions are made upon them by means of the pictures on the retina, some more links of the chain may be brought within our view, and a more general law of vision discovered: but while we know so little of the nature and office of these more immediate instruments of vision, it seems to be impossible to trace its laws beyond the pictures upon the retina.

Neither do I pretend to say, that there may not be diseases of the eye, or accidents, which may occasion our seeing objects in a direction somewhat different from that mentioned above. I shall beg leave to mention one instance of this kind that concerns myself.

In May, 1761, being occupied in making an exact meridian, in order to observe the transit of Venus, I rashly directed to the sun, by my right eye, the cross hairs of a small telescope. I had often done the like in my younger days with impunity; but I suffered by it at last, which I mention as a warning to others.

I soon observed a remarkable dimness in that eye; and for many weeks, when I was in the dark, or shut my eyes, there appeared before the right eye a lucid spot, which trembled much like the image of the sun seen by reflection from water. This appearance grew fainter and less frequent by degrees; so that now there are seldom any remains of it. But some other very sensible effects of this hurt still remain. For, first, The sight of the right eye continues to be more dim than that of the left. Secondly, The nearest limit of distinct vision is more remote in the right eye than in the other; although, before the time mentioned, they were equal in both these respects, as I had found by many trials. But, thirdly, What I chiefly intended to mention is, that a straight line, in some circumstances, appears to the right eye to have a curvature in it. Thus, when I look upon a music-book, and, shutting my left eye, direct the right to a point of the middle line of the five which compose the staff of music, the middle line appears dim indeed, at the point to which the eye is directed, but straight; at the same time the two lines above it, and the two below it, appear to be bent outwards, and to be more distant from each other, and from the middle line, than at other parts of the staff, to which the eye is not directed. Fourthly, Although I have repeated this experiment times innumerable, within these sixteen months, I do not find that custom and experience take away this appearance of curvature in straight lines. Lastly, This appearance of curvature is perceptible when I look with the right eye only, but not when I look with both eyes: yet I see better with both eyes together than even with the left eye alone.

I have related this fact minutely as it is, without regard to any hypothesis, because I think such uncommon facts deserve to be recorded. I shall leave it to others to conjecture the cause of this appearance. To me it seems most probable, that a small part of the retina towards the centre is shrunk, and that thereby the contiguous parts are drawn nearer to the centre, and to one another, than they were before; and that objects whose images fall on these parts appear at that distance from each other which corresponds, not to the interval of the parts in their present preternatural contraction, but to their interval in their natural and sound state.

XIII. *Of seeing objects single with two eyes.*—Another phenomenon of vision which deserves attention, is our seeing objects single with two eyes. There are two pictures of the object, one on each retina; and each picture by itself makes us see an object in a certain direction from the eye: yet both together commonly make us see only one object. All the accounts or solutions of this phenomenon given by anatomists and philosophers seem to be unsatisfactory. I shall pass over the opinions of Galen, of Gassendus, of Baptista Porta, and of Rohault. The reader may see these examined and refuted by Dr. Porterfield. I shall examine Dr. Porterfield's own opinion, Bishop Berkeley's, and some others. But it will be necessary first to ascertain the facts; for if we mistake the phenomena of single and double vision, it is ten to one but this mistake will lead us wrong in assigning the causes. This likewise we ought carefully to attend to, which is acknowledged in theory by all who have any true judgment or just taste in inquiries of this nature, but is very often overlooked in practice, namely, That in the solution of natural phenomena, all the length that the human faculties can carry us, is only this, that from particular phenomena, we may, by induction, trace out general phenomena, of which all the particular ones are necessary consequences. And when we have arrived at the most general phenomena we can reach, there we must stop. If it is asked, Why such a body gravitates towards the earth? all the answer that can be given is, Because all bodies gravitate towards the earth. This is resolving a particular phenomenon into a general one. If it should again be asked, Why do all bodies gravitate towards the earth? we can give no other solution of this phenomenon, but that all bodies whatsoever gravitate towards each other. This again is resolving a general phenomenon into a more general one. If it should be asked, Why all bodies gravitate to one another? we cannot tell; but if we could tell, it could only be by resolving this universal gravitation of bodies into some other phenomenon still more general, and of which the gravitation of all bodies is a particular instance. The most general phenomena we can reach, are what we call *laws of nature*. So that the laws of nature are nothing else but the most general facts relating to the operations of nature, which include a great many particular facts under them. And if in any case we should give the name of a law of nature to a general phenomenon, which human industry shall afterwards trace to one more general, there is no great harm done. The most general assumes the name of a law of nature, when it is discovered; and the less general is contained and comprehended in it. Having premised these things, we proceed to consider the phenomena of single and double vision, in order to discover some general principle to which they all lead, and of which they are the necessary consequences. If we can discover any such general principle, it must either be a law of nature, or the necessary consequence of some law of nature; and its authority will be equal, whether it is the first or the last.

1. We find, that when the eyes are sound and perfect, and the axes of both directed to one point, an object placed in that point is seen single: and here we observe, that in this case the two pictures which show the object single, are in the centres of the retinæ. When two pictures of a small object are formed upon points of the retinæ, if they show the object single, we shall, for the sake of perspicuity, call such two points of the retinæ *corresponding points;* and where the object is seen double, we shall call the points of the retinæ on which the pictures are formed, *points that do not correspond.* Now, in this first phenomenon it is evident, that the two centres of the retinæ are corresponding points.

2. Supposing the same things as in the last phenomenon, other objects at the same distance from the eyes as that to which their axes are directed, do also appear single. Thus, if I direct my eyes to a candle placed at the distance of ten feet; and, while I look at this candle, another stands at the same distance from my eyes, within the field of vision; I can, while I look at the first candle, attend to the appearance which the second makes to the eye; and I find that in this case it always appears single. It is here to be observed, that the pictures of the second candle do not fall upon the centres of the retinæ, but they both fall upon the same side of the centres, that is, both to the right, or both to the left, and both are at the same distance from the centres. This might easily be demonstrated from the principles of optics. Hence it appears, that in this second phenomenon of single vision, the corresponding points are points of the two retinæ, which are similarly situate with respect to the two centres, being both upon the same side of the centre, and at the same distance from it. It appears, likewise, from this phenomenon, that every point in one retina corresponds with that which is similarly situate in the other.

3. Supposing still the same things, objects which are much nearer to the eyes, or much more distant from them, than that to which the two eyes are directed, appear double. Thus, if the candle is placed at the distance of ten feet, and I hold my finger at arm's-length between my eyes and the candle, when I look at the candle, I see my finger double; and when I look at my finger, I see the candle double: and the same thing happens with regard to all other objects at like distances which fall within

the sphere of vision. In this phenomenon it is evident to those who understand the principles of optics, that the pictures of the objects which are seen double, do not fall upon points of the retinæ which are similarly situate, but that the pictures of the objects seen single do fall upon points similarly situate. Whence we infer, that as the points of the two retinæ which are similarly situate with regard to the centres, do correspond, so those which are dissimilarly situate do not correspond.

4. It is to be observed, that although in such cases as are mentioned in the last phenomenon, we have been accustomed from infancy to see objects double which we know to be single; yet custom, and experience of the unity of the object, never take away this appearance of duplicity.

5. It may however be remarked, that the custom of attending to visible appearances has a considerable effect, and makes the phenomenon of double vision to be more or less observed and remembered. Thus you may find a man that can say with a good conscience, that he never saw things double all his life. Yet this very man, put in the situation above mentioned, with his finger between him and the candle, and desired to attend to the appearance of the object which he does not look at, will, upon the first trial, see the candle double, when he looks at his finger; and his finger double, when he looks at the candle. Does he now see otherwise than he saw before? No, surely, but he now attends to what he never attended to before. The same double appearance of an object hath been a thousand times presented to his eye before now; but he did not attend to it; and so it is as little an object of his reflection and memory, as if it had never happened.

When we look at an object, the circumjacent objects may be seen at the same time, although more obscurely and indistinctly; for the eye hath a considerable field of vision, which it takes in at once. But we attend only to the object we look at. The other objects which fall within the field of vision are not attended to, and therefore are as if they were not seen. If any of them draws our attention, it naturally draws the eyes at the same time, (for in the common course of life, the eyes always follow the attention,) or if at any time, in a reverie, they are separated from it, we hardly at that time see what is directly before us. Hence we may see the reason, why the man we are speaking of thinks that he never before saw an object double. When he looks at any object, he sees it single, and takes no notice of other visible objects at that time, whether they appear single or double. If any of them draws his attention, it draws his eyes at the same time; and as soon as the eyes are turned towards it, it appears single. But in order to see things double, at least in order to have any reflection or remembrance that he did so, it is necessary that he should look at one object, and at the same time attend to the faint appearance of other objects which are within the field of vision. This is a practice which perhaps he never used, nor attempted; and therefore he does not recollect that ever he saw an object double. But when he is put upon giving this attention, he immediately sees objects double in the same manner, and with the very same circumstances, as they who have been accustomed, for the greatest part of their lives, to give this attention.

There are many phenomena of a similar nature, which show that the mind may not attend to, and thereby, in some sort, not perceive, objects that strike the senses. I had occasion to mention several instances of this in the second chapter; and I have been assured, by persons of the best skill in music, that in hearing a tune upon the harpsichord, when they give attention to the treble, they do not hear the bass; and when they attend to the bass, they do not perceive the air of the treble. Some persons are so near-sighted, that, in reading, they hold the book to one eye, while the other is directed to other objects. Such persons acquire the habit of attending in this case to the objects of one eye, while they give no attention to those of the other.

6. It is observable, that in all cases wherein we see an object double, the two appearances have a certain position with regard to one another, and a certain apparent or angular distance. This apparent distance is greater or less in different circumstances; but in the same circumstances, it is always the same, not only to the same, but to different persons.

Thus, in the experiment above mentioned, if twenty different persons, who see perfectly with both eyes, shall place their finger and the candle at the distances above expressed, and hold their heads upright, looking at the finger, they will see two candles, one on the right, another on the left. That which is seen on the right, is seen by the right eye, and that which is seen on the left, by the left eye; and they will see them at the same apparent distance from each other. If again they look at the candle, they will see two fingers, one on the right, and the other on the left; and all will see them at the same apparent distance; the finger towards the left being seen by the right eye, and the other by the left. If the head is laid horizontally to one side, other circumstances remaining the same, one appearance of the object seen double, will be directly above the other. In a word, vary the circumstances as you please, and the appearances are varied to all the spectators in one and the same manner.

7. Having made many experiments in order to ascertain the apparent distance of the two appearances of an object seen double, I have found, that in all cases this apparent distance is proportioned to the distance between the point of the retina, where the picture is made in one eye, and the point which is situate similarly to that on which the picture is made on the other eye.

So that as the apparent distance of two objects seen with one eye, is proportioned to the arch of the retina, which lies between their pictures; in like manner, when an object is seen double with the two eyes, the apparent distance of the two appearances is proportioned to the arch of either retina, which lies between the picture in that retina, and the point corresponding to that of the picture in the other retina.

8. As in certain circumstances we invariably see one object appear double, so in others we as invariably see two objects unite into one; and in appearance lose their duplicity. This is evident in the appearance of the binocular telescope. And the same thing happens when any two similar tubes are applied to the two eyes in a parallel direction; for in this case we see only one tube. And if two shillings are placed at the extremities of the two tubes, one exactly in the axis of one eye, and the other in the axis of the other eye, we shall see but one shilling. If two pieces of coin, or other bodies, of different colour, and of different figure, be properly placed in the two axes of the eyes, and at the extremities of the tubes, we shall see both the bodies in one and the same place, each as it were spread over the other, without hiding it; and the colour will be that which is compounded of the two colours.

9. From these phenomena, and from all the trials I have been able to make, it appears evidently, that in perfect human eyes, the centres of the two retinæ correspond and harmonize with one another; and that every other point in one retina, doth correspond and harmonize with the point which is similarly situate in the other; in such manner, that pictures falling on the corresponding points of the two retinæ, show only one object, even when there are really two; and pictures falling upon points of the retinæ which do not correspond, show us two visible appearances, although there be but one object. So that pictures upon corresponding points of the two retinæ, present the same appearance to the mind as if they had both fallen upon the same point of one retina; and pictures upon points of the two retinæ which do not correspond, present to the mind the same apparent distance and position of two objects, as if one of those pictures was carried to the point corresponding to it in the other retina. This relation and sympathy between corresponding points of the two retinæ, I do not advance as an hypothesis, but as a general fact or phenomenon of vision. All the phenomena before mentioned, of single or double vision, lead to it, and are necessary consequences of it. It holds true invariably in all perfect human eyes, as far as I am able to collect from innumerable trials of various kinds made upon my own eyes, and many made by others at my desire. Most of the hypotheses that have been contrived to resolve the phenomena of single and double vision, suppose

this general fact, while their authors were not aware of it. Sir Isaac Newton, who was too judicious a philosopher, and too accurate an observer, to have offered even a conjecture which did not tally with the facts that had fallen under his observation, proposes a query with respect to the cause of it, "Optics," quer. 15. The judicious Dr. Smith, in his "Optics," lib. 1. § 137, hath confirmed the truth of this general phenomenon from his own experience, not only as to the apparent unity of objects whose pictures fall upon the corresponding points of the retinæ, but also as to the apparent distance of the two appearances of the same object when seen double.

This general phenomenon appears, therefore, to be founded upon a very full induction, which is all the evidence we can have for a fact of this nature. Before we make an end of this subject, it will be proper to inquire, first, Whether those animals whose eyes have an adverse position in their heads, and look contrary ways, have such corresponding points in their retinæ? Secondly, What is the position of the corresponding points in imperfect human eyes, I mean in those that squint? And, in the last place, Whether this harmony of the corresponding points in the retinæ be natural and original, or the effect of custom? And if it is original, Whether it can be accounted for by any of the laws of nature already discovered? or whether it is itself to be looked upon as a law of nature, and a part of the human constitution?

XIV. *Of the laws of vision in brute animals.*—It is the intention of nature, in giving eyes to animals, that they may perceive the situation of visible objects, or the direction in which they are placed: it is probable, therefore, that in ordinary cases, every animal, whether it has many eyes or few, whether of one structure or of another, sees objects single and in their true and proper direction. And since there is a prodigious variety in the structure, the motions, and the number of eyes in different animals and insects, it is probable that the laws by which vision is regulated, are not the same in all, but various, adapted to the eyes which nature hath given them.

Mankind naturally turn their eyes always the same way, so that *the axes of the two eyes meet in one point.* They naturally attend to, or look at that object only which is placed in the point where the axes meet. And whether the object be more or less distant, the configuration of the eye is adapted to the distance of the object, so as to form a distinct picture of it.

When we use our eyes in this natural way, the two pictures of the object we look at, are formed upon the centres of the two retinæ; and the two pictures of any contiguous object are formed upon points of the retinæ which are similarly situate with regard to the centres. Therefore, in order to our seeing objects single, and in their proper direction, with two eyes, it is sufficient that we be so constituted, that objects whose pictures are formed upon the centres of the two retinæ, or upon points similarly situate with regard to these centres, shall be seen in the same visible place. And this is the constitution which nature hath actually given to human eyes.

When we distort our eyes from their parallel direction, which is an unnatural motion, but may be learned by practice; or when we direct the axes of the two eyes to one point, and at the same time direct our attention to some visible object much nearer or much more distant than that point, which is also unnatural, yet may be learned; in these cases, and in these only, we see one object double, or two objects confounded in one. In these cases, the two pictures of the same object are formed upon points of the retinæ which are not similarly situate, and so the object is seen double, or the two pictures of different objects are formed upon points of the retinæ which are similarly situate, and so the two objects are seen confounded in one place.

Thus it appears that the laws of vision in the human constitution are wisely adapted to the natural use of human eyes, but not to that use of them which is unnatural. We see objects truly when we use our eyes in the natural way; but have false appearances presented to us when we use them in a way that is unnatural. We may reasonably think, that the case is the same with other animals. But is it not unreasonable to think, that those animals which naturally turn one eye towards one object, and another towards another, must thereby have such false appearances presented to them, as we have when we do so against nature?

☞ Many animals have their eyes by nature placed adverse and immoveable, the axes of the two eyes being always directed to opposite points. Do objects painted on the centres of the two retinæ appear to such animals as they do to human eyes, in one and the same visible place? I think it is highly probable that they do not; and that they appear, as they really are, in opposite places.

If we judge from analogy in this case, it will lead us to think, that there is a certain correspondence between points of the two retinæ in such animals, but of a different kind from that which we have found in human eyes. The centre of one retina will correspond with the centre of the other, in such manner that the objects whose pictures are formed upon these corresponding points, shall appear not to be in the same place as in human eyes, but in opposite places. And in the same manner will the superior part of one retina correspond with the inferior part of the other, and the anterior part of one with the posterior part of the other.

Some animals, by nature, turn their eyes with equal facility, either the same way, or different ways, as we turn our hands and arms. Have such animals corresponding points in their retinæ, and points which do not correspond, as the human kind has? I think it is probable that they have not; because such a constitution in them could serve no other purpose but to exhibit false appearances.

If we judge from analogy, it will lead us to think that as such animals move their eyes in a manner similar to that in which we move our arms, they have an immediate and natural perception of the direction they give to their eyes, as we have of the direction we give to our arms, and perceive the situation of visible objects by their eyes, in a manner similar to that in which we perceive the situation of tangible objects with our hands.

We cannot teach brute animals to use their eyes in any other way than in that which nature hath taught them; nor can we teach them to communicate to us the appearances which visible objects make to them, either in ordinary or in extraordinary cases. We have not, therefore, the same means of discovering the laws of vision in them as in our own kind, but must satisfy ourselves with probable conjectures: and what we have said upon this subject is chiefly intended to show that animals to which nature hath given eyes differing in their number, in their position, and in their natural motions, may very probably be subjected to different laws of vision, adapted to the peculiarities of their organs of vision.

XV. *The phenomena of squinting considered hypothetically.*— Whether there be corresponding points in the retinæ of those who have an involuntary squint? and if there are, whether they be situate in the same manner as in those who have no squint? are not questions of mere curiosity. They are of real importance to the physician who attempts the cure of a squint, and to the patient who submits to the cure. After so much hath been said of the strabismus, or squint, both by medical and by optical writers, one might expect to find abundance of facts for determining these questions. Yet I confess I have been disappointed in this expectation, after taking some pains both to make observations, and to collect those which have been made by others.

Nor will this appear very strange, if we consider, that to make the observations which are necessary for determining these questions, knowledge of the principles of optics, and of the laws of vision, must concur with opportunities rarely to be met with.

Of those who squint, the far greater part have no distinct vision with one eye. When this is the case, it is impossible, and indeed of no importance, to determine the situation of the corresponding points. When both eyes are good, they commonly differ so much in their direction, that the same object cannot be seen by both at the same time: and in this case it will be very difficult to determine the situation of the corresponding points;

for such persons will probably attend only to the objects of one eye, and the objects of the other will be as little regarded as if they were not seen.

We have before observed, that when we look at a near object, and attend to it, we do not perceive the double appearances of more distant objects, even when they are in the same direction, and are presented to the eye at the same time. It is probable that a squinting person, when he attends to the objects of one eye, will, in like manner, have his attention totally diverted from the objects of the other; and that he will perceive them as little as we perceive the double appearances of objects when we use our eyes in the natural way. Such a person, therefore, unless he is so much a philosopher as to have acquired the habit of attending very accurately to the visible appearances of objects, and even of objects which he does not look at, will not be able to give any light to the questions now under consideration.

☞ It is very probable that hares, rabbits, birds, and fishes, whose eyes are fixed in an adverse position, have the natural faculty of *attending at the same time to visible objects placed in different, and even in contrary directions;* because, without this faculty, they could not have those advantages from the contrary direction of their eyes, which nature seems to have intended. But it is not probable that those who squint have any such natural faculty; because we find no such faculty in the rest of the species. We naturally attend to objects placed in the point where the axes of the two eyes meet, and to them only. To give attention to an object in a different direction is unnatural, and not to be learned without pains and practice.

A very convincing proof of this may be drawn from a fact now well known to philosophers: when one eye is shut, there is a certain space within the field of vision, where we can see nothing at all; the space which is directly opposed to that part of the bottom of the eye where the optic nerve enters. This defect of sight in one part of the eye, is common to all human eyes, and hath been so from the beginning of the world; yet it was never known, until the sagacity of the Abbé Mariotte discovered it in the last century. And now when it is known, it cannot be perceived, but by means of some particular experiments, which require care and attention to make them succeed.

What is the reason that so remarkable a defect of sight, common to all mankind, was so long unknown, and is now perceived with so much difficulty? It is surely this, that the defect is at some distance from the axis of the eye, and consequently in a part of the field of vision to which we never attend naturally, and to which we cannot attend at all, without the aid of some particular circumstances.

From what we have said it appears, that to determine the

situation of the corresponding points in the eyes of those who squint is impossible, if they do not see distinctly with both eyes; and that it will be very difficult, unless the two eyes differ so little in their direction, that the same object may be seen with both at the same time. Such patients I apprehend are rare; at least there are very few of them with whom I have had the fortune to meet; and therefore, for the assistance of those who may have happier opportunities, and inclination to make the proper use of them, we shall consider the case of squinting hypothetically, pointing out the proper articles of inquiry, the observations that are wanted, and the conclusions that may be drawn from them.

1. It ought to be inquired, whether the squinting person sees equally well with both eyes? and, if there be a defect in one, the nature and degree of that defect ought to be remarked. The experiments by which this may be done, are so obvious that I need not mention them. But I would advise the observer to make the proper experiments, and not to rely upon the testimony of the patient; because I have found many instances, both of persons that squinted, and others, who were found, upon trial, to have a great defect in the sight of one eye, although they were never aware of it before. In all the following articles it is supposed that the patient sees with both eyes so well, as to be able to read with either, when the other is covered.

2. It ought to be inquired, whether, when one eye is covered, the other is turned directly to the object? This ought to be tried in both eyes successively. By this observation, as a touchstone, we may try the hypothesis concerning squinting, invented by M. de la Hire, and adopted by Boerhaave, and many others of the medical faculty.

The hypothesis is, that in one eye of a squinting person, the greatest sensibility and the most distinct vision is not, as in other men, in the centre of the retina, but upon one side of the centre; and that he turns the axis of this eye aside from the object, in order that the picture of the object may fall upon the most sensible part of the retina, and thereby give the most distinct vision. If this is the cause of squinting, *the squinting eye will be turned aside from the object, when the other eye is covered, as well as when it is not.*

A trial so easy to be made, never was made, for more than forty years; but the hypothesis was very generally received. So prone are men to invent hypotheses, and so backward to examine them by facts. At last Dr. Jurin having made the trial, found that persons who squint, turn the axis of the squinting eye directly to the object, when the other eye is covered. This fact is confirmed by Dr. Porterfield; and I have found it verified in all the instances that have fallen under my observation.

3. It ought to be inquired, whether the axes of the two eyes follow one another, so as to have always the same inclination, or make the same angle, when the person looks to the right or to the left, upward or downward, or straight forward. By this observation we may judge, whether a squint is owing to any defect in the muscles which move the eye, as some have supposed. In the following articles we suppose that the inclination of the axes of the eyes is found to be always the same.

4. It ought to be inquired, whether the person that squints sees an object single or double?

If he sees the object double; and if the two appearances have an angular distance equal to the angle which the axes of his eyes make with each other, it may be concluded that he hath corresponding points in the retinæ of his eyes, and that they have the same situation as in those who have no squint. If the two appearances should have an angular distance which is always the same, but manifestly greater or less than the angle contained under the optic axes, this would indicate corresponding points in the retinæ, whose situation is not the same as in those who have no squint; but it is difficult to judge accurately of the angle which the optic axes make.

A squint too small to be perceived, may occasion double vision of objects: for if we speak strictly, every person squints more or less, whose optic axes do not meet exactly in the object which he looks at. Thus, if a man can only bring the axes of his eyes to be parallel, but cannot make them converge in the least, he must have a small squint in looking at near objects, and will see them double, while he sees very distant objects single. Again, if the optic axes always converge, so as to meet eight or ten feet before the face at farthest, such a person will see near objects single; but when he looks at very distant objects, he will squint a little, and see them double.

An instance of this kind is related by Aguilonius in his "Optics;" who says, that he had seen a young man to whom near objects appeared single, but distant objects appeared double.

Dr. Briggs, in his "Nova Visionis Theoria," having collected from authors several instances of double vision, quotes this from Aguilonius, as the most wonderful and unaccountable of all, in so much that he suspects some imposition on the part of the young man: but to those who understand the laws by which single and double vision are regulated, it appears to be the natural effect of a very small squint.

Double vision may always be owing to a small squint, when the two appearances are seen at a small angular distance, although no squint was observed: and I do not remember any instances of double vision recorded by authors, wherein any account is given of the angular distance of the appearances.

In almost all the instances of double vision, there is reason to suspect a squint or distortion of the eyes, from the concomitant circumstances, which we find to be one or other of the following, the approach of death, or of a deliquium, excessive drinking, or other intemperance, violent headach, blistering the head, smoking tobacco, blows or wounds in the head. In all these cases, it is reasonable to suspect a distortion of the eyes, either from spasm, or paralysis, in the muscles that move them. But although it be probable that there is always a squint greater or less where there is double vision; yet it is certain that there is not double vision always where there is a squint. I know no instance of double vision that continued for life, or even for a great number of years. We shall therefore suppose, in the following articles, that the squinting person sees objects single.

5. The next inquiry then ought to be, whether the object is seen with both eyes at the same time, or only with the eye whose axis is directed to it? It hath been taken for granted, by the writers upon the strabismus, before Dr. Jurin, that those who squint, commonly see objects single with both eyes at the same time; but I know not one fact advanced by any writer which proves it. Dr. Jurin is of a contrary opinion; and as it is of consequence, so it is very easy, to determine this point in particular instances, by this obvious experiment. While the person that squints looks steadily at an object, let the observer carefully remark the direction of both his eyes, and observe their motions; and let an opaque body be interposed between the object and the two eyes successively. If the patient, notwithstanding this interposition, and without changing the direction of his eyes, continues to see the object all the time, it may be concluded that he saw it with both eyes at once. But if the interposition of the body between one eye and the object, makes it disappear, then we may be certain, that it was seen by that eye only. In the two following articles we shall suppose the first to happen, according to the common hypothesis.

6. Upon this supposition it ought to be inquired, whether the patient sees an object double in those circumstances wherein it appears double to them who have no squint? Let him, for instance, place a candle at the distance of ten feet; and holding his finger at arm's length between him and the candle, let him observe, when he looks at the candle, whether he sees his finger with both eyes, and whether he sees it single or double; and when he looks at his finger, let him observe whether he sees the candle with both eyes, and whether single or double.

[By this observation, it may be determined, whether to this patient, the phenomena of double as well as of single vision are the same as to them who have no squint. If they are not the same; if he sees objects single with two eyes, not only in the cases wherein they appear single, but in those also wherein they appear double to other men; the conclusion to be drawn from this supposition is, that *his single vision does not arise from corresponding points in the retinæ of his eyes;* and that the laws of vision are not the same in him as in the rest of mankind.]

7. If, on the other hand, he sees objects double in those cases wherein they appear double to others, the conclusion must be, that he hath corresponding points in the retinæ of his eyes, but unnaturally situate; and their situation may be thus determined.

When he looks at an object, having the axis of one eye directed to it, and the axis of the other turned aside from it; let us suppose a right line to pass from the object through the centre of the diverging eye. We shall, for the sake of perspicuity, call this right line *the natural axis of the eye:* and it will make an angle with the real axis, greater or less, according as his squint is greater or less. We shall also call that point of the retina in which the natural axis cuts it, *the natural centre of the retina;* which will be more or less distant from the real centre, according as the squint is greater or less.

Having premised these definitions, it will be evident to those who understand the principles of optics, that in this person the natural centre of one retina corresponds with the real centre of the other, in the very same manner as the two real centres correspond in perfect eyes; and that the points similarly situate with regard to the real centre in one retina, and the natural centre in the other, do likewise correspond, in the very same manner as the points similarly situate with regard to the two real centres correspond in perfect eyes.

If it is true, as has been commonly affirmed, that one who squints sees an object with both eyes at the same time, and yet sees it single, the squint will most probably be such as we have described in this article. And we may farther conclude, that if a person affected with such a squint as we have supposed, could be brought to the habit of looking straight, his sight would thereby be greatly hurt. For he would then see every thing double which he saw with both eyes at the same time, and distant objects would appear to be confounded together. His eyes are made for squinting, as much as those of other men are made for looking straight; and his sight would be no less injured by looking straight, than that of another man by squinting. He can never see perfectly when he does not squint, unless the corresponding points of his eyes should by custom change their place; but how small the probability of this is, will appear in the seventeenth section.

Those of the medical faculty who attempt the cure of a squint, would do well to consider, whether it is attended with such symptoms as are above described. If it is, the cure would be worse than the malady: for every one will readily acknowledge, that it is better to put up with the deformity of a squint, than to purchase the cure by the loss of perfect and distinct vision.

8. We shall now return to Dr. Jurin's hypothesis, and suppose that our patient, when he saw objects single notwithstanding his squint, was found, upon trial, to have seen them only with one eye.

We would advise such a patient to endeavour, by repeated efforts, to lessen his squint, and to bring the axes of his eyes nearer to a parallel direction. We have naturally the power of making small variations in the inclination of the optic axes; and this power may be greatly increased by exercise.

In the ordinary and natural use of our eyes, we can direct their axes to a fixed star; in this case they must be parallel: we can direct them also to an object six inches distant from the eye; and in this case the axes must make an angle of fifteen or twenty degrees. We see young people in their frolics learn to squint, making their eyes either converge or diverge, when they will, to a very considerable degree. Why should it be more difficult for a squinting person to learn to look straight when he pleases? If once, by an effort of his will, he can but lessen his squint, frequent practice will make it easy to lessen it, and will daily increase his power. So that if he begins this practice in youth, and perseveres in it, he may probably, after some time, learn to direct both his eyes to one object.

When he hath acquired this power, it will be no difficult matter to determine, by proper observations, whether the centres of the retinæ, and other points similarly situate with regard to the centres, correspond, as in other men.

9. Let us now suppose that he finds this to be the case; and that he sees an object single with both eyes, when the axes of both are directed to it. It will then concern him to acquire the habit of looking straight, as he hath got the power, because he will thereby not only remove a deformity, but improve his sight: and I conceive this habit, like all others, may be got by frequent exercise. He may practise before a mirror when alone, and in company he ought to have those about him, who will observe and admonish him when he squints.

10. What is supposed in the 9th article is not merely imaginary; it is really the case of some squinting persons, as will appear in the next section. Therefore it ought further to be inquired, how it comes to pass, that such a person sees an object which he looks at only with one eye, when both are open. In order to answer this question, it may be observed, first, Whether, when he looks at an object, the diverging eye is not drawn so close to the nose, that it can have no distinct images? Or, secondly, Whether the pupil of the diverging eye is not covered

wholly, or in part, by the upper eye-lid? Dr. Jurin observed instances of these cases in persons that squinted, and assigns them as causes of their seeing the object only with one eye. Thirdly, it may be observed, Whether the diverging eye is not so directed, that the picture of the object falls upon that part of the retina where the optic nerve enters, and where there is no vision? This will probably happen in a squint wherein the axes of the eyes converge so as to meet about six inches before the nose.

11. In the last place, it ought to be inquired, whether such a person hath any distinct vision at all with the diverging eye, at the time he is looking at an object with the other?

It may seem very improbable that he should be able to read with the diverging eye when the other is covered; and yet, when both are open, have no distinct vision with it at all. But this perhaps will not appear so improbable, if the following considerations are duly attended to.

Let us suppose that one who saw perfectly gets, by a blow on the head, or some other accident, a permanent and involuntary squint. According to the laws of vision, he will see objects double, and will see distant objects confounded together: but such vision being very disagreeable, as well as inconvenient, he will do every thing in his power to remedy it. For alleviating such distresses, nature often teaches men wonderful expedients, which the sagacity of a philosopher would be unable to discover. Every accidental motion, every direction or conformation of his eyes, which lessens the evil, will be agreeable; it will be repeated until it be learned to perfection, and become habitual, even without thought or design. Now, in this case, what disturbs the sight of one eye, is the sight of the other; and all the disagreeable appearances in vision would cease, if the light of one eye was extinct: the sight of one eye will become more distinct and more agreeable in the same proportion as that of the other becomes faint and indistinct. It may therefore be expected, that every habit will, by degrees, be acquired, which tends to destroy distinct vision in one eye, while it is preserved in the other. These habits will be greatly facilitated, if one eye was at first better than the other; for in that case the best eye will always be directed to the object which he intends to look at, and every habit will be acquired which tends to hinder his seeing it at all or seeing it distinctly by the other at the same time.

I shall mention one or two habits that may probably be acquired in such a case; perhaps there are others which we cannot so easily conjecture. First, By a small increase or diminution of his squint, he may bring it to correspond with one or other of the cases mentioned in the last article. Secondly, The diverging eye may be brought to such a conformation as to be extremely short-sighted, and consequently to have no distinct vision of objects at a distance. I knew this to be the case of one person that squinted; but cannot say whether the short-sightedness of the diverging eye was original, or acquired by habit.

We see, therefore, that one who squints, and originally saw objects double by reason of that squint, may acquire such habits, that when he looks at an object, he shall see it only with one eye: nay, he may acquire such habits, that when he looks at an object with his best eye, he shall have no distinct vision with the other at all. Whether this is really the case, being unable to determine in the instances that have fallen under my observation, I shall leave to future inquiry.

I have endeavoured, in the foregoing articles, to delineate such a process as is proper in observing the phenomena of squinting. I know well by experience, that this process appears more easy in theory than it will be found to be in practice; and that, in order to carry it on with success, some qualifications of mind are necessary in the patient, which are not always to be met with. But if those who have proper opportunities, and inclination, to observe such phenomena, attend duly to this process, they may be able to furnish facts less vague and uninstructive than those we meet with, even in authors of reputation. By such facts, vain theories may be exploded, and our knowledge of the laws of nature which regard the noblest of our senses, enlarged.

XVI. *Facts relating to squinting.*— Having considered the phenomena of squinting hypothetically, and their connexion with corresponding points in the retinæ, I shall now mention the facts I have had occasion to observe myself, or to meet with in authors that can give any light to this subject.

Having examined above twenty persons that squinted, I found in all of them a defect in the sight of one eye. Four only had so much of distinct vision in the weak eye as to be able to read with it, when the other was covered. The rest saw nothing at all distinctly with one eye. Dr. Porterfield says that this is generally the case of people that squint: and I suspect it is so more generally than is commonly imagined. Dr. Jurin, in a very judicious dissertation upon squinting, printed in Dr. Smith's "Optics," observes, that those who squint, and see with both eyes, never see the same object with both at the same time; that when one eye is directed straight forward to an object, the other is drawn so close to the nose, that the object cannot at all be seen by it, the images being too oblique and too indistinct to affect the eye. In some squinting persons, he observed the diverging eye drawn under the upper eye-lid while the other was directed to the object. From these observations he concludes, that the eye is thus distorted, "not for the sake of seeing better with it, but rather to avoid seeing at all with it as much as possible." From all the observations he had made, he was satisfied that there is nothing peculiar in the structure of a squinting eye; that the fault is only in its wrong direction; and that this wrong direction is got by habit. Therefore he proposes that method of cure which we have described in the 8th and 9th articles of the last section. He tells us, that he had attempted a cure after this method, upon a young gentleman, with promising hopes of success, but was interrupted by his falling ill of the small pox, of which he died.

It were to be wished that Dr. Jurin had acquainted us whether he ever brought the young man to direct the axes of both eyes to the same object, and whether, in that case, he saw the object single, and saw it with both eyes: and that he had likewise acquainted us whether he saw objects double when his squint was diminished. But as to these facts he is silent.

I wished long for an opportunity of trying Dr. Jurin's method of curing a squint, without finding one; having always, upon examination, discovered so great a defect in the sight of one eye of the patient as discouraged the attempt.

But I have lately found three young gentlemen, with whom I am hopeful this method may have success, if they have patience and perseverance in using it. Two of them are brothers, and, before I had access to examine them, had been practising this method by the direction of their tutor, with such success, that the elder looks straight when he is upon his guard: the younger can direct both his eyes to one object; but they soon return to their usual squint.

A third young gentleman, who had never heard of this method before, by a few days' practice was able to direct both his eyes to one object, but could not keep them long in that direction. All the three agree in this, that when both eyes are directed to one object, they see it and the adjacent objects single; but when they squint, they see objects sometimes single and sometimes double. I observed of all the three, that when they squinted most, that is, in the way they had been accustomed to, the axes of their eyes converged so as to meet five or six inches before the nose. It is probable that in this case the picture of the object in the diverging eye, must fall upon that part of the retina where the optic nerve enters; and therefore the object could not be seen by that eye.

All the three have some defect in the sight of one eye, which none of them knew until I put them upon making trials; and when they squint, the best eye is always directed to the object, and the weak eye is that which diverges from it. But when the best eye is covered, the weak eye is turned directly to the object. Whether this defect of sight in one eye be the effect of its having been long disused, as it must have been when they squinted, or whether some original defect in one eye might be the occasion of their squinting, time may discover. The two brothers have found the sight of the weak eye improved by using to read with it while the other is covered. The elder can read an ordinary print with the weak eye; the other, as well as the third gentleman, can only read a large print with the weak eye.

I have met with one other person only who squinted, and yet could read a large print with the weak eye. He is a young man whose eyes are both tender and weak-sighted, but the left much weaker than the right. When he looks at any object, he always directs the right eye to it, and then the left is turned towards the nose so much, that it is impossible for him to see the same object with both eyes at the same time. When the right eye is covered, he turns the left directly to the object; but he sees it indistinctly, and as if it had a mist about it.

I made several experiments, some of them in the company and with the assistance of an ingenious physician, in order to discover whether objects that were in the axes of the two eyes were seen in one place confounded together, as in those who have no involuntary squint. The object placed in the axis of the weak eye was a lighted candle, at the distance of eight or ten feet. Before the other eye we placed a printed book, at such a distance as that he could read upon it. He said that while he read upon the book, he saw the candle, but very faintly. And from what we could learn, these two objects did not appear in one place, but had all that angular distance in appearance which they had in reality.

If this was really the case, the conclusion to be drawn from it is, that the corresponding points in his eyes are not situate in the same manner as in other men; and that if he could be brought to direct both eyes to one object, he would see it double. But considering that the young man had never been accustomed to observations of this kind, and that the sight of one eye was so imperfect, I do not pretend to draw this conclusion with certainty from this single instance.

All that can be inferred from these facts is, that of four persons who squint, three appear to have nothing preternatural in the structure of their eyes. The centres of their retinæ, and the points similarly situate with regard to the centres, do certainly correspond in the same manner as in other men. So that if they can be brought to the habit of directing their eyes right to an object, they will not only remove a deformity, but improve their sight. With regard to the fourth, the case is dubious, with probability of a deviation from the usual course of nature in the situation of the corresponding points of his eyes.

XVII. *Of the effect of custom in seeing objects single.*—It appears from the phenomena of single and double vision, recited in sect. 13, that our seeing an object single with two eyes, depends upon these two things. *First*, upon that mutual correspondence of certain points of the retinæ which we have often described. *Secondly*, upon the two eyes being directed to the object so accurately, that the two images of it fall upon corresponding points. These two things must concur in order to our seeing an object single with two eyes; and as far as they depend upon custom, so far only can single vision depend upon custom.

With regard to the second, that is, the accurate direction of both eyes to the object, I think it must be acknowledged that this is only learned by custom. Nature hath wisely ordained the eyes to move in such manner, that their axes shall always be nearly parallel; but hath left it in our power to vary their inclination a little, according to the distance of the object we look at. Without this power, objects would appear single at one particular distance only; and at distances much less, or much greater, would always appear double. The wisdom of nature is conspicuous in giving us this power, and no less conspicuous in making the extent of it exactly adequate to the end.

[*The parallelism of the eyes* in general, is therefore *the work of nature;* but that precise and *accurate direction*, which must be varied according to the distance of the object, is *the effect of custom.*] The power which nature hath left us of varying the inclination of the optic axes a little, is turned into a habit of giving them always that inclination which is adapted to the distance of the object.

But it may be asked, What gives rise to this habit? The only answer that can be given to this question is, that it is found necessary to perfect and distinct vision. A man who hath lost the sight of one eye, very often loses the habit of directing it exactly to the object he looks at, because that habit is no longer of use to him. And if he should recover the sight of his eye, he would recover this habit, by finding it useful. No part of the human constitution is more admirable than that whereby we acquire habits which are found useful, without any design or intention. Children must see imperfectly at first; but by using their eyes, they learn to use them in the best manner, and acquire, without intending it, the habits necessary for that purpose. Every man becomes most expert in that kind of vision which is most useful to him in his particular profession and manner of life. A miniature painter, or an engraver, sees very near objects better than a sailor; but the sailor sees very distant objects much better than they. A person that is short-sighted, in looking at distant objects, gets the habit of contracting the aperture of his eyes, by almost closing his eye-lids. Why?

For no other reason, but because this makes him see the object more distinct. In like manner, the reason why every man acquires the habit of directing both eyes accurately to the object, must be, because thereby he sees it more perfectly and distinctly.

It remains to be considered, whether that correspondence between certain points of the retinæ, which is likewise necessary to single vision, be the effect of custom, or an original property of human eyes.

A strong argument for its being an original property, may be drawn from the habit just now mentioned of directing the eyes accurately to an object. This habit is got by our finding it necessary to perfect and distinct vision. But why is it necessary? For no other reason but this,—because thereby the two images of the object falling upon corresponding points, the eyes assist each other in vision, and the object is seen better by both together, than it could be by one; but when the eyes are not accurately directed, the two images of an object fall upon points that do not correspond, whereby the sight of one eye disturbs the sight of the other, and the object is seen more indistinctly with both eyes, than it would be with one. Whence it is reasonable to conclude, that this correspondence of certain points of the retinæ, is prior to the habits we acquire in vision, and consequently is natural and original. We have all acquired the habit of directing our eyes always in a particular manner, which causes single vision. Now, if nature hath ordained that we should have single vision only when our eyes are thus directed, there is an obvious reason why all mankind should agree in the habit of directing them in this manner. But if single vision is the effect of custom, any other habit of directing the eyes would have answered the purpose; and no account can be given why this particular habit should be so universal; and it must appear very strange, that no one instance hath been found of a person who had acquired the habit of seeing objects single with both eyes, while they were directed in any other manner.

The judicious Dr. Smith, in his excellent system of optics, maintains the contrary opinion, and offers some reasonings and facts in proof of it. He agrees with Bishop Berkeley in attributing it entirely to *custom*, that *we see objects single with two eyes*, as well as that *we see objects erect by inverted images.* Having considered Bishop Berkeley's reasonings in the 11th section, we shall now beg leave to make some remarks on what Dr. Smith hath said upon this subject, with the respect due to an author to whom the world owes, not only many valuable discoveries of his own, but those of the brightest mathematical genius of this age, which, with great labour, he generously redeemed from oblivion.

He observes, that the question, Why we see objects single with two eyes? is of the same sort with this, Why we hear sounds single with two ears? and that the same answer must serve both. The inference intended to be drawn from this observation is, that as the second of these phenomena is the effect of custom, so likewise is the first.

Now I humbly conceive that the questions are not so much of the same sort, that the same answer must serve for both; and moreover, that our hearing single with two ears is not the effect of custom.

Two or more visible objects, although perfectly similar, and seen at the very same time, may be distinguished by their visible places: but two sounds perfectly similar, and heard at the same time, cannot be distinguished; for from the nature of sound, the sensations they occasion must coalesce into one, and lose all distinction. If, therefore, it is asked, Why we hear sounds single with two ears? I answer, Not from custom; but because two sounds which are perfectly like and synchronous, have nothing by which they can be distinguished. But will this answer fit the other question? I think not.

The object makes an appearance to each eye, as the sound makes an impression upon each ear; so far the two senses agree. But the visible appearances may be distinguished by place, when perfectly like in other respects; the sounds cannot be thus distinguished; and herein the two senses differ. Indeed, if the two appearances have the same visible place, they are, in that case, as incapable of distinction as the sounds were, and we see the object single. But when they have not the same visible place, they are perfectly distinguishable, and we see the object double. We see the object single only, when the eyes are directed in one particular manner; while there are many other ways of directing them within the sphere of our power, by which we see the object double.

Dr. Smith justly attributes to custom ☞ that well-known fallacy in feeling, whereby a button pressed with two opposite sides of two contiguous fingers laid across, is felt double. I agree with him, that the cause of this appearance is, that those opposite sides of the fingers have never been used to feel the same object, but two different objects, at the same time. And I beg leave to add, that as custom produces this phenomenon, so a contrary custom destroys it: for if a man frequently accustoms himself to feel the button with his fingers across, it will at last be felt single; as I have found by experience.

It may be taken for a general rule, that things which are produced by custom, may be undone or changed by disuse, or by a contrary custom. On the other hand, it is a strong argument, that an effect is not owing to custom, but to the constitution of nature, when a contrary custom, long continued, is found neither to change nor weaken it. I take this to be the best rule by which we can determine the question presently under consideration. I shall, therefore, mention two facts brought by Dr. Smith, to prove that the corresponding points of the retinæ have been changed by custom; and then I shall mention some facts tending to prove, that there are corresponding points in the retinæ of the eyes originally, and that custom produces no change in them.

"One fact is related, upon the authority of Martin Folkes, Esq., who was informed by Dr. Hepburn, of Lynn, that the Rev. Mr. Foster, of Clinchwharton, in that neighbourhood, having been blind for some years of a gutta serena, was restored to sight by salivation; and that upon his first beginning to see, all objects appeared to him double; but afterwards the two appearances approaching by degrees, he came at last to see single, and as distinctly as he did before he was blind."

Upon this case I observe, first, That it does not prove any change of the *corresponding points* of the eyes, unless we suppose, what is not affirmed, that Mr. Foster directed his eyes to the object at first, when he saw double, with the same accuracy, and in the same manner, that he did afterwards when he saw single. Secondly, If we should suppose this, no account can be given, why at first the two appearances should be seen at one certain angular distance rather than another: or why this angular distance should gradually decrease, until at last the appearances coincided. How could this effect be produced by custom? But, thirdly, Every circumstance of this case may be accounted for on the supposition that Mr. Foster had corresponding points in the retinæ of his eyes from the time he began to see, and that custom made no change with regard to them. We need only farther suppose, what is common in such cases, that by some years' blindness, he had lost the habit of directing his eyes accurately to an object, and that he gradually recovered this habit when he came to see.

The second fact mentioned by Dr. Smith is taken from Mr. Cheselden's anatomy, and is this: "A gentleman who, from a blow on the head, had one eye distorted, found every object appear double; but by degrees the most familiar ones became single; and in time all objects became so, without any amendment of the distortion."

I observe here, that it is not said that the two appearances gradually approached, and at last united, without any amendment of the distortion. This would indeed have been a decisive proof of a change in the corresponding points of the retinæ; and yet of such a change as could not be accounted for from custom. But this is not said: and if it had been observed, a circumstance so remarkable would have been mentioned by Mr. Cheselden, as it was in the other case by Dr. Hepburn. We may therefore take it for granted, that one of the appearances vanished by degrees, without approaching to the other. And this, I conceive, might happen several ways. First, The sight of the distorted eye might gradually decay by the hurt: so the appearances presented by that eye would gradually vanish. Secondly, A small and unperceived change in the manner of directing the eyes, might occasion his not seeing the object with the distorted eye, as appears from sect. 15, art. 10. Thirdly, By acquiring the habit of directing one and the same eye always to the object, the faint and oblique appearance presented by the other eye, might be so little attended to when it became familiar, as not to be perceived. One of these causes, or more of them, concurring, might produce the effect mentioned, without any change of the corresponding points of the eyes.

For these reasons, the facts mentioned by Dr. Smith, although curious, seem not to be decisive.

The following facts ought to be put in the opposite scale: First, In the famous case of the young gentleman couched by Mr. Cheselden, after having had cataracts on both eyes until he was thirteen years of age, it appears, that he saw objects single from the time he began to see with both eyes. Mr. Cheselden's words are—" And now being lately couched of his other eye, he says, that objects at first appeared large to this eye, but not so large as they did at first to the other; and looking upon the same object with both eyes, he thought it looked about twice as large as with the first couched eye only, but not double, that we can any ways discover."

Secondly, The three young gentlemen mentioned in the last section, who had squinted, as far as I know, from infancy; as soon as they learned to direct both eyes to an object, saw it single. In these four cases it appears evident, that the centres of the retinæ corresponded originally, and before custom could produce any such effect; for Mr. Cheselden's young gentleman had never been accustomed to see at all before he was couched; and the other three had never been accustomed to direct the axes of both eyes to the object.

Thirdly, From the facts recited in sect. 13, it appears, that from the time we are capable of observing the phenomenon of single and double vision, custom makes no change in them.

I have amused myself with such observations for more than thirty years; and in every case wherein I saw the object double at first, I see it so to this day, notwithstanding the constant experience of its being single. In other cases, where I know there are two objects, there appears only one, after thousands of experiments.

Let a man look at a familiar object through a polyhedron or

multiplying-glass every hour of his life, the number of visible appearances will be the same at last as at first: nor does any number of experiments, or length of time, make the least change.

Effects produced by habit, must vary according as the acts by which the habit is acquired are more or less frequent: but the phenomena of single and double vision are so invariable and uniform in all men, and so exactly regulated by mathematical rules, that I think we have good reason to conclude, that they are not the effect of custom, but of fixed and immutable laws of nature.

XVIII. *Of Dr. Porterfield's account of single and double vision.*—Bishop Berkeley and Dr. Smith seem to attribute *too much to custom* in vision, Dr. Porterfield *too little*.

This ingenious writer thinks that, by an original law of our nature, antecedent to custom and experience, we perceive visible objects in their true place, not only as to their direction, but likewise as to their distance from the eye; and therefore he accounts for our seeing objects single, with two eyes, in this manner: Having the faculty of perceiving the object with each eye in its true place, we must perceive it with both eyes in the same place; and consequently must perceive it single.

He is aware, that this principle, although it accounts for our seeing objects single with two eyes, yet does not at all account for our seeing objects double: and whereas other writers on this subject take it to be a sufficient cause for double vision, that we have two eyes, and only find it difficult to assign a cause for single vision; on the contrary, Dr. Porterfield's principle throws all the difficulty on the other side.

Therefore, in order to account for the phenomena of double vision, he advances another principle, without signifying whether he conceives it to be an original law of our nature, or the effect of custom. [It is—that our natural perception of the distance of objects from the eye, is not extended to all the objects that fall within the field of vision, but limited to that which we directly look at; and that the circumjacent objects, whatever be their real distance, are seen at the same distance with the object we look at, as if they were all in the surface of a sphere whereof the eye is the centre.]

Thus, single vision is accounted for by our seeing the true distance of an object which we look at; and double vision by a false appearance of distance in objects which we do not directly look at.

We agree with this learned and ingenious author, that it is by a natural and original principle that we see visible objects in a certain direction from the eye, and honour him as the author of this discovery: but we cannot assent to either of those principles by which he explains single and double vision, for the following reasons:—

1. Our having a natural and original perception of the distance of objects from the eye, appears contrary to a well-attested fact; for the young gentleman couched by Mr. Cheselden, imagined at first, that whatever he saw touched his eye, as what he felt touched his hand.

2. The perception we have of the distance of objects from the eye, whether it be from nature or custom, is not so accurate and determinate as is necessary to produce single vision. A mistake of the twentieth or thirtieth part of the distance of a small object, such as a pin, ought, according to Dr. Porterfield's hypothesis, to make it appear double. Very few can judge of the distance of a visible object with such accuracy. Yet we never find double vision produced by mistaking the distance of the object. There are many cases in vision, even with the naked eye, wherein we mistake the distance of an object by one half or more: why do we see such objects single? When I move my spectacles from my eyes toward a small object, two or three feet distant, the object seems to approach, so as to be seen at last at about half its real distance; but it is seen single at that apparent distance, as well as when we see it with the naked eye at its real distance. And when we look at an object with a binocular telescope, properly fitted to the eyes, we see it single, while it appears fifteen or twenty times nearer than it is. There are then few cases wherein the distance of an object from the eye is seen so accurately as is necessary for single vision, upon this hypothesis: this seems to be a conclusive argument against the account given of single vision. We find, likewise, that false judgments or fallacious appearances of the distance of an object, do not produce double vision. This seems to be a conclusive argument against the account given of double vision.

3. The perception we have of the *linear* distance of objects, seems to be wholly the effect of experience. This I think hath been proved by Bishop Berkeley and by Dr. Smith; and when we come to point out the means of judging of distance by sight, it will appear that they are all furnished by experience.

4. Supposing that by a law of our nature, the distance of objects from the eye were perceived most accurately, as well as their direction, it will not follow that we must see the object single. Let us consider what means such a law of nature would furnish for resolving the question, Whether the objects of the two eyes are in one and the same place, and consequently are not two, but one?

Suppose then two right lines, one drawn from the centre of one eye to its object, the other drawn, in like manner, from the centre of the other eye to its object. This law of nature gives us the direction or position of each of these right lines, and the length of each; and this is all that it gives. These are geometrical data, and we may learn from geometry what is determined by their means. Is it then determined by these data, whether the two right lines terminate in one and the same point, or not? No, truly. In order to determine this, we must have three other data. We must know whether the two right lines are in one plane: we must know what angle they make: and we must know the distance between the centres of the eyes. And when these things are known, we must apply the rules of trigonometry, before we can resolve the question, whether the objects of the two eyes are in one and the same place? and consequently whether they are two or one?

5. That false appearance of distance into which double vision is resolved, cannot be the effect of custom; for constant experience contradicts it: neither hath it the features of a law of nature; because it does not answer any good purpose, nor indeed any purpose at all but to deceive us. But why should we seek for arguments, in a question concerning what appears to us, or does not appear? The question is, at what distances do the objects presently in my eye appear? Do they all appear at one distance, as if placed in the concave surface of a sphere, the eye being in the centre? Every man surely may know this with certainty; and, if he will but give attention to the testimony of his eyes, needs not ask a philosopher, how visible objects appear to him. Now, it is very true, that if I look up to a star in the heavens, the other stars that appear at the same time, do appear in this manner: yet this phenomenon does not favour Dr. Porterfield's hypothesis; for the stars and heavenly bodies do not appear at their true distances when we look directly to them, any more than when they are seen obliquely: and if this phenomenon be an argument for Dr. Porterfield's second principle, it must destroy the first.

The true cause of this phenomenon will be given afterwards; therefore setting it aside for the present, let us put another case. I sit presently in my room, and direct my eyes to the door, which appears to be about sixteen feet distant: at the same time I see many other objects faintly and obliquely; the floor, floor-cloth, the table which I write upon, papers, standish, candle, &c. Now, do all these objects appear at the same distance of sixteen feet? Upon the closest attention, I find they do not.

XIX. *Of Dr. Briggs's theory, and Sir Isaac Newton's conjecture on this subject.*—I am afraid the reader, as well as the writer, is already tired of the subject of single and double vision. The multitude of theories advanced by authors of great name, and the multitude of facts, observed without sufficient skill in optics, or related without attention to the most material and decisive circumstances, have equally contributed to perplex it.

In order to bring it to some issue, I have, in the 13th section, given a more full and regular deduction than had been given heretofore, of the phenomena of single and double vision, in those whose sight is perfect; and have traced them up to one general principle, which appears to be a law of vision in human eyes that are perfect and in their natural state.

In the 14th section I have made it appear, that this law of vision, although excellently adapted to the fabric of human eyes, cannot answer the purposes of vision in some other animals; and therefore, very probably, is not common to all animals. The purpose of the 15th and 16th sections is, to inquire, whether there be any deviation from this law of vision in those who squint? a question which is of real importance in the medical art, as well as in the philosophy of vision; but which, after all that hath been observed and written on the subject, seems not to be ripe for a determination, for want of proper observations. Those who have had skill to make proper observations, have wanted opportunities; and those who have had the opportunities, have wanted skill or attention. I have therefore thought it worth while to give a distinct account of the observations necessary for the determination of this question, and what conclusions may be drawn from the facts observed. I have likewise collected, and set in one view, the most conclusive facts that have occurred in authors, or have fallen under my own observation.

It must be confessed that these facts, when applied to the question in hand, make a very poor figure; and the gentlemen of the medical faculty are called upon, for the honour of their profession, and for the benefit of mankind, to add to them.

All the medical, and all the optical writers, upon the strabismus, that I have met with, except Dr. Jurin, either affirm, or take it for granted, that squinting persons see the object with both eyes, and yet see it single. Dr. Jurin affirms, that squinting persons never see the object with both eyes; and that if they did, they would see it double. If the common opinion be true, the cure of a squint would be as pernicious to the sight of the patient, as the causing of a permanent squint would be to one who naturally had no squint: and therefore no physician ought to attempt such a cure; no patient ought to submit to it. But if Dr. Jurin's opinion be true, most young people that squint may cure themselves, by taking some pains; and may not only remove the deformity, but at the same time improve their sight. If the common opinion be true, the centres and other points of the two retinæ in squinting persons do not correspond as in other men, and nature in them deviates from her common rule. But if Dr. Jurin's opinion be true, there is reason to think, that the same general law of vision which we have found in perfect human eyes, extends also to those which squint.

It is impossible to determine, by reasoning, which of these opinions is true; or whether one may not be found true in some patients, and the other in others. Here, experience and observation are our only guides; and a deduction of instances is the only rational argument. It might therefore have been expected, that the patrons of the contrary opinions should have given instances in support of them that are clear and indisputable: but I have not found one such instance on either side of the question, in all the authors I have met with. I have given three instances from my own observation, in confirmation of Dr. Jurin's opinion, which admit of no doubt; and one which leans rather to the other opinion, but is dubious. And here I must leave the matter to further observation.

In the 17th section, I have endeavoured to show, that the correspondence and sympathy of certain points of the two retinæ, into which we have resolved all the phenomena of single and double vision, is not, as Dr. Smith conceived, the effect of custom, nor can be changed by custom, but is a natural and original property of human eyes: and in the last section, that it is not owing to an original and natural perception of the true distance of objects from the eye, as Dr. Porterfield imagined. After this recapitulation, which is intended to relieve the attention of the reader, shall we enter into more theories upon this subject?

That of Dr. Briggs, first published in English, in the "Philosophical Transactions," afterwards in Latin, under the title of "Nova visionis theoria," with a prefatory epistle of Sir Isaac Newton to the author, amounts to this, that the fibres of the optic nerves passing from corresponding points of the retinæ to the *thalami nervorum opticorum*, having the same length, the same tension, and a similar situation, will have the same tone; and therefore their vibrations excited by the impression of the rays of light will be like unisons in music, and will present one and the same image to the mind: but the fibres passing from parts of the retinæ which do not correspond, having different tensions and tones, will have discordant vibrations; and therefore present different images to the mind.

I shall not enter upon a particular examination of this theory. It is enough to observe in general, that it is *a system of conjectures* concerning things of which we are entirely ignorant; and that all such theories in philosophy deserve rather to be laughed at, than to be seriously refuted.

From the first dawn of philosophy to this day, it hath been believed that the optic nerves are intended to carry the images of visible objects from the bottom of the eye to the mind; and that the nerves belonging to the organs of the other senses have a like office. But how do we know this? we conjecture it: and taking this conjecture for a truth, we consider how the nerves may best answer this purpose. The system of the nerves, for many ages, was taken to be an hydraulic engine, consisting of a bundle of pipes which carry to and fro a liquor called *animal spirits*. About the time of Dr. Briggs, it was thought rather to be a stringed instrument, composed of vibrating chords, each of which had its proper tension and tone. But some, with as great probability, conceived it to be a wind instrument, which played its part by the vibrations of an elastic ether in the nervous fibrils.

These, I think, are all the engines into which the nervous system hath been moulded by philosophers, for conveying the images of sensible things from the organ to the sensorium. And for all that we know of the matter, every man may freely choose which he thinks fittest for the purpose; for from fact and experiment no one of them can claim preference to another. Indeed they all seem so unhandy engines for carrying images, that a man would be tempted to invent a new one.

Since, therefore, a blind man may guess as well in the dark as one that sees, I beg leave to offer another conjecture touching the nervous system, which I hope will answer the purpose as well as those we have mentioned, and which recommends itself by its simplicity. Why may not the optic nerves, for instance, be made up of empty tubes, opening their mouths wide enough to receive the rays of light which form the image upon the retina, and gently conveying them safe, and in their proper order, to the very seat of the soul, until they flash in her face? It is easy for an ingenious philosopher to fit the caliber of these empty tubes to the diameter of the particles of light, so as they shall receive no grosser kind of matter. And if these rays should be in danger of mistaking their way, an expedient may also be found to prevent this. For it requires no more than to bestow upon the tubes of the nervous system a peristaltic motion, like that of the alimentary tube.

It is a peculiar advantage of this hypothesis, that although all philosophers believe that the species or images of things are conveyed by the nerves to the soul, yet none of their hypotheses show how this may be done. For how can the images of sound, taste, smell, colour, figure, and all sensible qualities, be made out of the vibrations of musical chords, or the undulations of animal spirits, or of ether? We ought not to suppose means inadequate to the end. Is it not as philosophical, and more intelligible, to conceive, that as the stomach receives its food, so the soul receives her images by a kind of nervous deglutition? I might add, that we need only continue this peristaltic motion of the nervous tubes from the sensorium to the extremities of the nerves that serve the muscles, in order to account for muscular motion.

Thus nature will be consonant to herself; and as sensation will be the conveyance of the ideal aliment to the mind, so muscular motion will be the expulsion of the recrementitious part of it. For who can deny, that the images of things conveyed by sensation, may, after due concoction, become fit to be thrown off by muscular motion? I only give hints of these things to the ingenious, hoping that in time this hypothesis may be wrought up into a system as truly philosophical, as that of animal spirits, or the vibration of nervous fibres.

To be serious: in the operations of nature, I hold the theories of a philosopher, which are unsupported by fact, in the same estimation with the dreams of a man asleep, or the ravings of a madman. We laugh at the Indian philosopher, who, to account for the support of the earth, contrived the hypothesis of a huge elephant, and to support the elephant, a huge tortoise. If we will candidly confess the truth, we know as little of the operation of the nerves, as he did of the manner in which the earth is supported; and our hypotheses about animal spirits, or about the tension and vibrations of the nerves, are as like to be true, as his about the support of the earth. His elephant was an hypothesis, and our hypotheses are elephants. Every theory in philosophy which is built on pure conjecture is an elephant; and every theory that is supported partly by fact, and partly by conjecture, is like Nebuchadnezzar's image, whose feet were partly of iron, and partly of clay.

The great Newton first gave an example to philosophers, which always ought to be, but rarely hath been, followed, by distinguishing his conjectures from his conclusions, and putting the former by themselves, in the modest form of queries. This is fair and legal; but all other philosophical traffic in conjecture, ought to be held contraband and illicit. Indeed his conjectures have commonly more foundation in fact, and more verisimilitude, than the dogmatical theories of most other philosophers; and therefore we ought not to omit that which he hath offered concerning the cause of our seeing objects single with two eyes, in the 15th query annexed to his "Optics."

"Are not the species of objects seen with both eyes, united where the optic nerves meet before they come into the brain, the fibres on the right side of both nerves uniting there, and after union going thence into the brain in the nerve which is on the right side of the head, and the fibres on the left side of both nerves uniting in the same place, and after union going into the brain in the nerve which is on the left side of the head, and these two nerves meeting in the brain in such a manner that their fibres make but one entire species or picture, half of which on the right side of the sensorium comes from the right side of both eyes through the right side of both optic nerves to the place where the nerves meet, and from thence on the right side of the head into the brain, and the other half on the left side of the sensorium comes in like manner from the left side of both eyes? For the optic nerves of such animals as look the same way with both eyes (as men, dogs, sheep, oxen, &c.) meet before they come into the brain : but the optic nerves of such animals as do not look the same way with both eyes (as of fishes and of the chameleon) do not meet, if I am rightly informed."

I beg leave to distinguish this query into two, which are of very different natures: one being purely anatomical, the other relating to the carrying species or pictures of visible objects to the sensorium.

The first question is, Whether the fibres coming from corresponding points of the two retinæ, do not unite at the place where the optic nerves meet, and continue united from thence to the brain; so that the right optic nerve, after the meeting of the two nerves, is composed of the fibres coming from the right side of both retinæ, and the left, of the fibres coming from the left side of both retinæ.

This is undoubtedly a curious and rational question, because if we could find ground from anatomy to answer it in the affirmative, it would lead us a step forward in discovering the cause of the correspondence and sympathy which there is between certain points of the two retinæ. For although we know not what is the particular function of the optic nerves, yet it is probable that some impression made upon them, and communicated along their fibres, is necessary to vision : and whatever be the nature of this impression, if two fibres are united into one, an impression made upon one of them, or upon both, may probably produce the same effect. Anatomists think it a sufficient account of a *sympathy* between two parts of the body, when they are served by branches of the same nerve; we should therefore look upon it as an important discovery in anatomy, if it were found that the same nerve sent branches to the corresponding points of the retinæ.

But hath any such discovery been made? No, not so much as in one subject, as far as I can learn. But in several subjects, the contrary seems to have been discovered. Dr. Porterfield hath given us two cases at length from Vesalius, and one from Cæsalpinus, wherein the optic nerves, after touching one another as usual, appeared to be reflected back to the same side whence they came, without any mixture of their fibres. Each of these persons had lost an eye some time before his death, and the optic nerve belonging to that eye was shrunk, so that it could be distinguished from the other at the place where they met. Another case which the same author gives from Vesalius, is still more remarkable; for in it the optic nerves did not touch at all;

and yet, upon inquiry, those who were most familiar with the person in his lifetime, declared that he never complained of any defect of sight, or of his seeing objects double. Diemerbroek tells us, that Aquapendens and Valverda likewise affirm, that they have met with subjects wherein the optic nerves did not touch.

As these observations were made before Sir Isaac Newton put this query, it is uncertain whether he was ignorant of them, or whether he suspected some inaccuracy in them, and desired that the matter might be more carefully examined. But from the following passage of the most accurate Winslow, it does not appear that later observations have been more favourable to his conjecture. "The union of these [optic] nerves, by the small curvatures of their cornua, is very difficult to be unfolded in human bodies. This union is commonly found to be very close, but in some subjects it seems to be no more than a strong adhesion, in others to be partly made by an intersection or crossing of fibres. They have been found quite separate; and in other subjects, one of them has been found to be very much altered both in size and colour through its whole passage, the other remaining in its natural state."

When we consider this conjecture of Sir Isaac Newton by itself, it appears more ingenious, and to have more verisimilitude, than any thing that has been offered upon the subject; and we admire the caution and modesty of the author, in proposing it only as a subject of inquiry: but when we compare it with the observations of anatomists which contradict it, we are naturally led to this reflection, That if we trust to the conjectures of men of the greatest genius in the operations of nature, we have only the chance of going wrong in an ingenious manner.

The second part of the query is, Whether the two species of objects from the two eyes are not, at the place where the optic nerves meet, united into one species or picture, half of which is carried thence to the sensorium in the right optic nerve, and the other half in the left? and whether these two halves are not so put together again at the sensorium, as to make one species or picture?

Here it seems natural to put the previous question, What reason have we to believe, that pictures of objects are at all carried to the sensorium, either by the optic nerves, or by any other nerves? Is it not possible, that this great philosopher, as well as many of a lower form, having been led into this opinion at first by education, may have continued in it, because he never thought of calling it in question? I confess this was my own case for a considerable part of my life. But since I was led by accident to think seriously what reason I had to believe it, I could find none at all. It seems to be a mere hypothesis, as much as the Indian philosopher's elephant. I am not conscious of any pictures of external objects in my sensorium, any more than in my stomach: the things which I perceive by my senses, appear to be external, and not in any part of the brain; and my sensations properly so called, have no resemblance of external objects.

[*The conclusion* from all that hath been said, in no less than seven sections, upon our seeing objects single with two eyes, is this, That, by an original property of human eyes, objects painted upon the centres of the two retinæ, or upon points similarly situate with regard to the centres, appear in the same visible place; that the most plausible attempts to account for this property of the eyes, have been unsuccessful; and therefore, that it must be either a primary law of our constitution, or the consequence of some more general law which is not yet discovered.]

We have now finished what we intended to say, both of the visible appearances of things to the eye, and of the laws of our constitution by which those appearances are exhibited. But it was observed in the beginning of this chapter, that the visible appearances of objects serve only as signs of their distance, magnitude, figure, and other tangible qualities. The visible appearance is that which is presented to the mind, by nature, according to those laws of our constitution which have been explained. But the thing signified by that appearance, is that which is presented to the mind by custom.

When one speaks to us in a language that is familiar, we hear certain sounds, and this is all the effect that his discourse has upon us by nature: but by custom we understand the meaning of these sounds, and therefore we fix our attention, not upon the sounds, but upon the things signified by them. In like manner, we see only the visible appearance of objects by nature; but we learn by *custom* to interpret these appearances, and to understand their meaning. And when this visual language is learned, and becomes familiar, we attend only to the things signified; and cannot, without great difficulty, attend to the signs by which they are presented. The mind passes from one to the other so rapidly and so familiarly, that no trace of the sign is left in the memory, and we seem immediately, and without the intervention of any sign, to perceive the thing signified.

☞ When I look at the apple-tree which stands before my window, I perceive at the first glance its distance and magnitude, the roughness of its trunk, the disposition of its branches, the figure of its leaves and fruit. I seem to perceive all these things immediately. The visible appearance which presented them all to the mind, has entirely escaped me; I cannot, without great difficulty, and painful abstraction, attend to it, even when it stands before me. Yet it is certain that this visible appearance only is presented to my eye by nature, and that I learned by custom to collect all the rest from it. If I had never seen before now, I should not perceive either the distance or tangible figure of the tree, and it would have required the practice of seeing for many months, to change that original perception which nature gave me by my eyes, into that which I now have by custom.

[The objects which we see naturally and originally, as hath been before observed, *have length* and *breadth*, but *no thickness nor distance from the eye*. *Custom*, by a kind of legerdemain, withdraws gradually these original and proper objects of sight, and *substitutes* in their place *objects of touch*, which have length, breadth, and thickness, and a determinate distance from the eye.] By what means this change is brought about, and what principles of the human mind concur in it, we are next to inquire.

XX. *Of perception in general.*—Sensation and the perception of external objects by the senses, though very different in their nature, have commonly been considered as one and the same thing. The purposes of common life do not make it necessary to distinguish them, and the received opinions of philosophers, tend rather to confound them: but without attending carefully to this distinction, it is impossible to have any just conception of the operations of our senses. The most simple operations of the mind admit not of a logical definition: all we can do is to describe them, so as to lead those who are conscious of them in themselves, to attend to them, and reflect upon them: and it is often very difficult to describe them so as to answer this intention.

The same mode of expression is used to denote sensation and perception; and therefore we are apt to look upon them as things of the same nature. Thus, *I feel a pain; I see a tree:* the first denoteth a *sensation*, the last a *perception*. The grammatical analysis of both expressions is the same: for both consist of an active verb and an object. But if we attend to the thing signified by these expressions, we shall find that in the first, the distinction between the act and the object is not real, but grammatical; in the second, the distinction is not only grammatical but real.

The form of the expression, *I feel pain*, might seem to imply that the feeling is something distinct from the pain felt; yet, in reality, there is no distinction. As *thinking a thought*, is an expression which could signify no more than *thinking*, so *feeling a pain* signifies no more than *being pained*. What we have said of pain is applicable to every other mere sensation. It is difficult to give instances, very few of our sensations having names; and where they have, the name being common to the sensation, and to something else which is associated with it. But when we attend to the sensation by itself, and separate it from other things which are conjoined with it in the imagination, it appears to be something which can have no existence but in a sentient mind, no distinction from the act of the mind by which it is felt.

Perception, as we here understand it, hath always an object distinct from the act by which it is perceived; an object which may exist whether it be perceived or not. I perceive a tree that grows before my window; there is here an object which is perceived; and an act of the mind by which it is perceived; and these two are not only distinguishable, but they are extremely unlike in their natures. The object is made up of a trunk, branches and leaves; but the act of the mind by which it is perceived, hath neither trunk, branches, nor leaves. I am conscious of this act of my mind and I can reflect upon it; but it is too simple to admit of an analysis, and I cannot find proper words to describe it. I find nothing that resembles it so much as the remembrance of the tree, or the imagination of it. Yet both these differ essentially from perception; they differ likewise one from another. It is in vain that a philosopher assures me that the imagination of the tree, the remembrance of it, and the perception of it, are all one, and differ only in degree of vivacity. I know the contrary; for I am as well acquainted with all the three, as I am with the apartments of my own house. I know this also, that the perception of an object implies both a conception of its form, and a belief of its present existence. I know, moreover, that this belief is not the effect of argumentation and reasoning; it is the immediate effect of my constitution.

[I am aware that this belief which I have in perception, stands exposed to the strongest batteries of *scepticism*.] But they make no great impression upon it. The sceptic asks me, Why do you believe the existence of the external object which you perceive? This belief, Sir, is none of my manufacture; it came from the mint of nature; it bears her image and superscription; and if it is not right, the fault is not mine: I even took it upon trust, and without suspicion. Reason, says the sceptic, is the only judge of truth, and you ought to throw off every opinion and every belief that is not grounded on reason. Why, Sir, should I believe the faculty of reason more than that of perception? they came both out of the same shop, and were made by the same artist; and if he puts one piece of false ware into my hands, what should hinder him from putting another?

Perhaps the sceptic will agree to distrust reason, rather than give any credit to perception. For, says he, since by your own concession, the object which you perceive, and that act of your mind by which you perceive it, are quite different things, the one may exist without the other; and as the object may exist without being perceived, so the perception may be without an object. There is nothing so shameful in a philosopher as to be deceived and deluded; and therefore you ought to resolve firmly to withhold assent, and to throw off this belief of external objects, which may be all delusion. For my part, I will never attempt to throw it off; and although the sober part of mankind will not be very anxious to know my reasons, yet if they can be of use to any sceptic, they are these:—

First, Because it is not in my power: why then should I make a vain attempt? It would be agreeable to fly to the moon, and to make a visit to Jupiter and Saturn: but when I know that nature has bound me down by the law of gravitation to this planet which I inhabit, I rest contented, and quietly suffer myself to be carried along in its orbit. My belief is carried along by perception, as irresistibly as my body by the earth. And the greatest sceptic will find himself to be in the same condition. He may struggle hard to disbelieve the informations of his senses, as a man does to swim against a torrent; but ah! it is in vain. It is in vain that he strains every nerve, and wrestles with nature, and with every object that strikes upon his senses. For after all, when his strength is spent in the fruitless attempt, he will be carried down the torrent with the common herd of believers.

Secondly, I think it would not be prudent to throw off this belief, if it were in my power. If nature intended to deceive me, and impose upon me by false appearances, and I, by my great cunning and profound logic, have discovered the imposture; prudence would dictate to me in this case, even to put up with this indignity done me, as quietly as I could, and not to call her an impostor to her face, lest she should be even with me in another way. For what do I gain by resenting this injury? You ought at least not to believe what she says. This, indeed, seems reasonable, if she intends to impose upon me. But what is the consequence? I resolve not to believe my senses. I break my nose against a post that comes in my way; I step into a dirty kennel; and after twenty such wise and rational actions, I am taken up and clapped into a madhouse. Now I confess I would rather make one of the credulous fools whom nature imposes upon, than of those wise and rational philosophers who resolve to withhold assent at all this expense. If a man pretends to be a sceptic with regard to the informations of sense, and yet prudently keeps out of harm's way as other men do, he must excuse my suspicion, that he either acts the hypocrite, or imposes upon himself. For if the scale of his belief were so evenly poised, as to lean no more to one side than to the contrary, it is impossible that his actions could be directed by any rules of common prudence.

Thirdly, Although the two reasons already mentioned are perhaps two more than enough, I shall offer a third. I gave implicit belief to the informations of nature by my senses, for a considerable part of my life, before I had learned so much logic as to be able to start a doubt concerning them. And now, when I reflect upon what is past, I do not find that I have been imposed upon by this belief. I find, that without it I must have perished by a thousand accidents. I find, that without it I should have been no wiser now than when I was born. I should not even have been able to acquire that logic which suggests these sceptical doubts with regard to my senses. Therefore, I consider this instinctive belief as one of the best gifts of nature. I thank the Author of my being who bestowed it upon me, before the eyes of my reason were opened, and still bestows it upon me to be my guide, where reason leaves me in the dark. And now I yield to the direction of my senses, not from instinct only, but from confidence and trust in a faithful and beneficent Monitor, grounded upon the experience of his paternal care and goodness.

In all this, I deal with the Author of my being, no otherwise than I thought it reasonable to deal with my parents and tutors. I believed by instinct whatever they told me, long before I had the idea of a lie, or thought of the possibility of their deceiving me. Afterwards, upon reflection, I found they had acted like fair and honest people who wished me well. I found, that if I had not believed what they told me, before I could give a reason of my belief, I had to this day been little better than a changeling. And although this natural credulity hath sometimes occasioned my being imposed upon by deceivers, yet it hath been of infinite advantage to me upon the whole; therefore I consider it as another good gift of nature. And I continue to give that credit, from reflection, to those of whose integrity and veracity I have had experience, which before I gave from instinct.

[There is a much greater similitude than is commonly imagined, between the testimony of nature given by our senses, and the testimony of men given by language. The credit we give to both is at first the effect of instinct only.] When we grow up, and begin to reason about them, the credit given to human testimony is restrained and weakened by the experience we have of deceit. But the credit given to the testimony of our senses, is established and confirmed by the uniformity and constancy of the laws of nature.

[Our perceptions are of two kinds: some are natural and original; others acquired, and the fruit of experience.] When I perceive that this is the taste of cyder, that of brandy; that this is the smell of an apple, that of an orange; that this is the noise of thunder, that the ringing of bells; this the sound of a coach passing, that the voice of such a friend; these perceptions, and others of the same kind, are not original, they are acquired. But the perception which I have by touch of the hardness and softness of bodies, of their extension, figure, and motion, is not acquired, it is original.

In all our senses, the acquired perceptions are many more than the original, especially in sight. By this sense we perceive originally the visible figure and colour of bodies only, and their visible place: but we learn to perceive by the eye, almost every thing which we can perceive by touch. The original perceptions of this sense, serve only as signs to introduce the acquired.

The signs by which objects are presented to us in perception, are the language of nature to man; and as in many respects it hath great affinity with the language of man to man, so particularly in this, that both are partly natural and original, partly acquired by custom. Our original or natural perceptions are analogous to the natural language of man to man, of which we took notice in the fourth chapter; and our acquired perceptions are analogous to artificial language, which, in our mother-tongue, is got very much in the same manner with our acquired perceptions, as we shall afterwards more fully explain.

☞ Not only men, but children, idiots, and brutes, acquire by habit many perceptions which they had not originally. Almost every employment in life hath perceptions of this kind, that are peculiar to it. The shepherd knows every sheep of his flock, as we do our acquaintance, and can pick them out of another flock, one by one. The butcher knows by sight the weight and quality of his beeves and sheep before they are killed. The farmer perceives by his eye, very nearly, the quantity of hay in a rick, or of corn in a heap. The sailor sees the burthen, the build, and the distance of a ship at sea, while she is a great way off. Every man accustomed to writing, distinguishes his acquaintance by their handwriting, as he does by their faces. And the painter distinguishes, in the works of his art, the style of all the great masters. In a word, acquired perception is very different in different persons, according to the diversity of objects about which they are employed, and the application they bestow in observing them.

[Perception ought not only to be distinguished from sensation, but likewise from that knowledge of the objects of sense which is got by reasoning. There is *no reasoning in perception*, as hath been observed. The belief which is implied in it, is the effect of *instinct*.] But there are many things with regard to sensible objects which we can infer from what we perceive; and such conclusions of reason ought to be distinguished from what is merely perceived. When I look at the moon, I perceive her to be sometimes circular, sometimes horned, and sometimes gibbous. This is simple perception, and is the same in the philosopher and in the clown: but from these various appearances of her enlightened part, I infer that she is really of a spherical figure. This conclusion is not obtained by simple perception, but by reasoning. Simple perception has the same relation to the conclusions of reason drawn from our perceptions, as the axioms in mathematics have to the propositions. I cannot demonstrate, that two quantities which are equal to the same quantity, are equal to each other; neither can I demonstrate, that the tree which I perceive exists. But, by the constitution of my nature, my belief is irresistibly carried along by my apprehension of the axiom; and, by the constitution of my nature, my belief is no less irresistibly carried along by my perception of the tree. All reasoning is from principles. The first principles of mathematical reasoning are mathematical axioms and definitions; and the first principles of all our reasoning about existences, are our perceptions. The first principles of every kind of reasoning are given us by nature, and are of equal authority with the faculty of reason itself, which is also the gift of nature. The conclusions of reason are all built upon first principles, and can have no other foundation. Most justly, therefore, do such principles disdain to be tried by reason, and laugh at all the artillery of the logician, when it is directed against them.

When a long train of reasoning is necessary, in demonstrating a mathematical proposition, it is easily distinguished from an axiom, and they seem to be things of a very different nature. But there are some propositions which lie so near to axioms, that it is difficult to say, whether they ought to be held as axioms, or demonstrated as propositions. The same thing holds with regard to perception, and the conclusions drawn from it. Some of these conclusions follow our perceptions so easily, and are so immediately connected with them, that it is difficult to fix the limit which divides the one from the other.

Perception, whether original or acquired, implies no exercise of reason, and is common to men, children, idiots, and brutes. The more obvious conclusions drawn from our perceptions by reason, make what we call *common understanding;* by which men conduct themselves in the common affairs of life, and by which they are distinguished from idiots. The more remote conclusions which are drawn from our perceptions by reason, make what we commonly call *science* in the various parts of nature, whether in agriculture, medicine, mechanics, or in any part of natural philosophy. When I see a garden in good order, containing a great variety of things of the best kinds, and in the most flourishing condition, I immediately conclude from these signs, the skill and industry of the gardener. A farmer, when he rises in the morning, and perceives that the neighbouring brook overflows his field, concludes that a great deal of rain hath fallen in the night. Perceiving his fence broken, and his corn trodden down, he concludes that some of his own or his neighbours' cattle have broke loose. Perceiving that his stable-door is broke open, and some of his horses gone, he concludes that a thief has carried them off. He traces the prints of his horse's feet in the soft ground, and by them discovers which road the thief hath taken. These are instances of common understanding, which dwells so near to perception, that it is difficult to trace the line which divides the one from the other. In like manner, the science of nature dwells so near to common understanding, that we cannot discern where the latter ends and the former begins. I perceive that bodies lighter than water swim in water, and that those which are heavier sink. Hence I conclude, that if a body remains wherever it is put under water, whether at the top or bottom, it is precisely of the same weight with water. If it will rest only when part of it is above water, it is lighter than water. And the greater the part above water is, compared with the whole, the lighter is the body. If it had no gravity at all, it would make no impression upon the water, but stand wholly above it. Thus every man, by common understanding, has a rule by which he judges of the specific gravity of bodies which swim in water; and a step or two more leads him into the science of hydrostatics.

All that we know of nature, or of existences, may be compared to a tree, which hath its root, trunk, and branches. In this tree of knowledge, perception is the root, common understanding is the trunk, and the sciences are the branches.

XXI. *Of the process of nature in perception.*—Although there is no reasoning in perception, yet there are *certain means* and instruments, which, by the appointment of nature, must intervene between the object and our perception of it; and *by these, our perceptions are limited* and regulated. *First,* If the object is not in contact with the organ of sense, there must be some medium which passes between them. Thus, in vision, the rays of light; in hearing, the vibrations of elastic air; in smelling, the effluvia of the body smelt, must pass from the object to the organ; otherwise we have no perception. *Secondly,* There must be some action or impression upon the organ of sense, either by the immediate application of the object, or by the medium that goes between them. *Thirdly,* The nerves which go from the brain to the organ, must receive some impression by means of that which was made upon the organ; and probably, by means of the nerves, some impression must be made upon the brain. *Fourthly,* The impression made upon the organ, nerves, and brain, is followed by a sensation. And, *last* of all, this sensation is followed by the perception of the object.

Thus our perception of objects is the result of a train of operations; some of which affect the body only, others affect the mind. We know very little of the nature of some of these operations; we know not at all how they are connected together, or in what way they contribute to that perception which is the result of the whole: but by the laws of our constitution, we perceive objects in this, and in no other way.

There may be other beings, who can perceive external objects without rays of light, or vibrations of air, or effluvia of bodies; without impressions on bodily organs, or even without sensations: but we are so framed by the Author of nature, that even when we are surrounded by external objects, we may perceive none of them. Our faculty of perceiving an object lies dormant, until it is roused and stimulated by a certain corresponding sensation. Nor is this sensation always at hand to perform its office; for it enters into the mind only in consequence of a certain corresponding impression made on the organ of sense by the object.

Let us trace this correspondence of impressions, sensations, and perceptions, as far as we can; beginning with that which is first in order, the impression made upon the bodily organ. But, alas! we know not of what nature these impressions are, far less how they excite sensations in the mind.

We know that one body may act upon another by pressure, by percussion, by attraction, by repulsion, and probably in many other ways which we neither know, nor have names to express. But in which of these ways objects, when perceived by us, act upon the organs of sense, these organs upon the nerves, and the nerves upon the brain, we know not. Can any man tell me how, in vision, the rays of light act upon the retina, how the retina acts upon the optic nerve, and how the optic nerve acts upon the brain? No man can. When I feel the pain of the gout in my toe, I know that there is some unusual impression made upon that part of my body. But of what kind is it? Are the small vessels distended with some redundant elastic or unelastic fluid? Are the fibres unusually stretched? Are they torn asunder by force, or gnawed and corroded by some acrid humour? I can answer none of these questions. All that I feel is pain, which is not an impression upon the body, but upon the mind; and all that I perceive by this sensation is, that some distemper in my toe occasions this pain. But as I know not the natural temper and texture of my toe when it is at ease, I know as little what change or disorder of its parts occasions this uneasy sensation. In like manner, in every other sensation there is, without doubt, some impression made upon the organ of sense; but an impression of which we know not the nature. It is too subtile to be discovered by our senses, and we may make a thousand conjectures without coming near the truth. If we understood the structure of our organs of sense so minutely, as to discover what effects are produced upon them by external objects, this knowledge would contribute nothing to our perception of the object; for they perceive as distinctly who know least about the manner of perception, as the greatest adepts. It is necessary that the impression be made upon our organs, but not that it be known. Nature carries on this part of the process of perception, without our consciousness or concurrence.

But we cannot be unconscious of the next step in this process, the sensation of the mind, which always immediately follows the impression made upon the body. It is essential to a sensation to be felt, and it can be nothing more than we feel it to be. If we can only acquire the habit of attending to our sensations, we may know them perfectly. But how are the sensations of the mind produced by impressions upon the body? Of this we are absolutely ignorant, having no means of knowing how the body acts upon the mind, or the mind upon the body. When we consider the nature and attributes of both, they seem to be so different, and so unlike, that we can find no handle by which the one may lay hold of the other. There is a deep and a dark gulf between them, which our understanding cannot pass: and the manner of their correspondence and intercourse is absolutely unknown.

Experience teaches us that certain impressions upon the body are constantly followed by certain sensations of the mind; and that, on the other hand, certain determinations of the mind are constantly followed by certain motions in the body: but we see not the chain that ties these things together. Who knows but their connexion may be arbitrary, and owing to the will of our Maker? Perhaps the same sensations might have been connected with other impressions, or other bodily organs? Perhaps we might have been so made, as to taste with our fingers, to smell with our ears, and to hear by the nose. Perhaps we might have been so made, as to have all the sensations and perceptions which we have, without any impression made upon our bodily organs at all.

[However these things may be, if Nature had given us nothing more than impressions made upon the body, and sensations in our minds corresponding to them, we should in that case have been *merely sentient*, but *not percipient* beings.] We should never have been able to form a conception of any external object, far less a belief of its existence. Our sensations have no resemblance to external objects; nor can we discover, by our reason, any necessary connexion between the existence of the former and that of the latter.

We might perhaps, (1) have been made of such a constitution, as to have our present perceptions connected with other sensations. We might, perhaps, (2) have had the perception of external objects, without either impressions upon the organs of sense, or sensations. Or lastly, (3) The perceptions we have, might have been immediately connected with the impressions upon our organs, without any intervention of sensations. This last seems really to be the case in one instance, to wit, in our perception of the visible figure of bodies, as was observed in the fourth section of this chapter.

The process of nature in perception by the senses, may therefore be conceived as a kind of drama, wherein some things are performed behind the scenes, others are represented to the mind in different scenes, one succeeding another. The impression made by the object upon the organ, either by immediate contact, or by some intervening medium, as well as the impression made upon the nerves and brain, is performed behind the scenes, and the mind sees nothing of it. But every such impression, by the laws of the drama, is followed by a sensation, which is the first scene exhibited to the mind; and this scene is quickly succeeded by another, which is the perception of the object.

In this drama, nature is the actor, we are the spectators. We know nothing of the machinery by means of which every different impression upon the organ, nerves, and brain, exhibits its corresponding sensation; or of the machinery by means of which each sensation exhibits its corresponding perception. We are inspired with the sensation, and we are inspired with the corresponding perception, by means unknown. And because the mind passes immediately from the sensation to that conception and belief of the object which we have in perception, in the same manner as it passes from signs to the things signified by them, we have therefore called our sensations *signs of external objects;* finding no word more proper to express the function which nature hath assigned them in perception, and the relation which they bear to their corresponding objects.

There is no necessity of a resemblance between the sign and the thing signified: and indeed no sensation can resemble any external object. But there are two things necessary to our knowing things by means of signs. *First*, That a real connexion between the sign and thing signified be established, either by the course of nature, or by the will and appointment of men. When they are connected by the course of nature, it is a natural sign; when by human appointment, it is an artificial sign. Thus, smoke is a natural sign of fire; certain features are natural signs of anger: but our words, whether expressed by articulate sounds or by writing, are artificial signs of our thoughts and purposes.

Another requisite to our knowing things by signs is, that the appearance of the sign to the mind, be followed by the conception and belief of the thing signified. Without this the sign is not understood or interpreted; and therefore is no sign to us, however fit in its own nature for that purpose.

[Now, there are three ways in which the mind passes from the appearance of a natural sign to the conception and belief of the thing signified; by original principles of our constitution, by custom, and by reasoning.

Our original perceptions are got in the first of these ways, our acquired perceptions in the second, and all that reason discovers in the course of nature, in the third.] In the first of these ways, nature, by means of the sensations of touch, informs us of the hardness and softness of bodies; of their extension, figure, and motion; and of that space in which they move and are placed, as hath been already explained in the fifth chapter of this inquiry. And in the second of these ways she informs us, by means of our eyes, of almost all the same things which originally we could perceive only by touch.

In order, therefore, to understand more particularly how we learn to perceive so many things by the eye, which originally could be perceived only by touch, it will be proper, *first*, To point out the signs by which those things are exhibited to the eye, and their connexion with the things signified by them; and, *secondly*, To consider how the experience of this connexion produces that habit by which the mind, without any reasoning or reflection, passes from the sign to the conception and belief of the thing signified.

Of all the acquired perceptions which we have by sight, the most remarkable is the perception of the *distance of objects* from the eye; we shall therefore particularly consider the signs by which this perception is exhibited, and only make some general remarks with regard to the signs which are used in other acquired perceptions.

XXII. *Of the signs by which we learn to perceive distance from the eye.*—It was before observed in general, That the original perceptions of sight are signs which serve to introduce those that are acquired: but this is not to be understood as if no other signs were employed for that purpose. [There are several motions of the eyes, which, in order to distinct vision, must be varied, according as the object is more or less distant; and such motions being by *habit* connected with the corresponding distances of the object, become signs of those distances.] These motions were at first voluntary and unconfined; but as the intention of nature was, to produce perfect and distinct vision by their means, we soon learn by experience to regulate them according to that intention only, without the least reflection.

☞ A ship requires a different trim for every variation of the direction and strength of the wind: and, if we may be allowed to borrow that word, the eyes require a different trim for every degree of light, and for every variation of the distance of the object, while it is within certain limits. The eyes are trimmed for a particular object, by contracting certain muscles, and relaxing others; as the ship is trimmed for a particular wind, by drawing certain ropes, and slackening others. The sailor learns the trim of his ship, as we learn the trim of our eyes, by experience. A ship, although the noblest machine that human art can boast, is far inferior to the eye in this respect, that it requires art and ingenuity to navigate her; and a sailor must know what ropes he must pull, and what he must slacken, to fit her to a particular wind; but with such superior wisdom is the fabric of the eye, and the principles of its motion contrived, that it requires no art nor ingenuity to see by it. Even that part of vision which is got by experience, is attained by idiots. We need not know what muscles we are to contract, and what we are to relax, in order to fit the eye to a particular distance of the object.

But although we are not conscious of the motions we perform in order to fit the eyes to the distance of the object, we are conscious of the effort employed in producing these motions; and probably have some sensation which accompanies them, to which we give as little attention as to other sensations. And thus, an effort consciously exerted, or a sensation consequent upon that effort, comes to be conjoined with the distance of the object which gave occasion to it, and by this conjunction becomes a sign of that distance. Some instances of this will appear in considering the means or signs by which we learn to see the distance of objects from the eye. In the enumeration of these, we agree with Dr. Porterfield, notwithstanding that distance from the eye, in *his opinion*, is perceived *originally*, but, *in our opinion*, by *experience* only.

In general, when a near object affects the eye in one manner, and the same object placed at a greater distance, affects it in a different manner; these various affections of the eye become signs of the corresponding distances. The means of perceiving distance by the eye, will therefore be explained, by showing in what various ways objects affect the eye differently, according to their proximity or distance.

1. It is well known, that to see objects distinctly at various distances, the form of the eye must undergo some change. And nature hath given us the power of adapting it to near objects, by the contraction of certain muscles, and to distant objects by the contraction of other muscles. As to the manner in which this is done, and the muscular parts employed, anatomists do not altogether agree. The ingenious Dr. Jurin, in his excellent essay on distinct and indistinct vision, seems to have given the most probable account of this matter; and to him I refer the reader.

But whatever be the manner in which this change of the form of the eye is effected, it is certain that young people have commonly the power of adapting their eyes to all distances of the object, from six or seven inches to fifteen or sixteen feet; so as to have perfect and distinct vision at any distance within these limits. From this it follows, that the effort which we consciously employ to adapt the eye to any particular distance of objects within these limits, will be connected and associated with that distance, and will become a sign of it. When the object is removed beyond the farthest limit of distinct vision, it will be seen indistinctly; but more or less so, according as its distance is greater or less; so that the degrees of indistinctness of the object, may become the signs of distances considerably beyond the farthest limit of distinct vision.

[If we had *no other mean but this*, of perceiving the distance of visible objects, *the most distant would not appear to be above twenty or thirty feet from the eye,* and the tops of houses and trees would seem to touch the clouds; for in that case the signs of all greater distances being the same, they have the same signification, and give the same perception of distance.]

But it is of more importance to observe, that because the nearest limit of distinct vision in the time of youth, when we learn to perceive distance by the eye, is about six or seven inches, no object seen distinctly, ever appears to be nearer than six or seven inches from the eye. We can, by art, make a small object appear distinct, when it is in reality not above half an inch from the eye; either by using a single microscope, or by looking through a small pin-hole in a card. When by either of these means an object is made to appear distinct, however small its distance is in reality, it seems to be removed at least to the distance of six or seven inches, that is, within the limits of distinct vision.

This observation is the more important, because it affords the only reason we can give why an object is magnified either by a single microscope, or by being seen through a pin-hole; and the only mean by which we can ascertain the degree in which the object will be magnified by either. Thus, if the object is really half an inch distant from the eye, and appears to be seven inches distant, its diameter will seem to be enlarged in the same proportion as its distance, that is, fourteen times.

2. In order to direct both eyes to an object, the optic axes must have a greater or less inclination, according as the object is nearer or more distant. And although we are not conscious of this inclination, yet we are conscious of the effort employed in it. By this mean we perceive small distances more accurately than we could do by the conformation of the eye only. And therefore we find, that those who have lost the sight of one eye, are apt, even within arm's-length, to make mistakes in the distance of objects, which are easily avoided by those who see with both

eyes. Such mistakes are often discovered in snuffing a candle, in threading a needle, or in filling a tea-cup.

When a picture is seen with both eyes, and at no great distance, the representation appears not so natural as when it is seen only with one. The intention of painting being to deceive the eye, and to make things appear at different distances which in reality are upon the same piece of canvass, this deception is not so easily put upon both eyes as upon one; because we perceive the distance of visible objects more exactly and determinately with two eyes than with one. If the shading and relief be executed in the best manner, the picture may have almost the same appearance to one eye as the objects themselves would have, but it cannot have the same appearance to both. This is not the fault of the artist, but an unavoidable imperfection in the art. And it is owing to what we just now observed, that the perception we have of the distance of objects by one eye is more uncertain, and more liable to deception, than that which we have by both.

[The great impediment, and I think the only invincible impediment, to that agreeable deception of the eye which the painter aims at, is the perception which we have of the distance of visible objects from the eye, partly (1) by means of the conformation of the eye, but chiefly (2) by means of the inclination of the optic axes.] If this perception could be removed, I see no reason why a picture might not be made so perfect as to deceive the eye in reality, and to be mistaken for the original object. Therefore, in order to judge of the merit of a picture, we ought, as much as possible, to exclude these two means of perceiving the distance of the several parts of it.

In order to remove this perception of distance, the connoisseurs in painting use a method which is very proper. They look at the picture with one eye, through a tube which excludes the view of all other objects. By this method, the principal mean whereby we perceive the distance of the object, to wit, the inclination of the optic axes, is entirely excluded. I would humbly propose, as an improvement of this method of viewing pictures, that the aperture of the tube next to the eye should be very small. If it is as small as a pin-hole, so much the better, providing there be light enough to see the picture clearly. The reason of this proposal is, that when we look at an object through a small aperture, it will be seen distinctly whether the conformation of the eye be adapted to its distance or not, and we have no mean left to judge of the distance, but the light and colouring, which are in the painter's power. If, therefore, the artist performs his part properly, the picture will by this method affect the eye in the same manner that the object represented would do, which is the perfection of this art.

Although this second mean of perceiving the distance of visible objects be more determinate and exact than the first, yet it hath its limits, beyond which it can be of no use. For when the optic axes directed to an object are so nearly parallel, that in directing them to an object yet more distant, we are not conscious of any new effort, nor have any different sensation, there our perception of distance stops; and as all more distant objects affect the eye in the same manner, we perceive them to be at the same distance. This is the reason why the sun, moon, planets, and fixed stars, when seen not near the horizon, appear to be all at the same distance, as if they touched the concave surface of a great sphere. The surface of this celestial sphere is at that distance beyond which all objects affect the eye in the same manner. Why this celestial vault appears more distant towards the horizon, than towards the zenith, will afterwards appear.

3. The colours of objects, according as they are more distant, become more faint and languid, and are tinged more with the azure of the intervening atmosphere: to this we may add, that their minute parts become more indistinct, and their outline less accurately defined. It is by these means chiefly, that painters can represent objects at very different distances upon the same canvass. And the diminution of the magnitude of an object, would not have the effect of making it appear to be at a great distance, without this degradation of colour, and indistinctness of the outline, and of the minute parts. If a painter should make a human figure ten times less than other human figures that are in the same piece, having the colours as bright, and the outline and minute parts as accurately defined, it would not have the appearance of a man at a great distance, but of a pigmy or Lilliputian.

When an object hath a known variety of colours, its distance is more clearly indicated by the gradual dilution of the colours into one another, than when it is of one uniform colour. In the steeple which stands before me, at a small distance the joinings of the stones are clearly perceptible, the grey colour of the stone and the white cement are distinctly limited: when I see it at a greater distance, the joinings of the stones are less distinct, and the colours of the stone and of the cement begin to dilute into one another; at a distance still greater, the joinings disappear altogether, and the variety of colour vanishes.

In an apple-tree which stands at the distance of about twelve feet, covered with flowers, I can perceive the figure and the colour of the leaves and petals; pieces of branches, some larger, others smaller, peeping through the intervals of the leaves, some of them enlightened by the sun's rays, others shaded; and some openings of the sky are perceived through the whole. When I gradually remove from this tree, the appearance, even as to colour, changes every minute. First, the smaller parts, then the larger, are gradually confounded and mixed. The colours of leaves, petals, branches, and sky, are gradually diluted into each other, and the colour of the whole becomes more and more uniform. This change of appearance, corresponding to the several distances, marks the distance more exactly than if the whole object had been of one colour.

Dr. Smith, in his "Optics," gives us a very curious observation made by Bishop Berkeley, in his travels through Italy and Sicily. He observed, that in those countries, cities and palaces seen at a great distance, appeared nearer to him, by several miles, than they really were; and he very judiciously imputed it to this cause—that the purity of the Italian and Sicilian air, gave to very distant objects that degree of brightness and distinctness, which, in the grosser air of his own country, was to be seen only in those that are near. The purity of the Italian air hath been assigned as the reason why the Italian painters commonly give a more lively colour to the sky than the Flemish. Ought they not, for the same reason, to give less degradation of the colours, and less indistinctness of the minute parts, in the representation of very distant objects?

It is very certain, that as in air uncommonly pure, we are apt to think visible objects nearer, and less than they really are; so in air uncommonly foggy, we are apt to think them more distant and larger than the truth. Walking by the sea-side in a thick fog, I see an object which seems to me to be a man on horseback, and at the distance of about half a mile. My companion, who has better eyes, or is *more accustomed* to see such objects in such circumstances, assures me, that it is a sea-gull, and not a man on horseback. Upon a second view, I immediately assent to his opinion, and now it appears to me to be a sea-gull, and at the distance only of seventy or eighty yards. The mistake made on this occasion, and the correction of it, are both so sudden, that we are at a loss whether to call them by the name of *judgment*, or by that of *simple perception*.*

It is not worth while to dispute about names; but it is evident that my belief, both first and last, was produced rather by signs than by arguments: and that the mind proceeded to the conclusion in both cases by habit, and not by ratiocination. And the process of the mind seems to have been this: first, not knowing, or not minding, the effect of a foggy air on the visible appearance of objects, the object seems to me to have that degradation of colour, and that indistinctness of the outline, which objects have at the distance of half a mile; therefore, from the visible appearance as a sign, I immediately proceed to the belief that the object is half a mile distant. Then, this distance, toge-

* They are ideas of perception, or sensation, changed by the judgment.

ther with the visible magnitude, signify to me the real magnitude, which, supposing the distance to be half a mile, must be equal to that of a man on horseback; and the figure, considering the indistinctness of the outline, agrees with that of a man on horseback. Thus the deception is brought about. But when I am assured that it is a sea-gull, the real magnitude of a sea-gull, together with the visible magnitude presented to the eye, immediately suggest the distance, which in this case cannot be above seventy or eighty yards: the indistinctness of the figure likewise suggests the fogginess of the air as its cause: and now the whole chain of signs and things signified, seems stronger and better connected than it was before; the half-mile vanishes to eighty yards; the man on horseback dwindles to a sea-gull; I get a new perception, and wonder how I got the former, or what is become of it; for it is now so entirely gone, that I cannot recover it.

It ought to be observed, that in order to produce such deceptions from the clearness or fogginess of the air, it must be uncommonly clear, or uncommonly foggy; for we learn from experience, to make allowance for that variety of constitutions of the air which we have been accustomed to observe, and of which we are aware. Bishop Berkeley therefore committed a mistake, when he attributed the large appearance of the horizontal moon to the faintness of her light, occasioned by its passing through a larger tract of atmosphere: for we are so much accustomed to see the moon in all degrees of faintness and brightness, from the greatest to the least, that we learn to make allowance for it; and do not imagine her magnitude increased by the faintness of her appearance. Besides, it is certain that the horizontal moon seen through a tube which cuts off the view of the interjacent ground, and of all terrestrial objects, loses all that unusual appearance of magnitude.

4. We frequently perceive the distance of objects by means of intervening or contiguous objects whose distance or magnitude is otherwise known. When I perceive certain fields or tracts of ground to lie between me and an object, it is evident that these may become signs of its distance. And although we have no particular information of the dimensions of such fields or tracts, yet their similitude to others which we know, suggests their dimensions.

We are so much accustomed to measure with our eye the ground which we travel, and to compare the judgments of distances formed by sight, with our experience or information, that we learn by degrees, in this way, to form a more accurate judgment of the distance of terrestrial objects, than we could do by any of the means before mentioned. An object placed upon the top of a high building, appears much less than when placed upon the ground at the same distance. When it stands upon the ground, the intervening tract of ground serves as a sign of its distance; and the distance, together with the visible magnitude, serves as a sign of its real magnitude. But when the object is placed on high, this sign of its distance is taken away: the remaining signs lead us to place it at a less distance; and this less distance, together with the visible magnitude, becomes a sign of a less real magnitude.

The two first means we have mentioned, would never of themselves make a visible object appear above a hundred and fifty or two hundred feet distant; because, beyond that, there is no sensible change, either of the conformation of the eyes, or of the inclination of their axes: the third mean, is but a vague and indeterminate sign, when applied to distances above two or three hundred feet, unless we know the real colour and figure of the object: and the fifth mean, to be afterwards mentioned, can only be applied to objects which are familiar, or whose real magnitude is known. Hence it follows, that when unknown objects, upon, or near the surface of the earth, are perceived to be at the distance of some miles, it is always by this fourth mean that we are led to that conclusion.

Dr. Smith hath observed, very justly, that the known distance of the terrestrial objects which terminate our view, makes that part of the sky which is towards the horizon, appear more distant than that which is towards the zenith. Hence it comes to pass, that the apparent figure of the sky is not that of a hemisphere, but rather a less segment of a sphere. And hence likewise it comes to pass, that the diameter of the sun or moon, or the distance between two fixed stars, seen contiguous to a hill, or to any distant terrestrial object, appears much greater than when no such object strikes the eye at the same time.

These observations have been sufficiently explained and confirmed by Dr. Smith. I beg leave to add, that when the visible horizon is terminated by very distant objects, the celestial vault seems to be enlarged in all its dimensions. When I view it from a confined street or lane, it bears some proportion to the buildings that surround me: but when I view it from a large plain, terminated on all hands, by hills which rise one above another, to the distance of twenty miles from the eye, methinks I see a new heaven, whose magnificence declares the greatness of its Author, and puts every human edifice out of countenance; for now the lofty spires and the gorgeous palaces shrink into nothing before it, and bear no more proportion to the celestial dome, than their makers bear to its Maker.

5. There remains another mean by which we perceive the distance of visible objects, and that is, *the diminution* of their visible or *apparent magnitude*. By experience I know what figure a man, or any other known object, makes to my eye, at the dis-

tance of ten feet : I perceive the gradual and proportional diminution of this visible figure, at the distance of twenty, forty, a hundred feet, and at greater distances, until it vanish altogether. Hence a certain visible magnitude of a known object, becomes the sign of a certain determinate distance, and carries along with it the conception and belief of that distance.

In this process of the mind, the sign is not a sensation; it is an original perception. We perceive the visible figure and visible magnitude of the object, by the original powers of vision; but the visible figure is used only as a sign of the real figure, and the visible magnitude is used only as a sign either of the distance, or of the real magnitude, of the object; and therefore these original perceptions, like other mere signs, pass through the mind without any attention or reflection.

This last mean of perceiving the distance of known objects, serves to explain some very remarkable phenomena in optics, which would otherwise appear very mysterious. When we view objects of known dimensions through optical glasses, there is no other mean left of determining their distance, but this fifth. Hence it follows, that known objects seen through glasses, must seem to be brought nearer, in proportion to the magnifying power of the glass, or to be removed to a greater distance, in proportion to the diminishing power of the glass.

If a man who had never before seen objects through a telescope, were told, that the telescope which he is about to use, magnifies the diameter of the object ten times; when he looks through this telescope at a man six feet high, what would he expect to see? Surely he would very naturally expect to see a giant sixty feet high. But he sees no such thing. The man appears no more than six feet high, and consequently no bigger than he really is; but he appears ten times nearer than he is. The telescope indeed magnifies the image of this man upon the retina ten times in diameter, and must therefore magnify his visible figure in the same proportion; and as we have been accustomed to see him of this visible magnitude when he was ten times nearer than he is presently, and in no other case; this visible magnitude, therefore, suggests the conception and belief of that distance of the object with which it hath been always connected. We have been accustomed to conceive this amplification of the visible figure of a known object, only as the effect or sign of its being brought nearer: and we have annexed a certain determinate distance to every degree of visible magnitude of the object; and therefore any particular degree of visible magnitude, whether seen by the naked eye or by glasses, brings along with it the conception and belief of the distance which corresponds to it. This is the reason why a telescope seems not to magnify known objects, but to bring them nearer to the eye.

When we look through a pin-hole, or a single microscope, at an object which is half an inch from the eye, the picture of the object upon the retina is not enlarged, but only rendered distinct; neither is the visible figure enlarged: yet the object appears to the eye twelve or fourteen times more distant, and as many times larger in diameter, than it really is. Such a telescope as we have mentioned amplifies the image on the retina, and the visible figure of the object, ten times in diameter, and yet makes it seem no bigger, but only ten times nearer. These appearances had been long observed by the writers on optics; they tortured their invention to find the causes of them from optical principles; but in vain: they must be resolved into habits of perception, which are acquired by custom, but are apt to be mistaken for original perceptions. The Bishop of Cloyne first furnished the world with the proper key for opening up these mysterious appearances; but he made considerable mistakes in the application of it. Dr. Smith, in his elaborate and judicious treatise of "Optics," hath applied it to the apparent distance of objects seen with glasses, and to the apparent figure of the heavens, with such happy success, that there can be no more doubt about the causes of these phenomena.

XXIII. *Of the signs used in these acquired perceptions.*—The distance of objects from the eye, is the most important lesson in vision. Many others are easily learned in consequence of it. [The distance of the object, joined with its visible magnitude, is a sign of its real magnitude: and the distance of the several parts of an object, joined with its visible figure, becomes a sign of its real figure.] Thus, when I look at a globe which stands before me; by the original powers of sight I perceive only something of a circular form, variously coloured. The visible figure hath no distance from the eye, no convexity, nor hath it three dimensions; even its length and breadth are incapable of being measured by inches, feet, or other linear measures. But when I have learned to perceive the distance of every part of this object from the eye, this perception gives it convexity, and a spherical figure; and adds a third dimension to that which had but two before. The distance of the whole object makes me likewise perceive the real magnitude; for being accustomed to observe how an inch or a foot of length affects the eye at that distance, I plainly perceive by my eye the linear dimensions of the globe, and can affirm with certainty that its diameter is about one foot and three inches.

It was shown in the seventh section of this chapter, that the visible figure of a body may, by mathematical reasoning, be inferred from its real figure, distance, and position, with regard to the eye: in like manner we may, by mathematical reasoning, from the visible figure, together with the distance of the several parts of it from the eye, infer the real figure and position. But this last inference is not commonly made by mathematical reasoning, nor indeed by reasoning of any kind, but by custom.

The original appearance which the colour of an object makes to the eye, is a sensation for which *we have no name*, because it is used merely as a sign, and is never made an object of attention in common life: but this appearance, according to the different circumstances, signifies various things. If a piece of cloth, of one uniform colour, is laid so, that part of it is in the sun, and part in the shade; the appearance of colour, in these different parts, is very different: yet we perceive the colour to be the same; we interpret the variety of appearance as a sign of light and shade, and not as a sign of real difference in colour. But if the eye could be so far deceived, as not to perceive the difference of light in the two parts of the cloth, we should, in that case, interpret the variety of appearance to signify a variety of colour in the parts of the cloth.

Again, if we suppose a piece of cloth placed as before, but having the shaded part so much brighter in the colour, that it gives the same appearance to the eye as the more enlightened part; the sameness of appearance will here be interpreted to signify a variety of colour, because we shall make allowance for the effect of light and shade.

When the real colour of an object is known, the appearance of it indicates, in some circumstances, the degree of light or shade, in others, the colour of the circumambient bodies, whose rays are reflected by it; and in other circumstances it indicates the distance or proximity of the object, as was observed in the last section; and by means of these, many other things are suggested to the mind. Thus, an unusual appearance in the colour of familiar objects, may be the diagnostic of a disease in the spectator. The appearance of things in my room may indicate sunshine or cloudy weather, the earth covered with snow, or blackened with rain. It hath been observed, that the colour of the sky, in a piece of painting, may indicate the country of the painter, because the Italian sky is really of a different colour from the Flemish.

It was already observed, that the original and acquired perceptions which we have by our senses, are the language of nature to man, which, in many respects, hath a great affinity to human languages. The instances which we have given of acquired perceptions suggest this affinity, that as in human languages ambiguities are often found, so this language of nature in our acquired perceptions is not exempted from them. We have seen, in vision particularly, that the same appearance to the eye, may, in different circumstances, indicate different things. Therefore, when the circumstances are unknown upon which the interpretation of the signs depends, their meaning must be ambiguous; and when the circumstances are mistaken, the meaning of the signs must also be mistaken.

This is the case in all the phenomena which we call *fallacies of the senses*, and particularly in those which are called *fallacies in vision*. The appearance of things to the eye always corresponds to the fixed laws of nature; therefore, if we speak properly, there is no fallacy in the senses. Nature always speaketh the same language, and useth the same signs in the same circumstances: but we sometimes mistake the meaning of the signs, either through ignorance of the laws of nature, or through ignorance of the circumstances which attend the signs.

To a man unacquainted with the principles of optics, almost every experiment that is made with the prism, with the magic lantern, with the telescope, with the microscope, seems to produce some fallacy in vision. Even the appearance of a common mirror, to one altogether unacquainted with the effects of it, would seem most remarkably fallacious. For how can a man be more imposed upon, than in seeing that before him which is really behind him? How can he be more imposed upon, than in being made to see himself several yards removed from himself? Yet children, even before they can speak their mother-tongue, learn not to be deceived by these appearances. These, as well as all the other surprising appearances produced by optical glasses, are a part of the visual language; and, to those who understand the laws of nature concerning light and colours, are no wise fallacious, but have a distinct and true meaning.

XXIV. *Of the analogy between perception and the credit we give to human testimony.*—The objects of human knowledge are innumerable, but the channels by which it is conveyed to the mind are few. Among these, the perception of external things by our senses, and the informations which we receive upon human testimony, are not the least considerable: and so remarkable is the analogy between these two, and the analogy between the principles of the mind which are subservient to the one and those which are subservient to the other, that, without further apology, we shall consider them together.

In the testimony of nature given by the senses, as well as in human testimony given by language, things are signified to us by signs: and in one as well as the other, the mind, either by original principles, or by custom, passes from the sign to the conception and belief of the thing signified.

[We have distinguished our perceptions into original and acquired; and language, into natural and artificial. Between acquired perception and artificial language, there is a great analogy; but still a greater between original perception and natural language.]

The signs in original perception are sensations, of which nature hath given us a great variety, suited to the variety of the things signified by them. Nature hath established a real connexion between these signs and the things signified, and nature hath also taught us the interpretation of the signs; so that, previous to experience, the sign suggests the thing signified, and creates the belief of it.

The signs in natural language are features of the face, gestures of the body, and modulations of the voice; the variety of which is suited to the variety of the things signified by them. Nature hath established a real connexion between these signs, and the thoughts and dispositions of the mind which are signified by them; and nature hath taught us the interpretation of these signs; so that, previous to experience, the sign suggests the thing signified, and creates the belief of it.

☞ A man in company, without doing good or evil, without uttering an articulate sound, may behave himself gracefully, civilly, politely; or, on the contrary, meanly, rudely, and impertinently. We see the dispositions of his mind, by their natural signs in his countenance and behaviour, in the same manner as we perceive the figure and other qualities of bodies by the sensations which nature hath connected with them.

The signs in the natural language of the human countenance and behaviour, as well as the signs in our original perceptions, have the same signification in all climates and in all nations; and the skill of interpreting them is not acquired, but innate.

In acquired perception, the signs are either sensations, or things which we perceive by means of sensations. The connexion between the sign and the thing signified is established by nature: and we discover this connexion by experience; but not without the aid of our original perceptions, or of those which we have already acquired. After this connexion is discovered, the sign, in like manner as in original perception, always suggests the thing signified, and creates the belief of it.

In artificial language, the signs are articulate sounds, whose connexion with the things signified by them is established by the will of men: and in learning our mother-tongue we discover this connexion by experience; but not without the aid of natural language, or of what we had before attained of artificial language. And after this connexion is discovered, the sign, as in natural language, always suggests the thing signified, and creates the belief of it.

Our original perceptions are few, compared with the acquired; but without the former we could not possibly attain the latter. In like manner, natural language is scanty, compared with artificial; but without the former, we could not possibly attain the latter.

Our original perceptions, as well as the natural language of human features and gestures, must be resolved into particular principles of the human constitution. Thus, it is by one particular principle of our constitution, that certain features express anger; and by another particular principle that certain features express benevolence. It is in like manner, by one particular principle of our constitution, that a certain sensation signifies hardness in the body which I handle; and it is by another particular principle that a certain sensation signifies motion in that body.

But our acquired perceptions, and the information we receive by means of artificial language, must be resolved into general principles of the human constitution. When a painter perceives that this picture is the work of Raphael, that the work of Titian; a jeweller, that this is a true diamond, that a counterfeit; a sailor that this is a ship of five hundred ton, that, of four hundred: these different acquired perceptions are produced by the same general principles of the human mind, which have a different operation in the same person, according as they are variously applied, and in different persons according to the diversity of their education and manner of life. In like manner, when certain articulate sounds convey to my mind the knowledge of the battle of Pharsalia, and others, the knowledge of the battle of Pultowa; when a Frenchman and an Englishman receive the same information by different articulate sounds; the signs used in these different cases produce the knowledge and belief of the things signified, by means of the same general principles of the human constitution.

Now, if we compare the general principles of our constitution, which fit us for receiving information from our fellow-creatures by language, with the general principles which fit us for acquiring the perception of things by our senses, we shall find them to be very similar in their nature and manner of operation.

When we begin to learn our mother-tongue, we perceive, by the help of natural language, that they who speak to us use certain sounds to express certain things: we imitate the same sounds when we would express the same things, and find that we are understood.

But here a difficulty occurs which merits our attention, because the solution of it leads to some original principles of the human mind, which are of great importance, and of very extensive influence. We know by experience that men *have* used such words to express such things. But all experience is of the *past,* and can of itself give no notion or belief of what is *future.* How come we then to believe, and to rely upon it with assurance, that men who have it in their power to do otherwise will continue to use the same words when they think the same things?

Whence comes this knowledge and belief, this foresight, we ought rather to call it, of the future and voluntary actions of our fellow-creatures? Have they promised that they will never impose upon us by equivocation or falsehood? No, they have not. And if they had, this would not solve the difficulty: for such promise must be expressed by words, or by other signs; and before we can rely upon it, we must be assured that they put the same meaning upon those signs as they have used to do. No man of common sense ever thought of taking a man's own word for his honesty; and it is evident that we take his veracity for granted when we lay any stress upon his word or promise. I might add, that this reliance upon the declarations and testimony of men is found in children long before they know what a promise is.

There is therefore in the human mind an early anticipation, neither derived from experience, nor from reason, nor from any compact or promise, that our fellow-creatures will use the same signs in language, when they have the same sentiments.

This is, in reality, a kind of prescience of human actions; and it seems to me to be an original principle of the human constitution, without which we should be incapable of language, and consequently incapable of instruction.

The wise and beneficent Author of nature, who intended that we should be social creatures, and that we should receive the greatest and most important part of our knowledge by the information of others, hath, for these purposes, implanted in our natures two principles that tally with each other.

[The first of these principles is, *a propensity to speak truth*, and to use the signs of language, so as to convey our real sentiments.] This principle has a powerful operation, even in the greatest liars; for where they lie once, they speak truth a hundred times. Truth is always uppermost, and is the natural issue of the mind. It requires no art or training, no inducement or temptation, but only that we yield to a natural impulse. Lying, on the contrary, is doing violence to our nature; and is never practised, even by the worst men, without some temptation. Speaking truth is like using our natural food, which we would do from appetite, although it answered no end; but lying is like taking physic, which is nauseous to the taste, and which no man takes but for some end which he cannot otherwise attain.

If it should be objected, That men may be influenced by moral or political considerations to speak truth, and therefore that their doing so is no proof of such an original principle as we have mentioned; I answer, first, That moral or political considerations can have no influence, until we arrive at years of understanding and reflection; and it is certain from experience, that children keep to truth invariably, before they are capable of being influenced by such considerations. Secondly, When we are influenced by moral or political considerations, we must be conscious of that influence, and capable of perceiving it upon reflection. Now, when I reflect upon my actions most attentively, I am not conscious that in speaking truth, I am influenced on ordinary occasions by any motive moral or political. I find, that truth is always at the door of my lips, and goes forth spontaneously, if not held back. It requires neither good nor bad intention to bring it forth, but only that I be artless and undesigning. There may indeed be temptations to falsehood, which would be too strong for the natural principle of veracity, unaided by principles of honour or virtue; but where there is no such temptation, we speak truth by instinct: and this instinct is the principle I have been explaining.

By this instinct, a real connexion is formed between our words and our thoughts, and thereby the former become fit to be signs of the latter, which they could not otherwise be. And although this connexion is broken in every instance of lying and equivocation, yet these instances being comparatively few, the authority of human testimony is only weakened by them, but not destroyed.

[Another original principle implanted in us by the Supreme Being, is a disposition *to confide in the veracity of others*, and to believe what they tell us.] This is the counter-part to the former; and as that may be called *the principle of veracity*, we shall, for want of a more proper name, call this *the principle of credulity*. It is unlimited in children, until they meet with instances of deceit and falsehood: and it retains a very considerable degree of strength through life.

If nature had left the mind of the speaker in equilibrio, without any inclination to the side of truth more than to that of falsehood, children would lie as often as they speak truth, until reason was so far ripened, as to suggest the imprudence of lying, or conscience, as to suggest its immorality. And if nature had left the mind of the hearer in equilibrio, without any inclination to the side of belief more than to that of disbelief, we should take no man's word until we had positive evidence that he spoke truth. His testimony would, in this case, have no more authority than his dreams; which may be true or false, but no man is disposed to believe them, on this account, that they were dreamed. It is evident, that in the matter of testimony, the balance of human judgment is by nature inclined to the side of belief; and turns to that side of itself, when there is nothing put into the opposite scale. If it was not so, no proposition that is uttered in discourse would be believed, until it was examined and tried by reason; and most men would be unable to find reasons for believing the thousandth part of what is told them.

Such distrust and incredulity would deprive us of the greatest benefits of society, and place us in a worse condition than that of savages.

Children, on this supposition, would be absolutely incredulous; and therefore absolutely incapable of instruction: those who had little knowledge of human life, and of the manners and characters of men, would be in the next degree incredulous: and the most credulous men would be those of greatest experience, and of the deepest penetration; because, in many cases, they would be able to find good reasons for believing testimony, which the weak and the ignorant could not discover.

In a word, if credulity were the effect of reasoning and experience, it must grow up and gather strength, in the same proportion as reason and experience do. But if it is the gift of nature, it will be strongest in childhood, and limited and restrained by experience; and the most superficial view of human life shows, that the last is really the case, and not the first.

It is the intention of nature, that we should be carried in arms before we are able to walk upon our legs; and it is likewise the intention of nature, that our belief should be guided by the authority and reason of others, before it can be guided by our own reason. The weakness of the infant, and the natural affection of the mother, plainly indicate the former; and the natural credulity of youth, and authority of age, as plainly indicate the latter. The infant, by proper nursing and care, acquires strength to walk without support. Reason hath likewise her infancy, when she must be carried in arms: then she leans entirely upon authority, by natural instinct, as if she was conscious of her own weakness; and without this support, she becomes vertiginous. When brought to maturity by proper culture, she begins to feel her own strength, and leans less upon the reason of others; she learns to suspect testimony in some cases, and to disbelieve it in others; and sets bounds to that authority to which she was at first entirely subject. But still, to the end of life she finds a necessity of borrowing light from testimony where she has none within herself, and of leaning in some degree upon the reason of others, where she is conscious of her own imbecility.

And as in many instances reason, even in her maturity, borrows aid from testimony; so in others she mutually gives aid to it, and strengthens its authority. For as we find good reason to reject testimony in some cases, so in others we find good reason to rely upon it with perfect security, in our most important concerns. The character, the number, and the disinterestedness of witnesses, the impossibility of collusion, and the incredibility of their concurring in their testimony, without collusion, may give an irresistible strength to testimony, compared to which its native and intrinsic authority is very inconsiderable.

Having now considered the general principles of the human mind which fit us for receiving information from our fellow-creatures, by the means of language; let us next consider the general principles which fit us for receiving the information of nature by our acquired perceptions.

It is undeniable, and indeed is acknowledged by all, that when we have found two things to have been constantly conjoined in the course of nature, the appearance of one of them is immediately followed by the conception and belief of the other. The former becomes a natural sign of the latter; and the knowledge of their constant conjunction in time past, whether got by experience or otherwise, is sufficient to make us rely with assurance upon the continuance of that conjunction.

This process of the human mind is so familiar, that we never think of inquiring into the principles upon which it is founded. We are apt to conceive it as a self-evident truth, that what is to come must be similar to what is past. Thus, if a certain degree of cold freezes water to-day, and has been known to do so in all time past, we have no doubt but the same degree of cold will freeze water to-morrow, or a year hence. That this a truth, which all men believe as soon as they understand it, I readily admit; but the question is, Whence does its evidence arise? Not from comparing the ideas, surely. For when I compare the idea of cold with that of water hardened into a transparent solid body, I can perceive no connexion between them: no man can show the one to be the necessary effect of the other: no man can give a shadow of reason why nature hath conjoined them. But do we not learn their conjunction from experience? True; experience informs us that they have been conjoined in time *past:* but no man ever had any experience of what is *future:* and this is the very question to be resolved, How we come to believe that the *future* will be like the *past?* Hath the Author of nature promised this? Or were we admitted to his council, when he established the present laws of nature, and determined the time of their continuance? No surely. Indeed if we believe that there is a wise and good Author of nature, we may see a good reason why he should continue the same laws of nature, and the same connexions of things, for a long time; because, if he did otherwise, we could learn nothing from what is past, and all our experience would be of no use to us. But though this consideration, when we come to the use of reason, may confirm our belief of the continuance of the present course of nature, it is certain that it did not give rise to this belief; for children and idiots have this belief as soon as they know that fire will burn them. It must therefore be the effect of instinct, not of reason.

The wise Author of our nature intended that a great and necessary part of our knowledge should be derived from experience, *before we are capable of reasoning,* and he hath provided means perfectly adequate to this intention. For, first, He governs nature by fixed laws, so that we find innumerable connexions of things which continue from age to age. Without this stability of the course of nature, there could be no experience : or it would be a false guide, and lead us into error and mischief. If there were not a principle of veracity in the human kind, men's words would not be signs of their thoughts : and if there were no regularity in the course of nature, no one thing could be a natural sign of another. Secondly, He hath implanted in human minds an original principle by which we believe and expect the continuance of the course of nature, and the continuance of those connexions which we have observed in time past. It is by this general principle of our nature, that when two things have been found connected in time past, the appearance of the one produces the belief of the other.

I think the ingenious author of the " Treatise of Human Nature" first observed, that our belief of the *continuance* of the laws of nature cannot be founded either upon knowledge or probability : but, far from conceiving it to be an original principle of the mind, he endeavours to account for it from his favourite hypothesis, that belief is nothing but a certain degree of vivacity in the idea of the thing believed. I made a remark upon this curious hypothesis in the second chapter, and shall now make another.

[The belief which we have in perception, is a belief of the present existence of the object; that which we have in memory, is a belief of its past existence; the belief of which we are now speaking, is a belief of its future existence, and in imagination there is no belief at all.] Now I would gladly know of this author, how one degree of vivacity fixes the existence of the object to the present moment; another carries it back to time past; a third, taking a contrary direction, carries into futurity; and a fourth, carries it out of existence altogether. Suppose, for instance, that I see the sun rising out of the sea; I remember to have seen him rise yesterday; I believe he will rise to-morrow near the same place; I can likewise imagine him rising in that place, without any belief at all. Now, according to this sceptical hypothesis, this perception, this memory, this foreknowledge, and this imagination, are all the same idea, diversified only by different degrees of vivacity. The perception of the sun rising is the most lively idea; the memory of his rising yesterday, is the same idea a little more faint; the belief of his rising to-morrow is the same idea yet fainter; and the imagination of his rising, is still the same idea, but faintest of all. One is apt to think that this idea might gradually pass through all possible degrees of vivacity without stirring out of its place. But if we think so, we deceive ourselves; for no sooner does it begin to grow languid, than it moves backward into time past. Supposing this to be granted, we expect at least that as it moves backward by the decay of its vivacity, the more that vivacity decays, it will go back the farther, until it remove quite out of sight. But here we are deceived again; for there is a certain period of this declining vivacity, when, as if it had met an elastic obstacle in its motion backward, it suddenly rebounds from the past to the future, without taking the present in its way. And now having got into the regions of futurity, we are apt to think that it has room enough to spend all its remaining vigour: but still we are deceived; for, by another sprightly bound, it mounts up into the airy region of imagination. So that ideas, in the gradual declension of their vivacity, seem to imitate the inflection of verbs in grammar. They begin with the present, and proceed in order to the preterite, the future, and the indefinite. This article of the sceptical creed is indeed so full of mystery, on whatever side we view it, that they who hold that creed are very injuriously charged with incredulity: for to me it appears to require as much faith as that of Saint Athanasius.

However, we agree with the author of the "Treatise of Human Nature" in this, [that our belief of the continuance of nature's laws is not derived from reason. It is *an instinctive prescience* of the operations of nature, very like to that prescience of human actions which makes us rely upon the testimony of our fellow-creatures: and as, without the latter we should be incapable of receiving information from men by language; so without the former we should be incapable of receiving the information of nature by means of experience.]

All our knowledge of nature, beyond our original perceptions, is got by experience, and consists in the interpretation of natural signs. The constancy of nature's laws connects the sign with the thing signified, and by the natural principle just now explained, we rely upon the continuance of the connexions which experience hath discovered; and thus the appearance of the sign is followed by the belief of the thing signified.

Upon this principle of our constitution, not only acquired perception, but all inductive reasoning, and all our reasoning from analogy, is grounded: and therefore, for want of another name, we shall beg leave to call it *the inductive principle*. It is from the force of this principle that we immediately assent to that axiom upon which all our knowledge of nature is built, that effects of the same kind must have the same cause. For *effects* and *causes*, in the operations of nature, mean nothing but signs, and the things signified by them. We perceive no proper causality or efficiency in any natural cause, but only a connexion established by the course of nature between it and what is called its effect. Antecedently to all reasoning, we have, by our constitution, an anticipation that there is a fixed and steady course of nature ; and we have an eager desire to discover this course of nature. We attend to every conjunction of things which presents itself, and expect the continuance of that conjunction. And when such a conjunction has been often observed, we conceive the things to be naturally connected, and the appearance of one, without any reasoning or reflection, carries along with it the belief of the other.

If any reader should imagine that the inductive principle may be resolved into what philosophers usually call *the association of ideas,* let him observe, that by this principle, natural signs are not associated with the idea only, but with the belief of the things signified. Now, this can with no propriety be called an association of ideas, unless ideas and belief be one and the same thing. A child has found the prick of a pin conjoined with pain, hence he believes, and knows, that these things are naturally connected; he knows that the one will always follow the other. If any man will call this only an association of ideas, I dispute not about words, but I think he speaks very improperly. For if we express it in plain English, it is a prescience that things which he hath found conjoined in time past, will be conjoined in time to come. And this prescience is not the effect of reasoning, but of an original principle of human nature, which I have called *the inductive principle.*

This principle, like that of credulity, is unlimited in infancy, and gradually restrained and regulated, as we grow up. It leads us often into mistakes, but is of infinite advantage upon the whole. By it the child once burnt shuns the fire ; by it, likewise runs away from the surgeon, by whom he was inoculated. It is better that he should do the last than that he should not do the first.

But the mistakes we are led into by these two natural principles are of a different kind. Men sometimes lead us into mistakes, when we perfectly understand their language, by speaking lies. But nature never misleads us in this way : her language is always true ; and it is only by misinterpreting it that we fall into error. There must be many accidental conjunctions of things, as well as natural connexions; and the former are apt to be mistaken for the latter. Thus, in the instance above mentioned, the child connected the pain of inoculation with the surgeon; whereas it was really connected with the incision only. Philosophers, and men of science, are not exempted from such mistakes; indeed all false reasoning in philosophy is owing to them : it is drawn from experience and analogy, as well as just reasoning, otherwise it could have no verisimilitude : but the one is an unskilful and rash, the other, a just and legitimate interpretation of natural signs. If a child, or a man of common understanding, were put to interpret a book of science, wrote in his mother-tongue, how many blunders and mistakes would he be apt to fall into? Yet he knows as much of this language as is necessary for his manner of life.

The language of nature is the universal study; and the students are of different classes. Brutes, idiots, and children, employ themselves in this study, and owe to it all their acquired perceptions. Men of common understanding make a greater progress, and learn, by a small degree of reflection, many things of which children are ignorant.

Philosophers fill up the highest form in this school, and are critics in the language of nature. All these different classes have one teacher, experience enlightened by the inductive principle. Take away the light of this inductive principle, and experience is as blind as a mole: she may indeed feel what is present, and what immediately touches her; but she sees nothing that is either before or behind, upon the right hand or upon the left, future or past.

The rules of *inductive* reasoning, or of a just interpretation of nature, as well as the fallacies by which we are apt to misinterpret her language, have been, with wonderful sagacity, delineated by the great genius of Lord Bacon: so that his " Novum Organum" may justly be called *a grammar of the language of nature*. It adds greatly to the merit of this work, and atones for its defects, that at the time it was written, the world had not seen any tolerable model of inductive reasoning from which the rules of it might be copied. The arts of poetry and eloquence were grown up to perfection when Aristotle described them: but the art of interpreting nature was yet *in embryo* when Bacon delineated its manly features and proportions. Aristotle drew his rules from the best models of those arts that have yet appeared; but the best models of inductive reasoning that have yet appeared, which I take to be the third book of the " Principia" and the " Optics" of Newton, were drawn from Bacon's rules. The purpose of all those rules is, to teach us to distinguish seeming or apparent connexions of things in the course of nature, from such as are real.

They that are unskilful in inductive reasoning, are more apt to fall into error in their *reasonings* from the phenomena of nature, than in their *acquired perceptions;* because we often reason from a few instances, and thereby are apt to mistake accidental conjunctions of things for natural connexions: but that habit of passing, without reasoning, from the sign to the thing signified, which constitutes acquired perception, must be learned by many instances or experiments; and the number of experiments serves to disjoin those things which have been accidentally conjoined, as well as to confirm our belief of natural connexions.

From the time that children begin to use their hands, nature directs them to handle every thing over and over, to look at it while they handle it, and to put it in various positions, and at various distances from the eye. We are apt to excuse this as a childish diversion, because they must be doing something, and have not reason to entertain themselves in a more manly way. But if we think more justly, we shall find, that they are engaged in the most serious and important study; and if they had all the reason of philosophers, they could not be more properly employed. For it is this childish employment that enables them to make the proper use of their eyes. They are thereby every day acquiring habits of perception which are of greater importance than any thing we can teach them. The original perceptions which nature gave them are few, and insufficient for the purposes of life; and therefore she made them capable of acquiring many more perceptions by habit. And to complete her work, she hath given them an unwearied assiduity in applying to the exercises by which those perceptions are acquired.

This is the education which nature gives to her children. And since we have fallen upon this subject, we may add, that another part of nature's education is, that, by the course of things, children must often exert all their muscular force, and employ all their ingenuity, in order to gratify their curiosity, and satisfy their little appetites. What they desire is only to be obtained at the expense of labour and patience, and many disappointments. By the exercise of body and mind necessary for satisfying their desires, they acquire agility, strength, and dexterity in their motions, as well as health and vigour to their constitutions; they learn patience and perseverance; they learn to bear pain without dejection, and disappointment without despondence. The education of nature is most perfect in savages, who have no other tutor: and we see, that in the quickness of all their senses, in the agility of their motions, in the hardiness of their constitutions, and in the strength of their minds to bear hunger, thirst, pain, and disappointment, they commonly far exceed the civilized. A most ingenious writer, on this account, seems to prefer the savage life to that of society. But the education of nature could never of itself produce a Rousseau. It is the intention of nature, that human education should be joined to her institution, in order to form the man. And she hath fitted us for human education, by the natural principles of imitation and credulity, which discover themselves almost in infancy, as well as by others which are of later growth.

When the education which we receive from men does not give scope to the education of nature, it is wrong directed; it tends to hurt our faculties of perception, and to enervate both the body and mind. Nature hath her way of rearing men, as she hath of curing their diseases. The art of medicine is to follow nature, to imitate and to assist her in the cure of diseases; and the art of education is to follow nature, to assist and to imitate her in her way of rearing men. ☞ The ancient Balearides followed nature in the manner of teaching their children to be good archers, when they hung their dinner aloft by a thread, and left the younkers to bring it down by their skill in arching.

The education of nature, without any more human care than is necessary to preserve life, makes a perfect savage. Human education, joined to that of nature, may make a good citizen a skilful artizan, or a well-bred man. But reason and reflection must superadd their tutory, in order to produce a Rousseau, a Bacon, or a Newton.

Notwithstanding the innumerable errors committed in human education, there is hardly any education so bad, as to be worse than none. And I apprehend, that if even Rousseau were to choose whether to educate a son among the French, the Italians, the Chinese, or among the Esquimaux, he would not give the preference to the last.

When reason is properly employed, she will confirm the documents of nature, which are always true and wholesome; she will distinguish, in the documents of human education, the good from the bad, rejecting the last with modesty, and adhering to the first with reverence.

Most men continue all their days to be just what nature and human education made them. Their manners, their opinions, their virtues, and their vices, are all got by habit, imitation, and instruction; and reason has little or no share in forming them.

CHAPTER VII.

CONCLUSION.

Containing, reflections upon the opinions of philosophers on this subject.—THERE are two ways in which men may form their notions and opinions concerning the mind, and concerning its powers and operations. The first is the only way that leads to truth; but it is narrow and rugged, and few have entered upon it. The second is broad and smooth, and hath been much beaten, not only by the vulgar, but even by philosophers: it is sufficient for common life, and is well adapted to the purposes of the poet and orator; but, in philosophical disquisitions concerning the mind, it leads to error and delusion.

We may call the first of these ways, *the way of reflection.*

When the operations of the mind are exerted, we are conscious of them; and it is in our power to attend to them, and to reflect upon them, until they become familiar objects of thought. This is the only way in which we can form just and accurate notions of those operations. But this attention and reflection is *so difficult to man,* surrounded on all hands by external objects which constantly solicit his attention, that it has been very little practised, even by philosophers. In the course of this inquiry, we have had many occasions to show how little attention hath been given to the most familiar operations of the senses.

The second, and the most common way, in which men form their opinions concerning the mind and its operations, we may call *the way of analogy.* There is nothing in the course of nature so singular, but we can find some resemblance, or at least some analogy, between it and other things with which we are acquainted. *The mind naturally delights in* hunting after such *analogies,* and attends to them with pleasure. From them, poetry and wit derive a great part of their charms; and eloquence not a little of its persuasive force.

[Besides (1) the pleasure we receive from analogies, (2) they are of very considerable use both to facilitate the conception of things, when they are not easily apprehended without such a handle, and to lead us to probable conjectures about their nature and qualities, when we want the means of more direct and immediate knowledge.] ☞ When I consider that the planet Jupiter, in like manner as the earth, rolls round his own axis, and revolves round the sun, and that he is enlightened by several secondary planets, as the earth is enlightened by the moon; I am apt to conjecture from analogy, that as the earth by these means is fitted to be the habitation of various orders of animals, so the planet Jupiter is, by the like means, fitted for the same purpose: and having no argument more direct and conclusive to determine me in this point, I yield to this analogical reasoning a degree of assent proportioned to its strength. When I observe, that the potato-plant very much resembles the solanum in its flower and fructification, and am informed that the last is poisonous, I am apt from analogy to have some suspicion of the former: but in this case, I have access to more direct and certain evidence; and therefore ought not to trust to analogy, which would lead me into an error.

[Arguments from analogy are always at hand, and grow up spontaneously in a fruitful imagination, while arguments that are more direct, and more conclusive, often require painful attention and application: and therefore mankind in general have been very much disposed to trust to the former.] If one attentively examines the systems of the ancient philosophers, either concerning the material world, or concerning the mind, he will find them to be built solely upon the foundation of analogy. Lord Bacon first delineated the strict and *severe method of induction;* since his time it has been applied with very happy success in some parts of natural philosophy; and hardly in any thing else. But there is no subject in which mankind are so much disposed to trust to the analogical way of thinking and reasoning, as in what concerns the mind and its operations; because, to form clear and distinct notions of those operations in the direct and proper way, and to reason about them, requires a habit of attentive reflection, of which few are capable, and which, even by those few, cannot be attained without much pains and labour.

Every man is apt to form his notions of things difficult to be apprehended, or less familiar, from their analogy to things which are more familiar. Thus, if a man bred to the seafaring life, and accustomed to think and talk only of matters relating to navigation, enters into discourse upon any other subject; it is well known, that the language and the notions proper to his own profession are infused into every subject, and all things are measured by the rules of navigation: and if he should take it into his head to philosophize concerning the faculties of the mind, it cannot be doubted, but he would draw his notions from the fabric of his ship, and would find in the mind, sails, masts, rudder, and compass.

Sensible objects of one kind or other, do no less occupy and engross the rest of mankind, than things relating to navigation, the seafaring man. For a considerable part of life, we can think of nothing but the objects of sense; and to attend to objects of another nature, so as to form clear and distinct notions of them, is no easy matter, even after we come to years of reflection. The condition of mankind, therefore, affords good reason to apprehend, that their language, and their common notions, concerning the mind and its operations, will be analogical, and derived from the objects of sense; and that these analogies will be apt to impose upon philosophers, as well as upon the vulgar, and to lead them to materialize the mind and its faculties: and experience abundantly confirms the truth of this.

How generally men of all nations, and in all ages of the world, have conceived the soul, or thinking principle in man, to be some subtile matter, like breath or wind, the names given to it almost in all languages sufficiently testify. We have words which are proper, and not analogical, to express the various ways in which we perceive external objects by the senses; such as *feeling, sight, taste:* but we are often obliged to use these words analogically, to express other powers of the mind which are of a very different nature. And the powers which imply some degree of reflection, have generally no names but such as are analogical. The objects of thought are said to be *in the mind*, to be *apprehended, comprehended, conceived, imagined, retained, weighed, ruminated*.

It does not appear that the notions of the ancient philosophers, with regard to the nature of the soul, were much more refined than those of the vulgar, or that they were formed in any other way. We shall distinguish the philosophy that regards our subject into the *old* and the *new*. [The old reached down to Des Cartes, who gave it a fatal blow, of which it has been gradually expiring ever since, and is now almost extinct. Des Cartes is the father of the new philosophy that relates to this subject; but it hath been gradually improving since his time, upon the principles laid down by him.] The old philosophy seems to have been purely analogical: the new is more derived from reflection, but still with a very considerable mixture of the old analogical notions.

Because the objects of sense consist of *matter* and *form*, the ancient philosophers conceived every thing to belong to one of these, or to be made up of both. Some, therefore, thought that the soul is a particular kind of subtile matter, separable from our gross bodies; others thought that it is only a particular form of the body, and inseparable from it. For there seem to have been some among the ancients, as well as among the moderns, who conceived that a certain structure or organization of the body is all that is necessary to render it sensible and intelligent. The different powers of the mind were accordingly, by the last sect of philosophers, conceived to belong to different parts of the body, as the heart, the brain, the liver, the stomach, the blood.

They who thought that the soul is a subtile matter, separable from the body, disputed to which of the four elements it belongs, whether to earth, water, air, or fire. Of the three last, each had its particular advocates. But some were of opinion that it partakes of all the elements; that it must have something in its composition similar to every thing we perceive; and that we perceive earth by the earthy part; water, by the watery part; and fire, by the fiery part of the soul. Some philosophers, not satisfied with determining of what kind of matter the soul is made, inquired likewise into its figure, which they determined to be spherical, that it might be the more fit for motion. The most spiritual and sublime notion concerning the nature of the soul, to be met with among the ancient philosophers, I conceive to be that of the Platonists, who held that it is made of that celestial and incorruptible matter of which the fixed stars were made, and therefore has a natural tendency to rejoin its proper element. I am at a loss to say in which of these classes of philosophers Aristotle ought to be placed. He defines the soul to be, The first ἐντελέχεια of a natural body which has potential life. I beg to be excused from translating the Greek word, because I know not the meaning of it.

The notions of the ancient philosophers with regard to the operations of the mind, particularly with regard to perception and ideas, seem likewise to have been formed by the same kind of analogy.

[Plato, of the writers that are extant, first introduced the word *idea* into philosophy; but his doctrine upon this subject was somewhat peculiar.] He agreed with the rest of the ancient philosophers in this, that all things consist of matter and form; and that the matter of which all things were made, existed from eternity, without form: but he likewise believed, that there are eternal forms of all possible things which exist, without matter; and to these eternal and immaterial forms he gave the name of *ideas;* maintaining that they are the only object of true knowledge. It is of no great moment to us whether he borrowed these notions from Parmenides, or whether they were the issue of his own creative imagination. The later Platonists seem to have improved upon them, in conceiving those ideas, or eternal forms of things, to exist, not of themselves, but in the Divine mind, and to be the models and patterns according to which all things were made:

" Then lived th' Eternal One, then, deep retired
In his unfathomed essence, view'd at large
The uncreated images of things."

To these Platonic notions that of Malebranche is very nearly allied. This author seems, more than any other, to have been aware of the difficulties attending the common hypothesis concerning ideas, to wit, that ideas of all objects of thought are in the human mind; and, therefore, in order to avoid those difficulties, makes the ideas which are the immediate objects of human thought, to be the ideas of things in the Divine mind; who being intimately present to every human mind, may discover his ideas to it, as far as pleaseth him.

The Platonists and Malebranche excepted, all other philosophers, as far as I know, have conceived that there are ideas or images of every object of thought in the human mind, or at least in some part of the brain, where the mind is supposed to have its residence.

Aristotle had no good affection to the word *idea,* and seldom or never uses it but in refuting Plato's notions about ideas. He thought that matter might exist without form, but at the same time he taught, that there could be no sensation, no imagination, nor intellection, without forms, phantasms, or species in the mind; and that things sensible were perceived by sensible species, and things intelligible by intelligible species. His followers taught more explicitly, that these sensible and intelligible species are sent forth by the objects, and make their impressions upon the passive intellect; and that the active intellect perceives them in the passive intellect. And this seems to have been the common opinion while the Peripatetic philosophy retained its authority.

The Epicurean doctrine, as explained by Lucretius, though widely different from the Peripatetic in many things, is almost the same in this. He affirms, that slender films or ghosts (tenuia rerum simulacra) are still going off from all things, and flying about; and that these being extremely subtile, easily penetrate our gross bodies, and striking upon the mind, cause thought and imagination.

After the Peripatetic system had reigned above a thousand years in the schools of Europe, almost without a rival, it sunk before that of Des Cartes; the perspicuity of whose writings and notions, contrasted with the obscurity of Aristotle and his commentators, created a strong prejudice in favour of this new philosophy. [The characteristic of Plato's genius was sublimity, that of Aristotle's, subtilty; but Des Cartes far excelled both in perspicuity, and bequeathed this spirit to his successors.] The system which is now generally received, with regard to the mind, and its operations, derives not only its spirit from Des Cartes, but its fundamental principles; and after all the improvements made by Malebranche, Locke, Berkeley, and Hume, may still be called *the Cartesian system:* we shall therefore make some remarks upon its spirit and tendency in general, and upon its doctrine concerning ideas in particular.

1. It may be observed, That the method which Des Cartes pursued, naturally led him to attend more to the operations of the mind by accurate reflection, and to trust less to analogical reasoning upon this subject, than any philosopher had done before him. Intending to build a system upon a new foundation, he began with a resolution to admit nothing but what was absolutely certain and evident. He supposed that his senses, his memory, his reason, and every other faculty to which we trust in common life, might be fallacious; and resolved to disbelieve every thing, until he was compelled by irresistible evidence to yield assent.

In this method of proceeding, what appeared to him, first of all, certain and evident, was, that he thought, that he doubted, that he deliberated. In a word, the operations of his own mind, of which he was conscious, must be real, and no delusion; and though all his other faculties should deceive him, his consciousness could not. This therefore he looked upon as the first of all truths. This was the first firm ground upon which he set his foot, after being tossed in the ocean of scepticism; and he resolved to build all knowledge upon it, without seeking after any more first principles.

As every other truth, therefore, and particularly the existence of the objects of sense, was to be deduced by a train of strict argumentation from what he knew by consciousness, he was naturally led to give attention to the operations of which he was conscious, without borrowing his notions of them from external things.

It was not in the way of *analogy*, but of *attentive reflection*, that he was led to observe, that thought, volition, remembrance, and the other attributes of the mind, are altogether unlike to extension, to figure, and to all the attributes of body; that we have no reason, therefore, to conceive thinking substances to have any resemblance to extended substances; and that, as the attributes of the thinking substance are things of which we are conscious, we may have a more certain and immediate knowledge of them by *reflection*, than we can have of external objects by our senses.]

These observations, as far as I know, were first made by Des Cartes; and they are of more importance, and throw more light upon the subject, than all that had been said upon it before. They ought to make us diffident and jealous of every notion concerning the mind and its operations, which is drawn from sensible objects, in the way of analogy, and to make us rely only upon accurate reflection, as the source of all real knowledge upon this subject.

2. I observe, That as the Peripatetic system has a tendency to materialize the mind, and its operations; so the Cartesian has a tendency to spiritualize body, and its qualities. One error, common to both systems, leads to the first of these extremes in the way of analogy, and to the last, in the way of reflection. The error I mean is, that we can know nothing about body, or its qualities, but as far as we have sensations which resemble those qualities. Both systems agreed in this: but according to their different methods of reasoning, they drew very different conclusions from it; the Peripatetic drawing his notions of sensation from the qualities of body; the Cartesian, on the contrary, drawing his notions of the qualities of body from his sensations.

The Peripatetic, *taking it for granted that bodies* and their qualities *do really exist*, and are such as we commonly take them to be, inferred from them the nature of his sensations, and reasoned in this manner: our sensations are the impressions which sensible objects make upon the mind, and may be compared to the impression of a seal upon wax; the impression is the image or form of the seal, without the matter of it: in like manner, every sensation is the image or form of some sensible quality of the object. This is the reasoning of Aristotle, and it has an evident tendency to materialize the mind, and its sensations.

The Cartesian, on the contrary, thinks, *that the existence of body*, or of any of its qualities, *is not to be taken as a first principle;* and that we ought to admit nothing concerning it, but what, by just reasoning, can be deduced from our sensations; and he knows, that by reflection we can form clear and distinct notions of our sensations, without borrowing our notions of them by analogy from the objects of sense. The Cartesians, therefore, beginning to give attention to their sensations, first discovered that the sensations corresponding to secondary qualities, cannot resemble any quality of body. Hence Des Cartes and Locke inferred, that sound, taste, smell, colour, heat, and cold, which the vulgar took to be qualities of body, were not qualities of body, but mere sensations of the mind. Afterwards the ingenious Berkeley, considering more attentively the nature of sensation in general, discovered, and demonstrated, that no sensation whatever could possibly resemble any quality of an insentient being, such as body is supposed to be: and hence he inferred, very justly, that there is the same reason to hold extension, figure, and all the primary qualities, to be mere sensations, as there is to hold the secondary qualities to be mere sensations. Thus, by just reasoning upon the Cartesian principles, matter was stript of all its qualities; the new system, by a kind of metaphysical sublimation, converted all the qualities of matter into sensations, and spiritualized body, as the old had materialized spirit.

The way to avoid both these extremes, is, to admit the existence of what we see and feel as a first principle, as well as the existence of things whereof we are conscious; and to take our notions of the qualities of body, from the testimony of our senses, with the Peripatetics; and our notions of our sensations, from the testimony of consciousness, with the Cartesians.

3. I observe, That the modern scepticism is the natural issue of the new system; and that, although it did not bring forth this monster until the year 1739, it may be said to have carried it in its womb from the beginning.

The *old system admitted all the principles of common sense as first principles*, without requiring any proof of them; and therefore, though its reasoning was commonly vague, analogical, and dark, yet it was built upon a broad foundation, and had no tendency to scepticism.] We do not find that any Peripatetic thought it incumbent upon him to prove the existence of a material world; but every writer upon the Cartesian system attempted this, until Berkeley clearly demonstrated the futility of their arguments; and thence concluded, that there was no such thing as a material world; and that the belief of it ought to be rejected as a vulgar error.

[The new system admits only *one* of the *principles of common sense as a first principle;* and pretends, by strict argumentation, to deduce all the rest from it.] That our thoughts, our sensations, and every thing of which we are conscious, hath a real existence, is admitted in this system as a first principle; but every thing else must be made evident by the light of reason. Reason must rear the whole fabric of knowledge upon this single principle of consciousness.

There is a disposition in human nature to reduce things to as few principles as possible; and this, without doubt, adds to the beauty of a system, if the principles are able to support what rests upon them. The mathematicians glory very justly, in having raised so noble and magnificent a system of science, upon the foundation of a few axioms and definitions. This love of simplicity, and of reducing things to few principles, hath produced many a false system; but there never was any system in which it appears so remarkably as that of Des Cartes. His whole system concerning matter and spirit is built upon one axiom, expressed in one word, *cogito*. Upon the foundation of conscious thought, with ideas for his materials, he builds his system of the human understanding, and attempts to account for all its phenomena: and having, as he imagined, from his consciousness, proved the existence of matter; upon the existence of matter, and of a certain quantity of motion originally impressed upon it, he builds his system of the material world, and attempts to account for all its phenomena.

These principles with regard to the material system have been found insufficient; and it has been made evident, that besides matter and motion, we must admit gravitation, cohesion, corpuscular attraction, magnetism, and other centripetal and centrifugal forces, by which the particles of matter attract and repel each other. Newton, having discovered this, and demonstrated, that these principles cannot be resolved into matter and motion, was led by analogy, and the love of simplicity, to conjecture, but with a modesty and caution peculiar to him, that all the phenomena of the material world depended upon attracting and repelling forces in the particles of matter. But we may now venture to say, that this conjecture fell short of the mark. For, even in the unorganized kingdom, the powers by which salts, crystals, spars, and many other bodies, concrete into regular forms, can never be accounted for by attracting and repelling forces in the particles of matter. And in the vegetable and animal kingdoms, there are strong indications of powers of a different nature from all the powers of unorganized bodies. We see then, that although in the structure of the material world there is, without doubt, all the beautiful simplicity consistent with the purposes for which it was made, it is not so simple as the great Des Cartes determined it to be: nay, it is not so simple as the greater Newton modestly conjectured it to be. Both were misled by analogy, and the love of simplicity. One had been much conversant about extension, figure, and motion; the other had enlarged his views to attracting and repelling forces; and both formed their notions of the unknown parts of nature, from those with which they were acquainted, as the shepherd Tityrus formed his notion of the city Rome from his country-village:

> "Urbem quam dicunt Romam, Melibœe, putavi
> Stultus ego, huic nostræ similem, quo sæpe solemus
> Pastores ovium teneros depellere fœtus.
> Sic canibus catulos similes, sic matribus hædos
> Nôram: sic parvis componere magna solebam."

> Fool that I was, I thought imperial Rome
> Like Mantua, where on market days we come,
> And thither drive our tender lambs from home;
> So kids and whelps their sires and dams express:
> And so the great I measured by the less.

This is a just picture of the analogical way of thinking.

But to come to the system of Des Cartes concerning the human understanding; it was built, as we have observed, upon consciousness as its sole foundation, and with ideas as its materials; and all his followers have built upon the same foundation and with the same materials. They acknowledge that nature hath given us various simple ideas: these are analogous to the matter of Des Cartes' physical system. They acknowledge likewise a natural power by which ideas are compounded, disjoined, associated, compared: this is analogous to the original quantity of motion in Des Cartes' physical system. From these principles they attempt to explain the phenomena of the human understanding, just as in the physical system the phenomena of nature were to be explained by matter and motion. It must indeed be acknowledged, that there is great simplicity in this system as well as in the other. There is such a similitude between the two, as may be expected between children of the same father: but as the one has been found to be the child of Des Cartes, and not of nature, there is ground to think that the other is so likewise.

[That *the natural issue of this system is scepticism* with regard to every thing *except the existence of our ideas, and* of their necessary *relations* which appear upon comparing them, is evident: for ideas being the *only* objects of thought, and having *no existence but when we are conscious of them*, it necessarily follows, that there is no object of our thought which can have a continued and permanent existence.] Body and spirit, cause and effect, time and space, to which we were wont to ascribe an existence independent of our thought, are all turned out of existence by this short dilemma: either these things are ideas of sensation or reflection, or they are not: if they are ideas of sensation or reflection, they can have no existence but when we are conscious of them: if they are not ideas of sensation or reflection, they are words without any meaning.

Neither Des Cartes nor Mr. Locke perceived this consequence of their system concerning ideas. Bishop Berkeley was the first who discovered it. And what followed upon this discovery? Why, with regard to the material world, and with regard to space and time, he admits the consequence, that these things are mere ideas, and have no existence but in our minds: but with regard to the existence of spirits or minds, he does not admit the consequence; and if he had admitted it, he must have been an absolute sceptic. But how does he evade this consequence with regard to the existence of spirits? The expedient which the good Bishop uses on this occasion is very remarkable, and shows his great aversion to scepticism. He maintains, that we have no ideas of spirits; and that we can think, and speak, and reason about them, and about their attributes, without having any ideas of them. If this is so, my lord, what should hinder us from thinking and reasoning about bodies, and their qualities, without having ideas of them? The Bishop either did not think of this question, or did not think fit to give any answer to it. However, we may observe, that in order to avoid scepticism, he fairly starts out of the Cartesian system, without giving any reason why he did so in this instance, and in no other. This indeed is the only instance of a deviation from Cartesian principles which I have met with in the successors of Des Cartes; and it seems to have been only a sudden start, occasioned by the terror of scepticism; for in all other things Berkeley's system is founded upon Cartesian principles.

Thus we see, that Des Cartes and Locke take the road that leads to scepticism, without knowing the end of it; but they stop short for want of light to carry them farther. Berkeley, frighted at the appearance of the dreadful abyss, starts aside, and avoids it. But the author of the "Treatise of Human Nature," more daring and intrepid, without turning aside to the right hand or to the left, like Virgil's Alecto, shoots directly into the gulf:

> "Hic specus horrendum, et sævi spiracula Ditis
> Monstrantur: ruptoque ingens Acheronte vorago
> Pestiferas aperit fauces."
>
> There Pluto pants for breath from out his cell,
> And opens wide the grinning jaws of hell.

4. We may observe, that the account given by the new system, of that furniture of the human understanding which is the gift of nature, and not the acquisition of our own reasoning faculty, is extremely lame and imperfect.

The natural furniture of the human understanding is of two kinds; first, The *notions* or simple apprehensions which we have of things; and secondly, The *judgments* or the belief which we have concerning them. As to our notions, the new system reduces them to two classes; *ideas of sensation,* and *ideas of reflection;* the first are conceived to be copies of our sensations, retained in the memory or imagination; the second, to be copies of the operations of our minds whereof we are conscious, in like manner retained in the memory or imagination: and we are taught, that these two comprehend all the materials about which the human understanding is, or can be employed. As to our judgment of things, or the belief which we have concerning them, the new system allows no part of it to be the gift of nature, but holds it to be the acquisition of reason, and to be got by comparing our ideas, and perceiving their agreements or disagreements. Now I take this account, both of our notions, and of our judgments or belief, to be extremely imperfect; and I shall briefly point out some of its capital defects.

[The division of our notions into ideas of sensation, and ideas of reflection, is contrary to all rules of logic; because *the second member of the division includes the first.*] For, can we form clear and just notions of our sensations any other way than by reflection? Surely we cannot. Sensation is an operation of the mind of which we are conscious; and we get the notion of sensation, by reflecting upon that which we are conscious of. In like manner, doubting and believing are operations of the mind whereof we are conscious; and we get the notion of them by reflecting upon what we are conscious of. The ideas of sensation, therefore, are ideas of reflection, as much as the ideas of doubting, or believing, or any other ideas whatsoever.

But to pass over the inaccuracy of this division, it is extremely incomplete. For, since sensation is an operation of the mind, as well as all the other things of which we form our notions by reflection; when it is asserted, that all our notions are either ideas of sensation or ideas of reflection, the plain English of this is, that mankind neither do, nor can think of any thing but of the operations of their own minds. Nothing can be more contrary to truth, or more contrary to the experience of mankind. I know that Locke, while he maintained this doctrine, believed the notions which we have of body and of its qualities, and the notions which we have of motion and of space, to be ideas of sensation. But why did he believe this? Because he believed those notions to be nothing else but images of our sensations. If, therefore, the notions of body and its qualities, of motion and space, be not images of our sensations, will it not follow, that those notions are not ideas of sensation? Most certainly.

There is no doctrine of the new system which more directly leads to scepticism than this. And the author of the "Treatise of Human Nature," knew very well how to use it for that purpose: for, if you maintain that there is any such existence as body or spirit, time or place, cause or effect, he immediately catches you between the horns of this dilemma; your notions of these existences are either ideas of sensation, or ideas of reflection; if of sensation, from what sensation are they copied? if of reflection, from what operation of the mind are they copied?

It is indeed to be wished, that those who have written much about sensation, and about the other operations of the mind, had likewise thought and reflected much, and with great care, upon those operations: but is it not very strange, that they will not allow it to be possible for mankind to think of any thing else?

The account which this system gives of our judgment and belief concerning things, is as far from the truth as the account it gives of our notions or simple apprehensions. It represents our senses as having no other office, but that of furnishing the mind with notions or simple apprehensions of things; and makes [our judgment and belief concerning those things to be acquired by *comparing* our notions together, and *perceiving their agreements or disagreements.*]

We have shown, on the contrary, that every operation of the senses, in its very nature, implies judgment or belief, as well as simple apprehension. Thus, when I feel the pain of the gout in my toe, I have not only a notion of pain, but a belief of its existence, and a belief of some disorder in my toe which occasions it; and this belief is not produced by comparing ideas, and perceiving their agreements and disagreements; it is included in the very nature of the sensation. When I perceive a tree before me, my faculty of seeing gives me not only a notion or simple apprehension of the tree, but a belief of its existence, and of its figure, distance, and magnitude; and this judgment or belief is not got by comparing ideas, it is included in the very nature of the perception. We have taken notice of several original principles of belief in the course of this inquiry; and when other faculties of the mind are examined, we shall find more, which have not occurred in the examination of the five senses.

Such original and natural judgments are therefore a part of that furniture which nature hath given to the human understanding. They are the inspiration of the Almighty, no less than our notions or simple apprehensions. They serve to direct us in the common affairs of life, where our reasoning faculty would leave us in the dark. They are a part of our constitution, and all the discoveries of our reason are grounded upon them. They make up what is called *the common sense of mankind;* and what is manifestly contrary to any of those first principles, is what we call *absurd.* The strength of them is *good sense*, which is often found in those who are not acute in reasoning. A remarkable deviation from them, arising from a disorder in the constitution, is what we call *lunacy;* as when a man believes that he is made of glass. When a man suffers himself to be reasoned out of the principles of common sense by metaphysical arguments, we may call this *metaphysical lunacy;* which differs from the other species of the distemper in this, that it is not continued, but intermittent: it is apt to seize the patient in solitary and speculative moments; but when he enters into society, common sense recovers her authority. A clear explication and enumeration of the principles of common sense, is one of the chief desiderata in logic. We have only considered such of them as occurred in the examination of the five senses.

[5. The last observation that I shall make upon the new system is, That, although it professes to set out in the way of *reflection,* and *not of analogy,* it hath retained some of the old analogical notions concerning the operations of the mind; particularly, That things which do not presently exist in the mind itself, can only be perceived, remembered, or imagined, by means of ideas or images of them in the mind, which are the immediate objects of perception, remembrance, and imagination.] This doctrine appears evidently to be borrowed from the old system; which taught, that external things make impressions upon the mind, like the impressions of a seal upon wax; that it is by means of those impressions that we perceive, remember, or imagine them; and that those impressions must resemble the things from which they are taken. When we form our notions of the operations of the mind by analogy, this way of conceiving them seems to be very natural, and offers itself to our thoughts: for as every thing which is felt must make some impression upon the body, we are apt to think, that every thing which is understood must make some impression upon the mind.

[From such analogical reasoning, this opinion of the existence of ideas or images of things in the mind, seems to have taken its rise, and to have been so universally received among philosophers.] It was observed already, that Berkeley, in one instance, apostatizes from this principle of the new system, by affirming, that we have no ideas of spirits, and that we can think of them immediately, without ideas. But I know not whether in this he has had any followers. There is some difference, likewise, among modern philosophers, with regard to the ideas or images by which we perceive, remember, or imagine sensible things. For, though all agree in the existence of such images, they differ about their place; some placing them in a particular part of the brain, where the soul is thought to have her residence, and others placing them in the mind itself. Des Cartes held the first of these opinions; to which Newton seems likewise to have inclined; for he proposes this query in his " Optics:"

"Annon sensorium animalium est locus cui substantia sentiens adest, et in quem sensibiles rerum species per nervos et cerebrum deferuntur, ut ibi præsentes a præsente sentiri possint?" But Locke seems to place the ideas of sensible things in the mind: and that Berkeley, and the author of the "Treatise of Human Nature," were of the same opinion, is evident. The last makes a very curious application of this doctrine, by endeavouring to prove from it, that the mind either is no substance, or that it is an extended and divisible substance; because the ideas of extension cannot be in a subject which is indivisible and unextended.

[I confess I think his reasoning in this, as in most cases, is clear and strong. For whether the idea of extension be only another name for extension itself, as Berkeley and this author assert; or whether the idea of extension be an image and resemblance of extension, as Locke conceived; I appeal to any man of common sense, whether *extension*, or any *image* of extension, can be in an unextended and indivisible subject.] But while I agree with him in his reasoning, I would make a different application of it. He takes it for granted, that there are ideas of extension in the mind; and thence infers, that if it is at all a substance, it must be an extended and divisible substance. On the contrary, I take it for granted, upon the testimony of common sense, that my mind is a substance, that is, a permanent subject of thought; and my reason convinces me, that it is an unextended and indivisible substance; and hence I infer, that there cannot be in it any thing that resembles extension. If this reasoning had occurred to Berkeley, it would probably have led him to acknowledge, that we may think and reason concerning bodies, without having ideas of them in the mind, as well as concerning spirits.

I intended to have examined more particularly and fully this doctrine of the existence of ideas or images of things in the mind; and likewise another doctrine, which is founded upon it, to wit,—that judgment or belief is nothing but a perception of the agreement or disagreement of our ideas: but having already shown, through the course of this inquiry, that the operations of the mind which we have examined, give no countenance to either of these doctrines, and in many things contradict them, I have thought it proper to drop this part of my design. It may be executed with more advantage, if it is at all necessary, after inquiring into some other powers of the human understanding.

Although we have examined only the five senses, and the principles of the human mind which are employed about them, or such as have fallen in our way in the course of this examination; we shall leave the further prosecution of this inquiry to future deliberation. The powers of memory, of imagination, of taste, of reasoning, of moral perception, the will, the passions, the affections, and all the active powers of the soul, present a vast and boundless field of philosophical disquisition, which the author of this inquiry is far from thinking himself able to survey with accuracy. Many authors of ingenuity, ancient and modern, have made excursions into this vast territory, and have communicated useful observations: but there is reason to believe, that those who have pretended to give us a map of the whole, have satisfied themselves with a very inaccurate and incomplete survey. If Galileo had attempted a complete system of natural philosophy, he had, probably, done little service to mankind: but by confining himself to what was within his comprehension, he laid the foundation of a system of knowledge, which rises by degrees, and does honour to the human understanding. Newton, building upon this foundation, and in like manner confining his inquiries to the law of gravitation and the properties of light, performed wonders. If he had attempted a great deal more, he had done a great deal less, and perhaps nothing at all. Ambitious of following such great examples, with unequal steps, alas! and unequal force, we have attempted an inquiry only into one little corner of the human mind; that corner which seems to be most exposed to vulgar observation, and to be most easily comprehended; and yet, if we have delineated it justly, it must be acknowledged, that the accounts heretofore given of it, were very lame, and wide of the truth.

AN ESSAY ON QUANTITY:*

OCCASIONED BY READING A TREATISE IN WHICH SIMPLE AND COMPOUND RATIOS ARE APPLIED TO VIRTUE AND MERIT.

I. *What quantity is.*—SINCE mathematical demonstration is thought to carry a peculiar evidence along with it, which leaves no room for further dispute, it may be of some use, or entertainment at least, to inquire to what subjects this kind of proof may be applied.

Mathematics contain properly the doctrine of measure; and the object of this science is commonly said to be quantity; therefore quantity ought to be defined, what may be measured. Those who have defined quantity to be whatever is capable of more or less, have given too wide a notion of it, which, I apprehend, has led some persons to apply mathematical reasoning to subjects that do not admit of it.

Pain and pleasure admit of various degrees, but who can pretend to measure them? Had this been possible, it is not to be doubted but we should have had as distinct names for their various degrees as we have for measures of length or capacity; and a patient should have been able to describe the quantity of his pain, as well as the time it began, or the part it affected. To talk intelligibly of the quantity of pain, we should have some standard to measure it by; some known degree of it, so well ascertained, that all men, when they talked of it, should mean the same thing; we should also be able to compare other degrees of pain with this, so as to perceive distinctly, not only whether they exceed or fall short of it, but how far, or in what proportion,—whether by a half, a fifth, or a tenth.

Whatever has quantity, or is measurable, must be made up of parts, which bear proportion to one another and to the whole; so that it may be increased by addition of like parts, and dimin-

---

* This splendid specimen of metaphysical mathematics originally appeared in the xlvth vol. of the "Philosophical Transactions," and has never before been published in conjunction with the author's other Essays.

ished by subtraction, may be multiplied and divided, and, in a word, may bear any proportion to another quantity of the same kind, that one line or number can bear to another. That this is essential to all mathematical quantity, is evident from the first elements of algebra, which treats of quantity in general, or of those relations and properties which are common to all kinds of quantity. Every algebraical quantity is supposed capable not only of being increased and diminished, but of being exactly doubled, tripled, halved, or of bearing any assignable proportion to another quantity of the same kind. This then is the characteristic of quantity; whatever has this property may be adopted into mathematics, and its quantity and relations may be measured with mathematical accuracy and certainty.

II. *Of proper and improper quantity.*—There are some quantities which may be called *proper* and others *improper*. This distinction is taken notice of by Aristotle, but it deserves some explanation.

I call that proper quantity which is measured by its own kind, or which of its own nature is capable of being doubled or tripled, without taking in any quantity of a different kind as a measure of it. Thus a line is measured by known lines, as inches, feet, or miles; and the length of a foot being known, there can be no question about the length of two feet, or of any part or multiple of a foot. And this known length, by being multiplied or divided, is sufficient to give us a distinct idea of any length whatsoever.

Improper quantity is that which cannot be measured by its own kind; but to which we assign a measure by the means of some proper quantity that is related to it. Thus velocity of motion, when we consider it by itself, cannot be measured. We may perceive one body to move faster, another slower; but we can have no distinct idea of a proportion or ratio between their velocities, without taking in some quantity of another kind to measure them by. Having, therefore, observed that by a greater velocity a greater space is passed over in the same time, by a less velocity in a less space, and by an equal velocity in an equal space; we hence learn to measure velocity by the space passed over in a given time, and to reckon it to be in exact proportion to that space. And having once assigned this measure to it, we can then, and not till then, conceive one velocity to be exactly double, or half, or in any other proportion to another; we may then introduce it into mathematical reasoning without danger of confusion or error, and may also use it as a measure of other improper quantities.

All the kinds of proper quantity we know, may, I think, be reduced to these four: extension, duration, number, and proportion. Though proportion be measurable in its own nature, and therefore hath proper quantity, yet as things cannot have proportion which have not quantity of some other kind, it follows that whatever has quantity must have it in one or other of these three kinds, extension, duration, or number. These are the measure of themselves, and of all things else that are measurable.

Number is applicable to some things to which it is not commonly applied by the vulgar. Thus, by attentive consideration, lots and chances of various kinds appear to be made up of a determinate number of chances that are allowed to be equal; and by numbering these the values and proportions of those which are compounded of them may be demonstrated.

Velocity, the quantity of motion, density, elasticity, the *vis insita*, and *impressa*, the various kinds of centripetal forces, and different orders of fluxions, are all improper quantities, which, therefore, ought not to be admitted into mathematics without having a measure of them assigned. The measure of an improper quantity ought always to be included in the definition of it; for it is the giving it a measure that makes it a proper subject of mathematical reasoning. If all mathematicians had considered this as carefully as Sir Isaac Newton appears to have done, some labour had been saved both to themselves and to their readers. That great man, whose clear and comprehensive understanding appears even in his definitions, having frequent occasion to treat of such improper quantities, never fails to define them, so as to give a measure of them, either in proper quantities, or in such as had a known measure. This may be seen in the definitions prefixed to his " Princip. Phil. Nat. Math."

It is not easy to say how many kinds of improper quantity may in time be introduced into mathematics, or to what new subjects measures may be applied; but this, I think, we may conclude, that there is no foundation in nature for, nor can any valuable end be served by, applying measure to anything but what has these two properties. First, it must admit of degrees of greater and less. Secondly, it must be associated with, or related to something that has proper quantity, so as that when one is increased the other is increased, when one is diminished the other is diminished also; and every degree of the one must have a determinate magnitude or quantity of the other corresponding to it.

It sometimes happens that we have occasion to apply different measures to the same thing. Centripetal force, as defined by Newton, may be measured various ways; he himself gives different measures of it, and distinguishes them by different names, as may be seen in the above-mentioned definitions.

In reality, I conceive that the applying of measures to things that properly have not quantity, is only a fiction or artifice of the mind, for enabling us to conceive more easily and more distinctly to express and demonstrate the properties and relations of those things that have real quantity. The propositions contained in the two first books of Newton's " Principia," might, perhaps, be expressed and demonstrated without those various measures of motion, and of centripetal and impressed forces, which he uses. But this would occasion such intricate and perplexed circumlocutions, and such a tedious length of demonstrations, as would fright any sober person from attempting to read them.

III. *Corollary First.*—From the nature of quantity we may see what it is that gives mathematics such advantage over other sciences in clearness and certainty; namely, that quantity admits of a much greater variety of relations than any other subject of human reasoning; and, at the same time, every relation or proportion of quantities may, by the help of lines and numbers, be so distinctly defined as to be easily distinguished from all others, without any danger of mistake. Hence it is that we are able to trace its relations through a long process of reasoning, and with a perspicuity and accuracy which we in vain expect in subjects not capable of mensuration.

Extended quantities, such as lines, surfaces and solids, besides what they have in common with all other quantities, have this peculiar, that their parts have a particular place and disposition among themselves: a line may not only bear any assignable proportion to another, in length or magnitude, but lines of the same length may vary in the disposition of their parts; one may be straight, another may be part of a curve of any kind or dimension, of which there is an endless variety. The like may be said of surfaces and solids. So that extended quantities admit of no less variety with regard to their form than with regard to their magnitude; and as their various forms may be exactly defined and measured, no less than their magnitudes, hence it is that geometry, which treats of extended quantity, leads us into a much greater compass and variety of reasoning than any other branch of mathematics. Long deductions in algebra for the most part are made, not so much by a train of reasoning in the mind, as by an artificial kind of operation, which is built on a few very simple principles: but in geometry, we may build one proposition upon another, a third upon that, and so on, without ever coming to a limit which we cannot exceed. The properties of the more simple figures can hardly be exhausted, much less those of the more complex ones.

IV. *Coroll. 2.*—It may I think be deduced from what hath been above said, that mathematical evidence is an evidence sui generis, not competent to any proposition which does not express a relation of things measurable by lines or numbers. All proper quantity may be measured by these, and improper quantities must be measured by those that are proper.

There are many things capable of more and less, which perhaps are not capable of mensuration. Tastes, smells, the sensation of heat and cold, beauty, pleasure, all the affections and appetites of the mind, wisdom, folly, and most kinds of probability, with many other things too tedious to enumerate, admit of degrees, but have not yet been reduced to measure, nor, as I apprehend, ever can be. I say, most kinds of probability, because one kind of it, viz., the probability of chances, is properly measurable by number, as is above observed.

Although attempts have been made to apply mathematical reasoning to some of these things, and the quantity of virtue and merit in actions has been measured by simple and compound ratios; yet I do not think that any real knowledge has been struck out this way: it may perhaps, if discreetly used, be a help to discourse on these subjects, by pleasing the imagination, and illustrating what is already known; but until our affections and appetites shall themselves be reduced to quantity, and exact measures of their various degrees be assigned, in vain shall we essay to measure virtue and merit by them. This is only to ring changes upon words, and to make a show of mathematical reasoning, without advancing one step in real knowledge.

V. *Coroll. 3.*—I apprehend the account that hath been given of the nature of proper and improper quantity, may also throw some light upon the controversy about the force of moving bodies, which long exercised the pens of many mathematicians, and, for what I know, is rather dropped than ended; to the no small scandal of mathematics, which hath always boasted of a degree of evidence, inconsistent with debates that can be brought to no issue.

Though philosophers on both sides agree with one another, and with the vulgar in this, That the force of a moving body is the same while its velocity is the same, is increased when its velocity is increased, and diminished when that is diminished. But this vague notion of force, in which both sides agree, though perhaps sufficient for common discourse, yet is not sufficient to make it a subject of mathematical reasoning. In order to that, it must be more accurately defined, and so defined as to give us a measure of it, that we may understand what is meant by a double or a triple force. The ratio of one force to another cannot be perceived but by a measure; and that measure must be settled not by mathematical reasoning, but by a definition. Let any one consider force without relation to any other quantity, and see whether he can conceive one force exactly double to another; I am sure I cannot, nor shall, till I shall be endowed with some new faculty; for I know nothing of force but by its effects, and therefore can measure it only by its effects. Till force then is defined, and by that definition a measure of it assigned, we fight in the dark about a vague idea, which is not sufficiently determined to be admitted into any mathematical proposition. And when such a definition is given, the controversy will presently be ended.

VI. *Of the Newtonian measure of force.*—You say, the force of a body in motion is as its velocity; either you mean to lay this down as a definition as Newton himself has done; or you mean to affirm it as a proposition capable of proof. If you mean to lay it down as a definition, it is no more than if you should say, I call that a double force which gives a double velocity to the same body, a triple force which gives a triple velocity, and so on in proportion. This I entirely agree to; no mathematical definition of force can be given that is more clear and simple, none that is more agreeable to the common use of the word in language. For since all men agree, that the force of the body being the same, the velocity must also be the same; the force being increased or diminished, the velocity must be so also; what can be more natural or proper than to take the velocity for the measure of the force?

Several other things might be advanced to show, that this definition agrees best with the common popular notion of the word force. If two bodies meet directly with a shock, which mutually destroys their motion without producing any other sensible effect, the vulgar would pronounce, without hesitation, that they met with equal force; and so they do, according to the measure of force above laid down: for we find by experience, that in this case their velocities are reciprocally as their quantities of matter. In mechanics, where by a machine two powers or weights are kept in equilibrio, the vulgar would reckon, that these powers act with equal force; and so by this definition they do. The power of gravity being constant and uniform, any one would expect that it should give equal degrees of force to a body in equal times; and so by this definition it does. So that this definition is not only clear and simple, but it agrees best with the use of the word force in common language, and this, I think, is all that can be desired in a definition.

But if you are not satisfied with laying it down as a definition, that the force of a body is as its velocity, but will needs prove it by demonstration or experiment, I must beg of you, before you take one step in the proof, to let me know what you mean by force, and what by a double or a triple force. This you must do by a definition which contains a measure of force. Some primary measure of force must be taken for granted, or laid down by way of definition; otherwise we can never reason about its quantity. And why, then, may you not take the velocity for the primary measure, as well as any other? You will find none that is more simple, more distinct, or more agreeable to the common use of the word force: and he that rejects one definition that has these properties, has equal right to reject any other. I say, then, that it is impossible, by mathematical reasoning or experiment, to prove that the force of a body is as its velocity, without taking for granted the thing you would prove, or something else that is no more evident than the thing to be proved.

VII. *Of the Leibnitzian measure of force.*—Let us next hear the Leibnitzian, who says, that the force of a body is as the square of its velocity. If he lays this down as a definition, I shall rather agree to it, than quarrel about words, and for the future shall understand him, by a quadruple force, to mean that which gives a double velocity, by nine times the force that which gives three times the velocity, and so on in duplicate proportion. While he keeps by his definition, it will not necessarily lead him into any error in mathematics or mechanics. For, however paradoxical his conclusions may appear, however different in words from theirs who measure force by the simple ratio of the velocity, they will, in their meaning, be the same: just as he who would call a foot twenty-four inches, without changing other measures of length, when he says a yard contains a foot and a-half, means the very same as you do, when you say a yard contains three feet.

But though I allow this measure of force to be distinct, and cannot charge it with falsehood, for no definition can be false, yet I say, in the first place, it is less simple than the other; for why should a duplicate ratio be used, where the simple ratio will do as well? In the next place, this measure of force is less agreeable to the common use of the word force, as hath been shown above: and this, indeed, is all that the many laboured arguments and experiments, brought to overturn it, do prove. This also is evident, from the paradoxes into which it has led its defenders.

We are next to consider the pretences of the Leibnitzian, who will undertake to prove, by demonstration or experiment, that force is as the square of the velocity. I ask him first, what he lays down for the first measure of force? The only measure I remember to have been given by the philosophers of that side, and which seems first of all to have led Leibnitz into his notion of force, is this: the height to which a body is impelled by any impressed force, is, says he, the whole effect of that force, and therefore must be proportional to the cause; but this height is found to be as the square of the velocity, which the body had at the beginning of its motion.

In this argument, I apprehend that great man has been extremely unfortunate. For, first, Whereas all proof should be taken from principles that are common to both sides, in order to prove a thing we deny, he assumes a principle which we think further from the truth; namely, that the height to which the body rises is the whole effect of the impulse, and ought to be the whole measure of it. Secondly, His reasoning serves as well against him as for him. For may I not plead with as good reason, at least, thus? The velocity given by an impressed force, is the whole effect of that impressed force; and therefore the force must be as the velocity. Thirdly, Supposing the height to which the body is raised to be the measure of the force, this principle overturns the conclusion he would establish by it, as well as that which he opposes. For, supposing the first velocity of the body to be still the same, the height to which it rises will be increased, if the power of gravity is diminished; and diminished, if the power of gravity is increased. Bodies descend slower at the equator, and faster towards the poles, as is found by experiments made on pendulums. If, then, a body is driven upwards at the equator with a given velocity, and the same body is afterwards driven upwards at Leipsic with the same velocity, the height to which it rises in the former case will be greater than in the latter; and therefore, according to his reasoning, its force was greater in the former case; but the velocity in both was the same; consequently, the force is not as the square of the velocity, any more than as the velocity.

VIII. *Reflections on this controversy.*—Upon the whole, I cannot but think the controvertists on both sides have had a very hard task; the one to prove, by mathematical reasoning and experiment, what ought to be taken for granted; the other, by the same means, to prove what might be granted, making some allowance for impropriety of expression, but can never be proved.

If some mathematician should take it in his head to affirm, that the velocity of a body is not as the space it passes over in a given time, but as the square of that space, you might bring mathematical arguments and experiments to confute him; but you would never by these force him to yield, if he was ingenuous in his way; because you have no common principles left you to argue from, and you differ from one another, not in a mathematical proposition, but in a mathematical definition.

Suppose a philosopher has considered only that measure of centripetal force which is proportional to the velocity generated by it in a given time, and from this measure deduces several propositions: another philosopher, in a distant country, who has the same general notion of centripetal force, takes the velocity generated by it, and the quantity of matter together, as the measure of it. From this he deduces several conclusions, that seem directly contrary to those of the other. Thereupon, a serious controversy is begun, whether centripetal force be as the velocity, or as the velocity and quantity of matter taken together. Much mathematical and experimental dust is raised; and yet neither party can ever be brought to yield; for they are both in the right, only they have been unlucky in giving the same name to different mathematical conceptions. Had they distinguished these measures of centripetal force as Newton has done, calling the one "vis centripetæ quantitatis acceleratrix," the other, "quantitas motrix," all appearance of contradiction had ceased, and their propositions, which seem so contrary, had exactly tallied.

FINIS.

Tyler & Reed, Printers, Bolt-court, London.